Frommer's®

W9-BOM-694

Oregon

8th Edition

by Karl Samson

WILEY

John Wiley & Sons, Inc.

Published by:

JOHN WILEY & SONS, INC.

111 River St.

Hoboken, NJ 07030-5774

ISBN 978-1-118-09624-6 (paper); ISBN 978-1-118-22361-1 (ebk); ISBN 978-1-118-26196-5 (ebk);
ISBN 978-1-118-23694-9 (ebk)

Editor: Anuja Madar
Production Editor: Jana M. Stefanciosa
Cartographer: Andrew Dolan
Photo Editor: Richard Fox
Production by Wiley Indianapolis Composition Services
Front Cover Photo: Fishermen casting from a dock on a foggy morning with Mount Hood looming in
the distance ©Peter Carroll / First Light / Alamy Images
Back Cover Photo: Oregon, Willamette Valley: Autumn vineyards on the Red Hills ©Steve Terrill /
Jaynes Gallery / DanitaDelimont.com

For information on our other products and services or to obtain technical support, please contact our
Customer Care Department within the U.S. at 877/762-2974, outside the U.S. at 317/572-3993 or fax
317/572-4002.

Wiley also publishes its books in a variety of electronic formats. Some content that appears in print may
not be available in electronic formats.

Manufactured in the United States of America

5 4 3 2 1

CONTENTS

LIST OF MAPS

ABOUT THE AUTHOR

Karl Samson lives in Oregon, where he spends his time juggling his obsessions with traveling, gardening, outdoor sports, and wine. Each winter, to dry out his webbed feet, he flees the soggy Northwest and heads to Arizona, where he updates *Frommer's Arizona & the Grand Canyon*. Karl is also the author of *Frommer's Seattle* and *Frommer's Washington State*.

HOW TO CONTACT US

In researching this book, we discovered many wonderful places—hotels, restaurants, shops, and more. We're sure you'll find others. Please tell us about them, so we can share the information with your fellow travelers in upcoming editions. If you were disappointed with a recommendation, we'd love to know that, too. Please write to:

Frommer's Oregon, 8th Edition
John Wiley & Sons, Inc. • 111 River St. • Hoboken, NJ 07030-5774
frommersfeedback@wiley.com

ADVISORY & DISCLAIMER

Travel information can change quickly and unexpectedly, and we strongly advise you to confirm important details locally before traveling, including information on visas, health and safety, traffic and transport, accommodations, shopping, and eating out. We also encourage you to stay alert while traveling and to remain aware of your surroundings. Avoid civil disturbances, and keep a close eye on cameras, purses, wallets, and other valuables.

While we have endeavored to ensure that the information contained within this guide is accurate and up-to-date at the time of publication, we make no representations or warranties with respect to the accuracy or completeness of the contents of this work and specifically disclaim all warranties, including without limitation warranties of fitness for a particular purpose. We accept no responsibility or liability for any inaccuracy or errors or omissions, or for any inconvenience, loss, damage, costs, or expenses of any nature whatsoever incurred or suffered by anyone as a result of any advice or information contained in this guide.

The inclusion of a company, organization, or website in this guide as a service provider and/or potential source of further information does not mean that we endorse them or the information they provide. Be aware that information provided through some websites may be unreliable and can change without notice. Neither the publisher nor author shall be liable for any damages arising herefrom.

FROMMER'S STAR RATINGS, ICONS & ABBREVIATIONS

Every hotel, restaurant, and attraction listing in this guide has been ranked for quality, value, service, amenities, and special features using a **star-rating system**. In country, state, and regional guides, we also rate towns and regions to help you narrow down your choices and budget your time accordingly. Hotels and restaurants are rated on a scale of zero (recommended) to three stars (exceptional). Attractions, shopping, nightlife, towns, and regions are rated according to the following scale: zero stars (recommended), one star (highly recommended), two stars (very highly recommended), and three stars (must-see).

In addition to the star-rating system, we also use **seven feature icons** that point you to the great deals, in-the-know advice, and unique experiences that separate travelers from tourists. Throughout the book, look for:

Special finds—those places only insiders know about

Fun facts—details that make travelers more informed and their trips more fun

Best bets for kids and advice for the whole family

Special moments—those experiences that memories are made of

Places or experiences not worth your time or money

Insider tips—great ways to save time and money

Great values—where to get the best deals

The following **abbreviations** are used for credit cards:

AE	American Express	DISC	Discover	V	Visa
DC	Diners Club	MC	MasterCard		

TRAVEL RESOURCES AT FROMMERS.COM

Frommer's travel resources don't end with this guide. Frommer's website, **www.frommers. com**, has travel information on more than 4,000 destinations. We update features regularly, giving you access to the most current trip-planning information and the best airfare, lodging, and car-rental bargains. You can also listen to podcasts, connect with other Frommers.com members through our active-reader forums, share your travel photos, read blogs from guidebook editors and fellow travelers, and much more.

THE BEST OF OREGON

To 19th-century pioneers, Oregon was the promised land, and things haven't changed much in the ensuing 150 years. Native Oregonians and recent transplants are both envisioning new ways to make the state a better place. Farmers are pioneering sustainable farms close to urban centers, while urban pioneers are eschewing cars in favor of bicycles. This innovative outlook also expresses itself as a protectiveness of farmlands and forests, mountains and beaches. Together people and landscape spell the good life here, and for visitors, it is these same factors that make Oregon a great vacation destination.

CITIES

Portland is Oregon's only major metropolitan area, but the city, with its compact downtown, extensive streetcar and light-rail network, and vibrant outlying neighborhoods, is frequently held up as a model of livability. In central Oregon, **Bend** has become a wealthy boomtown surrounded by natural attractions. In the southern Oregon city of **Ashland,** the Oregon Shakespeare Festival takes center stage, while in **Hood River,** the lively downtown is full of outdoors types who come for the windsurfing and kiteboarding.

COUNTRYSIDE

While the ocean waters of the **Oregon coast** may be too cold for swimming, you can hike its rugged headlands and scan the Pacific for gray whales. On **Mount Hood,** there are miles of mountain trails, as well as year-round skiing and snowboarding. The **Willamette Valley,** which separates the Coast Range from the Cascades, is home to some of the nation's top pinot noir wineries. Slicing through the Cascades, the **Columbia River Gorge,** sculpted by massive ancient floods, is a spectacular landscape of cliffs, waterfalls, and lush forests.

EATING & DRINKING

Fresh, local, organic, sustainable . . . these are more than just buzzwords in Oregon. Here, people walk their talk. Whether you're eating at a wine-country bistro, a beach-town fish-and-chips shack, a burger joint, or a food cart, you'll likely be told where and how the ingredients in your meal were produced. Accompany your meal with a local craft ale or a glass of Oregon pinot noir (either of which might be organic), and you'll have a sense of how obsessed Oregonians are with their food and drinks.

THE OREGON COAST

Stretching for 300 miles, Oregon's Pacific shore is one of the nation's most dramatic and varied coastlines. Rugged headlands, often crowned by historic lighthouses, separate sandy stretches of beach, and dense forests of giant trees rise directly from the crashing waves, imbuing this coastline with a sense of mystery. Take in the coast's scenic wonders in **Cannon Beach,** along the **Three Capes Scenic Loop,** in the **Oregon Dunes National Recreation Area,** and in the **Samuel H. Boardman State Scenic Corridor.**

THE best NATURAL ATTRACTIONS

- **The Oregon Coast:** Rocky headlands, offshore islands and haystack rocks, natural arches, caves full of sea lions, giant sand dunes, and dozens of state parks make this one of the most spectacular coastlines in the country. The only drawback is that the water is too cold for swimming. See chapter 6.

- **Columbia Gorge National Scenic Area:** Carved by ice-age floodwaters up to 1,200 feet deep, the Columbia Gorge is a unique feature of the Oregon landscape. Waterfalls by the dozen cascade from the basalt cliffs of the gorge, and highways on both the Washington and Oregon sides of the Columbia River provide countless memorable views. See p. 234.

- **Mount Hood:** As Oregon's tallest mountain and the closest Cascade peak to Portland, Mount Hood is a recreational mecca 12 months a year. Hiking trails, lakes and rivers, and year-round skiing make this one of the most appealing natural attractions in the state. See p. 255.

- **Crater Lake National Park:** At 1,932 feet deep, Crater Lake is the deepest lake in the United States, and its sapphire-blue waters are a bewitchingly beautiful sight when seen from the rim of the volcanic caldera that forms the lake. See p. 268.

- **Central Oregon Lava Lands:** Throughout central Oregon and the central Cascades region, from the lava fields of McKenzie Pass to the obsidian flows of Newberry National Volcanic Monument, you'll find dramatic examples of the volcanic activity that gave rise to the Cascade Range. See chapters 8 and 10.

- **Hells Canyon:** Deeper than the Grand Canyon, this massive gorge along the Oregon-Idaho border is remote and inaccessible, and that is just what makes it fascinating. You can gaze down into it from on high, float its waters, or hike its trails. See p. 344.

THE best OUTDOOR ACTIVITIES

- **Biking the Oregon Coast:** With U.S. 101 clinging to the edge of the continent for much of its route through Oregon, this road has become one of the most popular cycling routes in the Northwest. The entire coast can be done in about a week, but there are also plenty of short sections that make good day trips. See p. 171.

- **Windsurfing and Kiteboarding in Hood River:** Summer winds blast through the Columbia Gorge and whip up white-capped standing waves that have turned this area into the windsurfing and kiteboarding capital of the United States. People come from around the world to ride the river here. See p. 242.

- **Fly-Fishing for Steelhead on the North Umpqua River:** Made famous by Zane Grey, the North Umpqua is the quintessential steelhead river, and for part of its length it's open to fly-fishing only. The river and the elusive steelhead offer a legendary fishing experience. See p. 266.

- **Rafting the Rogue River:** Of all the state's white-water-rafting rivers, none is more famous than the Rogue. Meandering through remote wilderness in the southern part of the state, this river has been popular with anglers since the early 20th century for its beauty and great fishing. Today you can splash through roaring white water by day and spend your nights in remote lodges that are inaccessible by car. See p. 294.

- **Mountain Biking in Bend:** Outside the town of Bend, in central Oregon, dry ponderosa pine forests are laced with trails that are open to mountain bikes. Routes pass by several lakes, and along the way you'll get great views of the Three Sisters, Broken Top, and Mount Bachelor. See p. 320.

- **Skiing Mount Bachelor:** With ski slopes dropping off the very summit of this extinct volcano, Mount Bachelor, in central Oregon, is the state's premier ski area. Seemingly endless runs of all ability levels make this a magnet for skiers and snowboarders from around the state, and lots of high-speed quad chairs keep people on the snow instead of standing in line. See p. 318.

THE best BEACHES

- **Cannon Beach/Ecola State Park:** With the massive monolith of Haystack Rock rising up from the low-tide line and the secluded beaches of Ecola State Park just north of town, Cannon Beach offers all the best of the Oregon coast. See p. 173.

- **Oswald West State Park:** At this state park south of Cannon Beach, it's a 15-minute walk through the woods to the beach, which keeps the sand from ever getting too crowded. The crescent-shaped beach is on a secluded cove backed by dense forest. This also happens to be a popular surfing spot. See p. 175.

- **Sunset Bay State Park:** Almost completely surrounded by sandstone cliffs, this little beach near Coos Bay is on a shallow cove. The clear waters here get a little bit warmer than unprotected waters elsewhere on the coast, so it's sometimes possible to actually go swimming. See p. 216.

- **Bandon:** It's difficult to imagine a more picturesque stretch of coastline than the beach in Bandon. Haystack rocks rise up from sand and sea as if strewn there by some giant hand. Motels and houses front this scenic beach, which ensures its popularity no matter what the weather. See p. 219.

- **The Beaches of Samuel H. Boardman State Scenic Corridor:** Some of the prettiest, most secluded, and least visited beaches on the Oregon coast are within this remote south-coast state park. Ringed by rocky headlands, the many little crescents of sand in this park provide an opportunity to find *the* perfect beach. See p. 227.

THE best HIKES

- **Cape Lookout State Park Trail:** Leading 2.5 miles through dense forests to the tip of this rugged cape on the north Oregon coast, this trail ends high on a cliff above the waters of the Pacific. Far below, gray whales can often be seen lolling in the waves, and the view to the south takes in miles of coastline. See p. 186.

- **John Dellenback Dunes Trail:** If you've ever dreamed of joining the French Foreign Legion or simply want to play at being Lawrence of Arabia, then the Oregon Dunes National Recreation Area is the place for you. Within this vast expanse of sand dunes, you'll find the highest dunes on the Oregon coast—some 500 feet tall. See p. 212.

- **Eagle Creek Trail:** This trail in the Columbia Gorge follows the tumbling waters of Eagle Creek and passes two spectacular waterfalls in the first 2 miles. Along the way, the trail climbs up the steep gorge walls, and in places it is cut right into the basalt cliffs. See p. 237.

- **Timberline Trail:** As the name implies, this trail starts at the timberline, high on the slopes of Mount Hood. Because the route circles Mount Hood, you can start in either direction and make a day, overnight, or multiday hike of it. Paradise Park, its meadows ablaze with wildflowers in July and August, is a favorite for both day hikes and overnight trips. See p. 255.

- **McKenzie River Trail to Tamolitch Pool:** The McKenzie River Trail stretches for 26 miles along the banks of this aquamarine river, but by far the most rewarding stretch of trail is the 2-mile hike to Tamolitch Pool, an astounding pool of turquoise waters formed as the McKenzie River wells up out of the ground after flowing underground for several miles. The trail leads through rugged, overgrown lava fields. See p. 262.

- **Deschutes River Trail:** The Deschutes River, which flows down from the east side of the Cascades, passes through open ponderosa pine forest to the west of Bend. This easy trail parallels the river and passes tumultuous waterfalls along the way. See p. 319.

THE best SCENIC DRIVES

- **Gold Beach to Brookings:** No other stretch of U.S. 101 along the Oregon coast is more breathtaking than the segment between Gold Beach and Brookings. This remote coastline is dotted with offshore islands, natural rock arches, sea caves, bluffs, and beaches. Take your time, stop at the many pull-offs, and make this a leisurely all-day drive. See p. 226.

- **Historic Columbia River Highway:** Built between 1914 and 1926 to allow automobiles access to the wonders of the Columbia Gorge, this narrow, winding highway east of Portland climbs up to the top of the gorge for a scenic vista before diving into forests where waterfalls, including the tallest one in the state, pour off of basalt cliffs. See p. 235.

- **The Santiam and McKenzie Pass Route:** This loop drive, which crosses the Cascade crest twice, takes in views of half a dozen major Cascade peaks, negotiates a bizarre landscape of lava fields, passes several waterfalls, and skirts aptly named Clear Lake, the source of the McKenzie River. This is one of the best drives in the state for fall color. See p. 260.

- **Crater Lake Rim Drive:** This scenic drive circles the rim of the massive caldera that holds Crater Lake. Along the way are numerous pull-offs where you can admire the sapphire-blue waters and the ever-changing scenery. See p. 269.

- **Cascade Lakes Highway:** This road covers roughly 100 miles as it loops out from Bend along the eastern slope of the Cascades. Views of Broken Top and the

Three Sisters are frequent, and along the way are numerous lakes, both large and small. See p. 320.

THE best MUSEUMS

- **Portland Art Museum:** The Portland Art Museum has an outstanding wing dedicated to contemporary and modern art. The museum also has respectable collections of Native American artifacts and Northwest contemporary art. See p. 88.
- **Evergreen Aviation & Space Museum** (McMinnville): Looking like a cross between a gigantic airplane hangar and a huge barn, this museum is home to Howard Hughes's "Spruce Goose," the largest wooden plane ever built. There are also plenty of smaller planes on display to provide a little perspective for this behemoth of the air. See p. 126.
- **Hallie Ford Museum of Art** (Salem): While this museum's large collection of Native American baskets is a highlight, there are also exhibits of Asian and European art, as well as exhibits of contemporary art. See p. 137.
- **Columbia River Maritime Museum** (Astoria): Located near the mouth of the Columbia River, this large museum has fascinating exhibits on the Coast Guard and the dangerous waters at the mouth of the river. See p. 164.
- **Favell Museum of Western Art and Indian Artifacts** (Klamath Falls): This museum houses an overwhelming assortment of Native American artifacts, including thousands of arrowheads, spear points, and other stone tools. See p. 272.
- **The Museum at Warm Springs** (Warm Springs Reservation): Set in a remote valley in central Oregon, this museum houses an outstanding collection of artifacts from the area's Native American tribes. See p. 307.
- **National Historic Oregon Trail Interpretive Center** (Baker City): The lives of 19th-century pioneers, who gave up everything to venture overland to the Pacific Northwest, are documented at this evocative museum. Set atop a hill in sagebrush country, the museum overlooks wagon ruts left by pioneers. See p. 333.

THE best FAMILY ATTRACTIONS

- **Oregon Museum of Science and Industry** (Portland): With an OMNIMAX theater, a planetarium, a submarine, and loads of hands-on exhibits, this Portland museum is fun for kids and adults alike. See p. 90.
- **Evergreen Wings & Waves Waterpark** (McMinnville): With water slides that start inside a Boeing 747 that sits on the roof of the waterpark building, this is not your average water park. In addition to all the water slides and the wave pool, there's a water museum.
- **Oregon Coast Aquarium** (Newport): This is the biggest attraction on the Oregon coast, and justly so. Tufted puffins and sea otters are always entertaining, while tide pools, jellyfish tanks, sharks, and a giant octopus also contribute to the appeal of this very realistically designed public aquarium. See p. 199.
- **Sea Lion Caves** (north of Florence): This massive cave, the largest sea cave in the country, is home to hundreds of Steller sea lions that lounge on the rocks beneath busy U.S. 101. See p. 209.

- **West Coast Game Park Safari** (Bandon): The opportunity to pet baby wild animals, including leopards and bears, doesn't come often, so it's hard to pass up this roadside attraction on the southern Oregon coast. See p. 220.
- **Wildlife Safari** (Winston): Giraffes peer in your window and rhinoceroses thunder past your car doors as you drive the family through this expansive wildlife park. The savanna-like setting is reminiscent of the African plains. See p. 301.
- **The High Desert Museum** (Bend): With its popular live-animal exhibits, this is more a zoo than a museum, but exhibits also offer glimpses into the history of the vast and little-known high desert that stretches from the Cascades eastward to the Rocky Mountains. See p. 316.

THE best FAMILY ACTIVITIES

- **Mt. Hood Adventure Park at Skibowl** (Mount Hood): Bungee jumping, zip lines, ski-lift-serviced downhill mountain biking, and an alpine slide (a sort of summertime bobsled) keep the kids thrilled at this summertime action park at Mount Hood's Skibowl ski area. See p. 256.
- **Feeding a Herd of Elk** (near Cannon Beach): Although the elk feedings at Jewell Meadows Wildlife Area only take place in the winter (and it isn't easy to get a reservation to participate), this is an unforgettable experience for the whole family. See p. 180.
- **Go Fly a Kite** (Lincoln City): The waters along the Oregon coast may be too cold and rough for swimming, but the winds that blow almost constantly along the beach are perfect for kite flying. Lincoln City's long stretches of beach make this one of the state's top kite-flying spots. See p. 189.
- **Oregon Dunes National Recreation Area** (Florence): With Sahara-size sand dunes that can be explored on dune-buggy rides, miles of hiking trails and unspoiled beaches, plus sandboarding (sort of like summertime snowboarding), this unusual area of giant shifting sand dunes is a fascinating place to explore with the kids. See p. 210.
- **Jetboating on the Rogue River** (Gold Beach and Grants Pass): In both Grants Pass and Gold Beach, large, shallow-draft jetboats take people roaring over rapids and shallow stretches of the river that seemingly couldn't float a toy boat. Tours out of Gold Beach sometimes pass bears along the river banks. See p. 225 and p. 294.
- **Rafting the Deschutes River** (Bend): Whether it's a quick splash-and-giggle trip down the Big Eddy run just outside Bend or a longer and more serious river trip on the lower Deschutes River, this central Oregon river is the state's premier whitewater-rafting river. See p. 252.

THE best HISTORICAL SITES

- **Lewis and Clark National Historical Park** (Astoria): This national park comprises numerous historic sites that explorers Lewis and Clark utilized during the winter of 1805–06. The sites are located around the mouth of the Columbia River. During the summer, costumed interpreters bring the history of Fort Clatsop, the explorers' winter home, to life. See p. 164.
- **Jacksonville:** With more than 80 buildings listed on the National Register of Historic Places, this 19th-century gold-mining town is the best preserved historic

community in Oregon. Here you'll also find two inns housed in buildings constructed in 1861, which makes these some of Oregon's oldest buildings being used as inns. See p. 287.

o **Oregon Trail Wagon Ruts** (Baker City): It's hard to believe that something as seemingly ephemeral as a wagon rut can last more than 150 years, but the path made by the thousands of pioneers who followed the Oregon Trail cut deep into the land. One place you can see ruts is near Baker City's National Historic Oregon Trail Interpretive Center. See p. 333.

o **Kam Wah Chung State Heritage Site** (John Day): This unusual little museum is way off the beaten path but is well worth a visit if you're anywhere in the vicinity. The museum preserves the home, office, and apothecary of a Chinese doctor who ministered to the local Chinese community in the early part of the 20th century. See p. 338.

THE best HOTELS FOR FAMILIES

o **Embassy Suites** (Portland; © 800/362-2779 or 503/279-9000): Unlike most other Embassy Suites, this is a historic hotel, but it still has those spacious suites that are great for families. Plus, there's a pool and video arcade down in the basement. See p. 58.

o **Hallmark Resort** (Cannon Beach; © 888/448-4449 or 503/436-1566): Set on a bluff with a great view of Cannon Beach's famous Haystack Rock, this is just about the most family-oriented hotel in town. There are two indoor pools. See p. 178.

o **Lake of the Woods Resort** (Klamath Falls; © 866/201-4194 or 541/949-8300): This old-fashioned lakefront lodge in the southern Oregon Cascades is a bit like a summer camp for the whole family. There's great swimming, and you can rent boats and mountain bikes. See p. 273.

o **Kah-Nee-Ta High Desert Resort & Casino** (Warm Springs; © 800/554-4786 or 541/553-1112): This remote resort is centered around a huge warm-springs-fed swimming pool that is a major magnet for vacationing families. You can also go kayaking and horseback riding. See p. 309.

o **Black Butte Ranch** (Sisters; © 866/901-2961 or 541/595-1252): With stunning views of the Three Sisters peaks, this central Oregon resort has a solid feel of being in the mountains. Five pools, a lake, horseback-riding stables, and bike paths provide plenty of options for keeping the kids entertained. See p. 312.

o **Seventh Mountain Resort** (© 877/765-1501 or 541/382-8711): Although this resort is close to the Mount Bachelor ski area and has an ice-skating rink in the winter, it is most popular with families in the summer, when kids flock to the pools and children's programs give parents some free time. See p. 323.

o **Sunriver Lodge & Resort** (Sunriver; © 800/801-8765): This resort south of Bend in Oregon's high desert is popular with families for its many miles of bike trails that meander through pine forests. There are also swimming pools, riding stables, and canoes and kayaks for rent on the gentle waters of the Deschutes River. See p. 324.

THE best B&BS

- **Portland's White House** (Portland; ✆ 800/272-7131 or 503/287-7131): From the circular drive to the portico reminiscent of that other White House to the grand foyer and spacious guest rooms, everything about this inn is impressive. Who needs a presidential suite when you can have the whole house? See p. 65.

- **Black Walnut Inn** (Dundee; ✆ 866/429-4114 or 503/429-4114): Set high in the hills above Dundee, this inn is designed to resemble a Tuscan villa and is a luxurious retreat amid wine-country vineyards. See p. 129.

- **Abbey Road Farm** (Carlton; ✆ 503/852-6278): This fantasy farm in the middle of wine country has the most unusual B&B building I've ever seen. The inn is a collection of metal farm silos that have been converted into one of the prettiest and most luxurious inns in the state. See p. 130.

- **Arch Cape Inn and Retreat** (Cannon Beach; ✆ 800/436-2848 or 503/436-2800): Designed to resemble a French château, this B&B may seem oddly out of place on the Oregon coast, but no one staying here seems to mind. It could be the huge guest rooms and castlelike ambience, or it could be the abundance of European antiques and original art. See p. 176.

- **Channel House** (Depoe Bay; ✆ 800/447-2140 or 541/765-2140): Situated on the cliff above the narrow channel into tiny Depoe Bay, this B&B offers one of the most striking settings on the Oregon coast. The contemporary design includes guest rooms made for romance—a hot tub on the balcony, a fireplace, and an unsurpassed view out the windows. See p. 196.

- **Heceta Head Lightstation** (Yachats; ✆ 866/547-3696 or 541/547-3696): Ever dreamed of staying at a lighthouse? Well, on the Oregon coast, your dream can come true at this former lighthouse keeper's home. The Victorian B&B, which claims one of the most spectacular locations on the entire coast, is set high on a hill above the crashing waves. See p. 207.

- **Ashland Mountain House B&B** (✆ 866/899-2744 or 541/482-2744): In a building that was constructed in 1852 and was once a stagecoach stop, this country inn is rich in details and preserves a fascinating piece of southern Oregon history. See p. 281.

THE best SMALL INNS & LODGES

- **Cannery Pier Hotel** (Astoria; ✆ 888/325-4996 or 503/325-4996): Located on a pier 600 feet out in the Columbia River, this luxury hotel fits in perfectly on the Astoria waterfront and looks as if it actually could have been a cannery at one time. See p. 167.

- **Stephanie Inn** (Cannon Beach; ✆ 800/633-3466 or 503/436-2221): Combining the look of a mountain lodge with a beachfront setting in Oregon's most artistic town, the Stephanie Inn is a romantic retreat that surrounds its guests with unpretentious luxury. See p. 177.

- **Coast Cabins** (Manzanita; ✆ 503/368-7113): Although not actually an inn or a lodge, this collection of five modern cottages is so thoroughly enchanting that I have to include it here. Beautiful perennial gardens surround the cottages. See p. 182.

- **Whale Cove Inn** (Depoe Bay; ✆ **800/628-3409** or 541/765-4300): Quite simply, nowhere else on the Oregon coast is there another hotel as luxurious and sophisticated as this. That it also has what might be the best view of any coastal hotel is just icing on the cake. See p. 197.

- **Tu Tu Tun Lodge** (Gold Beach; ✆ **800/864-6357** or 541/247-6664): Though some might think of this as a fishing lodge, it's far too luxurious for anglers to keep to themselves. A secluded setting on the lower Rogue River guarantees tranquillity, and choice guest rooms provide the perfect setting for forgetting about your everyday stresses. See p. 229.

- **Crater Lake Lodge** (Crater Lake National Park; ✆ **888/774-2728** or 541/594-2255): Perched on the rim of the caldera (not crater) that holds the blue waters of Crater Lake, this mountain lodge isn't actually a historic hotel, but it incorporates details from the original lodge that used to stand on this same site. The setting is breathtaking. See p. 270.

- **The Winchester Inn** (Ashland; ✆ **800/972-4991** or 541/488-1113): Located only 2 blocks from the theaters of the Oregon Shakespeare Festival, this place has the feel of a country inn although it's located right in town. Rooms are in three different buildings, including a modern Victorian cottage. See p. 283.

- **FivePine Lodge & Conference Center** (Sisters; ✆ **866/974-5900** or 541/549-5900): This collection of modern Craftsman-style cottages is set in the shade of ponderosa pines on the edge of Sisters. You'll find a spa, athletic club, movie theater, brewpub, and restaurant on the grounds. See p. 313.

- **The Lodge at Suttle Lake** (✆ **541/595-2628**): There simply is no more luxurious and enjoyable lakeside lodge in the state of Oregon. Grand log beams combine with modern creature comforts to create a mountain lodge worth seeking out. See p. 313.

THE best HISTORIC HOTELS & LODGES

- **The Benson** (Portland; ✆ **800/663-1144** or 503/228-2000): With its crystal chandeliers, walnut paneling, and ornate plasterwork ceiling in the lobby, this 1912 vintage hotel is Portland's most elegant lodging. See p. 58.

- **Hotel Elliott** (Astoria; ✆ **877/378-1924** or 503/325-2222): Originally opened in 1924, this hotel retains much of its original character, but now features lots of modern touches and contemporary styling. When it's time to relax, you'll have to choose between the rooftop garden and the cellar wine bar. See p. 167.

- **Columbia Gorge Hotel** (Hood River; ✆ **800/345-1921** or 541/386-5566): Opened in 1921 to handle the first automobile traffic up the Columbia Gorge, this Mission-style hotel commands a stunning view across the gorge and is surrounded by colorful gardens. See p. 246.

- **Timberline Lodge** (Mount Hood; ✆ **800/547-1406** or 503/272-3311): Built by the WPA during the Great Depression, this stately mountain lodge with a grand stone fireplace, exposed beams, and wide-plank floors showcases the skills of the craftspeople who created it. See p. 258.

- **Ashland Springs Hotel** (Ashland; ✆ **888/795-4545** or 541/488-1700): This historic high-rise hotel was originally built to cash in on Ashland's mineral springs, but today it is, instead, a superb choice for anyone attending the Oregon Shake-speare Festival. See p. 281.

o **Geiser Grand Hotel** (Baker City; ✆ **888/434-7374** or 541/523-1889): Originally opened in 1889 at the height of the Blue Mountains gold rush, this Baker City grand dame succeeds in capturing the feel of a Wild West luxury hotel without sacrificing any modern conveniences. See p. 337.

THE best DINING
WITH A VIEW

o **Chart House** (Portland; ✆ **503/246-6963**): Perched high on a hillside, this restaurant boasts the best view of any restaurant in Portland. The Willamette River is directly below, and off in the distance stand Mount Hood and Mount St. Helens. See p. 75.

o **Roseanna's Oceanside Cafe** (Oceanside; ✆ **503/842-7351**): You can expect a long wait to get a table here on a summer weekend, but the view of the haystack rocks just offshore makes this place an absolute legend on the Three Capes Scenic Loop. See p. 187.

o **Pelican Pub & Brewery** (Pacific City; ✆ **503/965-7007**): Creative pub food and good microbrews are usually enough to keep an Oregon brewpub packed, but this one also is right on the beach and has a head-on view of Pacific City's Haystack Rock. See p. 187.

o **Beck** (Depoe Bay; ✆ **503/765-3220**): With windows that look out to Whale Cove, one of the prettiest little coves on the Oregon coast, this stylish, modern restaurant is a foodie's dream come true—highly creative cuisine and a view to match. Sunset dinners are unforgettable. See p. 197.

o **Tidal Raves** (Depoe Bay; ✆ **541/765-2995**): When the surf's up, you can practically forget about getting a table at this oceanfront restaurant. The windows overlook a rugged shoreline known for putting on some of the coast's best displays of crashing waves. See p. 198.

o **Saffron Salmon** (Newport; ✆ **541/265-8921**): As you dine at this restaurant at the end of a short pier on the Newport bayfront, keep an eye out for sea lions and fishermen unloading their catch. See p. 204.

o **Lord Bennett's Restaurant and Lounge** (Bandon; ✆ **541/347-3663**): The beach in Bandon is strewn with dozens of huge monoliths that make this one of the most impressive stretches of shoreline in the state, and this restaurant has the perfect view for enjoying sunset over the sand, surf, and giant rocks. See p. 223.

o **Redfish** (Port Orford; ✆ **541/366-2200**): A glass-walled jewel box of a restaurant with some of the best food on the Oregon coast, Redfish sits high on a bluff with a view of both the beach and Battle Rock. See p. 230.

o **Multnomah Falls Lodge** (Columbia Gorge; ✆ **503/695-2376**): This historic lodge is at the base of Oregon's tallest waterfall, and although not every table has a view of the waterfall, there are plenty that do, especially in the summer when there is outside seating. See p. 241.

THE best OFF-THE-BEATEN-PATH RESTAURANTS

- **The Joel Palmer House** (Dayton; ☏ **503/864-2995**): Mushrooms are the chef's obsession at this wine-country restaurant, and you'll find them in almost every dish on the menu. The restaurant is quite formal, housed in an immaculately restored old home. See p. 133.
- **Nora's Table** (Hood River; ☏ **541/387-4000**): In a tiny basement restaurant on a Hood River side street, you'll find some of the most creative food in Oregon. The setting is casual, and the eclectic menu ranges from India to Mexico. See p. 248.
- **Cascade Dining Room** (Mount Hood; ☏ **503/272-3391**): Located inside the historic Timberline Lodge, the Cascade Dining Room is Oregon's premier mountain-lodge restaurant and has long kept skiers and other hotel guests happy. See p. 259.
- **New Sammy's Cowboy Bistro** (Ashland; ☏ **541/535-2779**): Long a hidden gem of the southern Oregon restaurant scene, this roadside bastion of culinary creativity serves meals driven by fresh produce from the restaurant's garden. The chef/owners started out in Napa Valley before moving north to Oregon. See p. 285.
- **Jen's Garden** (Sisters; ☏ **541/549-2699**): This little cottage in the central Oregon faux cowtown of Sisters is one of the best reasons to stay here in the area. With superb food and exquisite wines, dinner here is unforgettable. See p. 314.
- **Kokanee Cafe** (Camp Sherman; ☏ **541/595-6420**): Located amid the ponderosa pines on the banks of the Metolius River, near the Western theme town of Sisters, this rustic restaurant has the look of an upscale fishing lodge, but its clientele is much broader than just the fly anglers who come to test the waters of the Metolius. The trout is, of course, always a good bet. See p. 314.

THE best WINERIES

- **Archery Summit** (☏ **503/864-4300**): Big wines with a big reputation are produced from estate-grown pinot noir grapes at this impressive facility in the Dundee Hills. Pinot noir is the only wine they produce here. See p. 118.
- **Domaine Drouhin Oregon** (☏ **503/864-2700**): When a French winery starts making pinot noir in Oregon, you know it must be a good climate for wine. Certain vintages of Domaine Drouhin's Laurène pinot noir have been among the best pinots I've ever tasted. See p. 119.
- **Domaine Serene** (☏ **866/864-6555** or 503/864-4600): Producing pinot noir, chardonnay, and Syrah, this winery high in the Red Hills above Dundee is reliably consistent. See p. 119.
- **Lenné Estate** (☏ **503/956-2256**): If you've ever been to Tuscany or dreamed of going, this winery outside Yamhill is an absolute must. The stone-walled tasting room building seems lifted right from the hills of Chianti, and the estate-grown pinot noirs are excellent. See p. 122.
- **WillaKenzie Estate** (☏ **888/953-9463** or 503/662-3280): This 420-acre estate has more than 100 acres of grapevines and produces exclusively estate-grown wines. The hilltop setting is spectacular. This is a good place to sample rarely produced gamay noir and pinot meunier wines. See p. 123.

- **Methven Family Vineyards** (© 503/868-7259): One of the prettiest vineyards in the Willamette Valley surrounds the impressive hilltop tasting room of this winery. The vineyard views are spectacular. Look for well-balanced Riesling and exceptional reserve pinot noir. See p. 125.

- **Van Duzer Vineyards** (© 800/884-1927): Set high on a hilltop west of Salem and with a commanding 180-degree view, Van Duzer boasts one of the most magnificent settings in the Willamette Valley. The winery produces several different pinot noirs each vintage and even does a port-style wine. See p. 142.

- **King Estate Winery** (© 541/942-9874): Set amid 470 acres of organic vineyards, King Estate is one of the largest wineries in Oregon and boasts the most impressive and expansive setting. With an on-site restaurant, scheduled tours, and a wide selection of wines available for tasting, this winery is a superb introduction to Oregon wines. See p. 155.

- **Sarver Winery** (© 541/935-2979): This little Eugene-area winery is a hidden gem. Set on a vineyard that was planted in 1984, Sarver produces not only the expected pinot noir and pinot gris (from estate-grown grapes), but also Syrah made from Yakima Valley grapes. See p. 155.

- **Abacela** (© 541/679-6642): Set in the warm hills of southern Oregon's Umpqua Valley, the Abacela specializes in tempranillo, which it does in a variety of styles. Here you'll also find grenache, dolcetto, and malbec, all wines that are rarely produced in Oregon. See p. 301.

OREGON IN DEPTH

You've probably already heard the jokes: Oregonians have webbed feet and they don't tan, they rust. Even people otherwise unfamiliar with Oregon seem to know that it rains a lot here. There's simply no getting around the fact that few states receive as much rain or cloudy weather as Oregon (except Washington, Oregon's northern neighbor). You would think, then, that those infamous rains, which fall regularly for 8 months every year, would keep people away from Oregon. They don't. Why, then, is this state wedged between California and Washington such a popular destination?

It could be for the same reasons that early pioneers were willing to walk all the way across the continent to get here—the summers. The seductiveness of summer in Oregon is impossible to resist. Summer is a time of bounty, easily seen at farmers markets around the state and on the menus of restaurants that emphasize fresh, local, and organic cuisine. Strawberries, raspberries, blackberries, and blueberries ripen on Willamette Valley farms. Wineries release their rosés, Rieslings, and other summer sippers and patio wines. Wildflowers in mountain meadows burst into bloom. Beaches beckon along 300 miles of Pacific shoreline. Music festivals set up their outdoor stages. And in the evening, the sun doesn't go down until after 9 o'clock. Could it get any better?

OREGON TODAY

Although the recession hit Oregon a bit later than it hit many other states, Oregon fell hard when it finally did. By 2009, the state had one of the highest unemployment rates in the nation. Funny thing is, though, the high unemployment rate didn't stop people from moving to Oregon.

Portland, a city that has developed a reputation for being one of the hippest and most liberal cities on the West Coast, has been the main destination for most of the young creative types who have migrated to Oregon in recent years. The city's reputation for its youth culture has grown so large that the city has even been parodied on the IFC comedy network's series *Portlandia*.

Why would people continue moving to Oregon even when they know they won't be able to find a job? They move here for the same reason people many want to vacation here—the great outdoors. Oregon is a state dominated by those with a love of the outdoors, and this isn't surprising when you realize just how much nature dominates beyond the city limits.

From almost anywhere in Oregon, it's possible to look up and see green forests and snow-capped mountains, and a drive of less than 2 hours from any Willamette Valley city will get you to the mountains or the Pacific Ocean's beaches.

But what about all that rain? Well, Oregonians don't let the weather stand between them and the outdoors. The temptation is too great to head for the mountains, the river, or the beach—no matter the forecast. Consequently, life in Oregon's cities tends to revolve less around cultural venues and shopping than around parks, gardens, waterfronts, rivers, mountains, and beaches. Portland has its Forest Park, Rose Garden, Japanese Garden, Classical Chinese Garden, and Waterfront Park. Eugene has its miles of riverside parks, bike paths, and even a park just for rock climbing. In Hood River, the entire Columbia River has become a playground for windsurfers and kiteboarders, and when the wind doesn't blow, there are always the nearby mountain-bike trails and rivers for kayaking. In Bend, for example, mountain biking, downhill skiing, and snowboarding are a way of life. These outdoor areas are where people find tranquillity, where summer festivals are held, where locals take their visiting friends and relatives, and where Oregonians tend to live their lives when life isn't being interrupted by such inconveniences as work and sleep.

This is not to say, however, that the region is a cultural wasteland. Both Portland and Eugene have large, modern, and active performing-arts centers. During the summer months, numerous **festivals** take music, theater, and dance outdoors. Most impressive of these are southern Oregon's Britt Festivals and Oregon Shakespeare Festival. Many other festivals feature everything from chamber music to alternative rock.

Oregon has long had a reputation for being an environmentally aware state. Back in 1971 it was the first state to pass a bottle bill mandating a refundable deposit on beer and soft-drink cans and bottles. At about the same time, the state worked hard to clean up the heavily polluted Willamette River and passed legislation to protect its beautiful beaches. Today the state is trying to hold true to its 1970s ideals and identity, but the fact is that in the recent boom years prior to the collapse of the economy, rapid population growth and development began reshaping the core identity of the state.

As the population in urban areas of the Willamette Valley has expanded, a pronounced urban-rural political split has developed in Oregon. Citizens from the eastern part of the state argue that Salem and Portland are dictating to rural regions that have little in common with the cities, while urban dwellers, who far outnumber those living outside the Willamette Valley, argue that majority rule is majority rule. This split has pitted conservative voters (often from rural regions and the suburbs) against liberal voters (usually urban) on a wide variety of issues, and the reality of Oregon politics is now quite a bit different from the popular perception of a state dominated by liberal, forward-thinking environmentalists and former hippies. The growing urbanization of Portland, the state's population center, has led to a change in the focus of Oregon's political agendas. While the state remains a "blue" state, electing Democrats to many of the highest political offices, the state's political battles are no longer as focused on the environment as they once were.

While the environment is no longer at the political forefront, the state is not without its controversial political battles. In 1994, Oregon became the first state to legalize physician-assisted suicide. In 1998 the state passed the Oregon Medical Marijuana Act, which made it legal for people with a medical prescription to grow and possess marijuana. In 2004, Multnomah County, which is where Portland, Oregon's largest city, is located, began issuing marriage licenses to same-sex couples. Although the county soon reversed this policy, the state, in 2008, passed the Oregon Family

Fairness Act, which made it possible for same-sex couples to legally establish a domestic partnership.

LOOKING BACK: OREGON HISTORY

Early History

The oldest known inhabitants of what is now the state of Oregon lived along the shores of huge lakes in the Klamath Lakes Basin some 10,000 years ago. Here they fished and hunted ducks and left records of their passing in several caves. These people would have witnessed the massive eruption of Mount Mazama, which left a vast caldera that eventually filled with water and was named Crater Lake. Along the coast, numerous small tribes subsisted on salmon and shellfish. In the northeast corner of the state, the Nez Perce tribe became expert at horse breeding even before Lewis and Clark passed through the region at the start of the 19th century. In fact, the appaloosa horse derives its name from the nearby Palouse Hills of Washington.

However, it was the **Columbia River tribes** that became the richest of the Oregon tribes through their control of Celilo Falls, which was historically the richest salmon-fishing area in the Northwest. These massive falls on the Columbia River, east of present-day The Dalles, witnessed the annual passage of millions of salmon, which were speared and dipnetted by Native Americans, who then smoked the fish to preserve it for the winter. Today, Native Americans sometimes still fish for salmon as they once did, perched on precarious wooden platforms with dip nets in hand. However, Celilo Falls are gone, inundated by the water impounded behind The Dalles Dam, which was completed in 1957. Today little remains of what was once the Northwest's most important Native American gathering ground, a place where tribes from hundreds of miles away congregated every year to fish and trade.

Even before this amazing fishing ground was lost, a far greater tragedy had been visited upon Northwest tribes. Between the 1780s, when white explorers and traders began frequenting the Northwest coast, and the 1830s, when the first settlers began arriving, the Native American population of the Northwest was reduced to perhaps a tenth of its historic numbers. These people were not killed off by warfare but by European diseases—smallpox, measles, malaria, and influenza. The Native Americans had no resistance to these diseases, and entire tribes were soon wiped out by fast-spreading epidemics.

The Age of Exploration

Though a Spanish ship reached what is now southern Oregon in 1542, the Spanish had no interest in the gray and rainy coast. Nor did famed British buccaneer Sir Francis Drake, who in 1579 sailed his ship the *Golden Hind* as far north as the mouth of the Rogue River. Drake called off his explorations in the face of what he described as "thicke and stinking fogges."

However, when the Spanish found out that Russian fur traders dealing in sea-otter pelts had established themselves in Alaska and along the North Pacific coast, Spain took a new interest in the Northwest. Several **Spanish expeditions** sailed north from Mexico to reassert the Spanish claim to the region. In 1775, Spanish explorers Bruno de Heceta and Francisco de la Bodega y Quadra charted much of the Northwest coast, and though they found the mouth of the Columbia River, they did not

Did You Know?

- Oregon was home to America's first policewoman, Lola Greene Baldwin, who joined the Portland force in 1908.
- Portland is the site of the world's smallest dedicated park—Mill Ends Park—measuring only 24 inches in diameter.
- Oregon is one of the few states with no sales tax.

- The chanterelle is the official state mushroom and the hazelnut is the official state nut.
- Astoria, in the very northwest corner of the state, is the oldest American community west of the Mississippi.
- Oregon's Crater Lake is the deepest lake in the U.S.
- Hells Canyon is the deepest gorge in North America.

enter it. To this day, four of the coast's most scenic headlands—Cape Perpetua, Heceta Head, Cape Arago, and Cape Blanco—bear names from these early Spanish explorations.

It was not until 1792 that American trader and explorer Robert Gray risked a passage through the treacherous sandbars that guarded the mouth of the long-speculated-upon Great River of the West. Gray named this newfound river Columbia's River, in honor of his ship, the *Columbia Rediviva*. This discovery established the first American claim to the region. When news of the *Columbia's* discovery reached the United States and England, both countries began speculating on a northern water route across North America. Such a route, if it existed, would facilitate trade with the Northwest.

In 1793, Scotsman Alexander MacKenzie made the first overland trip across North America north of New Spain. Crossing British Canada on foot, MacKenzie arrived somewhere north of Vancouver Island. After reading MacKenzie's account of his journey, Thomas Jefferson decided that the United States needed to find a better route overland to the Northwest. To this end, he commissioned Meriwether Lewis and William Clark to lead an expedition up the Missouri River in hopes of finding a single easy portage that would lead to the Columbia River.

Beginning in 1804, the members of the **Lewis and Clark expedition** paddled up the Missouri, crossed the Rocky Mountains on foot, and then paddled down the Columbia River to its mouth. A French-Canadian trapper and his Native American wife, Sacagawea, were enlisted as interpreters, and it was probably the presence of Sacagawea that helped the expedition gain acceptance among Western tribes. After spending the wet and dismal winter of 1805–06 at the mouth of the Columbia at a spot they named **Fort Clatsop,** the expedition headed back east. Discoveries made by the expedition added greatly to the scientific and geographical knowledge of the continent. A replica of Fort Clatsop in the Lewis and Clark National Historical Park is one of the most interesting historical sites in the state. Outside of The Dalles, a campsite used by Lewis and Clark has also been preserved.

In 1819, the Spanish relinquished all claims north of the present California-Oregon state line, and the Russians gave up their claims to all lands south of Alaska. This left only the British and Americans dickering for control of the Northwest.

Fur Traders, Missionaries & the Oregon Trail

Only 6 years after Lewis and Clark spent the winter at the mouth of the Columbia, employees of John Jacob Astor's Pacific Fur Company managed to establish themselves at a nearby spot they called **Fort Astoria.** This was the first permanent settlement in the Northwest, but with the War of 1812 being fought on the far side of the continent, the fur traders at Fort Astoria, with little protection against the British, chose to relinquish control of their fort. In the wake of the war, the fort returned to American control, though the United States and Britain had not yet arrived at a firm decision regarding possession of the Northwest. The British still dominated the region, but American trade was tolerated.

The late-18th-century and early-19th-century traders who had come to the Northwest in search of sea otter pelts to sell in China quickly depleted the otter population, and British fur traders turned to beaver and headed inland up the Columbia River. For the next 30 years or so, fur-trading companies would be the sole authority in the region. Fur-trading posts were established throughout the Northwest, though most were on the eastern edge of the territory in the foothills of the Rocky Mountains. The powerful Hudson's Bay Company (HBC) eventually became the single fur-trading company in the Northwest.

In 1824 the HBC established its Northwest headquarters at **Fort Vancouver,** 100 miles up the Columbia near the mouth of the Willamette River, and in 1829 the HBC founded **Oregon City** at the falls of the Willamette River. Between 1824 and 1846, when the 49th parallel was established as the boundary between British and American northwestern lands, Fort Vancouver was the most important settlement in the region. A replica of the fort now stands in the city of Vancouver, Washington, across the Columbia River from Portland. In Oregon City, several homes from this period are still standing, including that of John McLoughlin, who was chief factor at Fort Vancouver and aided many of the early pioneers who arrived in the area after traveling the Oregon Trail.

By the 1830s, the future of the Northwest had arrived in the form of **American missionaries.** The first was Jason Lee, who established his mission in the Willamette Valley near present-day Salem. (Today the site is Willamette Mission State Park.) Two years later, in 1836, Marcus and Narcissa Whitman, along with Henry and Eliza Spaulding, made the overland trek to Fort Vancouver, and then backtracked into what is now eastern Washington and Idaho, to establish two missions. This journey soon inspired other settlers to make the difficult overland crossing.

In 1840, a slow trickle of American settlers began crossing the continent, a 2,000-mile journey. Their destination was the Oregon country, which had been promoted as a veritable Eden where land was waiting to be claimed. In 1843, Marcus Whitman, after traveling east to plead with his superiors not to shut down his mission, headed back west, leading 900 settlers on the **Oregon Trail.** Before these settlers ever arrived, the small population of retired trappers, missionaries, and HBC employees who were living at Fort Vancouver and in nearby Oregon City had formed a provisional government in anticipation of the land-claim problems that would arise with the influx of settlers to the region. Today the best place to learn about the experiences of the Oregon Trail emigrants is at the Oregon Trail Interpretive Center outside Baker City. In many places in the eastern part of the state, **Oregon Trail wagon ruts** can still be seen.

The Graveyard of the Pacific

Because of the many shipwrecks that have occurred over the years, the waters off the Oregon coast, near the mouth of the Columbia River, are known as "the graveyard of the Pacific." In Fort Stevens State Park, the rusting remains of the *Peter Iredale*, which ran aground in 1906, can still be seen. One ship- wreck even inadvertently led to the naming of an Oregon coast town: Cannon Beach takes its name from a cannon that washed ashore after the *U.S.S. Shark* sank in 1846. Two more cannons believed to have been from the *Shark* showed up on the same stretch of beach in 2008.

In 1844, Oregon City became the first incorporated town west of the Rocky Mountains. This outpost in the wilderness, a gateway to the fertile lands of the Willamette Valley, was the destination of the wagon trains that began traveling the Oregon Trail, every year bringing more and more settlers to the region. As the land in the Willamette Valley was claimed, settlers began fanning out to different regions of the Northwest so that during the late 1840s and early 1850s many new towns, including Portland, were founded.

Though the line between American and British land in the Northwest had been established in 1846 at the 49th parallel (the current U.S.-Canada border), Oregon was not given U.S. territorial status until 1848. It was the massacre of the missionaries at the Whitman mission in Walla Walla (now in Washington State) and the subsequent demand for territorial status and U.S. military protection that brought about the establishment of the first U.S. territory west of the Rockies.

The discovery of **gold** in eastern Oregon in 1860 set the stage for one of the saddest chapters in Northwest history. With miners pouring into eastern Oregon and Washington, conflicts with Native Americans over land were inevitable. Since 1805, when Lewis and Clark had first passed this way, the **Nez Perce tribe** (the name means "pierced nose" in French) had been friendly to the white settlers. However, in 1877, a disputed treaty caused friction. Led by Chief Joseph, 700 Nez Perce, including 400 women and children, began a march from their homeland to their new reservation. Along the way, several Nez Perce, in revenge for the murder of an older member of the tribe, attacked a white settlement and killed several people. The U.S. Army took up pursuit of the Nez Perce, who fled across Idaho and Montana, only to be caught 40 miles from the Canadian border and sanctuary.

Industrialization & the 20th Century

From the very beginning of white settlement in the Northwest, the region based its growth on an extractive economy. **Lumber** and **salmon** were exploited ruthlessly. The history of the timber and salmon-fishing industries ran parallel for more than a century and led to similar results in the 1990s.

The trees in Oregon grew to gigantic proportions. Nurtured on steady rains, such trees as Douglas fir, Sitka spruce, Western red cedar, Port Orford cedar, and hemlock grew tall (as much as 300 ft.) and straight. The first sawmill in the Northwest began operation near present-day Vancouver, Washington, in 1828, and between the 1850s and the 1870s, Northwest sawmills supplied the growing California market as well as a limited foreign market. When the transcontinental railroads arrived in the 1880s, a whole new market opened up, and mills began shipping to the eastern states.

Lumber companies developed a cut-and-run policy that leveled the forests. By the turn of the century, the government had gained more control over public forests in an attempt to slow the decimation of forestlands, and sawmill owners began buying up huge tracts of land. At the outbreak of World War I, more than 20% of the forest-land in the Northwest was owned by three companies—Weyerhaeuser, the Northern Pacific Railroad, and the Southern Pacific Railroad—and more than 50% of the workforce labored in the timber industry.

The timber industry, which has always been extremely susceptible to fluctuations in the economy, experienced a roller-coaster ride of boom and bust throughout the 20th century. Boom times in the 1970s brought on record-breaking production that came to a screeching halt in the 1980s, first with a nationwide recession and then with the listing of the **Northern spotted owl** as a threatened species. When the timber industry was born in the Northwest, there was a belief that the forests of the region were endless. However, by the latter half of the 20th century, big lumber companies realized that the forests were dwindling. Tree farms were planted with increasing frequency, but the large old trees continued to be cut faster than younger trees could replenish them. By the 1970s, environmentalists, shocked by the vast clear-cuts, began trying to save the last **old-growth trees.** The battle between the timber industry and environmentalists is today still one of the state's most heated debates.

In the Northwest, salmon was the mainstay of the Native American diet for thousands of years before the first whites arrived in the Oregon country, but within 10 years of the opening of the first salmon cannery in the Northwest, the fish population was decimated. In 1877, the first fish hatchery was developed to replenish dwindling runs of salmon, and by 1895 salmon canning had reached its peak on the Columbia River. Later, in the 20th century, salmon runs would be further reduced by the construction of numerous dams on the Columbia and Snake rivers. Though fish ladders help adult salmon make their journeys upstream, the young salmon heading downstream have no such help, and the turbines of hydroelectric dams kill a large percentage of fish. One solution to this problem has been the barging and trucking of young salmon downriver. Today the **salmon populations** of the Northwest have been so diminished that entire runs of salmon have been listed as threatened or endangered under the Endangered Species Act. Talk in recent years has focused on the removal of certain dams that pose insurmountable barriers to salmon. However, there has been great resistance to this.

The dams that have proved such a detriment to salmon populations have provided irrigation water and cheap electricity that have fueled both industry and farming. Using irrigation water, potato and wheat farms flourished in northeastern Oregon after the mid-20th century. The reservoirs behind the Columbia River dams have also turned this river into a waterway that can be navigated by huge barges, which often carry wheat downriver from ports in Idaho. Today the **regional salmon recovery plan** is attempting to strike a balance between saving salmon runs and meeting all the other needs that have arisen since the construction of these dams.

Manufacturing began gaining importance during and after World War II. In the Portland area, the Kaiser Shipyards employed tens of thousands of people in the construction of warships, but the postwar years saw the demise of the Kaiser facilities. In the 1980s and 1990s, there was a diversification into **high-tech industries,** with such major manufacturers as Intel, Epson, and Hewlett-Packard operating manufacturing facilities in the Willamette Valley.

However, it is in the area of **sportswear manufacturing** that Oregon businesses have gained the greatest visibility. Outdoor recreation is a way of life in this state, so it comes as no surprise that a few regional companies have grown into international giants. Chief among these is Nike, which is headquartered in the Portland suburb of Beaverton. Other familiar names include Jantzen, one of the nation's oldest swimwear manufacturers; Pendleton Woolen Mills, maker of classic wool shirts, Indian-design blankets, and other classic wool fashions; and Columbia Sportswear, which in recent years has become one of the country's biggest sports-related outerwear manufacturers.

OREGON IN POP CULTURE

Books

HISTORY

Although it is more than 20 years old now, Timothy Egan's *The Good Rain,* which uses a long-forgotten Northwest explorer as the springboard for an examination of all the forces that have made the Northwest what it is today, is still one of the best introductions to Oregon and the rest of the Northwest. Some of the more interesting episodes in Oregon history are highlighted in *It Happened in Oregon,* by James A. Crutchfield.

Nineteenth-century explorers Meriwether Lewis and William Clark spent the winter of 1805–06 in present-day Oregon (and had a miserable time). *The Journals of Lewis and Clark* is a fascinating account of the difficult 1804 to 1806 journey across the continent, and it includes a wealth of observations on Native Americans and North American flora and fauna. David Freeman Hawke's *Those Tremendous Mountains: The Story of the Lewis and Clark Expedition* is a more readable form of the journals and also has a considerable amount of background information.

If you're interested in learning more about the Oregon wine industry, read Paul Pintarich's *Boys Up North: Dick Erath and the Early Oregon Wine Makers,* which chronicles the early years of contemporary Oregon wine making.

NATURAL HISTORY & THE OUTDOORS

If you're a hiker and want some great trail recommendations, pick up one of William Sullivan's many hiking guides. These include *100 Hikes/Travel Guide: Oregon Coast & Coast Range, 100 Hikes in Northwest Oregon & Southwest Washington, 100 Hikes in the Central Oregon Cascades, 100 Hikes in Southern Oregon,* and *100 Hikes/Travel Guide: Eastern Oregon.* If, en route to the great outdoors, you want to learn about the rocks by the side of the road, pick up a copy of *Roadside Geology of Oregon* by David Alt and Donald Hyndman. Want color photos to go with that geology information? Get a copy of *In Search of Ancient Oregon* by Ellen Morris Bishop. Many more gorgeous photos are to be found in the coffee-table picture books by photographer Ray Atkeson. Among his many books are *Oregon, Oregon II,* and *Oregon III.*

In his book *Voyage of a Summer Sun: Canoeing the Columbia River,* Robin Cody writes of his 1,200-mile canoe journey down the Columbia River from its source in the Canadian Rockies.

FICTION

Oregon has not inspired a great deal of fiction. The best-known work of Oregon fiction is probably Ken Kesey's *Sometimes a Great Notion,* which presents an evocative portrayal of a logging family. Kesey also set his novel *The Last Go Round* among the cowboys and bucking broncos of the Pendleton Round-Up, in 1911. The life of a 19th-century mountain man is the subject of Don Berry's *Trask*.

In *The River Why*, David J. Duncan writes of the search for self along the rivers of Oregon. This book could best be described as a sort of "Zen and the Art of Fly-Fishing." Robin Cody's *Ricochet River* is a coming-of-age story set in the 1960s in a small Oregon logging town.

If you were a fan of the oenophilic film *Sideways*, then you might want to read author Rex Pickett's *Vertical*, which follows the same characters that appeared in *Sideways*. This time a road trip takes them to the Oregon wine country.

Film

Twilight, the film version of the hugely popular teen-vampire romance novel of the same name, is the most popular movie to have been shot in Oregon in recent years. Wait, you say, *Twilight* takes place in Forks, Washington. Well, yes, but it was filmed mostly in Oregon, with shots of the Columbia River Gorge and Multnomah Falls. The other films in the series, however, were shot elsewhere.

Oregon's role on the silver screen isn't new. Silent-screen star Buster Keaton shot his 1926 Civil War comedy *The General* near the town of Cottage Grove, south of Eugene. This same town later served as the backdrop for the 1986 movie *Stand by Me*, a story of boyhood pals on an adventure in 1950s Oregon. The hilarious John Belushi comedy classic *National Lampoon's Animal House* was also shot in Cottage Grove and nearby Eugene.

Gus Van Sant is Oregon's most acclaimed film director, and several of his highly rated, though often somewhat disturbing, films have been shot here. These include *Drugstore Cowboy*, *My Own Private Idaho*, and *Elephant*.

The town of Astoria, at the mouth of the Columbia River, has been the setting for several films, including the family cult film *The Goonies*, Arnold Schwarzenegger's *Kindergarten Cop*, and hit children's movies *Free Willy* and *Free Willy 2*. For a while, the orca whale star of the *Free Willy* films even resided at the Oregon Coast Aquarium. The 1971 Ken Kesey classic *Sometimes a Great Notion*, starring Paul Newman and Henry Fonda, was also shot on the Oregon coast, though in the Newport area rather than in Astoria.

Meek's Cutoff, released in 2010, is a historical drama that chronicles the fate of a wagon train that struck out across the desert of eastern Oregon in 1845. Based on an actual event, the film presents this historical narrative from the perspective of the women of the wagon train.

Other movies shot in Oregon include *One Flew Over The Cuckoo's Nest*, starring Jack Nicholson; *The River Wild*, starring Meryl Streep; *The Hunted*, starring Tommy Lee Jones and Benicio Del Toro; *Bandits*, starring Bruce Willis and Billy Bob Thornton; and *Without Limits*, a film about Oregon running phenomenon Steve Prefontaine. Timberline Lodge (p. 258) stood in for the hotel in the Jack Nicholson's horror movie *The Shining*.

EATING & DRINKING

Regional Specialties

Although there is no cuisine that can be specifically identified as Oregon cuisine, regional Northwest cooking is distinguished by its pairings of meats and seafood with local fruits and nuts. This cuisine features such regional produce as salmon, oysters, halibut, raspberries, blackberries, apples, pears, and hazelnuts. A classic Northwest dish might be raspberry chicken or halibut with a hazelnut crust.

Salmon is king of Oregon fish and has been for thousands of years, so it shows up on plenty of menus throughout the state in one shape or another. It's prepared in seemingly endless ways, but the most traditional method is what's known as **alder-planked salmon.** Traditionally, this Native American cooking style entailed preparing a salmon as a single filet, splaying it on readily available alder wood, and slow cooking it over hot coals. The result is a cross between grilling and smoking. Today, however, it's hard to find salmon prepared this way. Much more readily available, especially along the Oregon coast, is traditional **smoked salmon.** Smoked oysters are usually also available at smokehouses and are a treat worth trying.

With plenty of clean, cold water in many of its bays and estuaries, Oregon raises large numbers of **oysters,** especially in Tillamook and Coos bays. If you see an oyster burger listed on a menu, give it a try; there's no beef, just oysters. Plenty of mussels and clams also come from these waters. Of particular note are **razor clams,** which can be tough and chewy if not prepared properly, but which are eagerly sought after along north-coast beaches when the clamming season is open. After salmon, though, **Dungeness crab** is the region's other top seafood offering. Though not as large as a king crab, the Dungeness is usually big enough to make a meal for one or two people. Crab cakes are also ubiquitous on Oregon restaurant menus, and along the coast, you can still find a few old-fashioned crab shacks that boil up crabs on a daily basis.

The Northwest's combination of climate and abundant irrigation waters has also helped make this one of the nation's major fruit-growing regions. The Hood River Valley and the Medford area are two of the nation's top **pear-growing regions,** and just a few miles east of Hood River, around The Dalles, cherries reign supreme, with the blushing **Rainier cherry** a regional treat rarely seen outside the Northwest. The Willamette Valley, south of Portland, has become the nation's center for the production of **berries,** including strawberries, raspberries, and numerous varieties of blackberries. All these fruits show up in the summer months at farm stands, making a drive through the Willamette Valley at that time of year a real treat. Pick-your-own farms are also common in Oregon. So famed are this state's fruits that its produce is shipped all over the country.

When hunger strikes on the road, Oregon offers a regional potato preparation known as **jo-jos.** Consisting of potato wedges dipped in batter and fried, jo-jos are traditionally served with ranch dressing. These belly bombs are usually purchased as an accompaniment to fried or baked chicken.

Wild mushrooms are one last Northwest staple not to be overlooked. As you'd expect in such a rainy climate, mushrooms abound here. The most common wild mushrooms are morels, which are harvested in spring, and chanterelles, which are harvested in autumn. You'll find wild mushrooms on menus of better restaurants throughout the state.

Wine, Beer & Coffee

Oregon's thriving wine industry has been producing **award-winning varietal wines** for several decades. Oregon is on the same latitude as the French wine regions of Burgundy and Bordeaux, and thus produces similar wines. Oregon pinot noirs rank up there with those from France, and local pinot gris and other varietals are getting good press as well. Wineries throughout the state are open to the public for tastings, with the greatest concentrations to be found southwest of Portland in Yamhill County, just west of Salem, northwest of Roseburg, and west of Jacksonville.

Oregon is at the center of the national obsession with **craft beers,** and there are brewpubs in both cities and small towns all across the state. Such Oregon breweries as Bridgeport, Full Sail, and Widmer, which have long been at the forefront of the state's craft-brewing industry, have grown so large that the term "microbrewery" no longer applies to them. Portland is recognized as the nation's microbrewery mecca, and it has earned the nickname Beervana.

Local wines may be the state's preferred accompaniment to dinner, and microbrews the favorite social drink, but it's **coffee** that keeps Oregonians going through long, gray winters—and even through hot, sunny summers, for that matter. Although Seattle gets all the press for its espresso obsession, this dark and flavorful style of coffee is just as popular in Oregon. There may still be a few small towns in the state where you can't get an espresso, but you certainly don't have to worry about falling asleep at the wheel for want of a decent cup of java. In parking lots throughout the state, tiny espresso stands dispense all manner of coffee concoctions to the state's caffeine addicts.

WHEN TO GO

Summer is the peak season in Oregon, and during these months, hotel and car reservations are almost essential; the rest of the year, they're highly recommended, but not imperative. If you visit in one of the rainy months, between October and May, expect lower hotel rates. It will also be easier to get reservations, especially on the coast. However, you will have to bring good rain gear. Whenever you go, keep in mind that you usually get better rates by reserving at least a couple of weeks in advance, whether you're booking a plane, hotel, or rental car. Summer holiday weekends are the hardest times of year to get room (and restaurant) reservations, especially on the coast. You should book months in advance for Memorial Day, Fourth of July, and Labor Day.

Though Oregon is famous for its gray skies and mild temperatures, the state is actually characterized by a diversity of climates almost unequaled in the United States. For the most part, moist winds off the Pacific Ocean keep temperatures west of the Cascade Range mild year-round. However, summers in the Willamette Valley and southern Oregon can see temperatures over 100°F (38°C). On the coast, though, you're likely to need a sweater or light jacket at night, even in August. The Oregon rains that are so legendary fall primarily as a light—but almost constant—drizzle between October and early July. Sure, there are windows of sunshine during this period, but they usually last no more than a week or so. There are also, unfortunately, occasional wet summers, so be prepared for wet weather whenever you visit. Winters usually include one or two blasts of Arctic air that bring snow and freezing weather to the Portland area (usually right around Christmas or New Year's). Expect snow in the Cascades any time during the winter, and even some Coast Range passes can get icy.

If you visit the coast, expect grayer, wetter weather than in the Portland area. It can be quite cool here in the summer and is often foggy or rainy throughout the year. In fact, when the Willamette Valley is at its hottest, in July and August, you can be sure that the coast will be fogged in. The best month for the coast is usually September, with good weather often holding on into October.

Portland's Average Monthly Temperatures & Rainfall

	JAN	FEB	MAR	APR	MAY	JUNE	JULY	AUG	SEPT	OCT	NOV	DEC
Temp. (°F)	40	43	47	51	57	63	68	68.5	64	54	45	40
Temp. (°C)	4.5	6	8	10.5	14	17	20	20	18	12	7	4.5
Days of Rain	19	20	18	15	12	9	4	4	7	13	18	2

In the Cascades and eastern Oregon's Blue, Elkhorn, and Wallowa mountains, snowfall is heavy in the winter and skiing is a popular sport. Summer doesn't come until late in the year in these mountains, with snow lingering into July at higher elevations (for instance, the Timberline Lodge area at Mount Hood and the Eagle Cap Wilderness in the Wallowas). At such elevations, late July through August is the best time to see wildflowers in alpine meadows.

The region east of the Cascades is characterized by lack of rain and temperature extremes. This high desert area can be very cold in the winter, and at higher elevations it receives considerable amounts of snow. In summer the weather can be blazingly hot at lower elevations, though nights are often cool enough to require a sweater or light jacket.

If you're planning to go wine touring, avoid January and February, when many wineries are closed. Also keep in mind that many wineries are open daily during the summer months, but in spring and fall are open only on weekends.

HOLIDAYS

Banks, government offices, post offices, and many stores, restaurants, and museums are closed on the following legal national holidays: January 1 (New Year's Day), the third Monday in January (Martin Luther King, Jr., Day), the third Monday in February (Presidents' Day), the last Monday in May (Memorial Day), July 4 (Independence Day), the first Monday in September (Labor Day), the second Monday in October (Columbus Day), November 11 (Veterans' Day/Armistice Day), the fourth Thursday in November (Thanksgiving Day), and December 25 (Christmas). The Tuesday after the first Monday in November is Election Day, a federal government holiday in 2012 and in all presidential-election years (held every 4 years).

Oregon Calendar of Events

FEBRUARY

The Portland International Film Festival, Portland. Catch interesting foreign films and documentaries. Screenings are held at various theaters around the city. ℂ **503/221-1156;** www.nwfilm.org. Last 3 weeks of February.

Oregon Shakespeare Festival, Ashland. This 9-month-long repertory festival features about a dozen plays—some by Shakespeare and others by classical and contemporary playwrights. ℂ **800/219-8161** or 541/482-4331; www.osfashland.org. February through October.

Newport Seafood and Wine Festival, Newport. Taste local seafood dishes and wines while shopping for art. ℂ **800/262-7844** or 541/265-8801; www.newport chamber.org. Last full weekend in February.

MARCH

Tulip Fest, Woodburn. Bold swaths of color paint the landscape at the Wooden Shoe Tulip Farm's annual celebration of tulips. ℂ **800/711-2006** or 503/634-2243; www. woodenshoe.com. Late March to early May.

APRIL

Hood River Valley Blossom Festival, Hood River. The blossoming of the apple and pear orchards outside the town of Hood River is the reason for this annual festival. ℂ **800/366-3530** or 541/386-2000; www.hoodriver.org. Third weekend in April.

MAY

Mother's Day Rhododendron Show, Portland. At Crystal Springs Rhododendron Garden, blooming rhododendrons and azaleas transform the tranquil garden into a mass of blazing color. ✆ **503/771-8386.** Mother's Day.

UFO Festival, McMinnville. Held at McMenamins Hotel Oregon, this is a kooky celebration of a 1950 UFO sighting near McMinnville. A UFO costume parade and an alien costume ball poke fun at extraterrestrials, while various talks address more serious UFO issues. ✆ **888/472-8427** or 503/472-8427; www.ufofest.com. Mid-May.

Memorial Day Weekend in the Wine Country, throughout the wine country surrounding Portland. This is one of two weekends celebrated by Willamette Valley wineries with special tastings and events. Many wineries not usually open to the public put out the welcome mat on this weekend. ✆ **503/646-2985;** www.willamettewines. com. Memorial Day weekend.

Boatnik, Grants Pass. Jet boats and hydroplanes race on the Rogue River. There's also a parade and carnival. ✆ **800/547-5927;** www.boatnik.com. Memorial Day weekend.

JUNE

Sandcastle Day, Cannon Beach. Artistic sand-sculpted creations are created along the beach. ✆ **503/436-2623;** www.cannon beach.org. Early June.

Sisters Rodeo, Sisters. A celebration of the West in this duded-up Western-themed town near Bend. ✆ **800/827-7522** or 541/549-0121; www.sistersrodeo.com. Second weekend of June.

Portland Rose Festival, Portland. From its beginnings back in 1888, the Rose Festival has blossomed into Portland's biggest celebration. The festivities now span nearly a month and include the nation's second-largest all-floral parade, a starlight parade, rose queen contest, music festival, and dragon-boat races. ✆ **503/227-2681;** www. rosefestival.org. Most events (some of which are free) take place during the middle 2 weeks of June.

Britt Festivals, Jacksonville. Performing-arts festival with world-class jazz, pop, classical, folk, and country music, plus contemporary dance performances in a beautiful natural setting. ✆ **800/882-7488** or 541/773-6077; www.brittfest.org. June through mid-September.

Oregon Bach Festival, Eugene. One of the biggest Bach festivals in the country. Tickets go on sale in February. ✆ **800/457-1486** or 541/346-5666; www.oregonbachfestival. com. Late June to mid-July.

JULY

Waterfront Blues Festival, Portland. This is Portland's biggest summer party and takes place in Tom McCall Waterfront Park. Expect lots of big names in blues. ✆ **503/282-0555** [3378]; www.waterfrontbluesfest.com. Fourth of July weekend.

Oregon Country Fair, Eugene. Counterculture craft fair and festival for Deadheads young and old. Everything from circus performers to samba bands on a dozen stages in an idyllic wooded setting. ✆ **541/343-4298;** www.oregoncountryfair.org. Second weekend in July.

Sisters Outdoor Quilt Show, Sisters. During this large outdoor quilt show, the entire town gets decked out in colorful handmade quilts. ✆ **541/549-0989;** www.sistersoutdoor quiltshow.org. Second Saturday of July.

Da Vinci Days, Corvallis. Fun 3-day celebration of science and technology with a kinetic sculpture race, performances, art, children's activities, food, and wine. ✆ **541/757-6363;** www.davinci-days.org. Third weekend in July.

Salem Art Fair & Festival, Salem. The largest juried art fair in Oregon, under the trees in Bush's Pasture Park, with hundreds of artists, musical entertainment, and food booths. ✆ **503/581-2228;** www.salemart.org. Third weekend in July.

Oregon Brewers Festival, Portland. One of the country's largest festivals of independent craft brewers features lots of local and international craft beers as well as live music. ✆ **503/778-5917;** www.oregonbrewfest. com. Last weekend in July.

AUGUST

Oregon State Fair, Salem. A typical agricultural state fair, although with wine and home-brew competitions. ☏ **800/833-0011** or 503/947-3247; www.oregonstatefair.org. The 11 or 12 days before and including Labor Day.

SEPTEMBER

Eugene Celebration, Eugene. Street party celebrating the diversity of the community. Bed races are a fun highlight. ☏ **541/681-4108;** www.eugenecelebration.com. Early September.

Shrewsbury Renaissance Faire, Kings Valley (near Corvallis). Go back 500 years to celebrate the age of Elizabeth I and Shakespeare with jousting and period costumes in an Elizabethan village. www.shrewfaire.com. Second weekend of September.

Mount Angel Oktoberfest, Mount Angel. Biergarten, Bavarian-style oompah bands, and food booths. ☏ **855/899-6338;** www.oktoberfest.org. Second weekend after Labor Day.

Pendleton Round-Up, Pendleton. Rodeo, Native American pageant, country-music concert. ☏ **800/457-6336** or 541/276-2553; www.pendletonroundup.com. Mid-September.

OCTOBER

Fall Kite Festival, Lincoln City. Kite carnival including a wide and wild variety of kites, plus kite fights, kite-making demonstrations, and other activities. ☏ **800/452-2151** or 541/996-1274; www.oregoncoast.org. Mid-October.

Yachats Village Mushroom Festival, Yachats. In the tiny Oregon coast town of Yachats, the autumn's fungal abundance is celebrated with a weekend of walks, talks, and exhibits focusing on mushrooms. ☏ **800/929-0477** or 541/547-3530. www.yachats.org

Hood River Valley Harvest Fest, Hood River. Under tents set up on the waterfront, enjoy fruit products of the region, crafts, and entertainment; drive the Fruit Loop to visit farm stands and wineries. ☏ **800/366-3530** or 541/386-2000; www.hoodriver.org. Third weekend in October.

NOVEMBER

Stormy Weather Arts Festival, Cannon Beach. Celebration of the rainy season features lots of live music, a gallery walk, and a quick-draw art event in which artists have 1 hour to paint a picture. ☏ **503/436-2623;** www.cannonbeach.org. First weekend in November.

Wine Country Thanksgiving, Willamette Valley. About 30 miles outside of Portland, more than 100 wineries open their doors for tastings of new releases, usually with food and live music. ☏ **503/646-2985;** www.willamettewines.com. Thanksgiving weekend.

Holiday Lights and Open House at Shore Acres State Park, Charleston. Extravagantly decorated gardens near dramatic cliffs at the Oregon coast. ☏ **541/888-2472;** www.shoreacres.net. Thanksgiving through December.

Festival of Light, Ashland. More than a million lights decorate the town. ☏ **541/482-3486;** www.ashlandchamber.com. Thanksgiving through December.

DECEMBER

Holiday Parade of Ships, Willamette and Columbia rivers in the Portland area. Boats decked out in fanciful holiday lights parade and circle on the rivers after nightfall. www.christmasships.org. Mid-December.

THE LAY OF THE LAND

At 97,073 square miles (roughly 1.5 times the size of the New England region of the northeastern United States or 1.2 times the size of Great Britain), Oregon is the 10th-largest state in the Union, and it encompasses within its vast area an amazing diversity of natural environments—not only lush forests, but also deserts, glacier-covered peaks, grasslands, alpine meadows, sagebrush-covered hills, sand beaches, and rugged ocean shores. Together these diverse environments support a wide variety of natural life.

The **Oregon coast** stretches for nearly 300 miles from the redwood country of Northern California north to the mouth of the Columbia River, and for most of this length is only sparsely populated. Consequently, this coastline provides habitat not only for large populations of seabirds—such as cormorants, tufted puffins, and pigeon guillemots—but also for several species of marine mammals, including Pacific gray whales, Steller sea lions, California sea lions, and harbor seals.

Every year between December and April, more than 20,000 **Pacific gray whales** pass by the Oregon coast as they make their annual migration south to their breeding grounds off Baja California. These whales can often be seen from shore at various points along the coast, and numerous whale-watching tour boats operate out of different ports. Many gray whales also spend the summer in Oregon's offshore waters, and it is possible to spot these leviathans any month of the year. More frequently spotted, however, are **harbor seals** and Steller and California **sea lions,** which are frequently seen lounging on rocks. The Newport bayfront, Sea Lion Caves, and Cape Arago State Park, all on the central Oregon coast, are the best places to spot sea lions.

The **Coast Range,** which in places rises directly from the waves, gives the coastline its rugged look. However, even more than the mountains, it is **rain** that gives this coastline its definitive character. As moist winds from the Pacific Ocean rise up and over the Coast Range, they drop their moisture as rain and snow. The tremendous amounts of rain that fall on these mountains have produced dense forests that are home to some of the largest trees on earth. Although the south coast is the northern limit for the coast redwood, the **Douglas firs,** which are far more common and grow throughout the region, are almost as impressive in size, sometimes reaching 300 feet tall. Other common trees of these coastal forests include Sitka spruce, Western hemlocks, Port Orford cedars, Western red cedars, and, along the southern Oregon coast, evergreen myrtle trees. The wood of these latter trees is used extensively for carving, and myrtle-wood shops are common along the south coast.

More than a century of intensive **logging** has, however, left the state's forests of centuries-old trees shrunken to remnant groves scattered in largely remote and rugged areas. How much exactly is still left is a matter of hot debate between the timber industry and environmentalists, and the battle to save the remaining old-growth forests continues, with both sides claiming victories and losses with each passing year.

Among this region's most celebrated and controversial wild residents is the **Northern spotted owl,** which, because of its requirements for large tracts of undisturbed old-growth forest and its listing as a federally endangered species, brought logging of old-growth forests to a virtual halt in the 1990s. Since that time, barred owls, which compete for the same habitat as spotted owls, have been expanding their range and have had a negative impact on spotted-owl populations. Concern has also focused on the **marbled murrelet,** a small bird that feeds on the open ocean but nests exclusively in old-growth forests. Destruction of forests has also been partially blamed for the demise of trout, salmon, and steelhead populations throughout the region.

Roosevelt elk, the largest commonly encountered land mammal in the Northwest, can be found throughout the Coast Range, and there are even designated elk-viewing areas along the coast (one off U.S. 26 near Jewell and one off Ore. 38 near Reedsport).

To the east of the northern section of the Coast Range lies the **Willamette Valley,** which, because of its mild climate and fertile soils, was the first region of the state to be settled by pioneers. Today the Willamette Valley remains the state's most densely populated region and is home to Oregon's largest cities. It also still contains the most productive farmland in the state.

To the east of the Willamette Valley rise the mountains of the 700-mile-long **Cascade Range,** which stretches from Northern California to southern British Columbia. The most prominent features of the Oregon Cascades are their **volcanic peaks:** Hood, Jefferson, Three Fingered Jack, Washington, the Three Sisters, Broken Top, Thielsen, and McLoughlin. The eruption of Washington's Mount St. Helens on May 18, 1980, reminded Northwesterners that this is still a volcanically active region. However, here in Oregon, it is the remains of ancient Mount Mazama, which erupted with unimaginable violence 7,000 years ago, that provide the most dramatic reminder of the potential power of Cascade volcanoes. Today the waters of **Crater Lake** fill the shell of this long-gone peak. Near the town of Bend, geologically recent volcanic activity is also visible in the form of cinder cones, lava flows, lava caves, and craters. Much of this volcanic landscape near Bend is now preserved as **Newberry National Volcanic Monument.**

The same moisture-laden clouds that produce the near rainforest conditions in the Coast Range frequently leave the Cascades with heavy snows and, on the highest peaks (Mount Hood, Mount Jefferson, the Three Sisters), numerous glaciers. The most readily accessible glaciers are on **Mount Hood,** where ski lifts keep running right through the summer, carrying skiers and snowboarders to slopes atop the Palmer Glacier, high above the historic Timberline Lodge.

East of the Cascades, less than 200 miles from the damp Coast Range forests, the landscape becomes a desert. The **Great Basin,** which reaches its northern limit in central and eastern Oregon, comprises a vast, high-desert region that stretches east to the Rockies. Through this desolate landscape flows the **Columbia River,** which, together with its tributary, the Snake River, forms the second-largest river drainage in the United States. During the last ice age, roughly 13,000 years ago, glaciers repeatedly blocked the flow of the Columbia, forming huge lakes behind dams of ice. These vast prehistoric lakes repeatedly burst the ice dams, sending massive and devastating walls of water flooding down the Columbia. These floodwaters were sometimes 1,000 feet high and carried with them ice and rocks, which scoured out the **Columbia Gorge.** The gorge's many waterfalls are the most evident signs of these prehistoric floods.

Today it is numerous large, modern **dams** (built of concrete, not ice) that impound the Columbia, and these dams have become the focus of another of the region's environmental battles. The large dams, mostly built during the mid-20th century, present a variety of barriers both to adult **salmon** heading upstream and to young salmon heading downstream to the Pacific. Though many of the dams have fish ladders to allow salmon to return upriver to spawn, salmon must still negotiate an obstacle course of degraded spawning grounds, slower river flows in the reservoirs behind the dams, turbines that kill fish by the thousands, and irrigation canals that often confuse salmon into swimming out of the river and into farm fields. Overfishing for salmon canneries in the late 19th century struck the first major blow to salmon populations, and for more than a century these fish have continued to struggle against man-made and natural obstacles. Compounding the problems faced by wild salmon has been the use of fish hatcheries to supplement the wild fish populations (hatchery fish tend to be less vigorous than wild salmon).

Southcentral and southeastern Oregon are the most remote and unpopulated regions of the state. However, this vast desert area does support an abundance of wildlife. The **Hart Mountain National Antelope Refuge** shelters herds of pronghorn antelopes, which are the fastest land mammals in North America. This refuge also protects a small population of California bighorn sheep. At **Malheur National Wildlife Refuge,** more than 300 bird species frequent large shallow lakes and wetlands, and at the **Lower Klamath National Wildlife Refuge,** large numbers of bald eagles gather every winter. Several of the region's other large lakes, including Summer Lake and Lake Abert, also attract large populations of birds.

RESPONSIBLE TRAVEL

Oregon has long had a big reputation for being environmentally aware and eco-friendly, and today many businesses throughout the state are doing what they can to be sustainable and environmentally and socially responsible.

Many restaurants around the state have adopted the mantra of "fresh, local, organic," and with the incomparable bounties of the Willamette Valley and Oregon coast close at hand, it is very easy to adhere to these tenets of sustainability. Wild salmon? No problem. Organic beer and wine? Got it. Throughout this book I have made a point of highlighting restaurants that are doing their part for the environment. Check restaurant websites when you're planning your trip, and you'll likely find that other Oregon restaurants are also emphasizing sustainability.

Even bed-and-breakfast inns and major hotel chains are going green. The **Oregon Bed and Breakfast Guild** (www.obbg.org) has a green certification program. Major chains doing their part to become more sustainable include Starwood (Sheraton, W Hotels, Westin), Kimpton, and Hilton.

If you rent a car from Alamo or National, you can opt to pay a small additional amount to offset carbon dioxide emissions. You can also choose to rent a hybrid from Enterprise and other rental-car companies.

Of course, it's hard to get greener than by riding a bike, but if you're headed out on an organized bike tour, you'll still have a sag wagon. At **Escape Adventures** (*©* **800/596-2953;** www.escapeadventures.com), which offers both road and mountain-bike tours in Oregon, sag wagons are fueled by used cooking oil in an effort to be as carbon-neutral as possible. In Bend, Oregon's **Wanderlust Tours** (p. 316) offers great adventure tours in central Oregon and also does a great deal to be sustainable, including dedicating $1 of each tour to planting trees for the purpose of carbon sequestration.

Riding a bike in Oregon isn't just about touring the coast or bombing down a mountain single-track. Portland is one of the most bicycle-friendly cities in the U.S., and downtown Portland's **Hotel Monaco** (p. 59) even offers a "Carless Vacation" package. You can also just rent a bike and head out on your own. The city has a well-marked network of bike routes, including special bike lanes downtown. Of course, if you're not a cyclist, Portland also has a great public transit system that includes light rail, street cars, buses, and even an aerial tram.

Even wineries and vineyards in Oregon are doing their part to help the environment. More and more vineyards are choosing to grow their grapes organically or biodynamically, while others, by reducing runoff and erosion and otherwise improving salmon habitats in streams adjacent to vineyards, have received "Salmon Safe" certification from the organization **Salmon-Safe** (*©* **503/232-3750;** www.salmonsafe.org).

Many of the newer large wineries in the state are now using photovoltaic panels to generate electricity, and a number of them—including the Carlton Winemakers Studio, Stoller Vineyards, and Sokol Blosser Winery—have received LEED (Leadership in Energy and Environmental Design) certification from the U.S. Green Building Association.

Because the citizens of Corvallis, a college town 80 miles south of Portland, buy so much alternative energy, the city has been voted the nation's top Green Power Community by the Environmental Protection Agency (EPA).

For information on volunteer vacation opportunities, see "Volunteer & Working Trips," below.

TOURS

Academic Trips

If your personal interests run to art or the environment, be sure to check the calendar for seminars and classes offered by the **Sitka Center for Art and Ecology,** 56605 Sitka Dr., Otis, OR 97368 (✆ **541/994-5485;** www.sitkacenter.org), which is located on the northern Oregon coast on the slopes of rugged Cascade Head. The center runs classes and workshops on writing, painting, ecology, ceramics, and other topics.

Down in southern Oregon, a wide range of educational classes, seminars, and trips are offered by the **Siskiyou Field Institute,** 1241 Illinois River Rd. (P.O. Box 207), Selma, OR 97538 (✆ **541/597-8530;** www.thesfi.org). Offerings range from birdwatching trips to wildflower photography seminars. The emphasis is on the flora and fauna of the Siskiyous and adjoining areas of southern Oregon and Northern California.

Adventure Trips

The abundance of outdoor recreational activities is one of the main reasons people choose to live in and visit Oregon. With both mountains and beaches within a 90-minute drive of the major metropolitan areas, there are numerous choices for the active vacationer and numerous tour companies that specialize in providing people with Oregon adventures.

BICYCLING

The Oregon coast is one of the most popular bicycling destinations in the nation, and every summer it attracts thousands of dedicated pedalers. Expect to spend about a week pedaling the entire coast if you're in good shape and are traveling at a leisurely pace. During the summer months, it's best to travel from north to south along the coast due to the prevailing winds. Also keep in mind that many state parks have designated hiker/biker campsites. You can get a free Oregon coast bicycle map, as well as other bicycle maps for the state of Oregon, by contacting the Oregon Department of Transportation's Oregon Bicycle Map Hot Line (✆ **503/986-3556;** www.oregon.gov/odot/hwy/bikeped). Cyclists should also check out **Ride Oregon** (www.rideoregonride.com), a website that abounds with great information on cycling in Oregon.

Other regions popular with cyclists include the wine country of Yamhill County and other parts of the Willamette Valley. Portland, Salem, Corvallis, Eugene, Cottage Grove, and Central Point all have easy bicycle paths that either are in parks or connect parks. In addition, the region's national forests provide miles of logging roads and single-track trails for mountain biking. Among the most popular mountain-biking areas are the east side of Mount Hood, the Oakridge area southeast of Eugene, the Ashland area, and the Bend and Sisters areas of central Oregon.

If you're interested in a guided bike tour in the state, try **Bicycle Adventures,** 29700 SE High Point Way, Issaquah, WA 98027 (ⓒ **800/443-6060** or 425/250-5540; www.bicycleadventures.com), which has tours of the Oregon coast, the Willamette Valley wine country, the Columbia Gorge, and Crater Lake National Park. Tour prices range from $1,995 to $3,185 per person including room and meals.

Mountain bikers in search of Oregon adventures should check out the tours offered by **Cog Wild Mountain Bike Tours,** P.O. Box 1789, Bend, OR 97709 (ⓒ **866/610-4822** or 541/385-7002; www.cogwild.com), which offers 3-day trips, as well as trips exclusively for women. Tours range in price from $465 to $725. Guided bike tours are also offered by **Oregon Adventures,** P.O. Box 148, Oakridge, OR 97463 (ⓒ **541/968-5397;** www.oregon-adventures.com).

BIRD-WATCHING

Oregon offers many excellent bird-watching spots. Malheur National Wildlife Refuge, in central Oregon, is the state's premier bird-watching area and attracts more than 300 bird species. Nearby Summer Lake also offers good bird-watching, with migratory waterfowl and shorebirds most prevalent. There's also good bird-watching on Sauvie Island, outside Portland, where waterfowl, sandhill cranes, and eagles can be seen, and along the coast, where you can see tufted puffins, pigeon guillemots, and perhaps even a marbled murrelet. The Klamath Lakes region in the southern part of central Oregon is well known for its large population of bald eagles, which are best seen in the winter months.

Throughout the year, the National Audubon Society sponsors expeditions, outings, and field seminars. For more information, contact the **Audubon Society of Portland** (ⓒ **503/292-6855;** www.audubonportland.org). For the Rare Bird Report hot line, call ⓒ **503/233-3976.**

Birders should also check out Oregon Birding Trails (www.oregonbirdingtrails.org), a website with information on birding trail maps. Currently there are five maps that list birding hot spots around the state.

HIKING & BACKPACKING

Oregon is a hiker's paradise. The state has thousands of miles of hiking trails, including the Pacific Crest Trail, which runs along the spine of the Cascades from the Columbia River to the California line (and onward all the way to both Canada and Mexico). The state's hiking trails are concentrated primarily in national forests, especially in wilderness areas, in the Cascade Range. Along the length of the Pacific Crest Trail are such scenic hiking areas as the Mount Hood Wilderness, the Mount Jefferson Wilderness, the Three Sisters Wilderness, the Diamond Peak Wilderness, the Mount Thielsen Wilderness, and the Sky Lakes Wilderness. Many state parks also have extensive hiking-trail systems.

The Oregon Coast Trail is a designated route that runs the length of the Oregon coast. In most places it travels along the beach, but in other places it climbs up and over capes and headlands through dense forests and windswept meadows. The longest stretches of the trail are along the southern coast in Samuel H. Boardman State Park. There's also a long beach stretch in the Oregon Dunes National Recreation Area.

Get a Pass

Before heading out to a national forest anywhere in Oregon, be sure to get a Northwest Forest Pass. Most national-forest trail head parking areas in the state now require such a permit, and though they can sometimes be purchased from machines at the most popular trail heads, it's better to have one before heading out. To find out if you need a pass for your particular destination, contact the **Nature of the Northwest Information Center,** 800 NE Oregon St., Ste. 965, Portland, OR 97232 (© **971/673-2331;** www. naturenw.org). Passes are available at national-forest ranger stations throughout the state and also at many outdoors-supply stores, such as REI. Day passes cost $5 and annual passes are $30. In some cases such passes are required not just for trail heads but for other national-forest recreational areas as well.

Other coastal parks with popular hiking trails include Saddle Mountain State Park, Ecola State Park, Oswald West State Park, and Cape Lookout State Park. Silver Falls State Park, east of Salem and home to numerous beautiful waterfalls, is another of my favorite hiking spots. The many trails of the Columbia Gorge National Scenic Area are also well trodden, with Eagle Creek Trail being a longtime favorite. The trails leading out from Timberline Lodge on Mount Hood lead through forests and meadows at the tree line and, unfortunately, can be very crowded on summer weekends. For a quick hiking fix, Portlanders often head for the city's Forest Park.

If you'd like to do your hiking with a guide, contact **Oregon Peak Adventures,** P.O. Box 1, Seneca, OR 97873 (© **866/936-0910;** www.oregonpeakadventures. com). This company leads hikes in the Columbia Gorge, on the Oregon coast, and on Mount St. Helens and Mount Adams. Prices start at around $50 per person for a half-day hike.

KAYAKING & CANOEING

While Puget Sound, in Washington State, is the sea-kayaking capital of the Northwest, Oregonians have also taken to this sport. However, sea kayaks in Oregon very rarely make it to the sea, where waters are usually far too rough for kayaks. But numerous protected bays along the Oregon coast are popular paddling spots. Also, the Lewis & Clark National Wildlife Refuge on the Columbia River, not far from Astoria, offers miles of quiet waterways to explore.

White-water kayaking is popular on many of the rivers that flow down out of the Cascade Range in Oregon, including the Deschutes, the Clackamas, the Molalla, and the Sandy. Down in southern Oregon, the North Umpqua and the Rogue provide plenty of white-water action.

Sundance Kayak School (© **888/777-7557** or 541/386-1725; www.sundance river.com), which operates classes on southern Oregon's Rogue River, is one of the premier kayaking schools in the country. They offer an 8-day beginner's program ($1,695) that includes time on the wild and scenic section of the Rogue River.

Canoeing is popular on many of Oregon's lakes. Some of the best are Hosmer and Sparks lakes, west of Bend; Clear Lake, south of Santiam Pass; Waldo Lake, near Willamette Pass southeast of Eugene; and Upper Klamath Lake (where there's a designated canoe trail).

MOUNTAINEERING

Mount Hood and several other Cascades peaks offer challenging mountain climbing and rock climbing for both the novice and the expert. If you're interested in learning some mountain-climbing skills or want to hone your existing skills, contact **Timberline Mountain Guides,** P.O. Box 1167, Bend, OR 97709 (**℃ 541/312-9242;** www.timberlinemtguides.com), a company that offers a range of mountaineering and rock-climbing courses. They also lead summit climbs on Mount Hood. A 2-day Mount Hood mountaineering course with summit climb costs $485.

SKIING

Because the winter weather in Oregon is so unpredictable, the state is not known as a ski destination. Most of the state's ski areas are relatively small and cater primarily to local skiers. Mount Bachelor, in central Oregon outside of Bend, is the one exception. Because of its high elevation and location on the drier east side of the Cascades, it gets a more reliable snowpack and isn't as susceptible to midwinter warming spells, which tend to bring rain to west-side ski slopes with irritating regularity.

Ski areas in Oregon include Mount Hood Meadows, Mt. Hood Skibowl, Timberline, Cooper Spur Mountain Resort, and Summit Ski Area, all of which are on Mount Hood, outside Portland. Farther south are Hoodoo Ski Area (east of Salem), Willamette Pass Resort (east of Eugene), and Mount Bachelor (outside Bend). In the eastern part of the state, Anthony Lakes and Spout Springs Ski Resort provide a bit of powder skiing. Down in the south, Mount Ashland Ski Area is the only option.

Many downhill ski areas also offer groomed **cross-country ski trails.** Cross-country skiers will find an abundance of trails up and down the Cascades. Teacup Lake and Mount Hood Meadows, on Mount Hood, offer good groomed trails. Near and at Mount Bachelor, there are also plenty of groomed trails. Crater Lake is another popular spot for cross-country skiing. Backcountry skiing is also popular in the Wallowa Mountains in eastern Oregon.

WHITE-WATER RAFTING

Plenty of rain and snowmelt and lots of mountains combine to produce dozens of good white-water-rafting rivers in Oregon, depending on the time of year and water levels. Central Oregon's Deschutes River and southern Oregon's Rogue River are the two most popular rafting rivers. Other popular rafting rivers include the Clackamas, outside Portland; the McKenzie, outside Eugene; and the North Umpqua, outside Roseburg. Out in the southeastern corner, the remote Owyhee River provides adventurers with still more white water. See the respective regional chapters for information on rafting companies operating on these rivers.

WINDSURFING & KITEBOARDING

The Columbia River Gorge is one of the most renowned windsurfing and kiteboarding spots in the world. As the winds whip up the waves, skilled sailors rocket across the water and launch themselves skyward to perform aerial acrobatics. On calmer days and in spots where the wind isn't blowing so hard, opportunities are plentiful for novices to learn the basics. Summer is the best sailing season, and the town of Hood River is the center of the boarding scene, with plenty of windsurfing and kiteboarding schools and rental companies. The southern Oregon coast also has some popular spots, including Floras Lake, just north of Port Orford, and Meyers Creek in Pistol River State Park, south of Gold Beach.

Food & Wine Trips

Several small tour companies lead tours through Oregon wine country. See "The North Willamette Valley Wine Country" in chapter 5 and "Ashland" in chapter 9 for details.

Want to turn a trip to the beach into an opportunity to learn some new cooking techniques? You can take cooking classes in Cannon Beach at **EVOO,** 188 S. Hemlock St. (© **877/436-3866** or 503/436-8555; www.evoo.biz), which offers half-day and evening classes; and in Lincoln City, at **the Culinary Center,** 801 SW U.S. 101, Ste. 401 (© **541/557-1125;** www.oregoncoast.org/culinary), which has regularly scheduled half-day classes.

Wellness Trips

If you're looking for someplace in Oregon to do a spiritual retreat, check the calendar at **Breitenbush Hot Springs Retreat & Conference Center,** P.O. Box 578, Detroit, OR 97342 (© **503/854-3320;** www.breitenbush.com), a new-age center in the Oregon Cascades. Programs in meditation, Native American drumming, and tai chi are also offered on the southern Oregon coast at **WildSpring Guest Habitat,** 92978 Cemetery Loop (P.O. Box R), Port Orford, OR 97465 (© **866/333-9453;** www.wildspring.com).

Volunteer & Working Trips

Want to turn your vacation into an educational experience or give a little back by volunteering?

The Nature Conservancy is a nonprofit organization dedicated to the global preservation of natural diversity, and to this end it operates educational excursions, guided hikes, and work parties to its own nature preserves. For information about field trips in Oregon, contact the Nature Conservancy, 821 SE 14th Ave., Portland, OR 97214 (© **503/802-8100;** www.nature.org).

SUGGESTED OREGON ITINERARIES

Where should I go? What should I see? What's the best route? How do I make the most of my limited vacation time? This chapter should help you answer these questions. If you read through all these itineraries, you'll notice a bit of overlap. Indeed, there are some destinations and attractions that just should not be missed on any visit to the state. For example, a trip to Oregon should include at least 1 day in Portland, and, to really get a feel for the state, you have to explore both the mountains and the coast.

THE REGIONS IN BRIEF

Geography and climate play important roles in dividing Oregon into its various regions.

THE WILLAMETTE VALLEY This is Oregon's most densely populated region and site of the state's largest cities, including Portland, Eugene, and Salem, which is the state capital. In addition, the valley's fabled farmland grows the greatest variety of crops of any region of the United States. These include berries, hazelnuts, irises, tulips, Christmas trees, hops, mint, grass seed, and an immense variety of landscape plants. The Willamette Valley is also one of the nation's top wine regions, with vineyards up and down the length of the valley.

Summer, when farm stands pop up alongside rural highways, is by far the best time of year to visit the Willamette Valley. If you are interested in wine, though, you might also want to consider October, when vineyards pick and crush their grapes.

THE OREGON COAST Stretching for nearly 300 miles, the Oregon coast is one of the most spectacular coastlines in the country. Backed by the densely forested mountains of the Coast Range and alternating sandy beaches with rocky headlands, this rugged shoreline provides breathtaking vistas at almost every turn of the road. Haystack rocks—large monoliths on the beach or just offshore—give the coast an unforgettable drama and beauty. Along the central coast, huge dunes, some as much as 500 feet tall, have been preserved as the Oregon Dunes National Recreation Area. Small towns, some known as fishing ports and some as artists' communities, dot the coast. Unfortunately, waters are generally too cold for swimming, and a cool breeze often blows even in summer.

Oregon

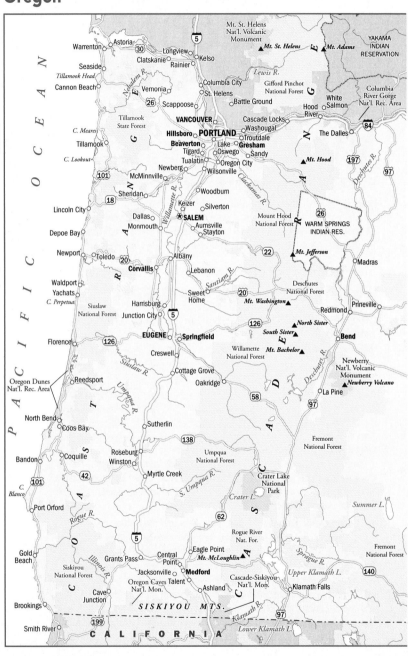

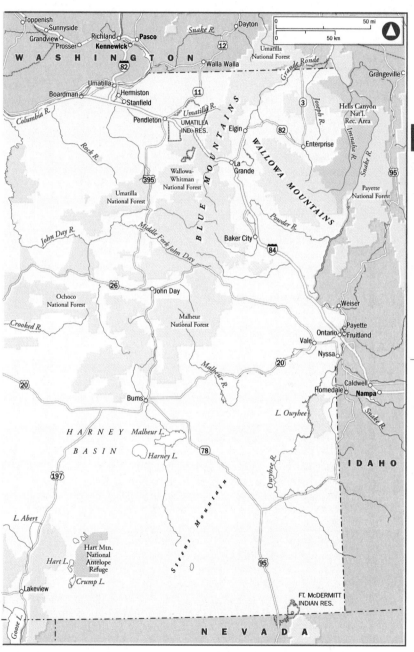

Of course, summer is the most popular time of year on the coast, and crowds can be daunting. In Seaside, Cannon Beach, Lincoln City, and Newport, traffic backups try the patience of many vacationers. The north coast, because of its proximity to Portland, is the most visited section of the coast, and, with its headlands, coves, and haystack rocks, is also one of the most dramatic. The south coast, where giant rocks dot the beaches and rocky islands break the waves not far from shore, is even more spectacular than the north. Also because of its distance from major metropolitan areas, the south coast is not nearly as crowded as other stretches of the coast. The central coast, though it boasts the Oregon Dunes National Recreation Area, is less spectacular than the north and south coasts, and while it is lined with long, sandy beaches, much of this coastline is inaccessible by car.

THE COLUMBIA GORGE Beginning just east of Portland, the Columbia Gorge is a place of immense beauty and natural diversity. Declared a national scenic area, the Gorge is the site of numerous waterfalls, including Multnomah Falls, the fourth highest in the country. As the only sea-level gap in the Cascade Range, the Gorge is also something of a wind tunnel, and the winds that regularly blast through the Gorge attract windsurfing enthusiasts from around the world. Consequently, the town of Hood River is now one of the world's top windsurfing spots. Rising above the waterfalls and basalt cliffs of the Gorge are the snowy slopes of Mount Hood.

Although the Gorge can be explored in a day or two, if you are an avid hiker or windsurfer, you might want to plan a longer visit. Spring is the best time of year to visit. March through May, countless wildflowers, some of which grow nowhere else but in the Columbia Gorge, burst into bloom, and Gorge wildflower hikes are annual rites of spring for many Oregonians.

THE CASCADE RANGE Stretching from the Columbia River in the north to the California state line in the south, this mountain range is a natural dividing line between eastern and western Oregon. Dominated by conical peaks of volcanic origin (all currently inactive), the Cascades are almost entirely encompassed by national forests that serve as both sources of timber and year-round recreational playgrounds. Within these mountains there are several designated wilderness areas in which all mechanized travel is prohibited. Among these, the Mount Hood Wilderness, the Mount Jefferson Wilderness, and the Three Sisters Wilderness are the most scenic. In the southern Cascades, an entire mountain once blew its top, leaving behind a huge caldera that is now filled by the sapphire-blue waters of Crater Lake, Oregon's only national park.

With little private property and few lodges other than rustic (and often run-down) cabin "resorts," the Cascades are primarily a camping destination during the warmer months. In winter several ski areas and many miles of cross-country ski trails attract skiers and snowboarders.

SOUTHERN OREGON Lying roughly midway between San Francisco and Portland, southern Oregon is a jumbled landscape of mountains and valleys through which flow two of the state's most famous rivers. The North Umpqua and the Rogue rivers have been fabled among anglers ever since Zane Grey popularized these waters in his writings. With a climate much drier than that of the Willamette Valley to the north, this region resembles parts of Northern California. In fact, several towns in the region are very popular with retired Californians. Among these are Ashland, site of the Oregon Shakespeare Festival, and Jacksonville, a historic gold-mining town that is the site of the Britt Festivals, an annual summer music festival. Also in the region are quite a few wineries that take advantage of the warm climate to produce Oregon's best cabernet sauvignon and merlot.

Although summer is the most popular time of year to visit this region, the Oregon Shakespeare Festival runs from spring through fall, which keeps Ashland busy almost year-round.

CENTRAL OREGON   When the rain on the west side of the Cascades becomes too much to bear, many of the state's residents flee to central Oregon, the drier and sunnier side of the state. Consisting of the east side of the Cascade Range from the Columbia River to just south of Bend, the region spans the eastern foothills of the Cascades and the western edge of the Great Basin's high desert. Known primarily for its lack of rain and proximity to the cities of the Willamette Valley, central Oregon is the state's second most popular summer vacation destination (after the coast), with resorts clustered around Sisters and Bend. The biggest and most popular resort is Sunriver, an entire community south of Bend. A volcanic legacy has left the region with some of the most fascinating geology in the state, much of which is preserved in Newberry National Volcanic Monument. Also in this region is the High Desert Museum, a combination museum and zoo that is among the state's most popular attractions.

Although summer is the peak season here, central Oregon is also quite popular in winter—Mount Bachelor ski area provides the best skiing in the Northwest.

EASTERN OREGON   Large and sparsely populated, eastern Oregon is primarily high desert interspersed with small mountain ranges. Despite the desert climate, the region is also the site of several large shallow lakes that serve as magnets for a wide variety of migratory birds. In the northeast corner of the region rise the Blue, Elkhorn, and Wallowa mountains, which are remote, though popular, recreation areas. Partially forming the border with Idaho is the Snake River and Hells Canyon, North America's deepest gorge. Throughout this region, signs of the Oregon Trail can still be seen.

Because this region is so remote from Portland and the Willamette Valley, it is little visited. However, the breathtaking Wallowa Mountains offer some of the finest backpacking in the state. The towns of Joseph and Enterprise, on the north side of these mountains, are also home to several bronze foundries.

OREGON IN 1 WEEK

Oregon is a big state, so don't expect to see it all in a week. However, if your vision of Oregon includes forests of towering trees, snowcapped volcanic peaks, and waves crashing on rugged shores, you're in luck: You can take in all of these, plus plenty of the state's famous wineries and brewpubs, during a 7-day visit—if you're willing to drive quite a bit. The following 1-week itinerary will allow you to experience many of the state's highlights.

Day 1: Portland ★★

Start your visit in Portland, Oregon's largest city and a model of livability. Head to Washington Park to visit the **Japanese Garden** (p. 92) and the **International Rose Test Garden** (p. 92). Hang out in a cafe, wine bar, or brewpub to find out how Portland relaxes. Ride the MAX or the Portland Streetcar (they're both free downtown) to visit some outlying neighborhoods. Wander around the Pearl District and stop by the **Saturday Market** (p. 104) if it happens to be the weekend. Stroll through **Tom McCall Waterfront Park** (p. 89) on the banks of the Willamette River, and then be sure to take a quick ride on the **Portland Aerial Tram** (p. 54).

Day 2: The Mount Hood Loop ★★★

On your second day, head east from Portland through the Columbia River Gorge and around Mount Hood. In the Gorge, drive the **Historic Columbia River Highway** (p. 235) and try to avoid straining your neck while gazing up at **Multnomah Falls** (p. 236) and the gorge's many other falls. Take a short hike on the **Eagle Creek Trail** (p. 237). Have lunch in **Hood River** (p. 241), a town that has become one of the world's premier windsurfing and kiteboarding spots. As you loop around snowcapped Mount Hood, Oregon's tallest peak, stop at the historic **Timberline Lodge** (p. 258). If it's July or August, be sure to go for a short hike through the wildflower meadows.

Day 3: Astoria ★★

Next, head west to the Oregon coast. Starting at the mouth of the Columbia River, you can explore **Astoria** (p. 161), a historic river port and home to the **Lewis and Clark National Historical Park** (p. 164). This town is still an active shipping and fishing port and has loads of character. Astoria's **Columbia River Maritime Museum** (p. 164) is one of the state's best museums. Don't miss it.

Day 4: Cannon Beach to the Three Capes Scenic Loop ★★★

The next day, head south from Astoria to **Cannon Beach** (p. 173), the most charming town on the coast and home to the impressive **Haystack Rock.** Just north of town, visit the rugged beaches of **Ecola State Park** (p. 174), and south of town, stop at **Hug Point** and **Arcadia waysides** (p. 174) as well as **Oswald West State Park** (p. 175). At this latter park, a short trail leads to one of the prettiest beaches in the state. Longer trails lead up onto rugged headlands. South of here, mellow out in **Manzanita** (p. 181) before continuing south to the **Three Capes Scenic Loop** (p. 186), which takes in Cape Meares, Cape Lookout, and Cape Kiwanda.

Day 5: Newport ★★

Continue driving south, through miles of traffic congestion in Lincoln City, to **Depoe Bay** (p. 194), where you'll find not only the smallest natural harbor on the coast but also, south of town, the **Otter Crest Scenic Loop** (p. 195) and **Devil's Punchbowl State Natural Area** (p. 196). Continuing south you'll come to **Newport** (p. 198), my personal favorite of the coast's family-vacation destinations. The big attraction here is the **Oregon Coast Aquarium** (p. 199). On the **Newport Bayfront** (p. 201), you'll find both fish-packing plants and souvenir shops. Here in Newport, you can also visit the **Yaquina Bay Lighthouse** (p. 200) and the **Yaquina Head Lighthouse** (p. 200).

Day 6: Crater Lake National Park ★★★

Today is your longest drive, so get an early start and spend some time at **Cape Perpetua Scenic Area** (p. 206), **Heceta Head Lighthouse State Scenic Viewpoint** (p. 209), and **Sea Lion Caves** (p. 209). Head inland at the historic river town of **Florence** (p. 210), perhaps after grabbing some lunch on the town's historic waterfront. Follow the beautiful blue waters of the North Umpqua River from Roseburg to **Crater Lake National Park** (p. 268). If you reach the national park early enough, drive the scenic road that circles the lake.

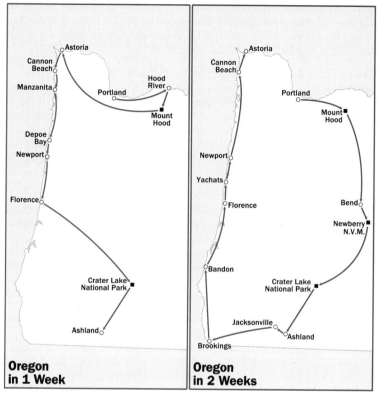

Day 7: Ashland ★★

This morning, take a **boat tour** (p. 269) on Crater Lake, then head down out of the mountains to the town of **Ashland** (p. 276), which is the home of the **Oregon Shakespeare Festival** (p. 276). It runs from February to October and is the state's premier performing-arts festival. Ashland has loads of great shops and restaurants. The next day, either drive back to Portland or fly out of Medford.

OREGON IN 2 WEEKS

Plan on spending 2 weeks in Oregon, and you'll get a much better sense of this state's diverse landscapes. You'll also get to spend more time exploring the great outdoors and taking interesting tours.

Days 1 & 2: Portland ★★

Start your Oregon vacation in Portland, where parks and gardens are the main attractions. Downtown, stroll through **Tom McCall Waterfront Park** (p. 89), ride the **Portland Aerial Tram** (p. 54), and visit the **Lan Su Chinese Garden** (p. 89). In

Washington Park, visit the **Japanese Garden** (p. 92) and the **International Rose Test Garden** (p. 92). If you're the outdoorsy type, go for a hike in **Forest Park** (p. 91) or paddle the Willamette River in a sea kayak (p. 99). Alternatively, do a jet-boat tour with **Willamette Jetboat Excursions** (p. 95). Go shopping in the Pearl District or on Nob Hill, and check out the **Portland Art Museum** (p. 88). Spend some time in a brewpub, wine bar, or cafe.

Days 3 & 4: The Mount Hood Loop ★★★
Spend the next 2 days circling snow-covered Mount Hood by way of the Columbia River Gorge. Drive the **Historic Columbia River Highway** (p. 235) and stop at **Multnomah Falls** (p. 236) and other waterfalls. Hike the **Eagle Creek Trail** (p. 237), and then relax on a river cruise aboard the **stern-wheeler** *Columbia Gorge* (p. 238). As you loop around snowcapped Mount Hood, Oregon's tallest peak, stop in Hood River or at the historic **Timberline Lodge** (p. 258) for the night. Go for a hike from Timberline Lodge, or perhaps at **Cooper Spur** (p. 259), on the northwest side of Mount Hood.

Days 5 & 6: Bend ★★
From Mount Hood, head south into central Oregon's high desert and ponderosa-pine landscapes. This region gets more sunshine than the west side of the Cascades and consequently has several golf resorts. Near the town of Bend, you can explore the lava fields, cinder cones, and volcanic crater of **Newberry National Volcanic Monument** (p. 317), go **white-water rafting** (p. 319), and hike beneath the jagged peaks of the **Three Sisters** (p. 310). In winter, go skiing or snowboarding at **Mount Bachelor** (p. 318).

Day 7: Crater Lake National Park ★★★
Continue south from the Bend area to **Crater Lake National Park** (p. 268), which preserves the deepest lake in the United States. Drive the scenic road around the lake and take a **boat tour** (p. 269). Do one or two short hikes to high points along the rim of the caldera that forms this gorgeous blue lake. Stay at **Crater Lake Lodge** (p. 270).

Days 8 & 9: Ashland & Jacksonville ★★
If you're a fan of Shakespeare or theater in general, you'll want to spend a couple of days in the hip little city of Ashland, where the **Oregon Shakespeare Festival** (p. 277) stages the Bard's works from February to October. Plenty of other playwrights also get equal time. When you aren't at the theater, shop the great boutiques, do a little wine touring, and eat out at the best restaurants in southern Oregon. Drive over to the historic town of Jacksonville, which is also home to the **Britt Festivals** (p. 288), a summer-long series that brings in great musicians.

Days 10 & 11: The Southern Oregon Coast ★★★
From Ashland, head to the southern Oregon coast (the highway will take you briefly into the redwood country of Northern California). The most scenic stretch of the coast is between Brookings and Gold Beach. Most of this area is preserved as the **Samuel H. Boardman State Scenic Corridor** (p. 227), which has lots of over-looks and also includes many stretches of the **Oregon Coast Trail** (p. 226). In Gold Beach, take a **jet-boat tour** (p. 226) up the Rogue River. Spend a night in **Bandon** (p. 219), where the beach is littered with monolithic haystack rocks.

Day 12: The Central Coast ★★★

North of Bandon, a trio of state parks—**Cape Arago, Sunset Bay,** and **Shore Acres** (p. 216)—should not be missed. These three parks are all within a few miles of each other, and you can easily visit all three in a few hours. North of Coos Bay, you drive through the **Oregon Dunes National Recreation Area** (p. 210), where some sand dunes are 500 feet tall. There are lots of hiking trails through the Sahara-like landscape. Stop for lunch in the historic river town of **Florence** (p. 210). North of Florence, the mountains once again meet the sea. Stop at **Sea Lion Caves** (p. 209) and the picturesque **Heceta Head Lighthouse** (p. 209) before exploring the rugged shoreline of **Cape Perpetua Scenic Area** (p. 206). Stay in **Yachats** (p. 205).

Day 13: The Three Capes Scenic Loop ★★★

From Yachats, drive north to Newport and visit the **Oregon Coast Aquarium** (p. 199). Then work your way through the traffic congestion of Lincoln City to reach the little fishing town of Pacific City, and the start of the Three Capes Scenic Loop. Climb the giant sand dune at **Cape Kiwanda Natural Area** (p. 186), then drive north to **Cape Lookout State Park** (p. 186) and, if you have time, hike out to the end of the cape. The last stop on this loop is **Cape Meares State Scenic Viewpoint** (p. 186).

Day 14: Astoria ★★

Continue north, stopping in **Manzanita** (p. 181) and artsy **Cannon Beach** (p. 173) to see two of my favorite Oregon coast towns. Also be sure to take the short hike to the beach at **Oswald West State Park** (p. 175). Finish your tour in **Astoria** (p. 161), a working port town with lots of grand old Victorian homes. Just outside of town, you'll find **Lewis and Clark National Historical Park** (p. 164), which commemorates the explorers who spent the winter of 1805–06 here at the mouth of the Columbia River. The next day, head back to Portland.

OREGON FOR FAMILIES

While Oregon doesn't have a major amusement park to attract families, it does have lots of great kid-oriented museums in Portland, and there are several other children's attractions in nearby Salem. Plus, the state has loads of the great outdoors, including wild ocean beaches, a dormant volcano with snow-skiing all summer, and an extinct volcano that really blew its top.

Days 1 & 2: Portland ★★

Start your Oregon family vacation in Portland, where you and the kids have lots of options for fun activities. For example, you can spend a whole day in Washington Park. Here you'll find the **Oregon Zoo** (p. 93), the **World Forestry Center Discovery Museum** (p. 93), and the **Portland Children's Museum** (p. 95). The next day, head to the **Oregon Museum of Science and Industry** (p. 90), where you can watch an OMNIMAX movie, see a planetarium show, and explore a submarine. Afterward you can head out on the Willamette River on a high-speed **jet-boat ride** (p. 95).

Days 3, 4 & 5: The Northern Oregon Coast ★★

From Portland, head west to the coast. Although the waters on the Oregon coast are too cold for most adults, children don't seem to mind the chilly temperatures at all. However, you'll be better off buying some kites and spending your time on the beach rather than in the water. **Seaside** is the north coast's premier family beach town and is full of arcades, saltwater-taffy stores, and places where you can rent unusual cycles (beach trikes, four-wheel surreys, tandems). However, I recommend staying in **Cannon Beach** (p. 173), a much prettier town. There you can explore the tide pools at the base of Haystack Rock, fly kites, and, as in Seaside, rent beach bikes. There are also several nearby state parks.

Day 6: Salem ★

After you've built enough sand castles, head back inland to the state capital of Salem, which has a great waterfront park that's home to **Salem's Riverfront Carousel** (p. 139), the fun **A. C. Gilbert's Discovery Village** (p. 139), and the *Willamette Queen* (p. 136) paddle wheeler. A few miles south of town, you'll find **Enchanted Forest** (p. 139), another great children's attraction.

Day 7: Crater Lake National Park ★★★

Although it's a long drive from Salem to **Crater Lake National Park** (p. 268), you shouldn't miss the opportunity to visit this amazing natural attraction that was created when a large volcano blew its top. If your kids can hike a mile downhill (and back up), or if you don't mind carrying the little ones, be sure to take the boat ride around the lake.

Days 8 & 9: Bend & Sunriver ★★

Next, head north to central Oregon, which is the state's favorite sunshine destination. Here, in Bend and Sunriver, you'll find several resorts that are geared toward keeping families entertained. There are big swimming pools, bikes, and lots of scheduled activities for kids of all ages. The short **white-water-rafting trips** (p. 319) on the Deschutes River just outside Bend are always a big hit with kids. The other must-visit attraction in the area is the **High Desert Museum** (p. 316), which is as much a zoo as it is a museum. You can also stop at **Newberry National Volcanic Monument** (p. 317) and the **Lava Lands Visitor Center** (p. 317).

Day 10: Mount Hood ★★★

Finally, head up to Mount Hood and try to stay at the historic **Timberline Lodge** (p. 258), where you just might bump into the lodge's Saint Bernard mascot. In winter this is a popular family ski area; in summer you can do a little skiing or snowboarding at **Timberline ski area** (p. 257), or check out all the fun rides and activities at the **Mt. Hood Adventure Park at Skibowl** (p. 257) in Government Camp. The trail to Mirror Lake is an easy hike that's popular with families.

A WEEK IN WILLAMETTE VALLEY WINE COUNTRY

Here's an itinerary for serious oenophiles. If you're a fan of pinot noir, then you definitely need to spend a week in wine country. Because there are so many wineries in

More Suggested Itineraries

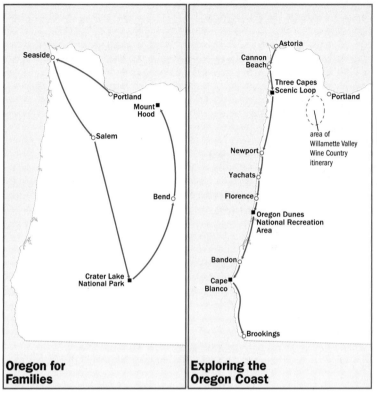

Oregon for Families

Exploring the Oregon Coast

Oregon's Willamette Valley, a week of wine tasting here can easily lead to a fabulous cellar full of Oregon wines.

Day 1: Portland
Start your wine tour in Portland. Here you should spend some time at **Oregon Wines on Broadway** (p. 110), a combination wine bar and wine shop specializing in Oregon wines. On any given day, you can sample 30 different Oregon pinot noirs and get an idea of which wineries you might want to visit.

Day 2: Dundee & the Red Hills
From Portland it is less than 45 minutes to the start of wine country. **Rex Hill Vineyards** (p. 118), just east of Newberg, is the first major winery you'll come to. A few miles farther on Ore. 99W, you'll come to Dundee, which is the heart of the wine country. The Red Hills north of town are covered with vineyards, and numerous wineries lie within a few miles of town. **Alexana Winery** (p. 118), **Dobbes Family Estate/Wine by Joe** (p. 119), **Lange Estate Winery & Vineyards** (p. 119), **Torii Mor** (p. 120), and **Winderlea Vineyard and Winery** (p. 120) are a few of my

favorite area wineries. Have dinner at one of Dundee's great restaurants or at **Jory** (p. 131), the restaurant at the luxurious Allison Inn in Newberg.

Day 3: West of Dundee

Today explore the hills west of Dundee, where you'll find some of the most highly regarded pinot noir producers in the state. **Archery Summit** (p. 118), **Domaine Drouhin Oregon** (p. 119), and **Domaine Serene** (p. 119) should not be missed. In this area, you'll also find **Sokol Blosser Winery** (p. 120). Don't pass up the opportunity to stop at some of the area's fruit stands. In the morning you might want to do some antiques shopping in Lafayette, stroll around downtown McMinnville, or visit the **Evergreen Aviation & Space Museum** (p. 126), which is home to Howard Hughes's "Spruce Goose."

Days 4 & 5: Carlton ★★

The little town of Carlton is home to some of Oregon's best wineries and deserves a couple of days of wine tasting. You won't want to miss the **Carlton Winemakers Studio** (p. 121), **Cana's Feast Winery** (p. 122), **Penner-Ash Wine Cellars** (p. 122), **Soléna** (p. 122), **Tyrus Evan** (p. 122), **Lenné** (p. 122), and **WillaKenzie Estate** (p. 123). Plan to have dinner at **Cuvée** (p. 134), Carlton's delightful little French restaurant; the next night, head to McMinnville for dinner.

Days 6 & 7: The Eola Hills & the West Valley ★★

South of McMinnville lie the Eola Hills and lots of good wineries. Be sure to visit **Amity Vineyards** (p. 124), one of the state's oldest wineries. Other wineries worth searching out include **Methven Family Vineyards** (p. 125), **Bethel Heights Vineyard** (p. 125), **St. Innocent Winery** (p. 125), **Cristom Vineyards** (p. 125), **Mystic** (p. 125), **Stangeland Vineyards** (p. 125), and **Witness Tree Vineyard** (p. 125). One morning, drive in to Salem to the **Hallie Ford Museum of Art** (p. 137). If you like chocolate, be sure to visit the **Brigittine Monks Priory** (p. 127) to buy some fudge.

EXPLORING THE OREGON COAST

While inland Oregon has loads to offer visitors, it's the coast that's the state's crown jewel. Oregon's beaches are not the lounge-chair and cold-beer beaches of Mexico and the Caribbean, but this coast is one of the most dramatic shorelines in America. Hiking, kite flying, and exploring tide pools are the top recreational activities on the Oregon coast, so come prepared for an active vacation.

Day 1: Astoria ★★

Start your Oregon coast vacation by flying into Portland and driving down the Columbia River to Astoria. You will be following the route of explorers Lewis and Clark, who spent the winter of 1805–06 near present-day Astoria. Visit the **Lewis and Clark National Historical Park** (p. 164), then head to **Fort Stevens State Park** (p. 166) at the mouth of the Columbia River. Also visit the **Columbia River Maritime Museum** (p. 164).

Day 2: Cannon Beach ★★★

Head south down the coast to the arts community of **Cannon Beach** (p. 173), which lies on the south side of Tillamook Head. Check out all the art galleries, and marvel at the massive **Haystack Rock,** which rises up from the beach in the middle of town. Just north of Cannon Beach, you can hike the trails of **Ecola State Park** (p. 174). To escape the crowds, head south of town to **Arcadia, Hug Point wayside** (p. 174), or the larger **Oswald West State Park** (p. 175).

Day 3: The Three Capes Scenic Loop ★★★

Drive around Tillamook Bay to the **Three Capes Scenic Loop** (p. 186). The first cape you'll come to on this drive is **Cape Meares State Scenic Viewpoint** (p. 186), which is a good place from which to spot gray whales. Farther south is **Cape Lookout State Park** (p. 186), where there is a trail through the forest to the end of the cape. The southernmost of the three capes is **Cape Kiwanda State Natural Area** (p. 186), where a giant sand dune rises up from the beach and the huge Haystack Rock (yes, it has the same name as the one in Cannon Beach) rises just offshore. Here at Cape Kiwanda you'll find a great hotel and brewpub.

Days 4 & 5: Newport & Yachats ★★★

Continue south through the sprawl and congestion of Lincoln City to Newport. En route, be sure to drive the **Otter Crest Scenic Loop** (p. 195), just south of Depoe Bay, and stop to marvel at the **Devil's Punchbowl** (p. 196). Newport's main attraction is the not-to-be-missed **Oregon Coast Aquarium** (p. 199). Outside of town, you can also visit the **Yaquina Bay Lighthouse** (p. 200) and the **Yaquina Head Lighthouse** (p. 200). South of Newport 24 miles is Yachats, one of the prettiest stretches of the central coast. Hike the rocky shoreline here, and visit **Cape Perpetua Scenic Area** (p. 206), **Heceta Head Lighthouse** (p. 209), and the **Sea Lion Caves** (p. 209).

Days 6 & 7: Oregon Dunes National Recreation Area to Bandon ★★★

South of Cape Perpetua, you leave the mountains behind and drive through 50 miles of forests, lakes, and giant sand dunes that have been preserved as the **Oregon Dunes National Recreation Area** (p. 210). Stop for lunch in historic **Florence** (p. 210), then continue on to visit **Sunset Bay, Shore Acres,** and **Cape Arago state parks** (p. 216) outside Coos Bay. Finish the day amid the dramatic boulders and haystack rocks that litter the beach at **Bandon** (p. 219).

Days 8 & 9: The Southern Oregon Coast ★★★

This is the most remote and least developed section of the coast, and it has numerous state parks and waysides. Wander the headlands at **Cape Blanco** (p. 225) and **Cape Sebastian** (p. 227). Explore the beach and Battle Rock in **Port Orford** (p. 225). In Gold Beach, take a **jet-boat tour** (p. 226) up the wild Rogue River. South of Gold Beach, stop to marvel at the monoliths at **Pistol River State Scenic Viewpoint** (p. 227) and hike segments of the Oregon Coast Trail within the **Samuel H. Boardman State Scenic Corridor** (p. 227). From Brookings, drive back north and then west to reach I-5, which is the fastest route back to Portland.

PORTLAND

ncontrovertibly hip and legendarily liberal, Portland is a magnet for young creatives who have been flocking to the city in droves despite the lack of available jobs. The city's youthful demographic, fueled by microroastery espresso and microbrewed beer, has transformed the city into a center for creativity and craftiness. Young foodie entrepreneurs have filled the city with food carts, and urban homesteaders have pioneered back-yard chicken farming in once decrepit neighborhoods that have now become hip hot spots. It's not the *Twilight Zone,* but it is the vibrant, alternative universe of *Portlandia.*

4

THINGS TO DO
If you've got a green thumb (or wish you did), spend time at Portland's trio of world-class gardens—**the Japanese Garden, Lan Su Chinese Garden,** and the **International Rose Test Garden.** Shop for colorful clocks, pottery, and other funky crafts at the **Portland Saturday Market,** or "window" shop the produce stalls at the **Portland Farmers Market.** Say hello to *Portlandia,* a giant hammered-bronze statue, and check the weather on **Pioneer Courthouse Square** at high noon.

ACTIVE PURSUITS
Portland is a city of cyclists. During rush hours, there is a constant stream of bicycle commuters rolling across the Hawthorne Bridge. There's no better way to tap into Portland's pulse (and get your own heart rate up) than by **renting a bike** and exploring the city on two wheels. Special lanes and signage make it easy to find your way around. The city also has a network of signed walking routes, and in the massive Forest Park, there are miles of hiking trails.

RESTAURANTS & DINING
From food carts to fine dining, Portland is a foodie's nirvana. The region's bounty provides restaurants with everything fresh and local, from blackberries and hazelnuts to wild salmon and foraged mushrooms. While French and Italian fine dining are still popular at such stalwarts as **Paley's Place** and **Genoa,** economic hard times have elevated sandwiches and burgers to haute cuisine at such places as **Bunk** and **Violetta.** Head to **Jake's** for crawfish, **Bamboo Sushi** for sustainably harvested seafood, or **Pok Pok** and **Ping** for Asian street food.

NIGHTLIFE & ENTERTAINMENT
You just won't find a better city in the country (some say anywhere on earth) for a brewpub crawl. Portland has more **breweries** than any other city in America, and for this reason, it has come to be called Beervana. If you're not a beer drinker, don't despair, all those nearby wineries keep

plenty of Portland **wine bars** pouring Oregon pinot noir. Want that beer or wine with an independent film? Portland has pioneered the **movie-theater pub** and movie-theater bar.

ORIENTATION

Arriving

BY PLANE

Portland International Airport (**PDX;** ✆ **877/739-4636** or 503/460-4234; www.flypdx.com) is located 10 miles northeast of downtown Portland, adjacent to the Columbia River. There are information booths in the baggage-claim area where you can pick up maps and brochures and find out about transportation into the city. Many hotels near the airport provide courtesy shuttle service to and from the airport; be sure to ask when you make a reservation.

GETTING INTO THE CITY BY CAR   If you've rented a car at the airport and want to reach central Portland, follow signs for downtown. These signs will point you first to I-205 and then west-bound I-84, which brings you to the Willamette River. Take the Morrison Bridge exit to cross the river. The trip takes about 20 minutes and is entirely on interstates. For more information on renting a car, see "Getting Around," p. 53.

GETTING INTO THE CITY BY TAXI, SHUTTLE, BUS, OR LIGHT RAIL   If you haven't rented a car at the airport, the best way to get into town is to take the Airport MAX (Red Line) light-rail line. The MAX operates daily roughly every 15 to 30 minutes between 5am and midnight, and the trip from the airport to Pioneer Courthouse Square in downtown Portland takes approximately 40 minutes. (Many downtown hotels lie within 4 or 5 blocks of the square; plan on walking since taxis in Portland don't generally cruise for fares. Folks arriving with a lot of luggage will be better off taking a cab or shuttle van from the airport.) The adult fare is $2.40. For information on this service, contact TriMet (✆ **503/238-7433;** www.trimet.org).

A **taxi** to downtown generally costs between $35 and $40.

BY TRAIN OR BUS

Amtrak trains stop at the historic **Union Station,** 800 NW Sixth Ave. (✆ **800/872-7245;** www.amtrak.com), about 10 blocks from the heart of downtown Portland. Taxis are usually waiting to meet trains and can take you to your hotel. Alternatively, you might be able to get your hotel to send a van to pick you up, or, if you are renting a car from a downtown car-rental office, the agency will usually pick you up at the station. The MAX Yellow and Green lines both run past Union Station and can take you into downtown Portland. Because Union Station is within the Free Rail Zone (see below), you don't have to pay to ride MAX into downtown.

The **Greyhound** bus station is at 550 NW Sixth Ave. (✆ **800/231-2222** or 503/243-2361; www.greyhound.com), on the north side of downtown near Union Station. As with getting into downtown from the train station, there is no charge to ride the MAX if you catch it outside the Greyhound terminal, which is within Portland's Free Rail Zone area (see below).

Although you could easily walk from the station into the heart of downtown, you have to pass through a somewhat rough neighborhood for a few blocks. Although this area is currently undergoing a renaissance and is not nearly as bad as it once was, I don't recommend walking, especially after dark.

Visitor Information

Travel Portland, 701 SW Sixth Ave. (𝒞 **877/678-5263** or 503/275-8355; www.travel portland.com), is in Pioneer Courthouse Square in downtown Portland. **Travel Oregon** (𝒞 **503/284-4620;** www.traveloregon.com), the state tourism office, has an information desk in the baggage claims area of the Portland Airport.

City Layout

Portland is in northwestern Oregon at the confluence of the Columbia and Willamette rivers. To the west are the West Hills, which rise to more than 1,000 feet. Some 90 miles west of the city are the spectacular Oregon coast and the Pacific Ocean. To the east are rolling hills that extend to the Cascade Range, about 50 miles away. The most prominent peak in this section of the Cascades is Mount Hood (11,235 ft.), a dormant volcanic peak that looms over the city on clear days. From many parts of Portland it's also possible to see Mount St. Helens, a volcano that erupted violently in 1980.

With about 2.2 million people in the entire metropolitan area, Portland remains a relatively small city. This is especially evident when you begin to explore the compact downtown area. Nearly everything is accessible on foot, and the city does everything it can to encourage walking and using public transit.

MAIN ARTERIES & STREETS

I-84 (**Banfield Fwy.** or **Expwy.**) enters Portland from the east. East of the city is **I-205,** which bypasses downtown Portland and runs past the airport. **I-5** runs through the city on a north-south axis, passing along the east bank of the Willamette River directly across from downtown. **I-405** circles around the west and south sides of downtown. **U.S. 26 (Sunset Hwy.)** leaves downtown heading west toward Beaverton and the coast. **Ore. 217** runs south from U.S. 26 in Beaverton and connects to I-5.

The most important artery within Portland is **Burnside Street.** This is the dividing line between north and south Portland. Dividing the city from east to west is the **Willamette River,** which is crossed by eight bridges in the downtown area. From north to south these bridges are the Fremont, Broadway, Steel, Burnside, Morrison, Hawthorne, Marquam, and Ross Island. Additional bridges beyond the downtown area include the Sellwood Bridge, located south of downtown near the city of Lake Oswego, and the St. John's Bridge, which connects Northwest Portland with north Portland.

For the sake of convenience, I have defined downtown Portland as the 300-block area within the **Free Rail Zone.** This is the area (shaded on the map "Portland Accommodations") in which you can ride for free on the city's MAX light-rail system and the Portland Streetcar. In downtown the Free Rail Zone is bounded by I-405 on the west and south, by Irving Street on the north, and by the Willamette River on the east. A Free Rail Zone extension also allows transit riders to travel free between downtown Portland and the Rose Quarter, Oregon Convention Center, and Lloyd Center mall.

FINDING AN ADDRESS

Finding an address in Portland can be easy. Almost all addresses in Portland, and for miles beyond, include a map quadrant—NE (northeast), SW (southwest), and so forth. The dividing line between east and west is the Willamette River; between north and south it's Burnside Street. Any downtown address will be labeled either SW (southwest) or NW (northwest). An exception to this rule is the area known as North

DID YOU KNOW?

- The flasher in the famous "Expose Yourself to Art" poster was none other than Bud Clark, the former mayor of Portland.
- Portland is the only city in the United States with an extinct volcano within the city limits (Mount Tabor).
- Matt Groening, creator of *The Simpsons,* got his start in Portland.

- More Asian elephants have been born in Portland (at the Oregon Zoo) than in any other city in North America.
- Twenty downtown water fountains were a gift to the city from early-20th-century timber baron and teetotaler Simon Benson, who wanted his mill workers to have something other than alcohol to drink during the day.

Portland, which is the area across the Willamette River from downtown going toward the Columbia River and Vancouver, Washington. Streets here have a plain "North" designation. Also, Burnside Street is designated either "East" or "West."

Avenues run north-south and streets run east-west. Many street names are the same on both sides of the Willamette River. Consequently, there is a SW Yamhill Street and a SE Yamhill Street. In Northwest Portland, street names are alphabetical going north from Burnside to Wilson. Naito Parkway is the street nearest the Willamette River on the west side, and Water Avenue is the nearest on the east side. Beyond these are numbered avenues. On the west side you'll also find Broadway and Park Avenue between Sixth Avenue and Ninth Avenue, respectively. With each block, the addresses increase by 100, beginning at the Willamette River for avenues and at Burnside Street for streets. Odd numbers are generally on the west and north sides of the street, and even numbers on the east and south sides.

Here's an example: You want to go to 1327 SW Ninth Ave. Because it's in the 1300 block, you'll find it 13 blocks south of Burnside and, because it's an odd number, on the west side of the street.

STREET MAPS

Stop by **Travel Portland,** 701 SW Sixth Ave. (✆ **877/678-5263** or 503/275-8355; www.travelportland.com), in Pioneer Courthouse Square in downtown Portland for a free map of the city.

Powell's City of Books, 1005 W. Burnside St. (✆ **800/878-7323** or 503/228-4651; www.powells.com), has an excellent free map of downtown that includes a walking-tour route and information on many of the sights you'll pass along the way.

Members of the **American Automobile Association (AAA)** can get a free map of the city at the AAA offices at 600 SW Market St. (✆ **503/222-6767;** www.aaaorid.com).

The Neighborhoods in Brief

Portland's neighborhoods are mostly dictated by geography. The Willamette River forms a natural dividing line between the eastern and western portions of the city, while the Columbia River forms a boundary with the state of Washington on the north. The West Hills, comprising Portland's prime residential neighborhoods, are a beautiful backdrop for this attractive city. Covered in evergreens, the hills rise to a height of 1,000 feet at the edge of downtown. Within these hills are the Oregon Zoo, the International Rose Test Garden, the Japanese Garden, and several other attractions.

For a map of Portland neighborhoods, see the "Portland Attractions" map, later in this chapter.

DOWNTOWN
This term usually refers to the business and shopping district south of Burnside and north of Jackson Street between the Willamette River and 13th Avenue. Here you'll find a dozen or more high-end hotels, dozens of restaurants of all types, and loads of shopping. Within downtown's **Cultural District** (along Broadway and the South Park blocks) are most of the city's performing-arts venues and a couple of museums.

SKIDMORE HISTORIC DISTRICT
Also known as Old Town, this is Portland's original commercial core and centers around SW Ankeny Street and SW First Avenue. Many of the restored buildings have become retail stores, but despite the presence of the **Portland Saturday Market,** the neighborhood has never become a popular shopping district, mostly because of its welfare hotels, missions, street people, and drug dealing. However, with its many clubs and bars, it is the city's main nightlife district. The neighborhood is safe during the day, but visitors should exercise caution at night.

CHINATOWN
Portland has had a Chinatown almost since its earliest days. This small area, with its numerous Chinese groceries and restaurants, is wedged between the Pearl District and Old Town and is entered through the colorful Chinatown Gate at West Burnside Street and Fourth Avenue. The neighborhood's main attraction is the impressive **Lan Su Chinese Garden.** Because of its proximity to bars on West Burnside Street and the homeless missions and welfare hotels in Old Town, this is not a good neighborhood to explore late at night. However, it has been undergoing something of a renaissance in recent years.

THE PEARL DISTRICT
This neighborhood of galleries, boutiques, restaurants, cafes, brewpubs, and residential and business lofts is bounded by the North Park blocks, Overton Street, I-405, and Burnside Street. Crowds of people come here for **First Thursday** (the first Thurs of every month), when art galleries and other businesses are open late. This is Portland's hip urban loft scene and one of the city's main upscale-restaurant neighborhoods.

NORTHWEST/NOB HILL
Located along NW 23rd and NW 21st avenues, this is one of Portland's two most fashionable neighborhoods. Here you'll find some of the city's best restaurants, as well as lots of cafes, boutiques, and national chain stores. Surrounding the two main business streets of the neighborhood are blocks of restored Victorian homes on shady tree-lined streets.

SOUTH WATERFRONT
This is the newest neighborhood in Portland and is a collection of high-rise offices and condominiums a half mile south of Tom McCall Waterfront Park. The South Waterfront is where you'll find the lower terminal for the Portland Aerial Tram.

IRVINGTON
Though neither as attractive nor as large as the Northwest/Nob Hill neighborhood, Irvington, centered around Broadway in northeast Portland, is almost as hip. For several blocks along Broadway (around NE 15th Ave.) you'll find interesting boutiques and numerous good, inexpensive restaurants.

HAWTHORNE DISTRICT
This southeast Portland neighborhood is full of eclectic boutiques, moderately priced restaurants, and hip college students from nearby **Reed College.** Just south of Hawthorne Boulevard, beginning at SE 12th Avenue, you'll find the interesting **Ladd's Addition** neighborhood, which has five rose gardens and a great pastry shop. Belmont Street, just north of Hawthorne Boulevard, and Division Street, to the south, are two of the city's hippest neighborhoods, and both areas are well worth exploring.

SELLWOOD & WESTMORELAND

Situated in southeast Portland, Sellwood is the city's antiques district and contains many restored Victorian houses. Just north of the antiques district, surrounding the intersection of SE Milwaukie Avenue and SE Bybee Boulevard, you'll find the heart of the Westmoreland neighborhood, home to numerous good restaurants.

ALBERTA ARTS DISTRICT

This neighborhood, a few miles north of downtown Portland and a mile to the east of I-5, is Portland's most multicultural and creative neighborhood. Because the old houses have character yet are fairly small, it's a popular neighborhood with young, liberal families. Neighborhood shops are full of alternative-lifestyle fashions, avant-garde art, and lots of the unexpected and the uncategorizable. Cafes, pubs, and inexpensive restaurants provide plenty of places for making the scene. On the **Last Thursday** of every month, the neighborhood throws a blocks-long art-oriented street party.

NORTH MISSISSIPPI DISTRICT

Anchored by the ReBuilding Center, a sort of warehouse-size thrift store full of recycled building materials, this quirky neighborhood 2 miles north of downtown Portland is another neighborhood favored by youthful and liberal-minded types. With plenty of good restaurants, a brewpub, popular music venues, and a couple of great coffeehouses, North Mississippi Avenue is a fun neighborhood to explore if you want to get a feel for what it's like to live in Portland.

GETTING AROUND

By Public Transportation

FREE RIDES   Portland is committed to keeping its downtown uncongested, and to this end it has invested heavily in its public transportation system. The single greatest innovation—as well as the best reason to ride the MAX light-rail system, and the Portland Streetcar—is that they're free within an area known as the **Free Rail Zone.**

There are 300 blocks of downtown included in the Free Rail Zone, and as long as you stay within the boundaries, you don't pay a cent. The Free Rail Zone covers the area between I-405 on the south and west, Hoyt Street on the north, and the Willamette River on the east. The Free Rail Zone extension also makes it possible to ride for free between downtown Portland and three destinations on the east side of the Willamette River in northeast Portland. These stops include the Rose Quarter (site of the Rose Garden Arena), the Oregon Convention Center, and the Lloyd District (site of the Lloyd Center mall).

BY BUS   TriMet buses operate daily over an extensive network. You can pick up individual route maps and time schedules or the *TriMet Schedule Book,* which lists all the bus routes with times, at the **TriMet Ticket Office,** 701 SW Sixth Ave. (© **503/238-7433;** www.trimet.org), which is behind and beneath the waterfall fountain at Pioneer Courthouse Square. The office is open Monday through Friday from 8:30am to 5:30pm. On Saturdays between 10am and 4pm, there are no attendants on duty, but you can still buy tickets from vending machines and pick up maps and schedule books. Bus and MAX passes and transit information are also available at Fred Meyer, Safeway, and most Albertsons grocery stores in the area.

Outside the Free Rail Zone, adult fares on TriMet buses, MAX light-rail trains, and Portland Streetcars are $2.10 or $2.40, depending on how far you travel. Seniors 65 years and older pay $1 with valid proof of age; children 7 through 17 pay $1.50. You can also make free transfers between the bus and both the MAX light-rail system and the Portland Streetcar. All-day tickets costing $5 are good for travel to all zones and are valid on buses, MAX, and streetcars. These tickets can be purchased from any bus driver, at MAX stops, and on board Portland Streetcars.

BY LIGHT RAIL The **Metropolitan Area Express (MAX)** is Portland's above-ground light-rail system that connects downtown Portland with the airport (Red Line), the eastern suburb of Gresham (Blue Line), the western suburbs of Beaverton (Red and Blue lines) and Hillsboro (Blue Line), North Portland (Yellow Line), and Clackamas (Green Line). MAX is basically a modern trolley, but there are also replicas of vintage trolley cars (✆ 503/323-7363; http://vintagetrolleys.com) that operate downtown on Sunday afternoons between May and late December. The Red and Blue lines operate along SW First Avenue and SW Morrison and SW Yamhill streets. The Yellow and Green lines operate along the Transit Mall, which is along SW Fifth and SW Sixth avenues. Transfers to the bus are free if you have paid a fare to ride the MAX. If you have only ridden within the Free Rail Zone, you'll have to buy a ticket when you board a bus.

MAX is free within the Free Rail Zone, which includes all the downtown area. A Free Rail Zone extension also makes it possible to ride the MAX between downtown Portland and the Oregon Convention Center, the Rose Quarter (site of the Rose Garden Arena), and the Lloyd District (site of the Lloyd Center mall). These three sites are all across the Willamette River in northeast Portland. If you are traveling outside of the Free Rail Zone, be sure to buy your ticket and stamp it in the time-punch machine on the platform before you board MAX. There are ticket-vending machines at all MAX stops that tell you how much to pay for your destination; some of these machines give change, but more and more of them take only credit and debit cards. The MAX driver cannot sell tickets. Fares are the same as on TriMet buses. There are ticket inspectors who randomly check to make sure passengers have stamped tickets.

The **Portland Streetcar** (✆ 503/238-7433; www.portlandstreetcar.org) operates from the South Waterfront District (site of the Portland Aerial Tram) south of downtown, through Portland State University, downtown, and the Pearl District to Northwest Portland. The route takes in not only the attractions of the Cultural District but also all the restaurants and great shopping in the Pearl District and along NW 21st and 23rd avenues, which makes this streetcar a great way for visitors to get from downtown (where most of the hotels are located) to the neighborhoods with concentrations of restaurants. Streetcar fares for trips outside the Free Rail Zone are $2.10 for adults, $1.50 for children 7 to 17, and $1 for seniors 65 and older. Note that these fares are valid all day.

Hospitals aren't usually considered tourist destinations, but in Portland's case, one medical center, the Oregon Health & Sciences University Hospital, has become something of an accidental tourist destination. The hillside hospital is connected to the newly developed South Waterfront District by the **Portland Aerial Tram** (www.portlandtram.org), and this tram has become a popular Portland excursion. There may not be much to do once you get to the hospital, but the ride up and back is fun and provides great views over the city. The tram's silvery, egg-shaped gondolas operate Monday through Friday from 5:30am to 9:30pm and Saturday from 9am to 5pm (June–Sept also Sun 1–5pm), with departures every 6 minutes. The round-trip fare is $4, and children 6 and under ride free. You'll find the lower terminal on SW Bond Street, a half mile south of downtown. The Portland Streetcar stops at the tram station, but keep in mind that this stop is one stop outside the Free Rail Zone. You can avoid having to pay for riding the streetcar by getting off at the SW River Parkway and SW Moody Street stop and walking the rest of the way.

By Car

CAR RENTALS   Portland is a compact city, and public transit will get you to most attractions within its limits. However, if you are planning to explore outside the city—and the Portland area's greatest attractions, such as Mount Hood and the Columbia River Gorge, lie in the countryside within an hour's drive—you'll definitely need a car.

The major car-rental companies are all represented in Portland and have desks at Portland International Airport, which is the most convenient place to pick up a car. However, the airport also has the most taxes and surcharges, so if at all possible, try to rent your car somewhere other than the airport (perhaps downtown Portland or even Beaverton, a suburb west of Portland). At press time, weekly rates for a compact car in July (high-season rates) were running anywhere from $192 to $430 ($252–$550 with taxes); it pays to shop around. Expect lower rates in the rainy months.

On the ground floor of the airport parking deck, across the street from the baggage-claim area, you'll find the following companies: **Avis** (© 800/331-1212 or 503/249-4950; www.avis.com), **Dollar** (© 800/800-3665 or 503/249-4792; www.dollar.com), **Enterprise** (© 800/261-7331 or 503/252-1500; www.enterprise.com), **Hertz** (© 800/654-3131 or 503/528-7900; www.hertz.com) and **National** (© 877/222-9058 or 503/249-4900; www.nationalcar.com). Outside the airport, but with desks adjacent to the other car-rental desks, are **Advantage** (© 800/777-5500 or 503/284-6064; www.advantage.com), **Alamo** (© 877/222-9075 or 503/249-4900; www.goalamo.com), **Budget** (© 800/527-0700 or 503/249-6331; www.budget.com), and **Thrifty** (© 800/847-4389 or 877/283-0898; www.thrifty.com).

PARKING   Throughout most of downtown Portland and the Pearl District, you won't find any individual parking meters on the streets. However, in the middle of every block, you will find an electronic parking meter that takes coins, credit cards, and debit cards. These machines issue little parking receipts that you then have to place on the curbside window of your car. Although a bit inconvenient, this system allows you to buy time while parked in one space and still use your remaining time if you move your car to another space. In most parts of town, you don't have to feed the meters after 7pm, but there are some exceptions, so be sure to read the meter where you park to be sure of the hours you will have to pay for parking. Also keep in mind that you must pay for parking on Sundays from 1 to 7pm in some parts of the city. The hourly rate is $1.60 in most neighborhoods.

The best parking deal in town is at the **Smart Park** garages, where the cost is $1.50 per hour for the first 4 hours (but after that the hourly rate jumps to $3 or $5, so you'd be well advised to move your car), $2 to $6 for the entire evening after 6pm. Look for the red, white, and black signs featuring the image of a parking attendant pointing at his head. You'll find Smart Park garages at First Avenue and Jefferson Street, Fourth Avenue and Yamhill Street, 10th Avenue and Yamhill Street, Third Avenue and Alder Street, O'Bryant Square, and Naito Parkway and Davis Street. Many downtown merchants validate Smart Park tickets for 2 hours if you spend at least $25, so don't forget to take your ticket along with you.

SPECIAL DRIVING RULES   You may turn right on a red light after a full stop, and if you are in the far left lane of a one-way street, you may turn left into the adjacent left lane of a one-way street at a red light after a full stop. Everyone in a moving vehicle is required to wear a seat belt.

By Taxi

Because most everything in Portland is fairly close, getting around by taxi can be economical. Although there are almost always taxis waiting in line at major hotels, you won't find them cruising the streets—you'll have to phone for one. **Broadway Cab** (✆ **503/227-1234;** www.broadwaycab.com) and **Radio Cab** (✆ **503/227-1212;** www.radiocab.net) charge $2.50 for the first mile, $2.50 for each additional mile, and $1 for additional passengers.

On Foot

City blocks in Portland are about half the size of most city blocks elsewhere, and the entire downtown area covers only about 13 blocks by 26 blocks. This makes Portland a very easy place to explore on foot. The sidewalks are wide and there are many fountains, works of art, and small parks with benches.

[FastFACTS] PORTLAND

AAA The **American Automobile Association** (✆ **800/452-1643;** www.aaaorid.com) has a Portland office at 600 SW Market St. (✆ **503/222-6767**), which offers free city maps to members.

Airport See section "Getting There," in chapter 12, and "Arriving," under "Orientation," earlier in this chapter.

Area Codes The Portland metro area has two area codes—503 and 971—and it is necessary to dial all 10 digits of a telephone number, even when making local calls.

Babysitters If your hotel doesn't offer babysitting services, call **Northwest Nannies** (✆ **503/245-5288;** www.nwnanny.com).

Car Rentals See "Getting Around," above.

Climate See "When to Go," in chapter 2.

Dentist Contact the **Multnomah Dental Society**

(✆ **503/513-5010;** www.multnomahdental.org) for a referral.

Doctor If you need a physician referral while in Portland, contact the **Legacy Referral Services** (✆ **503/335-3500;** www.legacyhealth.org).

Emergencies For police, fire, or medical emergencies, phone ✆ **911.**

Eyeglass Repair Check out **Visionworks,** 803 SW Morrison St. (✆ **503/226-6688;** www.binyons.com).

Hospitals Two conveniently located area hospitals are **Legacy Good Samaritan Medical Center,** 1015 NW 22nd Ave. (✆ **503/413-7711;** www.legacyhealth.org), and **Providence Portland Medical Center,** 4805 NE Glisan St. (✆ **503/215-1111;** www.providence.org).

Information See "Visitor Information," under "Orientation," earlier in this chapter.

Internet Access If you need to check e-mail while you're in Portland, first check with your hotel, or if you have your own laptop, find a cafe with Wi-Fi access. Otherwise visit a **FedEx Office.** There's one downtown at 221 SW Alder St. (✆ **503/224-6550;** www.fedex.com/us/office), and in Northwest Portland at 475 NW 23rd Ave. (✆ **503/222-4133**). You can also try the **Multnomah County Library,** 801 SW 10th Ave. (✆ **503/988-5123;** www.multcolib.org/agcy/cen.html), which is Portland's main library and offers online services.

Maps See "City Layout," under "Orientation," earlier in this chapter.

Newspapers & Magazines Portland's morning daily newspaper is **The Oregonian.** For arts and entertainment information and listings, consult the "A&E" section of the Friday *Oregonian,* or pick up a free copy of **Willamette Week** at

Powell's Books and other bookstores, convenience stores, cafes, and sidewalk newspaper boxes.

Pharmacies Convenient to most downtown hotels, **Central Drug,** 538 SW Fourth Ave. (℃ **503/226-2222;** www.centraldrug portland.com), is open Monday through Friday from 9am to 6pm.

Photographic Needs Camera World, 400 SW Sixth Ave. (℃ **503/205-5900;** www.camera world.com), is one of the largest camera and video stores in the city.

Police To reach the police, call ℃ **911.**

Post Offices The most convenient downtown post office is University Station, 1505 SW Sixth Ave. (℃ **800/275-8777** or 503/274-1362; www.usps.com), open Monday through Friday from 8am to 6pm, Saturday from 10am to 3pm.

Restrooms There are public restrooms underneath the Starbucks coffee shop in Pioneer Courthouse Square, in downtown shopping malls, and in hotel lobbies.

Safety Because of its small size and progressive emphasis on keeping the downtown alive and growing, Portland is still a relatively safe city. Take extra precautions, however, if you venture into the entertainment district along West Burnside Street and in the Chinatown and Old Town areas at night. If you plan to go hiking in Forest Park, don't leave anything valuable in your car. This holds true in the Skidmore Historic District (Old Town) as well.

Smoking Smoking indoors in public places is banned in Oregon.

Taxes Portland is a shopper's paradise—there's no sales tax. However, there's a

12.5% tax on hotel rooms within the city and a 17% tax on car rentals (plus additional fees if you pick up your rental car at the airport; these additional fees add anywhere from around 10%–16%). Outside the city, the room tax varies, as do car-rental taxes and fees.

Taxis See "Getting Around," above.

Time Zone Portland is on Pacific time, 3 hours behind the East Coast. In the summer, daylight saving time is observed and clocks are set forward 1 hour.

Transit Info For bus, MAX, and Portland Streetcar information, contact the **TriMet Customer Service Office** (℃ **503/238-7433;** www.trimet.org).

Weather If it's summer, it's sunny; otherwise there's a chance of rain. This rule of thumb almost always suffices, but for specifics, check **http://weather.cnn.com** or **www.weather.com**.

WHERE TO STAY

Whether you're looking for a downtown corporate high-rise, a restored historic hotel, a hip boutique hotel, a romantic B&B, or just something relatively inexpensive, you'll find it in Portland. You even have a couple of good choices for riverfront hotels.

If your budget won't allow for a first-class downtown business hotel, try near the airport or elsewhere on the outskirts of the city (Troutdale and Gresham on the east side; Beaverton and Hillsboro on the west; Wilsonville and Lake Oswego in the south; and Vancouver, Washington, in the north), where you're more likely to find inexpensive to moderately priced motels.

You'll find the greatest concentration of bed-and-breakfasts in the Irvington neighborhood of northeast Portland. This area is close to downtown and is generally quite convenient.

In the following listings, price categories are based on the rate for a double room in high season. (Most hotels charge the same for a single or double room.) Keep in mind that the rates listed do not include local room taxes, which vary between 7% and 12.5%.

For comparison purposes, I list what hotels call "rack rates," or walk-in rates—but you should never have to pay these highly inflated prices. Various discounts (Internet, advance purchase, AAA, senior, and corporate) often reduce these rates, so be sure to ask. In fact, you can often get a discounted corporate rate simply by flashing a business card (your own, that is). At inexpensive chain motels, there are almost always discounted rates for AAA members and seniors.

You'll also find that room rates are almost always considerably lower October through April (the rainy season), and large downtown hotels often offer weekend discounts of up to 50% throughout the year. Some of the large, upscale hotel chains have now gone to an airline-type rate system based on occupancy, so if you call early enough, before a hotel books up, you might get a really good rate. On the other hand, call at the last minute, and you might catch a cancellation and still be offered a low rate. However, it's always advisable to make reservations as far in advance as possible if you're planning to visit during the busy summer months. Also be sure to ask about special packages (romance, golf, or theater), which most of the more expensive hotels usually offer.

Most hotels offer nonsmoking rooms, and most bed-and-breakfasts are exclusively nonsmoking. The majority of hotels also offer wheelchair-accessible rooms.

Helping Hands

If you're having trouble booking a room, try **Travel Portland,** 701 SW Sixth Ave., Portland, OR 97205 (✆ **877/678-5263** or 503/275-9293; www.travelportland.com), which offers a reservation service for the Portland metro area.

For information on **bed-and-breakfasts** in the Portland area, contact the **Oregon Bed and Breakfast Guild** (✆ **800/944-6196;** www.obbg.org).

Downtown
EXPENSIVE

The Benson ★★   Built in 1912, The Benson exudes old-world sophistication and elegance. In the French baroque lobby, walnut paneling frames a marble fireplace, Austrian crystal chandeliers hang from the ornate plasterwork ceiling, and a marble staircase allows for grand entrances. These are the poshest digs in Portland, and guest rooms are luxuriously furnished in a plush Euro-luxe styling. Rooms vary considerably in size, and most of the deluxe kings are particularly spacious. However, the corner junior suites, which are large and have lots of windows, are the hotel's best deal. All the guest rooms have Tempur-Pedic mattresses. The hotel's **London Grill** is well known for its Sunday brunch, and El Gaucho, just off the lobby, serves some of the best steaks in Portland. In the lobby, the elegant Palm Court lounge has live music on Friday and Saturday evenings.

309 SW Broadway, Portland, OR 97205. www.bensonhotel.com. ✆ **800/663-1144** or 503/228-2000. Fax 503/471-3920. 287 units. $129–$229 double; $189–$299 junior suite; $450–$1,200 suite. Children 17 and under stay free in parent's room. AE, DC, DISC, MC, V. Valet parking $29. Pets accepted ($25 fee). **Amenities:** 3 restaurants; 2 lounges; babysitting; bikes; concierge; executive-level rooms; exercise room and access to nearby health club; room service. *In room:* A/C, TV, hair dryer, minibar, MP3 docking station, free Wi-Fi.

Embassy Suites ★ ☺ 🥄   Located in the restored former Multnomah Hotel, which originally opened in 1912, the Embassy Suites has a beautiful large lobby that is a masterpiece of gilded plasterwork. The accommodations here are primarily two-room suites, with the exception of a handful of studio suites. In keeping with the

Ace Hotel **7**
Avalon Hotel & Spa **16**
The Benson **8**
Crystal Hotel **5**
Embassy Suites **11**
Heron Haus **1**
Hotel deLuxe **4**
Hotel Fifty **14**
Hotel Lucia **9**
Hotel Modera **15**
Hotel Monaco **12**
Hotel Vintage Plaza **10**
Inn @ Northrup Station **3**
The Mark Spencer Hotel **6**
The Nines **13**
RiverPlace Hotel **16**
Silver Cloud Inn Northwest Portland **2**

----o---- Light rail/Streetcar line and stop

0   1/4 mi
0   1/4 km

historic nature of the hotel, the suites have classically styled furnishings. What's much more important, though, is that they give you lots of room to spread out, a rarity in downtown hotels.

319 SW Pine St., Portland, OR 97204. www.embassyportland.com. ☏ **800/362-2779** or 503/279-9000. Fax 503/497-9051. 276 units. $139–$209 double. Rates include full breakfast and nightly manager's reception. Children 18 and under stay free in parent's room. AE, DC, DISC, MC, V. Valet parking $30; self-parking $18. **Amenities:** Restaurant; lounge; exercise room; Jacuzzi; indoor pool; room service; sauna; day spa. *In room:* A/C, TV, fridge, hair dryer, Wi-Fi ($10 per day).

Hotel Monaco ★★   Located a block from Pioneer Courthouse Square and within a few blocks of the best downtown shopping, this playful yet sophisticated hotel is housed in what was originally a department store. Artwork by Northwest artists fills the lobby, and in the afternoon there are complimentary tastings of Northwest wines. Guest rooms, most of which are suites, are done in a whimsical decor—striped wall-paper, big padded headboards on the beds, red couches. In other words, colors and patterns everywhere, but it all comes together in a pleasantly theatrical fashion that makes these some of my favorite rooms in Portland. Plus, bathrooms have lots of counter space. In the suites, sliding French doors with curtains divide the living room from the bedrooms.

506 SW Washington St., Portland, OR 97204. www.monaco-portland.com. ✆ **888/207-2201** or 503/222-0001. Fax 503/222-0004. 221 units. $139–$289 double; $159–$459 suite. Children 18 and under stay free in parent's room. AE, DC, DISC, MC, V. Valet parking $35. Pets accepted. **Amenities:** Restaurant; lounge; bikes; concierge; exercise room and access to nearby health club; room service. *In room:* A/C, TV/DVD, CD player, fridge, hair dryer, minibar, MP3 docking station, free Wi-Fi.

The Nines ★★★   The Nines, the most stylish and sophisticated hotel in Port-land, is on the upper floors of the historic Meier & Frank Building, which on its lower floors houses Macy's. However, with a separate eighth-floor atrium lobby and a large collection of contemporary art, you'd never guess shoppers are searching for deals beneath your feet. Rooms here are done in a sort of hip interpretation of French Provincial styling, with great beds and well-designed marble bathrooms. A swanky rooftop lounge, a library with a billiard table, and glass-box seating areas in a lobby that combines contemporary art with rustic, bare-wood architectural accents give this place a distinctive feel. The Nines is very service oriented, and in the evenings it attracts Portland's beautiful people to its restaurant and lounge.

525 SW Morrison St., Portland, OR 97204. www.thenines.com. ✆ **877/229-9995.** Fax 503/222-9997. 331 units. $179–$449 double; $259–$2,500 suite. Children 18 and under stay free in parent's room. AE, DC, DISC, MC, V. Valet parking $39. Pets accepted ($30 fee). **Amenities:** 2 restaurants; 2 lounges; concierge; club-level rooms; exercise room; room service. *In room:* A/C, TV/DVD, hair dryer, minibar, MP3 docking station, free Wi-Fi.

RiverPlace Hotel ★★★   With the Willamette River at its back doorstep and the sloping lawns of Waterfront Park to one side, the RiverPlace is Portland's only down-town waterfront hotel. This alone would be enough to recommend the hotel, but its quiet boutique-hotel atmosphere would make it an excellent choice even if it weren't on the water. Understated contemporary furnishings and plush beds make this a comfortable choice, and more than half the rooms are suites, some of which have wood-burning fireplaces and whirlpool baths. However, the riverview standard king rooms are the best deal. The hotel's restaurant overlooks the river, and there's also a bar with a patio overlooking the river. All in all, what you're paying for here is primarily the waterfront locale.

1510 SW Harbor Way, Portland, OR 97201. www.riverplacehotel.com. ✆ **800/227-1333** or 503/228-3233. Fax 503/295-6190. 84 units. $199–$259 double; $229–$525 suite. Children 12 and under stay free in parent's room. AE, DC, DISC, MC, V. Valet parking $30. Pets accepted ($50 fee). **Amenities:** Restaurant; lounge; bikes; concierge; access to nearby health club; Jacuzzi; room service. *In room:* A/C, TV/DVD, CD player, fridge, hair dryer, free Wi-Fi.

MODERATE

Hotel deLuxe ★★   If you're a fan of 1930s to 1950s Hollywood movies, then this glamorous hotel should be your first choice in Portland. Not only are there old black-and-white photos of movie stars throughout the hotel, but the lobby, with its potted palms, gilded plasterwork ceiling, and crystal chandeliers, is primed for an entrance by Fred and Ginger. Guest rooms are equally classic, though with a hip aesthetic geared toward younger travelers. Sure, the basic rooms are small, but they're so pretty that it's easy to overlook the tight quarters. It's all delightfully playful, which is a welcome change from downtown's many sterile corporate business hotels.

729 SW 15th Ave., Portland, OR 97205. www.hoteldeluxe.com. © **866/895-2094** or 503/219-2094. Fax 503/219-2095. 130 units. $129–$219 double; $169–$389 suite. Children 18 and under stay free in parent's room. AE, DC, DISC, MC, V. Parking $25. Pets accepted ($45 fee). **Amenities:** Restaurant; lounge; concierge; exercise room; room service. *In room:* A/C, TV, hair dryer, minibar, MP3 docking station, Wi-Fi ($10 per night).

Hotel Fifty ★ 🐾   Overlooking Waterfront Park and located on the MAX light-rail line, this 1960s vintage hotel is a bit nondescript from the outside, but the inside has a contemporary look that makes it surprisingly stylish for an economically priced hotel. You are only steps from the Willamette River (although not actually on the water) and also close to businesses, fine restaurants, and shopping. Guest rooms are stylishly modern without being aggressively hip, and are much larger than the rooms at the Hotel Modera (Portland's hippest boutique hotel; see below).

50 SW Morrison St., Portland, OR 97204. www.hotelfifty.com. © **877/237-6775** or 503/221-0711. Fax 503/484-1417. 140 units. $119–$339 double; $199–$429 suite. Children 18 and under stay free in parent's room. AE, DISC, MC, V. Valet parking $27; self-parking $22. Pets accepted ($50 fee). **Amenities:** Restaurant; lounge; bikes; access to nearby health club; room service. *In room:* A/C, TV, hair dryer, MP3 docking station, free Wi-Fi.

Hotel Luⓧia ★★   Portland may not have a W Hotel, but it does have the Luⓧia, which is just as hip. Located across from the prestigious and very traditional Benson hotel, the Luⓧia is the Portland address of choice for young business travelers with a taste for contemporary style. There's a big emphasis on the visual arts here, with paintings by Northwest and national artists on the lobby walls, and black-and-white photos by famed White House photographer David Hume Kennerly throughout the hotel. Guest rooms are some of the prettiest in the city, with great beds and bathrooms that have lots of chrome and frosted-glass counters. The hotel's restaurant, **Typhoon!,** is one of Portland's best Thai restaurants.

400 SW Broadway, Portland, OR 97205. www.hotellucia.com. © **877/225-1717** or 503/225-1717. Fax 503/225-1919. 127 units. $129–$309 double; $249–$759 suite. Children 18 and under stay free in parent's room. AE, DC, DISC, MC, V. Parking $30. Pets accepted ($45 fee). **Amenities:** 2 restaurants; lounge; concierge; exercise room; room service. *In room:* A/C, TV, hair dryer, minibar, MP3 docking station, Wi-Fi ($10 per night).

Hotel Modera ★   The Modera is sexy and stylish, and its garden courtyard, with a living wall of greenery, is one of the prettiest hotel spaces in downtown Portland. A gravel patio with fire pits lends the restaurant's outdoor dining area the feel of an Arizona resort, and the lobby's utterly hip and bold contemporary decor will have young creative types feeling right at home. The drawback is that the basic rooms are absolutely tiny and don't even have a comfortable chair in which to relax. If you want to stay at this hip hotel and you want enough room for you and your suitcases, splurge on a suite.

515 SW Clay St., Portland, OR 97201. www.hotelmodera.com. © **877/484-1084** or 503/484-1084. Fax 503/226-0447. 174 units. $119–$209 double; $289–$309 suite. Children 17 and under stay free in parent's room. AE, DC, DISC, MC, V. Valet parking $27. **Amenities:** Restaurant; lounge; concierge; access to nearby 24 Hour Fitness; room service. *In room:* A/C, TV, fridge, hair dryer, MP3 docking station, free Wi-Fi.

Hotel Vintage Plaza ★★   This hotel, which was built in 1894, is on the National Register of Historic Places—it is *the* place to stay in Portland if you are a wine lover. A wine theme predominates the hotel's decor, and there are complimentary evening tastings of Northwest wines. A wide variety of room types are available, and though the standard rooms are worth recommending, the starlight rooms and bi-level suites are the real scene stealers. The starlight rooms in particular are truly extraordinary. Though small, they have solarium-style windows that provide very romantic views at night and let in floods of light during the day. The bi-level suites, some with Japanese soaking tubs, are equally attractive spaces. The hotel's Pazzo Ristorante is a sort of contemporary trattoria.

422 SW Broadway, Portland, OR 97205. www.vintageplaza.com. ℂ **800/263-2305** or 503/228-1212. Fax 503/228-3598. 117 units. $129–$305 double; $170–$440 suite. Children 18 and under stay free in parent's room. AE, DC, DISC, MC, V. Valet parking $35. Pets accepted. **Amenities:** Restaurant; lounge; concierge; exercise room; room service. *In room:* A/C, TV, fridge, hair dryer, minibar, free Wi-Fi.

The Mark Spencer Hotel 🏆   This economically priced downtown hotel just off West Burnside Street is ideally situated around the corner from both Powell's City of Books and Jake's Famous Crawfish (p. 68). The trendy Pearl District begins only a couple of blocks from the hotel, and the Portland Streetcar stops nearby. All the rooms and suites here have kitchenettes (and there's a Whole Foods only a block away). By the summer of 2012, this hotel's rooms and suites should be done with a major renovation. When you've had enough of wandering the city streets, head up to the hotel's rooftop garden deck for a different perspective on Portland. The Mark Spencer is a favorite of touring Broadway shows when they're in town.

409 SW 11th Ave., Portland, OR 97205. www.markspencer.com. ℂ **800/548-3934** or 503/224-3293. Fax 503/223-7848. 101 units. $99–$179 double; $109–$249 suite. Rates include continental breakfast and afternoon wine reception. Children 12 and under stay free in parent's room. AE, DC, DISC, MC, V. Parking $18. Pets accepted ($15 per day). **Amenities:** Concierge; exercise room and access to nearby health club; room service. *In room:* A/C, TV, hair dryer, kitchen, MP3 docking station (in suites), free Wi-Fi.

INEXPENSIVE

Ace Hotel ★   Bauhaus meets industrial salvage center at this überhip hotel a block away from Powell's City of Books. Young creative types will adore this fun and funky place that conjures up cheap European hotels of the past. In the lobby, a large, old industrial door serves as a giant coffee table, while over in the corner there's a vintage photo booth. Every guest room is different, with very unusual murals on the walls. There are Pendleton blankets on the platform beds, and, in rooms with private bathrooms, you might find an old wooden apple crate serving as a step up into the claw-foot tub. Book one of the larger rooms, and you can play old vinyl records on a genuine turntable. A hip espresso bar and eclectic restaurant are off the lobby. Ask for a room in back if you're a light sleeper.

1022 SW Stark St., Portland, OR 97205. www.acehotel.com. ℂ **503/228-2277.** Fax 503/228-2297. 78 units, 11 with shared bath. $95 double with shared bath, $155 double with private bath; $275 suite. AE, DISC, MC, V. Parking $25. Pets accepted. **Amenities:** 3 restaurants; lounge; bikes; concierge; access to nearby health club; room service. *In room:* A/C, TV, minibar, MP3 docking station, free Wi-Fi.

Crystal Hotel ★   With room decor inspired by songs and performances over the decades at the adjacent Crystal Ballroom, this funky downtown hotel is another playful lodging option from Portland's McMenamin's brothers. Guest rooms are dark and theatrical, with deeply colored walls, black-velvet drapes, and elaborate headboards with colorful music-related murals. Basically, the hotel is a celebration of the adjacent

family-friendly **HOTELS**

Aloft Portland Airport at Cascade Station (p. 66)   Although this hip airport hotel is a ways from downtown, it is right on the MAX light-rail line, which makes it easy to get to most of Portland's top kid-friendly attractions. Best of all, the hotel has an indoor pool, provides treats for kids, and also has games for them to play.

Embassy Suites (p. 58)   Located in the center of the city, this renovated historic hotel offers spacious rooms (mostly two-room suites). You and the kids will have room to spread out and can hang out by the indoor pool when you tire of exploring Portland.

Homewood Suites by Hilton Vancouver/Portland (p. 67)   This hotel is on the north side of the Columbia River, in Vancouver, Washington. A paved riverside trail, a fun family restaurant, and a brewpub—not to mention its location right across the street from the river—all add up to convenience for families. You'll get a one- or two-bedroom apartment with a full kitchen to make life on vacation that much easier.

The Lakeshore Inn (p. 64)   This reasonably priced inn is right on the shore of Lake Oswego, a short drive south of downtown Portland, and it also has a pool. The big rooms with kitchenettes are great for families; for more space, opt for a one- or two-bedroom suite.

performance hall, and, when you stay here, you are given the option of purchasing tickets to the Crystal Ballroom performance on the night of your visit. When the shows are sold out, this is a real plus of staying here. The wedge-shaped hotel takes up an entire block and is sort of Portland's own Flatiron building. With multiple bars and restaurants in the building and across the street, this is a great place for beer geeks, rock and rollers, and other young, artistic travelers.

303 SW 12th Ave., Portland, OR 97205. www.mcmenamins.com. © **855/205-3930** or 503/972-2670. 51 units. $85–$105 double with shared bath; $145–$165 double with private bath. Children 6 and under stay free in parent's room. AE, DC, DISC, MC, V. Parking $25. **Amenities:** 3 restaurants; 4 lounges; soaking pool. *In room:* MP3 docking station, free Wi-Fi.

Nob Hill & Northwest Portland
MODERATE
Heron Haus ★   A short walk from the bustling Nob Hill shopping and dining district of Northwest Portland, the Heron Haus B&B offers outstanding accommodations, spectacular views, and tranquil surroundings. Surprisingly, the house still features some of the original plumbing. In most places this would be a liability, but not here, since the same man who plumbed Portland's famous Pittock Mansion (p. 93) did the plumbing here. Many of that building's unusual bathroom features are also found at the Heron Haus—one shower has *seven* showerheads. In another room there's a modern whirlpool spa with excellent views of the city. All the rooms have fireplaces.

2545 NW Westover Rd., Portland, OR 97210. www.heronhaus.com. © **503/274-1846.** Fax 503/248-4055. 6 units. $140–$215 double. Rates include full breakfast. 2-night minimum. AE, DISC, MC, V. Free parking. *In room:* A/C, TV, hair dryer, free Wi-Fi.

MODERATE
Inn @ Northrup Station ★   Colorful, hip, retro . . . those are the words that best describe this hotel in the leafy Nob Hill neighborhood. On top of this high style,

the hotel has large rooms with kitchens or kitchenettes, and the Portland Streetcar stops right outside, which makes this a quiet, yet convenient, hotel for exploring many of the city's most interesting neighborhoods and nearby restaurants. The colorful retro decor really sets this all-suite hotel apart from more cookie-cutter corporate hotels around town, and if you appreciate bright colors and contemporary styling, this should be your first choice in town. Lots of the rooms here have balconies, and there's a rooftop terrace.

2025 NW Northrup St., Portland, OR 97209. www.northrupstation.com. © **800/224-1180** or 503/224-0543. Fax 503/273-2102. 70 units. $129–$199 double. Rates include continental breakfast. Children 12 and under stay free in parent's room. AE, DISC, MC, V. Free parking. **Amenities:** Access to nearby health club. In room: A/C, TV, fridge, hair dryer, MP3 docking station, free Wi-Fi.

Silver Cloud Inn Northwest Portland This hotel is on the edge of Portland's trendy Nob Hill neighborhood, and though it's also near an industrial area, it's still an attractive and comfortable place. While the rooms fronting Vaughn Street are well insulated against traffic noise, I still prefer the rooms on the other side of the building. Reasonable rates are the main draw here, but the rooms are also well designed. The minisuites have separate seating areas, which makes them good bets for families. The best thing about the hotel is its location within a 5-minute drive (or 15-min. walk) of both Forest Park and several of the city's best restaurants. To find the hotel, take I-405 to Ore. 30 W. and get off at the Vaughn Street exit.

2426 NW Vaughn St., Portland, OR 97210. www.silvercloud.com. © **800/205-6939** or 503/242-2400. Fax 503/242-1770. 82 units. $129–$179 double. Rates include full breakfast. Children 18 and under stay free in parent's room. AE, DC, DISC, MC, V. Free parking. **Amenities:** Concierge; exercise room and access to nearby health club. In room: A/C, TV, fridge, hair dryer, free Wi-Fi.

South of Downtown & Lake Oswego
EXPENSIVE

Avalon Hotel & Spa ★★★ This hotel sits right on the banks of the Willamette River a mile south of downtown and half a mile south of the South Waterfront District. Although this location is a bit inconvenient for exploring the city on foot, there is a riverside bike path right in front of the hotel, making this a good bet if you're a jogger or like to take leisurely walks. The Avalon's contemporary decor makes it one of the most stylish hotels in the city, and the riverfront rooms, most of which have balconies, provide good views and a chance to breathe in some fresh air. The hotel's stylish restaurant boasts the same great river views and walls of glass to make the most of the setting. A full-service spa gives this luxurious boutique hotel the feel of a much larger resort.

4650 SW Macadam Ave., Portland, OR 97239. www.avalonhotelandspa.com. © **888/556-4402** or 503/802-5800. Fax 503/802-5820. 99 units. $129–$209 double; $219–$499 suite. Rates include continental breakfast. Children 17 and under stay free in parent's room. AE, DC, DISC, MC, V. Valet parking $19. **Amenities:** Restaurant; lounge; babysitting; health club; room service; spa. In room: A/C, TV, CD player, hair dryer, MP3 docking station, free Wi-Fi.

INEXPENSIVE

The Lakeshore Inn 🛍 ☺ Considering that the town of Lake Oswego is Portland's most affluent bedroom community, this hotel is quite reasonably priced. It's right on the lake, is flanked by two parks, and has a pool right on the water's edge, which makes this hotel a great place to stay in summer. The large rooms were completely renovated in 2011, and all have kitchenettes and lakefront decks. There are also one- and two-bedroom suites. The 7-mile drive into downtown Portland follows the Willamette River and is quite pleasant. There are several restaurants and cafes within walking distance.

210 N. State St., Lake Oswego, OR 97034. www.thelakeshoreinn.com. © **800/215-6431** or 503/636-9679. Fax 503/636-6959. 31 units. May–Sept $99–$129 double, $129–$189 suite; Oct–Apr $89–$99 double, $109–$149 suite. Rates include continental breakfast. Children 3 and under stay free in parent's room. AE, DC, DISC, MC, V. Pets accepted ($10 per night). **Amenities:** Outdoor pool. *In room:* A/C, TV, hair dryer, kitchen, free Wi-Fi.

The Rose Quarter, Irvington & Southeast Portland

MODERATE

Lion and the Rose Victorian Bed & Breakfast Inn ★ This imposing Queen Anne–style Victorian inn, located in the historic Irvington District a block off Northeast Broadway, is a real gem. In the Lavonna Room, there's a turret sitting area and a Sleep Number bed, while in the Starina Room you'll find an imposing Edwardian bed and armoire. The Garden Room has a claw-foot tub. If you have problems climbing stairs, ask for the ground floor's Rose Room, which has a whirlpool tub, or the Victorian apartment, which is on the basement level. May through September, breakfasts are sumptuous affairs, great for lingering; October through April, a simpler buffet breakfast is served. You can even save a bit of money by opting not to have breakfast at all. Restaurants, cafes, eclectic boutiques, and a huge shopping mall are all within 4 blocks.

1810 NE 15th Ave., Portland, OR 97212. www.lionrose.com. © **800/955-1647** or 503/287-9245. Fax 503/287-9247. 8 units. $99–$219 double. Rates include full breakfast (lower rates without breakfast). 2-night minimum on holiday weekends. AE, DISC, MC, V. Children 11 and over welcome. **Amenities:** Concierge. *In room:* A/C, TV, hair dryer, free Wi-Fi.

McMenamins Kennedy School 🎒 The Kennedy School, which was an elementary school from 1915 to 1975, is owned by the same local brewing company that turned Portland's old poor farm into the most entertaining and unusual lodge in the state, McMenamins Edgefield (p. 239). In the guest rooms you'll still find the original blackboards and great big school clocks (you know, like the one you used to watch so expectantly). However, the classroom/guest rooms here now have their own bathrooms, so you won't have to raise your hand or walk down the hall. On the premises you'll also find a restaurant, a movie-theater pub, a cigar bar, and a big heated soaking pool. The Kennedy School is located north of the stylish Irvington neighborhood in an up-and-coming part of the city that dates from the early 20th century.

5736 NE 33rd Ave., Portland, OR 97211. www.mcmenamins.com. © **888/249-3983** or 503/249-3983. 35 units. $115–$145 double. Children 6 and under stay free. AE, DC, DISC, MC, V. Pets accepted ($15 per day). **Amenities:** Restaurant; 4 lounges; soaking pool; room service. *In room:* A/C, free Wi-Fi.

Portland's White House ★★ With massive columns framing the portico, a circular driveway, and, in the front garden, a bubbling fountain, this imposing Greek-revival mansion bears more than a passing resemblance to its namesake in Washington, D.C. Behind the mahogany front doors, a grand foyer with original hand-painted wall murals is flanked by a parlor and the formal dining room, where the large breakfast is served beneath sparkling crystal chandeliers. A double staircase leads past a large stained-glass window to the second-floor accommodations. Canopy beds, four-poster beds, antique furnishings, and bathrooms with claw-foot or whirlpool tubs further the feeling of luxury here. Request the balcony room, and you can gaze out past the Greek columns and imagine you're in the Oval Office. There are also three rooms in the restored carriage house.

1914 NE 22nd Ave., Portland, OR 97212. www.portlandswhitehouse.com. ℰ **800/272-7131** or 503/287-7131. Fax 503/249-1641. 8 units. $135–$235 double. Rates include full breakfast. DISC, MC, V. **Amenities:** Concierge. *In room:* A/C, TV/DVD, CD player, hair dryer, MP3 docking station, free Wi-Fi.

INEXPENSIVE

Everett Street Guesthouse 🎒 No teddy bears, no frilly curtains, no pot-pourri—that's the mantra at this gorgeous little hideaway on a quiet residential street in northeast Portland. Innkeeper Terry Rusinow has an impeccable eye for interior decor, so public spaces and guest rooms here are beautifully decorated. This little inn has two rooms and a gorgeous little cottage with a kitchenette in the backyard. When you stay in the main house, you almost feel as though you've rented the entire place. Note that this is a nonsmoking and perfume-free house, and there is a resident cat. There are loads of great restaurants within walking distance.

2306 NE Everett St., Portland, OR 97232. www.everettstreetguesthouse.com. ℰ **503/230-0211** or 503/830-0650. 3 units. $85 double; $105 cottage. Rates include continental breakfast (except in cottage). 2-night minimum (3 nights in cottage). MC, V. No children. **Amenities:** Bikes; concierge. *In room:* No phone, Wi-Fi.

Jupiter Hotel 🎒 Although this place calls itself a boutique hotel, it's really more of a boutique motel. Once an aging midcentury motel, the Jupiter is the outcome of an extreme makeover and is now an überhip address for the Portland arts crowd and those in town to participate in the city's hip scene. With its log-cabin-swank Doug Fir Lounge restaurant/bar/nightclub, the Jupiter is also a popular spot for partying Portlanders, so don't plan on getting much sleep if you stay here. Platform beds, photo murals on the walls, and lots of retro accents provide guest rooms with plenty of hip styling for young travelers on a tight budget.

800 E. Burnside St., Portland, OR 97214. www.jupiterhotel.com. ℰ **877/800-0004** or 503/230-9200. 81 units. $99–$149 double; $350–$400 suite. Children 21 and under stay free in parent's room. AE, DC, DISC, MC, V. Parking $8. Pets accepted ($30 per night). **Amenities:** Restaurant; 2 lounges; bikes; concierge; access to nearby health club; room service. *In room:* A/C, TV/DVD, hair dryer, MP3 docking station, free Wi-Fi.

The Airport Area & Vancouver, Washington

Moderately priced hotels abound in the airport area, which makes this a good place to look for a room if you arrive with no reservation. Vancouver, Washington, just across the Columbia River from Portland, is another economical area from which to explore Portland.

MODERATE

Aloft Portland Airport at Cascade Station ★ ☺ 🌶 Sort of a kinder, gentler W hotel, the Aloft is hip and playful without being in your face. This location, just outside the airport, may not put you in the heart of Portland, but you can get to downtown easily on the MAX light rail and won't even need a car. Because this is primarily a business hotel, the guest rooms are wired to the max, and with 9-foot ceilings and big windows, the rooms feel quite spacious. With treats for kids and games in the lounge, this hotel is also a good choice for families.

9920 NE Cascades Pkwy., Portland, OR 97220. www.aloftportland.com. ℰ **877/462-5638** or 503/200-5678. Fax 503/200-5244. 136 units. $109–$199 double. Children 18 and under stay free in parent's room.

AE, DC, DISC, MC, V. Pets accepted. **Amenities:** Lounge; free airport transfers; bikes; exercise room; indoor pool. *In room:* A/C, TV, fridge, hair dryer, MP3 docking station, free Wi-Fi.

Homewood Suites by Hilton Vancouver/Portland ☺ Located across the street from the Columbia River, this modern all-suite hotel is a great choice for families. The hotel charges surprisingly reasonable rates for large apartment-like accommodations that include full kitchens. Rates include not only a large breakfast, but afternoon snacks as well (Mon–Thurs). These snacks are substantial enough to pass for dinner if you aren't too hungry. The hotel is right across the street from both a beach-themed restaurant and a brewpub. Across the street, you'll also find a paved riverside path that's great for walking or jogging. The only drawback is that it's a 15- to 20-minute drive to downtown Portland.

701 SE Columbia Shores Blvd., Vancouver, WA 98661. www.homewoodsuites.com. ℂ **800/225-5466** or 360/750-1100. Fax 360/750-4899. 104 units. $139–$209 double. Rates include full breakfast. Children 18 and under stay free in parent's room. AE, DC, DISC, MC, V. Free parking. Pets accepted ($25 per night). **Amenities:** Free airport transfer; exercise room; Jacuzzi; outdoor pool. *In room:* A/C, TV/DVD, hair dryer, kitchen, free Wi-Fi.

INEXPENSIVE

Clarion Hotel Conveniently located right outside the airport, this hotel has one of the best backyards of any hotel in the Portland area. A lake, lawns, and trees create a tranquil setting despite the proximity of both the airport and a busy nearby road. Rooms are designed primarily for business travelers, but even if you aren't here on an expense account, they are a good value, especially those with whirlpool tubs or gas fireplaces. Best of all, almost every room has a view of the lake. An indoor pool is another big plus. To find this hotel, take the complimentary airport shuttle or head straight out of the airport, drive under the I-205 overpass, and watch for the hotel sign ahead on the left.

11518 NE Glenn Widing Dr., Portland, OR 97220. www.choicehotels.com. ℂ **877/424-6423** or 503/252-2222. Fax 503/257-7008. 101 units. $79–$129 double. Rates include full breakfast. Children 17 and under stay free in parent's room. AE, DC, DISC, MC, V. Free parking. **Amenities:** Free airport transfers; exercise room; Jacuzzi; indoor pool. *In room:* A/C, TV, fridge, hair dryer, free Wi-Fi.

WHERE TO EAT

The Portland restaurant scene is hot, and it's not just because of all the wood ovens that have been cranking out perfect pizzas for the past few years. The city has a national reputation for having great restaurants. Driving this renaissance are lots of creative young chefs and their affinity for local produce and wines from Willamette Valley wineries. Bounteous ingredients can be sourced locally, including organic fruits and vegetables, hazelnuts and walnuts, wild mushrooms, even Oregon truffles. And, of course, pinot noir, pinot gris, and pinot blanc. The list goes on and on.

The only catch to the Portland dining scene is that it's spread out, and some of the most talked-about restaurants are basically neighborhood spots in residential districts away from the city center. While the neighborhood locations are inconvenient for visitors unfamiliar with navigating Portland, even more inconvenient is that these restaurants often don't take reservations. For this reason, I'm still partial to the less hyped but more reliable restaurants downtown and in the Pearl District and the Nob Hill/Northwest neighborhoods. Call me old-fashioned, but I'm just not interested in waiting 2 hours for a table when I'm going to spend $60 or more on dinner.

Downtown (Including the Skidmore Historic District & Chinatown)

EXPENSIVE

The Heathman Restaurant and Bar ★★★ NORTHWEST/FRENCH   Serving Northwest cuisine with a French accent, the Heathman Restaurant is Portland's grande dame nouvelle/regional restaurant. Philippe Boulot, a James Beard Foundation Award winner, changes his menu daily, but one thing remains constant: The ingredients used are the freshest of Oregon and Northwest seafood, meat, wild game, and produce. The interior is Art Deco–inspired, the atmosphere bistrolike. An extensive wine list spotlights Oregon wines. The Heathman Hotel has an extensive collection of classic and contemporary art, and on the restaurant walls you'll find Andy Warhol's *Endangered Species* series.

In the Heathman Hotel, 1001 SW Broadway. ☏ **503/790-7752.** www.heathmanrestaurantandbar. com. Reservations recommended. Main courses $11–$19 lunch, $19–$39 dinner. AE, DISC, MC, V. Mon–Thurs 6:30–11am, 11:30am–2pm, and 5:30–10pm; Fri 6:30–11am, 11:30am–2pm, and 5:30–11pm; Sat 6:30am–2pm, and 5:30–11pm; Sun 6:30am–2pm and 5:30–10pm.

Higgins ★★ NORTHWEST/MEDITERRANEAN   Higgins strikes a perfect balance between contemporary and classic in both decor and cuisine. The menu, which changes frequently, explores contemporary culinary horizons, while the decor in the tri-level dining room opts for wood paneling and elegant place settings. Despite all this, the restaurant remains unpretentious, and portions can be surprisingly generous for a high-end restaurant. Flavors change with the season, but are often both subtle and earthy. Pork lovers should keep an eye out for the braised "whole pig" plate. The steamed mussels are always a good starter, and in the bar, the burger is delicious. If you happen to be a beer lover, you'll be glad to know that Higgins has one of the most interesting beer selections in town (and plenty of good wine, too).

1239 SW Broadway. ☏ **503/222-9070.** http://higginsportland.com. Reservations recommended. Main courses $9–$22 lunch, $20–$37 dinner. AE, DC, DISC, MC, V. Mon–Fri 11:30am–2pm and 5–10:30pm; Sat–Sun 5–10:30pm; bistro menu served in the bar daily until midnight.

Jake's Famous Crawfish ★ SEAFOOD   Jake's has been a Portland institution since 1909 and boasts a back bar that came all the way around Cape Horn in 1880. Much of the rest of the decor looks just as old and well worn as the bar, and therein lies this restaurant's charm. Unfortunately, prices here are in keeping with some of the city's most creative restaurants, while the dishes are not nearly so memorable. There's a daily menu listing a dozen or more specials, but there's really no question about what to eat at Jake's: crawfish, which is always on the menu and served several different ways. Monday through Thursday from 3 to 6pm and 9pm to midnight, and Friday and Saturday from 10pm to midnight, bar appetizers are $1.95 to $4.95. The noise level after work, when local businesspeople pack the bar, can be high, and the wait for a table can be long if you don't make a reservation, but don't let these obstacles put you off.

401 SW 12th Ave. ☏ **503/226-1419.** www.jakesfamouscrawfish.com. Reservations recommended. Main courses $8–$20 lunch, $15–$45 dinner. AE, DC, DISC, MC, V. Mon–Thurs 11:30am–10pm; Fri–Sat 11:30am–midnight; Sun 3–10pm.

Veritable Quandary ★★ NEW AMERICAN   With the prettiest garden patio in downtown Portland, the VQ, as it's known to locals, is a historic gem of a restaurant and should not be missed on a summer visit. The restaurant is conveniently located

Downtown Portland Dining

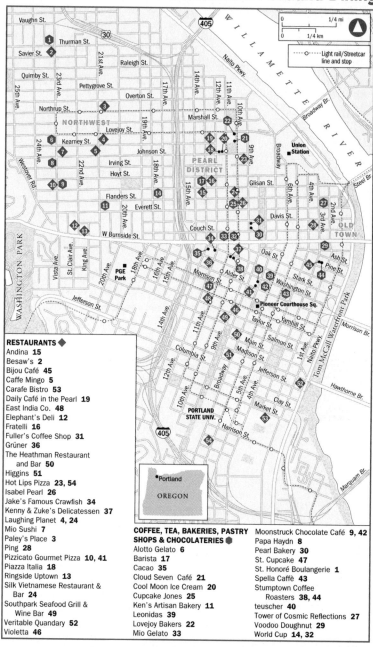

RESTAURANTS ◆
Andina **15**
Besaw's **2**
Bijou Café **45**
Caffe Mingo **5**
Carafe Bistro **53**
Daily Café in the Pearl **19**
East India Co. **48**
Elephant's Deli **12**
Fratelli **16**
Fuller's Coffee Shop **31**
Grüner **36**
The Heathman Restaurant
  and Bar **50**
Higgins **51**
Hot Lips Pizza **23, 54**
Isabel Pearl **26**
Jake's Famous Crawfish **34**
Kenny & Zuke's Delicatessen **37**
Laughing Planet **4, 24**
Mio Sushi **7**
Paley's Place **3**
Ping **28**
Pizzicato Gourmet Pizza **10, 41**
Piazza Italia **18**
Ringside Uptown **13**
Silk Vietnamese Restaurant &
  Bar **24**
Southpark Seafood Grill &
  Wine Bar **49**
Veritable Quandary **52**
Violetta **46**

**COFFEE, TEA, BAKERIES, PASTRY
SHOPS & CHOCOLATERIES ●**
Alotto Gelato **6**
Barista **17**
Cacao **35**
Cloud Seven Café **21**
Cool Moon Ice Cream **20**
Cupcake Jones **25**
Ken's Artisan Bakery **11**
Leonidas **39**
Lovejoy Bakers **22**
Mio Gelato **33**

Moonstruck Chocolate Café **9, 42**
Papa Haydn **8**
Pearl Bakery **30**
St. Cupcake **47**
St. Honoré Boulangerie **1**
Spella Caffè **43**
Stumptown Coffee
  Roasters **38, 44**
teuscher **40**
Tower of Cosmic Reflections **27**
Voodoo Doughnut **29**
World Cup **14, 32**

4

PORTLAND | Where to Eat

in an old brick building just a block off Tom McCall Waterfront Park, and windows and the patio look out on a small tree-shaded pocket park. The menu changes daily, but keep an eye out for the grilled prawns, and don't pass up the *osso buco*. The chef here pulls in all kinds of influences, so don't be surprised if you find bacon-wrapped dates stuffed with goat cheese and almonds, or duck-confit spring rolls served with wasabi-ginger sauce.

1220 SW First Ave. ✆ **503/227-7342.** www.veritablequandary.com. Reservations recommended. Main courses $11–$16 lunch, $19–$29 dinner. AE, DC, DISC, MC, V. Mon–Fri 11:30am–3pm and 5–10pm; Sat–Sun 9:30am–3pm and 5–10pm.

MODERATE

There's an outpost of **Typhoon!** at 410 SW Broadway (✆ **503/224-8285**), in the Hotel Lucia (for the complete review, see below).

Carafe Bistro ★ FRENCH With its small zinc bar, wicker patio chairs, and warm interior hues, Carafe feels just the way you'd expect a neighborhood bistro in Paris to feel. The menu is simple bistro fare (everything from baked escargot to croquet monsieur). With many appetizers, salads, and side dishes, you can easily assemble a thoroughly Gallic meal. On top of all this, Carafe is right across the street from Keller Auditorium.

200 SW Market St. ✆ **503/248-0004.** www.carafebistro.com. Main courses $9–$13 lunch, $11–$22 dinner. AE, DC, DISC, MC, V. Mon 11:30am–2:30pm; Tues–Fri 11:30am–8:30pm; Sat 5–9pm.

East India Co Grill & Bar ★ INDIAN With a convenient location directly behind downtown's main library, this large, pretty space serves superb Indian food at reasonable prices. Be sure to start with the fragrant and flavorful *papdi chaat*, a sort of Indian Napoleon. The menu includes lots of great dishes, including tandoori grilled fish and creamy *malai kofta* (dumplings stuffed with nuts and raisins and cooked in creamy gravy). This is the sort of place you eat at once and then have to return to as soon as possible (perhaps lunch the next day) for more of those great exotic flavors. The bar mixes some interesting cocktails.

821 SW 11th Ave. ✆ **503/227-8815.** www.eastindiacopdx.com. Reservations recommended. Main courses $9–$16 lunch, $13–$25 dinner. AE, MC, V. Mon–Sat 11:30am–2:30pm and 5–9:30pm.

Grüner ★★ AUSTRIAN/GERMAN Starkly minimalist, yet with a relaxed feel, this restaurant takes the dishes of middle Europe and gives them a fresh Northwestern spin. Start with a mushroom-hazelnut soup, an Alsatian "pizza," or duck terrine with pickled fiddleheads. Though Grüner serves dishes from a region known for its meat-heavy meals, salads here are always a highlight. Be sure to ask your server about the size of the salad you intend to order; some, such as the Grüner salad, are big enough to feed two. The house-made sausages are always a good bet, but you might also encounter spaetzle (German pasta) with morels and Riesling-braised chicken. The wine list leans heavily toward Germany, Austria, and Switzerland, and you might want to consider having a crisp Grüner Veltliner with your meal.

527 SW 12th Ave. ✆ **503/241-7163.** www.grunerpdx.com. Reservations recommended. Main courses $9–$12 lunch, $14–$22 dinner. Mon–Thurs 11:30am–2pm and 5–9:30pm; Fri 11:30am–2pm and 5–10:30pm; Sat 5–10:30pm.

Southpark Seafood Grill & Wine Bar ★ 🍴 MEDITERRANEAN/SEAFOOD With its high ceiling, long heavy drapes, and interesting wall mural, the wine bar here is a contemporary interpretation of late-19th-century Paris, and the main dining room is both comfortable and classy. For a starter, don't pass up the fried calamari served with the savory sauce of the moment. Equally delicious is the butternut squash–and-ricotta-filled ravioli with toasted hazelnuts, which comes in a rich Marsala wine sauce that begs to be sopped up with the crusty bread. An extensive wine list presents some compelling choices, and the desserts are consistently excellent. Southpark has been certified by the Green Restaurant Association.

901 SW Salmon St. (℮ **503/326-1300.** www.southparkseafood.com. Reservations recommended. Main courses $9.50–$17 lunch, $16–$28 dinner. AE, DISC, MC, V. Sun–Thurs 11:30am–10pm; Fri–Sat 11:30am–11pm.

INEXPENSIVE

Bijou Cafe ★ ☺ NATURAL FOODS   Although the Bijou is ostensibly just a breakfast joint, the folks who run the restaurant take food very seriously. The fresh oyster hash is an absolutely unforgettable way to start the day, as is the brioche French toast. Other big hits include the sautéed potatoes and muffins, which come with full breakfasts; don't leave without trying them. Local and organic products are used as often as possible at this comfortably old-fashioned, yet thoroughly modern, cafe.

132 SW Third Ave. (℮ **503/222-3187.** Breakfast and lunch $7–$15. MC, V. Mon–Fri 7am–2pm; Sat–Sun 8am–2pm.

Kenny & Zuke's Delicatessen ★ DELI   If you've ever been to a New York deli, then you know what to expect from this Portland deli. Kenny & Zuke's goes out of its way to channel the spirit of the Big Apple. The big hits here (with the emphasis on big) are the pastrami sandwiches and the Reubens. The latter can be ordered with either corned beef or pastrami. The meats are cured in-house, piled high and thick between the bread. Because this is Portland, a city that likes to be different, you can also get pastrami cheese fries, which are exactly what they sound like. There are also latkes and blintzes, and you can wash everything down with an egg cream.

1038 SW Stark St. (℮ **503/222-3354.** www.kennyandzukes.com. Reservations not accepted. Main courses $7–$16. DISC, MC, V. Mon–Thurs 7am–8pm; Fri–Sat 7am–10pm; Sun 8am–8pm.

Ping ★★ PAN-ASIAN   I've spent a lot of time in Southeast Asia, and, with one exception, no other restaurant I've ever been to on this side of the Pacific comes as close to a Southeast Asian dining experience as Ping (the exception is Ping's southeast Portland sister restaurant, Pok Pok, p. 79). The menu here is long, packed with dishes you've likely never heard of or tasted before, and, best of all, cheap. This place is for adventurous diners (baby octopus skewers; shrimp chips; quail-egg skewers; deep-fried tiny fish).

102 NW Fourth Ave. (℮ **503/229-7464.** www.pingpdx.com. Reservations recommended. Main courses $8–$12. AE, DISC, MC, V. Tues–Sat 11am–10pm.

Violetta ★ ☺ AMERICAN   With the motto "slow food, fast," Violetta is not your average burger joint. That becomes apparent as soon as you see this casual restaurant, a little glass cube beneath the glass roof of downtown Portland's Director Park, one of the city's newest and most popular public spaces. Violetta emphasizes local produce and ingredients as much as possible (try something with Oregonzola blue cheese). That you can also get a glass of wine or a pint of local microbrew also helps set Violetta apart from most other burger joints. They also serve Hot Lips sodas, locally produced fruit sodas that are positively addictive. Best of all, when you eat here, you can dine on the huge covered patio that takes up a quarter of Director Park.

877 SW Taylor St. (℮ **503/233-3663.** www.violettapdx.com. Reservations not accepted. Main courses $5–$8.50. AE, DISC, MC, V. Spring–summer Mon–Thurs 11am–10pm, Fri–Sat 11am–11pm, Sun 11am–9pm; fall–winter Sun–Thurs 11am–9pm, Fri–Sat 11am–10pm.

4

PORTLAND | Where to Eat

Northwest Portland (Including the Pearl District & Nob Hill)

VERY EXPENSIVE

RingSide Uptown ★ STEAK   Despite the location on a rather unattractive stretch of West Burnside Street, RingSide has been a favorite Portland steakhouse for more than 60 years. Boxing may be the main theme of the restaurant, but the name is a two-fisted pun that also refers to the incomparable onion rings that are an essential part of any meal here. Have your rings with a side order of one of the perfectly cooked steaks for a real knockout meal. The three-course prix-fixe dinners are only $35 if you order before 5:45pm or after 9pm.

2165 W Burnside St. ✆ **503/223-1513.** www.ringsidesteakhouse.com. Reservations recommended. Steaks $30–$68; other main courses $25–$66. AE, DC, MC, V. Mon–Wed 5–11:30pm; Thurs–Sat 5pm–midnight; Sun 4–11:30pm.

EXPENSIVE

Andina ★★ PERUVIAN   Whether you've tried Peruvian food before or not, don't miss an opportunity to eat at Andina. I've been known to eat here several times in the same week because I can't get enough of the spicy bread-dipping sauces, the grilled octopus, and the beautifully presented *causa* (mashed purple potatoes flavored with lime and layered with savory fillings). Because there is so much on the menu, I suggest sticking with the small plates and trying lots of them. Also, be sure to have a glass of *chicha morada,* a juice made from purple corn.

1314 NW Glisan St. ✆ **503/228-9535.** www.andinarestaurant.com. Reservations recommended. Main courses $12–$15 lunch, $18–$30 dinner. AE, DISC, MC, V. Sun–Thurs 11:30am–2:30pm and 5–9:30pm (tapas until 11pm); Fri–Sat 11:30am–2:30pm and 5–10:30pm (tapas until midnight).

Paley's Place ★★ NORTHWEST/FRENCH   Located in a Victorian-era house, Paley's is another favorite of Portland foodies. Year after year, James Beard–award-winning Chef Vitaly Paley continues to receive accolades. The menu relies extensively on local organic ingredients and ranges from traditional bistro fare to dishes with complex flavors. Whether you're in the mood for scallops and morel mushrooms in a saffron beurre blanc, rabbit ravioli, or escargots à la Bordelaise, you'll certainly find something that appeals to you. If you've never tried sweetbreads, this is the place to do so, and there is also an extensive charcuterie list. The signature *frites,* with a mustard aioli, are not to be missed. Big on wines, Paley's offers wine tastings on Wednesdays. For dessert, I can't pass up the warm chocolate soufflé cake with outrageously rich house-made ice cream.

1204 NW 21st Ave. ✆ **503/243-2403.** www.paleysplace.net. Reservations recommended. Main courses $15–$39. AE, DISC, MC, V. Mon–Thurs 5:30–10pm; Fri–Sat 5:30–11pm; Sun 5–10pm.

MODERATE

Caffe Mingo ★★ 🍴 ITALIAN   This intimate little neighborhood restaurant has terrific food at relatively reasonable prices. The only problem with this immensely popular place is that because they only take reservations for large parties, you almost always have to wait for a table. The solution? Get here as early as possible. The menu is short and focuses on painstakingly prepared Italian comfort food. Just about all the items on the menu are winners, from the antipasto platter, which might include roasted fennel, fresh mozzarella, and roasted red pepper, to an unusual penne pasta dish with tender beef braised in Chianti and espresso. The *panna cotta* dessert ("cooked cream" with fruit) is reason enough to come back again and again.

breakfast: THE MOST IMPORTANT MEAL OF THE DAY

If you're a breakfast person and are desperately seeking sustenance in the morning, check out the following places.

In business since 1903, **Besaw's**, 2301 NW Savier St. (℃ **503/228-2619;** www.besaws.com), is a Portland institution and a great place to get a filling breakfast before heading out for a hike in Forest Park. Try the wild-salmon scramble.

Founded in Portland in 1953, **the Original Pancake House,** 8601 SW 24th Ave. (℃ **503/246-9007;** www.originalpancakehouse.com), has lines out the door every weekend. Maybe you've got one of these places in your city (they're in 26 states), but this is the *original* Original Pancake House. Get the apple pancake or the Dutch baby. Open Wednesday to Sunday from 7am to 3pm.

Isabel Pearl, 330 NW 10th Ave. (℃ **503/222-4333;** www.isabelscantina.com), a glass-walled jewel box of a restaurant in the Pearl District, serves big, creative breakfasts. Try the coconut French toast or pesto scramble.

If biscuits and gravy are your breakfast of choice, then head to southeast Portland and **Pine State Biscuits,** 3640 SE Belmont St. (℃ **503/236-3346;** http://pinestatebiscuits.com), which also does a variety of unusual biscuit sandwiches. There's a second Pine State Biscuits at 2204 NE Alberta St. (℃ **503/477-6605**), and they can also be found every Saturday at the Portland Farmers Market in the South Park Blocks near Portland State University.

The **Bijou Cafe** (p. 71), **Daily Cafe** (p. 74), and **Fuller's Coffee Shop** (p. 74) also serve excellent breakfasts.

807 NW 21st Ave. ℃ **503/226-4646.** www.caffemingonw.com. Reservations accepted only for parties of 6 or more. Main courses $12–$28. AE, DISC, MC, V. Mon–Thurs 5–10pm; Fri–Sat 5–10:30pm; Sun 4:30–9:30pm.

Fratelli ★★ REGIONAL ITALIAN   In this rustic-yet-chic restaurant, cement walls provide a striking contrast to dramatic draperies and softly glowing candles. Dishes are consistently good, with surprisingly moderate prices for the Pearl District. Be sure to start with the mix-and-match antipasto plate, which might include chicken-liver mousse on crostini; frittata with seasonal vegetables; and grilled asparagus with shaved fennel and honey-lemon dressing. The polenta with wild mushrooms and the seared chicken wrapped in prosciutto are longtime favorites. This restaurant's aesthetic and menu are similar to Caffe Mingo's, but at Fratelli you can make reservations.

1230 NW Hoyt St. ℃ **503/241-8800.** www.fratellicucina.com. Reservations recommended. Main courses $7–$10 lunch, $17–$23 dinner. AE, MC, V. Sun–Mon 5–9pm; Tues–Thurs 11:30am–2pm and 5–9pm; Fri 11:30am–2pm and 5–10pm; Sat 11:30am–4pm and 5–10pm.

Silk Vietnamese Restaurant & Bar ★ VIETNAMESE   This is one of the most stylish restaurants in town, with rippling walls of back-lit glass and decor drawing on a modern Asian aesthetic. The prices, however, are quite reasonable, especially for the Pearl District. You can get flavorful *pho* soup (a Vietnamese staple), but I prefer the more substantial entrees, as well as such unusual dishes as banana-flower salad and the clay-pot pork.

1012 NW Glisan St. ℂ **503/248-2172.** www.silkbyphovan.com. Reservations recommended. Main courses $8–$24 lunch, $10–$24 dinner. AE, DISC, MC, V. Mon–Sat 11am–3pm and 5–10pm.

Typhoon! On Everett ★ THAI This Thai restaurant is one of my favorites for its unusual menu offerings that generally aren't available at other Portland Thai restaurants. Be sure to start a meal with the *miang kum,* which consists of dried shrimp, tiny chilies, ginger, lime, peanuts, shallots, and toasted coconut drizzled with a sweet-and-sour sauce and wrapped up in a spinach leaf. (I first had this in Thailand and waited years to get it in the United States.) The whole front wall of the restaurant slides away for Thai-style open-air dining in the summer.

There's another **Typhoon!** at 410 SW Broadway (ℂ **503/224-8285**), in the Hotel Lucia.

2310 NW Everett St. ℂ **503/243-7557.** www.typhoonrestaurants.com. Reservations recommended. Main courses $13–$26. AE, DISC, MC, V. Mon–Thurs 11am–2pm and 4–9pm; Fri 11am–2pm and 4–10pm; Sat 4–10pm; Sun noon–9pm.

INEXPENSIVE

Daily Cafe in the Pearl AMERICAN Healthy, flavorful breakfasts and creative sandwiches are the mainstays of this hip-yet-casual urban cafe in the heart of the Pearl District. On sunny days, take your meal out onto the converted loading dock and ogle all the buff people coming and going from the neighborhood gym. This is primarily a lunch spot, serving the likes of spicy Italian roast pork sandwiches, but dinners are also served. Other locations can be found in southeast Portland inside Rejuvenation House Parts, 1100 SE Grand Ave. (ℂ **503/234-8189**), and in the south waterfront district in the OHSU Center for Health and Healing, 3355 SW Bond Ave. (ℂ **503/224-9691**).

902 NW 13th Ave. ℂ **503/242-1916.** www.dailycafe.net. Main courses $7–$10 lunch, $17–$21 dinner. AE, MC, V. Mon–Fri 7am–9pm; Sat 8am–4pm; Sun 9am–2pm.

Elephant's Delicatessen DELI This is definitely not your corner deli, and it pushes the boundaries of what can even be considered a deli. Elephant's is a behemoth, which of course makes the name appropriate, and it's mouthwateringly diverse in its food offerings. Whether you want some pastrami to go or a full gourmet meal, you can get it here, and this is the best place in town to put together a picnic before heading up to Washington Park. Want a cocktail? Elephant's has a full bar and plenty of good appetizers to accompany the drinks. Be sure to check out the economical Monday night fireside dinners.

115 NW 22nd Ave. ℂ **503/299-6304.** www.elephantsdeli.com. Reservations not accepted. Main courses $6.75–$18. AE, MC, V. Mon–Sat 7am–7:30pm; Sun 9:30am–6:30pm.

Fuller's Coffee Shop AMERICAN Restaurants made to look like old diners can be found all over the country, but *genuine* old-fashioned diners are a bit harder to come by; Fuller's is just such an authentic diner. Grab a stool at the long zig-zagging counter and prepare to time travel. Fuller's is known primarily for its filling breakfasts, especially its omelets, but you can also get a pig in a blanket (sausage rolled in a German pancake) or a hot-cake sandwich. The lunch menu includes such diner classics as sloppy joe and chicken-fried steak, but also includes fried oysters and fired razor clams. The milkshakes are legendary around these parts.

136 NW Ninth Ave. ℂ **503/222-5608.** Reservations not accepted. Main courses $4–$9.50. No credit cards. Mon–Fri 6am–3pm; Sat 7am–2pm; Sun 8am–2pm.

Piazza Italia ★★ ITALIAN   Portland has more than its fair share of good Italian restaurants, but none feels as much like a trip to Italy as this one. The staff speaks Italian most of the time, and the TV over the bar is usually tuned to Italian soap operas and soccer matches. Just inside the front door is a glass case full of the imported meats, cheeses, and olives that go into the antipasto plate. This place is small and has a very limited menu, but it's always bustling. Try the simple linguine *squarciarella,* made with eggs, prosciutto, onions, and Parmesan cheese. During the summer, the tables on the sidewalk are in high demand.

1129 NW Johnson St. ✆ **503/478-0619.** www.piazzaportland.com. Main courses $9–$14 lunch, $11–$20 dinner. Reservations recommended. AE, DISC, MC, V. Mon–Thurs 11:30am–3pm and 5–9pm; Fri–Sat 11:30am–3pm and 5–10pm; Sun 11:30am–3pm and 5–8pm.

Southwest Portland
EXPENSIVE

Chart House ★★ SEAFOOD   Although this place is part of a chain with lots of outposts all over California and the rest of the West, it also happens to have the best view of any restaurant in Portland. On top of that, it serves the best New England clam chowder in the state. While you savor your chowder, you can marvel at the views of the Willamette River, Mount Hood, and Mount St. Helens. Fresh fish—grilled, baked, or blackened—is the house specialty. You'll also find a selection of excellent steaks. No dinner here is complete without the hot chocolate lava cake, which has to be ordered at the start of your meal. Because the views are so great, I recommend coming here for lunch or the early-bird dinner specials, which cost $19 to $22 and are available Monday through Thursday between 5 and 6pm. Because the Chart House is a 10-minute drive from downtown Portland, call ahead and get driving directions.

5700 SW Terwilliger Blvd. ✆ **503/246-6963.** www.chart-house.com. Reservations recommended. Main courses $10–$27 lunch, $20–$47 dinner. AE, DC, DISC, MC, V. Mon–Thurs 11:30am–2pm and 5–9:30pm; Fri 11:30am–2pm and 5–10pm; Sat 5–10pm; Sun 5–9pm.

North & Northeast Portland
MODERATE

Pambiche 🎁 CUBAN   Driving past this tiny hole-in-the-wall, painted garish tropical colors, you'd never guess that it's one of Portland's most popular restaurants. The food is straight out of Havana, with taro-root fritters, codfish-and-potato cro-quettes, fried yucca root, and fried bananas. Don't fill up on all those tasty little tropi-cal treats, though; the main dishes, such as Creole chicken, pepper-pot stew, and oxtail braised in red wine, are all served in huge portions.

2811 NE Glisan St. ✆ **503/233-0511.** www.pambiche.com. Reservations not accepted. Main courses $8–$13 lunch, $9–$20 dinner. MC, V. Mon–Thurs 11am–10pm; Fri 11am–midnight; Sat 8am–midnight; Sun 8am–10pm.

Toro Bravo ★★★ SPANISH   I don't usually applaud for a meal, but the first time I ate at this neighborhood tapas restaurant, my dinner companions and I just couldn't help ourselves. Perhaps it was the brandy-soaked prunes stuffed with foie gras, bacon-wrapped dates, olive-oil cake with strawberry caramel, or maybe a crepe filled with lemon curd. Every plate is a revelation—spicy octopus-and-prawn stew, smoked pork rillettes with orange marmalade and toast, sautéed snap peas with ham and mint. Just be sure to order the house-smoked coppa steak—phenomenal. Tapas prices are low, but you'll likely eat enough that the tab will add up. If you're feeling

family-friendly RESTAURANTS

Bijou Cafe (p. 71)   Parents who care about the food their children eat will want to bring the family to this cozy old-fashioned diner that serves great breakfasts made with organic ingredients.

Violetta (p. 71)   Serving "fast slow food," this fresh-and-local burger joint is in a glass cube under a glass roof on downtown's Director Park, which, in summer, has a play fountain for the kids. Burgers and splashing water? Doesn't get any better than that.

Old Wives' Tales (p. 79)   This place has been keeping young, liberal-minded families contentedly dining out for 3 decades now. A dining room with an attached children's playroom assures Mom and Dad of an enjoyable evening out.

adventurous, order the $25 chef's tasting menu, and let the kitchen make the decisions for you.

120 NE Russell St. ⓒ **503/281-4464.** www.torobravopdx.com. Reservations accepted only for parties of 7 or more and only Sun–Thurs. Small plates $1–$13; large plates $8–$20. AE, DISC, MC, V. Sun–Thurs 5–10pm; Fri–Sat 5–11pm.

INEXPENSIVE

Screen Door ★ SOUTHERN   This casual restaurant, just a few blocks from the restaurant-heavy crossroads of East Burnside Street and 28th Avenue, serves down-home Southern comfort food—shrimp and grits, fried green tomatoes, Carolina pulled-pork barbecue, po' boys—in huge portions, and the Northwesterners who eat here seem to love it. Since this is Portland, though, you can get a side of organic vegetables from a weekly list of half a dozen different sides/starters. Be sure to order cornbread and the sweet-potato fries.

2337 E. Burnside St. ⓒ **503/542-0880.** www.screendoorrestaurant.com. Reservations not accepted. Main courses $11–$16. AE, DISC, MC, V. Tues–Fri 5:30–10pm; Sat 9am–2:30pm and 5:30–10pm; Sun 9am–2:30pm and 5:30–9pm.

Southeast Portland

EXPENSIVE

Genoa ★★ ITALIAN   Sometimes a restaurant needs a bit of refocusing to sustain popularity for decades on end, and so, after closing in 2008, Genoa, long Portland's premier Italian restaurant, reinvented itself. Lighter and brighter, less formal, yet every bit as committed to serving the best Italian-inspired cuisine in the city. Each night there are two five-course menu options, and, because this is Portland, one is a pescetarian/vegetarian feast. The menu changes monthly, but you can expect such dishes as pheasant breast stuffed with prosciutto and taleggio cheese, venison loin wrapped in house-cured bacon, and tagliatelle pasta with duck-leg ragu. Genoa also operates the adjacent **Accanto,** 2838 SE Belmont St. (ⓒ **503/235-4900;** www.accantopdx.com), a casual cafe and wine bar emphasizing pastas and small plates.

2832 SE Belmont St. ⓒ **503/238-1464.** www.genoarestaurant.com. Reservations highly recommended. 5-course prix fixe menu $65. AE, DISC, MC, V. Sun and Tues–Thurs 5:30–9pm; Fri–Sat 5:30–9:30pm.

Laurelhurst Market ★★ STEAKS   The popularity of this combination steakhouse and butcher shop is proof that not everyone in Portland has become a vegan, yet. By day, Laurelhurst Market is an upscale butcher shop, but in the evening it takes

COFFEE, TEA, BAKERIES, PASTRY SHOPS & CHOCOLATERIES ●

Alma Chocolate **12**
Palio Dessert & Espresso House **25**
Pix Patisserie **17**
Rimsky-Korsakoffee House **6**
Staccato Gelato **11**
Stumptown Coffee Roasters **21, 24**
Tao of Tea **22**
Voodoo Doughnut **8**
Water Avenue Coffee **5**

RESTAURANTS ◆

Bamboo Sushi **16**
Beaker & Flask **3**
Bunk Sandwiches **4**
Genoa **19**
Hot Lips Pizza **18**
Ken's Artisan Pizza **15**
Laughing Planet **20**
Laurelhurst Market **14**
Lauro Mediterranean Kitchen **26**
Mio Sushi **23**
Nicholas **2**
Old Wives' Tales **7**
Olympic Provisions **1**
Pambiche **10**
Pizzicato Gourmet Pizza **13**
Pok Pok **27**
Screen Door **9**

the casual Portland aesthetic, adds perfectly prepared cuts of beef, and makes magic with meat. However, don't get the idea that this place is only about steaks. Peruse the butcher case before taking your seat (perhaps out on the front patio if it's summer), and ask your server if you can get some of the interesting cured meats you saw in the case. Such dishes as marrow bones, house-made mozzarella, crispy veal sweetbreads, salt-cured foie gras, and mussels with fries make it clear that this place can do more than just cook a decent steak. Keep an eye out for dishes with the house-made pickles, which are delicious.

3155 E. Burnside St. ℂ **503/206-3097.** www.laurelhurstmarket.com. Reservations recommended. Main courses $12–$38. AE, MC, V. Sun–Thurs 5–10pm; Fri–Sat 5–11pm.

MODERATE

Bamboo Sushi JAPANESE   Bamboo was the first certified sustainable sushi restaurant in the world, so if you want to feast on fresh sushi and still have a clear conscience, order your California roll here. Wild salmon is something of a specialty here (I like the spicy salmon roll). There are also plenty of other good seafood dishes on the menu (albacore carpaccio, Hawaiian-style tuna *poke*, made with seaweed and sesame sauce), plus vegetarian and vegan dishes, too. Look for good deals during happy hour.

310 SE 28th Ave. ℂ **503 232-5255.** www.bamboosushipdx.com. Reservations accepted for parties of 7 or more Sun–Thurs. Main course $11–$25. AE, DISC, MC, V. Daily 4:30–10pm.

Beaker & Flask ★★ NEW AMERICAN   The food and cocktails here are superb. Start with the mushroom appetizer—chanterelles perfectly cooked, with a dash of melt-in-your-mouth bone marrow. Follow with the grilled and smoked mackerel atop potato salad and Dungeness crab—at once creamy, smoky, and oily. Top it off with a Sazerac cocktail (a New Orleans staple said to be the original American cocktail), and don't pass on the pork cheeks with pickled octopus.

727 SE Washington St. ℂ **503/235-8180.** www.beakerandflask.com. Reservations recommended. Main courses $14–$24. DISC, MC, V. Mon–Sat 5pm–midnight.

Ken's Artisan Pizza ★ PIZZA   The heavenly aromas of wood smoke and pizza hit you as soon as you walk in the front door of this casual neighborhood restaurant. Start your meal with the wood oven–roasted vegetable plate, which comes with a trio of seasonal veggies that are wonderfully sauced. You could make a meal on this platter alone, but since this is a pizza place, you have to have a pie. The pizza with fennel sausage and roasted onions is wonderful, but the *amatriciana,* with house-cured pancetta, is good, too.

304 SE 28th Ave. (at Pine St.). ℂ **503/517-9951.** http://kensartisan.com. Reservations not accepted. Main courses $11–$14. MC, V. Mon–Sat 5–10pm; Sun 4–9pm.

Lauro Mediterranean Kitchen ★★ MEDITERRANEAN   Dark, romantic, and stylish, this sleek southeast Portland restaurant, in one of the city's best restaurant districts, is well worth the drive from downtown. The menu changes seasonally, but the paella, which is always on the menu, is a good bet. You might start with Moroccan soup made with lamb, chick peas, spinach, and rice, or roasted asparagus with flavorful romesco sauce. Prices here are considerably lower than they would be for comparable food in the Pearl District, so Lauro represents a pretty good value.

3377 SE Division St. ℂ **503/239-7000.** www.laurokitchen.com. Reservations recommended. Main courses $12–$22. AE, DISC, MC, V. Wed–Thurs and Sun–Mon 5–9pm; Fri–Sat 5–10pm.

INEXPENSIVE

Bunk Sandwiches AMERICAN To find this hole-in-the-wall sandwich shop, just watch for the ever-present line out the door. Why would anyone wait 30 minutes or more for a sandwich? Because they're big, they're filling, and they're packed with flavor. Oh, and, of course, most of the ingredients are locally sourced, including the albacore tuna used in the tasty tuna melt. Other hits here include the pork-belly cubano and the pulled pork with apple-cabbage slaw. You can also get Bunk sandwiches at the affiliated Bunk Bar, 1028 SE Water Ave. (𝒞 **503/894-9708**), not far from the Oregon Museum of Science and Industry.

621 SE Morrison St. 𝒞 **503/477-9515.** www.bunksandwiches.com. Main courses $5–$10. DISC, MC, V. Daily 8am–3pm.

Nicholas 👶 MIDDLE EASTERN This little hole in the wall on an unattractive stretch of Grand Avenue is usually packed at mealtimes, and it's not the decor or ambience that pulls people in. The big draw is the great food and cheap prices. In spite of the heat from the pizza oven and the crowded conditions, the customers and waitstaff still manage to be friendly. My favorite dish is the *manakish*, a Mediterranean pizza with *za'atar* (a mix of thyme, oregano, sesame seeds, olive oil, and lemony-flavored sumac). Also available are a creamy hummus, falafel, and kabobs. There's another Nicholas at 3223 NE Broadway (𝒞 **503/445-4700**).

318 SE Grand Ave. (between Pine and Oak sts.). 𝒞 **503/235-5123.** www.nicholasrestaurant.com. Reservations not accepted. Main courses $6.25–$14. MC, V. Mon–Sat 11am–9pm; Sun noon–9pm.

Old Wives' Tales 😊 INTERNATIONAL This restaurant has been feeding liberal, counterculture families for 3 decades now, and continues to be a favorite as much for its soul-satisfying food as for its children's play area. While the kids entertain themselves in the playroom, parents can enjoy such perennial favorites as spanakopita, Greek pasta, burritos, and enchiladas. There are also soup and salad bars, lots of good sandwiches, and plenty of interesting side dishes. Vegetarians and the gluten-intolerant get lots of choices. The children's menu is, of course, the most extensive in town.

1300 E. Burnside St. 𝒞 **503/238-0470.** www.oldwivestalesrestaurant.com. Reservations recommended. Main courses $6–$14. AE, DISC, MC, V. Sun–Thurs 8am–8pm; Fri–Sat 8am–9pm.

Olympic Provisions ★★ 👶 NEW AMERICAN *Sopressata, finocchiona, saucisson sec, chorizo.* If these words have you salivating, then you must be a salami aficionado, and if you are, then you won't want to leave Portland without searching out this hidden chapel of charcuterie. Olympic Provisions produces a wide range of salamis, as well as terrines, rillettes, and pâtés. There are also unusual and delicious house-made pickles to accompany the various salamis. A variety of vegetable and seafood dishes and other small plates are also available, so you can piece together a meal of small plates. There's a second Olympic Provisions in Northwest Portland at 1632 NW Thurman St. (𝒞 **503/894-8136**).

107 SE Washington St. 𝒞 **503/954-3663.** www.olympicprovisions.com. Reservations recommended on weekends. Main courses $7–$9 lunch, $14–$15 dinner. AE, DISC, MC, V. Mon–Sat 11am–10pm.

Pok Pok ★ THAI I spent part of my childhood in Thailand and have returned many times as an adult, so trust me when I say that Pok Pok is the most authentic Thai restaurant I've ever eaten at outside of Thailand. Not only are the flavors of the dishes here some of the most vibrant and exotic you'll ever taste, but also the whole atmosphere conjures casual restaurants on the beaches of Thailand. Get the *kai yang* (grilled chicken) and papaya Pok Pok for an absolute classic straight off the streets of Bangkok. Some people fault this place for serving skimpy portions, but it's the same way in Thailand. Just order another dish; you'll be glad you did.

3226 SE Division St. ☎ **503/232-1387.** www.pokpokpdx.com. Reservations accepted for parties of 5 or more. Main courses $9–$14. DISC, MC, V. Daily 11:30am–10pm.

Coffee, Tea, Bakeries, Pastry Shops & Chocolateries
CAFES

If you're in search of Portland's cafe culture or just need a good cup of coffee, you're never very far from a good cappuccino or latte. I recommend the following places:

Downtown Portland is surprisingly short on places to get really good espresso. If you're doing a bit of downtown shopping or have been checking out the scene at Pioneer Courthouse Square, you can get one of Portland's best cappuccinos just 3 blocks from the square at **Spella Café,** 520 SW Fifth Ave. (☎ **503/752-0264;** http://spellacaffe.com), which started out as a food cart before moving into its closet-size brick-and-mortar space. Because this place is too small to have tables and chairs, you'll have to get your coffee to go.

Many a Portlander swears by the coffee at **Stumptown Coffee Roasters,** 128 SW Third Ave. (☎ **503/295-6144;** www.stumptowncoffee.com), a big, trendy cafe with an art-school aesthetic. Whether you go for the French press or a double shot of espresso, you're sure to be satisfied. There's another Stumptown in the lobby of the Ace Hotel, 1026 SW Stark St. (☎ **503/224-9060**). Over on the east side of the Willamette River are Stumptown's two original cafes: 4525 SE Division St. (☎ **503/230-7702**) and 3356 SE Belmont St. (☎ **503/232-8889**), which both tend to attract a young, hip clientele.

With an upscale interior decor and a social conscience, **World Cup,** 1740 NW Glisan St. (☎ **503/228-4152;** www.worldcupcoffee.com), in the Nob Hill neighborhood, is a coffee haven for the politically correct. There's another World Cup inside Powell's City of Books, 1005 W. Burnside St. (☎ **503/228-4651,** ext. 1234).

If you've just spent longer than you expected at OMSI (the Oregon Museum of Science and Industry), head down SE Water Avenue to **Water Avenue Coffee,** 1028 SE Water Ave. (☎ **503/808-7084;** www.wateravenuecoffee.com), which is affiliated with a barista-training school and is positively obsessive about coffee.

If you've been shopping your way through the Pearl District for hours and desperately need a place to sit down for a latte, head to **Cloud Seven Café,** 901 NW 10th Ave. (☎ **503/336-1335;** www.cloudsevencafe.com), the neighborhood's most stylish coffee lounge. Right outside the front door is the popular Jamison Square park, where all summer long, kids splash in the wading-pool fountain. Alternatively, there's **Barista,** 539 NW 13th Ave. (☎ **503/579-6678;** www.baristapdx.com), which some people claim makes the best coffee in Portland. You can get vacuum-pot coffee here, and the baristas have even won awards for their espresso drinks.

Up in north Portland, **Ristretto Roasters,** 3808 N. Williams Ave. (☎ **503/288-8667;** http://ristrettoroasters.com), is *the* place to get espresso made from freshly roasted coffee. There's a second Ristretto at 3520 NE 42nd Ave. (☎ **503/284-6767**).

Not a coffee drinker? Try the funky **Tao of Tea,** 3430 SE Belmont St. (☎ **503/736-0119;** www.taooftea.com), which feels like it could be in some Kathmandu back alley and specializes in traditional Chinese tea service. There's a second tea room, called the **Tower of Cosmic Reflections,** inside the Lan Su Chinese Garden, 239 NW Everett St. (© 503/224-8455).

All you chocoholics out there will be relieved to know that Portland is a fabulous town for chocolate addicts. Whether you're looking for a handmade truffle, a fair-trade chocolate bar, or a cup of drinking chocolate, there's a chocolatier in town for you. If hot chocolate, not coffee, is your cup of choice, then be sure to stop by **Moonstruck Chocolate Café,** 608 SW Alder St. (© 503/241-0955; www.moon struckchocolate.com), where you can choose from a wide variety of hot chocolate drinks. There's another Moonstruck in the Nob Hill neighborhood at 526 NW 23rd Ave. (© 503/542-3400). **Cacao,** 414 SW 13th Ave. (© 503/241-0656; www.cacao drinkchocolate.com), just off West Burnside Street, offers a variety of chocolate confections from some of the Northwest's most noteworthy purveyors. There's a second Cacao just off the lobby of the Heathman Hotel, 712 SW Salmon St. (© 503/274-9510). **Alma Chocolate,** 140 NE 28th Ave. (© 503/517-0262; www.almachocolate. com), uses fair-trade and organic ingredients in its chocolates. Even big European chocolatiers have shops here in town. From Belgium come the pralines, butter-creams, and ganaches of **Leonidas,** 607 SW Washington St. (© 503/224-9247; www.leonidasportland.com), and from Switzerland come the truffles of **teuscher,** 531 SW Broadway (© 503/827-0587; www.teuscherportland.com). From mid-March through early December, it's even possible to take a chocolate walking tour with **Chocolate Tasting & More** (www.chocolatetastingandmore.com). Tours are $49 per person. Chocolate tastings are also available.

BAKERIES & PASTRY SHOPS

Pearl Bakery ★★, 102 NW Ninth Ave. (© **503/827-0910;** www.pearlbakery. com), in the heart of the Pearl District, is famous in Portland for its breads and European-style pastries. The *gibassier,* a chewy sweet roll fragrant with anise and orange, is an absolute revelation. The gleaming bakery/cafe is also good for sandwiches, such as a roasted eggplant and tomato pesto on crusty bread. On the other side of the Pearl District, near Jamison Park, you'll find **Lovejoy Bakers,** 939 NW Tenth Ave. (© **503/208-3113;** http://lovejoybakers.com), and more good pastries and sandwiches, plus a pretty sidewalk seating area.

Say the words "Papa Haydn" to a Portlander, and you'll see a blissful smile appear. What is it about this little bistro that makes locals start gushing superlatives? The desserts. The chocolate-hazelnut torte, raspberry gâteau, chocolate truffle cake, and marjolaine at **Papa Haydn West ★★,** 701 NW 23rd Ave. (© **503/228-7317;** www.papahaydn.com), are legendary. There's another location at 5829 SE Milwaukie Ave. (© **503/232-9440**) in the Westmoreland neighborhood.

Also in the Nob Hill neighborhood, you'll find **Ken's Artisan Bakery,** 338 NW 21st Ave. (© **503/248-2202;** www.kensartisan.com). Ken's doesn't do a wide variety of pastries, but what it does do, it does very well. Try the fruit tarts. However, my current favorite bakery in the neighborhood is the utterly Gallic **St. Honoré Boulangerie,** 2335 NW Thurman St. (© **503/445-4342;** www.sainthonorebakery. com); not only does this place turn out awesome pastries and breads, but you can peruse the latest issue of *Le Monde* while eating your croissant.

Located in Ladd's Addition, an old neighborhood full of big trees and Craftsman-style bungalows, **Palio Dessert & Espresso House ★,** 1996 SE Ladd Ave. (© **503/232-9412;** www.palio-in-ladds.com), is a very relaxed place with a timeless

European quality. To get there, take Hawthorne Boulevard east to the corner of 12th and Hawthorne, and then go diagonally down Ladd Avenue.

The **Rimsky-Korsakoffee House ★**, 707 SE 12th Ave. (② **503/232-2640**), a classic old-style coffeehouse, has been one of Portland's favorite dessert hangouts for more than 25 years. Live classical music and great desserts keep patrons loyal. It's open from 7pm to midnight Sunday through Thursday and 7pm until 1am Friday and Saturday.

If doughnuts are your guilty pleasure, then don't miss Portland's **Voodoo Doughnut,** 22 SW Third Ave. (② **503/241-4704;** www.voodoodoughnut.com). Open 24 hours a day and boasting that "the magic is in the hole," this downtown nightlife-district hole-in-the-wall is not your usual doughnut shop. There are voodoo-doll doughnuts, bacon-topped maple bars, vegan doughnuts, and even X-rated doughnuts. There's a second Voodoo Doughnut across the river at 1501 NE Davis St. (② **503/ 235-2666**).

Cupcake lovers should head to **Cupcake Jones,** 307 NW Tenth Ave. (② **503/222-4404;** www.cupcakejones.net), not far from Powell's Books. Alternatively, there's **Saint Cupcake,** 1138 SW Morrison St. (② **503/997-3674;** http://saintcupcake. com). There's a second Saint Cupcake in southeast Portland at 3300 SE Belmont St. (② **503/235-0078**).

I've saved the best for last: **Pix Patisserie,** 3402 SE Division St. (② **503/232-4407;** www.pixpatisserie.com), makes by far the most decadent pastries in Portland. Every sweet little jewel here is a work of art, and it can sometimes be a real challenge to desecrate these creations with a fork. Go ahead, take a bite—you won't soon forget the experience. There's a second Pix at 3901 N. Williams Ave. (② **503/282-6539**).

If it's hot out and nothing will do but something cold and creamy, check out one of Portland's gelaterias. These Italian-style frozen-dessert parlors have taken Portland by storm. In the Nob Hill neighborhood, there's **Alotto Gelato,** 931 NW 23rd Ave. (② **503/228-1709;** www.alottogelato.biz); in the Pearl District, there's **Mio Gelato,** 25 NW 11th Ave. (② **503/226-8002**); and in northeast Portland, just off East Burnside Street, there's **Staccato Gelato,** 232 NE 28th Ave. (② **503/231-7100;** www. staccatogelato.com). Alternatively, for old-school ice cream, it's hard to beat **Cool Moon Ice Cream,** 1105 NW Johnson St. (② **503/224-2021;** www.coolmoon icecream.com), which is right across the street from Jamison Park, the Pearl District's supercool kid magnet. If you're overheated and in need of a creamy treat in north Portland, head to **Ruby Jewel Scoops,** 3713 N. Mississippi Ave. (② **503/505-9314;** www.rubyjewel.net).

Quick Bites & Cheap Eats

If you're just looking for something quick, cheap, and good to eat, Portland abounds with great little local chains. Keep an eye out for any of the following places while you're exploring the city. Designer pizzas topped with anything from roasted eggplant to wild mushrooms to Thai peanut sauce can be had at **Pizzicato Gourmet Pizza ★** (www.pizzicatopizza.com). Find them downtown at 705 SW Alder St. (② 503/226-1007), in Northwest Portland at 505 NW 23rd Ave. (② 503/242-0023), and in southeast Portland at 2811 E. Burnside St. (② 503/236-6045). However, if you find yourself near a **Hot Lips Pizza** (www.hotlipspizza.com), give it a try. They're located at SE Hawthorne Blvd. and SE 22nd Ave. (② 503/234-9999), in the EcoTrust building at NW 10th Ave. and NW Irving St. (② 503/595-2342), and SW Sixth Ave. at SW Hall St. (② 503/224-0311). For inexpensive sushi, stop by one of Portland's

As in most cities, restaurants in downtown Portland tend to be either cheap lunch spots for the cubical crowd or expense-account places for management. If your vacation budget falls closer to the former category, then you may want to eat "a la cart." Portland has become legendary for its hundreds of food carts. You'll find these carts (mostly trailers, actually) in parking lots all over town, with concentrations at the corner of SW Stark Street and SW Fifth Avenue and the corners of SW Alder Street and both SW Ninth Avenue and SW Tenth Avenue. The following are some of my personal favorites. For cart-loads of information on Portland food carts, go to **www.foodcartsportland.com**.

I used to write about Amsterdam and Brussels for Frommer's guides, and in both cities, I lived on the exquisite fries. You can now get those great *frites* here in Portland at **Potato Champion,** SE 12th Avenue and Hawthorne Boulevard (www.potatochampion.com), which stays open late and also serves *poutine,* the national dish of Quebec.

As rainy as it is in Portland most of the year, it is not surprising that grilled-cheese sandwiches (almost as comforting as mac and cheese) are immensely popular. In the converted school bus that now serves as home for the **Grilled Cheese Grill,** 1027 NE Alberta Ave (© **503/206-8959;** http://grilledcheese grill.com), you can get all manner of these gooey, greasy belly bombs, including the legendary Original Cheesus

burger, which comes on two grilled-cheese sandwiches instead of a bun. There's a second Grilled Cheese Grill with a double-decker bus at 113 SE 28th Ave (© **503/206-7018**).

Waffle sandwiches. Try the sausage and maple at Old Town's **Flavour Spot,** at the corner of SW Third Avenue and SW Ash Street (© **503/704-4961;** www. flavourspot.com). There's another Flavour Spot at the corner of North Mississippi Avenue and N Fremont Street (© **503/282-9866**).

At **Nong's Khao Man Gai,** SW Alder Street and SW 10th Avenue (© **971/ 255-3480;** www.khaomangai.com), simple ingredients—a pile of rice, a heap of boiled chicken, a cup of broth with vegetables—become the stuff of Portland legends. How? The sauce. It is heavenly. Order extra.

It's cold. It's rainy. It's time for hot soup, and **Savor Soup House,** SW Alder Street and SW 10th Avenue (© **503/ 764-1415;** www.savorsouphouse.com), is the place to take the chill off. Pair your soup with a grilled cheese sandwich for the ultimate comfort meal. Now where did I leave my blanket?

What, more waffles? **Waffle Window,** SE 36th Avenue and SE Hawthorne Boulevard (© **503/239-4756;** www.waffle window.com), isn't officially a cart, but it is a window in the side of a building, which sort of counts. Waffles with jam and *panna cotta,* waffles with bacon, brie, and basil. What's not to love?

many outposts of **Mio Sushi** (www.miosushi.com). Locations include 1317 NW Hoyt St. (© 503/224-7905), in the Pearl District; 2271 NW Johnson St. (© 503/221-1469), in the Nob Hill neighborhood; and 3962 SE Hawthorne Blvd. (© 503/230-6981), and 4204 NE Halsey St. (© 503/288-4778), in the Hollywood District. For fast, organic, and mostly vegetarian food, search out a **Laughing Planet** (www. laughingplanetcafe.com). You'll find them at 721 NW Ninth Ave. (© 503/505-5020), 922 NW 21st Ave. (© 503/445-1319), 3320 SE Belmont St. (© 503/235-6472), and 3765 N. Mississippi St. (© 503/467-4146).

KEEP PORTLAND weird

"Keep Portland weird," an often-seen bumper sticker here in Stumptown, has become something of a mantra for many Portlanders. This town attracts a lot of independent thinkers, counterculturalists, and artistic types, a fact that has been parodied in the IFC comedy cable network's series *Portlandia*. Not surprisingly, some of the city's residents have chosen to share their personal passions through small, private museums. Here are some of my favorites.

○ **The Hat Museum** (📞 **503/232-0433;** www.thehatmuseum.com): Hundreds of hats, and lots more. Tours by costumed museum owner. Open daily 10am to 6pm; admission is $15, and reservations are required.

○ **Mike's Movie Memorabilia Collection,** 4320 SE Belmont St. (📞 **503/234-4363;** www.movie madnessvideo.com): Costumes and props from Hollywood movies inside a video-rental store. Open Sunday to Thursday noon to 11pm, Friday and Saturday noon to midnight; admission is free.

○ **Stark's Vacuum Museum,** 107 NE Grand Ave. (📞 **503/232-4101;** www.starks.com): A vacuum-cleaner store with vacuums dating from the 1880s to the 1960s. Open Monday to Friday 8am to 7pm, Saturday 9am to 5pm, Sunday 11am to 5pm; admission is free.

○ **3D Center of Art and Photography,** 1928 NW Lovejoy St. (📞 **503/227-6667;** www.3d center.us): Contemporary and vintage 3-D photos and art. Open Thursday to Saturday 11am to 5pm, Sunday 1 to 5pm; on first Thursday of the month, also open 6 to 9pm (with free admission). Admission is $5.

○ **Wells Fargo History Museum,** 1300 SW Fifth Ave. (📞 **503/886-1102;** www.wellsfargohistory.com): Stagecoaches in the soggy Northwest? Yee-haw. Open Monday to Friday 9am to 6pm; admission is free.

SEEING THE SIGHTS

Most American cities boast about their museums, their historic buildings, or their shopping districts; Portland, as always, is a little bit different. Ask a Portlander about the city's must-see attractions, and you'll probably be directed to the Japanese Garden, the International Rose Test Garden, and the Lan Su Chinese Garden. Gardening is a Portland obsession, and thanks to the weather here, you'll find some of the finest public gardens in the country. There are not only the three world-class public gardens already mentioned, but also plenty of other noteworthy public gardens and parks as well. Visiting all the city's noteworthy parks and gardens can easily take up 2 or 3 days of touring, so leave plenty of time in your schedule if you have a green thumb.

This isn't to say that the Portland Art Museum, which often hosts blockbuster exhibits, isn't worth visiting. However, when it comes to museums, Portland is just a little bit out of the ordinary. There's a museum of 3-D photography, a museum dedicated to vacuum cleaners, a hat museum, and a Wells Fargo museum. These little

Portland Attractions

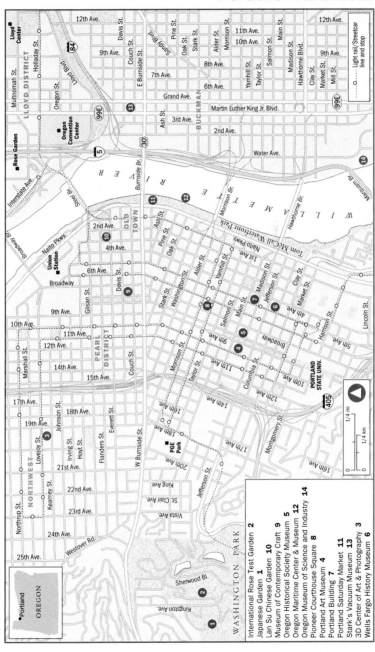

International Rose Test Garden **2**
Japanese Garden **1**
Lan Su Chinese Garden **10**
Museum of Contemporary Craft **9**
Oregon Historical Society Museum **5**
Oregon Maritime Center & Museum **12**
Oregon Museum of Science and Industry **14**
Pioneer Courthouse Square **8**
Portland Art Museum **4**
Portland Building **7**
Portland Saturday Market **11**
Stark's Vacuum Museum **13**
3D Center of Art & Photography **3**
Wells Fargo History Museum **6**

4

PORTLAND | Seeing the Sights

FROMMER'S FAVORITE PORTLAND experiences

o **Strolling the Grounds at the Japanese Garden.** This is the best Japanese garden in the United States, perhaps the best anywhere outside of Japan. My favorite time to visit is in June when the Japanese irises are in bloom. There's no better stress reducer in the city.

o **Beer Sampling at Brewpubs.** They may not have invented beer here in Portland, but they've certainly turned it into an art form. Whether you're looking for a cozy corner pub or an upscale taproom, you'll find a brewpub where you can feel comfortable sampling what local brewmeisters are concocting.

o **Kayaking Around Ross Island.** Seattle may be the sea-kayaking capital of the Northwest, but Portland's not a bad spot for pursuing this sport. You can paddle on the Columbia or Willamette rivers, but my favorite easy kayak outing is around Ross

Island in the Willamette River, about a quarter-mile from the downtown high-rises. You can even paddle past the submarine at the Oregon Museum of Science and Industry and pull out at Tom McCall Waterfront Park.

o **Mountain Biking the Leif Erickson Road.** Forest Park is one of the largest forested city parks in the country, and running its length is unpaved Leif Erickson Road. The road is closed to cars and extends for 12 miles. Along the way, there are occasional views of the Columbia River. This is a long but relatively easy ride, without any strenuous climbs.

o **Hanging Out at Powell's.** They don't call Powell's the City of Books for nothing. This bookstore, which sells both new and used books, is so big you have to get a map at the front door. No matter how much time I spend here, it's never enough.

museums can be a lot of fun to visit, and you should try to slip a visit to one or two of them into your busy vacation schedule.

Once you've seen the city's main attractions, it's time to start learning why everyone loves living here so much. Portlanders for the most part are active types who enjoy bicycling around the city, hiking in Forest Park and other urban forests, and paddling kayaks on the city's rivers and lakes, so no visit to Portland would be complete without getting a little exercise while exploring the city. However, for those who prefer urban activities, the museums and parks listed below should satisfy.

Downtown Portland's Cultural District
STROLLING AROUND DOWNTOWN

Any visit to Portland should start at the corner of SW Broadway and Yamhill Street on **Pioneer Courthouse Square.** The brick-paved square is an outdoor stage for everything from flower displays to concerts to protest rallies, but just a few decades ago this beautiful area was nothing but a parking lot. The parking lot had been created in 1951 (in the days before historic preservation) when the Portland Hotel, an architectural gem of a Queen Anne–style château, was torn down.

An in-store cafe makes it all that much easier to while away the hours.

○ **Free Rides on the Vintage Trolleys.** MAX light-rail trolleys and Portland Streetcars are all free within a large downtown area known as the Free Rail Zone. That alone should be enough to get you on some form of public transit while you're in town, but if you're really lucky, you might catch one of the vintage trolley cars that operate on downtown's Portland Transit Mall MAX line on Sundays from May through December. There aren't any San Francisco–style hills, but the old streetcars are still fun to ride.

○ **An Afternoon at the Portland Saturday Market.** This large arts-and-crafts market is an outdoor showcase for hundreds of the Northwest's creative artisans. You'll find one-of-a-kind clothes, jewelry, kitchenwares, musical instruments, and much, much more. The food stalls serve up some great fast food, too.

○ **Summertime Concerts at the Washington Park Zoo.** Summertime in Portland means partying with the pachyderms. Throughout the summer you can catch live music at the zoo's amphitheater. Musical styles include blues, rock, bluegrass, folk, Celtic, and jazz. Sometimes for nothing more than the regular zoo admission, you can catch the concert and tour the zoo (if you arrive early enough). Picnics are encouraged, and beer and wine are for sale during concerts.

○ **First Thursday Art Walk.** On the first Thursday of every month, Portland goes on an art binge. People get dressed up and go gallery hopping from art opening to art opening. There are usually hors d'oeuvres and wine available, and sometimes there's even live music. The galleries stay open until 9pm.

Today the square, with its waterfall fountain and freestanding columns, is Portland's favorite gathering spot, especially at noon, when the **Weather Machine ★**, a mechanical sculpture, forecasts the weather for the next 24 hours. Amid a fanfare of music and flashing lights, the Weather Machine sends up clouds of mist followed by a sun (clear weather), a dragon (stormy weather), or a blue heron (clouds and drizzle).

Keep your eyes on the square's brick pavement, too. Every brick contains a name (or names) or statement, and some are rather curious. Also on the square, you'll find the **Travel Portland** visitor's information center and a Starbucks. Unfortunately, you'll also find plenty of street kids hanging out here all hours of the day and night, so don't be surprised if they ask you for spare change.

A block away, at the corner of SW Park Avenue and SW Yamhill Street, you'll find **Director Park,** downtown Portland's newest and one of its most popular public spaces. With a glass roof high above one corner of the plaza (to keep the rain off diners sitting at the tables of an outdoor cafe), a play fountain that's a huge hit with kids on hot summer days, and a giant chess board that gets set up for several hours each day, Director Park is a fascinating place to sit and observe life in Portland.

Also not to be missed in this neighborhood are *Portlandia* **★★** and the **Portland Building,** 1120 SW Fifth Ave. The symbol of the city, *Portlandia* is the second-largest hammered bronze statue in the country (the largest is the Statue of Liberty). The massive kneeling figure holds a trident in one hand and reaches toward the street with the other. This classically designed figure perches incongruously above the entrance to architect Michael Graves' controversial Portland Building, considered to be the first postmodern structure in the United States. Today anyone familiar with the bizarre constructions of Los Angeles architect Frank Gehry would find it difficult to understand how such an innocuous and attractive building could have ever raised such a fuss, but it did just that in the early 1980s.

The **Ira Keller Fountain,** 5 blocks from *Portlandia,* at the corner of SW Third Avenue and SW Clay Street, is one of Portland's most unusual public spaces. The fountain, which was designed to resemble a mountain waterfall, and its surrounding gardens take up an entire city block. In summer, the roar of the waters cascading over the cement walls of the fountain transport visitors to the nearby Cascade Range.

Shopping for produce may not be on your usual vacation itinerary, but the **Portland Farmers Market** (✆ **503/241-0032;** www.portlandfarmersmarket.org), which can be found in this neighborhood's South Park blocks, between SW Harrison and SW Montgomery streets, is a quintessential Portland experience. Fresh berries, wild mushrooms and other foraged produce, salmon, oysters, pastries, artisan breads, hazelnuts, local wines—you'll find all of this and more here at the market. Live music and cooking demonstrations by local chefs add to the market's appeal. The market is held on Saturdays from 8:30am to 2pm between mid-March and mid-December, and from 8:30am to 2pm in November and December.

DOWNTOWN MUSEUMS

Oregon Historical Society Museum ★   In the mid-19th century, the Oregon Territory was a land of promise and plenty. Thousands of hardy individuals set out along the Oregon Trail, crossing a vast and rugged country to reach the fertile valleys of this region. Still others came by ship around Cape Horn. If you'd like to learn about the people who discovered Oregon before you, visit this well-designed museum. Fascinating exhibits chronicle Oregon's history from before the arrival of the first Europeans to well into the 20th century. You can't miss this museum—look for the eight-story-high *trompe l'oeil* mural stretching across the front.

1200 SW Park Ave. ✆ **503/306-5198.** www.ohs.org. Admission $11 adults, $9 students and seniors, $5 children 6–18, free for children 5 and under. Tues–Sat 10am–5pm; Sun noon–5pm. Bus: 6 or 8. MAX (Green or Yellow line): SW Sixth Ave. and Madison St. station or SW Jefferson St. and Fifth Ave. station. Portland Streetcar: Art Museum (northbound); 11th Ave. and Jefferson St. (southbound).

Portland Art Museum ★★   This is the oldest art museum in the Northwest, and it has an excellent collection of modern and contemporary art. This collection begins with European Impressionists and moves right up to the present. However, the best reason to visit is to see the extensive collection of Native American art and artifacts. There's also a good collection of Northwest contemporary art that includes a fascinating two-story wall of "artifacts" by glass artist William Morris. Other collections include European, Asian, and American art, and there's a small sculpture court. The Portland Art Museum is frequently the Northwest stop for touring blockbuster exhibits.

1219 SW Park Ave. ✆ **503/226-2811.** www.portlandartmuseum.org. Admission $15 adults, $12 seniors and college students, free for children 17 and under. Tues–Wed and Sat 10am–5pm; Thurs–Fri 10am–8pm; Sun noon–5pm. Bus: 6. MAX (Green or Yellow line): SW Sixth Ave. and Madison St. station or SW Jefferson St. and Fifth Ave. station. Portland Streetcar: Art Museum (northbound); 11th Ave. and Jefferson St. (southbound).

Skidmore Historic District, Chinatown, the Pearl District & the Willamette River Waterfront

If Pioneer Courthouse Square is the city's living room, **Tom McCall Waterfront Park ★**, along the Willamette River, is the city's front-yard play area. There are acres of lawns, shade trees, sculptures, and fountains, and the paved path through the park is popular with bicyclists and joggers. This park also serves as the site of numerous festivals every summer. Also in the park is the Japanese-American Historical Plaza, dedicated to Japanese Americans who were sent to internment camps during World War II.

Just north of this plaza, at the north end of Waterfront Park, a pedestrian walkway crosses the Steel Bridge to the east side of the Willamette River and the **Vera Katz Eastbank Esplanade,** which stretches for about 1½ miles along the east bank of the river. Although this paved multiuse path gets a lot of traffic noise from the adjacent freeway, it offers great views of the Portland skyline. Along the route are small parks and gardens, interesting sculptures, and benches for sitting and soaking up the view. The highlight of this path is a section that floats right on the river and is attached to pilings in much the same way that a floating dock is constructed.

Lan Su Chinese Garden ★★   This classically styled Chinese garden takes up an entire city block and is the largest of its type outside of China. The walls surrounding the garden in Portland's Chinatown separate the urban 21st century from the timeless Chinese landscape within. It is designed to evoke the wild mountains of China and to create a tranquil oasis within an urban setting. The garden is centered around a small pond, which at one end has a rock wall meant to conjure the sort of images often seen in Chinese scroll paintings. Numerous pavilions, a small bridge, and a winding pathway provide ever-changing views of the garden. With its many paved paths and small viewing pavilions, this garden has a completely different feel from the Japanese Garden. Try to visit as soon as the garden opens in the morning; when the crowds descend and the guided tours start circulating—well, so much for tranquillity. On the other hand, if you want to learn more about the garden, you can join a guided tour at noon or 1pm. Be sure to stop and have a cup of tea and maybe a snack in the garden's tearoom.

NW Everett St. and NW Third Ave. ✆ **503/228-8131.** www.lansugarden.org. Admission $8.50 adults, $7.50 seniors, $6.50 students and children 6–18, free for children 5 and under. Apr–Oct daily 10am–6pm; Nov–Mar daily 10am–5pm. Bus: 4, 8, 33, or 77. MAX (Blue or Red line): Old Town/ Chinatown Station.

Museum of Contemporary Craft ★★   Founded in 1937, this is one of the country's finest museums of contemporary craft. Throughout the year, works from the permanent collection share space with changing exhibits that might focus on an individual artist or a single theme. Cutting-edge ceramics and jewelry are always highlights of exhibits here, but you might catch a show focusing on crafts incorporating bamboo or an exhibition of artist-made books. From the museum, it is just a few blocks to the art galleries in the Pearl District.

724 NW Davis St. ✆ **503/223-2654.** www.museumofcontemporarycraft.org. Admission $3 adults, $2 students and seniors. Tues–Sat 11am–6pm (first Thurs of the month until 8pm). Bus: 9 or 17. MAX (Green or Yellow line): NW Sixth and Davis station or NW Fifth Ave. and Couch St. station.

Oregon Maritime Center & Museum   This floating museum is housed in the historic steam-powered stern-wheeler *Portland,* which is docked at Tom McCall

Waterfront Park. Inside are models of ships that once plied the Columbia and Willamette rivers. Also on display are early navigation instruments, artifacts from the battleship *Oregon,* old ship hardware, and other maritime memorabilia. However, the main reason to visit this museum is for the free guided tours of the *Portland.*

SW Pine St. and SW Naito Pkwy. ✆ **503/224-7724.** www.oregonmaritimemuseum.org. Admission $5 adults, $4 seniors, $3 youths 6–17, free for children 5 and under. Wed–Sat 11am–4pm; Sun 12:30–4:30pm. Bus: 12, 19, or 20. MAX: Skidmore Fountain Station.

Oregon Museum of Science and Industry (OMSI) ★ ☺ Located on the east bank of the Willamette River across from the south end of Waterfront Park, this modern science museum has six huge halls, and both kids and adults find the exhibits fun and fascinating. This is a hands-on museum, and everyone is urged to get involved with displays, from a science playground for young children to physics and chemistry labs for older children. There's plenty of pure entertainment at the **OMNI-MAX theater** and the **Kendall Planetarium,** which features laser-light shows and astronomy presentations. The USS *Blueback* submarine (used in the film *The Hunt for Red October*) is docked here, and tours are given daily.

A paved pathway runs beside OMSI and heads north to the Vera Katz Eastbank Esplanade and south 3 miles to Oaks Bottom amusement park. Along the pathway beside the museum, several interesting informational plaques tell the history of Portland and its relationship to the Willamette River. OMSI is also the departure point for several different boat cruises up and down the Willamette River.

1945 SE Water Ave. ✆ **800/955-6674** or 503/797-4000. www.omsi.edu. Museum $12 adults, $9 seniors and children 3–13; OMNIMAX shows $6–$8.50 adults, $5–$6.50 seniors and children 3–13; submarine tours, planetarium shows, and matinee laser-light shows $5.75; evening laser shows $7.50; discounted combination tickets available. Mid-June to early Sept daily 9:30am–7pm; early Sept to mid-June Tues–Sun 9:30am–5:30pm. Bus: 4, 14, or 33.

Portland Saturday Market ★★ The Portland Saturday Market (actually held on both Sat and Sun) is arguably the city's best-loved event. For decades the Northwest has attracted artists and craftspeople, and every weekend more than 300 of them can be found selling their creations here. In addition to the dozens of crafts stalls, you'll find ethnic and unusual foods and lots of free entertainment. This is one of the best places in Portland to shop for one-of-a-kind gifts. The atmosphere is always cheerful and the crowds colorful. Located on the riverfront adjacent to the historic Skidmore District, Portland Saturday Market makes an excellent starting or finishing point for a walk around Portland's downtown historic neighborhood.

By the west end of the Burnside Bridge along SW Naito Pkwy. ✆ **503/222-6072.** www.portland saturdaymarket.com. Free admission. First weekend in Mar to Christmas Eve Sat 10am–5pm and Sun 11am–4:30pm. Bus: 12, 19, or 20. MAX (Blue or Red line): Skidmore Fountain Station.

Washington Park & Portland's West Hills

Portland is justly proud of its green spaces, and foremost among them are **Washington Park** and **Forest Park.**

Within Washington Park, you'll find **the Japanese Garden** and **International Rose Test Garden,** which are adjacent to one another on the more developed east side of the park (see the listings below). On the west side of the park (farther from the city center), you'll find not only the Hoyt Arboretum but also the Oregon Zoo, World Forestry Center Discovery Museum, and the Portland Children's Museum.

The 187-acre **Hoyt Arboretum** ★, 4000 SW Fairview Blvd. (✆ **503/865-8733;** www.hoytarboretum.org), includes more than 1,100 species of trees and shrubs from

GREAT photo OPS

If you've seen a photo of Portland with conical snow-covered Mount Hood looming in the background and you want to snap a similar photo while you're in town, there are several places to try. Most popular are probably the terraces of the **International Rose Test Garden** (p. 92) and from behind the pavilion at the **Japanese Garden** (p. 92). Another great view can be glimpsed from the grounds of the **Pittock Mansion** (p. 93).

One other not-to-be-missed vista is located atop Council Crest, a hilltop park in Portland's West Hills. To reach this park, take the Sylvan exit off U.S. 26 west of downtown Portland, turn south and then east (left) on Humphrey Boulevard, and then follow the signs. Alternatively, you can follow SW Broadway south out of downtown Portland and follow the signs. This road winds through attractive hillside neighborhoods for a ways before reaching Council Crest.

temperate regions around the world, and has several miles of hiking trails. At the south end of the arboretum, adjacent to the World Forestry Center Discovery Museum and the Oregon Zoo, is the **Vietnam Veterans Living Memorial.** At the arboretum's visitor center (Mon–Fri 9am–4pm; Sat 9am–3pm), you can pick up maps and guides to the arboretum. The arboretum can be reached either from the Oregon Zoo/World Forestry Center Discovery Museum/Portland Children's Museum area or by following the arboretum signs from West Burnside Street.

To the north of Hoyt Arboretum is **Forest Park ★★** (𝄢 **503/823-7529**), which, with more than 5,000 acres of forest, is one of the largest forested city parks in the United States. Within the park are more than 74 miles of trails and old fire roads for hiking, jogging, and mountain biking. More than 100 species of birds call this forest home, making it a great spot for urban bird-watching. Along the forest trails, you can see huge old trees and find quiet picnic spots tucked away in the woods. One of the most convenient park access points is at the top of NW Thurman Street (just keep heading uphill until the road dead-ends). You can also park at the Hoyt Arboretum visitor center or the Audubon Society at 5151 NW Cornell Rd., pick up a map of Forest Park, and head out from either of these locations.

Adjacent to Forest Park, the **Portland Audubon Society,** 5151 NW Cornell Rd. (𝄢 **503/292-6855;** www.audubonportland.org), has a couple of miles of hiking trails on its forested property. In keeping with its mission to promote enjoyment, understanding, and protection of the natural world, these nature trails are open to the public. You can also visit the Nature Store or wildlife care center here. To find this facility from downtown Portland, first drive to NW 23rd Avenue, and then head uphill on NW Lovejoy Street, which becomes NW Cornell Road. (**Warning:** Car break-ins are commonplace at the parking area just down the road from the Audubon Society, so don't leave anything of value in your car.)

By car, the easiest route to the Washington Park attractions from downtown Portland is to take SW Jefferson Street west, turn right onto SW 18th Avenue, left on SW Salmon Street, right on SW King Street, and then left onto SW Park Place. Although this sounds confusing, you'll find most of the route well marked with SCENIC DRIVE signs. Alternatively, you can drive west on West Burnside Street and watch for signs to the arboretum, or take the zoo exit off U.S. 26. All of these attractions can also be reached via bus no. 63. You can also take the MAX line to the Washington Park

Station, which is adjacent to the Oregon Zoo, World Forestry Center Discovery Museum, Portland Children's Museum, and Hoyt Arboretum. From here it is possible (in the summer months) to take a bus shuttle to the Japanese Garden and International Rose Test Garden. There's also a miniature train that runs from the zoo to a station near the two public gardens. However, to ride this train, you must first pay zoo admission.

International Rose Test Garden ★★

Covering more than 5 acres of hillside in the West Hills above downtown Portland, these are among the largest and oldest rose test gardens in the United States and are the only city-maintained test gardens to bestow awards on every year's best roses. The gardens were established in 1917 by the American Rose Society and are used as a testing ground for new rose varieties. Though you will probably see some familiar roses in the Gold Medal Garden, most of the 400 varieties on display are new hybrids. Among the various gardens here, which have blooms from late spring through early winter, you'll find a separate garden of miniature roses and a Shakespeare Garden that includes flowers mentioned in the Bard's works. After seeing these acres of roses, you'll understand why Portland is known as the City of Roses and why the Rose Festival in June is the city's biggest annual celebration. The small Rose Garden Store, 850 SW Rose Garden Way (℃ **503/227-7033**), is packed with rose-inspired products.

 All Aboard!

The **Washington Park and Zoo Railway** travels between the zoo and the International Rose Test Garden and Japanese Garden. Tickets for the miniature railway are $5 (free for children 2 and under). There's also a shorter route that just loops around the zoo.

400 SW Kingston Ave. (in Washington Park). ℃ **503/823-3636.** www.rosegardenstore.com. Free admission (donations accepted). Daily 7:30am–9pm. Bus: 63.

The Japanese Garden ★★★

Considered the finest example of a Japanese garden in North America, this exquisitely manicured green space should not be missed. Not only are there five different styles of Japanese gardens scattered over 5½ acres, but there's also a view of volcanic Mount Hood, which bears a strong resemblance to Mount Fuji.

Although Japanese gardens are traditionally not designed with colorful floral displays, this garden definitely has its seasonal highlights. In early spring there are the cherry trees, in midspring there are the azaleas, in late spring a huge wisteria bursts into bloom, and in early summer, large Japanese irises color the banks of a pond. Amid the gardens, there's a beautiful and very realistic waterfall.

This is a very tranquil spot and is even more peaceful on rainy days, when the crowds stay away, so don't pass up a visit just because of inclement weather. Also, April through October, on the third Saturday of each month, there's a demonstration of the Japanese tea ceremony in the garden's teahouse. During these same months, there are daily free guided tours of the gardens.

611 SW Kingston Ave. (in Washington Park). ℃ **503/223-1321.** www.japanesegarden.com. Admission $9.50 adults, $7.75 seniors and college students, $6.75 children 6–17, free for children 5 and under. Apr–Sept Mon noon–7pm, Tues–Sun 10am–7pm; Oct–Mar Mon noon–4pm, Tues–Sun 10am–4pm. Bus: 63. MAX (Blue or Red line): Washington Park Station (then, in summer months, take the shuttle bus or the zoo train).

THE WORLD'S smallest park

Don't blink as you cross the median strip on Naito Parkway at the corner of SW Taylor Street, or you might just walk right past Mill Ends Park, the smallest public park in the world.

Covering a whopping 452 square inches of land, this park was the whimsical creation of local journalist Dick Fagen. After a telephone pole was removed from the middle of Naito Parkway (then known as Front Ave.), Fagen dubbed the phone-pole hole Mill Ends Park (Mill Ends, a lumber-mill term, was the name of

Fagen's newspaper column). The columnist, whose office looked down on the hole in the middle of Front Avenue, peopled the imaginary park with leprechauns and would often write of the park's goings-on in his column. On St. Patrick's Day 1976, it was officially designated a Portland city park. Rumor has it that despite its diminutive size, the park has been the site of several weddings (although the parks department has never issued a wedding permit for it).

Oregon Zoo ★ ☺   The Oregon Zoo is best known for its elephants and has the most successful breeding herd of elephants in captivity. However, the zoo has plenty of other great exhibits, too. The Africa exhibit, which includes a very lifelike rainforest and a savanna populated by zebras, rhinos, giraffes, hippos, and other animals, is one of the most realistic habitats you'll ever see at a zoo. Equally impressive is the Alaskan tundra exhibit, with grizzly bears, wolves, and musk oxen. The Cascade Crest exhibit includes a mountain goat habitat, and in the Steller Cove exhibit, you can watch the antics of Steller sea lions and sea otters. Don't miss the bat house or the Amazon Flooded Forest exhibit. In the summer, there are **outdoor concerts** in the zoo's amphitheater; admission prices vary.

4001 SW Canyon Rd. (in Washington Park). ✆ **503/226-1561.** www.oregonzoo.org. Admission $11 adults, $9 seniors, $7.50 children 3–11, free for children 2 and under (admission $4 2nd Tues of each month). Late May to early Sept daily 9am–6pm; early Sept to Dec and Mar to late May daily 9am–4pm; Jan–Feb 10am–4pm. Bus: 63. MAX (Blue or Red line): Washington Park Station.

Pittock Mansion ★   At nearly the highest point in the West Hills, 1,000 feet above sea level, stands the most impressive mansion in Portland. Once slated to be torn down to make way for new housing, this grand château, built by the founder of Portland's *Oregonian* newspaper, is fully restored and open to the public. Built in 1914 in a French Renaissance style, the mansion featured many innovations, including a built-in vacuum system and amazing multiple showerheads in the baths. Today it's furnished with 18th- and 19th-century antiques, much as it might have been at the time the Pittocks lived here. With an expansive view over the city to the Cascade Range, the lawns surrounding the mansion are great for picnics. You can also access Forest Park's Wildwood Trail from here.

3229 NW Pittock Dr. ✆ **503/823-3623.** www.pittockmansion.org. Admission $8 adults, $7 seniors, $5 children 6–18. July–Aug daily 10am–5pm; Sept–Dec and Feb–June daily 11am–4pm. Closed Jan.

World Forestry Center Discovery Museum ★   Although Oregon depends less and less on the timber industry with each passing year, this museum is still busy educating visitors about the importance of forest resources around the world. Among the main exhibits are installations focusing on the forests of Russia, China, South Africa, and the Amazon. One exhibit lets you practice being a smoke jumper (firefighter), while in another area, you can go on a video raft ride. There are also interesting temporary exhibits staged here throughout the year, from photographic exhibits to displays of the woodworker's art.

4033 SW Canyon Rd. ✆ **503/228-1367.** www.worldforestry.org. Admission $8 adults, $7 seniors, $5 children 3–18, free for children 2 and under. Daily 10am–5pm. Bus: 63. MAX (Blue or Red line): Washington Park Station.

Portland's Other Public Gardens

For Portland's two best-loved public gardens, the **International Rose Test Garden** and the **Japanese Garden,** see "Washington Park & Portland's West Hills," above.

If roses are your passion, you'll also want to check out the **Peninsula Park Rose Garden** at the corner of North Portland Boulevard and North Albina Avenue (take the Portland Blvd. exit off I-5, and go 2 blocks east), which has even more rose bushes than the International Rose Test Garden.

Crystal Springs Rhododendron Garden ★   Nowhere do rhododendrons do better than in the cool, rainy Northwest, and nowhere in Portland is there a more impressive planting of rhodies than at Crystal Springs. Eight months out of the year, this is a tranquil garden, with a waterfall, a lake, and ducks to feed. But when the rhododendrons and azaleas bloom from March to June, it becomes a spectacular mass of blazing color. The Rhododendron Show and Plant Sale is held here on Mother's Day weekend.

SE 28th Ave. (1 block north of SE Woodstock Blvd.). ✆ **503/771-8386.** www.portlandonline.com/parks. Admission $3 Mar to Labor Day Thurs–Mon 10am–6pm; free at other times. Apr–Sept daily 6am–10pm; Oct–Mar daily 6am–6pm. Bus: 19.

Elk Rock Gardens of the Bishop's Close ★   Set on a steep hillside above the Willamette River between Portland and Lake Oswego, this was once a private garden but was donated to the local Episcopal bishop of Oregon on the condition that it be opened to the public. The mature gardens are at their best through the spring and early summer. There's also an excellent view of Mount Hood from the grounds.

11800 SW Military Lane. ✆ **800/452-2562** or 503/636-5613. www.elkrockgarden.com. Free admission. Daily 8am–5pm. Bus: 35.

The Grotto—The National Sanctuary of Our Sorrowful Mother   Although this forested 62-acre sanctuary is first and foremost a Catholic religious shrine (with a marble replica of Michelangelo's Pietà set in a shallow rock cave at the foot of a cliff), the grounds are quite beautiful. The gardens here are at their best in the early summer and during the Christmas season, when half a million lights illuminate the grounds after dark. An elevator ride to the top of the bluff offers panoramic views of the Cascade Range, the Columbia River, and Mount St. Helens. There are also a couple of chapels on the grounds, a gift shop, and a coffee shop. The Grotto is open to visitors of all faiths.

8840 NE Skidmore St. (NE 85th Ave. and Sandy Blvd.) ✆ **503/254-7371.** www.thegrotto.org. Free admission (except during Christmas Festival of Lights: $8 adults, $4 children 3–12, free for children 2 and under); elevator $4 adults, $3 seniors, $2.50 children 6–11. Daily summer 9am–8pm; daily winter 9am–4, 5, or 6pm (call ahead); spring and fall 9am–6:30pm. Closed Thanksgiving and Christmas. Bus: 12.

ESPECIALLY FOR KIDS

In addition to the attractions listed below, kids will especially enjoy the **Oregon Museum of Science and Industry** (p. 90), which has lots of hands-on exhibits, and the **Oregon Zoo** (see above). From inside the zoo, it's possible to take a small train through Washington Park to the International Rose Test Garden, below which sits the **Rose Garden Children's Park,** a colorful play area for younger children. The **Salmon Street Springs fountain,** in downtown's Tom McCall Waterfront Park (at SW Naito Pkwy. and SW Salmon St.), is another fun place to take the kids. During hot summer months, lots of happy kids play in the jets of water that erupt from the pavement here. There are also big lawns in **Waterfront Park,** so the kids can run off plenty of excess energy, and a splashy play-pond at **Jamison Square** in the Pearl District.

Oaks Park Amusement Center ☺   Covering more than 44 acres, this amusement park first opened in 1905 to coincide with the Lewis and Clark Exposition. Beneath the shady oaks for which the park is named, you'll find waterfront picnic sites, miniature golf, and plenty of thrilling rides. Here in the park, you'll also find one of the largest roller-skating rinks in the West, and an organist still plays a Wurlitzer pipe organ for the skaters.

7805 SE Oaks Park Way (east end of the Sellwood Bridge). ✆ **503/233-5777.** www.oakspark.com. Free admission; individual-ride tickets $2.25, limited-ride bracelet $12, deluxe-ride bracelet $15. Rides open Apr to early Oct; skating rink open year-round. Hours vary seasonally; call for details. Bus: 70.

Portland Children's Museum ★ ☺   Located across the parking lot from the Oregon Zoo, this large, modern children's museum includes exhibits for children from newborns to 13 year olds. Kids can explore an indoor "wilderness," go shopping in a kid-size grocery store, or help build a house. However, it is the Water Works exhibit that is likely to make the biggest splash with your kids. There are also studios with changing exhibits and opportunities for exploring the visual, literary, and performing arts. Combined with the nearby zoo, this museum makes for an easy all-day kid-oriented outing.

4015 SW Canyon Rd. ✆ **503/223-6500.** www.portlandcm.org. Admission $9 adults and children, $8 seniors, free for children under age 1 (free for all on 1st Fri of each month 4–8pm). Mar to mid-Sept Fri–Wed 9am–5pm, Thurs 9am–8pm; mid-Sept to Feb Tues–Wed and Fri–Sun 9am–5pm, Thurs 9am–8pm. Bus: 63. MAX (Blue or Red line): Washington Park Station.

ORGANIZED TOURS

Cruises

With two large rivers winding through the city, Portland is a town that needs to be seen from the water. Try the ***Portland Spirit*** (✆ **800/224-3901** or 503/224-3900; www.portlandspirit.com), a 150-foot yacht that specializes in meal cruises. Lunch, brunch, and dinner cruises feature Northwest cuisine with views of the city skyline. There are also basic sightseeing cruises, and on Friday nights July through September, a Friday afternoon cocktail cruise features a live band. Call for reservations and schedule. Prices range from $28 to $68 for adults and $18 to $63 for children. This company also operates jet-boat tours that go up the Columbia River to the Bonneville Dam and down the Columbia to Astoria. Shorter jet-boat tours that focus on the history of Portland's many bridges are also offered. Tours leave from Waterfront Park at the foot of SW Salmon Street.

For a high-speed boat adventure up the Willamette River, book a tour with **Willamette Jetboat Excursions** ★ (✆ **888/538-2628** or 503/231-1532; www.willamettejet.com). These high-powered open-air boats blast their way from downtown

Portland to the impressive Willamette Falls in Oregon City. The 2-hour tours, which start at OMSI, are $37 for adults, $24 for children 4 to 11, and free for children 3 and under. Tours are offered May through September. There are also less expensive 1-hour tours, but these do not go upriver to the falls.

Bus Tours

If you just want to get an overview of Portland highlights, hop a ride on the **Big Pink Sightseeing's** trolley bus, which is operated by **Gray Line of Portland** (℃ **503/241-7373**; www.graylineofportland.com). This trolley bus makes 12 stops around Portland, and after you buy an all-day ticket ($24 for adults, $12 for children 6–12), you can hop on and off the bus all day. Each stop has service every 45 to 60 minutes. The trolley, which starts at Pioneer Courthouse Square, operates from late May to mid-October.

When you're ready to get out of town and see some of the Oregon countryside, contact **Eco Tours of Oregon** (℃ **888/868-7733** or 503/245-1428; www.ecotours-of-oregon.com), which offers bus tours to the Oregon coast, wine country, and up the Columbia River Gorge. Tour prices range from $50 to $90.

Portland supposedly has more breweries than any other city in the world and has come to be known as Beervana. If you're a beer geek and want to learn more about the local microbrewing scene here in Beervana, you can book a tour with **Brewvana Portland Brewery Tours** (℃ **503/729-6804**; www.experiencebrewvana.com), which charges $60 to $74 per person for tours that include transportation, tastings, and food. Tours are offered Friday, Saturday, and Sunday. Brewpub tours are also offered by the **Portland BrewBus** (℃ **503/647-0021**; www.brewbus.com), which heads out on Saturday afternoons and charges $45 per person. Slightly more economical brewery tours that utilize TriMet's light-rail line and the Portland streetcar line are offered by **Pubs of Portland Tours** (℃ **512/917-2464**; www.pubsofportlandtours.com). Tours, which stop at four or more breweries or pubs, cost $27 to $30, but you'll also have to purchase a TriMet all-day pass.

Walking Tours

Peter's Walking Tours of Portland (℃ **503/704-7900**; www.walkportland.com), led by Peter Chausse, are a great way to learn more about the city. The walking tours of downtown last 3 hours and take in fountains, parks, historic places, art, and architecture. Tours are by reservation and cost $15 for adults and $10 for teens (free for children 12 and under with a paying adult).

The seamy underbelly of history is laid bare on **Portland Underground Tours ★** (℃ **503/622-4798**), which are operated by the Cascade Geographic Society and head down below street level in the historic Old Town neighborhood. On these

PORTLAND | Organized Tours

unusual tours, which are only for those who are steady on their feet and able to duck under pipes and joists and such, you'll hear tales of the days when Portland was known as one of the most dangerous ports on the Pacific Rim. Sailors were regularly shanghaied (kidnapped) from bars and brothels in this area, and a vast network of tunnels and underground rooms was developed to support the shanghaiing business. Tours cost $13 for adults and $8 for children 11 and under, and are available by reservation only.

OUTDOOR PURSUITS

If you're planning ahead for a visit to Portland, contact **Metro,** 600 NE Grand Ave., Portland, OR 97232 (✆ **503/797-1850;** www.metro-region.org/parks), for its *Metro GreenScene* publication that lists tours, hikes, classes, and other outdoor activities and events being held in the Portland metro area.

Biking

Portland is one of America's most bicycle-friendly cities, and you'll notice plenty of cyclists on the streets. Because many of those cyclists commute to and from work on their bikes, the morning and evening rush hours are particularly busy with bikes, especially on the Hawthorne Bridge, which connects downtown Portland with the residential neighborhoods on the east side of the Willamette River. Both commuters and recreational cyclists avail themselves of the many miles of paved bike paths around the city. There are also some good mountain-biking areas as well.

Riding a bike around town is one of the best ways to understand why young creative types have been flocking to Portland in droves. On a bike, you'll definitely feel like a local, and you can explore out-of-the-way neighborhoods, pedal along the banks of the Willamette River, and visit bike-friendly businesses. If you'd like to explore Portland's riverfront bike paths, stop in at **Waterfront Bicycles,** 10 SW Ash St., Ste. 100 (✆ **503/227-1719;** www.waterfrontbikes.com), where you can rent a bike for $9 to $15 per hour or $40 to $100 per day. From here, head through Tom McCall Waterfront Park, cross the Steel Bridge, and ride down the Vera Katz Eastbank Esplanade path. This trail leads 4 miles south to the upscale Sellwood neighborhood. In Tom McCall Waterfront Park, at the foot of SW Salmon Street, you can rent a variety of unusual, family-friendly cycles from **Kerr Bikes** (✆ **503/808-9955;** www.kerr bikes.org), which rents three-wheeled and four-wheeled cycles and surreys (complete with fringe on top). These latter cycles carry as many as four adults. Rates range from $7 to $15 per hour. Kerr Bikes is open from March through October; hours vary with the month. Proceeds from cycle rentals here benefit the Albertina Kerr Centers, which provide support for people with mental health challenges and developmental disabilities.

At **Bike Gallery,** 1001 SW Tenth Ave. (✆ **503/222-3821;** www.bikegallery.com), you can rent a classic commuter bike (complete with fenders in case it rains) and feel like a local as you explore the city on two wheels. Got the kids along? You can even rent a bike trailer. Bikes rent for $20 for 4 hours or $35 for 24 hours.

For mountain-bike rentals, head to **Fat Tire Farm,** 2714 NW Thurman St. (✆ **503/222-3276;** www.fattirefarm.com), where bikes go for $40 to $125 for a 24-hour rental. Straight up Thurman Street from this bike shop, you'll find the trail head for **Leif Erickson Drive,** an old gravel road that is Forest Park's favorite route for cyclists and runners (the road is closed to motor vehicles); the trail is 12 miles long.

Want to be part of the Portland bike scene, but don't want to do it on your own? Book a bike tour with **Pedal Bike Tours,** 133 SW Second Ave. (© **503/243-2453;** http://pedalbiketours.com), which offers a wide range of bike tours, including those that focus on Portland history, brewpubs, and food and coffee. Farther afield, they operate tours of wine country, the Oregon coast, and the Columbia Gorge. Prices for in-town tours range from $49 to $69 per person, while tours outside the city are $89. Alternatively, there's **Portland Bicycle Tours,** 345 NW Everett St. (© **503/360-6815;** www.portlandbicycletours.com), which has a basic city tour, as well as tours that focus on Portland green-built buildings, Portland's bikeability, and, of course, brewpubs. Tours cost $40 per person.

Golf

If you're a golfer, don't forget to bring your clubs along on a trip to Portland. There are plenty of public courses around the area, and green fees at municipal courses range from $22 to $42 for 18 holes. Municipal golf courses operated by the Portland Bureau of Parks and Recreation include **RedTail Golf Course,** 8200 SW Scholls Ferry Rd. (© **503/646-5166;** www.golfredtail.com); **Eastmoreland Golf Course,** 2425 SE Bybee Blvd. (© **503/775-2900;** www.eastmorelandgolfcourse.com), which is the second-oldest golf course in the state (this one gets my vote for best municipal course); **Heron Lakes Golf Course,** 3500 N. Victory Blvd. (© **503/289-1818;** www.heronlakesgolf.com), which has two courses designed by Robert Trent Jones; and **Rose City Golf Course,** 2200 NE 71st Ave. (© **503/253-4744;** www.rosecitygc.com), on the site of a former country club.

If you want to tee off where the pros play, head west from Portland 20 miles to **Pumpkin Ridge Golf Club ★★**, 12930 Old Pumpkin Ridge Rd., North Plains (© **503/647-4747;** www.pumpkinridge.com), a 36-hole course that has hosted the U.S. Women's Open. Green fees in summer range from $90 to $150 on the one course that is open to the public.

Also west of the city, on the south side of Hillsboro, you'll find **the Reserve Vineyards and Golf Club ★★**, 4805 SW 229th Ave., Aloha (© **503/649-8191;** www.reservegolf.com). Green fees in summer range from $49 to $85 depending on the day of the week and time of day.

Hiking

Hiking opportunities abound in the Portland area. For shorter hikes, you don't even have to leave the city; just head to **Forest Park.** Bordered by West Burnside Street on the south, Newberry Road on the north, St. Helens Road on the east, and Skyline Road on the west, this is one of the largest forested city parks in the country. Within this urban wilderness, you'll find more than 70 miles of trails. One of my favorite access points is at the top of NW Thurman Street in Northwest Portland. (After a hike, you can stop for a post-exercise payoff at a neighborhood brewpub, an espresso bar, or a bakery along NW 23rd Ave. or NW 21st Ave.) The 30-mile Wildwood Trail is the longest trail in the park and along its length offers lots of options for loop hikes. For a roughly 2.5-mile hike, head up Leif Erickson Drive, make a left onto the Wild Cherry Trail, a right onto the Wildwood Trail, a right onto the Dogwood Trail, and then a right on Leif Erickson Drive to get you back to the trail head. There are also good sections of trail to hike in the vicinity of the Hoyt Arboretum. To reach the arboretum's **visitor center,** 4000 SW Fairview Blvd. (Mon–Fri 9am–4pm; Sat

9am–3pm), drive west on West Burnside Street from downtown Portland and follow signs to the arboretum. You can get a trail map at the visitor center.

About 5 miles south of downtown, off Terwilliger Boulevard, you'll find **Tryon Creek State Natural Area.** This park is similar to Forest Park and is best known for its displays of trillium flowers in the spring. There are several miles of walking trails within the park, and a bike path to downtown Portland starts here.

You can buy hiking gear and or even rent camping equipment from **REI Co-Op,** 1405 NW Johnson St. (✆ **503/221-1938;** www.rei.com). This huge outdoor recreation supply store also sells books on hiking in the area.

Sea Kayaking

If you want to check out the Portland skyline from water level, arrange for a sea-kayak tour through the **Portland Kayak Company ★★,** 6600 SW Macadam Ave. (✆ **503/459-4050;** www.portlandrivercompany.com), which operates tours out of the RiverPlace Marina at the south end of Tom McCall Waterfront Park. A 2½-hour tour that circles nearby Ross Island costs $45 to $47 per person. This company also rents sea kayaks (to experienced paddlers) for $10 to $20 per hour.

SPECTATOR SPORTS

The Rose Garden arena is home to the Portland Trail Blazers and is the main focal point of Portland's **Rose Quarter.** This sports-and-entertainment neighborhood includes the Rose Garden, Memorial Coliseum, and several restaurants and bars. Tickets to events at the Rose Garden arena and Memorial Coliseum are sold through the **Rose Quarter** box office (✆ **503/797-9619;** www.rosequarter.com). To reach the Rose Garden or adjacent Memorial Coliseum, take the Rose Quarter exit off I-5. Parking is expensive, so you might want to consider taking the MAX light-rail line from downtown Portland (the Rose Quarter stop is in the Free Rail Zone).

Basketball

The NBA's **Portland Trail Blazers** (✆ **503/797-9600;** www.nba.com/blazers) do well enough every year to have earned a very loyal following. Unfortunately, they have a habit of not quite making it all the way to the top. The Blazers pound the boards at the Rose Garden arena. Call for current schedule and ticket information. Most tickets are in the $22 to $150 range. If the Blazers are doing well, you can bet that tickets will be hard to come by.

Soccer

Major League Soccer's **Portland Timbers** (✆ **503/553-5550;** www.portland timbers.com), who play at downtown's JELD-WEN Field, have become immensely popular in Portland. Tickets go for $17 to $90.

DAY SPAS

If you prefer massages and facials to hikes in the woods, consider spending a few hours at a day spa. These facilities typically offer massages, facials, body wraps, and the like. Portland day spas include the **Spa at the Avalon,** 4650 SW Macadam Ave. (✆ **888/556-4402;** www.avalonhotelandspa.com); and **Salon Nyla—the Day Spa,** 327 SW Pine St. (✆ **503/228-0389;** www.salonnyla.com), which is adjacent to the Embassy Suites hotel. In the Pearl District, try **Aequis,** 422 NW 13th Ave. (☎ **503/223-7847;** www.aequisspa.com), which is an Asian-inspired retreat. Expect to pay about $75 or $135 for a 1-hour massage and $160 to more than $1,150 for a multitreatment spa package.

SHOPPING

Portland has no sales tax, making it a popular shopping destination for Washingtonians, who cross the Columbia River to avoid paying their state's substantial sales tax.

The Shopping Scene

The **blocks around Pioneer Courthouse Square** are the heartland of upscale shopping in Portland. It's here that you'll find Nordstrom, Macy's, NIKETOWN, Tiffany, Pioneer Place shopping mall, and numerous upscale boutiques and shops.

However, Portland's hippest shopping districts are the **Pearl District** and **Nob Hill/Northwest,** both of which are in Northwest Portland. Most of the Pearl District's best shopping is along NW 10th and 11th avenues going north from West Burnside Street. Here you'll find all kinds of trendy boutiques, art galleries, and home-furnishing stores. The best Nob Hill shopping is along NW 23rd Avenue going north from West Burnside Street. Both neighborhoods have block after block of interesting, hip boutiques and, along NW 23rd Avenue, a few national chains such as Gap, Urban Outfitters, and Pottery Barn.

For shops with a more down-to-earth, funky flavor, head out to the **Hawthorne District,** which is the city's counterculture shopping area (lots of tie-dye and imports). Other youth-oriented shopping neighborhoods include NE Alberta Street and North Mississippi Street.

Most small stores in Portland are open Monday through Saturday from 9 or 10am to 5 or 6pm. Shopping malls are usually open Monday through Friday from 9 or 10am to 9pm, Saturday from 9 or 10am to between 6 and 9pm, and Sunday from 11am until 6pm. Many department stores stay open past 6pm. Most art galleries and antiques stores are closed on Monday.

Shopping A to Z
ANTIQUES

The **Sellwood/Westmoreland** neighborhood (south of downtown at the east end of the Sellwood Bridge) is Portland's main antiques-shopping district, with about a dozen antiques shops and antiques malls along SE 13th Avenue and SE Milwaukie Avenue. With its old Victorian homes and 19th-century architecture, Sellwood and Westmoreland are the ideal setting for these shops. There are plenty of good restaurants in the area in case it turns into an all-day outing.

You'll also find two large antiques malls (under the same ownership) nearby on Milwaukie Avenue: **Stars,** 7027 SE Milwaukie Ave. (☎ **503/239-0346;** www.stars antique.com); and **Stars & Splendid,** 7030 SE Milwaukie Ave. (☎ **503/235-5990**).

ART GALLERIES

On the **first Thursday of the month,** galleries in downtown Portland and the Pearl District schedule coordinated openings in the evening. Stroll from one gallery to the next, meeting artists and perhaps buying an original work of art. On the last Thursday of every month, shops and galleries in the NE Alberta Street neighborhood stage a similar event. This latter event tends to attract a young and culturally diverse crowd.

THE CITY OF books

Portland's own **Powell's City of Books,** 1005 W. Burnside St. (✆ **800/878-7323** or 503/228-4651; www.powells.com), is the bookstore to end all bookstores. Powell's, which covers an entire city block three floors deep, claims to be the world's largest bookstore selling new and used books. At any given time, the store has roughly a million books on the shelves. Both new and used books are shelved side by side, which is why browsing is what Powell's is all about.

Once inside the store, be sure to pick up a store map, which will direct you to the color-coded rooms. Serious book collectors won't want to miss a visit to the Rare Book Room.

One warning: If you haven't got at least an hour of free time, enter at your own risk. It's so easy to lose track of time at Powell's that many customers miss meals and end up in the store's in-house cafe.

Believe it or not, City of Books is even bigger than what you see here; it has several satellite stores, including **Powell's Books for Home and Garden,** 3747 SE Hawthorne Blvd.; **Powell's Books on Hawthorne,** 3723 SE Hawthorne Blvd.; and **Powell's Books at PDX,** Portland International Airport, 7000 NE Airport Way, Ste. 2250.

To find NE Alberta Street, drive north from downtown Portland on I-5 and watch for the NE Alberta Street exit.

Augen Gallery   When it opened nearly 20 years ago, the Augen Gallery focused on internationally recognized artists such as Jim Dine, Andy Warhol, and David Hockney. Today the gallery has expanded its repertoire to regional contemporary painters and printmakers as well. 716 NW Davis St. ✆ **503/546-5056.** www.augengallery.com. Also at 817 SW Second Ave. (✆ **503/224-8182**).

The Bullseye Connection Gallery   Located in the Pearl District, the Bullseye Gallery is Portland's premier art-glass gallery and shows the work of internationally acclaimed glass artists. 300 NW 13th Ave. ✆ **503/227-0222.** www.bullseyegallery.com.

The Laura Russo Gallery   The focus here is on Northwest contemporary artists, showcasing talented emerging artists as well as the estates of well-known regional artists. This gallery has been in business for more than 25 years and is highly respected. 805 NW 21st Ave. ✆ **800/925-7152** or 503/226-2754. www.laurarusso.com.

Portland Art Museum Rental Sales Gallery   This downtown gallery has a wide selection of works by more than 250 Northwest artists. Sales here help support the Portland Art Museum. 1237 SW 10th Ave. ✆ **503/224-0674.** www.portlandartmuseum.org.

Pulliam Gallery   This gallery represents a long list of both talented newcomers and masters from the Northwest. Solo shows and salon-style group shows are held here. 929 NW Flanders St. ✆ **503/228-6665.** www.pulliamgallery.com.

Quintana Galleries   This large, bright space is a virtual museum of Native American art, selling everything from Northwest Coast Indian masks to Navajo rugs to contemporary paintings and sculptures by Native American artists. They also carry a smattering of Native American artifacts from both the Northwest and the Southwest. The jewelry selection is outstanding. 124 NW Ninth Ave. ✆ **800/321-1729** or 503/223-1729. www.quintanagalleries.com.

BOOKS

There's a **Barnes & Noble** at 1317 Lloyd Center (✆ **503/249-0800;** www.barnes andnoble.com), in northeast Portland, and another at 1720 N. Jantzen Beach Center (✆ **503/283-2800**), in north Portland. For information on Portland's massive Powell's City of Books, see the box below.

CRAFTS

For the largest selection of local crafts, visit the **Portland Saturday Market** (see "Markets," below), which is a showcase for local crafts.

The Gallery at Museum of Contemporary Craft   In business since 1937, and located on the North Park blocks, which are on the edge of the Pearl District, this is the nation's oldest not-for-profit art gallery. It shows only works of clay, glass, fiber, metal, and wood. The bulk of the large gallery is filled with glass and ceramic pieces. There are also several cabinets of jewelry. 724 NW Davis St. ✆ **503/546-2654.** http://gallery.museumofcontemporarycraft.org.

Hoffman Gallery   The Hoffman Gallery is on the campus of the Oregon College of Art and Craft, one of the nation's foremost crafts education centers since 1906. The gallery hosts installations and group shows by local, national, and international artists. The adjacent gift shop has a good selection of handcrafted items. 8245 SW Barnes Rd. ✆ **503/297-5544.** www.ocac.edu.

The Real Mother Goose   This is Portland's premier fine-crafts shop and one of the top such shops in the United States. It showcases only the very best contemporary American crafts, including imaginative ceramics, colorful art glass, intricate jewelry, exquisite wooden furniture, and sculptural works. Hundreds of craftspeople and artists from all over the United States are represented here. 901 SW Yamhill St. ✆ **503/223-9510.** www.therealmothergoose.com. Also at Portland International Airport, Main Terminal (✆ 503/284-9929).

Twist   This large store has quite a massive selection of wildly colorful and imaginative furniture, crockery, glassware, and lamps, and also a limited but impressive selection of handmade jewelry by artists from around the United States. 30 NW 23rd Place. ✆ **503/224-0334.** www.twistonline.com.

DEPARTMENT STORES

Macy's   Completely renovated and remodeled in 2007, this department store is in a historic building overlooking Pioneer Courthouse Square. If you didn't find it at Nordstrom, across the square, maybe you'll find it here. 621 SW Fifth Ave. ✆ **503/223-0512.** www.macys.com.

Nordstrom   Directly across the street from Pioneer Courthouse Square, Nordstrom is a top-of-the-line department store that originated in Seattle and takes great pride in its personal service and friendliness. 701 SW Broadway. ✆ **503/224-6666.** www.nordstrom.com. Also at 1001 Lloyd Center (✆ 503/287-2444) and 9700 SW Washington Square Rd., Tigard (✆ 503/620-0555).

FASHION
Sportswear
Columbia Sportswear Company   This flagship store is surprisingly low-key, given that the nearby Nike flagship store and REI in Seattle are designed to knock your socks off. Displays showing Columbia Sportswear's well-made outdoor clothing

and sportswear are rustic, with lots of natural wood. The most dramatic architectural feature of the store is the entryway—a very wide tree trunk seems to support the roof. 911 SW Broadway. © **503/226-6800.** www.columbia.com.

Columbia Sportswear Company Factory Outlet Store 🔥 This outlet store in the Sellwood neighborhood south of downtown and across the river sells remainders and past-season styles from the above-mentioned sportswear company, which is one of the Northwest's premier outdoor-clothing manufacturers. You'll pay 30% to 50% less here than you will at the downtown flagship store. 1323 SE Tacoma St. © **503/238-0118.** www.columbia.com.

Nike Factory Company Store 🔥 The Nike outlet is one season behind the current season at NIKETOWN (see below), selling swoosh-brand running, aerobic, tennis, golf, basketball, kids, and you-name-it shoes; sports clothing; and accessories, all at discounted prices. 2650 NE Martin Luther King Jr. Blvd. © **503/281-5901.** www.nike.com.

NIKETOWN Portland Sure, you may have a NIKETOWN back home, but this one is the closest to Nike's headquarters in nearby Beaverton, which somehow makes it just a little bit special. A true shopping experience. SW Fifth Ave. and SW Morrison St. © **503/221-6453.** www.nike.com.

Men's & Women's

Langlitz Leathers This family-run shop produces the Rolls-Royce (or should I say Harley-Davidson) of leather jackets. Even though there may be a wait of several months for custom leathers, the shop also has ready-to-wear leather jackets available. 2443-A SE Division St. © **503/235-0959.**

Portland Outdoor Store In business since 1919, this westernwear store is a Portland institution that feels little changed from decades ago. The big neon sign out front and the old general-store atmosphere is enough to pull in even people who aren't into playing cowboy or cowgirl. 304 SW Third Ave. © **503/222-1051.**

The Portland Pendleton Shop Pendleton wool is as much a part of life in the Northwest as forests and salmon. This company's fine wool fashions for men and women define the country-club look in the Northwest and in many other parts of the United States. Pleated skirts and tweed jackets are de rigueur here, as are the colorful blankets that have warmed generations of Northwesterners through long, chilly winters. 900 SW Fifth Ave. © **503/242-0037.** www.pendleton-usa.com.

Women's

CHANGES/Designs to Wear This shop specializes in handmade clothing, including hand-woven scarves, jackets, shawls, hand-painted silks, and other wearable art. 927 SW Yamhill St. © **503/223-3737.** www.therealmothergoose.com.

Imelda's Ooooh! Look at those, and those, and those! That's the usual response when women first gaze through the window of Imelda's. If you live for shoes, do not miss Imelda's. 935 NW Everett St. © **503/595-4970.** www.imeldasandlouies.com. Also at 3426 SE Hawthorne Blvd. (© 503/233-7476).

Men's

John Helmer Haberdasher Whether you're looking for a felt fedora, a Panama hat or a top hat, you'll find it at this classic haberdashery, which first opened in 1921. There are also plenty of men's suits, slacks, and sports jackets. 969 SW Broadway © **866/855-4976** or 503/223-4976. www.johnhelmer.com.

FOOD

The **Made in Oregon** shops offer the best selection of local food products. See "Gifts & Souvenirs," below, for details.

The Meadow A store that sells gourmet finishing salts, fresh flowers, wine, and chocolate? How very Portland. This store should not be missed. The blocks of pink Himalayan salt are fascinating. 3731 N. Mississippi Ave. © **503/288-4633.** www.themeadow.net.

Mr. Green Beans Here's another novel only-in-Portland sort of a shop. Mr. Green Beans specializes not in *haricot vert* as you might expect but, rather, in unroasted "green" coffee beans. The shop also sells all the paraphernalia necessary for roasting your own coffee beans at home, plus supplies for soap making, cheese making, pickling, and canning. 3932 N. Mississippi Ave. © **503/288-8698.** http://mrgreen beanspdx.com.

GIFTS & SOUVENIRS

For unique locally made souvenirs, your best bet is the **Portland Saturday Market** (see "Markets," below, for details).

Cargo I've been attracted to funky import stores since I bought my first Indonesian batiked shirt back in high school. Since then, the world of imports has changed immensely, and at this warehouse-size Pearl District store, you'll find all manner of curious cargo. 380 NW 13th Ave. © **503/209-8349.** www.cargoimportspdx.com.

Made in Oregon This is your one-stop shop for all manner of made-in-Oregon gifts, food products, and clothing. Every product sold is either grown, caught, or made in Oregon. You'll find smoked salmon, filberts, jams and jellies, Pendleton woolens, and Oregon wines. All branches are open daily, but hours vary from store to store. 340 SW Morrison St., Ste. 1300 (in Pioneer Place). © **866/257-0938** or 503/241-3630. www.madein oregon.com. Also at Portland International Airport (© 503/282-7827) and Lloyd Center mall (© 503/282-7636).

Oblation Papers & Press Although this little Pearl District print shop is primarily known for its wedding invitations, it also has racks full of beautiful greeting cards, often by local artists. The shop also sells beautiful wrapping papers and even makes its own papers. 516 NW 12th Ave. © **503/223-1093.** www.oblationpapers.com.

JEWELRY

For some of the most creative jewelry in Portland, visit **Twist,** the **Hoffman Gallery,** the **Gallery at Museum of Contemporary Craft,** and **the Real Mother Goose.** See "Crafts," above.

MALLS & SHOPPING CENTERS

Pioneer Place Just a block from Pioneer Courthouse Square, this is Portland's most upscale shopping center. Pioneer Place is filled with stores selling designer fashions and expensive gifts. 700 SW Fifth Ave. (between Third and Fifth aves.). © **503/228-5800.** www.pioneerplace.com.

MARKETS

Portland Saturday Market The Portland Saturday Market (held on both Sat and Sun) is a Portland tradition. Every weekend more than 300 artists and crafts-people can be found selling their creations at this open-air market beside the Burn-side Bridge in Waterfront Park. In addition to the dozens of crafts stalls, you'll find ethnic and unusual foods, and lots of free entertainment. This is one of the best places in Portland to shop for one-of-a-kind gifts that are small enough to fit into your suitcase. The market is open from the first weekend in March to Christmas Eve, Saturdays 10am to 5pm and Sundays 11am to 4:30pm. Waterfront Park and Ankeny Plaza, SW Naito Pkwy. ✆ **503/222-6072.** www.portlandsaturdaymarket.com.

TOYS

Finnegan's Toys and Gifts   This is the largest toy store in downtown Portland and appeals to the kid in all of us. It'll have your inner child kicking and screaming if you don't buy that silly little toy you never got when you were young. 820 SW Washington St. ✆ **503/221-0306.** www.finneganstoys.com.

WINE & SPIRITS

Just as Portland is a center for craft brewing, it has recently also become a center for microdistilleries. In southeast Portland, you'll find Distillery Row, an area that is home to six small distilleries, all of which are open for tastings at least 1 day a week. To learn more, go to **www.distilleryrowpdx.com**. For information on a pedal-powered, eco-friendly tour of Portland's microdistilleries, see the box "Green Beer Tours" on p. 96.

Clear Creek Distillery   The Portland area is known not only for microbrews and pinot noir, but also some outstanding liquors. This distillery in Northwest Portland produces astonishingly fragrant and flavorful fruit spirits in a variety of European styles. There are apple and pear brandies (with or without fruit in the bottles), grappas, eau de vie, and fruit liqueurs. You can sample them all at this tasting room. 2389 NW Wilson St. ✆ **503/248-9470.** www.clearcreekdistillery.com.

Oregon Wines on Broadway   This cozy wine bar/shop is located diagonally across from the Hotel Vintage Plaza in downtown Portland. Here you can taste some of Oregon's fine wines, including 30 different pinot noirs, as well as pinot gris and chardonnay, and a few cabernet sauvignons, merlots, and Syrahs that are mostly from eastern Washington. 515 SW Broadway. ✆ **800/943-8858** or 503/228-0126. www.oregonwines onbroadway.com.

PORTLAND AFTER DARK

Portland is Oregon's cultural mecca, and the city's symphony orchestra, ballet, and opera are all well regarded. A lively theater scene includes plenty of mainstream and fringe theater companies that offer classic and contemporary plays. In summer, festivals move the city's cultural activities outdoors.

To find out what's going on during your visit, pick up a copy of *Willamette Week,* Portland's free weekly arts-and-entertainment newspaper. The *Oregonian,* the city's daily newspaper, also publishes lots of entertainment-related information in its Friday "A&E" section and also in the Sunday edition of the paper.

The Performing Arts

For the most part, the Portland performing-arts scene revolves around the **Portland Center for the Performing Arts (PCPA),** 1111 SW Broadway (✆ **503/248-4335;** www.pcpa.com), which comprises five performance spaces in three buildings. The **Arlene Schnitzer Concert Hall,** 1037 SW Broadway, known locally as the Schnitz, is an immaculately restored 1920s movie palace that still displays the original Portland theater sign and marquee out front and is home to the Oregon Symphony. This hall also hosts popular music performances, lectures, and many other special events. Directly across Main Street from the Schnitz, at 1111 SW Broadway, is the glass jewel box known as **Antoinette Hatfield Hall.** This building houses the **Newmark** and **Dolores Winningstad theaters** and **Brunish Hall.** The two theaters host stage productions by local and visiting companies. Free tours of these theaters are held Wednesdays at 11am and Saturdays every half hour between 11am and 1pm.

A few blocks away from this concentration of venues is the 3,000-seat **Keller Auditorium,** 222 SW Clay St., the largest of the four halls and the home of the Portland Opera and the Oregon Ballet Theatre. The auditorium was constructed shortly after World War I and completely remodeled in the 1960s. In addition to the resident companies mentioned above, these halls host numerous visiting companies every year, including touring Broadway shows.

The PCPA's box office is open for ticket sales Monday through Saturday from 10am to 5pm. Tickets to PCPA performances, and performances at many other venues around the city, are also sold through either **Ticketmaster** (© **800/745-3000** or 800/982-2787; www.ticketmaster.com), which has outlets at area Fred Meyer stores, or **Tickets West** (© **503/224-8499;** www.ticketswest.com), which has outlets at area Safeway stores. The PCPA also has a **Half-Price Ticket Hotline** (© **503/432-2960**) that sells day-of-show, half-price tickets.

One other performing-arts venue worth checking out is **the Old Church,** 1422 SW 11th Ave. (© **503/222-2031;** www.oldchurch.org). Built in 1883, this wooden Carpenter Gothic church is a Portland landmark. It incorporates a grand traditional design, but was constructed with spare ornamentation. Today the building serves as a community facility, and every Wednesday at noon it hosts free lunchtime concerts. There are also many other performances held here throughout the year.

Opera & Classical Music

Founded in 1896, the **Oregon Symphony** (© **800/228-7343** or 503/228-1353; www.orsymphony.org), which performs at the Arlene Schnitzer Concert Hall, 1037 SW Broadway, is the oldest symphony orchestra on the West Coast and is currently under the baton of conductor Carlos Kalmar. Each year between September and May, the symphony stages several series, including classical, pops, and children's concerts. Ticket prices mostly range from $25 to $125 (students may purchase $10 tickets 2 hrs. before classical and pops concerts).

Every season, the **Portland Opera** (© **503/241-1802;** www.portlandopera.org), which performs primarily at Keller Auditorium, 222 SW Clay Street, offers five different productions that include both grand opera and light opera. The season runs September through May. Ticket prices range from $20 to $135.

Summer is the time for Portland's annual chamber-music binge. **Chamber Music Northwest** (© **503/294-6400;** www.cmnw.org) is a month-long series that starts in late June and attracts the world's finest chamber musicians. Performances are held at Reed College and St. Mary's Cathedral (tickets $25–$50).

Theater

Portland Center Stage (© **503/445-3700;** www.pcs.org), Portland's largest professional theater company, holds performances in the Pearl District's converted Portland Armory building, 128 NW 11th Ave., which now goes by the name Gerding Theater at the Armory. They stage a combination of as many as 10 classic and contemporary plays during their September-to-June season (tickets $39–$69).

Portland's other main theater company, **Artists Repertory Theatre,** 1515 SW Morrison St. (© **503/241-1278;** www.artistsrep.org), often stages more daring plays. They can be hit or miss, but they're frequently very thought provoking. The season often includes a world premiere. Tickets run $25 to $45.

If it's musicals you want, check the calendar of the **Broadway Across America** series (© **503/241-1802;** www.broadwayacrossamerica.com), which is staged at the Keller Auditorium. Tickets mostly range from around $25 to $65, but some shows are more expensive.

Dance

The **Oregon Ballet Theatre** (© **888/922-5538** or 503/222-5538; www.obt.org), which performs at the Keller Auditorium and the Newmark Theatre (see above), is best loved for its performances of *The Nutcracker* every December. The rest of the season includes performances of classic and contemporary ballets (tickets $23–$140).

Fans of modern dance should be sure to check what's being staged by **White Bird** (© **503/245-1600;** www.whitebird.org). This organization brings in such celebrated companies as Twyla Tharp Dance, the Merce Cunningham Dance Company, the Paul Taylor Dance Company, and the Alvin Ailey American Dance Theater.

Also keep an eye out for performances by **Imago Theatre,** 17 SE Eighth Ave. (© **503/231-9581;** www.imagotheatre.com), which, though it is also a live theater company, is best known for its wildly creative productions of *Frogz, Big Little Things,* and *ZooZoo,* all of which are fanciful dance performances that appeal to both adults and children. **Do Jump,** Echo Theatre, 1515 SE 37th Ave. (© **503/231-1232;** www.dojump.org), is another highly creative dance company worth watching for. Their performances incorporate dance, acrobatics, aerial work, and plenty of humor.

Performing-Arts Series

When summer hits, Portlanders like to head outdoors to hear music. The city's top outdoor music series is held at the **Oregon Zoo,** 4001 SW Canyon Rd. (© **503/226-1561;** www.oregonzoo.org), which brings in the likes of Joan Baez, Indigo Girls, and Ladysmith Black Mambazo. Ticket prices range from $14 to $39.

The Club & Music Scene

ROCK, BLUES & FOLK

Aladdin Theater   This former movie theater now serves as one of Portland's main venues for touring performers such as Richard Thompson, Bruce Cockburn, Judy Collins, and Greg Brown. The very diverse musical spectrum represented includes blues, rock, ethnic, country, folk, and jazz. 3017 SE Milwaukie Ave. © **503/234-9694.** www.aladdin-theater.com. Tickets $12–$35 (sometimes higher).

Crystal Ballroom   The Crystal Ballroom first opened in 1914 and has since hosted performers ranging from early jazz musicians to James Brown, Marvin Gaye, and the Grateful Dead. The McMenamin Brothers (of local brewing fame) renovated the Crystal Ballroom in 1997 and refurbished its dance floor, which, due to its mechanics, feels as if it's floating. The ballroom now hosts a variety of performances and special events nearly every night of the week. **Lola's Room,** a smaller version of the Ballroom, is on the second floor and also has a floating dance floor. You'll find **Ringlers Pub** (a colorful brewpub) on the ground floor. 1332 W. Burnside St. © **503/225-0047.** www.danceonair.com. Cover $5–$30.

Doug Fir Lounge North-woods log-cabin styling meets Scandinavian modern at this eclectic underground alt-rock club in the lower Burnside neighborhood of southeast Portland. The club is associated with the überhip Jupiter Hotel. 830 E. Burnside St. *C* **503/231-9663.** www.dougfirlounge.com. Cover free–$25.

Mississippi Studios This little performance space in north Portland has become one of the city's premier alternative-music venues, and the calendar here is both eclectic and affordable. 3939 N. Mississippi Ave. *C* **503/288-3895.** www.mississippistudios. com. Cover free–$20.

Wonder Ballroom Originally opened in 1914 as the hall for the Ancient Order of Hibernians and now on the National Register of Historic Places, the Wonder Ballroom is another of Portland's restored ballrooms that now serves as a popular venue for everything from hip-hop to swing to bluegrass. Best of all, Toro Bravo (p. 75), one of my favorite Portland restaurants, is on the same block. 128 NE Russell St. *C* **503/284-8686.** www.wonderballroom.com. Cover $10–$25.

JAZZ

Jimmy Mak's This Pearl District club is the best place in Portland to catch some live jazz and is considered one of the best jazz clubs in the country. With great resident groups performing on weeknights and guest performers on weekends, Jimmy Mak's showcases some of Portland's best jazz musicians. 221 NW 10th Ave. *C* **503/295-6542.** www.jimmymaks.com. Cover free–$10 (sometimes higher).

The Secret Society ★★ Gypsy jazz, vintage jazz, Texas swing, big band, jug band music, klezmer—you just won't find a more eclectic blend of music than at this second-floor nightclub in north Portland. Not only does this place showcase some of Portland's most distinctive acts, but it also does free 6pm shows several nights a week. 116 NE Russell St. *C* **503/493-3600.** http://secretsociety.net. Cover none–$15.

CABARET

Darcelle's XV In business since 1967 and run by Portland's best-loved crossdresser, this cabaret is a campy Portland institution with a female-impersonator show that has been a huge hit for years. There are shows Wednesday through Saturday. 208 NW Third Ave. *C* **503/222-5338.** www.darcellexv.com. Cover $15. Reservations recommended.

DANCE CLUBS

See also the listing for **Saucebox** under "The Bar & Pub Scene," below; this restaurant and bar becomes a dance club most nights when DJs begin spinning tunes.

Andrea's Cha-Cha Club Located in the basement of the Grand Cafe and open Wednesday through Saturday nights, this is Portland's premier dance spot for fans of Latin dancing. Whether it's cha-cha, salsa, or the latest dance craze from south of the border, they'll be doing it here. Lessons are available starting at 9pm. 832 SE Grand Ave. *C* **503/230-1166.** Cover $2–$4.

The Bar & Pub Scene

BARS

Departure ★★ This rooftop bar and restaurant is atop the historic Meier & Frank department-store building, which is now home to both a Macy's and, on its upper floors, Tte Nines, Portland's swankiest hotel. This futuristic lounge has two patios with fabulous views over the rooftops of Portland. People definitely get dressed up to make the scene here. 525 SW Morrison St. *C* **503/802-5370.** www.departureportland.com.

Huber's   No night out on the town in Portland is complete until you've stopped in at Huber's, Portland's oldest restaurant, for a Spanish coffee. These potent pick-me-ups are made with rum, Kahlúa, Triple Sec, coffee, and cream, and the preparation of each drink is an impressive show. 411 SW Third Ave. ✆ **503/228-5686.** www.hubers.com.

Jake's Famous Crawfish   In business since 1892, Jake's is a Portland institution and should not be missed; see the full review on p. 68. The bar is one of the busiest in town when the downtown offices let out. 401 SW 12th Ave. ✆ **503/226-1419.** www.jakesfamouscrawfish.com.

Mint/820   Mixologist Lucy Brennan, owner of this swanky place, single-handedly turned Portland into a town full of cocktail connoisseurs. Using fresh fruit juices, purées, and unusual ingredients, Brennan reinvented the cocktail and set in motion the city's craft cocktail obsession. How about a beet-infused martini or a creamy avocado cocktail? 816 N. Russell St. ✆ **503/284-5518.** www.mintand820.com.

¡Oba!   One of the Pearl District's most popular drinking spots, this big bar/Nuevo Latino restaurant has a tropical feel despite the warehouse-district locale. After work the bar is always packed with the stylish and the upwardly mobile taking advantage of great happy-hour deals. Don't miss the tropical-fruit margaritas! 555 NW 12th Ave. ✆ **503/228-6161.** www.obarestaurant.com.

Portland City Grill   Located way up on the 30th floor, this restaurant/bar has the best view in downtown Portland. Come for the great happy hour so you can catch the sunset and a little live piano music. This is definitely a singles scene. Unico/U.S. Bancorp Tower, 111 SW Fifth Ave. ✆ **503/450-0030.** www.portlandcitygrill.com.

Saucebox   Popular with the city's dressed-in-black hipsters, this downtown restaurant/bar is a large, dramatically lit dark box that can be very noisy. DJs spin music most nights, transforming this downtown bar into a dance club. Great cocktails. 214 SW Broadway. ✆ **503/241-3393.** www.saucebox.com.

PUBS

Bailey's Tap Room   This downtown beer shrine is far more sophisticated than the east side's Green Dragon, but it always has an equally eclectic lineup of kegs on tap. The location, in the heart of the hotel district, makes it a very convenient place to sample some of Oregon's best beers. 213 SW Broadway. ✆ **503/295-1004.** www.baileystaproom.com.

Green Dragon   This warehouselike inner-southeast pub is the quintessential Portland beer-geek hangout. Although it is owned by Rogue Brewing, it pours beers from lots of other breweries from around the country and has its own brewery, too. 928 SE Ninth St. ✆ **503/517-0660.** www.rogue.com.

Horse Brass Pub   If not for the Horse Brass Pub, which has been in business since 1976, Portland might not now be referred to as Beervana. Under the guidance of now-deceased founding publican Don Younger, many of Portland's early brewers got exposed to quality beers. The Horse Brass is as authentic an English pub as you'll find anywhere on this side of "the pond." 4534 SE Belmont St. ✆ **503/232-2202.** www.horsebrass.com.

WINE BARS

Coppia   Located in the heart of the Pearl District, this is Portland's swankiest wine bar and has lots of good wines as well as a very creative full menu. Coppia owner Timothy Nishimoto is also a member of Portland's popular eclectic little jazz orchestra Pink Martini. 417 NW 10th Ave. ✆ **503/295-9536.** www.coppiaportland.com.

MetroVino With nearly 100 wines available by the glass, this Pearl District wine bar is an oenophile's dream come true. A blackboard lists interesting wine flights, and the kitchen turns out good food to accompany your wine. The decor is very conservative, which seems to attract the neighborhood's moneyed set. 1139 NW 11th Ave. *C* **503/517-7778.** www.metrovinopdx.com.

Noble Rot Located on the fourth floor of a modern Lower Burnside building, this stylish wine bar has a killer view of the downtown Portland skyline. You can get various wine flights, and there are plenty of Oregon wines available. The wine bar also serves excellent food. By the way, noble rot is a type of grape fungus that is utilized in the production of sweet dessert wines. 1111 E. Burnside St. *C* **503/233-1999.** www.noblerotpdx.com.

Oregon Wines on Broadway ★ With just a handful of stools at the bar and a couple of cozy tables, this tiny place is the best spot in Portland to learn about Oregon wines. On any given night there will be 30 Oregon pinot noirs available by the glass, and five white wines as well. 515 SW Broadway. *C* **800/943-8858** or 503/228-4655. www.oregonwinesonbroadway.com.

BREWPUBS

Here in Portland, they're brewing beers the likes of which you won't taste in too many other places this side of the Atlantic. This is the heart of the Northwest craft-brewing explosion, and if you're a beer geek, you owe it to yourself to go directly to the source.

Brewpubs have become big business in Portland, and there are now glitzy upscale pubs as well as warehouse-district locals. No matter what vision you have of the ideal brewpub, you're likely to find it. Whether you're wearing bike shorts or a three-piece suit, there's a pub in Portland where you can enjoy a handcrafted beer, a light meal, and a convivial atmosphere.

With dozens of brewpubs in the Portland metropolitan area, the McMenamins chain is Portland's biggest brewpub empire. The owners think of themselves as court jesters, mixing brewing fanaticism with a Deadhead aesthetic. Throw in historic preservation and a strong belief in family-friendly neighborhood pubs, and you'll understand why these joints are so popular.

Downtown

Ringlers Pub With mosaic pillars framing the bar, Indonesian antiques, and big old signs all around, this cavernous place is about as eclectic a brewpub as you'll ever find. A block away are the two associated pubs of **Ringlers Annex,** 1223 SW Stark St. (*C* **503/384-2700**), which is in a flat-iron building. One of these pubs is below street level with a beer-cellar feel, and the other has walls of multipaned glass. These three pubs get my vote for most atmospheric alehouses in town. 1332 W. Burnside St. *C* **503/225-0627.** www.mcmenamins.com.

Northwest Portland

BridgePort Brewpub This stylish brewpub and restaurant is one of Portland's oldest brewpubs. On any given day, you'll find eight or more Bridgeport beers on tap. This place is loud, but the beers (and the food) are good. Don't miss the upstairs bar area. 1313 NW Marshall St. *C* **503/241-3612.** www.bridgeportbrew.com.

Deschutes Brewing ★ This brewpub is a satellite of my favorite central Oregon brewery, and although it's located in a converted industrial space, the pub has a mountain-lodge style similar to that of the famous Timberline Lodge on Mount Hood. There is always a wide range of beers on tap. 210 NW 11th Ave. *C* **503/296-4906.** www.deschutesbrewery.com.

Rogue Distillery & Public House ★   This Pearl District pub is an outpost of a popular microbrewery headquartered in the Oregon coast community of Newport. Rogue produces just about the widest variety of beers in the state and, best of all, keeps lots of them on tap at this pub. If you're a fan of barleywines, don't miss their Old Crustacean. 1339 NW Flanders St. ✆ **503/222-5910.** www.rogue.com.

Southeast

Burnside Brewing Co.   With an industrial-chic vibe and some of the most creative beers in the city, this big pub stands out from other Portland brewpubs by serving highly creative food, which makes this the city's only genuine gastro-brewpub. 701 E. Burnside St. ✆ **503/946-8151.** http://burnsidebrewco.com.

Cascade Barrel House   While Portland breweries have long been known for their exceedingly hoppy beers, this brewery bucks that trend and instead focuses on sour beers. If you aren't familiar with these unusual styles of beer, which originate in Belgium and southern Germany, then you'll need to stop by here and educate yourself. 939 SE Belmont St. ✆ **503/265-8603.** http://cascadebrewingbarrelhouse.com.

Hair of the Dog Brewing Company   This is Portland's most legendary craft brewery, producing several strong, Belgian-style ales that enjoy cult status and command surprisingly high prices. Here at the brewery's tasting room, you can sample a wide range of the complex beers. Note that, because this place is a tasting room and not a pub, hours are limited (Wed–Sun 2–8pm). 61 SE Yamhill St. ✆ **503/232-6585.** www.hairofthedog.com.

The Lucky Labrador Brew Pub   With a warehouse-size room, industrial feel, and picnic tables on the loading dock out back, this brewpub is a classic of southeast Portland. The crowd is young, and dogs are welcome. (They don't even have to be Labs.) 915 SE Hawthorne Blvd. ✆ **503/236-3555.** www.luckylab.com.

Northeast & North Portland

Amnesia Brewing Company   With the look of an old warehouse and a "beer garden" in the parking lot, this little north Portland brewpub is another of the city's old-school brewpubs, which means laid-back in the extreme. The beers are good, but the food is pretty limited. 832 N. Beech St. ✆ **503/281-7708.**

McMenamins Kennedy School   Never thought they'd ever start serving beer in elementary school, did you? In the hands of the local McMenamins brewpub empire, an old northeast Portland school is now a sprawling complex complete with brewpub, beer garden, movie-theater pub, and even a bed-and-breakfast. Order up a pint and wander the halls to check out all the cool artwork. 5736 NE 33rd Ave. ✆ **503/249-3983.** www.kennedyschool.com.

Migration Brewing   Sort of a sports brewpub, this casual place is popular with fans of the Portland Timbers soccer team. Even if you're not a Timbers fan, you'll likely enjoy the picnic tables out front or the dart boards in back. The Old Silenus, an old English-style ale, is a personal favorite. 2828 NE Glisan St. ✆ **503/206-5221.** http://migrationbrewing.com.

Widmer Brewing and Gasthaus   Located on the edge of a rapidly reviving industrial area just north of the Rose Garden arena, this place has the feel of a classic blue-collar pub. This pub is part of Portland's largest craft-brewing company, which is best known for its hefeweizen wheat beer. German and American food is served. 955 N. Russell St. ✆ **503/281-3333.** www.widmer.com.

A Portland Original: The Theater Pub

Portland brewpub magnates the McMenamin brothers (www.mcmenamins.com) have a novel way to sell their craft ales—in movie pubs. Although it's often hard to concentrate on the screen, it's always a lot of fun to attend a show. The movies are usually recent releases that have played the main theaters but have not yet made it onto DVD. Theaters include the **Bagdad Theater,** 3702 SE Hawthorne Blvd. (🕭 **503/249-7474**), a restored classic Arabian-nights movie palace; the **Mission Theater,** 1624 NW Glisan St. (🕭 **503/223-4527**), which was the first McMenamins theater pub; and the **Kennedy School Theater,** 5736 NE 33rd Ave. (🕭 **503/249-3983**), in a former elementary school. You can also have beer and pizza with your movie at the **Laurelhurst Theater,** 2735 E. Burnside St. (🕭 **503/232-5511;** www.laurelhurst theater.com), which is not a McMenamins establishment. At the **Living Room The-ater,** 341 SW Tenth Ave. (🕭 **971/222-2010;** http://pdx.livingroomtheaters.com), a block away from Powell's Books, there is a full bar and an extensive menu.

The Gay & Lesbian Nightlife Scene

DANCE CLUBS

Boxxes/Redcap Garage Billing itself as Portland's original gay dance club, Boxxes and the connected Redcap Garage together provide a dynamic duo of dance floors. You can work up an appetite from all that dancing, and then head to the club's Fish Grotto Seafood Restaurant for a meal. 1025 SW Stark St. 🕭 **503/226-4171.** www.boxxes.com. Cover free–$5.

C.C. Slaughters Popular with a young crowd, this big Old Town nightclub spins different dance sounds every night, with Tuesday currently the club's lesbian night. 219 NW Davis St. 🕭 **503/248-9135.** www.ccslaughterspdx.com.

The Embers Avenue Though primarily a gay disco, Embers is also popular with straights. There are always lots of flashing lights and sweaty bodies until the early morning. 110 NW Broadway. 🕭 **503/222-3082.** Cover free–$5.

BARS

Crush Bar This big, hip bar is over in southeast Portland and attracts a very diverse crowd that includes not only gay men but lesbians and straights as well. DJs spin dance tunes Friday and Saturday nights. 1400 SE Morrison St. 🕭 **503/235-8150.** www.crushbar.com.

Scandal's In business for more than 30 years, this bar/restaurant is both literally and figuratively at the center of the Portland gay bar scene. Try to get a window seat so you can people-watch. 1125 SW Stark St. 🕭 **503/227-5887.** www.scandalspdx.com.

A SIDE TRIP TO OREGON CITY & THE AURORA COLONY

Oregon City

When the first white settlers began crossing the Oregon Trail in the early 1840s, their destination was Oregon City and the fertile Willamette Valley. At the time, Portland had yet to be founded, and Oregon City, set beside powerful Willamette Falls, was the largest town in Oregon. However, with the development of Portland and the shifting of the capital to Salem, Oregon City began to lose its importance. Today it is primarily an industrial town, though one steeped in Oregon history and worth a visit. To get here from downtown Portland, drive south on SW First Avenue and continue on SW Macadam Avenue, which is Ore. 43. Follow this road for roughly 12 miles to reach Oregon City. (It should take 30–45 min.) You can also take I-5 S. to I-205 E.

Once in Oregon City, your first stop should be just south of town at the **Willamette Falls overlook ★** on Ore. 99 E. Though the falls have been much changed by industry over the years, they are still an impressive sight.

McLoughlin House Oregon City's most famous citizen, retired Hudson's Bay Company chief factor John McLoughlin, helped found this mill town on the banks of the Willamette River in 1829. By the 1840s, immigrants were pouring into Oregon, and McLoughlin provided food, seeds, and tools to many of them. Upon retirement in 1846, McLoughlin moved to Oregon City, where he built what was at that time the most luxurious home in Oregon. Today McLoughlin's house is a National Historic Site and is furnished as it would have been when McLoughlin lived there. Many of the pieces on display are original to the house.

713 Center St., Oregon City. ✆ **503/656-5151.** www.mcloughlinhouse.org. Free admission. Wed–Sat 10am–4pm. Closed Dec 22–Jan 31.

The Aurora Colony

An interesting chapter in Oregon pioneer history is preserved 13 miles south of Oregon City in the town of Aurora, which was founded in 1855 as a Christian communal society. The Aurora Colony lasted slightly more than 20 years. Today Aurora is a National Historic District, and the large old homes of the community's founders have been restored. Many of the old commercial buildings now house antiques stores. You can learn the history of Aurora at the **Old Aurora Colony Museum,** 15018 Second St. NE (✆ **503/678-5754;** www.auroracolony.org). February through December, the museum is open Tuesday through Saturday from 11am to 4pm and on Sunday from noon to 4pm. The museum is closed in January. Admission is $6 for adults, $5 for seniors, and $2 for students (free for children 5 and under).

A Rockin' Museum

One of the Portland area's most unusual museums can be found 30 minutes west of the city, off U.S. 26 north of the city of Hillsboro (take exit 61). **Rice NW Museum of Rocks & Minerals,** 26385 NW Groveland Dr., Hillsboro (✆ **503/647-2418;** www.ricenwmuseum.org), houses a private collection of fascinating, beautiful, and often rare minerals, as well as meteorites, specimens of petrified wood, and fluorescent minerals that glow in the presence of ultraviolet light. The museum is open Wednesday through Sunday from 1 to 5pm; admission is $7 for adults, $6 for seniors, and $5 for students.

THE WILLAMETTE VALLEY: THE BREAD (& WINE) BASKET OF OREGON

For more than 150 miles, from south of Eugene to the Columbia River at Portland, the Willamette River (pronounced "Wih-lam-it") flows between Oregon's two major mountain ranges. Tempered by cool moist air from the Pacific Ocean, yet protected from winter winds by the Cascade Range to the east, the Willamette Valley enjoys a mild climate that belies its northerly latitudes. It was because of this relatively benign climate and the valley's rich soils that the region's first settlers chose to put down roots here. Today the valley is home to Oregon's largest cities, its most productive farmlands, the state capital, and the state's two major universities.

Despite the many hardships, families were willing to walk 2,000 miles across the continent for a chance at starting a new life in the Willamette Valley. The valley very quickly became the breadbasket of the Oregon country, and today it still produces an agricultural bounty unequaled in its diversity. Throughout the year, you can sample the produce of this region at farms, produce stands, and wineries. In spring, commercial fields of tulips and irises paint the landscape with bold swaths of color. In summer, farm stands pop up near almost every town, and many farms will let you pick your own strawberries, raspberries, blackberries, peaches, apples, cherries, and plums. In autumn you can sample the filbert and walnut harvest, and at any time of year, you can do a bit of wine tasting at dozens of wineries.

THE NORTH WILLAMETTE VALLEY WINE COUNTRY

McMinnville: 38 miles SW of Portland, 26 miles NW of Salem

Were it not for Prohibition, wine connoisseurs might be comparing California wines to those of Oregon rather than vice versa. Oregon wines had already gained a national reputation back in the days when Oregon became one of the earliest states to vote in Prohibition. It would be a few years before more liberal California would outlaw alcohol, and in the interim, the Golden State got the upper hand. When Prohibition was rescinded, California quickly went back to wine production, but no one bothered to revive Oregon's wine-producing potential until the 1970s. By then Napa Valley had popped the cork on its wine dominance. Perhaps one day Willamette Valley wineries will be as well known as those in California—for fans of pinot noir, however, those days have already arrived. Oregon's pinot noirs have gained such international attention that even some French wineries have planted vineyards here and begun producing their own Oregon wines.

The north Willamette Valley wine country begins in the town of Newberg and extends south to the Salem area. The majority of the region's wineries are within a few miles of Ore. 99W, and a drive down this rural highway will turn up dozens of blue signs pointing to wineries within a few miles of the road. To the south of Salem, there are more wineries in the Corvallis and Eugene areas, and those wineries are dealt with in the appropriate sections of this chapter. To the north of Ore. 99W, still more wineries can be found in Washington County, which is actually in the drainage of the Tualatin River, a tributary of the Willamette. These latter wineries are included in this section.

The most important wine-growing areas within this region, and the areas that produce the best wines, are the Red Hills above the town of Dundee, the slopes outside the town of Carlton, and the Eola Hills northwest of Salem. Throughout this region, you'll find good restaurants and inns, so you never have too far to go from wining to dining or sipping to sleeping.

Essentials

GETTING THERE You'll find the heart of wine country between Newberg and McMinnville along Ore. 99W, which heads southwest out of Portland.

VISITOR INFORMATION Contact the **McMinnville Area Chamber of Commerce,** 417 NW Adams St., McMinnville, OR 97128 (℮ **503/472-6196;** www.mcminnville.org), or the **Chehalem Valley Chamber of Commerce,** 415 E. Sheridan St., Newberg, OR 97132 (℮ **503/538-2014;** www.chehalemvalley.org). The **Willamette Valley Visitors Association** (℮ **866/548-5018;** www.oregonwinecountry.org) is another good source of information on this area.

FESTIVALS The most prestigious festival of the year is the **International Pinot Noir Celebration,** P.O. Box 1310, McMinnville, OR 97128 (℮ **800/775-4762** or 503/472-8964; www.ipnc.org), held every year on the last weekend in July or first weekend in August. The 3-day event includes tastings, food, music, and seminars. Tickets, which currently start at $900 per person, can be purchased nearly a year in advance. Passport to Pinot, a separate event held during the celebration, is only $150.

Touring the Wineries

Forget pretentiousness, grand villas, celebrity wineries, and snobbish waiters—this is not Napa Valley. Oregon wineries, for the most part, are still small establishments. Even the wineries right on Ore. 99W (wineries that seem calculated to provide beach-bound vacationers with a bit of distraction and some less-than-impressive wine for the weekend) are still small affairs compared to the wineries of Napa. Although in recent years more and more well-capitalized wineries have been opening with the sole purpose of producing high-priced pinot noir, many of the region's wineries are still family owned and operated and produce moderately priced wines.

most part, you can forget about cabernet sauvignon, merlot, and zinfandel
re here. The Willamette Valley just isn't hot enough to produce these vari-
_ the exception of southern Oregon wineries and a few Willamette Valley
wineries that buy their grapes from warmer regions (the Columbia Gorge, southern
Oregon, California, and Washington's Yakima Valley), Oregon wineries have, thank-
fully, given up on trying to produce cabs and zins to compete with those of California.
The wines of the Willamette Valley are primarily the cooler-climate varietals traditionally produced in Burgundy, Alsace, and Germany. Pinot noir is the uncontested leader
of the pack, with pinot gris running a close second. However, gewürztraminer and
riesling are also produced, and with the introduction of early ripening Dijon-clone
chardonnay grapes, the region is finally beginning to produce chardonnays that can
almost compete with those of California. A handful of wineries also make sparkling
wines, which are often made from pinot noir and chardonnay grapes.

Wine country begins only a few miles west and southwest of Portland. Approaching the town of Newberg on Ore. 99W, you leave the urban sprawl behind and enter
the rolling farm country of Yamhill County. These hills form the northern edge of the
Willamette Valley and provide almost ideal conditions for growing wine grapes. The
views from these hills take in the Willamette Valley's fertile farmlands as well as the
snowcapped peaks of the Cascades.

Between Newberg and Rickreall, you'll find dozens of wineries and tasting rooms
that are open on a regular basis. There are concentrations of wineries in Dundee's
Red Hills and in the Eola Hills northwest of Salem, and if you head north from Ore.
99W, you'll find many wineries near Carlton, Yamhill, Hillsboro, and Forest Grove.
Each of these groupings of wineries makes a good day's tasting route, and they have
been organized here so that you can easily link them together as such.

Most, but not all, wineries maintain tasting rooms that are usually open between
11am or noon and 5pm. During the summer, most tasting rooms are open daily, but
in other months they may be open only on weekends or by appointment. Wineries
located right on Ore. 99W are usually open throughout the year. Many wineries also
have a few picnic tables or a patio with tables, so if you bring some goodies with you
and then pick up a bottle of wine, you'll be set for a great picnic.

For anyone simply interested in tasting a little Oregon wine, the wineries along the
highway are a good introduction. If you have more than a passing interest in wine, you'll
want to explore the wineries that are located up in the hills a few miles off Ore. 99W.

Many of the best wineries, however, are open only by appointment or on Memorial
Day and Thanksgiving weekends. If you're serious about your wine, you might want
to make appointments to visit some of these more exclusive wineries or plan a visit to
coincide with Thanksgiving or Memorial Day weekend. Oenophiles, especially pinot
noir fans, are likely to uncover some rare gems and discover a few new favorite wineries this way.

At most wineries, you'll be asked to pay a tasting fee, usually $5, but this fee is
often waived if you buy some wine. In the past few years, as pinot noir prices have
risen into the $40 to $60 range, tasting-room fees have also been creeping up. At
some of the more prestigious wineries, you may have to pay a tasting fee between $10
and $20. Many wineries have celebrations, festivals, music performances, and pic-
nics throughout the summer, and during these celebrations there is often a fee to
cover the cost of the appetizers and wine that are served. The Memorial Day and
Thanksgiving weekend tastings usually carry a fee between $5 and $20.

For more information about the Oregon wine scene, including a calendar of winery events, pick up a copy of *Oregon Wine Press*, a monthly magazine available at area wine shops and wineries (P.O. Box 727, McMinnville, OR 97128; www.oregonwine press.com). **Willamette Valley Wineries Association** (P.O. Box 25162, Portland, OR 97298; 𝓒 **503/646-2985;** http://willamettewines.com), a regional wineries association, publishes a free map and guide to the local wineries. You can pick up a copy at almost any area winery. You can also find out about new wineries and double-check tasting-room hours at a few winery-association websites: **Dundee Hills Winegrowers Association** (www.dundeehills.org), **Chehalem Mountains Winegrowers** (www.chehalemmountains.org), **North Willamette Vintners** (www.north willamettevintners.org), and **Sip 47** (www.sip47.com).

Newberg

Adelsheim Vineyard ★   If you're from out of state and you're at all familiar with Oregon pinot noir, you've probably had some Adelsheim wine. This winery has been around since the 1970s and consistently produces well-regarded pinots. The single-vineyard wines here are the standouts. If you'd like to tour a winery, this is a good choice; call ahead to arrange your tour ($40–$150).

16800 NE Calkins Lane. 𝓒 **503/538-3652.** www.adelsheim.com. Tasting fee $15. Daily 11am–4pm.

Bergström Wines ★★   The wines produced by winemaker Josh Bergström are among the most lauded and sought after in Oregon, and they have the prices to prove it ($48–$78 for most bottles). The various vineyard-designate pinot noirs produced here showcase wines with intriguingly distinctive flavor profiles. Chardonnay, gewürz-traminer, and riesling are also produced here. Winery tours ($20–$40) are available by reservation.

18215 NE Calkins Lane. 𝓒 **503/554-0468.** www.bergstromwines.com. Tasting fee $15–$40. Daily 10am–4pm.

Chehalem   At this tasting room, on the eastern edge of downtown Newberg, you can sample the wines of one of Oregon's most respected wineries. Reliable pinot noirs can be found here, as can good chardonnay, pinot gris, and pinot blanc, a less common white wine that has become a favorite of mine. You'll also find riesling and grüner veltliner here. Tours ($25) of the nearby winery are offered Wednesday through Saturday at 11am; reservations are required.

106 S. Center St. 𝓒 **503/538-4700.** www.chehalemwines.com. Tasting fee $15. Daily 11am–5pm.

J.K. Carriere ★★   This winery is a bit off the main wine-tour circuit and is only open a couple of days a week, but the wines, an assortment of pinot noirs and a chardonnay, are noteworthy for complexity, and in the case of the pinot noirs, age worthiness. Many of the pinot noirs here are vineyard-designate bottlings priced at $65, but there are also a couple of less expensive wines.

9995 NE Parrett Mountain Rd., Newberg. 𝓒 **503/554-0721.** www.jkcarriere.com. Tasting fee $10. Fri–Sat 11am–4pm.

Medici Vineyards/Dark Horse Wine Bar ★★   This small wine-tasting room, in a nondescript shopping plaza on the northern edge of downtown Newberg, makes an excellent first stop on a wine tour of this area. The tasting room pours the wines of Sineann Winery (one of my favorite Oregon wineries) as well as those of Medici

Vineyards and Ferraro Cellar. Sineann winemaker Peter Rosback is one of Oregon's most talented and prolific winemakers.

1505 Portland Rd., Newberg. © **503/538-2427.** www.sineann.com. Tasting fee $10. Mon and Wed–Fri 11:30am–5:30pm; Sat–Sun 11am–5pm.

Rex Hill Vineyards   One of the oldest wineries in Oregon, Rex Hill is owned by A to Z, the largest wine producer in Oregon. Here at Rex Hill they are focusing on higher-end pinot noir, which can be outstanding. Also look for good chardonnay and pinot gris for less than $20. This winery is set amid mature vineyards on the outskirts of Newberg and is a good first stop in wine country if you are heading out from Portland on Ore. 99W.

30835 N. Ore. 99W. © **800/739-4455.** www.rexhill.com. Tasting fee $10. Daily 10am–5pm.

Trisaetum Vineyards ★   Few Willamette Valley wineries produce riesling, but here at Trisaetum, it's one of the specialties. In any given vintage, the winery will produce several styles of riesling, from dry to sweet. Good pinot noir is also produced. Try to get a look at the winery's impressive barrel caves.

18401 Ribbon Ridge Rd. © **503/538-9898.** www.trisaetum.com. Tasting fee $10. Wed–Mon 11am–4pm.

Utopia Vineyards ★   This little vineyard and winery is within the Ribbon Ridge American Viticultural Area (AVA), which is the smallest in Oregon. Neighboring wineries produce some of the most highly regarded pinot noirs in the state, so the wines here, though mostly priced between $38 and $48, are good values compared to what the neighbors charge for wine from these same slopes.

177445 NE Ribbon Ridge Rd., Newberg. © **503/687-1671.** http://utopiawine.com. Tasting fee $10. Sat–Sun 11am–6pm.

The Dundee Hills

Alexana ★★   The wines at Alexana are made by Lynn Penner-Ash, one of Oregon's top winemakers (her own winery is just a short drive away), and they are every bit as good as the wines from her own label. The 2010 estate riesling was one of the best in the region. Pinot noirs include an estate bottling and a Shea vineyards pinot noir. This latter vineyard is considered one of the best vineyards in the state.

12001 NE Worden Hill Rd., Newberg. © **503/537-3100.** www.alexanawinery.com. Tasting fee $15. Daily 11am–5pm.

Archery Summit ★★★   With big wines, a big winery, and a big reputation, Archery Summit is one of Oregon's premier producers of pinot noir. Only pinot noir is produced, and the grapes all come from Archery Summit's own vineyards. Wines are aged almost exclusively in new-oak barrels and spend time in some of the only barrel-aging caves in the state. Prices are in the $50 to $85 range.

18599 NE Archery Summit Rd., Dayton. © **503/864-4300.** www.archerysummit.com. Tasting fee $15–$45. Daily 10am–4pm. West of Dundee on Ore. 99W; turn right on Archery Summit Rd.

Argyle Winery ★★   Located right on the highway in Dundee, this winery is best known for its sparkling wines ($30–$50) and chardonnay, but also produces pinot noir ($40–$50). If you're in the state for a special occasion, be sure to pick up a bottle of bubbly here. Due to traffic congestion in Dundee, this winery is best visited when heading east on Ore. 99W.

691 Ore. 99W, Dundee. © **888/427-4953** or 503/538-8520. www.argylewinery.com. Tasting fee $10–$22. Daily 11am–5pm.

Bella Vida Vineyard   This little winery in the Dundee Hills is unusual in that it hires three winemakers from other wineries to make pinot noir from its own estate-grown grapes. Each winemaker gives the wine a slightly different character. Bella Vida also produces a very enjoyable pinot gris---riesling blend called Gris-ling.

9380 NE Worden Hill Rd., Dundee. ✆ **503/538-9821.** www.bellavida.com. Tasting fee $10. Thurs–Sun 11am–5pm.

De Ponte Cellars ★★   This small winery, neighbor to acclaimed Archery Summit, produces pinot noir in a variety of prices, and these wines can be absolutely exquisite. This is also one of the only wineries in the state (and in the country, for that matter) that produces melon, a white wine that is made not from melons but from a French grape that goes by the name *melon de Bourgogne.*

17545 NE Archery Summit Rd., Dayton. ✆ **503/864-3698.** www.depontecellars.com. Tasting fee $10. Daily 11am–5pm.

Dobbes Family Estate ★   This tasting room right in Dundee pours the wines of both Dobbes Family Estate and the affiliated Wine by Joe. These are both labels of winemaker Joe Dobbes, one of Oregon's top winemakers. The Dobbes Family label offers some superb, highly extracted pinot noirs and syrahs, while the Wine by Joe label is all about good values.

240 SE Fifth St., Dundee. ✆ **503/538-1141.** www.dobbesfamilyestate.com. Tasting fee $10. Daily 11am–5pm. Just south of Ore. 99W in Dundee.

Domaine Drouhin Oregon ★★★   Years ago, when France first heard that Oregon wineries were making pinot noir, most French winemakers scoffed. Not Maison Joseph Drouhin of Burgundy; the family bought land in the Red Hills of Dundee and planted vines. Today the Burgundian-style wines of Domaine Drouhin Oregon are superb examples of old-world winemaking—silky, seductive, and well balanced. Tours of the winery ($25) are available by reservation.

6750 Breyman Orchards Rd., Dayton. ✆ **503/864-2700.** www.domainedrouhin.com. Tasting fee $10. July–harvest (Oct) daily 11am–4pm; other months Wed–Sun 11am–4pm. West of Dundee on Ore. 99W; turn right on McDougall Rd. and right again onto Breyman Orchards Rd.

Domaine Serene ★★   Located across the road from Domaine Drouhin Oregon, this is another of Oregon's top wineries, with an impressive winemaking facility and impressive prices ($42–$75) to prove it. Great ratings from *Wine Spectator* have made these wines some of the most sought after in the state. Pinot noir, chardonnay, and Syrah are produced here.

6555 NE Hilltop Lane, Dayton. ✆ **866/864-6555** or 503/864-4600. www.domaineserene.com. Tasting fee $15–$60. Wed–Mon 11am–4pm. West of Dundee on Ore. 99W; turn right on McDougall Rd. and right again onto Breyman Orchards Rd.

Erath Winery ★   In business since 1972, Erath Vineyards, set high in the Red Hills of Dundee, was founded by Dick Erath, one of the pioneers of modern Oregon winemaking. A wide variety of wines is produced here, and you can usually sample a half dozen or more during your visit to the tasting room. Today this winery is owned by Washington State's Chateau Ste. Michelle Winery.

9409 NE Worden Hill Rd., Dundee. ✆ **800/539-9463** or 503/538-3318. www.erath.com. Tasting fee $10. Daily 11am–5pm. In Dundee, go north on Ninth St., which becomes Worden Hill Rd.

Lange Estate Winery & Vineyards ★★   Superb pinot noirs are the hallmark of this small winery. The estate wines produced here are among the best pinot noirs in the state and tend to be priced from $40 to $60. Lange also produces a few wines (mostly pinot gris and chardonnay) in the $16 to $22 range. Domaine Trouvere, Lange's second label, produces, among other wines, tempranillo and syrah.

18380 NE Buena Vista Dr., Dundee. ℂ **503/538-6476.** www.langewinery.com. Tasting fee $10. Daily 11am–5pm. In Dundee, go north on Ninth St. and follow signs.

Ponzi Tasting Room & Wine Bar ★ Ponzi Vineyards was one of Oregon's wine pioneers, and though it's original tasting room is north of here near Beaverton, this tasting room and wine bar is a more convenient place to sample Ponzi wines. Expect excellent pinot gris and chardonnay, and be sure to sample the arneis, an Italian varietal dry white wine that is aged in oak and is rarely planted in this area. Also don't miss the Vino Gelato, a dessert wine made from frozen grapes.

100 SW Seventh St., Dundee. ℂ **503/554-1500.** www.ponziwinebar.com. Tasting fee $10–$12. Daily 11am–5pm (in summer Fri–Sat until 7pm).

Sokol Blosser Winery Another of the big Oregon wineries, Sokol Blosser sits high on the slopes above the west end of Dundee. Off-dry whites are a strong point here, and the Evolution, a blend of nine different grapes, shouldn't be missed. A walk-through showcase vineyard provides an opportunity to learn about the growing process, and tours of the winery ($20) are given on Saturday and Sunday by reservation.

5000 Sokol Blosser Lane, Dundee. ℂ **800/582-6668** or 503/864-2282. www.sokolblosser.com. Tasting fee $5–$15. Daily 10am–4pm. Southwest of Dundee off Ore. 99W.

Stoller Vineyards ★★ This large, LEED-certified winery produces not only good chardonnay and pinot noir, but with an array of photovoltaic panels on the roof, it also produces electricity. The owners are also co-owners of Chehalem Winery, one of the most highly respected wineries in the state. Stoller also has a cottage ($295 per night) and farmhouse ($395) that they rent out (2-night minimum).

16161 NE McDougall Rd., Dayton. ℂ **503/864-3404.** www.stollervineyards.com. Tasting fee $10–$15. Daily 11am–5pm. Southwest of Dundee off Ore. 99W.

Torii Mor Winery ★★ With the Japanese-inspired name (*torii* means "gate" in Japanese) and Japanese gardens outside the tasting room, you might expect this winery to produce sake, but Torii Mor actually produces some of the region's best pinot noirs. Expect to pay between $50 and $60 for one of this winery's single-vineyard pinot noirs. Tours ($25) can be arranged.

18323 NE Fairview Dr., Dundee. ℂ **503/538-2279.** www.toriimorwinery.com. Tasting fee $10. Daily 11am–5pm. In Dundee, go north on Ninth St. (which becomes Worden Hill Rd.) and then turn right on Fairview Rd.

Winderlea Vineyard & Winery ★ Set high in the Red Hills of Dundee, this winery is surrounded by one of the oldest and most highly regarded vineyards in the area. The grapes from this vineyard are coveted by area winemakers, and after tasting what Winderlea does with its own grapes, you'll understand why.

8905 NE Worden Hill Rd., Dundee. ℂ **888/554-5990** or 503/554-5900. www.winderlea.com. Tasting fee $10. Feb to mid-Dec Thurs–Mon 11am–4pm. Closed mid-Dec to Jan.

The McMinnville Area

For a selection of area wines, stop by **Wednesday Wines,** 250 NE Third St., McMinnville (ℂ **503/857-5665;** www.wednesdaywines.com), a small shop selling wine, cheese, and other gourmet picnic items. Also in downtown McMinnville, you'll find the **Willamette Valley Vineyards Wine Center,** 300 NE Third St. (✆ 503/883-9012; www.wvv.com/visit/wine_center), which has interesting displays on wine-growing in the region and also serves as a tasting room for the winery.

The Eyrie Vineyards   This winery is the oldest producer of pinot noir in Oregon and was responsible for putting Oregon on the international wine map when its 1975 pinot noir won major competitions in France in 1979 and 1980. Eyrie was also the first vineyard in America to produce pinot gris, which has since become one of Oregon's top white wines.

935 NE 10th Ave. ✆ **888/440-4970** or 503/472-6315. www.eyrievineyards.com. Tasting fee $5. Wed–Sun noon–5pm.

Panther Creek Cellars ★★   To find out just how different pinot noirs from various vineyards can be, stop in at Panther Creek's facility in downtown McMinnville. In any given year, this winery produces four or more vineyard-designate pinot noirs, and some of these wines have been rated among the best in the world.

455 N. Irvine St., McMinnville. ✆ **503/472-8080.** www.panthercreekcellars.com. Tasting fee $5. Daily noon–5pm.

Walnut City WineWorks ★★   This winemaking facility near downtown McMinnville houses five separate wineries, and in the little tasting room, you can sample wines from all of them (the best part of a stop here). The Z'Ivo wines are always my favorites.

475 NE 17th St. (at Evans St.), McMinnville. ✆ **503/472-3215.** www.walnutcitywineworks.com. Tasting fee $5–$10. Thurs–Sun 11am–4:30pm. From Ore. 99W in McMinnville, drive south on Evans St.

The Yamhill & Carlton Area ★★

With more than a dozen wineries and tasting rooms within a 6-block area, the tiny town of Carlton has the highest concentration of tasting rooms in the state. Many of these tasting rooms seem to serve as testing rooms; if the wines do well, the wineries move into other, larger facilities. Consequently, although I have had some excellent wines at Carlton tasting rooms, I hesitate to recommend by name any of the smaller wineries because they may have moved on by the time you visit. However, rest assured that a walk around Carlton will provide ample wine-sampling opportunities.

If you're searching for rare and expensive boutique wines from the area, stop in at **The Tasting Room,** 105 W. Main St. (✆ 503/852-6733; www.pinot-noir.com), which specializes in wines from wineries not usually open to the public. Most wines featured here are from wineries in the immediate vicinity of Carlton. The tasting room is open Thursday through Monday from noon to 5pm. Also here in Carlton, you'll find the **Carlton Winemakers Studio,** 801 N. Scott St. (✆ 503/852-6100; www.winemakersstudio.com), which represents numerous wineries, including Andrew Rich Vintner and Hamacher Wines. This tasting room is open daily from 11am to 5pm.

Anne Amie Vineyards   Set amid nearly 100 acres of vines and located high on a hill with one of the best views in the area, this winery has a large tasting room and does a few respectable white wines, which usually sell for less than $20. The winery also produces several vineyard-designate pinot noirs.

6580 NE Mineral Springs Rd., Carlton. ✆ **503/864-2991.** www.anneamie.com. Tasting fee $10. Mar–Dec daily 10am–5pm; Jan–Feb Fri–Sun 10am–5pm. Take Ore. 99W to Lafayette and go north on Mineral Springs Rd.

Cana's Feast Winery ★ If you like assertive red wines, don't miss this small winery. Cabernet sauvignon, sangiovese, and syrah all show up here, making this a distinctly different stop in this region of pinot noirs. Between June and December, lunch and dinner are served on Friday and Saturday, and brunch is served on Sunday; contact the winery for details.

750 W. Lincoln St., Carlton. ℂ **503/852-0002.** www.canasfeastwinery.com. Tasting fee $10. Daily 11am–5pm. Located just off Ore. 47 on the north side of town.

Lemelson Vineyards ★★ This has long been one of my favorite Oregon wineries, and it is one of the area's most enjoyable wineries to visit. If you're lucky, you'll have an opportunity to sample several different pinot noirs from a couple of vintages. Grapes here are organically and sustainably grown, and the winery has a huge array of photovoltaic panels.

12020 NE Stag Hollow Rd., Carlton. ℂ **503/852-6619.** www.lemelsonvineyards.com. Tasting fee $7–$10. Thurs–Mon 11am–4pm.

Lenné Estate ★★ With a tasting room in a beautiful little stone building that seems transported straight from an estate in Tuscany, this winery is a hidden gem of a place to stop and taste some wine. With 20 acres of vineyards surrounding the tasting room, the views are just spectacular. The wine, exclusively pinot noir, is made from estate-grown grapes and is very good (although priced in the $45–$55 range), which makes Lenné a must on any wine tour of the Yamhill-Carlton area.

18760 NE Laughlin Rd., Yamhill. ℂ **503/956-2256.** www.lenneestate.com. Tasting fee $5. May–Oct Thurs–Sun noon–5pm; other months Sat–Sun noon–5pm. From Yamhill, go east on Ore. 240 and turn left on NE Laughlin Rd.

Penner-Ash Wine Cellars ★★ Winemaker Lynn Penner-Ash has been on the Oregon wine scene for years, and her winery between Newberg and Yamhill is one of the more impressive facilities in the area. Set high on a hill with a stupendous view, it would be worth a visit even if Penner-Ash didn't produce excellent wines. The pinot noirs and syrahs here are some of the best in the state. Tours are offered on Saturday and Sunday at 10am.

15771 NE Ribbon Ridge Rd., Newberg. ℂ **503/554-5545.** www.pennerash.com. Tasting fee $10–$15. Wed–Sun 11am–5pm. From Ore. 240 between Newberg and Yamhill, drive north on NE Ribbon Ridge Rd.

Soléna Estate ★ Highly extracted pinot noirs that look more like syrah than pinot are the hallmark of this large and impressive estate winery outside Yamhill. Along with that deep, dark color comes plenty of tannin, which means these are wines for your cellar. Husband-and-wife team Laurent Montalieu and Danielle Andrus Montalieu worked for some of Oregon's top wineries before starting their own.

17100 NE Woodland Loop Rd., Yamhill. ℂ **503/852-0082.** www.solenaestate.com. Tasting fee $15. Daily 11am–5pm.

Tyrus Evan ★ Located in Carlton's old railroad depot and operated by the celebrated Ken Wright Cellars winery, Tyrus Evan specializes in Bordeaux blends (here referred to as clarets) and syrahs. These wines tend to be big and juicy, and the winery is a must for anyone who is not a fan of pinot noir.

120 N. Pine St., Carlton. ℂ **503/852-7010.** Tasting fee $15–$20. Sun–Thurs 11am–5pm; Fri–Sat 11am–6pm.

WillaKenzie Estate ★★ Situated on a 420-acre estate above the Chehalem Valley, this winery produces primarily pinot noir, pinot gris, pinot blanc, and pinot meunier, plus a bit of chardonnay in its gravity-fed facility. There's a nice picnic area with good views. This is one of the prettiest spots in all of wine country, and the wines are excellent.

19143 NE Laughlin Rd., Yamhill. ✆ **888/953-9463** or 503/662-3280. www.willakenzie.com. Tasting fee $15. May–Oct daily 11am–5pm; Nov–Apr daily 11am–4pm. From Ore. 240 just east of Yamhill, drive north on NE Laughlin Rd.

The Hillsboro & Beaverton Area

Cooper Mountain Vineyards Now nearly surrounded by upscale suburbs, this mountaintop winery is one of the few in the state that uses only organic grapes. The pinot gris is moderately priced and can be quite good. Chardonnays, which go light on the oak, can also be good. Pinot noirs are decent, and for those who like dessert wines, be sure to try the delicious Vin Glace.

9480 SW Grabhorn Rd., Beaverton. ✆ **503/649-0027.** www.coopermountainwine.com. Tasting fee $6–$10. Daily noon–5pm. From Ore. 217 on the west side of Portland, take Ore. 210 (Scholls Ferry Rd.) west approximately 5 miles, turn right on Tile Flat Rd., and right again on Grabhorn Rd.

Ponzi Vineyards Although Ponzi Tasting Room & Wine Bar on Ore. 99W in Dundee is more convenient for most people touring wine country, it is also possible to taste wines here at the Ponzi's original winery site. Although there are no views, the quiet setting and old shade trees make this a good spot for a picnic. See the listing on p. 120 for information on wines produced by this pioneering Oregon winery.

14665 SW Winery Lane, Beaverton. ✆ **503/628-1227.** www.ponziwines.com. Tasting fee $10. Daily 10am–5pm. From Ore. 217 on the west side of Portland, take Ore. 210 (Scholls Ferry Rd.) west 4½ miles to a left on Vandermost Rd.

Raptor Ridge This small winery produces several old-world-style vineyard-designate and reserve pinot noirs, usually in the $35 to $45 range, as well as a more moderately priced Willamette Valley pinot noir, a rosé, a pinot gris, and sometimes even a Grüner Veltliner (a wine rarely produced in Oregon).

18700 SW Hillsboro Hwy., Newberg. ✆ **503/628-8463.** www.raptoridge.com. Tasting fee $10. Mid-Mar to mid-Dec Thurs–Mon 11am–4pm; mid-Jan to mid-Mar Sat–Sun 11am–4pm; mid-Dec to mid-Jan by appointment. From Hillsboro, go south on Ore. 219 toward Newberg.

The Gaston & Forest Grove Area

In downtown Forest Grove, you can sample a wide variety of local wines at **Urban Decanter,** 2030 Main St. (✆ **503/359-7678;** www.urbandecanter.com), a wine bar open Monday from 4 to 7pm, Tuesday through Thursday from 11am to 9pm, and Friday and Saturday from 11am to 10pm.

David Hill Winery This winery overlooks the forested foothills of the Coast Range and has its tasting room in a picturesque farmhouse. Here you'll usually find more than a dozen wines available for tasting. The sparkling wine and dessert wines (including a port) are particularly noteworthy. For the most part, wines here are very reasonably priced, with quite a few wines for less than $20.

46350 NW David Hill Rd., Forest Grove. ✆ **877/992-8545** or 503/992-8545. www.davidhillwinery.com. Tasting fee $5. Daily 11am–5pm. West of Forest Grove off Ore. 8.

Elk Cove Vineyards ★ In business since 1974 and located in an idyllic setting in the hills above the community of Gaston, this is another of the state's larger

Sake It to Me, Baby

When you've had it with wine, why not try a little sake? In Forest Grove, you'll find **Saké One**, 820 Elm St., off Ore. 47 (℗ **800/550-7253** or 503/357-7056; www.sakeone.com), which is the world's only American-owned sake brewery and produces premium sakes that are meant to be served cold. The tasting room is open daily from 11am to 5pm, excluding major holidays. The tasting fee ranges from $3 to $10.

wineries. Pinot noir and pinot gris make up the bulk of the wine produced here, and the Roosevelt pinot noir, although expensive, can be very good. The Ultima dessert wine is delicious.

27751 NW Olson Rd., Gaston. ℗ **877/355-2683** or 503/985-7760. www.elkcove.com. Tasting fee $5. Daily 10am–5pm. From Ore. 47 in Gaston, go west on Olson Rd.

Montinore Estate ★   This is another of Oregon's big wineries, and as at several other of the state's large wineries, the wines are often somewhat lacking. White wines are the specialty, and prices are quite reasonable. The vineyard setting, with an old farmhouse that seems straight out of the antebellum South, is quite picturesque.

3663 SW Dilley Rd., Forest Grove. ℗ **888/359-5012** or 503/359-5012. www.montinore.com. Tasting fee $5. Daily 11am–5pm. South of Forest Grove off Ore. 47 at Dilley Rd.

Patton Valley Vineyard ★   Using only estate-grown grapes, this small winery produces exclusively pinot noir and usually has four different pinots to taste. My personal preference is for the West Block pinots, which can be decidedly different from this winery's East Block wines. The prices run from $20 to around $70, and grapes are sustainably grown.

9449 Old Ore. 47, Gaston. ℗ **503/985-3445.** www.pattonvalley.com. Tasting fee $10. Thurs–Sun 11am–5pm (shorter hours in winter). From Forest Grove, drive 6 miles south on Ore. 47 and turn right at the PATTON VALLEY/CHERRY GROVE sign and right again on Old Ore. 47.

The Eola Hills Area ★★

Some people claim the best pinot noirs in Oregon come from the Eola Hills, northwest of Salem. Why not decide for yourself?

Amity Vineyards ★   Founded in 1974, this was one of the oldest wineries in Oregon and helped set the stage for the Willamette Valley becoming one of the world's top pinot noir–producing regions. Amity Vineyards is one of the few wineries in the state producing gamay noir, and it also produces unsulfited pinot noir from organically grown grapes. Pinot noirs are usually in the $30 to $40 range and are often excellent. The late-harvest and dessert wines are delicious.

18150 Amity Vineyards Rd., Amity. ℗ **888/264-8966** or 503/835-2362. www.amityvineyards.com. Reserve wines tasting fee $8. June–Sept daily 11am–6pm; Oct–May daily noon–5pm. In Amity, go east on Rice Lane.

Arcane Cellars ★★   This casual, laid-back winery on the banks of the Willamette River is a real sleeper. Winemaker Jason Silva produces a wide range of varietals, including the expected pinot noir and pinot gris, but also pinot blanc, riesling, cabernet sauvignon, cabernet franc, merlot, and other Bordeaux blends. The wines are generally well balanced, and prices for many of the wines are quite reasonable.

22350 Magness Rd. NW, Salem. ℂ **503/868-7076.** www.arcanecellars.com. Sat–Sun noon–4pm. From I-5, take exit 263, drive west on Brooklake Rd. to a right on Wheatland Rd. and then, after crossing the Willamette River on the Wheatland Ferry, turn right on gravel Magness Rd. From Dayton, drive south on Ore. 221 and turn right on Wheatland Rd.

Bethel Heights Vineyard ★

Set high on a hill and surrounded by more than 50 acres of grapes, Bethel Heights primarily produces chardonnays and pinot noirs. Most of their pinot noirs are in the $40 to $50 range, while their chardonnays, which can be very good, are around $25.

6060 Bethel Heights Rd. NW, Salem. ℂ **503/581-2262.** www.bethelheights.com. Tasting fee $5. Feb–Nov Tues–Sun 11am–5pm; Dec Sat–Sun 11am–5pm; Jan by appointment. From Ore. 221 in Lincoln, take Zena Rd. west and turn right on Bethel Heights Rd.

Cristom Vineyards ★

With a beautiful setting high in the Eola Hills, this winery is an ideal place for a picnic. For every vintage, a wide range of pinot noirs, in a variety of styles and price ranges, is produced here. Cristom is also one of the few wineries in the region producing syrah from estate-grown grapes.

6905 Spring Valley Rd. NW, Salem. ℂ **503/375-3068.** www.cristomwines.com. Tasting fee $5. Tues–Sun 11am–5pm. From Ore. 221 in Lincoln, take Zena Rd. west and turn right on Spring Valley Rd., or take Spring Valley Rd. west from Ore. 221 north of Lincoln.

Methven Family Vineyards ★★

Set on a gorgeous estate on the east side of the Eola Hills, this is one of the prettiest vineyards in the Willamette Valley. That the reserve pinot noirs produced here can also be outstanding makes this a great place to do some tasting and perhaps have a picnic on the patio. They also do delicious, well-balanced riesling.

11400 Westland Lane, Dayton. ℂ **503/868-7259.** http://methvenfamilyvineyards.com. Tasting fee $5. Daily 11am–5pm.

Mystic Wines ★

This little winery on the north side of the Eola Hills bucks the Oregon pinot noir trend by producing excellent syrah, zinfandel, cabernet sauvignon, and merlot with grapes that come from near the Oregon town of The Dalles, as well as from Washington state. Prices are mostly in the $20 to $30 range.

11931 SE Hood View Rd., Amity. ℂ **503/581-2769.** www.mysticwine.com. Late May–Nov Fri–Sun noon–5pm. Off Ore. 221, about 1 mile north of Hopewell.

St. Innocent Winery ★

This large and impressive winery produces very drinkable white wines as well as some excellent pinot noirs. The latter are made with grapes from some of the most prestigious vineyards in Oregon.

5657 Zena Rd. NW, Salem. ℂ **503/378-1526.** www.stinnocentwine.com. Tasting fee $5. Apr–Nov Tues–Sun 11am–4pm; Dec–Mar Fri–Sun 11am–4pm. From Ore. 221 in Lincoln, take Zena Rd. west.

Stangeland Vineyards ★

With an attractive stone-walled tasting room, this small family-owned winery north of Salem is a good place to start a wine tour of the Eola Hills. Stangeland produces some excellent fruit-forward pinot noirs in a variety of price ranges, and has won numerous national and international awards.

8500 Hopewell Rd. NW, Salem. ℂ **800/301-9482** or 503/581-0355. www.stangelandwinery.com. Tasting fee $5. Thurs–Sun noon–5pm. From West Salem, go north on Ore. 221 for 9 miles and turn left on Hopewell Rd.

Witness Tree Vineyard ★

Named for a tree used by surveyors in the 19th century, this unpretentious winery produces estate-grown chardonnays and pinot noirs. In a region of high-priced pinots, Witness Tree is noteworthy for offering very

If you're interested in learning more about Oregon wines, contact **Grape Escape** (📞 **503/283-3380;** www.grapeescapetours.com), which offers in-depth winery tours of the Willamette Valley. All-day tours include stops at several wineries, appetizers, lunch, and dessert, and pickup and drop-off at your hotel.

For people with less time, half-day afternoon trips take in three wineries. Call for rates. **Oregon Wine Tours** (📞 **503/681-9463;** www.orwinetours.com) operates similar all-day tours that stop at four or five wineries. These tours cost $160 each if there are just two of you.

drinkable bottles at around $20 (though they also produce pricier vintage select pinots that are often very good). Witness Tree is also one of the only wineries in the region producing Dolcetto and Viognier from estate-grown grapes.

7111 Spring Valley Rd. NW, Salem. 📞 **503/585-7874.** www.witnesstreevineyard.com. Tasting fee $5. May–Sept Tues–Sun 11am–5pm; Mar–Apr and Oct to early Dec Sat–Sun 11am–5pm; early Dec to Feb limited hours and dates. From Ore. 221 in Lincoln, take Zena Rd. west and turn right on Spring Valley Rd., or take Spring Valley Rd. west from Ore. 221 north of Lincoln.

Other Wine Country Activities

Evergreen Aviation & Space Museum ★★   The middle of wine country may seem an odd landing place for Howard Hughes's famous "Spruce Goose" flying boat, but that's exactly what you'll find in this massive, barnlike museum. Designed during World War II as a flying troop transport, the "Spruce Goose" wasn't completed until 1947, at which point it was no longer needed. The plane flew only once, with Howard Hughes at the controls. The massive wooden plane rests in the company of many smaller planes. Among these are an SR-71A Blackbird spy plane, a Ford Trimotor, a P-51D Mustang, and a Spitfire. The term "Spruce Goose" is actually a misnomer; most of the plane is made of birch. A second museum focuses on space exploration. There is also an IMAX theater and the indoor Wings & Waves Waterpark.

500 NE Capt. Michael King Smith Way, McMinnville. 📞 **503/434-4185.** www.evergreenmuseum. org. Admission to museums $20 adults, $19 seniors, $18 children 5–16, free for children 4 and under (combination tickets available). Admission to waterpark $30 for those over 42" tall, $25 for those under 42" tall. Daily 9am–5pm. On Ore. 18 (the McMinnville bypass).

GETTING OUTDOORS IN WINE COUNTRY

You can see wine country from the air on a hot-air balloon ride with **Vista Balloon Adventures** (📞 **800/622-2309** or 503/625-7385; www.vistaballoon.com), which charges $189 per person for a 1-hour flight (that includes brunch at the end of the flight).

Seven miles south of Newberg off Ore. 219, on the banks of the Willamette River, is **Champoeg State Park** (pronounced "Sham-*poo*-ee"; 📞 **503/678-1251;** www. oregon.gov/oprd/parks). The park includes a campground, a bike path, disc-golf course, picnic area, historic home, log cabin, and a visitor center that traces Champoeg's history from its days as a Native American village up through its pioneer farming days. Park admission is $5.

Shopping in the Area

The Willamette Valley wine country is not just about wine. It also produces quite a few other crops, and a tour of this region can include stops at a variety of interesting roadside stands and farms.

South of Hillsboro there is a wonderful grouping of farms in the community of Scholls. To reach this area, which is on the northern edge of wine country, take U.S. 26 west from Portland, go south on Ore. 217, and then take the Scholls Ferry Road (Ore. 210) exit and drive southwest for about 8 miles. Here you'll find the **Hoffman Farms Store,** 22242 SW Scholls Ferry Rd. (© **503/628-5418;** www.hoffman farmsstore.com), where in the summer you can buy fresh berries. Across the road from this farm stand you'll find **Oregon Heritage Farms,** 22801 SW Scholls Ferry Rd. (© **503/628-2775;** www.oregonheritagefarm.com), which sells apples and cider in the autumn months. During the summer—peak season is the month of July—you can pick your own berries at **Rowell Brothers U-Pick,** 24100 SW Scholls Ferry Rd. (© **503/628-0431;** www.rowellbros.com). This farm also sells prepicked berries. More berries, plus gourmet foods and lots more, can be found at **Smith Berry Barn Farm and Garden Market,** 24500 SW Scholls Ferry Rd. (© **503/628-2172;** www.smithberrybarn.com). Across the street from this big red barn, you'll find the **South Store Café** (p. 135), my favorite area lunch spot. Scholls Ferry Road becomes Hillsboro Highway (Ore. 219) at this point and leads over Chehalem Mountain to the heart of the wine country. A little ways up this road, you'll come to **Mountainside Lavender Farm,** 17805 SW Hillsboro Hwy. (© **503/936-6744;** www.mountainsidelavender.com), where you can pick your own lavender during the summer. The little shop here sells lots of lavender products. In early July, this farm participates in the Oregon Lavender Festival.

Between Dundee and McMinnville, there are several other good places to stop. **Firestone Farms,** 18400 N. Ore. 99W, Dayton (© **503/864-2672**), just west of Dundee, sells a wide selection of local produce, wines, and gourmet foods. For fresh local fruit, don't miss **Sweet Oregon Berry Farm** (© **503/864-2897**), which is at the junction of Ore. 18 and Ore. 99W, between Dundee and Lafayette. Dried flowers, herbs, soaps, and other garden-related gifts can also be found at the beautiful **Red Ridge Farms,** 5510 NE Breyman Orchards Rd., Dayton (© **866/828-4372** or 503/864-8502; www. redridgefarms.com), a nursery and gift shop high in the hills west of Dundee and near **Domaine Drouhin Oregon** and **Domaine Serene** (both on p. 119). Call for directions and hours. Red Ridge Farms is also home to the **Oregon Olive Mill,** which produces olive oil from olive trees growing here at the farm. Tours of the Oregon Olive Mill can be arranged ($15–$25 per person with a four-person minimum).

Southwest of McMinnville, off Ore. 18, you can buy fresh produce from spring through fall at **Farmer John's Produce,** 15000 SW Oldsville Rd., McMinnville (© **503/474-3514;** www.farmerjohnsproduce.com). If you like chocolate, head to nearby Amity and stop in at the **Brigittine Monks Priory,** 23300 Walker Lane (© **503/835-8080;** www.brigittine.org), which is known for its heavenly fudge. The fudge and truffles are for sale at the guest reception area, which is open Monday through Saturday from 9am to 5pm and Sunday from 1 to 5pm.

South of Dayton, at the eastern base of the Eola Hills near the community of Hopewell, you should be sure to stop at **Willamette Valley Cheese Company,** 8105

Wallace Rd. (℗ **503/399-9806;** www.wvcheeseco.com), which produces more than 30 different cheeses, including gouda, cheddar, brie, fontina, and other farmstead cheeses. The tasting room here is open Tuesday to Saturday from 10am to 5pm.

Where to Stay

NEWBERG

The Allison Inn & Spa ★★★   This is the only wine-country resort in Oregon, and what a place it is. The Allison is both gorgeous and green built. With lots of natural wood and stone both inside and out, the hotel has a distinctly Northwest feel. Guest rooms are large, with plush headboards and big soaking tubs with walls that roll back to let you gaze at the gas fireplace. Window seats and balconies let you enjoy the views of the green Oregon landscape. Over the indoor pool, which has a huge door that rolls back to give it the feel of being outdoors, there is a living roof (a roof covered with live plants that reduce runoff), and elsewhere on the hotel's main roof, there are photovoltaic panels. The hotel's restaurant, Jory (see below), is one of the finest in wine country and should not be missed.

2525 Allison Lane, Newberg, OR 97132. www.theallison.com. ℗ **877/294-2525** or 503/554-2525. 85 units. $305–$375 double; $450–$1,100 suite. Children 12 and under stay free in parent's room. AE, DC, DISC, MC, V. Pets accepted ($50 fee). **Amenities:** Restaurant; lounge; babysitting; concierge; exercise room; Jacuzzi; indoor pool; room service; spa. *In room:* A/C, TV, fridge, hair dryer, MP3 docking station, free Wi-Fi.

Chehalem Ridge Bed & Breakfast ★★   If you revel in mountain-top views, this inn should not be missed. Built on a steep slope high above the heart of the Willamette Valley wine country, Chehalem Ridge boasts the most spectacular views in the region. Stretched out far below your room and its balcony is a patchwork quilt of vineyards and orchards that is unsurpassed. Rooms here are a bit small, but the views more than compensate for this shortcoming, as do the wonderful bathrooms, one of which has a two-person jetted tub.

28700 Mountain Top Rd., Newberg, OR 97132. www.chehalemridge.com. ℗ **503/538-3474.** 4 units. $120–$180 double. Rates include full breakfast. DISC, MC, V. Children 12 and over welcome. **Amenities:** Concierge. *In room:* A/C, CD player, hair dryer, no phone, free Wi-Fi.

Le Puy A Wine Valley Inn ★★   On a hillside surrounded by farms and with a view that encompasses some of the region's top vineyards, Le Puy is one of the most elegant, luxurious, and tasteful of wine country's B&Bs. Rooms vary in size and price range, but it's worth splurging on one with a view. Even better, most of these rooms also have a patio or deck. If you don't spring for a view room, you can still take in the scenery from the beautiful living room or one of the inn's patios. For a luxurious bathroom, check into the Lake suite, or for an outdoor spa tub, opt for the Mountain suite. The Heaven suite has the feel of a room in a Santa Fe adobe and comes with spa tub and gas fireplace.

20300 NE Ore. 240, Newberg, OR 97132. http://lepuy-inn.com. ℗ **503/554-9528.** 8 units. $195–$345 suite. Rates include full breakfast. AE, DISC, MC, V. Children 13 and over welcome. **Amenities:** Concierge. *In room:* A/C, TV/DVD, fridge, hair dryer, MP3 docking station, no phone, free Wi-Fi.

The Lion's Gate Inn ★   The town of Newberg has in the past couple of years become something of a wine-country town, and this pretty B&B, in one of the oldest—and prettiest—homes in town, is a good bet for a place to stay. With its wide veranda and attractive gardens, this Craftsman bungalow has lots of beautiful interior woodwork. Guest rooms, which take their themes from the four seasons, are not all that large, but they have plush beds and a contemporary elegance. Bathrooms gorgeous, and three of the rooms have gas fireplaces. Restaurants, a wine bar, and tasting room are all within walking distance. The inn also rents a fairy-tale house out in the middle of wine country.

401 N. Howard St. (P.O. Box 1060), Newberg, OR 97132. www.distinctivedestination.net. © **503/ 476-2211.** 4 units. $150–$200 double. Rates include full breakfast. AE, MC, V. Children 12 and over welcome. **Amenities:** Concierge. In room: A/C, TV, hair dryer, MP3 docking station, Wi-Fi.

THE DUNDEE HILLS

Black Walnut Inn ★★★   Perched high in the Red Hills of Dundee, with a view that seems to take in all of Oregon wine country, this inn looks as if it were transported here from Tuscany. Guest rooms are luxuriously homey and gorgeously decorated, and a few are absolutely huge. There are rooms with antique furnishings and others that are more contemporary—something for everyone. Some rooms have a soaking tub, and all have a balcony or patio. The gardens and patios here are the perfect place to sip a glass of wine at sunset.

9600 NE Worden Hill Rd., Dundee, OR 97115. www.blacknutwalnut-inn.com. © **866/429-4114** or 503/429-4114. Fax 503/538-4194. 9 units. $295–$550 suite. Rates include full breakfast and afternoon appetizers. AE, MC, V. Children 12 and over welcome. **Amenities:** Concierge. In room: A/C, TV/DVD, fridge, hair dryer, free Wi-Fi.

Inn at Red Hills ★   Although it's located right alongside busy Oregon 99W on the edge of Dundee, this modern inn is built in an attractive château style that conjures the French countryside. The roadside setting isn't exactly romantic, but the large guest rooms, with big windows and Sleep Number beds, certainly are. Guest rooms are all on the second floors of two adjacent buildings, and downstairs you'll find a wine bar, deli, and cafe. With a couple of good restaurants within walking distance, the Inn at Red Hills is a good choice for a wine-country getaway.

1410 N. Ore. 99W, Dundee, OR 97115. www.innatredhills.com. © **503/538-7666.** 20 units. $119– $279 double. AE, DC, DISC, MC, V. Pets accepted ($25 fee). **Amenities:** Restaurant; lounge; concierge. In room: A/C, TV, hair dryer, MP3 docking station; free Wi-Fi.

Red Ridge Farm Suite ★★   There are only a cottage and a huge suite available at this luxurious little place, and it is such a quintessential wine-country retreat that you should make this your first choice if you're looking for a romantic hideaway in the hills. The suite takes up the entire second floor of a gorgeous building that has a garden-oriented gift shop on the ground floor. Access is via a spiral staircase up the building's turret (in which lavender hangs to dry in summer). The modern styling, big windows, and wine-country views make this the sort of place you'd see in *Sunset* magazine. The cottage, which is even larger than the suite and surrounded by vineyards, offers a bit more privacy.

5510 NE Breyman Orchards Rd., Dayton, OR 97114. www.redridgefarms.com. © **503/864-8502.** Fax 503/864-8391. 2 units. $200–$225 suite; $350–$375 cottage. DISC, MC, V. In room: A/C, TV, CD player, hair dryer, kitchen, free Wi-Fi.

Wine Country Farm Bed & Breakfast   Surrounded by vineyards on 13 acres high in the hills between Dundee and Lafayette, this B&B has one of the best views in the area. The inn is a restored French-style farmhouse that was built in 1906, and inside you'll find attractively appointed rooms, many of which have decks, views, and fireplaces. If you happen to stay in a room without a view, you can soak up the scenery from the deck that runs the length of the house. You can also hang out in the gazebo

, bocce ball, or horseshoes. The inn also has a vacation-rental home
arby. In addition, there is a winery and tasting room on the grounds,
ides can be arranged.

...ards Rd., Dayton, OR 97114. www.winecountryfarm.com. ℭ **800/261-3446** or
...-3446. Fax 503/864-3109. 9 units. $150–$225 double; $400 vacation home. Rates include
full breakfast (except in vacation home). MC, V. Children 12 and over welcome. **Amenities:** Concierge; Jacuzzi; sauna. In room: A/C, hair dryer, free Wi-Fi.

THE MCMINNVILLE AREA

Joseph Mattey House B&B and Vineyard   This restored 1892 Queen Anne
Victorian farmhouse sits on an acre of farmland behind 1½ acres of grapevines. This
is a grand old house, and up on the second floor, you'll find a tiny balcony overlooking
the vineyard. It's the perfect spot for a glass of wine in the afternoon. Guest rooms
are decorated in country Victorian style, with antique beds. The Riesling Room, with
its claw-foot bathtub, is my favorite. Innkeepers Jack and Denise Seed are always glad
to help you plan your day's explorations.

10221 NE Mattey Lane, McMinnville, OR 97128. www.josephmatteyhouse.com. ℭ **877/434-5058** or
503/434-5058. Fax 503/434-6667. 4 units. $155–$185 double. Rates include full breakfast. AE, MC, V.
Children 10 and over welcome. **Amenities:** Concierge. In room: A/C, hair dryer, no phone, free Wi-Fi.

McMenamins Hotel Oregon ★   This restored historic hotel in downtown
McMinnville is operated by a Portland-based chain of brewpubs, nightclubs, and
unusual hotels that are all filled with interesting artwork. Guest rooms here are done
in a simple, classic style, with antique and reproduction furniture. The corner king
rooms with private baths and big windows on two sides are the nicest. While most
rooms here have shared bathrooms, this inconvenience is offset by the hotel's genuinely historic feel. The ground-floor brewpub/dining room, cellar bar, and rooftop bar
and deck overlooking McMinnville and the Yamhill Valley all help make the Hotel
Oregon eminently recommendable. There are also a couple of good restaurants
within a few blocks.

310 NE Evans St., McMinnville, OR 97128. www.mcmenamins.com. ℭ **888/472-8427** or 503/472-
8427. 42 units, 6 with private bathroom. $60–$115 double with shared bathroom; $115–$145 double with private bathroom. Children 6 and under stay free in parent's room. AE, DC, DISC, MC, V.
Amenities: 2 restaurants; 2 lounges; free Wi-Fi. In room: A/C.

Youngberg Hill Inn ★★   Set on a 50-acre farm that includes 22 acres of organically grown pinot noir and pinot gris vineyards, this is the quintessential wine-country
inn. A mile-long driveway leads to the inn, which sits atop a hill with commanding
views of the Willamette Valley, snowcapped Cascades peaks, and the Coast Range.
Large decks wrap around both floors of the inn, and some of the rooms have their
own fireplaces. Gourmet breakfasts get visitors off to a good start every morning. Pull
up a chair on the porch, pour a glass of the inn's own pinot noir, and gaze out over
the rolling hills, and you'll probably start thinking about cashing in your retirement
funds to start a vineyard of your own.

10660 SW Youngberg Hill Rd., McMinnville, OR 97128. www.youngberghill.com. ℭ **888/657-8668**
or 503/472-2727. Fax 503/472-1313. 8 units. $200–$230 double; $260–$350 suite. Rates include full
breakfast and wine-tasting reception. MC, V. Children 8 and over welcome. **Amenities:** Concierge;
Jacuzzi. In room: A/C, hair dryer, MP3 docking station, free Wi-Fi.

THE YAMHILL & CARLTON AREA

Abbey Road Farm ★★   This is one of the most unusual bed-and-breakfasts in
Oregon and should be one of your top choices for a wine-country getaway. The large

and luxurious guest rooms are located in a building that was constructed from three large metal silos. The silos have been transformed into an architectural gem of a building, a testament to the imagination of owners John and Judi Stuart. The large guest rooms have whirlpool tubs, memory-foam beds, contemporary country decor, and bucolic views. When you're not out wine touring, you can visit with the goats, sheep, llamas, chickens, and other farm animals that live here. A three-bedroom farmhouse is also available for rent.

10501 NE Abbey Rd., Carlton, OR 97111. www.abbeyroadfarm.com. © **503/852-6278.** 5 units. $210 double; $375 house. Rates include full breakfast (except in farmhouse). 2-night minimum (all week for house, on weekends only for double). AE, DISC, MC, V. No children. **Amenities:** Concierge; free Wi-Fi. In room: A/C, CD player, hair dryer, MP3 docking station.

Brookside Inn on Abbey Road ★   With 22 acres of woods, parklike grounds, fields, and a pretty pond complete with weeping willows growing along the shore, this inn, formerly a religious retreat, is wonderfully tranquil. In the main lodge, there's a lovely great room with lots of windows and a stone fireplace. Various decks provide plenty of outdoor gathering spaces. The inn has rooms both in the lodgelike main house and in a separate carriage house. My favorite room is the Kyoto, which has several windows overlooking the garden. Rooms, which have beautiful hardwood furnishings, are not as large as at some area inns, but you'll likely want to spend your time wandering the beautiful grounds and not sitting in your room.

8243 NE Abbey Rd., Carlton, OR 97111. www.brooksideinn-oregon.com. © **503/852-4433.** 9 units. $185–$300 double; $350 suite. Rates include full breakfast. AE, DISC, MC, V. Pets accepted ($40 fee). Children 12 and over welcome. **Amenities:** Bikes; concierge; access to nearby health club. In room: A/C, hair dryer, free Wi-Fi.

THE GASTON & FOREST GROVE AREA

McMenamins Grand Lodge ★   Housed in a former Masonic retirement home, this sprawling lodge is part of a local microbrewery chain and has a decidedly countercultural feel. Although only five of the rooms here have private baths, there are plenty of well-appointed bathrooms, and most rooms do have sinks. There's also lots of colorful artwork incorporated into the design of the building. The hotel is brimming with entertainment, including a movie theater, a bar with a pool table, numerous lounges, and, outside on the huge lawn that surrounds the hotel, a disc-golf course. There are also lots of picnic tables set up on the lawns outside the hotel's pub.

3505 Pacific Ave., Forest Grove, OR 97116. www.mcmenamins.com. © **877/922-9533** or 503/992-9533. 77 units, 5 with private bathroom. $45–$105 double with shared bathroom; $125–$215 double with private bathroom. Children 6 and under stay free in parent's room. AE, DC, DISC, MC, V. **Amenities:** 2 restaurants; 4 lounges; soaking pool; day spa; free Wi-Fi. In room: No phone.

Where to Eat

NEWBERG

If wine tasting has made you sleepy and you need a good latte, head to the **Coffee Cottage,** 808 E. Hancock St., Newberg (© **503/538-5126;** www.coffeecottage cafe.net).

Jory Restaurant ★★ NORTHWEST   "Fresh from the farm" is the focus at this elegant restaurant in the luxurious **Allison Inn** (see above), Oregon's only wine-country resort. The menu is driven by the seasons, and if you visit during the fall, you'll likely find a variety of wild mushrooms on the menu. I recommend ordering them in as many dishes as you can; they are the stars of an autumn meal in wine country. The dining room has walls of glass looking south across the valley; if it's already dark and there are only two of you, I recommend sitting at the counter facing the open, show-case kitchen. It's absolutely fascinating to watch the chefs prepare the evening's many meals. A delightful terrace makes an inviting spot for alfresco summer meals.

In the Allison Inn & Spa, 2525 Allison Lane, Newberg. (℃ **503/554-2526.** www.theallison.com. Reservations recommended. AE, DC, DISC, MC, V. Main courses $14–$20 lunch, $23–$45 dinner. Mon–Sat 6:30–10:30am, 11:30am–2pm, and 5:30–9pm; Sun 6:30am–2pm and 5:30–9pm.

The Painted Lady ★★ FRENCH/NORTHWEST Located just off Ore. 99W in a restored Victorian home in downtown Newberg, the Painted Lady brings sophistication and creativity to a town that has long thought of Chinese and Mexican as exotic foods. Chef/owner Allen Routt, whose credentials include studying at the prestigious Culinary Institute of America, serves three-course prix-fixe dinners that nonetheless offer plenty of choices. The menu changes with the seasons, but a recent night featured, among other offerings, wild-salmon carpaccio, potato gnocchi with wild-mushroom ragout, hazelnut-crusted halibut with sunchoke purée, rabbit roulade on butternut squash–cau-liflower purée, and chevre cheesecake with blueberry compote for dessert.

201 S. College St., Newberg. (℃ **503/538-3850.** www.thepaintedladyrestaurant.com. Reservations recommended. Prix-fixe menus $60 ($100 with wine). AE, DC, DISC, MC, V. Wed–Mon 5–10pm.

Recipe a Neighborhood Kitchen ★★ 🎒 NEW AMERICAN In a historic Victorian house at the west end of Newberg, you'll find one of the north Willamette Valley's hidden gems. Recipe, which sources as much as possible from local farms, invokes lots of French influences in its menu, so you might find escargot served with nettles, black-truffle butter, and the airiest little gnocchi you've ever eaten. There's also a range of house-made charcuterie offerings, including creamy duck-liver mousse that's topped with port-wine *gelee*. The entree menu is fairly short, with only six offer-ings, but that short list might include duck breast with toasted farro salad, hazelnut *aillade* (sort of like aioli), and roasted grapes, or tomato-fennel braised pork with Calabrian chilies and grana padano cheese. With its casual wine-country sophistica-tion and reasonable prices, this place is an absolute must.

115 N. Washington St. (℃ **503/487-6853.** www.recipeaneighborhoodkitchen.com. Reservations recommended. Main courses $6–$13 lunch, $17–$25 dinner. AE, DISC, MC, V. Tues–Thurs 11:30am–9pm; Fri–Sat 11:30am–10pm.

THE DUNDEE HILLS

For gourmet picnic supplies, a sandwich, gourmet meals to go, or a good pizza at the end of the day, stop by the **Red Hills Market,** 115 SW Seventh St., Dundee (℃ **971/832-8414;** www.redhillsmarket.com). The market also stocks a great selec-tion of local wines and beers. You'll find the market a half-block off the highway in the center of Dundee. The market is open daily from 7am to 8pm (sometimes later).

The Dundee Bistro ★ 🍷 NORTHWEST Located in the same building as the **Ponzi Wine Bar** (p. 120), this chic eatery would be right at home in Portland's trendy Pearl District. The bistro's hip, urban style, however, also epitomizes a modern wine-country aesthetic, which makes this place quite popular with people touring the area wineries. The menu is relatively short and changes on a regular basis to reflect the region's best seasonal ingredients, which translates into the likes of oyster mush-room pizza with spinach, sweet onions, and provolone; pork loin with grilled peaches; and line-caught Oregon king salmon with spring-onion purée. The wine list focuses on area wines.

100-A SW Seventh St., Dundee. ✆ **503/554-1650.** www.dundeebistro.com. Reservations recommended. Main courses $11–$24. AE, DISC, MC, V. Daily 11:30am–9pm.

Red Hills Provincial Dining ★ CONTINENTAL/NORTHWEST   Housed in a 1920s Craftsman bungalow, this restaurant sums up the Oregon wine-country appeal with both its setting and its food. The dinner menu changes regularly, and you can be sure it will always include plenty of fresh local produce, as well as Northwest meats and seafood. The menu leans toward European classics such as filet of coq au vin, pork tenderloin in riesling sauce, and filet mignon with porcini-mushroom demi-glace, but the wild mushroom pasta with dark rum and sherry cream is a perennial favorite. There's a very good selection of wines available (local wines are featured), and dishes are calculated to pair well with the wines of the region.

276 N. Ore. 99W, Dundee. ✆ **503/538-8224.** http://redhills-dining.com. Reservations recommended. Main courses $24–$32. AE, DISC, MC, V. Tues–Sat 5–9pm; Sun 5–8pm.

Tina's ★★ CONTINENTAL/NORTHWEST   Despite its rather small and nondescript building right on the highway in Dundee, Tina's has long been one of the Yamhill County wine country's premier restaurants, and with its contemporary menu and decor, it's my favorite place to eat in the area. The menu changes regularly and features a balance between the traditional (rack of lamb with red-wine sauce) and the less familiar (coffee-dusted tenderloin with porcini mushroom demi-glace), with the most creative dishes to be found among the appetizers. The wine list, of course, emphasizes local wines.

760 Ore. 99W, Dundee. ✆ **503/538-8880.** www.tinasdundee.com. Reservations recommended. Main courses $11–$14 lunch, $26–$39 dinner. AE, DISC, MC, V. Tues–Fri 11:30am–2pm and 5–9pm; Sat–Sun 5–9pm.

THE MCMINNVILLE AREA

For casual and inexpensive meals, try the **McMenamins Pub,** Hotel Oregon, 310 NE Evans St. (✆ **503/472-8427;** www.mcmenamins.com), which serves decent pub fare, plus good microbrews and regional wines. More pub fare, microbrews, and local wines can be had at the **Golden Valley Brewery & Pub,** 980 NE Fourth St. (✆ **503/472-2739;** www.goldenvalleybrewery.com). Good sandwiches and baked goods can be had at the **Red Fox Bakery & Café,** 328 NE Evans St. (✆ **503/434-5098;** www.redfoxbakery.net). For espresso, drop by **Union Block Coffee,** 403 NE Third St. (✆ **503/472-0645**).

The Joel Palmer House ★★★ FRENCH/NORTHWEST   If you love mushrooms in all their earthy guises, then you'll find culinary nirvana in this downtown Dayton restaurant, east of McMinnville. Chef Christopher Czarnecki, son of restaurant founder Jack Czarnecki, is as obsessed with mushrooms as his father was, and nearly every dish here has mushrooms in it. Start your meal with the extraordinary wild-mushroom soup made with suillis mushrooms, then move on to the filet mignon with porcini sauce or the beef stroganoff with wild mushrooms. Mushroom lovers should simply opt for the Mushroom Madness six-course dinner, which even incorporates mushrooms into dessert. The restaurant, which is in a house built in the 1850s, is quite formal and has an extensive wine list dominated by Oregon wines.

600 Ferry St., Dayton. ✆ **503/864-2995.** www.joelpalmerhouse.com. Reservations recommended. Main courses $21–$40; prix-fixe menu $75. AE, DISC, MC, V. Tues–Sat 5–9pm. Closed Jan 1–late Jan.

La Rambla Restaurant & Bar ★★ SPANISH   Located right in downtown McMinnville, La Rambla has a gorgeous dining room with a long bar down one side, and it is here that I like to sit, sipping wine and noshing on tapas. From the long menu of small plates, you might order some Spanish cheeses or cured meats, lobster croquettes, pan-seared tuna in a caper-and-honey marinade with fig-and-olive tapenade, or chorizo empanadas. However, if you're more inclined to a formal dinner, they've got a few good entree choices that range from a burger to paella.

238 NE Third St., McMinnville. ℂ **503/435-2126.** www.laramblaonthird.com. Reservations recommended. Main courses $13–$27; tapas $4–$12. AE, DC, DISC, MC, V. Mon–Thurs 11:30am–2:30pm and 5–9pm; Fri 11:30am–2:30pm and 5–10pm; Sat 11:30am–10pm; Sun 11:30am–9pm.

Nick's Italian Café ★ NORTHERN ITALIAN   Nick's is a McMinnville institution with a loyal following, especially among the older winemakers in the region. For many years, the restaurant only served a prix fixe menu, but these days, you can get a pizza, a panini, or a five-course dinner. The restaurant's minestrone with pesto is a must-have, as is the lasagna with Dungeness crab, pine nuts, and local mushrooms. However, there are always lots of other great house-made pastas as well. There's also always a daily lamb entree, and few dishes go better with Oregon pinot noir than lamb. The restaurant's wood-fired oven turns out excellent pizzas, too.

521 NE Third St., McMinnville. ℂ **503/434-4471.** www.nicksitaliancafe.com. Reservations recommended. Main courses $10–$25; 5-course tasting menu $65. AE, DISC, MC, V. Tues–Sat 11am–2pm and 5–9pm.

Thistle ★ NEW AMERICAN   With barely a handful of tables and a kitchen too small to swing a sauce pan, Thistle is a tiny place with a big reputation. The side-street location, shabby-chic decor, and superb food will have you imagining you're dining at an old friend's loft kitchen. The menu, driven by the seasons, changes daily and is so limited that it's written on a blackboard. Preparations tend to be simple, letting the flavor of the individual ingredients shine. You might find gnocchi prepared with sautéed sheep cheese and black-trumpet mushrooms; duck breast with bacon, cabbage, and black truffles; or a venison with winter squash, kale, and a peppercorn sauce. Desserts, such as apple-huckleberry-filbert crisp, should not be missed.

228 NE Evans St., McMinnville. ℂ **503/472-9623.** www.thistlerestaurant.com. Reservations recommended. Main courses $22–$24. MC, V. Tues–Thurs 5:30–10pm; Fri–Sat 5:30–11pm.

THE YAMHILL & CARLTON AREA

If you want to have a picnic at one of the Carlton-area wineries, be sure to stop first at **the Horse Radish,** 211 W. Main St., Carlton (ℂ **503/852-6656;** www.the horseradish.com), a combination wine bar and gourmet deli that sells wonderful cheeses, cured meats, and artisan breads. There are also small plates to go with the wine they serve here. The Horse Radish is open Monday through Thursday from noon to 4pm, Friday and Saturday from noon to 10pm, and Sunday from 1 to 5pm. Alternatively, you can get good sandwiches at **the Filling Station Deli,** 305 W. Main St., Carlton (ℂ **503/852-6687;** www.fillingstationdeli.com), which is open Thursday through Tuesday from 7am to 3:30pm (closed Jan–mid-Feb). On weekends between April and September, you can get lunch or dinner at **Cana's Feast,** 750 W. Lincoln St., Carlton (ℂ **503/852-0002;** www.canasfeastwinery.com).

Cuvée FRENCH   While Carlton is the cutest little town in wine country and is packed with wineries and tasting rooms, it is surprisingly short on good places to eat. This little French restaurant is your best bet for much of the year. The menu is short, with an emphasis on seafoods that pair well with local pinot gris and chardonnay.

However, you might also find boeuf bourguignon or rib-eye steak on the menu. Be sure to start your meal with some oysters or sautéed wild mushrooms.

214 W. Main St., Carlton. (C) **503/852-6555.** www.cuveedining.com. Reservations recommended. Main courses $21–$24. AE, DISC, MC, V. Wed–Sat 5:30–9pm; Sun 5–8pm.

THE HILLSBORO & BEAVERTON AREA

The South Store Café 🍴 COMFORT FOOD   I have a weakness for old general stores, and this cafe in a century-old building on the northern edge of wine country holds a special place in my heart. I always start my wine tours here. If it's early, I come for cappuccino and owner Lee Thompson's incomparable pastries. If it's lunchtime, I can't resist the soups. The chicken-artichoke soup is so good that customers beg for the recipe (don't bother asking, the recipe is a secret). On Fridays there is often clam chowder that would make any Oregon-coast restaurant jealous. Be sure to check the sandwich board for the day's sandwich special, which might be a tasty turkey pesto or New Orleans–style muffaletta.

24485 SW Scholls Ferry Rd., Hillsboro. (C) **503/628-1920.** www.southstorecafe.com. Soups, salads, and sandwiches $6–$8.25. AE, DISC, MC, V. Tues–Fri 7:30am–2pm; Sat–Sun 9am–3pm.

THE GASTON & FOREST GROVE AREA

You can get decent pub food at the **Ironwork Grill,** McMenamins Grand Lodge, 3505 Pacific Ave. ((C) **503/992-9533;** www.mcmenamins.com), in Forest Grove. This hotel also has picnic tables on the lawn in the summer.

SALEM ★ & THE MID-WILLAMETTE VALLEY

47 miles S of Portland, 40 miles N of Corvallis, 131 miles W of Bend, 57 miles E of Lincoln City

Although it's the state capital, the third-largest city in the state, and home to Willamette University, Salem feels more like a small Midwestern college town than a Pacific Rim capital. Founded by a Methodist missionary, the city still wears its air of conservatism like a minister's collar. No one has ever accused Salem of being too raucous or rowdy. Even when both the school and the legislature are in session, the city hardly seems charged with energy. The quiet conservatism does, however, give the city a certain charm that's not found in the other cities of the Willamette Valley. Although there are some interesting museums and the state capitol building to be visited here, it is the countryside surrounding Salem that's the real attraction. Within 20 to 25 miles of Salem, you'll find the Oregon Garden, Silver Falls State Park (one of the most beautiful state parks in Oregon), wineries, commercial flower fields, and several quaint small towns (Silverton, Mt. Angel, Independence, and Monmouth) that conjure the Willamette Valley's pioneer past.

Salem's roots date from 1834, when Methodist missionary Jason Lee, who had traveled west to convert the area's Native Americans, made it the first American settlement in the Willamette Valley. In 1842, a year before the first settlers crossed the continent on the Oregon Trail, Lee founded the Oregon Institute, the first school of higher learning west of the Rockies. In 1857 the first textile mill west of the Mississippi opened here, giving Salem a firm industrial base. However, despite all these historic firsts, Oregon City and Portland grew much faster and quickly became the region's population centers. Salem seemed doomed to backwater status until 1859, when Oregon became a state and Salem was chosen as its capital.

Essentials

GETTING THERE Salem is on I-5 at the junction of Ore. 22, which heads west to connect with Ore. 18 from Lincoln City and southeast to connect with U.S. 20 from Bend.

Amtrak has passenger rail service to Salem. The station is at 500 13th St. SE, between Leslie and Bellevue streets.

VISITOR INFORMATION Contact **Travel Salem,** 181 High St. NE, Salem, OR 97301 (℃ 800/874-7012 or 503/581-4325; www.travelsalem.com). For more information on the Silverton area, contact the **Silverton Chamber of Commerce,** 426 S. Water St. (P.O. Box 257), Silverton, OR 97381 (℃ 503/873-5615; www.silverton chamber.org).

FESTIVALS Two of the biggest events of the year in Salem are the **Oregon State Fair** (℃ 800/833-0011 or 503/947-3247; www.oregonstatefair.org), which is held from late August to Labor Day, and the **Salem Art Fair & Festival** (℃ 503/581-2228; www.salemart.org), which is the largest juried art fair in Oregon and is held the third weekend in July.

Every year on the second weekend after Labor Day, the town of Mt. Angel is the site of the huge **Mt. Angel Oktoberfest ★** (℃ 855/899-6338; www.oktoberfest. org). With polka bands from around the world, beer and wine gardens, German food, and dancing in the streets, this is just about the biggest party in the state.

Salem

SEEING THE SIGHTS

Though it is sometimes easy to forget, Salem is a river town. On the western edge of downtown, you'll find Salem's Riverfront Park, which features a state-of-the-art playground, amphitheater, carousel, and meandering pathways. It is also home to the **A. C. Gilbert Discovery Village** (see below). Here in the park, you'll also find the dock for the **Willamette Queen** (℃ 503/371-1103; www.willamettequeen.com), a paddle wheeler that cruises the Willamette River. Cruises range from basic 1-hour outings to lunch, brunch, and dinner cruises. Prices range from $12 ($6 for children 4–10) for a 1-hour cruise to $48 ($28 for children 4–10) for a 2-hour dinner or brunch cruise. Reservations are required.

From the carousel, a stroll up State Street will take you past some of Salem's most interesting shops and boutiques. To see the work of local artists, stop in at **Mary Lou Zeek Gallery,** 335 State St. (℃ 503/581-3229; www.zeekgallery.com).

Bush Barn Art Center The Salem Art Association's Bush Barn Art Center includes a sales gallery as well as exhibition spaces that feature changing art exhibits. The focus is on local and regional artists, and the quality is quite high. Every year on the third weekend in July, Bush's Pasture Park is the site of the Salem Art Fair & Festival, one of the most popular art festivals in the Northwest.

600 Mission St. SE (at Bush and High sts.). ℃ **503/581-2228.** www.salemart.org. Free admission. Tues–Fri 10am–5pm; Sat–Sun 11am–5pm.

Bush House Museum ★ Set at the top of a shady hill in the 100-acre Bush's Pasture Park, this imposing Italianate Victorian home dates back to 1878. Inside you can see the original furnishings, including 10 fireplaces and the original wallpaper. At the time it was built, this home had all the modern conveniences—indoor plumbing,

Salem

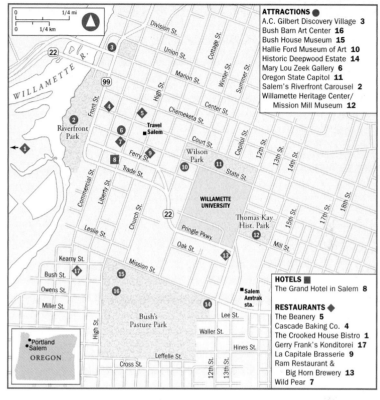

ATTRACTIONS ●
A.C. Gilbert Discovery Village **3**
Bush Barn Art Center **16**
Bush House Museum **15**
Hallie Ford Museum of Art **10**
Historic Deepwood Estate **14**
Mary Lou Zeek Gallery **6**
Oregon State Capitol **11**
Salem's Riverfront Carousel **2**
Willamette Heritage Center/
    Mission Mill Museum **12**

HOTELS ■
The Grand Hotel in Salem **8**

RESTAURANTS ◆
The Beanery **5**
Cascade Baking Co. **4**
The Crooked House Bistro **1**
Gerry Frank's Konditorei **17**
La Capitale Brasserie **9**
Ram Restaurant &
    Big Horn Brewery **13**
Wild Pear **7**

gas lights, and central heating. Adjacent to the house is Oregon's oldest greenhouse conservatory.

600 Mission St. SE. ☎ **503/363-4714.** www.salemart.org. Admission $4 adults, $3 students and seniors, $2 children 6–12. Wed–Sun noon–5pm.

Hallie Ford Museum of Art ★★   This is one of the three top art museums in Oregon and features collections of Native American art and artifacts and Northwest, European, and Asian art. The first-floor galleries are devoted to contemporary art and feature changing exhibitions. Upstairs you'll find one gallery filled with Native American artifacts and baskets from Northwestern tribes. Other galleries contain artifacts ranging from an ancient Egyptian coffin mask to 19th-century Chinese porcelain.

700 State St. ☎ **503/370-6855.** www.willamette.edu/museum_of_art. Admission $3 adults, $2 seniors and students; free admission Tues. Tues–Sat 10am–5pm; Sun 1–5pm. Closed Easter, July 4, Thanksgiving, day after Thanksgiving, and Dec 24–Jan 1.

Historic Deepwood Estate ★   Set on 5½ acres of English-style gardens and woodlands, this Queen Anne Victorian home is a delicate jewel box of a house. The house, with its many stained-glass windows, golden-oak moldings, and numerous lightning-rod-topped peaked roofs and gables, was built in 1894, and the gardens, designed by the Northwest's first women-owned landscape architecture firm, were added in the 1930s.

1116 Mission St. SE. © **503/363-1825.** www.historicdeepwoodestate.org. Admission $4 adults, $3 seniors and students, $2 children 6–12. Grounds daily dawn–dusk; guided house tours May to mid-Oct Wed–Mon 9am–noon, mid-Oct to Apr Wed–Thurs and Sat 11am–3pm.

Oregon State Capitol   Where's the dome? That's the first thing that strikes most visitors to the Oregon State Capitol, which looks as if construction was never completed (perhaps due to a lack of funds in the state budget). However, it was actually designed without a dome, and consequently the building, which opened in 1938, has a stark appearance (not unlike that of a mausoleum). If you look closer, though, you'll recognize the pared-down lines of Art Deco design aesthetics in this building. *The Oregon Pioneer,* a 23-foot-tall gilded statue, tops the building, which is faced with white Italian marble. Outside the building, there are numerous sculptures and attractive gardens; murals of historic Oregon scenes embellish the inside. Tours of the capitol are available. There are also changing art exhibits and videos about the history of the building and the state. Here on the grounds of the capitol, you'll also find a Douglas fir tree that was grown from a seed that went to the moon in 1971 on the Apollo 14 mission. You'll find this tree just north of the flags on Court Street.

900 Court St. NE. © **503/986-1388.** www.leg.state.or.us. Free admission. Building Mon–Fri 7:30am–5pm. Tours Memorial Day to Labor Day Mon–Fri 9am–3pm; other months by appointment.

Willamette Heritage Center/Mission Mill Museum ★   The sprawling red Thomas Kay Woolen Mill, a water-powered mill built in 1889, is one of the most fascinating attractions in Salem. The restored buildings house exhibits on every stage of the wool-making process, and in the main mill building, the water-driven turbine is still in operation, producing electricity for the buildings. Also on these neatly manicured grounds are a cafe, a collection of interesting shops, and several other old structures, including the Jason Lee House, which was built by Salem's founder in 1841 and is the oldest frame house in the Northwest. The **Marion County Historical Society Museum** (© 503/364-2128; www.oregonlink.com/historical_society/index.html), also on the grounds, houses exhibits on the history of the area, with a particularly interesting section on the local Kalapuya Indians. This museum is open Tuesday through Saturday from noon to 4pm; admission is $4 for adults, $3.50 for seniors, and $2.50 for children.

1313 Mill St. SE. © **503/585-7012.** www.missionmill.org. Free admission to grounds; museum admission $6 adults, $5 seniors, $4 students, $3 children 6–17, free Tues. Mon–Sat 10am–5pm.

A NEARBY STATE PARK & TWO WILDLIFE REFUGES

Eight miles north of Salem, you'll find **Willamette Mission State Park** (© 503/393-1172; www.oregon.gov/oprd/parks), which preserves the site of the first settlement in the Willamette Valley. It was here that Methodist missionary Jason Lee and four assistants established their first mission in 1834. Today there are 8 miles of walking, biking, and horseback-riding paths through the park, which is also home to the largest black cottonwood tree in the country.

If it's bird-watching that interests you, two national wildlife refuges in the area are excellent places to observe ducks, geese, swans, and raptors. **Ankeny National Wildlife Refuge** is 12 miles south of Salem off I-5 at exit 243. **Basket Slough**

National Wildlife Refuge is northwest of the town of Rickreall on Ore. 22, which passes through the north end of downtown Salem. Fall through spring is the best time of year for birding here. For more information, contact the **Willamette Valley National Wildlife Refuge Complex** (℃ **541/757-7236;** www.fws.gov/willamette valley/complex).

ESPECIALLY FOR KIDS

In addition to the two attractions listed below, the younger ones will likely enjoy a ride on **Salem's Riverfront Carousel ★**, 101 Front St. NE (℃ **503/540-0374;** www. salemcarousel.org), which is a modern carousel with 42 hand-carved horses. The carousel has its own building in Riverfront Park and is within walking distance of A. C. Gilbert Discovery Village. June through September, the carousel operates Monday through Saturday from 10am to 7pm, and Sunday from 11am to 6pm; other months the carousel closes 1 hour earlier Sunday through Thursday. Rides are $1.50.

A. C. Gilbert's Discovery Village ★ ☺ Known as the "man who saved Christmas," Salem's A. C. Gilbert may not be familiar to most people, but the toy he invented, the Erector Set, certainly is. Erector Sets have inspired generations of budding engineers, and it was during World War I that Gilbert saved Christmas. It seems Congress wanted to turn his toy factory into a munitions factory, but after taking Erector Sets to Congress, he convinced the legislators that America needed to prime its next generation of inventors just as much as it needed to prime its war machine. Here, in two Queen Anne Victorian homes, a few other small historic buildings, and a half-acre outdoor play/recreation center, the 21st century's inventors can let loose their own creative energies. Among the many interactive exhibits here are plenty of Erector Set constructions and a bubble room.

116 Marion St. NE. (℃ **800/208-9514** or 503/371-3631. www.acgilbert.org. Admission $7 adults and children 3 and over, $5.50 seniors, $3.50 children 1–2; free for children under 1. Mon–Sat 10am–5pm; Sun noon–5pm. Closed New Year's Day, Easter, Thanksgiving, and Christmas.

Enchanted Forest ☺ Classic children's stories come to life at this amusement park for kids. In addition to Storybook Lane, English Village, and Western Town, there's a haunted house, a bobsled run, a log-flume ride, and a comedy theater. Rides cost extra.

8462 Enchanted Way SE, Turner. (℃ **503/371-4242.** www.enchantedforest.com. Admission $9.95 adults, $8.95 seniors and children 3–12, free for children 2 and under. Days and hours vary monthly. Closed late Sept to mid-Mar. Take I-5 7 miles south of Salem to exit 248.

Wings of Wonder With a greenhouse filled with the fluttering of colorful butterflies, this live butterfly exhibit is a big hit with kids. The butterflies are free to fly about a greenhouse full of tropical flowers. It will all feel like an exotic adventure to your kids, especially when you have to take a tiny car ferry across the Willamette River to get to the little community of Buena Vista, southwest of Salem. If the kids want to take some butterflies home, there are kits available that let you raise your own caterpillars.

5978 Willamette Ferry St., Independence. (℃ **503/838-0976.** www.wingsofwonder.us. Admission $8.50 adults, $8 seniors, $6 ages 4–10. Mid-Mar to mid-Oct Wed–Sat 11am–4pm, Sun noon–4pm. From downtown Salem, drive south on Commercial St. to Liberty Rd. to Buena Vista Rd.

Silverton

Set in the foothills of the Cascade Range, Silverton is a quaint community on the banks of Silver Creek. The creek-side setting gives the town something of the feel of an old New England mill town, and although the area's major attractions—Silver Falls State Park and the Oregon Garden—are both outside of town, the downtown, where a pedestrian-covered bridge leads to a pleasant, shady park, is also worth a stroll. While in Silverton, be sure to wander around town and admire the many murals. For local art you can take home with you, stop by **Lunaria Gallery,** 113 N. Water St. (✆ **503/873-7734;** www.lunariagallery.com).

WATERFALLS & DISPLAY GARDENS

The Oregon Garden ★★ The Oregon Garden is one of the largest public display gardens in the Northwest and was created to showcase the state's horticultural heritage and the wide variety of plants grown in Oregon's commercial plant nurseries. In addition to an incredible array of plantings, the numerous display gardens include several water features and ponds, terraced gardens, a sensory garden, a children's garden, and a native oak grove. During the summer months, concerts are held in the garden's amphitheater.

The Oregon Garden is also home to the **Gordon House** (✆ **503/874-6006;** www.thegordonhouse.org), the only building in Oregon designed by Frank Lloyd Wright. The home was moved to this site after it was rescued from being destroyed. Today the Gordon House is open for tours ($10) daily from noon to 4pm (although tours are usually unavailable Tues–Wed). Reservations are recommended.

879 W. Main St., Silverton. ✆ **877/674-2733** or 503/874-8100. www.oregongarden.org. Admission Apr–Oct $10 adults, $9 seniors, $8 students 8–17; Nov–Mar $7 adults, $6 seniors, $5 students 8–17. May–Sept daily 9am–6pm; Oct–Apr daily 10am–4pm.

Silver Falls State Park ★★ Located 26 miles east of Salem on Ore. 214, this is the largest state park in Oregon and one of the most popular. Hidden in the lush canyons and dark old-growth forests of the park are 10 silvery waterfalls ranging in height from 27 to 177 feet. The trails are some of the most enjoyable in the state and can usually be hiked any time of year. Although the best hike is the 7-mile loop trail that links all the falls, shorter hikes are also possible. You can even walk behind the South, Lower South, and North falls. You can spend an afternoon or several days exploring the park. Camping (for reservations, contact **ReserveAmerica** ✆ **800/452-5687;** www. reserveamerica.com), swimming, picnicking, and biking are all popular activities.

15 miles southeast of Silverton on Ore. 214. ✆ **503/873-8681.** www.oregon/gov/oprd/parks. Admission $5 per car. Daily dawn–dusk.

Mt. Angel

Mt. Angel is best known as the site of Oregon's most popular Oktoberfest celebration, which is held the second weekend after Labor Day. But should you be here any other time of year, you might want to visit the **Mount Angel Abbey,** 1 Abbey Dr. (✆ **503/845-3303;** www.mountangelabbey.org), which was established by Benedictine monks in 1882 and stands atop a 300-foot bluff on the edge of town. There are peaceful gardens, a museum (with the world's largest porcine hair ball), and a gift shop. The abbey's library, designed by famous Finnish architect Alvar Aalto, contains an interesting collection of rare books. The museum is open daily from 10 to 11:30am and from 1 to 5pm; the library is open Monday through Friday from 9am to 4pm and Saturday from 10am to 4pm. The abbey is also the site of the annual **Abbey Bach Festival** (✆ **800/845-8272** or 503/845-3066), which takes place every year on the last Wednesday, Thursday, and Friday in July. Last-minute tickets are sometimes available.

Salem & the Mid-Willamette Valley

THE WILLAMETTE VALLEY

Wine Touring

For information on the many wineries in the Eola Hills northwest of Salem, see "The North Willamette Valley Wine Country," earlier in this chapter.

SOUTH OF TOWN

Ankeny Vineyard   Located south of Salem, not far from Willamette Valley Vineyards, this small family-run winery overlooks a national wildlife refuge and is surrounded by neighboring vineyards. Pinot noir and pinot gris are the specialties here, but they also produce Marechal Foch, a rarely seen red varietal. Prices are generally reasonable. In summer, the tasting room stays open until 8pm on Friday and Saturday, and food is available.

2565 Riverside Dr. S., Salem. *Ⓒ* **503/378-1498.** www.ankenyvineyard.com. Tasting fee $5. Daily 11am–5pm. From Salem, drive south on I-5, take exit 243 and continue 5 miles west.

Willamette Valley Vineyards ★   Willamette Valley Vineyards, one of the largest wine producers in the state, sits high on a hill overlooking the Willamette Valley, and with its large facility and fabulous views, it's about as close to a Napa Valley wine-tasting experience as you'll find in Oregon. With more than a dozen wines usually available for tasting and several separate labels represented, Willamette Valley manages to produce wines to please almost every palate and pocketbook. Tours ($15) are offered daily at noon, and private tours ($20) can also be arranged.

8800 Enchanted Way SE, Turner. *Ⓒ* **800/344-9463** or 503/588-9463. www.wvv.com. Tasting fee free–$10. Daily 11am–6pm. Take exit 248 or 244 off I-5.

WEST OF TOWN

Eola Hills Wine Cellars   Well known in the area for its Sunday brunches, this winery on the outskirts of Rickreall offers everything from cabernet sauvignon to zinfandel—almost all at reasonable prices. While many of the wines here are made with California grapes and seem to be crafted for the grocery-store market, there are the occasional gems.

501 S. Pacific Hwy., Rickreall. *Ⓒ* **800/291-6730** or 503/623-2405. www.eolahillswinery.com. Daily 10am–5pm. On Ore. 99W between Rickreall and Monmouth.

Left Coast Cellars   This winery, set amid large vineyards 13 miles northwest of Salem, is conveniently located right on Ore. 99W north of Rickreall. While they do produce pinot gris and chardonnay here, it is the pinot noirs, including the Latitude 45, that are the real reason to visit. This winery has a small cafe with a limited menu, so if you forgot to pack a lunch for your winery tour, this place makes a good lunch stop.

4225 N. Pacific Hwy., Rickreall. *Ⓒ* **503/831-4916.** www.leftcoastcellars.com. Tasting fee $5. Sun–Thurs 11am–5pm; Fri–Sat 11am–7pm. Take Ore. 22 west from Salem, then go north on Ore. 99W for 4 miles.

Redhawk Vineyard and Winery 🍷   Redhawk is mostly known in the area for its inexpensive ($15) and very drinkable Grateful Red pinot noir. The winery, located close to downtown Salem, with big views across the valley, also does several other slightly more expensive pinot noirs, as well as gamay noir, pinot gris, riesling, and an inexpensive Bordeaux blend.

2995 Michigan City Ave. NW, Salem. *Ⓒ* **503/362-1596.** www.redhawkwine.com. Tasting fee $5. Daily 11am–5pm. From downtown Salem, cross the Willamette River, immediately exit right and drive 4 miles north on Wallace Rd. NW.

blossom TIME

Every year between mid-May and early June, the countryside around Salem bursts into color as commercial iris fields come into bloom. During blossom time, the biggest growers open up their farms to the public.

Schreiner's Iris Gardens, 3625 Quinaby Rd. NE, Salem (℃ **800/525-2367** or 503/393-3232; www.schreiners gardens.com), has 200 acres of iris fields and a 10-acre display garden with 500 varieties of irises. To reach Schreiner's, take the Brooks exit (exit 263) off I-5 north of Salem, drive west on Brooklake Road, turn left on River Road, and, in 1 mile, left onto Quinaby Road. The display gardens here are open daily from dawn to dusk.

Also in the area are **Adelman Peony Gardens,** 5690 Brooklake Rd. NE, Salem (℃ **503/393-6185;** www.peonyparadise. com), which has 8 acres of fields and sells more than 160 varieties of peonies. Bloom season is from May to late June, and during this time, the farm is open daily from 9am to 6pm. From the Brooks exit, go east on Brooklake Road.

From late March to early May, you can see more than 40 acres of tulips and daffodils in bloom at **Wooden Shoe Tulip Farm,** 33814 S. Meridian Rd., Woodburn (℃ **800/711-2006** or 503/634-2243; www.woodenshoe.com). Throughout the blossom season, there are wooden shoe–making seminars, steam-tractor demonstrations, live music, and lots of other activities.

Van Duzer Vineyards ★★ Producing several different pinot noirs as well as pinot gris, this winery is built on the side of an oak-shaded knoll with a commanding view across the valley to the Eola Hills. The tasting room is a beautiful, big facility that takes full advantage of the tremendous views to be had from the top of the knoll. The reserve pinot noirs ($45) are often outstanding. Although this winery is 3 miles down a gravel road, it is well worth the dusty drive.

11975 Smithfield Rd., Dallas. ℃ **800/884-1927.** www.vanduzer.com. Tasting fee $7–$10. Mar–Dec daily 11am–5pm; other months by appointment. North of Rickreall off Ore. 99W, take graveled Smithfield Rd. 3 miles west.

Where to Stay

SALEM
The Grand Hotel in Salem ★★ From the moment you drive into the slate-walled portico at this large downtown conference hotel, it's obvious that this is by far the best hotel in Salem. Although the Grand Hotel is primarily a place for conference attendees to stay, the rooms here are just too nice to be left to business travelers. With beautiful leather couches and chairs in the large guest rooms and suites, this place is not your standard corporate hotel. Although the huge lobby might make you wonder when the crowds are going to descend, the Grand Hotel is often a very laid-back and relaxed place. The hotel has also been certified for its sustainability programs.

201 Liberty St. SE, Salem, OR 97301. www.grandhotelsalem.com. ℃ **877/540-7800** or 503/540-7800. Fax 503/540-7830. 193 units. $129–$139 double; $149–$399 suite. Rates include full breakfast. Children 17 and under stay free in parent's room. AE, DC, DISC, MC, V. **Amenities:** Restaurant; lounge; concierge; exercise room; Jacuzzi; indoor pool; room service. *In room:* A/C, TV, fridge, hair dryer, free Wi-Fi.

THE WILLAMETTE VALLEY | Salem & the Mid-Willamette Valley

SILVERTON

Oregon Garden Resort ★★   The Oregon Garden is one of the Willamette Valley's star attractions, and this casual little resort, with the garden right outside, is just the place to stay if you want to stop for the night and smell the flowers. Rooms here are in 17 buildings (each with six rooms), and all have gas fireplaces and patios or balconies. Because of the parking lots surrounding the buildings, some rooms have better views than others, so be sure to ask for one with a good view. With its big stone fireplace and wood floor, the resort's lounge has a rustic feel, while the dining room has a good view of the adjacent gardens. By the way, when you stay here, admission to the gardens is included in the room rate, and hotel guests can stay after the gardens close.

895 W. Main St., Silverton, OR 97381. www.oregongardenresort.com. 🕾 **800/966-6490** or 503/874-2500. 103 units. $89–$199 double. Rates include full breakfast. Children 7 and under stay free in parent's room. AE, DISC, MC, V. Pets accepted ($15 per night). **Amenities:** Restaurant; lounge; concierge; exercise room; Jacuzzi; outdoor pool; full-service spa. In room: A/C, TV, fridge, hair dryer, free Internet.

Where to Eat

SALEM

If you have a sweet tooth, you won't want to miss **Gerry Frank's Konditorei,** 310 Kearney St. SE (🕾 **503/585-7070;** www.gerryfranksconditorei.com), which has an amazing selection of extravagant cakes and pastries. For artisan breads and simpler pastries, try downtown's **Cascade Baking Co.,** 229 State St. (🕾 **503/589-0491;** www.cascadebaking.com). For a good cup of espresso (or a sandwich), head to **the Beanery,** 220 Liberty St. NE (🕾 **503/399-7220;** www.allannbroscoffee.com). If you're looking for a microbrew and a burger, try **Ram Restaurant & Big Horn Brewery,** 515 12th St. SE (🕾 **503/363-1905;** www.theram.com). For Sunday brunch, consider **Eola Hills Wine Cellars,** 501 S. Pacific Hwy., Rickreall (🕾 **800/291-6730** or 503/623-2405; www.eolahillswinery.com), which serves gourmet omelets, pan-fried oysters, pasta, Belgian waffles, sparkling wine, and more for $20. Reservations recommended.

The Crooked House Bistro ★ FRENCH   This romantic little bistro, across the river from downtown Salem, serves up the most imaginative meals in town. The menu here is short, running to only half a dozen entrees, and changes every few days. Wild game, such as elk and venison, is an emphasis, and such rarely encountered dishes as pan-seared frog legs with ratatouille, Spanish-style octopus, and seafood cassoulet often show up regularly. All in all, this is some of the most daring French cuisine available in the Oregon wine country. The wine list is dominated by French wines and wines from the nearby Eola Hills.

1142 Edgewater St. NW 🕾 **503/385-8851.** www.crookedhousebistro.com. Reservations recommended. Main courses $21–$29. AE, DISC, MC, V. Tues–Thurs 5–9pm; Fri–Sat 5–9:30pm.

La Capitale Brasserie ★ FRENCH   This casual French brasserie is your best bet for dinner in downtown Salem, and it's a good lunch choice, too. The menu is fairly short but has several French classics, including onion soup, escargot, and rotisserie chicken. Steak *frites,* another French classic, gets an American spin here at lunch by featuring buffalo flank steak. The house-made charcuterie plate (hams, salami, and sausage) makes an excellent starter. Even those with simple tastes will enjoy a meal here; the menu includes a burger and *pomme frites.*

508 State St. ϕ **503/585-1975.** www.lacapitalesalem.com. Reservations recommended. Main courses $8.50–$12 lunch, $12–$20 dinner. AE, DC, DISC, MC, V. Mon–Thurs 11am–2pm and 5–9pm; Fri 11am–2pm and 5–9:30pm; Sat noon–3pm and 5–9:30pm.

Wild Pear ★ NEW AMERICAN   Although this is mostly a downtown lunch spot, it serves some of the most creative food in town. For a satisfying lunch, try the seasonal soup (perhaps coconut-curry butternut squash) and the wild pear salad (made with chicken, candied pecans, pears, and blue cheese). If you're in the mood for something more substantial, there's a lobster-and-seafood melt on focaccia. Wild Pear is also open for dinner on the first Wednesday of each month and sometimes the third or fourth Sunday of the month

372 State St. ϕ **503/378-7515.** www.wildpearcatering.com. Main courses $7–$13. MC, V. Mon–Sat 10am–5:30pm.

SILVERTON

For a quick pick-me-up, try the **Silver Creek Coffee House,** 111 N. Water St. (ϕ **503/874-9600**), which has a deck overlooking Silver Creek and also serves wine.

Silver Grille Cafe & Wines ★ MEDITERRANEAN   This dark, romantic restaurant in an old storefront in downtown Silverton is a welcome outpost of urban culinary aesthetics in this small town. The menu, which changes regularly, is short and preparations are fairly simple, but flavors are big. You might start with shiitake-mushroom bisque or chilled tomato soup that's topped with basil pesto. Among the entrees, there are always good pastas such as goat-cheese cavatelli with lamb ragout. The wine list features some of the small wineries in the Silverton area.

206 E Main St. ϕ **503/873-8000.** www.silvergrille.com. Main courses $14–$23. AE, DISC, MC, V. Wed–Sun 5–9:30pm.

Salem After Dark

There are regularly scheduled performances by touring companies at the historic **Elsinore Theater,** 170 High St. SE (ϕ **503/375-3574;** www.elsinoretheatre.com). Since 1954, **Pentacle Theatre,** 145 Liberty St. SE (ϕ **503/485-3000;** www. pentacletheatre.org), which actually has its theater the in West Salem hills at 324 52nd Ave. NW, has been bringing live theater to the state capital.

CORVALLIS & ALBANY

40 miles S of Salem, 45 miles N of Eugene, 55 miles E of Newport

In Latin, Corvallis means "heart of the valley," and that is exactly where this college town is located. Set in the middle of the Willamette Valley and surrounded by farmlands, Corvallis is home to Oregon State University (OSU), a noted center for agricultural research. Life in this town revolves around the university, but the lively downtown, with its riverfront setting, makes this a pleasant base for exploring nearby wine country and the historic town of Albany. Numerous walking and bicycling paths add to the appeal of a stay here.

In addition to being home to OSU, Corvallis is at the center of the Willamette Valley's grass-seed fields. Area farms produce much of the nation's grass-seed crop. Visitors should note that in late summer, after the seed has been harvested, the remaining stubble has traditionally been burned off. The field burnings can blanket

Corvallis

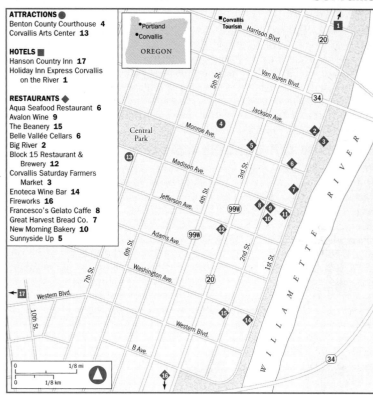

ATTRACTIONS ●
Benton County Courthouse 4
Corvallis Arts Center 13

HOTELS ■
Hanson Country Inn 17
Holiday Inn Express Corvallis
   on the River 1

RESTAURANTS ◆
Aqua Seafood Restaurant 6
Avalon Wine 9
The Beanery 15
Belle Vallée Cellars 6
Big River 2
Block 15 Restaurant &
   Brewery 12
Corvallis Saturday Farmers
   Market 3
Enoteca Wine Bar 14
Fireworks 16
Francesco's Gelato Caffe 8
Great Harvest Bread Co. 7
New Morning Bakery 10
Sunnyside Up 5

the valley with dense black smoke, making driving quite difficult along certain roads. So don't be too alarmed if you encounter smoky skies in the area in August.

Nearby Albany, 13 miles northeast, was a prosperous town in territorial days. Located on the banks of the Willamette River, the town made its fortune as a shipping point in the days when the river was the main transportation route for the region. More than 500 historic homes make Albany the best preserved historic town in the state, but owing to the large wood-pulp mill that was the town's biggest employer until it closed in 2009, the city has never really been able to cash in on its historic character.

Essentials

GETTING THERE   Albany is on I-5 at the junction with U.S. 20, which heads east to Bend and west to Newport. Corvallis is 12 miles west of I-5 at the junction of U.S. 20, Ore. 99W, and Ore. 34.

VISITOR INFORMATION   Contact **Corvallis Tourism,** 553 NW Harrison St., Corvallis, OR 97330 (© **800/334-8118** or 541/757-1544; www.visitcorvallis.com), or the **Albany Visitors Association,** 250 Broadalbin St. SW, Ste. 110 (P.O. Box 965), Albany, OR 97321 (© **800/526-2256** or 541/928-0911; www.albanyvisitors.com).

5

THE WILLAMETTE VALLEY

Corvallis & Albany

145

GETTING AROUND   Public bus service around the Corvallis area is provided by the **Corvallis Transit System** (© **541/766-6998;** www.ci.corvallis.or.us/pw/cts). Buses are free.

FESTIVALS   DaVinci Days (© **541/757-6363;** www.davinci-days.org), held each year in mid-July, is Corvallis's most fascinating festival. The highlight of this celebration of art, science, and technology is the **Kinetic Sculpture Race,** in which competitors race homemade, people-powered vehicles along city streets, through mud and sand, and down the Willamette River. Prizes are given for engineering and artistry. Another offbeat celebration, the **Shrewsbury Renaissance Faire** (© **541/ 929-4897;** www.shrewfaire.com), is held each year in the community of Kings Valley (north of nearby Philomath) in mid-September.

Exploring Off-Campus Corvallis

The tree-shaded streets of downtown Corvallis are well worth a wander. Here you'll find lots of interesting shops, as well as the stately **Benton County Courthouse,** 120 NW Fourth St., built in 1888 and still in use today. A few blocks away, you'll find the **Corvallis Arts Center,** 700 SW Madison Ave. (© **541/754-1551;** www. theartscenter.net), which is housed in an old church and schedules rotating exhibits of works by regional artists. The gift shop has a good selection of crafts. The center is open Tuesday through Saturday from noon to 5pm; admission is free.

Corvallis's pretty Riverfront Commemorative Park stretches for 10 blocks along the Willamette River in downtown Corvallis and includes walkways and lawns, river-viewing decks and plazas, sculpture, and a fountain that doubles as a map of the region's rivers. On Saturday mornings from late April through late November, the park is also the site of the **Corvallis Saturday Farmers Market** (http://locallygrown. org). The park's pathways connect to Corvallis's extensive network of biking paths, one of which crosses a covered bridge.

Exploring Historic Albany

Albany is a hidden jewel right on I-5 that is often overlooked because until 2009, the only thing visible from the interstate was a smoke-belching wood-pulp mill. While the mill is no longer operating, the mill's buildings still loom beside the freeway, hiding from passersby a quiet town that evokes days of starched crinolines and straw boaters. Throughout the mid- to late 19th century, Albany prospered, shipping agricultural and wood products downriver to Oregon City and Portland. Though every style of architecture popular during that period is represented in downtown Albany's historic districts, it is the town's many elegant Victorian homes that are the most compelling. Every year on the last Saturday of July, many of the historic homes are opened to the public for a **Historic Interior Homes Tour,** and on the second Sunday in December, homes are opened for a **Christmas Parlour Tour.** For a guide to the historic buildings and information on the tours, contact the **Albany Visitors Association.**

Among the town's more noteworthy buildings are two sparkling white 1890s churches—the **Whitespires Church** and **St. Mary's Church**—both built in the Gothic revival style. The **Monteith House,** 518 Second Ave. SW (© **541/928-0911**), built in 1849, is the town's oldest frame building. The house is open from mid-June to mid-September Wednesday through Sunday from noon to 4pm; admission is free. To learn more about Albany's past, stop in at the **Albany Regional Museum,** 136 Lyon St. S. (© **541/967-7122;** www.armuseum.com), open Monday through Friday from noon to 4pm and Saturday from 10am to 2pm; admission is by donation.

Fans of vintage carousels should be sure to stop by the **Historic Carousel & Museum,** 503 First Ave. W. (© **541/791-3340;** www.albanycarousel.com), in downtown Albany. Exhibits here focus primarily on the carousels of Gustave Dentzel, and for nearly a decade now, volunteers have been carving and painting 54 new animals to go on the 1909-vintage carousel mechanism. The museum is open Monday through Saturday from 10am to 4pm (Wed until 9pm), and admission is free.

South of Albany, off 99E near the town of Shedd, you can visit a historic 150-year-old flour mill. **Thompson's Mills State Heritage Site** (© **541/491-3611;** www. oregonstateparks.org/park_256.php) preserves the oldest water-powered grain mill in Oregon. The mill site is open daily from 9am to 4pm, and there are guided tours Monday through Friday at 10am and 2pm, and Saturday and Sunday at 10am, noon, and 2pm.

Wine Touring

Downtown Corvallis has several places worth checking out if you're in the area. **Avalon Wine,** 201 SW Second St. (© **541/752-7418;** www.avalonwine.com), is one of the best wine shops in Oregon and has a fabulously informative website focusing on Northwest wines. In the same area, you'll find **Enoteca Wine Bar,** 136 SW Washington Ave. (© **541/758-9095;** www.enotecawinebar.com), a stylish place to sample a variety of regional wines. If you'd prefer to have someone else do the driving, contact **Beviamo Wine Tours** (© **541/250-0747;** www.beviamowinetours.com), which has regularly scheduled tours ($55 per person) every other Saturday. These tours visit three local wineries.

Airlie Winery   This winery is quite a distance from the main wine-touring routes, but its setting in a narrow valley surrounded by forested hills is idyllic. There's a large pond and a covered picnic area, making it a good place to stop for a picnic lunch. They produce a wide variety of wines, but their müller-thurgaus and gewürztraminers, which are usually very good values, are highlights.

15305 Dunn Forest Rd., Monmouth. © **503/838-6013.** www.airliewinery.com. Mar–Dec Sat–Sun noon–5pm. From Ore. 99W between Corvallis and Monmouth, go 7 miles west on Airlie Rd., turn left on Maxfield Creek Rd., and continue another 3 miles.

Belle Vallée Cellars   This small downtown tasting room, facing Riverfront Commemorative Park, is a good place to begin a wine tour of the area. The winery produces a wide range of reds and whites, although, as you would expect, the emphasis is on pinot noir, which they produce in a wide range of prices. If you're not a pinot drinker, try their Syrah, cabernet sauvignon, and merlot.

151 NW Monroe St., Corvallis. © **541/757-9463.** www.bellevallee.com. Tasting fee $5. Tues–Sat noon–9pm; Sun noon–5pm.

Cardwell Hill Cellars ★   You may have heard of this little winery before; its 2006 estate pinot noir unexpectedly made *Wine Spectator's* Top 100 wines list. Although you can't get that particular wine anymore, you can get other vintages of pinot noir, pinot noir rosé, and pinot gris.

24241 Cardwell Hill Dr., Philomath. © **541/929-9463.** www.cardwellhillwine.com. Tasting fee $1 per taste. Early May to Thanksgiving daily noon–5:30pm; call for hours other months. Drive west on U.S. 20 through Philomath, turn right on Kings Valley Hwy. (Ore. 223), and then turn right onto Cardwell Hill Dr.

Emerson Vineyards   This little family winery doesn't produce much wine, but what it does make can be very good. So if you happen to be in the area on a Saturday or Sunday, be sure to stop by. Prices for pinot gris, riesling, and even pinot noir are very reasonable. This winery is quite close to Airlie Winery.

11665 Airlie Rd., Monmouth. ℂ **503/838-0944.** www.emersonvineyards.com. Tasting fee $5. May–Dec daily noon–5pm; call for hours other months. Drive north on Ore. 99W for 13 miles, turn left on Airlie Rd., and continue 2¼ miles.

Spindrift Cellars ✍   This little winery, located in an industrial area of downtown Philomath, may not have a beautiful wine-country setting, but it produces reliable and reasonably priced wines. Grapes for Spindrift's wines come from certified sustainably managed vineyards. The gewürztraminer, riesling, pinot gris, and pinot blanc are priced in the $14 to $16 range, making them some of the best wine values in the state. There are even decent pinot noirs here for $20.

810 Applegate St., Philomath. ℂ **541/929-6555.** www.spindriftcellars.com. Tasting fee $7. May–Nov Wed–Sun noon–5pm; other months by appointment.

Tyee Wine Cellars ★   The Tyee Wine Cellars tasting room is in an old milking barn from the days when this was a dairy farm. Although Tyee usually does a decent pinot noir, their real strength lies in the consistency of their whites—pinot gris, pinot blanc, chardonnay, and gewürztraminer all tend to be dry and light. The winery here is now powered by photovoltaic panels. Be sure to walk the 1.5-mile trail through farm and forest.

26335 Greenberry Rd., Corvallis. ℂ **541/753-8754.** www.tyeewine.com. Tasting fee $5. Apr to mid-June and early Sept to Dec Sat–Sun noon–5pm; mid-June to Labor Day Fri–Mon noon–5pm. From Corvallis, go 7 miles south on Ore. 99W and then 2⅓ miles west on Greenberry Rd.

A Covered-Bridge Tour

If you're a fan of covered bridges, don't pass up an opportunity to drive the back roads east of Albany. Here you'll find eight wooden covered bridges dating mostly from the 1930s. For a map to these covered bridges, contact the **Albany Visitors Association.** A ninth covered bridge, the Irish Bend Bridge, can be found in Corvallis on a pedestrian/bicycle path on the west side of the university campus.

Outdoor Activities

If you're a bird-watcher, the **William L. Finley National Wildlife Refuge** (ℂ **541/757-7236;** www.fws.gov/willamettevalley/finley/index.html), 12 miles south of Corvallis on Ore. 99W, is a good place to add a few more to your list. This refuge has three short, easy hiking trails that provide the region's best glimpse of what the Willamette Valley looked like before the first settlers arrived.

For superb views of the valley and a moderately strenuous hike, head west 16 miles from Corvallis on Ore. 34 to 4,097-foot **Mary's Peak,** the highest peak in the Coast Range. A road leads to the top of the mountain, but there is also a trail that leads from the campground up through a forest of old-growth noble firs to the meadows at the summit. For more information, contact the **Siuslaw National Forest,** 4077 SW Research Way (P.O. Box 1148), Corvallis, OR 97339 (ℂ **541/750-7000;** www.fs.fed.us/r6/siuslaw).

Where to Stay

IN CORVALLIS

Hanson Country Inn ★ Situated atop a knoll on the western edge of town and surrounded by fields and forests, this B&B feels as if it's out in the country, yet is within walking distance of the university. The Dutch colonial-style farmhouse was built in 1928 and features loads of built-in cabinets, interesting woodwork, and lots of windows. Plenty of antiques fill the rooms and lend the inn a feeling appropriate to its age. Two of the rooms have large balconies. The two-bedroom cottage, ideal for families, sits behind the main house and is tucked back in the trees.

795 SW Hanson St., Corvallis, OR 97333. www.hcinn.com. (℃ **541/752-2919.** 4 units, including a cottage. $145–$175 double. Rates include full breakfast. Children 12 and under stay free in parent's room. AE, DC, DISC, MC, V. Take Western Blvd. to West Hills Rd.; Hanson St. is on the right just past the fork onto West Hills Rd. Pets accepted ($20 per night). *In room:* A/C, TV, hair dryer, free Wi-Fi.

Holiday Inn Express-Corvallis on the River Just a few blocks north of the heart of downtown Corvallis, this modern hotel is, as the name implies, on the banks of the Willamette River and is the best hotel in town. Rooms are stylish and modern, and half of them have river views; these are definitely worth requesting. A paved path runs along the back of the hotel, and closer to downtown, you can pick up the bike path that leads all the way to the university campus.

781 NE Second St., Corvallis, OR 97330. www.hiexpress.com. (℃ **888/465-4329** or 541/752-0800. Fax 541/752-0060. 93 units. $130–$170 double. Rates include continental breakfast. Children 19 and under stay free in parent's room. AE, DC, DISC, MC, V. Pets accepted ($25 per night). **Amenities:** Concierge; exercise room and access to nearby health club; Jacuzzi; indoor pool. *In room:* A/C, TV, hair dryer, free Wi-Fi.

Where to Eat

IN CORVALLIS

When you just have to have a jolt of java and a pastry, drop by **the Beanery,** 500 SW Second St. (℃ 541/753-7442; www.allannbroscoffee.com), or **New Morning Bakery,** 219 SW Second St. (℃ 541/754-0181; http://members.peak.org/~newmorning). For great breakfasts, head to **Sunnyside Up,** 116 NW Third St. (℃ 541/758-3353; www.sunnyside-up-cafe.com). If you're looking for some picnic fare, stop by **Great Harvest Bread Co.,** 134 SW First St. (℃ 541/754-9960; www.greatharvest.com). On hot summer days, head to **Francesco's Gelato Caffe,** 208 SW Second St. (℃ 541/752-1326), for creamy gelato. For locally brewed beers, you've got a couple of options. Right on the riverfront, there's **Flat Tail Brewing,** 202 SW First St. (℃ 541/758-2229; www.flattailcorvallis.com), a combination sports bar and brewpub. A couple of blocks off the river, there's **Block 15 Restaurant & Brewery,** 300 SW Jefferson Ave. (℃ 541/758-2077; http://block15.com).

Aqua Seafood Restaurant ★ ☺ PACIFIC RIM Big and casual, Aqua brings the flavors of the South Pacific to the Willamette Valley. The restaurant has a prime location inside the Water Street Market with walls of glass overlooking Riverfront Commemorative Park. There are also a couple of big aquariums to distract you (and the kids) while you dine. I like to order two or three pupus (kalua pork spring rolls, lemon grass–teriyaki chicken skewers, grilled fish salad) and call it a meal. Although the menu leans heavily toward the flavors of Hawaii, you can also get a good beef tenderloin with Dungeness crab. There are special three-course meals for kids.

151 NW Monroe Ave. © **541/752-0262.** www.aquacorvallis.com. Reservations recommended. Main courses $22–$30. AE, DISC, MC, V. Daily 4:30–9 or 9:30pm.

Big River NORTHWEST/ITALIAN   Housed in a renovated warehouselike space across the street from the Willamette River, this big, lively place serves a mix of Italian dishes and creative Northwest offerings. The brick-oven pizzas and calzones are popular with college students, while such dishes as wild salmon with pea purée and roasted vegetables are hits with patrons who have more money and more sophisticated palates. There are always a few creative vegetarian dishes as well. The restaurant uses lots of fresh local produce (often organic), local wines, wild-caught seafood, and organic meats. Though Big River is a big place, you probably won't be able to miss the case full of tempting desserts. Be forewarned that this restaurant is very noisy.

101 NW Jackson St. © **541/757-0694.** www.bigriverrest.com. Reservations recommended. Main courses $10–$16 lunch, $17–$36 dinner. AE, DISC, MC, V. Mon–Thurs 11am–2pm and 5–9:30pm; Fri 11am–2pm and 5–11:30pm; Sat 5–11:30pm (Fri–Sat until 10:30pm in winter).

Del Alma ★ NUEVO LATINO   Bold south-of-the-border flavors in a stylish, contemporary setting make Del Alma the most distinctive and upscale restaurant in Corvallis. While the big bar has the best view of the riverfront park across the street, there is also seating on three more levels of terraced dining rooms, which give this place a very theatrical feel. The menu ranges from traditional dishes such as Yucatecan *cochinita pibil* (slow-roasted pork) to a nightly lamb special that might be leg of lamb ragout with lobster mushrooms, ancho chilies, and saffron-scented pasta. Keep an eye out for dishes made with wild mushrooms. The menu includes lots of small plates, and the bar serves some very creative cocktails.

136 SW Washington Ave., Suite 102. © **541/753-2222.** http://delalmarestaurant.com. Reservations recommended. Main courses $18–$30. AE, DISC, MC, V. Tues–Thurs 5–10pm; Fri–Sat 5–11pm.

Fireworks ★ 🍴 INTERNATIONAL   This place is just so Oregon it should not be missed. The menu is eclectic, the ingredients are usually organic and locally grown, and the wood-fired oven and patio are made of mud. (Actually, the owners of the restaurant like to call it earth, not mud.) If you're intrigued, come by for a meal and order something from the 9-foot-tall earth oven. Pizzas and burgers make up the bulk of the menu, but there are also a few more substantial entrees.

1115 SE Third St. © **541/754-6958.** www.intabas.com. Reservations recommended. Main courses $8–$18 lunch, $7–$25 dinner. AE, DISC, MC, V. Daily 4–10pm.

EUGENE & SPRINGFIELD

40 miles S of Salem, 71 miles N of Roseburg, 61 miles E of Florence

Although Eugene, with more than 150,000 residents, is the third-largest city in Oregon, tie-dyed T-shirts are more common than silk ties on downtown streets. This laid-back character is due in large part to the presence of the University of Oregon, the state's liberal-arts university. Although downtown does have a small historic district with restaurants and interesting shops, much of downtown is dominated by parking garages and the characterless buildings of 1970s urban renewal. Consequently, life in Eugene tends not to revolve around downtown but rather around the

Eugene

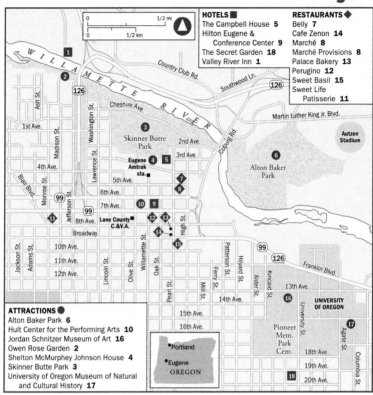

HOTELS ■
The Campbell House **5**
Hilton Eugene &
    Conference Center **9**
The Secret Garden **18**
Valley River Inn **1**

RESTAURANTS ◆
Belly **7**
Cafe Zenon **14**
Marché **8**
Marché Provisions **8**
Palace Bakery **13**
Perugino **12**
Sweet Basil **15**
Sweet Life
    Patisserie **11**

ATTRACTIONS ●
Alton Baker Park **6**
Hult Center for the Performing Arts **10**
Jordan Schnitzer Museum of Art **16**
Owen Rose Garden **2**
Shelton McMurphey Johnson House **4**
Skinner Butte Park **3**
University of Oregon Museum of Natural
    and Cultural History **17**

5

THE WILLAMETTE VALLEY | Eugene & Springfield

university. For this reason, you'll want to spend time on the school's tree-shaded 250-acre campus, where you'll find both an excellent art museum and a small natural-history museum.

Eugene has for years been home to liberal-minded folks who have adopted alternative lifestyles. At the **Saturday Market,** a weekly outdoor craft market, you can see the works of many of these colorful and creative spirits. Adding to the city's diverse cultural scene is the grandiose, glass-gabled **Hult Center for the Performing Arts,** which schedules a wide range of performances throughout the year. Throw in a couple of beautiful riverfront parks with miles of bike paths, several excellent restaurants, brewpubs, nearby wineries, and proximity to both mountains and coast, and you have a decent base for exploring a good chunk of the state.

Essentials

GETTING THERE   Eugene is located just off I-5 at the junction with I-105, which connects Eugene and Springfield, and Ore. 126, which leads east to Bend and west to Florence. Ore. 58 leads southeast from Eugene to connect with U.S. 97 between Klamath Falls and Bend. Ore. 99W is an alternative to I-5.

151

The **Eugene Airport,** 28801 Lockheed Dr. (✆ **541/682-5544;** www.eugene
airport.com), is 9 miles northwest of downtown off Ore. 99W. Allegiant Air, Delta
Connection, Alaska/Horizon Air, and United Express fly here. There's service to Portland, Seattle, San Francisco, Oakland, Los Angeles, Las Vegas, Denver, Salt Lake
City, and Phoenix.

Amtrak (✆ **800/872-7245**) passenger trains stop in Eugene. The station is at 433
Willamette St.

VISITOR INFORMATION   Contact **Travel Lane County Oregon,** 754 Olive St.,
Eugene, OR 97401 (✆ **800/547-5445** or 541/484-5307; www.visitlanecounty.org).

GETTING AROUND   Car rentals are available at the Eugene airport from **Alamo**
(✆ **877/222-9075;** www.goalamo.com), **Avis** (✆ **800/331-1212;** www.avis.com),
Budget (✆ **800/527-0700;** www.budget.com), **Enterprise** (✆ **800/261-7331;**
www.enterprise.com), **Hertz** (✆ **800/654-3131;** www.hertz.com), and **National**
(✆ **877/222-9058;** www.nationalcar.com).

FESTIVALS   Eugene's two biggest and most important music festivals are the
Oregon Bach Festival (✆ **800/457-1486** or 541/346-5666; www.oregonbach
festival.com) and the **Oregon Festival of American Music** (✆ **541/687-6526** or
541/434-7000 for tickets; www.ofam.org). The former is just what its name implies
and is held the last week in June and the first week in July. The latter is a celebration
of everything from blues to gospel to jazz, and is held in late July and early August.
The **Eugene Celebration** (✆ **541/681-4108;** www.eugenecelebration.com), held
in late August or early September, is a 3-day celebration that includes a wacky parade
and lots of live music. Also in August, there is the annual **SLUG Queen Competi-
tion and Coronation** (www.slugqueen.com). On the second weekend in July, all the
region's hippies, both young and old, show up in nearby Veneta for the **Oregon
Country Fair ★★** (✆ **541/343-4298;** www.oregoncountryfair.org), a showcase for
alternative music and unusual crafts. Also of note is Junction City's **Scandinavian
Festival** (✆ **541/998-9372;** www.scandinavianfestival.com), which celebrates the
region's Scandinavian heritage and is held each year on the second weekend in
August. Junction City is 14 miles northwest of Eugene.

Seeing the Sights
MUSEUMS, HISTORIC BUILDINGS & SUCH

Cascades Raptor Center   Whether you're an avid birder or not, this raptor
rehabilitation center, in the hills on the south side of town, is a fascinating place to
visit. There are more than 30 species of raptors on display here, ranging from diminutive pygmy owls to bald and golden eagles. For one reason or another, whether due to
injuries or human imprinting, none of the birds here can be released into the wild.
The large outdoor aviaries are set under a dense canopy of shady trees.

32275 Fox Hollow Rd. ✆ **541/485-1320.** www.eraptors.org. Admission $7 adults, $6 seniors and
teens, $4 children 11 and under. Apr–Oct Tues–Sun 10am–6pm; Nov–Mar Tues–Sun noon–5pm.

Conger Street Clock Museum ★ 📷   If you need a break, take some time to
stop by this timeless private museum. The hundreds of old clocks on display fill the
museum with a soothing ticking that is wonderfully relaxing. One of the oldest clocks
is a water clock dating to 1551. There's also an impressive tower clock from 1750. In
addition to the old clocks, there are displays of old cameras, telephones, model cars
and trains, and lots of other unusual collectibles.

THE bridges OF LANE COUNTY

Built of wood and covered to protect them from the rain and extend their life, the more than 50 covered bridges of Oregon are found primarily in the Willamette Valley, where early farmers needed safe river and stream crossings to get their crops to market. The highest concentration of covered bridges (20) is found in Lane County, which stretches from the crest of the Cascade Range all the way to the Pacific Ocean.

You can get a map and guide to Lane County's covered bridges from **Travel Lane County,** 754 Olive St., Eugene, OR 97401 (📞 **800/547-5445** or 541/484-5307; www.visitlanecounty.org).

730 Conger St. 📞 **541/344-6359.** http://conger-street-clock-museum.com. Admission free. Mon–Sat 10am–5:30pm. West of downtown off 11th Ave./Ore. 126.

Jordan Schnitzer Museum of Art ★★   An extensive Asian arts collection and exhibits of contemporary art are the main focus of this large art museum on the campus of the University of Oregon. Among the highlights of the Asian arts collection are a 9-foot-tall jade pagoda, a royal throne room, and ornate embroidered silk pieces, including Chinese imperial robes. Keep an eye out for the exhibit on foot-binding in China. You'll also find a small exhibit of paintings by Northwest artist Morris Graves.

1430 Johnson Lane. 📞 **541/346-3027.** http://jsma.uoregon.edu. Admission $5 adults, $3 seniors, free for children 18 and under (free for all on 1st Fri of each month). Tues and Thurs–Sun 11am–5pm; Wed 11am–8pm. Closed major holidays. East of 14th Ave. and Kincaid St. on the U of O campus.

Shelton McMurphey Johnson House ★   Built in 1888, this ornate Queen Anne Victorian home stands on the south slope of Skinner Butte on the north edge of downtown Eugene and was long referred to as the "Castle on the Hill." Tours of the beautiful old home focus on the families that lived here over the century that it was a private residence.

303 Willamette St. 📞 **541/484-0808.** www.smjhouse.org. Admission $6 adults, $3 children 12 and under. Tues–Fri 10am–1pm; Sat–Sun 1–4pm.

University of Oregon Museum of Natural and Cultural History ★   This small museum is housed in a building designed to vaguely resemble a traditional Northwest Coast Indian longhouse. The ancient peoples and even more ancient animals that once roamed the Northwest are the main focus of the museum's exhibits. Geology, botany, and archaeology topics also get plenty of display space here.

1680 E. 15th Ave. 📞 **541/346-3024.** http://natural-history.uoregon.edu. Admission $3 adults, $2 seniors and youths 3–18. Wed–Sun 11am–5pm.

Parks & Gardens

Alton Baker Park, on the north bank of the Willamette River, is Eugene's most popular park and offers jogging and biking trails. Across the river, **Skinner Butte Park,** on the north side of downtown Eugene, has more paved paths. Nearby is the **Owen Rose Garden.** At the **Mount Pisgah Arboretum,** 34901 Frank Parrish Rd. (📞 541/747-3817; www.mountpisgaharboretum.org), south of town, you can hike 7 miles of trails through meadows and forests. There are good views along the way, but watch out for poison oak.

Set beneath towering fir trees high on a hill overlooking the city, **Hendricks Park and Rhododendron Garden,** 2200 Summit Ave. (© 541/682-5324), is one of the prettiest parks in the city, especially in the spring when the rhododendrons bloom. You'll find this park in southeast Eugene off Franklin Boulevard (U.S. 99). Take Walnut Street to Fairmount Boulevard, and then turn east on Summit Avenue. If you're crazy about rhododendrons (as so many Northwesterners are), be sure to schedule a visit to **Greer Gardens,** 1280 Goodpasture Island Rd. (© 800/548-0111 or 541/686-8266; www.greergardens.com), one of the Northwest's most celebrated nurseries.

Wine Touring

Eugene is at the southern limit of the Willamette Valley wine region, and there are half a dozen wineries within 30 miles of the city. For a good introduction to the wines of the region, stop in at **Oregon Wine Merchants,** 2441 Hilyard St. (© 800/679-4637 or 541/687-9463; www.orwines.com), which claims to have the world's largest selection of Oregon wines.

WEST & NORTHWEST OF TOWN

Benton-Lane Winery   Benton-Lane has a big reputation in Oregon, and it is well worth searching out this off-the-beaten-path winery and tasting room. They focus primarily on pinot noir and do a superb job. The wide range of prices means there's a pinot for every budget. The valley views from the tasting room are great.

23924 Territorial Hwy., Monroe. © **541/847-5792.** www.benton-lane.com. Mar–Dec daily 11am–5pm; Jan–Feb Mon–Fri 11am–5pm. Take Ore. 126 west to Ore. 99E, heading north; turn onto Ore. 99W, drive north to Monroe, and turn left on Territorial Hwy.

Domaine Meriwether Winery   This is one of only a handful of wineries in Oregon that produces sparkling wines, and during a visit here, you'll usually be able to sample four different sparkling wines, all of which are produced by the traditional *méthode champenoise.* Prices range from $20 to $40.

88324 Vineyard Lane, Veneta. © **541/935-9711.** www.meriwetherwines.com. Daily noon–5pm. Take Ore. 126 west past Veneta.

High Pass Winery   This small winery was founded in 1984 by Dieter Boehm, who produces several different vineyard-designate pinot noirs. However, the winery is most noteworthy for its unusual huxelrebe and scheurebe dessert wines, which are made from grapes that were developed in Germany. These grapes are intensely floral and very distinctive.

24757 Lavell Rd., Junction City. © **541/998-1447.** www.highpasswinery.com. May to Thanksgiving Fri–Sun noon–5pm. Take Ore. 126 west to Veneta, and then go north on Territorial Hwy., west on High Pass Rd., and north again on Lavell Rd.

LaVelle Vineyards ★   Consistently good white wines (fruit forward, but not too much residual sugar) are the hallmark here. The pinot gris and riesling are usually quite good. LaVelle also operates Club Room, a tasting room/wine bar/bistro in downtown Eugene at the 5th Street Public Market, 296 E. Fifth Ave. (© **541/338-9875**). This latter facility is a good place to start a wine tour of the area.

89697 Sheffler Rd., Elmira. © **541/935-9406.** www.lavellevineyards.com. Tasting fee $5. Vineyard: Mon–Thurs noon–5pm, Fri noon–9pm, Sat–Sun noon–6pm. Club Room: Sat and Mon noon–6pm, Wed–Fri noon–8pm, Sun noon–5pm. Take Ore. 126 west to Veneta; go north on Territorial Hwy., west on Warthen Rd., and north on Scheffler Rd.

SOUTHWEST OF TOWN

Chateau Lorane ★   Chateau Lorane produces a greater variety of wines than just about any other winery in the state, and many of these you won't find at other Oregon wineries. Some of the more unusual wines include huxelrebe, marechal foch, baco noir, and fruit-flavored meads (honey wines). Several wines here are made from organic grapes.

27415 Siuslaw River Rd., Lorane. *(C)* **541/942-8028.** www.chateaulorane.com. Tasting fee $2. May–Sept daily noon–5pm; Oct–Apr Sat–Sun noon–5pm. Take Ore. 126 west to Veneta, turn left on Territorial Rd., and go south through Crow to Lorane.

King Estate Winery ★   Set in an idyllic valley southwest of Eugene, this is one of the largest and most impressive wineries in the state. The winery, part of a 1,000-acre estate, is surrounded by hundreds of acres of certified organic vineyards and features a huge, châteaulike facility. If you want to tour a winery, this is one of the best to visit. The winery also has a restaurant, so if you're out this way wine tasting, plan to stay for lunch or dinner.

80854 Territorial Rd., Eugene. *(C)* **541/942-9874.** www.kingestate.com. Tasting fee free to $5. Daily 11am–9pm. Take Ore. 126 west to Veneta, turn left on Territorial Rd., and go south through Crow almost to Lorane.

Sarver Winery ★★   Set on a vineyard that was planted in 1984, this family-run winery high on a hillside southeast of Eugene opened in 2010 and has become my favorite area winery. The wines, including pinot noir, pinot gris, syrah, petite syrah, and a Bordeaux blend, are exceptional. The view from the tasting room is beautiful, and a limited selection of snacks are available should you decide that you want to stay and enjoy some wine on the patio.

25600 Mayola Lane, Eugene. *(C)* **541/935-2979.** www.sarverwinery.com. Tasting fee $5. Mon–Thurs noon–5pm; Fri–Sun noon–8pm. Take Ore. 126 west toward Veneta and turn left on Central Rd.

Silvan Ridge ★   If you like sweet wines, you'll definitely want to drop by this winery. The semisparkling muscat here is outstanding, the perfect summer sipper. There are also respectable merlots and cabernet sauvignons with grapes from southern Oregon, and the pinot gris can be quite good. All in all, Silvan Ridge is one of the most reliable wineries in the state. You'll usually find a few wines for less than $20.

27012 Briggs Hill Rd., Eugene. *(C)* **866/574-5826** or 541/345-1945. www.silvanridge.com. Sun–Thurs noon–5pm; Fri–Sat noon–9pm. Take Ore. 126 west to Bertelsen Rd. and go south to Spencer Creek Rd.; turn right and continue for 2 miles; turn left on Briggs Hill Rd. and continue 3½ miles.

Sweet Cheeks Winery   Set high on a hill across Crow Valley from Silvan Ridge winery and with an impressive, big tasting room, Sweet Cheeks is one of the area's newest wineries. Visit for award-winning white wines and reasonable prices. The twilight tastings are a very pleasant way to spend a summer evening.

27007 Briggs Hill Rd., Eugene. *(C)* **877/309-9463** or 541/349-9463. www.sweetcheekswinery.com. Sat–Thurs noon–6pm; Fri noon–9pm. Take Ore. 126 west to Bertelsen Rd. and go south to Spencer Creek Rd.; turn right and continue for 2 miles; turn left on Briggs Hill Rd. and continue 3½ miles.

Outdoor Activities

Eugene has long been known as Tracktown, USA, and if you want to follow in the footsteps of Steve Prefontaine, there are plenty of routes around town for doing some running. At **Travel Lane County** (p. 152), you can pick up a map of area running trails. These jogging routes include the popular **Pre's Trail,** a 3.9-mile system of loops in Alton Baker Park, which is just across the Willamette River from downtown Eugene. You'll find Hayward Field off Agate Street in the southeast corner of the campus.

Shopping

You can shop for one-of-a-kind crafts at Eugene's **Saturday Market** (☏ 541/686-8885; www.eugenesaturdaymarket.org), which covers more than 2 downtown blocks beginning at the corner of Eighth Avenue and Oak Street. The bustling market was founded in 1970 and is something of a bastion of hippie crafts. There are also food vendors, fresh produce, and live music. The market, held April through mid-November, takes place on Saturdays from 10am to 5pm.

Other days of the week, you can explore the **Market District,** a 6-block area of restored buildings that houses unusual shops, galleries, restaurants, and nightclubs. The **5th Street Public Market,** 296 E. Fifth Ave. (☏ 541/484-0383; www.5stmarket.com), at the corner of Fifth Avenue and High Street, is the centerpiece of the area. Also nearby is **Down to Earth,** 532 Olive St. (☏ 541/342-6820; www.home2garden.com), a fascinating garden-and-housewares shop housed in an old granary building.

Where to Stay

The Campbell House ★★   Located only 2 blocks from the Market District and set at the base of Skinner's Butte overlooking the city, this large Victorian home was built in 1892 and now offers luxury, convenience, and comfort. The guest rooms here vary considerably in size and price, but you're sure to find something you like in your price range. Several of the guest rooms on the first floor have high ceilings, and on the lower level there's a pine-paneled room with a fishing theme and another with a golf theme. The upstairs rooms have plenty of windows, and in the largest room you'll find wood floors and a double whirlpool tub. A separate carriage house contains some of the inn's most luxurious and most thoughtfully designed rooms. Breakfasts are served in a room with a curving wall of glass.

252 Pearl St., Eugene, OR 97401. www.campbellhouse.com. ☏ **800/264-2519** or 541/343-1119. Fax 541/343-2258. 18 units. May–Oct $129–$299 double, $189–$389 suite; Nov–Apr $99–$199 double, $189–$349 suite. Rates include full breakfast. AE, DC, DISC, MC, V. Pets accepted ($50). **Amenities:** Restaurant; lounge; concierge; room service. *In room:* A/C, TV/VCR/DVD, hair dryer, free Wi-Fi.

Hilton Eugene & Conference Center   This is Eugene's only downtown corporate high-rise convention hotel, and it caters primarily to business travelers and conventioneers. However, with the Hult Center for the Performing Arts next door and lots of restaurants and cafes within a few blocks, it's also a good choice if you want to take in a show or explore downtown Eugene on foot. Guest rooms can be hit and miss, but are generally comfortable. Try to get a room on an upper floor so you can enjoy the views.

66 E. Sixth Ave., Eugene, OR 97401. www.eugene.hilton.com. ☏ **800/445-8667** or 541/342-2000. Fax 541/342-6661. 269 units. $119–$219 double. Children 18 and under stay free in parent's room. AE, DC, DISC, MC, V. Self-parking $15; valet parking $20. Pets accepted ($50). **Amenities:** Restaurant; lounge; free airport transfers; bikes; concierge; exercise room; Jacuzzi; indoor pool; room service; free Wi-Fi. *In room:* A/C, TV, hair dryer, MP3 docking station, Wi-Fi ($10 per night).

The Secret Garden ★ 🎁   This large inn just off the University of Oregon campus is a good choice for anyone coming to town specifically to visit the university. The B&B was once the home of Eugene pioneer Alton Baker and was later a sorority house. Rooms, most of which are quite large, feature classic styling, and many have antique reproductions. My favorite room is the Scented Garden, which has a bit of exotic Asian styling. And yes, the inn is surrounded by gardens, both secret and otherwise.

1910 University St., Eugene, OR 97403. www.secretgardenbbinn.com. © **888/484-6755** or 541/484-6755. Fax 541/431-1699. 10 units. May–Nov and holidays $130–$245 double; Dec–Apr $120–$225 double. Rates include full breakfast. AE, DISC, MC, V. **Amenities:** Access to nearby health club. *In room:* A/C, TV/DVD, fridge, hair dryer, free Wi-Fi.

Valley River Inn ★★   Although this lushly landscaped low-rise hotel sits on an enviable location on the banks of the Willamette River, the rates are aimed at those with expense accounts, not at vacationers. However, if you can get any sort of substantial discount, this might be a good choice. The hotel is only a few minutes' drive from downtown and the university, and is adjacent to Eugene's largest shopping mall. All the rooms are large and have a balcony or patio, but the riverside rooms have the best views. The hotel's restaurant has a long wall of glass overlooking the river.

1000 Valley River Way, Eugene, OR 97401. www.valleyriverinn.com. © **800/543-8266** or 541/743-1000. Fax 541/683-5121. 257 units. $149–$199 double; $189–$259 suite. Children 18 and under stay free in parent's room. AE, DC, DISC, MC, V. Pets accepted. **Amenities:** Restaurant; lounge; free airport transfers; bikes; concierge; executive-level rooms; exercise room and access to nearby health club; Jacuzzi; outdoor pool; room service; sauna. *In room:* A/C, TV, hair dryer, free Wi-Fi.

Where to Eat

For artisan breads and cheeses, pastries, pizza, and picnic supplies, I always go to **Marché Provisions,** 296 E. Fifth Ave. (© **541/743-0660;** www.marcheprovisions. com), which is inside the 5th Street Public Market and is affiliated with Marché, my favorite Eugene restaurant (see below). For rustic breads, breakfast pastries, and desserts, you can also try the **Palace Bakery,** 844 Pearl St. (© **541/484-2435;** www. full-city.com). If you've got a sweet tooth, don't miss out on **Sweet Life Patisserie,** 755 Monroe St. (© **541/683-5676;** www.sweetlifedesserts.com), which bakes the best pastries in Eugene. For good espresso and pastries, stop by downtown's **Perugino,** 767 Willamette St. (© **541/687-9102**).

EXPENSIVE

King Estate Restaurant ★★ NORTHWEST   King Estate is the biggest and most beautiful wine estate in the Willamette Valley, and its restaurant, inside the winery tasting room, is the quintessential wine-country restaurant. People drive from miles around to eat here, and I have to say it is well worth it. Creative Northwest cuisine is prepared using organic produce grown here on the estate, and wines served are from grapes that grow only a few feet from your table. The menu changes with the seasons, but I've had a wonderfully subtle dish of Pacific cod atop creamy potatoes accompanied by saffron aioli, and a smoked and roasted chicken with chanterelle mushrooms that was one of the best chicken dishes I've ever had. Service is excellent, and the views from the patio are gorgeous.

80854 Territorial Hwy. © **541/942-9874.** www.kingestate.com. Reservations recommended. Main courses $10–$14 lunch, $23–$32 dinner. AE, DISC, MC, V. Daily 11am–9pm. See winery listing on p. 155 for directions.

Marché ★★ MEDITERRANEAN Marché, located in the 5th Street Public Market, is the quintessential urban American bistro, and, with its hip decor, tiny (but popular) bar, patio, and display kitchen with a few settings for solo diners, the restaurant pulls in a wide range of customers, from couples to pretheater parties and even families. The menu is as creative as you'll find in Eugene, and preparations are fairly reliable. As often as possible, ingredients are organic and non-GMO (genetically modified). There's an extensive list of reasonably priced wines, plus plenty of wines by the glass. This restaurant also has a more casual cafe in the same building.

296 E. Fifth Ave. ☏ **541/342-3612.** www.marcherestaurant.com. Reservations recommended. Main courses $11–$18 lunch, $21–$32 dinner. AE, DC, DISC, MC, V. Mon–Sat 11:30am–10pm; Sun 11:30am–9pm.

MODERATE

Belly ★★ MEDITERRANEAN This is just the sort of restaurant I always dream of finding: a casual hole in the wall with fabulous food at reasonable prices. The first time I ate here, I wanted everything on the menu, and I was nearly despondent that I didn't have a half-dozen dinner companions with me so we actually could order everything. If you can resist the *gougeres* (French cheese puffs), you have more self-control than I do. So that I can taste as many dishes as possible, I usually stick to small plates such as their popular pork-shoulder confit with cherries and polenta. Take some friends or a big appetite. Currently Sunday and Monday nights are taco nights.

291 E. Fifth Ave. ☏ **541/683-5896.** www.eatbelly.com. Reservations accepted for parties of 4 or more. Main courses $16–$19. MC, V. Mon–Thurs 5:30–9pm; Fri–Sat 5:30–10pm.

Cafe Zenon ★ INTERNATIONAL Sister restaurant to ever-popular Café Soriah, Zenon has long been a Eugene favorite for its eclectic menu and reasonable prices. The setting is fairly stark, though with some raw wood for warmth. The menu is fairly long and ranges from around the globe, with an emphasis on the flavors of the Mediterranean. The Oregon lox mousse is a good bet for a starter, as is the grilled halloumi cheese served with a Greek salad. Entrees include such dishes as teasmoked duck breast, Portuguese lamb stew, cashew yellow curry, and pork saltimbocca (a classic Italian dish). Zenon's dessert case flaunts irresistible cakes, pies, tortes, and other pastries.

898 Pearl St. ☏ **541/684-4000.** www.zenoncafe.com. Reservations accepted for parties of 6 or more. Main courses $7–$14 lunch, $16–$22 dinner. AE, DISC, MC, V. Mon–Thurs 11am–9pm; Fri 11am–10pm; Sat 10am–10pm; Sun 9:30am–2pm and 5–10pm.

INEXPENSIVE

Sweet Basil ◢ THAI With its chic urban decor, zesty flavors, artful presentation, and reasonable prices, this upscale Thai restaurant serves some of the best Thai food I've had in Oregon. The *pad phet gai* (chicken and vegetables with homemade curry sauce) is a riot of vibrant flavors. They even do a good job with the *pad thai*, a dish that can often be rather insipid at some Thai restaurants. On sunny days, try to get a sidewalk table.

941 Pearl St. ☏ **541/284-2944.** www.sweetbasileug.com. Reservations recommended. Main courses $8–$12 lunch, $11–$24 dinner. AE, DISC, MC, V. Mon–Thurs 11:30am–3pm and 5–9pm; Fri–Sat 11:30am–3pm and 5–10pm; Sun 5–9pm.

Eugene After Dark

With its two theaters and nonstop schedule, the **Hult Center for the Performing Arts,** One Eugene Center, at Seventh Avenue and Willamette Street (© 541/682-5746 or 682-5000 for tickets; www.hultcenter.org), is the heart and soul of this city's performing-arts scene. The center's huge glass gables are unmistakable, and every year this sparkling temple of the arts puts together a first-rate schedule of performances by the Eugene Symphony, the Eugene Ballet Company, the Eugene Opera, and other local and regional companies, as well as visiting companies and performers. During the summer, the center hosts the Oregon Bach Festival. Also be sure to see what the **Shedd Institute for the Arts,** 868 High St. (© 541/687-6526 or 541/434-7000 for tickets; www.theshedd.org), has scheduled. Summer concerts by popular rock bands are held at **Cuthbert Amphitheater** (© 541/762-8099; www.thecuthbert.com) in Alton Baker Park.

You'll find plenty of microbreweries in Eugene. These include the **High Street Brewery & Cafe,** 1243 High St. (© 541/345-4905; www.mcmenamins.com), in an old house near downtown; the **East 19th Street Cafe,** 1485 E. 19th Ave. (© 541/342-4025; www.mcmenamins.com), adjacent to the university campus; **North Bank,** 22 Club Rd. (© 541/343-5622; www.mcmenamins.com), which has a pretty location right on the river; **Steelhead Brewing Co.,** 199 E. Fifth Ave. (© 541/686-2739; www.steelheadbrewery.com); and **Rogue Ales Public House,** 844 Olive St. (© 541/345-4155; www.rogue.com), the most conveniently located pub if you're staying downtown.

The building housing the **Oregon Electric Station,** 27 E. Fifth Ave. (© 541/485-4444; www.oesrestaurant.com), dates from 1912, and with a wine cellar in an old railroad car, lots of oak, and a back bar that requires a ladder to access all the bottles of premium spirits, it's the poshest bar in town.

Eugene's top two rock concert venues are **WOW Hall,** 291 W. Eighth Ave. (© 541/687-2746; www.wowhall.org), the former Woodmen of the World Hall, and **McDonald Theatre,** 1010 Willamette St. (© 541/345-4442; www.mcdonald theatre.com), a historic downtown theater owned by the family of the late Ken Kesey, a longtime resident of the area.

To find out what's happening, pick up a copy of the free *Eugene Weekly* (www.eugeneweekly.com), which is available at restaurants and shops around town.

6

THE OREGON COAST

Extending from the mouth of the Columbia River in the north to California's redwood country in the south, the Oregon coast is a shoreline of jaw-dropping natural beauty. Yes, it's often rainy or foggy, and, yes, the water is too cold and rough for swimming, but the coastline more than makes up for these shortcomings with its drama and grandeur. Wave-pounded rocky shores; dense, dark forests; lonely lighthouses; rugged headlands—these all set this shoreline apart.

In places the mountains of the Coast Range rise straight from the ocean's waves to form rugged, windswept headlands that still bear the colorful names given them by early explorers—Cape Blanco, Cape Perpetua, Cape Foulweather. With roads and trails that scale these heights, these capes provide ideal vantage points for surveying the wave-washed coast. Between these rocky headlands stretch miles of sandy beaches. In fact, on the central coast there's so much sand that dunes rise as high as 500 feet.

Wildlife-viewing opportunities along the Oregon coast are outstanding. From the beaches and the waters just offshore rise countless haystack rocks, rocky islets, monoliths, and other rock formations that serve as homes to birds, sea lions, and seals. Harbor seals loll on isolated sand spits, and large colonies of Steller and California sea lions lounge on rocks and docks, barking incessantly and entertaining people with their constant bickering. The best places to observe sea lions are on the Newport waterfront, at Sea Lion Caves north of Florence, and at Cape Arago State Park outside of Coos Bay. Hundreds of gray whales also call these waters home, and twice each year, in late winter and early spring, thousands more can be seen during their annual migrations between the Arctic and the waters off Baja California. They pass close by the coast and can be easily spotted from headlands such as Tillamook Head, Cape Meares, Cape Lookout, and Cape Blanco. In coastal meadows, majestic elk graze contentedly, and near the town of Reedsport, the Dean Creek meadows have been set aside as an elk preserve. It's often possible to spot 100 or more elk grazing here. The single best introduction to the aquatic flora and fauna of the Oregon coast is Newport's Oregon Coast Aquarium, where you can learn about the animals and plants that inhabit the diverse aquatic environments of the Oregon coast.

Rivers, bays, and offshore waters are also home to some of the best **fishing** in the country. The rivers, though depleted by a century of overfishing, are still home to salmon, steelhead, and trout, most of which are now hatchery raised. Several charter-boat marinas up and down the coast offer saltwater-fishing for salmon and bottom fish. Few anglers return

The Cost of the Coast

State parks, county parks, national-forest recreation areas, outstanding natural areas—along the Oregon coast, numerous state and federal access areas now charge day-use fees. You can either pay these fees as you encounter them or purchase an Oregon Pacific Coast Passport for $10. These passes are good for 5 days and get you into all state and federal parks and recreation areas along the coast. (However, you'll still have to pay campsite fees.) A $35 annual pass is also available. Passports are available at most state parks that charge a day-use fee. For more information, contact **Oregon State Parks Information Center** (☎ **800/551-6949**).

from these trips without a good catch. **Crabbing** and **clamming** are two other productive coastal pursuits that can turn a trip to the beach into a time for feasting.

To allow visitors to enjoy all the beauties of the Oregon coast, the state has created nearly 80 state parks, waysides, recreation areas, and scenic viewpoints between Fort Stevens State Park in the north and McVay Rock State Recreation Site in the south. Among the more popular activities at these parks are kite flying and beachcombing (but not swimming; the water is too cold).

As I've already mentioned, it rains a lot here. Bring a raincoat, and don't let a little moisture prevent you from enjoying one of the most beautiful coastlines in the world. In fact, the mists and fogs add an aura of mystery to the coast's dark, forested mountain slopes. Contrary to what you might think, the hot days of July and August are not always the best time to visit. When it's baking inland, the coast is often shrouded in fog. The best months to visit tend to be September and early October, when the weather is often fine and the crowds are gone.

ASTORIA ★★

95 miles NW of Portland; 20 miles S of Long Beach, WA; 17 miles N of Seaside

Astoria, situated on the banks of the Columbia River just inland from the river's mouth, is the oldest American community west of the Mississippi. More a river port than a beach town, Astoria's greatest attraction lies in its hillsides of restored Victorian homes and the scenic views across the Columbia to the hills of southwestern Washington. The combination of historical character, scenic vistas, a lively arts community, and some interesting museums make this one of the most intriguing towns on the Oregon coast. Although it still has seamy sections of waterfront, the town has been busy the past few years developing something of a tourist-oriented waterfront character.

Astoria's Euro-American history got its start in the winter of 1805–06 when Lewis and Clark built a fort near here and established an American claim. Five years later, in 1811, fur traders working for John Jacob Astor arrived at the mouth of the Columbia River to set up a fur-trading fort that was named Fort Astoria. During the War of 1812, the fort was turned over to the British, but by 1818 it reverted to American hands. When the salmon-canning boom hit in the 1880s, Astoria became a bustling little city—the second largest in Oregon—and wealthy merchants began building the ornate, Victorian-style homes that today give Astoria its historic character.

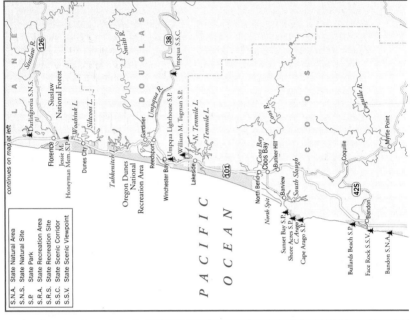

continues on map at left

S.N.A.	State Natural Area
S.N.S.	State Natural Site
S.P.	State Park
S.R.A.	State Recreation Area
S.R.S.	State Recreation Site
S.S.C.	State Scenic Corridor
S.S.V.	State Scenic Viewpoint

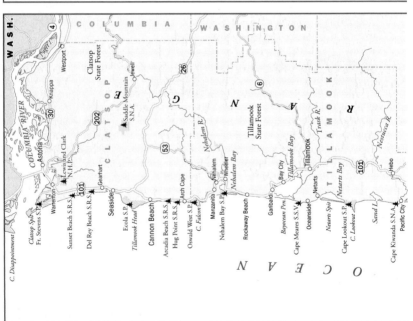

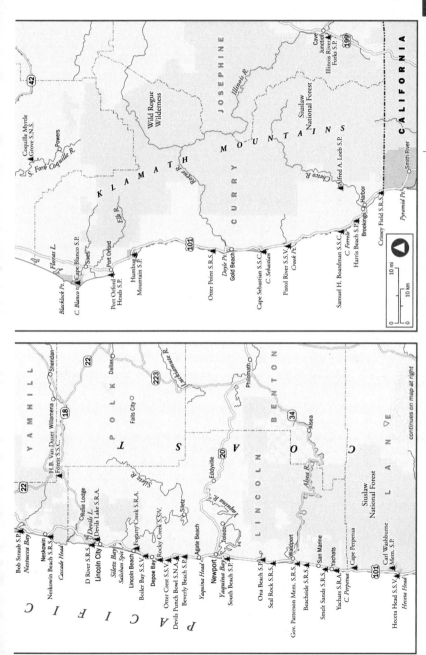

continues on map at right

163

Essentials

GETTING THERE   From Portland, take U.S. 30 west. From the north or south, take U.S. 101.

VISITOR INFORMATION   Contact the **Astoria-Warrenton Area Chamber of Commerce,** 111 W. Marine Dr. (P.O. Box 176), Astoria, OR 97103 (✆ **800/875-6807** or 503/325-6311; www.oldoregon.com).

FESTIVALS   You've probably heard of cowboy poetry, but have you heard of fisher poetry? Astoria's annual **Fisher Poets Gathering** (✆ **503/338-2438;** www.clatsopcc. edu/fisherpoets), held in late February, celebrates the poetry of commercial fishermen and women. In late April, there's the **Astoria Warrenton Crab, Seafood & Wine Festival.** The **Astoria Regatta** (✆ **800/535-8767** or 503/861-2288; www.astoria regatta.org), held every year in mid-August, is the city's biggest festival and includes lots of sailboat races.

Delving Into Astoria History

Columbia River Maritime Museum ★★   The Columbia River, the second-largest river (in volume) in the United States, was the object of centuries of exploration in the Northwest, and, since its discovery in 1792, it has been essential to the region. This boldly designed museum, built to resemble waves on the ocean, tells the story of the river's maritime history. High seas and constantly shifting sands make this one of the world's most difficult rivers to enter; displays of shipwrecks, lighthouses, and historical lifesaving missions testify to the danger. The Coast Guard, fishing, navigation, and naval history are also subjects of museum exhibits; a dramatic Coast Guard motor lifeboat display is a highlight of the museum. Docked beside the museum and open to visitors is the lightship *Columbia,* the last seagoing lighthouse ship to serve on the West Coast. This is one of the best museums in the state.

1792 Marine Dr. ✆ **503/325-2323.** www.crmm.org. Admission $10 adults, $8 seniors, $5 children 6–17. Daily 9:30am–5pm. Closed Thanksgiving and Christmas.

Flavel House Museum ★   The Flavel House, owned and operated by the Clatsop County Historical Society, is the grandest and most ornate of Astoria's many Victorian homes. This Queen Anne–style Victorian mansion was built in 1885 by Capt. George Flavel, who made his fortune operating the first pilot service over the Columbia River Bar and was Astoria's first millionaire. When constructed, this house was the envy of every Astoria resident. Along with much ornate woodwork, the home's high-ceilinged rooms are beautifully appointed with period furnishings.

441 Eighth St. ✆ **503/325-2203.** www.cumtux.org. Admission $5 adults, $4 seniors and students, $2 children 6–17. May–Sept daily 10am–5pm; Oct–Apr daily 11am–4pm.

Heritage Museum   Housed in Astoria's former city hall, this small museum chronicles the history of Astoria and surrounding Clatsop County. The main exhibits consist of Native American and pioneer artifacts, as well as historic photos.

1618 Exchange St. ✆ **503/325-2203.** www.cumtux.org. Admission $4 adults, $3 seniors, $2 children 6–17. May–Sept daily 10am–5pm; Oct–Apr Tues–Sat 11am–4pm.

Lewis and Clark National Historical Park ★★   During the winter of 1805–06, Meriwether Lewis, William Clark, and the other members of the Corps of Discovery camped at a spot near the mouth of the Columbia River. They built a log stockade and named their encampment Fort Clatsop after the local Clatsop Indians who had befriended them. A replica of the fort provides an insightful glimpse into

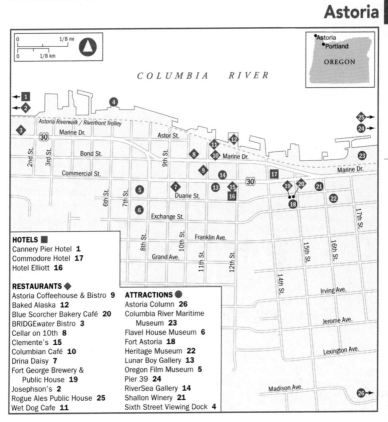

HOTELS ■
Cannery Pier Hotel **1**
Commodore Hotel **17**
Hotel Elliott **16**

RESTAURANTS ◆
Astoria Coffeehouse & Bistro **9**
Baked Alaska **12**
Blue Scorcher Bakery Café **20**
BRIDGE*water* Bistro **3**
Cellar on 10th **8**
Clemente's **15**
Columbian Café **10**
Drina Daisy **7**
Fort George Brewery &
  Public House **19**
Josephson's **2**
Rogue Ales Public House **25**
Wet Dog Cafe **11**

ATTRACTIONS ●
Astoria Column **26**
Columbia River Maritime
  Museum **23**
Flavel House Museum **6**
Fort Astoria **18**
Heritage Museum **22**
Lunar Boy Gallery **13**
Oregon Film Museum **5**
Pier 39 **24**
RiverSea Gallery **14**
Shallon Winery **21**
Sixth Street Viewing Dock **4**

what life was like that dreary, wet winter more than 200 years ago. This historical park includes not only the fort, but also the 6.5-mile Fort to Sea Trail, and several sites in Washington State. Over on the Washington side of the Columbia, there are two installations by celebrated artist Maya Lin. From mid-June through Labor Day, park rangers clad in period clothing give demonstrations of historical activities, including flintlock use, buckskin preparation, and candle making.

92343 Fort Clatsop Rd. (off U.S. 101, 5 miles southwest of Astoria). (*C*) **503/861-2471.** www.nps. gov/lewi. Admission $3 adults, free for children 15 and under. Mid-June to Labor Day daily 9am–6pm; Labor Day to mid-June daily 9am–5pm.

Oregon Film Museum ☺ Housed in the former Clatsop county jail, which figured prominently in the cult kids' film *The Goonies*, this interactive museum is a celebration of the history of filmmaking in Oregon. Why here? Well, because in addition to *The Goonies*, numerous other movies were filmed here. As you might expect, the museum is heavy on *Goonies* exhibits, but there are also plenty of props and exhibits on other movies that have been shot in Oregon. Visitors to the museum even get to make and edit their own short film, which makes this place a fun place to bring the kids.

732 Duane St. (*C*) **503/325-2203.** http://oregonfilmmuseum.org. Admission $4 adults, $2 children 6–17. Daily 10am–5pm.

Other Astoria Activities & Attractions

Atop Coxcomb Hill, which is reached by driving up 16th Street and following the signs, you'll find the **Astoria Column** (© 503/325-2963; www.astoriacolumn.org). Built in 1926, the column was patterned after Trajan's Column in Rome and stands 125 feet tall. On the exterior wall, a mural depicts the history of the area. There are 164 steps up to the top of the column, and on a clear day the view makes the climb well worth the effort. The column is open daily from dawn to dusk, and admission is by suggested $1 per-car donation. On the way to the Astoria Column, stop by **Fort Astoria,** on the corner of 15th and Exchange streets. A log blockhouse and historical marker commemorate the site of the trading post established by John Jacob Astor's fur traders.

There are several places in downtown where you can linger by the riverside atop the docks that once made up much of the city's waterfront. Stop by the **Sixth Street Viewing Dock,** where a raised viewing platform, as well as a fishing dock, enables you to gaze out at the massive Astoria-Megler Bridge, stretching for more than 4 miles across the mouth of the river. Also keep an eye out for sea lions. The best way to see the waterfront is aboard the restored 1913 streetcar operated by **Astoria Riverfront Trolley** (© 503/325-8790; http://homepage.mac.com/cearl/trolley). This trolley operates daily from noon to 7pm between Memorial Day and Labor Day and on a limited schedule other months. Rides are $1.

The Astoria waterfront is rapidly turning into a shoreline of waterfront condos and hotels, but you can still catch a glimpse of the old days on the waterfront at the east end of town on **Pier 39,** 100 39th St. (© 503/325-2502; www.pier39-astoria.com). Originally built in 1875, this cannery was home to Bumble Bee Seafoods, which was founded in Astoria. Today the old cannery is the largest and oldest building on the waterfront, and inside you'll find displays on the cannery's history. The pier is also home to a brewpub and a coffeehouse. On the breakwater adjacent to Pier 39, sea lions can often be seen and heard.

Right in downtown Astoria, you'll find one of the most unusual wineries in the state. **Shallon Winery,** 1598 Duane St. (© 503/325-5978; www.shallon.com), specializes in fruit wines, but it is the unique whey wines that are winemaker Paul van der Veldt's greatest achievement. The Cran du Lait, made with local cranberries and whey from the Tillamook cheese factory, is surprisingly smooth and drinkable. Also look for the amazing chocolate-orange wine, a thick nectar that will make a chocoholic of anyone.

If you'd like to see what regional artists are up to, stop by the **RiverSea Gallery,** 1160 Commercial St. (© 503/325-1270; www.riverseagallery.com). At **Lunar Boy Gallery,** 1133 Commercial St. (© 866/395-1566; www.lunarboygallery.com), you'll find a truly bizarre selection of art derived from the worlds of graphic design, cartoons, and animated films.

Outdoor Activities

Fort Stevens State Park (© 503/861-1671; www.oregon.gov/oprd/parks), 8 miles from Astoria at the mouth of the Columbia, preserves a fort that was built during the Civil War to protect the Columbia River and its important port cities. Though Fort Stevens had the distinction of being the only mainland military reservation to be fired on by the Japanese, the fort was deactivated after World War II. Today the fort's extensive grounds include historic buildings and gun emplacements, and the **Fort Stevens State Park Military Museum** (© 503/861-2000). Throughout the summer, the museum operates tours of the fort in a military surplus truck. There are also miles of bicycle paths, beaches, a campground, and a picnic area. Park admission is $5. At the north end of the park, you can climb to the top of a viewing tower and get a good look at the South Jetty, which was built to make navigating the mouth of the Columbia easier. Also within the park you can see the wreck of the *Peter Iredale,* one ship that did not make it safely over the sandbars at the river's mouth.

A few miles south of Fort Stevens on U.S. 101, you'll find **Sunset Beach State Recreation Area;** it provides beach access and is the western end of the 6.5-mile Fort to Sea Trail, which stretches from here to Fort Clatsop in Lewis and Clark National Historical Park.

A few miles east of town on Ore. 30, bird-watchers will find a roadside viewing platform overlooking the marshes of the **Twilight Creek Eagle Sanctuary.** Take Burnside Road off Ore. 30 between the John Day River and Svenson.

Where to Stay

Cannery Pier Hotel ★★   This hotel is one of my favorite lodgings on the Oregon coast, although it is actually on the Columbia River and not the Pacific Ocean. In fact, this hotel isn't just on the waterfront, it's *in* the river. Built 600 feet out in the river on an old cannery pier, this modern hotel fits in perfectly with the old wooden waterfront buildings around Astoria. Guest rooms are exceedingly comfortable, with window seats, little balconies, gas fireplaces, and superplush beds. In the bathrooms, you'll find a claw-foot tub, from which you can gaze out at the river while you soak. Your view will take in not only the waters of the mighty Columbia River, but also the Astoria-Megler Bridge looming high overhead and tankers and cruise ships rumbling up and down the river.

10 Basin St., Astoria, OR 97103. www.cannerypierhotel.com. ✆ **888/325-4996** or 503/325-4996. Fax 503/325-8350. 46 units. Summer $289–$329 double, $350–$575 suite; other months $169–$219 double, $299–$575 suite. Rates include continental breakfast and evening wine and appetizers. Children 18 and under stay free in parent's room. AE, DISC, MC, V. Pets accepted ($25 per night). **Amenities:** Bikes; exercise room; sauna; spa. *In room:* TV, fridge, hair dryer, free Wi-Fi.

Commodore Hotel   With its interesting mid-20th-century downtown, Astoria attracts a surprising number of artists and other young people seeking to carve out a niche in an urban setting. So it comes as no surprise that this city at the mouth of the Columbia River now has a hip budget hotel comparable to the Ace Hotel in downtown Portland. The renovation of this old hotel was done on a tight budget, and rooms are minimalist and modern. Basic rooms are tiny and have only sinks, not full bathrooms, but have a very hip feel. There are also larger rooms with attached bathrooms, at least one of which has a river view. The lobby has a cool 3-D wall collage of salvaged objects and old books and maps. Be forewarned that some rooms get a lot of street noise. Definitely an urban experience for young, heavy sleepers.

258 14th St., Astoria, OR 97103. www.commodoreastoria.com. ✆ **503/325-4747.** 18 units, 12 with shared bathroom. $69–$89 double with shared bath; $89–$189 double with private bath. AE, DISC, MC, V. *In room:* TV/DVD, MP3 docking station, free Wi-Fi.

Hotel Elliott ★   Historic hotels are few and far between on the Oregon coast, but even if they were a dime a dozen, this beautiful hotel would be the best. The Elliott blends a vintage feel with a thoroughly modern interior decor. Rooms have lots of nice touches, including heated tile floors in the bathrooms, handblown glass globes on reading lights, regional artwork, furniture with comfortable contemporary styling, plush feather-top beds, and, in suites, granite-topped wet bars. Down in the cellar there's a weekend wine bar, and up on the roof there's a garden with fire pits and grand views.

357 12th St., Astoria, OR 97103. www.hotelelliott.com. ✆ **877/378-1924** or 503/325-2222. 32 units. Summer $169–$229 double, $239–$650 suite; other months $139–$189 double, $179–$650 suite. Rates include continental breakfast. Children 18 and under stay free in parent's room. AE, DISC, MC, V. **Amenities:** Lounge; exercise room; free Wi-Fi. *In room:* TV, hair dryer, Internet.

CAMPGROUNDS
Fort Stevens State Park, on the beach at the mouth of the Columbia River, is one of the largest and most popular state-park campgrounds on the Oregon coast. For reservations, contact **ReserveAmerica** (✆ **800/452-5687;** www.reserveamerica.com).

Where to Eat
In addition to the restaurants listed below, you should be sure to stop by **Joseph-son's,** 106 Marine Dr. (✆ 800/772-3474 or 503/325-2190; www.josephsons.com), a local seafood-smoking company that sells smoked salmon by the pound and has a take-out deli counter with clam chowder, smoked seafood on rolls, and more. If you're looking for some local ale, you've got several excellent choices in Astoria. Downtown on the waterfront, there's the **Wet Dog Cafe,** 144 11th St. (✆ 503/325-6975; www.wetdogcafe.com), and at the east end of town, there's the **Rogue Ales Public House,** Pier 39, 100 39th St. (✆ 503/325-5964; www.rogue.com), where you can sometimes watch sea lions just outside the window. Some of the most unusual brews in town are on tap at the **Fort George Brewery & Public House,** 1483 Duane St. (✆ 503/325-7468; www.fortgeorgebrewery.com). This latter pub is right next door to the **Blue Scorcher Bakery Café,** 1493 Duane St. (✆ 503/338-7473; www.bluescorcher.com), Astoria's best bakery. You can also get good espresso at the hip **Astoria Coffeehouse & Bistro,** 243 11th St. (✆ 503/325-1787; www.astoriacoffeehouse.com). If it's wine you're after, stop by **the Cellar on 10th,** 1004 Marine Dr. (✆ 503/325-6600; www.thecellaron10th.com), a well-stocked wine shop that has weekly tastings and occasional winemaker dinners.

Baked Alaska NORTHWEST   Built on a pier in downtown Astoria, this restaurant isn't just on the waterfront, it's over the waves. Not only are there great views (keep an eye out for sea lions), but the menu includes both comfort food and creative dishes. This place started out as a mobile soup trailer in Alaska, and when the chef/owner and his wife decided to settle down, they picked Astoria. Begin with the soup in a sourdough bread bowl—it's what got this place started. Beyond soup, try the campfire salmon, blackened New York steak, or the unusual thundermuck tuna (seared tuna dusted with ground coffee). Be sure to finish with the half-baked Alaska.

1 12th St. ✆ **503/325-7414.** www.bakedak.com. Reservations recommended. Main courses $10–$18 lunch, $18–$35 dinner. AE, DISC, MC, V. Daily 11am–10pm.

BRIDGEwater Bistro ★★ NORTHWEST   Located inside a restored cannery building with the Astoria-Megler Bridge looming overhead and the Cannery Pier Hotel just across the water, this restaurant sums up the new Astoria. Melding a historic cannery building with a contemporary design aesthetic, the BRIDGE*water* offers casual sophistication and creative cuisine. The menu here is long, with lots of small plates and a variety of both traditional fare and more creative regional dishes.

There's something for everyone, from oyster shooters and seafood cakes to gnocchi with clams and mussels and spice-encrusted duck with wild blackberries

20 Basin St. ✆ **503/325-6777.** www.bridgewaterbistro.com. Reservations recommended. Main courses $8–$22 lunch, $11–$32 dinner. AE, MC, V. Mon–Sat 11:30am–8 or 9pm; Sun 11am–8 or 9pm.

Clemente's ★ MEDITERRANEAN/SEAFOOD   This casual place may ostensibly be a Mediterranean restaurant specializing in seafood, but lots of people know it for its great fish and chips, which are available with a variety of seafoods, including salmon, albacore tuna, shrimp, and oysters. However, they also do a good cioppino. At dinner, try the pesto halibut or the sole piccata. Clemente's also works hard to reduce its carbon footprint, purchases local ingredients as much as possible, and has its waste oil converted to biodiesel.

1198 Commercial St. ✆ **503/325-1067.** www.clementesrestaurant.com. Reservations recommended. Main courses $10–$16 lunch, $12–$34 dinner. AE, DISC, MC, V. Tues–Sun 11am–3pm and 5–9pm.

Columbian Café 🍴 VEGETARIAN/SEAFOOD   With offbeat and eclectic decor, this tiny place looks a bit like a cross between a college hangout and a seaport diner, and the clientele reflects this atmosphere. There are only a handful of booths and a lunch counter, and the cafe's reputation for good vegetarian fare keeps the seats full. Crepes are the house specialty and come with a variety of fillings, including avocado, tomato, and cheese, or curried bananas. Dinner offers a bit more variety, with an emphasis on seafood, and there are always lots of specials. Even the condiments here, including pepper jelly and garlic jelly, are homemade. Because the kitchen is so small and everything is cooked to order, it can take a while to get your meal. Next door, and affiliated with the cafe, are the Voodoo Room nightclub and the Columbian Theater movie theater.

1114 Marine Dr. ✆ **503/325-2233.** www.columbianvoodoo.com. Main courses $6–$16 breakfast or lunch, $12–$25 dinner. No credit cards. Wed–Thurs 8am–2pm and 5–8pm; Fri 8am–2pm and 5–9pm; Sat 9am–2pm and 5–9pm; Sun 9am–2pm.

Drina Daisy BOSNIAN   Ever had Bosnian food? Probably not, but here in Astoria, you can give it a try. The specialty here is whole spit-roasted lamb, but it's not always available, so call ahead to see if it will be on the menu. Even if there's no lamb roasting on the spit when you're in town, there are plenty of other tasty dishes to try, including beef in phyllo dough, stuffed cabbage with beef or vegetables, and Bosnian goulash flavored with paprika. Be sure to finish your meal with a cup of thick, Sarajevo-style coffee or Bosnian espresso, which is topped with whipped cream.

915 Commercial St. ✆ **503/338-2912.** www.drinadaisy.com. Main courses $10–$17 lunch, $15–$24 dinner. DISC, MC, V. Wed–Sun 11am–10pm.

Astoria After Dark

If you're here in the summer, try to catch a performance of *Shanghaied in Astoria,* a musical melodrama that is staged each year by the **Astor Street Opry Company,** 129 W. Bond St. (✆ **503/325-6104;** www.shanghaiedinastoria.com). Performances are usually held from early July to mid-September. Also be sure to check the schedule of the **Liberty Theater,** 1203 Commercial St. (✆ **503/325-5922;** www.liberty-theater.org), a beautifully restored 1920s movie palace.

6 | **SEASIDE**

17 miles S of Astoria, 79 miles W of Portland, 7 miles N of Cannon Beach

Seaside is the northern Oregon coast's top family-vacation destination. The town is one of the oldest beach resorts on the coast (dating from 1899) and is filled with quaint historic cottages and tree-lined streets. However, it is better known for its miniature golf courses, bumper boats, video arcades, and souvenir shops.

This is not the sort of place most people imagine when they dream about the Oregon coast, and if you're looking for a quiet, romantic weekend getaway, Seaside is *not* the place. As one of the closest beaches to Portland, crowds and traffic are a way of life on summer weekends. The town is also a very popular conference site, and several of the town's largest hotels cater primarily to this market (and have the outrageous rates to prove it). However, the nearby community of Gearhart, which has long been a retreat for wealthy Portlanders, is as quiet as any town you'll find on this coast.

Essentials

GETTING THERE   Seaside is on U.S. 101 just north of the junction with U.S. 26, which connects to Portland.

VISITOR INFORMATION   Contact the **Seaside Visitors Bureau,** 7 N. Roosevelt Dr., Seaside, OR 97138; (℃ **888/306-2326** or 503/738-3097; www.seasideor.com).

FESTIVALS   The weekend before Labor Day weekend, the **Hood to Coast Run** celebration is held in Seaside.

Enjoying the Beach & Seaside's Other Attractions

Seaside's centerpiece is its 2-mile-long beachfront **Promenade** (or Prom), built in 1921. At the west end of Broadway, the Turnaround divides the walkway into the North Prom and the South Prom. Here a bronze statue marks the official end of the trail for the Lewis and Clark expedition. South of this statue on Lewis & Clark Way between the Promenade and Beach Drive, 8 blocks south of Broadway, you'll find the **Lewis and Clark Salt Works,** a reconstruction of a fire pit used by members of the famous expedition. During the winter of 1805–06, while the expedition was camped at Fort Clatsop, near present-day Astoria, Lewis and Clark sent several men southwest 15 miles to a good spot for making salt from seawater. It took three men nearly 2 months to produce four bushels of salt for the return trip east. Five kettles were used for boiling seawater, and the fires were kept stoked 24 hours a day.

History is not what attracts most people to Seaside, though. Rather, it's the miles of **white-sand beach** that begin just south of Seaside at the foot of the imposing Tillamook Head and stretch north to the mouth of the Columbia River. Though the waters here are quite cold and only a few people venture in farther than knee deep, there are lifeguards on duty all summer, which is one reason Seaside is popular with families. At the south end of Seaside beach is one of the best surf breaks on the north coast. You can rent a board and wetsuit at **Cleanline Surf,** 60 N. Roosevelt Dr. (℃ **503/738-7888;** www.cleanlinesurf.com). A complete rental package runs $35 a day. Don't know how to surf? You can take lessons from **Oregon Surf Adventures,** 1116 S. Roosevelt Dr. (℃ **503/436-1481;** www.oregonsurfadventures.com).

Because of the cold water, nonaquatic activities such as kite flying and beach cycling prove far more popular than swimming or surfing. All over town there are places that rent four-wheeled bicycles, called surreys, and three-wheeled cycles

The Oregon coast is one of the nation's best-known bicycle tour routes, ranking right up there with the back roads of Vermont, Napa Valley, and the San Juan Islands. Cyclists will find breathtaking scenery, interesting towns, parks and beaches to explore, wide shoulders, and well-spaced places to stay. You can stay in campgrounds (all state-park campgrounds have hiker/biker campsites) or in hotels. If you can afford it, an inn-to-inn pedal down this coast is the way to go; as you slowly grind your way up hill after hill, you'll appreciate not having to carry camping gear.

The entire route, from Astoria to California, covers between 368 and 378 miles (depending on your route) and includes a daunting 16,000 total feet of climbing. Although most of the route is on U.S. 101, which is a 55-mph highway for most of its length, the designated coast route leaves the highway for less crowded and more scenic roads whenever possible.

During the summer, when winds are generally out of the northwest, you'll have the wind at your back if you ride from north to south. In the winter (when you'll likely get very wet), you're better off riding from south to north to take advantage of winds out of the southwest. Planning a trip along the coast in winter is not advisable; even though there is less traffic, winter storms frequently blow in with winds of up to 100 mph.

For a map and guide to bicycling the Oregon coast, contact the **Oregon Department of Transportation** (© **503/ 986-3555;** www.oregon.gov/odot/hwy/ bikeped).

(funcycles) for pedaling on the beach. The latter are the most popular and the most fun, but can really be used only when the tide is out and the beach is firm enough to pedal on. Cycles go for between $10 and $20 an hour, and multipassenger surreys rent for between $20 and $30 an hour. Try **Wheel Fun Rentals,** 407 S. Holladay Dr. (© **503/738-8447;** www.wheelfunrentals.com).

If you prefer hiking to cycling, head south of town to the end of Sunset Boulevard, where you'll find the start of the **Tillamook Head Trail,** which leads 6 miles over the headland to Indian Beach in **Ecola State Park.** This trail goes through shady forests of firs and red cedars with a few glimpses of the Pacific along the way.

Golfers can play a round at the 9-hole **Seaside Golf Club,** 451 Ave. U (© **503/ 738-5261;** www.cannon-beach.net/seasidegolf), which charges $15 to $17 for 9 holes; another 9-hole course, **the Highlands at Gearhart,** 33260 Highlands Lane, Gearhart (© **503/738-5248;** www.highlandsgolfgearhart.com), also charges $16 for 9 holes. However, the area's best course is the **Gearhart Golf Links,** 1157 N. Marion Ave., Gearhart (© **503/738-3538;** www.gearhartgolflinks.com), where you'll pay $35 to $65 for 18 holes. This course was established in 1892, which makes it the oldest golf course in Oregon.

The small, privately owned **Seaside Aquarium,** 200 N. Promenade (© **503/738- 6211;** www.seasideaquarium.com), where you can feed seals, is one of the town's most popular family attractions. Admission is $7.50 for adults, $6.25 for seniors, and $3.75 for children ages 6 to 13. In a big case visible from outside the aquarium, there is a 36-foot-long gray whale skeleton. Kids will also enjoy the gaudily painted **carousel** at the **Seaside Carousel Mall,** 300 Broadway (© **503/738-6728;** www.seaside carouselmall.com).

Where to Stay

IN SEASIDE

The Gilbert Inn ★ One block from the beach and 1 block south of Broadway, on the edge of both the shopping district and one of Seaside's old residential neighborhoods, the Gilbert Inn is a big yellow Queen Anne–style Victorian house with a pretty little yard. Alexander Gilbert, who had this house built in 1892, was once the mayor of Seaside, and he built a stately home worthy of someone in such a high position. Gilbert made good use of the area's plentiful fir trees; the interior walls and ceilings are constructed of tongue-and-groove fir planks. The inn is decorated in country French decor that enhances the Victorian ambience.

341 Beach Dr., Seaside, OR 97138. www.gilbertinn.com. ⓒ **800/410-9770** or 503/738-9770. 6 units. $89–$159 double. 2-night minimum on weekends; 3-night minimum on holiday weekends. AE, DISC, MC, V. *In room:* TV, hair dryer, free Wi-Fi.

Inn of the Four Winds You'll find this little oceanfront hotel up at the north end of the Promenade, away from all the activity in the center of town but still only a short walk from good restaurants. Most guest rooms have balconies, ocean views, and gas fireplaces. There are also large suites. All the rooms have a vaguely Italianate style, though it's obvious the decorator was on a tight budget. Keep in mind that although this hotel is right on the beach, it's a very wide beach.

820 N. Promenade, Seaside, OR 97138. www.innofthefourwinds.com. ⓒ **800/818-9524** or 503/738-9524. 14 units. $109–$169 double; $169–$269 suite. AE, DISC, MC, V. **Amenities:** Access to nearby health club. *In room:* TV/DVD, fridge, hair dryer, MP3 player, free Wi-Fi.

IN GEARHART

Gearhart Ocean Inn 🍃 This old motor-court-style motel has been turned into a collection of cottagelike rooms, which offer modest and economical accommodations that have been renovated with the sort of care usually reserved for historic homes. A taupe exterior with blue-and-white trim gives the two rows of wooden buildings a touch of sophistication, and roses, Adirondack chairs, and little pocket gardens add character to the grounds. The rooms have been decorated in a mix of country cute and casual contemporary; some have kitchens and/or fireplaces.

67 N. Cottage Ave. (P.O. Box 2161), Gearhart, OR 97138. www.gearhartoceaninn.com. ⓒ **800/352-8034** or 503/738-7373. 12 units. $80–$160 double. 2–3 night minimum summer, weekends, and holidays. Children 6 and under stay free in parent's room. DISC, MC, V. Pets accepted ($15 per night). **Amenities:** Bikes; concierge. *In room:* TV/DVD, CD player, hair dryer, kitchen, MP3 docking station, free Wi-Fi.

Where to Eat

IN SEASIDE

If you're looking for a quick meal, some picnic food, or something to take back and cook in your room, drop by the old-timey **Bell Buoy of Seaside,** 1800 S. Roosevelt Dr. (ⓒ **800/529-2722** or 503/738-6354; www.bellbuoyofseaside.com), which sells cooked Dungeness crabs, award-winning chowder, smoked salmon, fresh seafood, and shrimp or crab melts.

Yummy Wine Bar & Bistro ★ NEW AMERICAN "I'm moving in, and I'm not leaving," I once overheard a customer say at this stylish wine bar in downtown Seaside. That sums up how well appreciated this place is in a town very short on good places to eat. With its hip, retro decor, casual attitude, and long wine list, Yummy is a fun place not only for a glass of wine and a snack, but also for a full meal. The menu changes seasonally, and there are always interesting specials, but you might start with an onion

tartlet made with Montrachet cheese and then move on to pistachio gnocchi, prosciutto-wrapped ling cod, or pan-roasted scallops on cauliflower purée. If you're just
here for wine and something light, try to grab one of the couches by the fireplace.

831 Broadway. ⓒ **503/738-3100.** www.yummywinebarbistro.com. Reservations recommended.
Main courses $10–$24. MC, V. Summer Thurs–Mon 3–10pm; shorter hours other months.

IN GEARHART

McMenamins Sand Trap AMERICAN   This oceanside outpost of the McMenamins brewpub empire overlooks the oldest golf course in Oregon and melds a
classic country-club atmosphere with the McMenamins' Deadhead aesthetic. The
menu sticks mostly to tried-and-true pub standards, including burgers, pizzas, and
fish and chips. However, since this is the beach, you can also get steamer clams, crab
cakes, and cedar-plank roasted salmon. There are usually half a dozen or more
McMenamins beers on tap.

1157 N. Marion Ave. ⓒ **503/717-8150.** www.mcmenamins.com. Main courses $6–$21. AE, DISC,
MC, V. Mon–Tues 11am–10pm; Wed–Thurs 11am–11pm; Fri 11am–midnight; Sat 8am–midnight;
Sun 8am–10pm.

Pacific Way Bakery & Cafe ★ ▮SANDWICHES/NORTHWEST   This former mom-and-pop grocery store is in the center of Gearhart and has such a classic
old-fashioned Cape Cod–style beach feel that it's well worth searching out. The
vintage interior of the restaurant harkens to the 1930s. At lunch, there are appetizing
sandwiches and salads. In the evening, try the wild-mushroom macaroni and cheese
or the prosciutto-wrapped scallops, if either is on the menu. There's an adjacent
bakery open Thursday through Monday from 7am to 1pm (call for winter hours).

601 Pacific Way. ⓒ **503/738-0245.** www.pacificwaybakery-cafe.com. Main courses $9–$13 lunch,
$10–$30 dinner. MC, V. Thurs–Mon 11am–3:30pm and 5–9pm.

CANNON BEACH ★★★

7 miles S of Seaside, 112 miles N of Newport, 79 miles W of Portland

When most people dream of a vacation on the Oregon coast, chances are they're
thinking of a place such as **Cannon Beach:** weathered cedar-shingle buildings,
picket fences behind drifts of nasturtiums, quiet gravel lanes, interesting little art
galleries, and massive rock monoliths rising from the surf just off the wide sandy
beach. If it weren't for all the other people who think Cannon Beach is a wonderful
place, this town would be perfect. However, Cannon Beach is suffering from its own
quaintness and the inevitable upscaling that ensues when a place begins to gain
national recognition. Once the Oregon coast's most renowned artists' community,
Cannon Beach is now going the way of California's Carmel—lots of upscale shopping
tucked away in utterly tasteful plazas along a neatly manicured main street. Despite
the crowds, it still has a village atmosphere, and summer throngs and traffic jams can
do nothing to assault the fortresslike beauty of the rocks that lie just offshore.

Essentials

GETTING THERE   Cannon Beach is on U.S. 101 just south of the junction with
U.S. 26.

VISITOR INFORMATION   Contact the **Cannon Beach Chamber of Commerce,** 207 N. Spruce St. (P.O. Box 64), Cannon Beach, OR 97110 (ⓒ **503/436-
2623;** www.cannonbeach.org).

cannon beach TRIVIA

o Cannon Beach was named for a cannon that washed ashore after the U.S. Navy schooner *Shark* wrecked on the coast north of here in 1846.

o Cannon Beach's Haystack Rock, which rises 235 feet above the water, is the most photographed monolith on the Oregon coast.

o The area's offshore rocks are protected nesting grounds for sea birds. Watch for tufted puffins, something of a Cannon Beach mascot.

o Tillamook Rock is the site of the **Tillamook Rock Lighthouse** (aka "Terrible Tilly"), which was frequently battered by huge storm waves that occasionally sent large rocks crashing through the light, 133 feet above sea level. The lighthouse was decommissioned in 1957 and is now used as a columbarium (a vault for the interment of the ashes of people who have been cremated).

GETTING AROUND   The **Cannon Beach Shuttle,** which provides van service up and down the length of town, operates daily with seasonal hours. Watch for signed shuttle stops. The fare is $1.

FESTIVALS   In early June, the **Sandcastle Day** contest turns the beach into one vast canvas for sand sculptors from all over the region, and in early November, the **Stormy Weather Arts Festival** celebrates the arrival of winter storms.

Hitting the Beach

Ecola State Park ★★★ (© 800/551-6949 or 503/436-2844; www.oregon.gov/ oprd/parks), just north of the town of Cannon Beach, marks the southernmost point that Lewis and Clark explored on the Oregon coast. The park offers the area's most breathtaking vantage point from which to soak up the view of Cannon Beach, Haystack Rock, and the Tillamook Rock Lighthouse. The park also has several picnic areas perched on bluffs high above the crashing waves and a trail that leads 6 miles over Tillamook Head to Seaside. The 1-mile stretch of trail between the main blufftop picnic area and Indian beach is particularly rewarding, passing through oldgrowth forests and offering good views of the ocean and beaches far below. There's also the 2.5-mile Clatsop Loop Trail, which leads through dense forest to a viewpoint high on Tillamook Head. The day-use fee is $5 per vehicle.

Kite flying and beachcombing are the most popular Cannon Beach pastimes, but you can also enjoy the beach in a variety of other ways, too. Between Memorial Day and Labor Day, guided horseback rides to Cove Beach and Haystack Rock are offered by **Sea Ranch Stables,** 415 Fir St. (© 503/436-2815; www.cannon-beach.net/ searanch), which is at the north entrance to Cannon Beach. Rides cost $65 to $130.

Another great way to see the beach is from a funcycle, a three-wheeled beach cycle. These cycles enable you to ride up and down the beach at low tide. Funcycles can be rented from **Mike's Bike Shop,** 248 N. Spruce St. (© 800/492-1266 or 503/436-1266; www.mikesbike.com), for $14 for 90 minutes. Mountain bikes and road bikes are also available for rent from Mike's.

Three miles south of town is **Arcadia Beach State Recreation Site ★★**, one of the prettiest little beaches on the north coast; and another mile farther south you'll

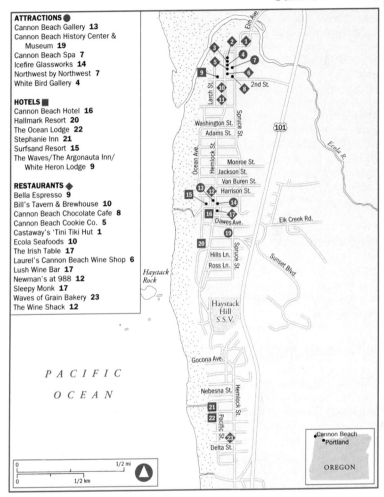

ATTRACTIONS ●
Cannon Beach Gallery **13**
Cannon Beach History Center &
   Museum **19**
Cannon Beach Spa **7**
Icefire Glassworks **14**
Northwest by Northwest **7**
White Bird Gallery **4**

HOTELS ■
Cannon Beach Hotel **16**
Hallmark Resort **20**
The Ocean Lodge **22**
Stephanie Inn **21**
Surfsand Resort **15**
The Waves/The Argonauta Inn/
   White Heron Lodge **9**

RESTAURANTS ◆
Bella Espresso **9**
Bill's Tavern & Brewhouse **10**
Cannon Beach Chocolate Cafe **8**
Cannon Beach Cookie Co. **5**
Castaway's 'Tini Tiki Hut **1**
Ecola Seafoods **10**
The Irish Table **17**
Laurel's Cannon Beach Wine Shop **6**
Lush Wine Bar **17**
Newman's at 988 **12**
Sleepy Monk **17**
Waves of Grain Bakery **23**
The Wine Shack **12**

PACIFIC

OCEAN

Elm Ave.

Larch St.

Spruce St.

2nd St.

Washington St.

Adams St.

101

Ecola R.

Ocean Ave.

Hemlock St.

Monroe St.

Jackson St.

Van Buren St.

Harrison St.

Dawes Ave.

Elk Creek Rd.

*Haystack
Rock*

Hills Ln.

Ross Ln.

Spruce St.

Sunset Blvd.

Haystack
Hill
S.S.V.

Gocona Ave.

Nebesna St.

Hemlock St.

Pacific St.

Delta St.

● Cannon Beach
● Portland

OREGON

0   1/2 mi
0   1/2 km

find **Hug Point State Recreation Site ★★**, which has picnic tables, a sheltered beach, and the remains of an old road that was cut into the rock face of this headland. **Oswald West State Park ★★**, 10 miles south of Cannon Beach, is one of my favorites of all the parks on the Oregon coast. A short trail leads to a driftwood-strewn cobblestone beach on a small cove. Headlands on either side of the cove can be reached by hiking trails that offer splendid views. The waves here are popular with surfers, and there's a walk-in campground.

If you want to try riding the wild (and very cold) surf, you can rent a surfboard and wetsuit from **Cannon Beach Surf,** 1088 S. Hemlock St. (© **503/436-0475;** www. cannonbeachsurf.com). A board and wetsuit rent for $30 to $35 per day.

Exploring the Town

For many Cannon Beach visitors, **shopping** is the town's greatest attraction. In the heart of town, along Hemlock Street, you'll find dozens of densely packed small shops and galleries offering original art, fine crafts, unusual gifts, and casual fashions. Galleries worth seeking out include **Northwest by Northwest,** 232 N. Spruce St. (✆ **800/494-0741** or 503/436-0741; www.nwbynwgallery.com), which features works by established Northwest artists; **White Bird Gallery,** 251 N. Hemlock St. (✆ **503/436-2681;** www.whitebirdgallery.com), a good gallery for colorful contemporary art and fine crafts; **Icefire Glassworks,** 116 E. Gower St. (✆ **888/423-3545** or 503/436-2359; http://cbgallerygroup.com/icefire-glassworks), a glassblowing studio south of downtown; and **Cannon Beach Gallery,** 1064 S. Hemlock St. (✆ **503/436-0744;** www.cannonbeacharts.org), which is operated by a local arts organization and mounts shows in a wide variety of styles not usually seen in other Cannon Beach galleries (which tend to be heavy on beach landscapes). On the surface, Cannon Beach may not look as though it has much history, but from Lewis and Clark's visit to the story of the cannon that gave the town its name, there is a bit to learn about this town's past. Visit the **Cannon Beach History Center & Museum,** 1387 S. Spruce St. (✆ **503/436-9301;** www.cbhistory.org), where modern, well-designed exhibits tell the story of the town's past, including the history of tourism here. A hands-on reproduction of a Native American longhouse is a hit with kids. The museum is open Wednesday through Monday from 1 to 5pm, and admission is free.

Want to turn a Cannon Beach getaway into a truly relaxing escape? Book a massage or a skin or hydrotherapy treatment at the **Cannon Beach Spa,** 232 N. Spruce St. (✆ **888/577-8772** or 503/436-8772; www.cannonbeachspa.com). Prices run between $80 and $105 for an hour-long massage.

Where to Stay

If you're heading here with the whole family or plan to stay a while, consider renting a house, a cottage, or an apartment. Offerings range from studio apartments to large luxurious oceanfront houses, and prices span an equally wide range. Contact **Cannon Beach Property Management,** 3188 S. Hemlock St. (P.O. Box 231), Cannon Beach, OR 97110 (✆ **877/386-3402;** www.cbpm.com), for more information.

EXPENSIVE

Arch Cape Inn and Retreat ★★ 🏠
Not only is this country inn a gorgeous interpretation of a French château, but it is one of the most luxurious lodgings on the entire coast. Each of the rooms fulfills a different fantasy of the perfect romantic escape. There is the Tower Room, with its circular breakfast nook and soaking tub; the Tapestry Room, with a stained-glass ceiling and a soaking tub; and the Tuscan spa, with a stone sink and private sauna. Lavish three-course breakfasts are served in the conservatory, and a dining room serves full dinners on a seasonal basis. So luxurious is this place that the fact that you aren't right on the beach doesn't even seem to matter.

31970 E. Ocean Lane, Arch Cape, OR 97102. www.archcapeinn.com. ✆ **800/436-2848** or 503/436-2800. Fax 503/436-1206. 10 units. $149–$399 double. Rates include full breakfast and evening wine social hour. AE, DC, DISC, MC, V. Pets accepted ($50 fee). No children 16 and under. **Amenities:** Restaurant; concierge; room service; sauna. *In room:* TV/VCR, fridge, hair dryer, free Wi-Fi.

The Ocean Lodge ★★★
Located right next door to the Stephanie Inn, this lodge is every bit as deluxe, but boasts a more laid-back, vintage Northwest feel. The

lobby has huge rough-cut timber beams and warm wood tones. All rooms are spacious suites with fireplaces and decks, most have in-room Jacuzzis, and some boast good views of Haystack Rock; if you can afford the premium, the views are well worth requesting. Ground-floor oceanfront rooms also have direct access to the beach. The lodge's beach bungalows are across the street, and some are up two flights of stairs.

2864 S. Pacific St. (P.O. Box 1037), Cannon Beach, OR 97110. www.theoceanlodge.com. © **888/777-4047** or 503/436-2241. 45 units. Late June to mid-Oct $249–$349 double, $299–$369 suite; mid-Oct to late June $189–$289 double, $289–$309 suite. Rates include continental breakfast. AE, DC, DISC, MC, V. Pets accepted ($15 per night). **Amenities:** Concierge; access to nearby health club. In room: A/C, TV/DVD, CD player, fridge, hair dryer, kitchen (some rooms), free Wi-Fi.

Stephanie Inn ★★★   The Stephanie Inn is the most classically romantic inn on the Oregon coast—the perfect place for a special weekend away. With flower boxes beneath the windows and neatly manicured gardens by the entry, the inn is reminiscent of New England's country inns, but the beach out the back door is definitely of Pacific Northwest origin. Inside, the lobby feels warm and cozy with its river-rock fireplace, huge wood columns, and beamed ceiling. The guest rooms, all individually decorated, are equally cozy, and all have double whirlpool tubs and gas fireplaces. The higher you go in the three-story inn, the better the views and the more spacious the outdoor spaces (patios, balconies, and decks). A bounteous breakfast buffet is served each morning, and complimentary afternoon wine and evening nightcaps are also served. The inn's elegant dining room serves creative Northwest cuisine. Various spa services are offered.

2740 S. Pacific St. (P.O. Box 219), Cannon Beach, OR 97110. www.stephanie-inn.com. © **800/633-3466** or 503/436-2221. 41 units. $369–$509 double; $539–$609 suite. Rates include full breakfast. AE, DC, DISC, MC, V. Children 12 and over welcome. **Amenities:** Restaurant; access to nearby health club; room service. In room: A/C, TV/DVD, fridge, hair dryer, free Wi-Fi.

Surfsand Resort ★★   This sprawling resort, a sister property to the Stephanie Inn, is a beautiful blend of Northwest-lodge styling on the exterior and bold, contemporary interior design in the guest rooms. There are wall-hung flatscreen TVs, separate tubs and showers, gas fireplaces, and lots of other welcome details that make these rooms great for romantic getaways. However, with an indoor pool and many room types, it is also a good choice for families. Best of all, the resort is almost right in front of Haystack Rock.

148 W. Gower St. (P.O. Box 219), Cannon Beach, OR 97110. www.surfsand.com. © **800/547-6100** or 503/436-2274. Fax 503/436-9116. 97 units. $279–$339 double; $389–$449 suite. Children 18 and under stay free in parent's room. AE, DC, DISC, MC, V. Pets accepted ($15 per night). **Amenities:** Restaurant; lounge; children's programs; concierge; exercise room; Jacuzzi; indoor pool; room service; sauna. In room: TV/DVD, fridge, hair dryer, MP3 docking station, free Wi-Fi.

MODERATE

Cannon Beach Hotel   Although not in the town's best location (there are parking lots all around), this hotel, in a cute historic building, manages to capture Cannon Beach's spirit economically. A white fence, black shutters, and cedar-shingle siding give the hotel plenty of character. Inside you'll find attractively furnished rooms that vary in size and price. The best rooms, though, are those with fireplaces and claw-foot soaking tubs, and two of these have partial ocean views. Rooms are also available in three nearby buildings, with some of these rooms being more luxurious than those in the main hotel. Rooms in the Courtyard have gas fireplaces, kitchenettes, whirlpool tubs, and balconies. The 1940s vintage McBee Cottages are good for families and those traveling with a pet. Rooms in the Hearthstone Inn have a rustic Northwest styling.

1116 S. Hemlock St. (P.O. Box 943), Cannon Beach, OR 97110. www.cannonbeachhotel.com. © **800/238-4107** or 503/436-1392. Fax 503/436-1396. 37 units. Mid-June to Sept $140–$240 double; Oct–Nov and Mar to mid-June $85–$195 double; Dec–Feb $70–$175 double. Rates include continental breakfast (for rooms in hotel only). Children 12 and under stay free in parent's room. AE, DISC, MC, V. Pets accepted ($20 per night). **Amenities:** Restaurant; concierge. *In room:* TV/DVD, hair dryer, free Wi-Fi.

Hallmark Resort ★ ☺ Situated on a bluff with a head-on view of Haystack Rock, the Hallmark appeals primarily to families, and a wide range of rates reflects the variety of rooms available. The lowest rates are for nonview standard rooms, and the highest rates are for oceanfront two-bedroom suites. Between these extremes are all manner of rooms, studios, and suites. The best values are the limited-view rooms, many of which have fireplaces and comfortable chairs set up to take in what little view there might be. Some rooms also have kitchens.

1400 S. Hemlock St., Cannon Beach, OR 97110. www.hallmarkinns.com. © **888/448-4449** or 503/436-1566. Fax 503/436-0324. 129 units. Summer $129–$319 double, $214–$389 suite; other months $89–$219 double, $129–$239 suite. AE, DISC, MC, V. Pets accepted ($20). **Amenities:** Exercise room; 2 Jacuzzis; 2 indoor pools; sauna; spa. *In room:* TV/DVD, fridge, hair dryer, kitchen (some rooms), free Wi-Fi.

The Waves/the Argonauta Inn/White Heron Lodge ★ Variety is the name of the game in eclectic Cannon Beach, and the Waves plays the game better than any other accommodations in town. This lodge, only a block from the heart of Cannon Beach, consists of more than four dozen rooms, suites, cottages, and beach houses. The Garden Court rooms (renovated in 2011) are the least expensive, though they don't have ocean views. My favorites are the Argonauta Inn's cottages. Surrounded by beautiful flower gardens in the summer, these old cottages (many of which are oceanfront) capture the spirit of Cannon Beach. There are fireplaces in some rooms and whirlpool spas overlooking the ocean. If you want to get away from the crowds, ask for a suite at the White Heron Lodge. The Waves itself offers contemporary accommodations, some of which are right on the beach and have great views.

188 W. Second St. (P.O. Box 3), Cannon Beach, OR 97110. www.thewavesmotel.com. © **800/822-2468** or 503/436-2205. Fax 503/436-1490. 55 units. The Waves $99–$179 double, $189–$429 suite; White Heron Lodge $199–$299 suite; Argonauta $99–$429 suite. 3-night minimum July–Aug; 2-night minimum on weekends Sept–June. Children 6 and under stay free in parent's room. DISC, MC, V. **Amenities:** Jacuzzi. *In room:* TV/DVD, hair dryer, kitchen (some rooms), free Wi-Fi.

Where to Eat

For pastries, cookies, and wraps, head south of downtown Cannon Beach to the Tolovana Park neighborhood, where you'll find the cozy little **Waves of Grain Bakery,** 3116 S. Hemlock St. (© **503/436-9600;** www.wavesofgrainbakery.com). The **Cannon Beach Cookie Co.,** 239 Hemlock St. (© **503/436-1129**), is another good place to indulge a sweet tooth. For good espresso, head south from the main part of town to the area known as midtown, where you'll find **Sleepy Monk,** 1235 S. Hemlock St. (© **503/436-2796;** www.sleepymonkcoffee.com), a coffee roaster specializing in organic coffee. Alternatively, try **Bella Espresso,** 231 N. Hemlock St. (© **503/436-2595;** www.bella-espresso.com), in the main part of town. Chocoholics should not miss the **Cannon Beach Chocolate Café,** 232 N. Spruce St. (© **503/436-8772;** www.cannonbeachspa.com/chocolate-cafe.html), which sells a wide range of chocolates and hot chocolate, and is associated with the Cannon Beach Spa.

If you're looking for a pleasant place to have a glass of wine and some appetizers, check out **Lush Wine Bar,** 1235 S. Hemlock St. (© **503/436-8500;** www.lush winebar.com), located next door to The Irish Table, one of Cannon Beach's best restaurants. The wine bar is a great place to wait for seating at The Irish Table. For a bottle of wine to take back to your room and enjoy on the balcony overlooking the beach, stop in at **The Wine Shack,** 124 Hemlock St. (© **800/787-1765** or 503/436-1100; www.beachwine.com), or **Laurel's Cannon Beach Wine Shop,** 263 N. Hemlock St. (© **503/436-1666**). For good locally brewed beer, visit **Bill's Tavern & Brewhouse,** 188 N. Hemlock St. (© **503/436-2202**).

Also, foodies should consider booking a cooking class at **EVOO Cannon Beach Cooking School,** 188 S. Hemlock St. (© **877/436-3866** or 503/436-8555; www. evoo.biz).

Castaways 'Tini Tiki Bar ★ CARIBBEAN/INTERNATIONAL   The water in Cannon Beach may be too cold for swimming, but at least here at Castaways you can eat as if you're on a warm, tropical beach. At this little cottage restaurant at the north end of town, spicy flavors dominate the menu, spanning the globe from Thailand and Hawaii to Jamaica and the Bahamas. Dishes, such as the crab fritters, are packed with a range of flavors and often look like plated fiestas. The macaroni and cheese with andouille sausage gives a tropical spin to the classic comfort food and is a big hit. Save room for the mango flambé. The rum punch is sure to put you in an island state of mind.

316 N. Fir St. © **503/436-8777.** Reservations accepted for parties of 6 or more. Main courses $16–$23. DISC, MC, V. Wed–Sun 5–9pm.

Ecola Seafoods SEAFOOD   This casual place is both a seafood market and restaurant, and since the owners are commercial fishermen, you can count on the fish here being fresh. It's strictly counter service, and in summer the place can be so crowded, you just might want to get your meal to go (a beach picnic, perhaps?). While there are all kinds of fish and chips (salmon, albacore, oysters, halibut), I'm partial to the crab dinner and the smoked-salmon-salad sandwich.

208 N. Spruce St. © **503/436-9130.** www.ecolaseafoods.com. Main courses $7–$18. DISC, MC, V. Summer daily 9am–9pm; other months daily 10am–7pm or later (in spring and fall).

The Irish Table ★ IRISH   With its low, open-beamed ceiling and abundance of wood, this little restaurant in midtown Cannon Beach feels just like a cottage in County Cork. The food, although only vaguely Irish, tends to rich, creamy dishes, including wonderful pasties and shepherd's pie. You'll also find steaks and pork chops on the short menu (four entrees plus a daily special). It's the specials that are often the most interesting—perhaps sturgeon with wild mushrooms. The restaurant takes over the space occupied during the day by the Sleepy Monk coffee roastery, and this portion of the restaurant feels a lot like a cabin in an old sailing ship. Because this cozy restaurant is so popular, plan on being in line for a table at opening.

1235 S. Hemlock St. © **503/436-0708.** Reservations accepted for parties of 4 or more. Main courses $17–$24. MC, V. Fri–Tues 5:30–9pm.

Newman's at 988 ★★ FRENCH/ITALIAN   Chef/owner John Newman was for many years the executive chef at Cannon Beach's Stephanie Inn, and here, in his own restaurant, he continues to wow both new and longtime customers. The restaurant, inside a cottage, is small, dark, and very romantic, the perfect place for a special night out. The menu is short, but you can expect such delicacies as duck breast with foie gras and a truffle-oil drizzle, rack of lamb with wild mushrooms, and the ever-popular lobster ravioli with hazelnuts and Marsala cream sauce.

988 S. Hemlock St. © **503/436-1151.** www.newmansat988.com. Reservations recommended. Main courses $19–$29. AE, DISC, MC, V. July 4–Oct 15 daily 5:30–9pm; Oct 16–July 3 Tues–Sun 5:30–9pm. Closed mid-Jan to early Feb.

En Route to or from Portland

If you'd like to see a large herd of **Roosevelt elk,** watch for the Jewell turnoff about 37 miles before reaching Cannon Beach on U.S. 26. From the turnoff, continue 10 miles north, following the wildlife-viewing signs to the **Jewell Meadows Wildlife Area ★** (© 503/755-2264; www.dfw.state.or.us/resources/visitors/jewell_meadows_wildlife_area.asp), where there's a large pasture frequented in the cooler months by up to 300 elk. Although November through March are the best months to see the elk, September and October are rutting season and, at this time, big bulls can often be heard bugling and seen locking antlers. Summer is not usually a reliable time for seeing the elk, but in June you may see elk cows with calves. During the winter, the elk are provided with supplemental hay to keep the herd healthy, and it is possible to assist in the daily feeding. Participants are taken out into the meadows on a flatbed trailer loaded with hay, which is then tossed out to the expectant elk. To participate, however, you'll need to call on the morning of December 1 to make your reservation. (Weekends fill up the fastest.)

Twelve miles past the U.S. 26 turnoff for Jewell, you'll find **Saddle Mountain State Natural Area ★★**, which is a favorite day hike in the area. A strenuous 2.5-mile trail leads to the top of Saddle Mountain, from which there are breathtaking views up and down the coast. In the spring, rare wildflowers are abundant along this trail. The trail is steep and rocky, so wear sturdy shoes or boots, and carry water.

WHERE TO EAT

Camp 18 Restaurant AMERICAN   There is no better place than this combination restaurant/logging museum to learn how logging was done in the days before clear-cutting. The restaurant is in a huge log lodge with lots of chain-saw art, axes for door handles, and a hollowed-out stump for a hostess desk. The restaurant's 85-foot-long ridge pole (the log beam that runs along the inside of the peak of the roof) is supposedly the largest of its kind in the country and weighs 25 tons. There are also stone fireplaces and lots of old logging photos. After tucking into logger-size meals (don't miss the marionberry cobbler), you can wander the grounds studying old steam logging equipment. Oh, and the food? Basic steak and seafood, mostly fried, with a few pasta and chicken dishes thrown in.

42362 U.S. 26 (Milepost 18, 22 miles east of Seaside), Elsie. © **800/874-1810** or 503/755-1818. www.camp18restaurant.com. Main courses $8–$13 lunch, $16–$24 dinner. AE, DISC, MC, V. Daily 7am–8pm.

TILLAMOOK COUNTY

75 miles W of Portland, 51 miles S of Seaside, 44 miles N of Lincoln City

Although this is one of the closest stretches of coast to Portland, it is not a major destination because there are no large beachfront towns in the area. The town of Tillamook, which lies inland from the Pacific at the south end of Tillamook Bay, is the area's commercial center, but it is the surrounding farmland that has made Tillamook famous in Oregon. Ever since the first settlers arrived in the area in 1851, dairy farming has been the mainstay of the economy, and today large herds of contented cows graze in the area's odiferous fields. With no beaches to attract visitors, the town of Tillamook has managed to turn its dairy industry into a tourist attraction. No, this isn't the cow-watching capital of Oregon, but the town's cheese factory is now one of the most popular stops along the Oregon coast. Most of the milk produced by area cows goes to the Tillamook County Creamery Association's cheese factory, which turns out a substantial share of the cheese consumed in Oregon.

Although the town of Tillamook has no beaches, there are a few beachside hamlets in the area that offer a variety of accommodations, activities, and dining options. Tillamook is also the starting point for the scenic Three Capes Loop, which links three state parks and plenty of great coastal scenery. By the way, Tillamook is a mispronunciation of the word *Killamook,* which was the name of the Native American tribe that once lived in this area. The name is now applied to a county, a town, and a bay.

Essentials

GETTING THERE Tillamook is on U.S. 101 at the junction with Ore. 6, which leads to Portland.

VISITOR INFORMATION For more information on the area, contact the **Tillamook Area Chamber of Commerce,** 3705 U.S. 101 N., Tillamook, OR 97141 (℃ **503/842-7525;** www.tillamookchamber.org), or the **Nehalem Bay Area Chamber of Commerce,** P.O. Box 601, Wheeler, OR 97147 (℃ **877/368-5100;** www.nehalembaychamber.com).

Manzanita

As the crowds have descended on Cannon Beach, people seeking peace and quiet and a slower pace have migrated south to the community of Manzanita. Located south of Neahkanie Mountain, Manzanita enjoys a setting similar to Cannon Beach, but without the many haystack rocks. There isn't much to do except walk on the beach and relax, which is exactly why most people come here.

The beach at Manzanita stretches for 5 miles, from the base of Neahkanie Mountain to the mouth of the Nehalem River, and is a favorite of both surfers and windsurfers. The latter have the option of sailing either in the oceanfront waves or in the quieter waters of Nehalem Bay, which is just across Nehalem Spit from the ocean. Access to both the bay and the beach is provided at **Nehalem Bay State Park** (℃ **503/368-5154;** www.oregon.gov/oprd/parks), which is just south of Manzanita and encompasses all of Nehalem Spit. The park, which includes a campground (and an airstrip), has a 1¾-mile paved bike path, a horse camp, and horse trails. The day-use fee is $5. During the summer, horseback rides are usually available here in the park through **Oregon Beach Rides** (℃ **971/237-6653;** www.oregonbeachrides.com). Out at the south end of the spit, more than 50 harbor seals can often be seen basking on the beach. To reach the seal area requires a 5-mile round-trip hike. Alternatively, you can take a brief seal-watching boat excursion through **Jetty Fishery** (see "Wheeler," below).

WHERE TO STAY

If you want to rent a vacation house in Manzanita, contact **Manzanita Rental Company,** 686 Manzanita Ave. (P.O. Box 162), Manzanita, OR 97130 (℃ **800/579-9801** or 503/368-6797; www.manzanitarentals.com).

Coast Cabins ★★ 🎁   These six modern cabins are set back a ways from the beach but are the most impressive cabins on the entire coast. Done in a sort of modern interpretation of Scandinavian cabins, these accommodations are designed as romantic getaways for couples. Two of the cabins are tall two-story structures, and the second-floor bedrooms have walls of windows. The cabin interiors are well designed and artfully decorated, with such touches as Tibetan carpets, original art, and unusual lighting fixtures. Now imagine the burnished glow of the cabins' cedar exteriors accented by lovely terraced perennial gardens, and you'll have an idea of just how the perfect getaway on the Oregon coast should look. Several cabins have outdoor spa tubs and one also has a sauna. Three vacation-rental homes are also available.

635 Laneda Ave., Manzanita, OR 97130. www.coastcabins.com. © **503/368-7113.** 5 units. $125–$395 double. 2-night minimum on weekends and throughout the summer. AE, MC, V. Pets accepted ($30 deposit, plus $25 per night). **Amenities:** Access to nearby health club. *In room:* TV/VCR/DVD, CD player, hair dryer, kitchen, MP3 docking station, free Wi-Fi.

The Inn at Manzanita ★   Searching for an unforgettably romantic spot for a weekend getaway? This is it. Right in the heart of town, the Inn at Manzanita is a great place to celebrate a special event. All the rooms have double whirlpool tubs and fireplaces, and most rooms have balconies. The weathered cedar-shingle siding blends unobtrusively with the natural vegetation, and the grounds are planted with beautiful flowers for much of the year.

67 Laneda Ave. (P.O. Box 243), Manzanita, OR 97130. www.innatmanzanita.com. © **503/368-6754.** Fax 503/368-5941. 14 units. $179–$199 double (Oct–May $129–$149 midweek); $385 penthouse suite (Oct–May $295 midweek). 2-night minimum on weekends and July to Labor Day; 3-night minimum on some holidays. AE, DC, DISC, MC, V. Pets accepted ($15 per night). **Amenities:** Concierge; access to nearby health club; Wi-Fi. *In room:* TV/DVD, fridge, hair dryer, kitchen (some rooms), free Wi-Fi.

WHERE TO EAT

For lattes and the latest news, head to **Manzanita News & Espresso,** 500 Laneda Ave. (© **503/368-7450**). At the end of the day, wind down at **Vino Manzanita,** 387-D Laneda Ave. (© **503/368-8466**), a hip little wine bar.

Bread and Ocean NORTHWEST   Do not visit Manzanita without at least buying some bread, pastries, or a sandwich from this little hole-in-the-wall restaurant. Deservedly Manzanita's most popular lunch spot, Bread and Ocean also serves decent dinners, but they are only available Friday through Sunday nights. The menu changes with the seasons and utilizes organic ingredients as often as possible.

154 Laneda Ave. © **503/368-5823.** www.breadandocean.com. Reservations not accepted. No credit cards. Main courses $8–$8.50 lunch, $15–$24 dinner. Wed–Thurs 7:30am–2pm; Fri–Sat 7:30am–2pm and 5–9pm; Sun 8am–2pm and 5–8pm.

Wheeler

Located on Nehalem Bay, this wide spot in the road has long been popular for crabbing and fishing. However, it's also a favorite for sea kayaking. The marshes of the bay provide plenty of meandering waterways to explore, and several miles of the Nehalem River can also be easily paddled if the tides are in your favor. You can rent a sea kayak at **Wheeler Marina,** 278 Marine Dr. (© **503/368-5780**), right on the waterfront in Wheeler. Expect to pay around $22 per hour or $44 per day; higher rates are for double kayaks.

If you're interested in trying your hand at crabbing, contact **Jetty Fishery,** 27550 U.S. 101 N., Rockaway Beach (© **503/368-5746;** www.jettyfishery.com), located just south of Wheeler at the mouth of the Nehalem River. They rent boats and crab rings and offer dock crabbing. The folks here also offer a ferry service ($10 per person) across the river to Nehalem Bay State Park, where you can often see dozens of harbor seals lying on the beach. You can also sometimes see seals close up if you sit on the jetty rocks at nearby Neadonna, which is just south of Jetty Fishery.

WHERE TO STAY

The Nehalem River Inn 🛏️ The Oregon coast is not just about beaches and rocky headlands; it's also about meandering tidal rivers, and this country inn is set on just such a river. Situated a couple of miles off U.S. 101 between Nehalem and Wheeler, the inn is a hideaway par excellence. You can choose among rooms, suites, or a cottage, and all of the accommodations have a stylish contemporary look. The inn has an excellent restaurant that uses organic ingredients as much as possible. One caveat: This valley has dairy farms and, to be polite, the air can be somewhat fragrant at times.

34910 Ore. 53, Nehalem, OR 97131. www.nehalemriverinn.com. ✆ **503/368-7708.** 5 units. May 15–Oct 15 $105–$185 double; Oct 16–May 14 $100–$160 double. MC, V. **Amenities:** Restaurant. *In room:* TV/VCR/DVD, hair dryer, free Wi-Fi.

Old Wheeler Hotel This delightfully old fashioned second-floor walk-up hotel may be right on busy U. S. 101, but it has so much character that it is one of the most enjoyable places to stay in the area. The building, painted a pretty Tuscan yellow, has a very old-world feel, and in fact the entire hotel feels very European. You'll find plush beds and comfortable furnishings in all the rooms, but be aware that the two cheapest rooms have private bathrooms down the hall. Several rooms have views of Nehalem Bay, which is just across the highway, and these rooms are worth requesting. Rooms are well insulated against traffic noise.

495 N. U.S. 101, Wheeler, OR 97147. www.oldwheelerhotel.com. ✆ **877/653-4683** or 503/368-6000. 8 units. May–Sept $119–$160 double; Oct–Apr $99–$149 double. Rates include continental breakfast. AE, DISC, MC, V. Children 12 and over welcome. *In room:* TV/DVD; free Wi-Fi.

Wheeler on the Bay Lodge & Marina Located right on the shore of Nehalem Bay, this is one of the north coast's most economical waterfront lodges. It's not fancy, but the bayfront location is great. The Honeymoon Room, the best room here, has walls of glass looking onto the bay, a private deck, a fireplace, and, best of all, a whirlpool tub with great views. Six of the rooms have spas, and most of these have water views. All the rooms have distinctive decor. Kayak rentals make this an ideal spot for active vacationers.

580 Marine Dr., Wheeler, OR 97147. www.wheeleronthebay.com. ✆ **800/469-3204** or 503/368-5858. 11 units. May 16–Oct $90–$155 double, $110–$225 suite; Nov–May 15 $72–$124 double, $88–$180 suite. Rates include continental breakfast. 2-night minimum on holidays. Children 13 and under stay free in parent's room. DISC, MC, V. **Amenities:** Kayak rentals. *In room:* TV/VCR/DVD, fridge, hair dryer, free Wi-Fi.

WHERE TO EAT

If you like smoked salmon, don't miss **Karla's Smokehouse** ★, 2010 U.S. 101 N. (✆ **503/355-2362;** www.karlassmokehouse.com), which is at the north end of nearby Rockaway Beach and sells some of the best smoked fish and oysters on the coast. For the best breakfasts in Tillamook County, head to **Wanda's Café & Bakery,** 12870 U.S. 101 (✆ **503/368-8100**), which is in Nehalem (watch for it on the left as you come down the hill from Manzanita).

Nehalem River Inn ★ 🍴 FRENCH/NORTHWEST   Set on the banks of the Nehalem River, this restaurant, part of a secluded country inn, serves some of the best food on the Oregon coast. The menu is contemporary, and although it changes with the seasons, you might start your meal with heirloom tomato soup with manchego cheese and white-truffle oil, or roasted quail with lentils, chorizo, and tart cherry syrup. For an entree, try the succulent steak, which might be accompanied by truffled penne pasta and a balsamic reduction. The hidden-away location and high caliber of the meals make this restaurant a real find.

34910 Ore. 53 (less than 3 miles off U.S. 101), Nehalem. ℂ **503/368-7708.** www.nehalemriverinn. com. Reservations highly recommended. Main courses $27–$30. MC, V. Call for hours. No children 12 and under.

Rising Star Cafe ★ 🍴 SEAFOOD/NEW AMERICAN   With a view that often takes in the setting sun, this Wheeler hole-in-the-wall is indeed one of the Oregon coast's rising stars. Fresh seafood is the specialty, and each week, the chef finds something fresh off the boats that catches his fancy and builds the menu around that. While seafood specials are the mainstay of the menu, you might also find lamb shanks or other meaty preparations. Thursday is currently Pasta Night, when you can get a simple pasta dinner with your choice of sauce for only $10. Weekend brunches are also popular and make this a good stop if you're planning to continue along the coast.

92 Rorvik St., Wheeler. ℂ **503/368-3990.** www.risingstarcafe.com. Reservations recommended on weekends. Main courses $10–$20. No credit cards. Wed–Thurs and Sat noon–3pm and 5–8pm; Fri 5–8pm; Sun 10am–3pm.

Garibaldi

Named (by the local postmaster) in 1879 for Italian patriot Giuseppe Garibaldi, this little town is at the north end of Tillamook Bay and is the region's main sportfishing and crabbing port. If you've got an urge to do some salmon or bottom fishing, this is the place to book a trip. Try **Garibaldi Charters** (ℂ **800/900-4665** or 503/322-0007; www.garibaldicharters.com), which charges between $95 and $125 for a full day of salmon fishing. Deep-sea halibut fishing will run you about $185 per day. **Whale-watching** and **sailing** excursions are also offered. At the **Garibaldi Marina,** 302 Mooring Basin Rd. (ℂ **800/383-3828** or 503/322-3312; www.garibaldi marina.com), you can rent boats and crab rings if you want to do some fishing or crabbing on your own.

Garibaldi is also where you'll find the depot for the **Oregon Coast Scenic Railroad,** 403 American Way (ℂ **503/842-7972;** www.ocsr.net), an excursion train that runs along some of the most scenic portions of this section of coast. The train usually runs weekends in June and September and daily July through Labor Day. Call to see if it's operating when you visit. The fare for the 90-minute excursions is $16 for adults and $9 for children ages 3 to 10.

If you're interested in regional history, I highly recommend visiting the fascinating **Garibaldi Museum** ★, 112 Garibaldi Ave., U.S. 101 (ℂ **503/322-8411;** www. garibaldimuseum.com), a small, privately owned maritime museum that focuses on the history of Tillamook Bay and Captain Robert Gray, the American ship captain who discovered the Columbia River. The museum is open April through November, Thursday through Monday from 10am to 4pm. Admission is $3 for adults and $2.50 for seniors and children 5 to 18.

Tillamook

Tillamook has long been known as one of Oregon's foremost dairy regions, and Tillamook cheese is ubiquitous in the state. So it's no surprise that the **Tillamook Cheese Factory,** 4175 U.S. 101 N. (© **800/542-7290** or 503/815-1300; www.tillamookcheese.com), located just north of Tillamook, is the most popular tourist attraction in town. Visitors can observe the cheese-making process (cheddars are the specialty), and there's also a large store where all manner of cheeses and other edible gifts are available. From mid-June to Labor Day, the factory is open daily from 8am to 8pm, and from Labor Day to mid-June, it's open 8am to 6pm.

If the Tillamook Cheese Factory seems too crowded for you, head back toward town a mile and you'll see the **Blue Heron French Cheese Company,** 2001 Blue Heron Dr. (© **800/275-0639** or 503/842-8281; www.blueheronoregon.com), which is on the same side of U.S. 101 as the Tillamook Cheese Factory. Located in a big old dairy barn with a flagstone floor, this store stocks the same sort of comestibles as the Tillamook Cheese Factory, though the emphasis here is on brie (which, however, is not made locally). Farm animals make this a good stop for kids. Blue Heron is open daily from 8am to 8pm in summer and 9am to 6pm in winter.

Quilters and other fiber-arts aficionados will want to visit the **Latimer Quilt & Textile Center,** 2105 Wilson River Loop Rd. (© **503/842-8622;** www.latimer quiltandtextile.com), which is housed in a 1930s schoolhouse. The center has a large collection of textiles and mounts a variety of exhibits throughout the year. April through October, the center is open Monday through Saturday from 10am to 5pm and Sunday from noon to 4pm; November through March, it's open Monday through Saturday from 10am to 4pm. Admission is $3 (free for children 5 and under). The **Tillamook County Pioneer Museum,** 2106 Second St. (© **503/842-4553;** www.tcpm.org), is also worth a visit for its reproduction tree-stump house and interesting natural-history exhibit. The museum is open Tuesday through Saturday from 10am to 4pm. Admission is $4 for adults, $3 for seniors, and $1 for children age 10 to 17.

To learn more about the forests and 20th-century forest fires in the nearby Coast Range, visit the fascinating **Tillamook Forest Center,** 45500 Wilson River Hwy. (© **866/930-4646** or 503/815-6800; www.tillamookforestcenter.org). This modern interpretive center tells the story of massive forest fires that devastated this area four times in the middle of the 20th century. After the fires, it took decades of intensive replanting to bring these forests back to the lush woodlands you see today. At the center, there is a reproduction of a fire lookout tower and access to the Wilson River Trail. The center is open March to November daily from 10am to 5pm.

A hangar built during World War II for a fleet of navy blimps is 2 miles south of town off U.S. 101 and lays claim to being the largest freestanding wooden building in the world. Statistics bear this out: It's 296 feet wide, 1,072 feet long, and 192 feet tall. The blimp hangar now houses the **Tillamook Air Museum,** 6030 Hangar Rd. (© **503/842-1130;** www.tillamookair.com), which contains more than 30 restored vintage planes, including a P-51 Mustang, an F4U-7 Corsair, and an F-14A Tomcat. The museum is open daily from 9am to 5pm. Admission is $9 for adults, $8 for seniors, and $5 for youths 6 to 17.

You can also go up in a small plane to see this section of the coast, and you may even see whales. Contact **Tillamook Air Tours** (© **503/842-1942;** www.tillamook airtours.com), which offers tours in a restored 1942 Stinson Reliant V-77 plane. Flights start at $85 per person if you have four people in your group.

Anglers interested in going after salmon or steelhead in Tillamook Bay or area rivers should contact **Fishing Oregon** (© 503/842-5171; www.fish-oregon.com). If you'd rather just paddle the area's waterways in a sea kayak, contact **Kayak Tillamook** (© 503/866-4808; http://kayaktillamook.com), which charges $65 for 2½- to 3½-hour tours.

WHERE TO EAT

If you need to stock up your larder for the beach house or are on your way back from a weekend at the beach, don't miss an opportunity to stop in at **Bear Creek Artichokes** (© 503/398-5411; www.bearcreekartichokes.com), which is located 11 miles south of Tillamook on U.S. 101. This is one of the few commercial artichoke farms in Oregon and usually has fresh artichokes throughout the summer and fall. The farm stand has lots of other great produce, as well as jams, mustards, and salsas.

The Three Capes Scenic Loop ★★★

The **Three Capes Scenic Loop** begins just west of downtown Tillamook and leads past Cape Meares, Cape Lookout, and Cape Kiwanda. Together these capes offer some of the most spectacular views on the northern Oregon coast. All three capes are state parks, and all make great whale-watching spots in the spring or storm-watching spots in the winter. To start the loop, follow Third Street out of town and watch for the right turn for Cape Meares State Scenic Viewpoint. This road will take you along the shore of Tillamook Bay and around the north side of Cape Meares, where the resort town of Bayocean once stood. Built early in the 20th century by developers with a dream to create the Atlantic City of the West, Bayocean was constructed at the end of a sand spit that often felt the full force of winter storms. When Bayocean homes began falling into the ocean, folks realized that this wasn't going to be the next Atlantic City. Today there's no sign of the town, but the long sandy beach along the spit is a great place for a walk and a bit of bird-watching.

Just around the tip of the cape, you'll come to **Cape Meares State Scenic Viewpoint,** which is the site of the **Cape Meares Lighthouse.** April through October, the lighthouse is open daily from 11am to 4pm. The views from atop this rocky headland are superb. Continuing around the cape, you come to the residential community of **Oceanside,** from where you have an excellent view of the **Three Arch Rocks** just offshore. The beach at Oceanside is a popular spot and is often protected from the wind in the summer. At the north end of the beach, a pedestrian tunnel leads under a headland to a secluded beach.

Three miles south of Oceanside, you'll come to tiny **Netarts Bay,** which is known for its excellent clamming and crabbing. Continuing south, you come to **Cape Lookout State Park ★★** (© 503/842-4981; www.oregon.gov/oprd/parks), which has a campground, picnic areas, beaches, and several miles of hiking trails. The most breathtaking trail leads 2.5 miles out to the end of Cape Lookout, where, from several hundred feet above the ocean, you can often spot gray whales in the spring and fall. There is a $5 day-use fee here.

Cape Kiwanda ★★, which lies just outside the town of Pacific City, is the last of the three capes and is preserved as Cape Kiwanda State Natural Area. At the foot of the cape's sandstone cliffs, you'll find sand dunes and tide pools, and it's possible to scramble up a huge sand dune to the top of the cape for dramatic views of this rugged piece of shoreline. At the base of the cape is the staging area for Pacific City's beach-launched dory fleet. These flat-bottomed commercial fishing boats are launched from the beach and plow through crashing breakers to get out to calmer waters beyond. When the day's fishing is done, the dories roar into shore at full throttle and come to a grinding stop as high up on the beach as they can. This is Oregon's only such fishing fleet and is celebrated each year during the annual Dory Days Festival on the third weekend in July. If you'd like to go out in one of these dories and fish for salmon or albacore tuna, contact **Haystack Fishing** (© **866/965-7555** or 503/965-7555; www.haystackfishing.com), which charges $180 per person (two-person minimum) for a day of fishing. Trips are offered June through September.

WHERE TO STAY
In Pacific City
Inn at Cape Kiwanda ★★ 🛍️ Although it's across the street from the beach (and Cape Kiwanda State Natural Area), this modern, cedar-shingled, three-story hotel has one of the best views on the Oregon coast: Directly offshore rises Haystack Rock, a huge jug-handled monolith. Since a great view isn't quite enough, the hotel was designed with contemporary rooms, all of which have balconies and fireplaces. A few have whirlpool tubs, and there is also a very luxurious suite. The corner rooms are my favorites. The inn also rents out modern fractional-ownership cottages that are right on the beach. The inn is affiliated with the Pelican Pub & Brewery (see below), which is right across the street, and on the inn's ground floor there is an art gallery and an espresso bar.

33105 Cape Kiwanda Dr., Pacific City, OR 97135. www.innatcapekiwanda.com. © **888/965-7001** or 503/965-7001. Fax 503/965-7002. 35 units. $139–$329 double; $229–$359 suite. 2-night minimum on holidays, and on weekends July–Aug. Children 18 and under stay free in parent's room. AE, DISC, MC, V. Pets accepted ($20). **Amenities:** 2 restaurants; lounge; bikes; concierge; exercise room. *In room:* TV/DVD, CD player, fridge, hair dryer, free Wi-Fi.

WHERE TO EAT
In Oceanside
Roseanna's Oceanside Cafe SEAFOOD/INTERNATIONAL Roseanna's is such a Scenic Loop legend that people come from miles around to eat here and don't seem to mind the dated decor or the long waits to get a table. What lures them are the views of the beach and offshore rocks, and the selection of big desserts. Appetizers and entrees often seem to be just an afterthought. Lunch prices are reasonable, with such offerings as cioppino and oyster sandwiches. At dinner, entrees include a shellfish or fish offering with a choice of sauces (ginger-lime butter, lemon-herb butter, or aioli, for example). The wait for a table can be long, so if you just want dessert or a quick snack, grab a stool at the counter.

1490 Pacific Ave. © **503/842-7351.** www.roseannascafe.com. Reservations not accepted. Main courses $7–$13 lunch, $15–$30 dinner. MC, V. Summer daily 9am–9pm; call for hours other months.

In Pacific City
For tasty baked goods and lunches, stop in at **The Grateful Bread Bakery & Restaurant,** 34805 Brooten Rd. (© **503/965-7337**), with tables both inside and outside on a deck. If you're in need of good coffee, stop by **Stimulus Espresso Cafe,** 33105 Cape Kiwanda Dr. (© **503/965-4661;** www.stimuluscafe.com), which is located on the ground floor of the Inn at Cape Kiwanda.

Pelican Pub & Brewery ★ PUB FOOD With massive Haystack Rock looming just offshore and the huge dune of Cape Kiwanda just up the beach, this oceanfront brewpub claims the best view of any pub in Oregon. There's a good selection of brews, including Tsunami Stout and, my personal favorite, the Doryman's Dark Ale.

187

Sandwiches, burgers, great fish and chips, and pizzas are the menu mainstays here. Kids are welcome, and the beach location makes this a great spot for lunch or dinner if you're hanging out on the beach all day.

33180 Cape Kiwanda Dr. (② **503/965-7007.** www.pelicanbrewery.com. Main courses $12–$24. AE, DISC, MC, V. Sun–Thurs 8am–10pm; Fri–Sat 8am–11pm.

The Riverhouse AMERICAN   This tiny place is built on the banks of the Nestucca River and has great river views out its many windows. With its casual, friendly atmosphere, The Riverhouse has the feel of a place that time and contemporary fads have passed by. Although burgers and sandwiches are the order of the day at lunch, the dinner menu features prawns in a creamy wine sauce; fresh fish amandine; halibut basted with butter, lemon pepper, and dill; filet mignon; and crepes Florentine.

34450 Brooten Rd. (② **503/965-6722.** www.riverhousefoods.com. Main courses $8–$29. DISC, MC, V. Summer daily 11am–9pm; other months Wed–Thurs and Sun 11am–8pm, Fri–Sat 11am–9pm.

Neskowin

The quaint community of Neskowin is nestled at the northern foot of Cascade Head, 12 miles north of Lincoln City. Inland families have spent their summers in these tiny cottages along tree-lined lanes for decades. Quiet vacations are the norm in Neskowin, where you'll find only condominiums and rental houses. The beach is accessible at **Neskowin Beach State Recreation Site,** which faces Proposal Rock, a tree-covered haystack rock bordered by Neskowin Creek. On the beach, keep an eye out for the stumps of trees that died hundreds of years ago when an earthquake lowered the shoreline in this area.

If you're interested in art, check out the **Hawk Creek Gallery,** 48460 U.S. 101 S. (② **503/392-3879;** www.michaelschlicting.com), which features the paintings of Michael Schlicting, a master watercolorist.

Just to the south of Neskowin is rugged, unspoiled **Cascade Head.** Rising 1,770 feet above sea level, this is one of the highest headlands on the coast. Lush forests of Sitka spruce and windswept cliff-top meadows thrive here and are home to such diverse flora and fauna that the Nature Conservancy purchased much of the headland. Trails onto Cascade Head start about 2 miles south of Neskowin. The Nature Conservancy's preserve has been set aside primarily to protect the habitat of the rare Oregon silverspot butterfly; the upper trail is closed from January 1 to July 15 due to the timing of the butterflies' life cycle. However, a lower trail, reached from Three Rocks Road (park at Knight Park and walk up Savage Rd. to the trail head), is open year-round.

On the south side of Cascade Head, you'll find the **Sitka Center for Art and Ecology,** P.O. Box 65, Otis, OR 97368 (② **541/994-5485;** www.sitkacenter.org), which runs classes and workshops on writing, painting, ecology, ceramics, and other topics.

WHERE TO STAY

There are numerous vacation cottages and beach houses for rent in Neskowin. Contact **Sea View Vacation Rentals,** 6340 Pacific Ave. (P.O. Box 1049), Pacific City, OR 97135 (② **888/701-1023** or 503/965-7888; www.seaview4u.com), or **Grey Fox Vacation Rentals,** P.O. Box 364, Neskowin, OR 97149 (② **888/720-2154** or 503/392-4850; www.oregoncoast.com/greyfox).

LINCOLN CITY & GLENEDEN BEACH

88 miles SW of Portland, 44 miles S of Tillamook, 25 miles N of Newport

Lincoln City is the Oregon coast's number-one family destination, and despite the name, it is not really a city at all. It's a collection of five small towns that grew together over the years and now stretch for miles along the coast. Today there's no specific downtown, and though there may be more motel rooms here than anywhere else on the Oregon coast, there's little to distinguish most of the thousands of rooms. However, families looking for a long beach and steady winds for flying kites will likely enjoy Lincoln City. Motel rates here, though often high for what you get, are generally better than those in beach towns that are longer on charm. You'll also find an abundance of vacation homes for rent here. Likewise, restaurants catering to big families and small pocketbooks are the norm. Such restaurants purvey hot meals rather than haute cuisine, and you can eat your fill of seafood (usually deep-fried) without going broke.

Once referred to as "20 miracle miles," the stretch of the Oregon coast from Otis to Depoe Bay, which includes Lincoln City, is no longer the miracle it once was. Miracle miles have become congested sprawl, and a summer weekend in Lincoln City can mean coping with bumper-to-bumper traffic. Not surprisingly, many have come to think of this as "20 miserable miles" (although the traffic congestion really only stretches for 5 miles or so). If at all possible, come during the week or during the off season to avoid the crowds.

Once you get off U.S. 101, though, Lincoln City has neighborhoods as charming as any on the coast, and at the south end of town, in the Taft District, the city has been working hard to bring back a historical character and provide an attractive, pedestrian-friendly area. In Gleneden Beach, just south of Lincoln City, you'll find the coast's most prestigious resort, while just north of town, in an area known as Road's End, you'll find a long, uncrowded beach with spectacular views to the north. Also in the Lincoln City area are some of Oregon's best art galleries and some interesting artists' studios.

Essentials

GETTING THERE Ore. 22 from Salem merges with Ore. 18 before reaching the junction with U.S. 101. From Portland, take Ore. 99W to McMinnville and then head west on Ore. 18.

VISITOR INFORMATION For more information on the area, contact the **Lincoln City Visitor and Convention Bureau,** 540 NE U.S. 101, Lincoln City, OR 97367 (© **800/452-2151** or 541/996-1274; www.oregoncoast.org).

FESTIVALS Annual **kite festivals** include the Summer Kite Festival in late June and the Fall Kite Festival in early to mid-October. In addition, Lincoln City has an annual **Sandcastle Building Contest** each year in early August. On the nearby Siletz Indian Reservation, the **Nesika Illahee,** the annual Siletz Pow Wow, takes place on the second weekend in August.

Enjoying the Beach & the Outdoors

Lincoln City's 7½-mile-long **beach** is its main attraction. However, cold waters and constant breezes conspire to make swimming a pursuit for Polar Bear Club members only. The winds, on the other hand, make this beach the best kite-flying spot on the Oregon coast. Among the better beach-access points are the D River State Wayside, on the south side of the river, and the Road's End State Wayside, up at the north end of Lincoln City. Road's End is also a good place to explore some tide pools. You'll find more tide pools on the beach at NW 15th Street.

Adding to the appeal of Lincoln City's beach is **Devil's Lake,** which drains across the beach by way of the D River, the world's shortest river. Formerly called Devil's River, the D River is only 120 feet long, flowing from the outlet of Devil's Lake, under U.S. 101, and across the beach to the Pacific Ocean. Boating, sailing, water-skiing, windsurfing, swimming, fishing, and camping are all popular Devil's Lake activities. Access points on the west side of the lake include **Devil's Lake State Recreation Area (West),** 1452 NE Sixth Drive (© **541/994-2002;** www.oregonstateparks.org), which has a campground, and **Regatta Grounds Park,** which is off West Devil's Lake Road and has a boat ramp and picnic tables. On the east side, you'll find the **East Devil's Lake day-use area** 2 miles east on East Devil's Lake Road, and **Sand Point Park** on NE Loop Drive near the north end of NE East Devil's Lake Road. Both of these parks have picnic tables and swimming areas. If you don't have your own boat, you can rent canoes, kayaks, paddleboats, and various motorboats at **Blue Heron Landing,** 4006 W. Devil's Lake Rd. (© **541/994-4708;** www.blueheron landing.net). Rates range from $12 an hour for a kayak to $140 for a 2-hour motor-boat rental.

If you're a gardener or enjoy visiting public gardens, schedule time to visit the **Connie Hansen Garden,** 1931 NW 33rd St. (© **541/994-6338;** www.connie hansengarden.com). This cottage garden was created over a 20-year period and abounds in primroses, irises, and rhododendrons, making it a great place to visit in the spring. The gardens are open daily from dawn to dusk. Call for directions.

Golfers have two options. The top choice is the Scottish-inspired (though solidly Northwestern in character) **Salishan Golf Links** ★, 7760 U.S. 101, Gleneden Beach (© **541/764-3632;** www.salishan.com), which charges $79 to $119 for 18 holes. This resort course is a longtime Oregon coast favorite. The town's other main course is the **Chinook Winds Golf Resort,** 3245 NE 50th St. (© **541/994-8442;** www.chinookwindscasino.com), which is affiliated with Chinook Winds Casino. This course charges $40 to $55 for 18 holes (with a cart).

If you want to challenge the waves, you can rent a wetsuit, surfboard, or body board down at the south end of town at the **Lincoln City Surf Shop,** 4792 SE U.S. 101 (© **541/996-7433;** www.lcsurfshop.com), or the **Oregon Surf Shop,** 3001 SW U.S. 101 (© **877/339-5672;** www.oregonsurfshop.com).

Hikers should head inland approximately 10 miles to **Drift Creek Falls Trail** ★, which leads through coastal forest to a 240-foot-long suspension bridge above a 75-foot-tall waterfall. From the bridge you have a bird's-eye view not only of the falls but of the treetops as well. It's a 1.3-mile hike to the bridge, and the route is moderately difficult. To find the trail head (Northwest Forest Pass is required), head east from U.S. 101 on Drift Creek Road, which is just north of Salishan Lodge at the south end of Lincoln City. Turn right onto South Drift Creek Road and then left onto Forest Road 17 (not Anderson Creek Rd.), and continue 10 miles on this single-lane road.

Sharing a name with this hiking trail is a historic covered bridge—the **Drift Creek Bridge,** a 66-foot-long covered bridge that was built in 1933. In 2000 the bridge was moved and reconstructed at its current location in a privately owned park that is open

Each year between mid-October and Memorial Day, Lincoln City hides more than 2,000 art-glass balls, similar to the much-prized Japanese handblown glass fishing floats that sometimes drift ashore on this coast. Look above the high-tide line for the colorful globes of glass. Some are hidden each week.

to the public. To find the bridge, drive east from Lincoln City on Ore. 18; at milepost 4.9, turn south onto Bear Creek Road, and continue 1 mile to the bridge.

Indoor Pursuits

These days the hottest thing in town is the **Chinook Winds Casino Resort,** 1777 NW 44th St. (𝒸 **888/244-6665** or 541/996-5825; www.chinookwindscasino.com), a massive casino run by the Confederated Tribes of Siletz Indians and located right on the beach at the north end of town. The casino offers blackjack, poker, slot machines, keno, and bingo. There's plenty of cheap food, as well as a video-game room for the kids. Big-name entertainers help attract folks who might not otherwise consider visiting a casino.

You can catch live music at **Eden Hall,** 6645 Gleneden Beach Loop Rd., Gleneden Beach (𝒸 **541/764-3826;** www.edenhall.com), a big club and restaurant just south of the Salishan Lodge.

The casino may actually be second in popularity to the **Tanger Outlet Center,** 1500 SE E. Devil's Lake Rd. (𝒸 **541/996-5000;** www.tangeroutlet.com), which is on the corner of U.S. 101.

Lincoln City has a surprising number of interesting art galleries and artists' studios. At the north end of town, the first gallery you'll come to is the **Ryan Gallery,** 4270 N. U.S. 101 (𝒸 **541/994-5391;** www.ryanartgallery.com). South of Lincoln City proper, you'll find the impressive **Freed Gallery,** 6119 SW U.S. 101 (𝒸 **541/994-5600;** www.freedgallery.com), which has an excellent selection of art glass and ceramic work, as well as sculpture and paintings in a wide variety of styles. Just off U.S. 101, north of Salishan Lodge, you'll find **Alderhouse Glass,** 611 Immonen Rd. (𝒸 **541/994-6485;** www.alderhouse.com), the oldest glassblowing studio in Oregon. The shop and studio are open daily from 10am to 5pm between mid-March and Thanksgiving weekend. Nearby you'll also find **Mossy Creek Pottery,** 483 S. Immonen Rd. (𝒸 **541/996-2415;** www.mossycreekpottery.com), with an eclectic selection of porcelain and stoneware by Oregon potters.

Where to Stay

In addition to the town's many hotels and motels, Lincoln City has plenty of vacation rental houses and apartments offering good deals, especially for families. For information, contact **Horizon Rentals** (𝒸 **800/995-2411** or 541/994-2226; www.horizon-rentals.com) or **Pacific Retreats** (𝒸 **800/473-4833** or 541/994-4833; www.pacific retreats.com). Rates generally range from around $75 to $250 nightly for houses for 4 to 12 people.

EXPENSIVE

Salishan Spa & Golf Resort ★★★ ☺ The largest resort on the coast, Salishan is nestled amid towering evergreens on a hillside at the south end of Siletz Bay.

However, because the resort is almost half a mile from the beach and on the inland side of U.S. 101, it's more of a golf resort and spa than a traditional beach resort. An extensive network of walking paths meanders through the 760-acre grounds, and there are plenty of activities for kids. Guest rooms come in three sizes. Whichever size you opt for, try to get a second-floor room; most of these have cathedral ceilings and stone fireplaces. For breathtaking views, you'll have to shell out top dollar for a deluxe or premier room. The Salishan Dining Room is one of the most upscale restaurants on the entire coast and has a superb wine collection.

7760 U.S. 101 N., Gleneden Beach, OR 97388. www.salishan.com. ℂ **800/452-2300** or 541/764-3600. 205 units. $160–$230 double. Children 16 and under stay free in parent's room. AE, DISC, MC, V. Pets accepted ($35). **Amenities:** 4 restaurants; 2 lounges; exercise room and access to nearby health club; 18-hole golf course; Jacuzzi; indoor pool; room service; sauna; spa; 3 tennis courts. *In room:* TV, fridge, hair dryer, Wi-Fi ($5 per night).

Starfish Manor Hotel ★ This modern inn is located in a quiet neighborhood at the north end of Lincoln City, away from the crowds and traffic, which gives it one of the best locations in town as far as I'm concerned. Large suites with gas fireplaces, two-person oceanview whirlpool tubs, and double-headed showers are perfect for romantic getaways. My favorite suites have their whirlpool tubs out on the balcony, where you can listen to the crashing waves. This hotel is also affiliated with the nearby Nelscott Manor, Nantucket Inn, and the Beachfront Manor Hotel, all of which are equally good options.

2735 NW Inlet Ave., Lincoln City, OR 97367. www.onthebeachfront.com. ℂ **800/972-6155** or 541/996-9300. 17 units. $159–$425 suite. AE, DISC, MC, V. No children 12 and under. *In room:* TV/DVD/VCR, hair dryer, kitchen, free Wi-Fi.

MODERATE

Looking Glass Inn ★ Located in the historic Taft District and across the street from Siletz Bay, the Looking Glass, with its cedar shingles and white trim, has a classic Cape Cod feel. Rooms are available with both ocean and bay views, and there are rooms with whirlpool tubs, balconies, or gas fireplaces. While most hotels that claim to be pet-friendly simply tolerate dogs, this hotel welcomes them with a basket with water and food bowls, sheets, towels, and doggy treats.

861 SW 51st St., Lincoln City, OR 97367. www.lookingglass-inn.com. ℂ **800/843-4940** or 541/996-3996. 36 units. July to Labor Day $129–$159 double, $149–$269 suite; Labor Day to June $79–$134 double, $89–$154 suite. Rates include continental breakfast. Children 5 and under stay free in parent's room. AE, DC, DISC, MC, V. Pets accepted ($10 per night). *In room:* TV/DVD, fridge, hair dryer, kitchen (some rooms), free Wi-Fi.

The O'dysius Hotel ★★ This hotel offers the sort of luxury you would expect from a downtown Portland historic hotel, but with a beach right across the street. Traditional European styling dominates, and the lobby, with its antique furniture, has the feel of a very classy living room. It's here that the hotel serves its complimentary afternoon wine. Guest rooms have lots of nice touches, including slate entries, down comforters, Art Nouveau lamps, gas fireplaces, and DVDs. All the rooms have ocean views, and most have balconies. If you enjoy luxury but aren't into the golf-resort scene, this is definitely the place for you. For the best view, ask for a room on the fifth floor.

120 NW Inlet Court, Lincoln City, OR 97367. www.odysius.com. ℂ **800/869-8069** or 541/994-4121. Fax 541/994-8160. 30 units. $109–$149 double; $195–$269 suite. Rates include continental breakfast. DC, DISC, MC, V. Pets accepted ($25 per night). **Amenities:** Concierge; access to nearby health club. *In room:* TV/DVD, hair dryer, kitchen (some rooms), free Wi-Fi.

Siletz Bay Lodge   Located at the south end of Lincoln City right on Siletz Bay, this modern motel is a particularly good choice for families but is also a good option for couples. Although the motel isn't on the ocean, it is on a driftwood-strewn beach that has quiet waters that are perfect for kids, and across the bay you can often see harbor seals lounging on the beach. About half of the standard rooms have balconies. Spa rooms and spa suites are also available if you happen to be in town for a romantic getaway.

1012 SW 51st St. (P.O. Box 952), Lincoln City, OR 97367. www.siletzbaylodge.com. © **888/430-2100** or 541/996-6111. Fax 541/996-3992. 44 units. Summer $128–$165 double, $155 suite; off season $79–$140 double, $130 suite. Rates include continental breakfast. Children 12 and under stay free in parent's room. AE, DC, DISC, MC, V. **Amenities:** Jacuzzi. In room: TV/DVD, fridge, hair dryer, kitchen (some rooms), free Wi-Fi.

Where to Eat

If you're looking for some good smoked salmon or smoked oysters, stop by **Mr. Bill's Village Smokehouse,** 2981 SW U.S. 101 (© **888/672-4557;** www.mrbillsvillage smokehouse.com). For fish tacos, mojitos, and margaritas, don't miss **Tiki's at 51st,** 1005 SW 51st St. (© **541/996-4200;** www.tikisat51st.com), a Polynesian-themed beach shack in the Taft District at the south end of Lincoln City.

EXPENSIVE

Bay House ★★ NORTHWEST   With a big wall of glass overlooking Siletz Bay and Salishan Spit, the Bay House, between Lincoln City and Gleneden Beach, provides fine dining and dramatic sunsets (and good bird-watching, if you're interested). There are snowy linens on the tables, and service is gracious. The menu here is the most creative on the central coast and changes seasonally to take advantage of fresh ingredients. A recent menu included whole quail with arugula–blood orange salad; cod with a beet purée, French lentils, and a pineapple–pea tendril salad; and scallops with preserved kumquats, red mustard, and beurre blanc. Any time of year, however, the crab cakes should not be missed.

5911 SW U.S. 101. © **541/996-3222.** www.thebayhouse.org. Reservations recommended. Main courses $28–$45. AE, DISC, MC, V. Wed–Sun 5:30–9pm.

MODERATE

Blackfish Cafe ★ SEAFOOD   Located near the north end of Lincoln City, this restaurant has a big reputation for such a casual and unpretentious spot. The Dungeness crab cocktail and the local Yaquina Bay oysters on the half shell both make great starters. The menu includes everything from fish and chips to grilled duck breast with a conserve of blackberries and port wine. While dinners here are very good, lunches just might be the best on the entire coast. Lunch or dinner, the house-smoked salmon pasta is a good bet.

2733 NW U.S. 101. © **541/996-1007.** www.blackfishcafe.com. Reservations recommended. Main courses $8.75–$14 lunch, $12–$27 dinner. AE, DISC, MC, V. Wed–Mon 11:30am–9pm.

Kyllo's Seafood Grill SEAFOOD   Providing a lively "beach party" atmosphere on a family-oriented beach, Kyllo's is housed in an architecturally unusual contemporary building with curved walls that make the restaurant impossible to miss. Inside you'll find a big copper fireplace, plenty of deck space, and a facade of glass to take in the view of the D River and the ocean. If all this sounds like you're going to be paying for the atmosphere, think again. Prices are reasonable, and while none of the food is all that memorable, this is still the best oceanfront dining in town. Expect to wait for a table if you come here on a summer evening.

1110 NW First Court. ✆ **541/994-3179.** www.kyllosrestaurant.com. Reservations not accepted. Main courses $8.50–$30. AE, DISC, MC, V. Daily 11:30am–9pm.

Side Door Café ★ NEW AMERICAN Affiliated with Eden Hall, which is one of the premier performing-arts venues on the coast, the Side Door Café is a great, untouristy choice whether you are on your way to a concert or not. The big, high-ceilinged space has a bit of a fern-bar feel, and the menu is sort of counterculture gourmet (good vegetarian options). Soups are good bets, and there are always plenty of fresh seafood dishes on the menu, which changes regularly. Be sure to finish your meal with one of the Side Door's award-winning chocolate desserts. As much as possible, ingredients used here are organic.

6645 Gleneden Beach Loop Rd., Gleneden Beach. ✆ **541/764-3825.** www.sidedoorcafe.com. Reservations recommended. Main courses $8–$14 lunch, $8–$32 dinner. AE, DISC, MC, V. Wed–Mon 11:30am–9pm.

INEXPENSIVE

Right across the street from the Otis Café (below), you'll find another great alternative for a quick bite on the way to or from the beach. **Pronto Pup,** 1252 Salmon River Hwy., Otis (✆ **541/996-4844**), a roadside hot dog stand that opened in 1946, is legendary among Oregonians for its corn dogs. The original Pronto Pup, which, some say, is where the corn dog was invented in 1939, was in the town of Rockaway Beach on the northern Oregon coast. For good breakfasts at the south end of Lincoln City, head to the **Beach Dog Cafe,** 1266 SW 50th St. (✆ **541/996-3647**), which is also well known for its hot dogs and sausages.

Otis Café 🍴 AMERICAN If you've ever seen the determination with which urbanites flock to the beach on summer weekends, you can understand what a feat it is to get cars to stop before they have sand in the treads of their tires. This tiny roadside diner, 5 miles north of Lincoln City and 4 miles shy of the beach, manages to do just that with its black bread, cinnamon rolls, and fried red potatoes. The homemade mustard and salsa are also favorites. Pies—marionberry, strawberry/rhubarb, or walnut—have crusts to be savored only by people unconcerned with cholesterol and are memorable even in a region of numerous perfect pies. Expect a line out the door, even in the rainy season.

1259 Salmon River Hwy. (Ore. 18), Otis. ✆ **541/994-2813.** Main courses $5.25–$14. DISC, MC, V. Daily 7am–8pm.

DEPOE BAY

13 miles S of Lincoln City, 13 miles N of Newport, 70 miles W of Salem

Depoe Bay calls itself the smallest harbor in the world, and though the tiny harbor covers only 6 acres, it's home to more than 100 fishing boats. These boats must all enter the harbor through a narrow rock-walled channel, little more than a crack in the coastline's solid rock wall. During stormy seas, it's almost impossible to get in or out of the harbor safely.

Shell mounds and kitchen middens around the bay indicate that Native Americans long ago called this area home. In 1894, the U.S. government deeded the land surrounding the bay to a Siletz Indian known as Old Charlie Depot, who had taken his name from an army depot at which he had worked. Old Charlie later changed his name to DePoe, and when a town was founded here in 1927, it took the name Depoe Bay. Though most of the town is a bit off the highway, you'll find a row of garish souvenir shops right on U.S. 101, which sadly mar the beauty of this rocky section of coast. Among these shops are several family restaurants and charter-fishing and whale-watching companies.

Essentials

GETTING THERE   From the north, the most direct route is Ore. 99W/18 to Lincoln City, and then south on U.S. 101. From the south, take U.S. 20 from Corvallis to Newport, and then go north on U.S. 101.

VISITOR INFORMATION   Contact the **Depoe Bay Chamber of Commerce,** 223 SW U.S. 101, Ste. B (P.O. Box 21), Depoe Bay, OR 97341 (© **877/485-8348** or 541/765-2889; www.depoebaychamber.org).

FESTIVALS   Memorial Day is time for the **Fleet of Flowers,** during which local boats carry flower wreaths out to sea in memory of loved ones. In mid-September the town holds its annual **Salmon Bake,** which is a great opportunity to enjoy some traditionally prepared salmon. Contact the chamber of commerce for details.

Depoe Bay Activities & Attractions

Aside from standing on the highway bridge watching the boat traffic passing in and out of the world's smallest harbor, the most popular activity here, especially when the seas are high, is watching the **spouting horns** across U.S. 101 from Depoe Bay's souvenir shops. Spouting horns, which are similar to blowholes, can be seen all along the coast, but nowhere are they more spectacular than here. These geyserlike plumes occur in places where water is forced through narrow channels in basalt rock. As the channels become more restricted, the water shoots skyward under great pressure and can spray 60 feet into the air. If the surf is really up, the water can carry quite a ways, and more than a few unwary visitors have been soaked.

Be sure to stop in at Depoe Bay's **Whale Watching Center,** 119 U.S. 101 (© **541/765-3304;** www.oregon.gov/oprd/parks), which is perched on the cliff above the entrance to the harbor. There are displays about whales, and rangers and volunteers are on hand to point out gray whales if they happen to be visible. Memorial Day to Labor Day, the center is open daily from 9am to 5pm; other months, open Wednesday through Saturday from 10am to 4pm and Sunday from noon to 4pm.

At **Fogarty Creek State Recreation Area,** a couple of miles north of Depoe Bay, you'll find a beautiful little cove with basalt cliffs at one end and a creek flowing across the beach. The parking area is on the east side of U.S. 101. **Boiler Bay State Scenic Viewpoint,** a mile north of Depoe Bay, is a good picnic spot from which to look for gray whales. There are also tide pools among the rocks in some small coves here. Although the beach itself is not accessible from the state park pull-off, about midway between Boiler Bay and Fogarty Creek, a mile north of here, there's a trail that leads down to the beach.

South of Depoe Bay, U.S. 101 winds through scenes of rugged splendor, passing several small, picturesque coves. Just south of town, **Rocky Creek State Scenic Viewpoint,** with windswept lawns, picnic tables, and great views of buff-colored cliffs and spouting horns, is a good picnic spot. In a few more miles you'll come to the Otter Crest Scenic Loop, which leads to Cape Foulweather and the **Otter Crest State Scenic Viewpoint.** Named by Capt. James Cook in 1778, the cape was his first glimpse of land after leaving the Sandwich Islands (Hawaii). The cape frequently lives up to its name, with winds often gusting to more than 100 mph. However, the views are quite stupendous. Keep an eye out for the sea lions that sun themselves on offshore rocks near Cape Foulweather. A historic building houses the **Lookout Gift Shop** (© 541/765-2270; www.lookoutgiftshop.com), which provides a protected glimpse of the sea from atop Cape Foulweather.

At the south end of the Otter Crest Scenic Loop, you'll find an overlook at **Devil's Punchbowl State Natural Area** ★★. The overlook provides a glimpse into a collapsed sea cave that during high tides or stormy seas becomes a churning cauldron of foam. Adjacent to Devil's Punchbowl, in a small cove, you'll find numerous tide pools that can be explored at low tide. From this cove, you can also explore inside the Devil's Punchbowl. South of Devil's Punchbowl State Natural Area lies **Beverly Beach State Park** (© 541/265-9278; www.oregon.gov/oprd/parks), which has a large campground and is a popular surfing spot. Here at the Devil's Punchbowl, you'll also find **Mo's Chowder House,** 122 First St., Otter Rock (© 541/765-2442; www.moschowder.com), and the **Flying Dutchman Winery,** 915 First St., Otter Rock (© 541/765-2553; www.dutchmanwinery.com).

If you're interested in **sportfishing** or **whale-watching** ★★, contact **Tradewinds Charters** (© 800/445-8730 or 541/765-2345; www.tradewindscharters.com), at the north end of the bridge, or **Dockside Charters** (© 800/733-8915 or 541/765-2545; www.docksidedepoebay.com), down by the marina. Whale-watching trips run $16 to $35, depending on the type of boat you go out on and how long you stay out. Fishing trips run from $75 for 5 hours to $210 or $250 for a day of tuna fishing.

Where to Stay

Channel House ★★ The Channel House, one of the Oregon coast's most romantic and luxurious boutique hotels, perches dramatically on a cliff above the narrow channel into tiny Depoe Bay. A contemporary building with lots of angles and windows, the Channel House has large rooms, and the gas fireplaces and private decks with whirlpool tubs make it one of the most romantic inns on the coast. You can sit and soak as fishing boats navigate their way through the channel below you.

35 Ellingson St. (P.O. Box 56), Depoe Bay, OR 97341. www.channelhouse.com. © **800/447-2140** or 541/765-2140. Fax 541/765-2191. 12 units. Apr–Oct $100–$330 double; Nov–Mar $100–$250 double. Rates include continental breakfast. AE, DISC, MC, V. Children 16 and over welcome. **Amenities:** Concierge. *In room:* TV/DVD, CD player, fridge, hair dryer, free Wi-Fi.

Inn at Arch Rock 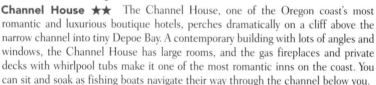 You just won't find a better view from any hotel on the Oregon coast. This collection of renovated Cape Cod–style buildings sits above the cliffs on the north side of Depoe Bay, and you can sit in your room and watch the waves crashing against the rocks. When you want to get your feet wet in the summer, follow the flight of stairs that leads down to a tiny beach. Guest rooms have a simple cottage decor, and some have kitchens or fireplaces. On the lawn overlooking the ocean, you'll find a fire pit, which is a popular gathering spot on summer evenings. The inn is just around the corner from the Tidal Raves restaurant.

70 NW Sunset St. (P.O. Box 1516), Depoe Bay, OR 97341. www.innatarchrock.com. © **800/767-1835** or 541/765-2560. 13 units. $79–$299 double; lower rates in winter. Rates include continental breakfast. Children 12 and under stay free in parent's room. AE, DC, DISC, MC, V. Pets accepted ($10 per night). *In room:* TV/DVD, fridge.

An Ocean Paradise Whales Rendezvous B&B ★★ If you got any closer to the ocean than the Whales Rendezvous, you'd be sleeping with the fishes. As it is, you'll feel as though you have the entire Pacific Ocean to yourself. You can easily sit in your room gazing out to sea for hours, and chances are good that you'll see plenty of whales just offshore. With only two suites, both of which have private entrances and oceanfront outdoor areas, this B&B has a very private feel. With plush beds, fireplaces, comfortable seating areas, and walls of windows, these luxurious accommodations are definitely made for romantic getaways. In winter the storm watching here is the best in the state.

147 NW U.S. 101, Depoe Bay, OR 97341. www.whalesrendezvous.com. ☎ **541/765-3455.** 2 units. $365–$385 suite. Discounts for stays of 2 or more nights. Rates include full breakfast. AE, DISC, MC, V. *In room:* TV/DVD, CD player, hair dryer, kitchen, free Wi-Fi.

The Surfrider Though it has been around for many years and is nothing fancy, this low-rise motel, just north of Depoe Bay, claims an enviable location and view and has long been a family favorite. It's hidden from the highway, which gives it a secluded feel, and great views unfold from the open bluff-top setting. You can choose between basic motel rooms and rooms with fireplaces, kitchens, or whirlpool tubs. At the foot of a long staircase is the wide beach of Fogarty Creek State Recreation Area, which is on a pretty little cove. The dining room and lounge have great views of this cove.

3115 NW U.S. 101, Depoe Bay, OR 97341. www.surfriderresort.com. ☎ **800/662-2378** or 541/764-2311. Fax 541/764-4634. 55 units. Late June to early Sept $109–$159 double, $149–$199 suite; mid-Mar to late June and early Sept to mid-Oct $89–$129 double, $109–$159 suite; mid-Oct to mid-Mar $69–$109 double, $94–$139 suite. Children 11 and under stay free in parent's room. AE, DISC, MC, V. **Amenities:** Restaurant; lounge; exercise room; Jacuzzi; indoor pool; sauna; free Wi-Fi. *In room:* TV/DVD, fridge, hair dryer.

Whale Cove Inn ★★★ Quite simply, there is nothing else like this boutique inn anywhere on the Oregon coast. Looking like it could have been transported directly from Malibu, the Whale Cove Inn is the most sophisticated and contemporary small inn on the coast. Huge rooms with king-size Tempur-Pedic beds, gas fireplaces, and outdoor Jacuzzis on private decks are exquisitely sumptuous and romantic. That the inn also has what just might be the most jaw-dropping view on the coast seems only befitting of such luxury. Be sure to keep an eye out for harbor seals, bald eagles, and whales. As befits such an inn, the dining room is the finest on the coast. If you can afford a room here, you will experience the best that Oregon's shore has to offer.

2345 S. U.S. 101, Depoe Bay, OR 97341. www.whalecoveinn.net. ☎ **800/628-3409** or 541/765-4300. Fax 541/765-3409. 8 units. $395–$795 suite; lower rates in winter. 2-night minimum on holidays. Rates include continental breakfast. AE, DISC, MC, V. Children 16 and over welcome. **Amenities:** Restaurant (Beck; see below); concierge. *In room:* TV/DVD, CD player, fridge, hair dryer, free Wi-Fi.

Where to Eat

If you're in need of a pick-me-up while passing through Depoe Bay, stop by the **Pirate Coffee Company,** 10 Vista St. (☎ **541/765-4373;** www.piratecoffeecompany.com).

Beck ★★★ NORTHWEST Located on the ground floor of the luxurious Whale Cove Inn, this sophisticated restaurant boasts one of the most spectacular settings of any restaurant on the Oregon coast. The menu is short and changes almost daily to take advantage of fresh seasonal ingredients. Chef Justin Wills, a graduate of the Culinary Institute of America in Hyde Park, New York, prepares some of the most memorable and unusual meals on the Oregon coast. This place is a foodie's paradise. Expect to find such dishes as pork belly and pork tenderloin with sweet-corn ice cream, arugula, and dauphine-style potatoes (airy potato dumplings); stinging-nettle pasta with ham-hock broth and Japanese-style eel; and scallops with cucumber, green almond, pea shoots, pink peppercorns, rhubarb pickle, and spring pea broth.

At Whale Cove Inn, 2345 S. US. 101. 🕿 **541/765-3220.** www.restaurantbeck.com. Reservations recommended. Main courses $26–$31. AE, DISC, MC, V. Daily 5–9pm.

Tidal Raves ★★ 🍴 SEAFOOD   With a tasteful modern decor and big windows for taking in the wave-carved sandstone cliffs outside, Tidal Raves, located at the north end of Depoe Bay's strip of tourist shops, is the most dramatically situated restaurant on the Oregon coast. This place has had folks raving for years now, and on days when the surf's up, it's hard to take your eyes off the wave-pounded cliffs outside the window and concentrate on your food. The menu offers plenty of straightforward seafood (razor clams are a good bet), but it also includes some creative preparations such as green curry with halibut, seafood linguine with a choice of sauces, and Thai barbecued shrimp. For light eaters, entrees are available a la carte.

279 NW U.S. 101. 🕿 **541/765-2995.** www.tidalraves.com. Reservations recommended. Main courses $8–$24. AE, MC, V. Daily 11am–9pm.

NEWPORT ★★

23 miles S of Lincoln City, 58 miles W of Corvallis, 24 miles N of Yachats

As Oregon coast towns go, Newport has a split personality. Dockworkers unloading fresh fish mingle with vacationers licking ice-cream cones, and both fishing boats and pleasure craft ply the waters of the bay. The air smells of fish and shrimp, and free-loading sea lions doze on the docks while they wait for their next meal. Directly across the street, art galleries and souvenir shops stand side by side. Across Yaquina Bay from the waterfront, you'll find the Oregon Coast Aquarium (the coast's top tourist attraction) and the Hatfield Marine Science Center. If you're looking for a balance of the old and the new on the Oregon coast, Newport is the place.

Newport got its start in the late 1800s as both an oystering community and one of the earliest Oregon beach resorts, and many of the old cottages and historic buildings can still be seen in the town's Nye Beach neighborhood. Although Nye Beach has the feel of a 19th-century resort, the downtown bayfront is, despite its souvenir shops, galleries, and restaurants, still a working port and home to the largest commercial fishing fleet on the Oregon coast. Oysters are also still important to the local economy and are raised in oyster beds along Yaquina Bay Road, east of town.

Though in recent years it has come close to matching the overdevelopment of Lincoln City, this fishing port on the shore of Yaquina Bay still manages to offer a balance of industry, history, culture, beaches, and family attractions.

Essentials

GETTING THERE   Newport is on U.S. 101 at the junction with U.S. 20, which leads to Corvallis.

VISITOR INFORMATION   Contact the **Greater Newport Chamber of Commerce,** 555 SW Coast Hwy., Newport, OR 97365 (🕿 **800/262-7844** or 541/265-8801; www.newportchamber.org).

FESTIVALS   In February there's the **Seafood and Wine Festival;** contact the Newport Chamber of Commerce for information.

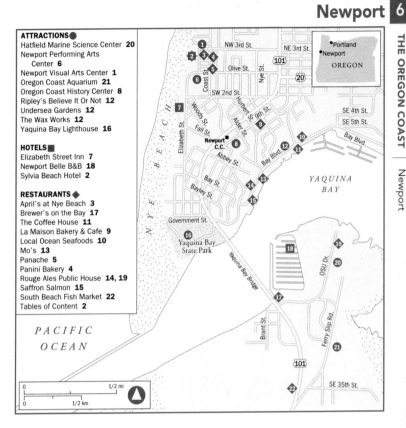

ATTRACTIONS●
Hatfield Marine Science Center **20**
Newport Performing Arts
   Center **6**
Newport Visual Arts Center **1**
Oregon Coast Aquarium **21**
Oregon Coast History Center **8**
Ripley's Believe It Or Not **12**
Undersea Gardens **12**
The Wax Works **12**
Yaquina Bay Lighthouse **16**

HOTELS■
Elizabeth Street Inn **7**
Newport Belle B&B **18**
Sylvia Beach Hotel **2**

RESTAURANTS◆
April's at Nye Beach **3**
Brewer's on the Bay **17**
The Coffee House **11**
La Maison Bakery & Cafe **9**
Local Ocean Seafoods **10**
Mo's **13**
Panache **5**
Panini Bakery **4**
Rouge Ales Public House **14, 19**
Saffron Salmon **15**
South Beach Fish Market **22**
Tables of Content **2**

PACIFIC
OCEAN

YAQUINA
BAY

0   1/2 mi
0   1/2 km

Fins & Flippers

Hatfield Marine Science Center Visitor Center ★ ☺   This facility, though primarily a university research center, also contains displays that are open to the public. Exhibits are not as impressive as those at the Oregon Coast Aquarium, but they do highlight current topics in marine research and include an octopus aquarium and a touch tank. Interpretive exhibits explain life in the sea. It's a worthwhile adjunct to a visit to the Oregon Coast Aquarium.

2030 SE Marine Science Dr. ⓒ **541/867-0226.** http://hmsc.oregonstate.edu. Admission by suggested $5 donation. Memorial Day to Labor Day daily 10am–5pm; Labor Day to Memorial Day Thurs–Mon 10am–4pm.

Oregon Coast Aquarium ★★★ ☺   Considered one of the top aquariums in the country, the Oregon Coast Aquarium focuses primarily on sea life native to the Oregon coast. There are so many fascinating displays here that it's easy to spend the better part of a day enjoying the many exhibits. The stars are the playful sea otters, but the clown-faced tufted puffins, which are kept in a walk-through aviary, are big favorites as well. The sea lions sometimes rouse from their naps to put on impromptu shows, and the lucky visitor even gets a glimpse of a giant octopus with an arm span of nearly 20 feet. Artificial waves surge in a tank that reproduces, on a speeded-up scale, life in a rocky intertidal zone. And so far, you haven't even made it to the indoor displays. One of the most fascinating exhibits here is a walk-through deep-sea shark tank featuring a 200-foot-long acrylic walkway. There are examples of sandy beaches, rocky shores, salt marshes, kelp forests, and the open ocean. Because this is the most popular attraction on the Oregon coast, lines to get in can be very long. Arrive early if you're visiting on a summer weekend.

2820 SE Ferry Slip Rd. © **541/867-3474.** www.aquarium.org. Admission $16 adults, $14 seniors and children 13–17, $9.95 children 3–12. Memorial Day to Labor Day daily 9am–6pm; Labor Day to Memorial Day daily 10am–5pm.

Seeing the Lights

Newport is home to two historic lighthouses, which are just 3 miles apart. The **Yaquina Bay Lighthouse** began operation in 1871, but in 1874 was replaced by the **Yaquina Head Lighthouse.** The latter was supposed to be built on Cape Foulweather, farther to the north, but heavy seas made it impossible to land there. Instead the light was built on Yaquina Head, and so powerful was the light that it supplanted the one at Yaquina Bay.

At 93 feet tall, the **Yaquina Head Lighthouse,** 3 miles north of Newport and still a functioning light, is the tallest lighthouse on the Oregon coast. The lighthouse lies within the **Yaquina Head Outstanding Natural Area** (© **541/574-3100;** www. blm.gov/or/resources/recreation/yaquina/index.php), and adjacent to the lighthouse, you'll find the **Yaquina Head Interpretive Center,** which houses displays covering everything from the life of lighthouse keepers and their families to the sea life of tide pools. Cormorants and pigeon guillemots can be seen roosting on the steep slopes, and harbor seals lounge on the rocks. In early winter and spring, you may spot gray whales migrating along the coast. On the cobblestone beach below the lighthouse, you can explore tide pools at low tide, and there is even a wheelchair-accessible tidepool trail in a cove that was the site of a rock quarry. In summer the interpretive center is open daily from 9am to 5pm, and the lighthouse is open daily from 11am to 4pm (call for hours in other months). Admission to Yaquina Head is $7 per car.

The older of the two lighthouses, **Yaquina Bay Lighthouse** is now part of **Yaquina Bay State Recreation Site,** 846 SW Government St. (© **800/551-6949;** www.oregon.gov/oprd/parks), which can be found just north and west of the Yaquina Bay Bridge. This 1871 lighthouse is the oldest building in Newport, and it is unusual in that the light is in a tower atop a two-story wood-frame house. The building served as both home and lighthouse, and supposedly is haunted. The lighthouse is open from Memorial Day weekend to the end of September daily from 11am to 5pm; from October to Memorial Day weekend, it's open daily from noon to 4pm. Entrance is free. For more information on both of these lighthouses, visit **www.yaquinalights.org**.

Beaches

Beaches in the Newport area range from tiny rocky coves to long, wide stretches of sand perfect for kite flying. Right in town, north and west of the Yaquina Bay Bridge, you'll find **Yaquina Bay State Recreation Site,** which borders on both the ocean and the bay. North of Newport is **Agate Beach,** which was once known for the beautiful agates that could be found there. However, sand now covers the formerly

If you haven't had any luck finding a glass float along the Oregon coast, how about blowing one of your own? You've got a couple of options on the central coast. At the **Jennifer Sears Glass Art Studio**, 4821 SW U.S. 101 ((C) **541/996-2569;** www.jennifersearsglassart.com), which is at the south end of Lincoln City in the Taft District, you can try your hand (actually, your lungs) at blowing a glass float. These glass-blowing classes cost $65, and you'll need to make an appointment. You can also take a glass-blowing class at **The Edge Art Gallery**, 3916 S. Coast Hwy., South Beach ((C) **541/867-4198;** www.theedgeartgallery.com), which is located a half-mile south of the Yaquina Bay Bridge in Newport.

rocky beach, hiding the stones from rock hunters. This beach has a stunning view of Yaquina Head. Two miles south of Newport, you'll find **South Beach State Park** ((C) **541/867-4715;** www.oregon.gov/oprd/parks), a wide sandy beach with picnic areas and a large campground (that also rents yurts).

Six miles south of Newport is **Ona Beach State Park,** a sandy beach with a picnic area under the trees. Beaver Creek, a fairly large stream, flows through the park and across the beach to the ocean. During the summer, the state park offers guided kayak tours on Beaver Creek. For information or reservations, call (C) **541/867-6590.** Another 2 miles south will bring you to **Seal Rock State Recreation Site,** where a long wall of rock rises from the waves and sand and creates numerous tide pools and fascinating nooks and crannies to explore.

The Bayfront

The Bayfront is tourist central for Newport. Here you'll find ice-cream parlors, salt-water-taffy stores, chowder houses, and souvenir shops. The Bayfront is also home to commercial fishermen, seafood processing plants, and art galleries, and in its waters are numerous sea lions, which love to sleep on the floating docks adjacent to Undersea Gardens. From the adjacent pier, you can observe the sea lions at close range. Their bickering and barking make for great free entertainment.

As one of the coast's most popular family-vacation spots, Newport has all the tourist traps one would expect. Billboards up and down the coast advertise the sorts of places that kids have to visit. Tops on this list are **Ripley's Believe It or Not!** and **The Wax Works.** Across the street from these you'll find **Undersea Gardens,** where a scuba diver feeds fish in a large tank beneath a boat moored on the Bayfront. All three attractions are on the Bayfront and share the same address and phone number: **Mariner Square,** 250 SW Bay Blvd. ((C) **541/265-2206;** www.marinersquare. com). Admission for each is $12 for adults and $7 for children 5 to 12, or $24 for adults and $14 for children to visit all three attractions.

The Bayfront is also the place to arrange **whale-watching tours** and **fishing trips.** Two-hour whale-watching tours are given throughout the year by **Marine Discovery Tours,** 345 SW Bay Blvd. ((C) **800/903-2628** or 541/265-6200; www. marinediscovery.com), which charges $36 for adults, $34 for seniors, and $18 for kids ages 4 to 13. You can charter a fishing boat on the Bayfront at **Newport Tradewinds,** 653 SW Bay Blvd. ((C) **800/676-7819** or 541/265-2101; www.newporttradewinds. com). Salmon, tuna, halibut, and bottom fish can all be caught off the coast here depending on the season. Fishing trips cost anywhere from $69 to $185.

Nye Beach

Newport was one of the earliest beach vacation destinations in Oregon, and it was in Nye Beach that the first hotels and vacation cottages were built. Today this neighborhood, north of the Yaquina Bay Bridge along the beach, is slowly being renovated and has both historic and hip hotels, good restaurants, some interesting shops, and, of course, miles of sandy beach. There's public parking at the turnaround on Beach Drive.

The works of local and regional artists are showcased at the **Newport Visual Arts Center,** 777 NW Beach Dr. (© **541/265-6540;** www.coastarts.org). The center is open Tuesday through Sunday from 11am to 6pm. Just a few blocks away, the **Newport Performing Arts Center,** 777 W. Olive St. (© **541/265-2787;** www.coast arts.org), hosts local and nationally recognized performers.

Other Newport Activities & Attractions

If you'd like to delve into local history, stop by the **Oregon Coast History Center,** 545 SW Ninth St. (© **541/265-7509;** www.oregoncoast.history.museum), which consists of two historic buildings—the Burrows House and the Log Cabin. The Burrows House was built in 1895 as a boardinghouse and now contains exhibits of Victorian household furnishings and fashions. The Log Cabin houses Siletz Indian artifacts from the area, as well as exhibits on logging, farming, and maritime history. The Burrows House is open Tuesday to Saturday from 11am to 4pm, while the Log Cabin is open Thursday to Saturday from 11am to 4pm. Admission is by suggested $2 donation.

Take a drive east from the bayfront along scenic Yaquina Bay Road, and you'll come to **Toledo,** a small town that is something of an art community. In downtown Toledo, you'll find several artists' studios and galleries. For more information, contact the **Toledo Chamber of Commerce** (© **541/336-3183;** www.visittoledooregon.com).

Where to Stay

EXPENSIVE

Starfish Point ★★   Located north of town in a grove of fir trees on the edge of a cliff, the Starfish Point condominiums, although a bit dated in their decor, are among my favorite rooms in the area. Each of the six condos has two bedrooms and two baths spaced over two floors. Between the two floors you'll find a cozy sitting area in an octagonal room that's almost all windows. This little sunroom is in addition to the spacious living room with a fireplace and stereo. The bathrooms here are extravagant, with two-person whirlpool tubs and skylights or big windows. A path leads down to the beach, and to the north is Yaquina Head, one of the coast's most dramatic headlands.

140 NW 48th St., Newport, OR 97365. www.starfishpoint.com. © **800/870-7795** or 541/265-3751. Fax 541/265-3040. 6 units. $200–$225 double; lower weekday rates in off season. 2-night minimum on weekends. Children 5 and under stay free in parent's room. AE, DISC, MC, V. Pets accepted ($20 per night). **Amenities:** Bikes; Jacuzzi. In room: TV/VCR/DVD, CD player, hair dryer, kitchen, free Wi-Fi.

MODERATE

Elizabeth Street Inn   Located in the Nye Beach area and within walking distance of Yaquina Bay State Park, this modern oceanfront hotel, with its stone foundation wall, cedar-shingle facade, and white trim, has a classic beachy feel. There's a nautical theme throughout, and all rooms have ocean views, balconies, and fireplaces; some also have whirlpool tubs. The hotel is perched on a bluff above the beach, and several good restaurants lie within walking distance.

2332 SW Elizabeth St. (P.O. Box 1342), Newport, OR 97365. www.elizabethstreetinn.com. © **877/265-9400** or 541/265-9400. Fax 541/265-9551. 68 units. $160–$210 double; lower rates Oct–Mar. Rates include continental breakfast. Children 17 and under stay free in parent's room. AE, DISC, MC, V. Pets accepted ($25 fee). **Amenities:** Exercise room; Jacuzzi; indoor pool. *In room:* TV/DVD, fridge, hair dryer, free Wi-Fi.

Newport Belle Bed & Breakfast ★ This 100-foot-long modern sternwheeler is one of the most unusual B&Bs on the Oregon coast. It's docked in the Newport Marina in Yaquina Bay, within walking distance of the Oregon Coast Aquarium, Hatfield Marine Science Center, and Rogue Brewery. The guest rooms (staterooms) here are small, as you'd expect on any boat, but they all have big windows, private bathrooms, and wood floors. A salon on the main deck serves as a gathering space and dining room with a wonderful view of the harbor, and a solarium with floor-to-ceiling walls of glass is the perfect spot for taking in sunsets.

2126 SE OSU Dr., Newport, OR 97365. www.newportbelle.com. © **800/348-1922** or 541/867-6290. 5 units. $145–$165 double; lower rates in winter. Rates include full breakfast. MC, V. Closed Dec to mid-Feb. Pets accepted ($25 per night). Children not accepted. **Amenities:** Concierge; access to nearby health club. *In room:* Fridge, hair dryer, no phone, free Wi-Fi.

Sylvia Beach Hotel This eclectic, century-old hotel pays homage to literature. The guest rooms are named for different authors, and in each you'll find memorabilia, books, and decor that reflect the authors' lives, times, and works. The Agatha Christie Room seems full of clues, while in the J.K. Rowling Room, there's Harry Potter's bed from Hogwarts, his owl, Hedwig, in a cage by the window, and a Firebolt flying broom hanging from the ceiling. Among the writers represented are Shakespeare, Tolkien, John Steinbeck, Ernest Hemingway, Mark Twain, Jane Austen, F. Scott Fitzgerald, and Emily Dickinson. The hotel's **Tables of Content** dining room is a local favorite (see below).

267 NW Cliff St., Newport, OR 97365. www.sylviabeachhotel.com. © **888/795-8422** or 541/265-5428. 20 units. $70–$193 double. Rates include full breakfast. 2-night minimum on weekends. AE, DISC, MC, V. **Amenities:** Restaurant. *In room:* No phone.

Tyee Lodge ★ Located just south of Yaquina Head, this oceanfront bed-and-breakfast sits atop a high bluff surrounded by tall sitka spruce trees. Guest rooms are large and all have good ocean views, as do the living and dining rooms. There are gas fireplaces in all the rooms, and the house has a modern look with Native American accents. In summer, you can spend time in the lovely gardens, and on cooler days, there's a fire in the garden fire pit. A private trail leads down to the beach.

4925 NW Woody Way, Newport, OR 97365. www.tyeelodge.com. © **888/553-8933** or 541/265-8953. 5 units. $120–$210 double. Rates include full breakfast. AE, DC, DISC, MC, V. Children 12 and over welcome. *In room:* Hair dryer, free Wi-Fi.

Where to Eat

For an espresso, a slice of pizza, or a good sandwich, drop by **Panini Bakery,** 232 NW Coast St. (© **541/265-5033**), in Nye Beach. For pastries and artisan breads, search out **La Maison Bakery & Cafe,** 315 SW Ninth St. (© **541/265-8812;** www.lamaisoncafe.com), which is just off U.S. 101. On a hot summer day, nothing tastes better than a pint of microbrew ale at **Rogue Ales Public House,** 748 SW

Bay Blvd. (© **541/265-3188;** www.rogue.com). There's a second Rogue pub, **Brewer's on the Bay** over near the Oregon Coast Aquarium at 2320 OSU Dr. (© **541/867-3664**). For coffee, grab a table on the deck at **The Coffee House,** 156 SW Bay Blvd. (© **541/265-6263;** www.thecoffeehousenewport.com), and you'll have a front-row seat for watching all the action on the bayfront.

MODERATE

April's at Nye Beach ★ MEDITERRANEAN Located in the historic Nye Beach neighborhood, this restaurant is your best bet in the area for a romantic evening out. Popular both with the hip young crowd that likes to vacation in Nye Beach and patrons of the nearby Newport Center for the Performing Arts, the restaurant dishes up good contemporary Italian fare amid artistic surroundings. The afternoon light here is fabulous, so try to schedule your dinner for sunset (and ask for a table with an ocean view). Much of the produce used here comes from the restaurant owners' own farm. There's also an excellent selection of regional wines at reasonable prices.

749 NW Third St. © **541/265-6855.** http://aprilsatnyebeach.com. Reservations recommended. Main courses $16–$28. MC, V. Wed–Sun 5–9pm. Closed late Nov–Jan.

Panache NORTHWEST Located across the street from the Performing Arts Center, this elegant restaurant is the perfect spot for a pretheater dinner. Big and bright, Panache brings a highly refined dining experience to the funky Nye Beach neighborhood. Start your meal with the local Yaquina Bay oysters, and then move on to the pan-seared salmon with pomegranate glaze. The menu usually includes a couple of vegetarian entrees.

614 W. Olive St. © **541/265-2929.** www.panachenewport.com. Reservations recommended. Main courses $17–$29. AE, DISC, MC, V. Daily 4:30–9pm.

Saffron Salmon ★★ NORTHWEST With its walls of glass, bold contemporary styling, and location at the end of a pier on the bayfront, the Saffron Salmon is my favorite restaurant in Newport. As you dine on grilled wild salmon and fresh Dungeness crab, you'll watch commercial fishermen unloading their catch just outside the window. Seafood just doesn't get any fresher than this. Keep an eye out for sea lions, too. At lunch, go for the saffron salmon sandwich. Although the menu is dominated by creatively prepared seafood, there are also burgers and fries, so this makes a good compromise for foodie parents with finicky children.

859 SW Bay Blvd. © **541/265-8921.** www.saffronsalmon.com. Reservations recommended. Main courses $7.50–$22 lunch, $10–$28 dinner. AE, MC, V. Thurs–Tues 11:30am–2:15pm and 5–8:30pm. Closed early to late Nov.

Tables of Content ★ 🎁 INTERNATIONAL Located in the Sylvia Beach Hotel, this restaurant serves delicious and very reasonably priced four-course dinners. Although on any given night you'll have limited choices, if you enjoy creative cookery and eclectic combinations, you'll leave contented. Expect dishes such as mushroom saute, Greek salad, salmon dijonnaise, and black-bean cakes. Be forewarned, however, that dinners here are designed to foster interactions between guests. You'll be seated at a table for eight, and after dinner, guests participate in a game called "two truths and a lie." If you're outgoing and thrive on fiction, dinner here is unforgettable. On the other hand, if you're looking for a quiet, romantic evening out, this is definitely not the place.

In the Sylvia Beach Hotel, 267 NW Cliff St. ✆ **541/265-5428.** www.sylviabeachhotel.com. Reservations required. Fixed-price 4-course dinner $24. AE, DISC, MC, V. Summer and holidays seatings daily 7pm; other months Sun–Thurs 6pm, Fri–Sat 7pm.

INEXPENSIVE

Local Ocean Seafoods ★ 🍴 SEAFOOD   If you want fresh, sustainably harvested seafood, this casual fish-market-style eatery is the place. The modern space, with big windows, is located directly across the street from the water, so you can watch fishing boats coming and going, and know that the fish on your plate was caught only hours ago. The tuna mignon (bacon-wrapped albacore tuna) and the fishwives stew are excellent, but you can also get a simple whole crab or a crab po' boy. There are also plenty of oyster and shrimp dishes as well.

213 SE Bay Blvd. ✆ **541/574-7959.** www.localocean.net. Main courses $9–$25. MC, V. Summer Sun–Thurs 11am–9pm, Fri–Sat 11am–9:30pm; other months daily 11am–8pm.

Mo's SEAFOOD   Established in 1942, Mo's has become such an Oregon coast institution that it has spawned five other restaurants up and down the coast. Clam chowder is what made Mo's famous, and you can get it by the bowl, by the cup, or family style. **Be forewarned, though:** Some people think this clam chowder is the best, and others think it's awful. (I'd put it somewhere in between the two extremes.) Basic seafood dinners are fresh, large, and inexpensive, and the seafood-salad sandwiches are whoppers. There are also such dishes as cioppino, oyster stew, and slumgullion (clam chowder with shrimp). Expect a line out the door. Mo's Annex, across the street, has the same food and better views.

622 SW Bay Blvd. ✆ **541/265-2979.** www.moschowder.com. Complete dinner $4.50–$18. DISC, MC, V. Daily 11am–10pm.

South Beach Fish Market DELI   If you're looking for the best fish and chips on the Oregon coast, be sure to sample the offerings at this roadside stand near the Oregon Coast Aquarium. You can get salmon and chips, halibut and chips, oysters and chips, shrimp and chips, or the basic house fish and chips, which is made with whatever fresh inexpensive fish is available that day. Okay, so the chips aren't the best, but the fish is very lightly battered, which lets its flavor shine through. They also do smoked salmon, tuna, and oysters.

3640 S. U.S. 101. ✆ **541/867-6800.** www.southbeachfishmarket.com. Main dishes $6–$23. AE, DISC, MC, V. Daily 7am–9pm.

YACHATS ★★★

24 miles S of Newport, 26 miles N of Florence, 138 miles SE of Portland

Located on the north side of 800-foot-high Cape Perpetua, the village of Yachats (pronounced "*Yah*-hots") is something of an artists' community that also attracts a good number of counterculture types. When you get your first glimpse of the town's setting, you, too, will likely agree that there's more than enough beauty here to inspire anyone to artistic pursuits. Yachats is an Alsi Indian word meaning "dark waters at the foot of the mountains," and that sums up perfectly the setting of this small community, one of the few on the Oregon coast that could really be considered a village. The tiny Yachats River flows into the surf on the south edge of town, and to the east stand steep, forested mountains. The shoreline on which the town stands is rocky, with little coves here and there where you can find agates among the pebbles paving the beach. Tide pools offer hours of exploring, and in winter, storm waves create a spectacular show. Uncrowded beaches, comfortable motels, and a couple of good restaurants add up to a great spot for a quiet getaway.

Essentials

GETTING THERE   From the north, take Ore. 34 west from Corvallis to Waldport, and then head south on U.S. 101. From the south, take Ore. 126 west from Eugene to Florence, and then head north on U.S. 101.

VISITOR INFORMATION   Contact the **Yachats Area Chamber of Commerce,** 241 U.S. 101 (P.O. Box 728), Yachats, OR 97498 (© **800/929-0477** or 541/547-3530; www.yachats.org).

FESTIVALS   Each year in mid-October, Yachats celebrates its fungal abundance with the **Yachats Village Mushroom Fest** (© **800/929-0477** or 541/547-3530; www.yachats.org/MFest2011.html).

Yachats Area Activities & Attractions

Looming over tiny Yachats is the impressive bulk of 800-foot-high Cape Perpetua, the highest spot on the Oregon coast. Because of the cape's rugged beauty and diversity of natural habitats, it has been designated the **Cape Perpetua Scenic Area ★★★**. The **Cape Perpetua Visitor Center,** 2400 U.S. 101 (© **541/547-3289;** www. fs.fed.us/r6/siuslaw), is on a steep road off U.S. 101 and houses displays on the natural history of the cape and the Native Americans who for thousands of years harvested its bountiful seafood. Mid-June to mid-September, the visitor center is open daily from 10am to 5:30pm; mid-September to mid-November and mid-February to mid-June, it's open daily from 10am to 4pm; mid-November to mid-February, it's open Wednesday through Sunday from 10am to 4pm. Admission is $5 per vehicle. Within the scenic area are 26 miles of hiking trails, tide pools, ancient forests, scenic overlooks, and a campground. Guided hikes are offered (weather permitting) when the visitor center is open. If you're here on a clear day, be sure to drive to the top of the cape for one of the finest vistas on the coast. Waves and tides are a year-round source of fascination along these rocky shores, and Cape Perpetua's tide pools are some of the best on the coast. There's good access to the tide pools at the pull-off at the north end of the scenic area. However, it is the more dramatic interactions of waves and rocks that attract most people to walk the short oceanside trail here: At the **Devil's Churn,** a spouting horn caused by waves crashing into a narrow fissure in the basalt shoreline sends geyserlike plumes of water skyward, and waves boil through a narrow opening in the rocks.

Right in Yachats, be sure to visit **Yachats State Recreation Area,** which is at the southern end of the .75-mile historic 804 Trail that leads north along a rocky stretch of coastline to **Smelt Sands State Recreation Site.** Along the route of the trail, there are little pocket beaches (where smelts spawn) and tide pools. At the north end of the trail, a wide, sandy beach stretches northward. Just across the bridge at the south end of town, you'll find the **Yachats Ocean Road State Natural Site,** another good beach access.

Gray whales also come close to shore near Yachats. You can see them in the spring from Cape Perpetua, and throughout the summer several take up residence at the mouth of the Yachats River. South of Cape Perpetua, Neptune State Scenic Viewpoint, at the mouth of Cummins Creek, and Strawberry Hill Wayside are other good places to spot whales, as well as sea lions, which can be seen lounging on the rocks offshore at Strawberry Hill.

A couple of historic buildings in the area are also worth a visit. Built in 1927, the **Little Log Church & Museum,** 328 W. Third St. (✆ **541/547-3976;** http://ci.yachats.or.us/Little%20Log%20Church.htm), is now a museum housing displays on local history. The museum is open Friday through Wednesday from noon to 3pm.

The Yachats area has several crafts galleries, the most interesting of which is **Earthworks Gallery,** 2222 U.S. 101 N. (✆ **541/547-4300**), located north of town and focusing on glass and ceramic art.

Where to Stay

In addition to the hotels listed below, plenty of rental homes are available in Yachats. Contact **Ocean Odyssey,** 261 N. U.S. 101 (P.O. Box 491), Yachats, OR 97498 (✆ **800/800-1915** or 541/547-3637; www.ocean-odyssey.com), or **Yachats Village Rentals,** 230 Aqua Vista Loop (P.O. Box 44), Yachats, OR 97498 (✆ **888/288-5077** or 541/547-3501; www.97498.com). Rates for most vacation homes range from around $140 to $225 per night.

EXPENSIVE

Heceta Head Lightstation ★★ Thanks to a spectacular setting on a forested headland, the Heceta Head Lighthouse is the most photographed lighthouse on the Oregon coast. And although you can't spend the night in the lighthouse itself, you can stay in the former lighthouse keeper's home, a white-clapboard Victorian building high atop an oceanfront bluff and set behind a picket fence. The house is a National Historic Site and has been preserved much the way it might have been when it was active. Breakfasts are elaborate seven-course meals. Because this is one of the most popular B&Bs on the coast, you'll need to book your room 2 to 3 months in advance for a weekday stay and 5 to 6 months in advance for a weekend stay in the summer. Oh, and by the way, the inn is haunted.

92072 U.S. 101 S., Yachats, OR 97498. www.hecetalighthouse.com. ✆ **866/547-3696** or 541/547-3696. 6 units, 4 with private bathroom. Summer $209–$219 double with shared bathroom, $257–$315 double with private bathroom; winter $133–$148 double with shared bathroom, $174–$234 double with private bathroom. Rates include full breakfast. DISC, MC, V. 2-night minimum on weekends. Children 10 and over are welcome. **Amenities:** Free Wi-Fi. *In room:* No phone.

Overleaf Lodge ★★ Overlooking the rocky shoreline at the north end of Yachats, this modern hotel offers some of the most luxurious and tastefully decorated rooms on the central coast. Built in a sort of modern interpretation of the traditional Victorian beach cottage, the lodge caters primarily to couples seeking a romantic escape. Guest rooms all have ocean views, and most have patios or balconies. For a truly memorable stay, book one of the Restless Waters rooms, which have whirlpool tubs overlooking the crashing waves below. If you don't want to spring for one of these rooms, you can still curl up in a sunny little window nook beside your balcony and watch the waves in relative comfort. Many rooms also have fireplaces. The lodge also rents out some attractive cottages that are adjacent to the lodge.

280 Overleaf Lodge Lane, Yachats, OR 97498. www.overleaflodge.com. ✆ **800/338-0507** or 541/547-4880. 54 units. July–Aug $190–$275 double, $290–$499 suite; Sept–June $130–$270 double, $260–$280 suite. Rates include continental breakfast. Children 6 and under stay free in parent's room. AE, DISC, MC, V. **Amenities:** Exercise room; Jacuzzi; sauna; spa. *In room:* TV/DVD, CD player, fridge, hair dryer, MP3 docking station, free Wi-Fi.

INEXPENSIVE

The Fireside Motel Affiliated with the far more luxurious Overleaf Lodge next door, this economical oceanfront hotel is, like its sister property, on one of the prettiest stretches of coastline anywhere in Oregon. The Fireside is set far back from busy U.S. 101, and fronts on the pretty stretch of coastal trail that runs through Yachats. Most guest rooms here are simply furnished in motel-modern style and are comfortable enough. However, the more expensive oceanfront rooms with fireplaces are surprisingly nice.

1881 U.S. 101 N., Yachats, OR 97498. www.firesidemotel.com. **800/336-3573** or 541/547-3636. 43 units. $60–$149 double. Children 6 and under stay free in parent's room. AE, DISC, MC, V. Pets accepted ($10 per night). **Amenities:** Access to adjacent spa. *In room:* TV/DVD, fridge, free Wi-Fi.

Ocean Haven If you're looking for a good value, great views, and rooms that are a little bit unusual, the rustic and cozy Ocean Haven is the place. Opt for either the North View or the South View room, and you'll find yourself with two walls of glass overlooking the ocean. Stay in the Shag's Nest cabin, which is perched on the edge of the bluff and is my favorite room here, and you can lie in bed and gaze out to sea with a fire crackling in the fireplace. The beach and some of the best tide pools around are just a short walk away. This place is very enviro-friendly (no Hummers or smokers allowed on premises), and there are a few nature-friendly house rules. A minimum stay may apply.

94770 U.S. 101, Yachats, OR 97498. www.oceanhaven.com. **541/547-3583.** 5 units. $105–$135 double. AE, DISC, MC, V. **Amenities:** Concierge. *In room:* CD player, kitchen, no phone, free Wi-Fi.

Where to Eat

At **Green Salmon Coffee and Tea House,** 220 U.S. 101 N. (**541/547-3077;** www.thegreensalmon.com), you can get organic, fair-trade coffee, baked goods, and other sustainably produced light meals.

Adobe Restaurant and Lounge AMERICAN Let me make this perfectly clear. You don't eat at this restaurant for the food (mediocre) or the decor (vintage 1970s). You eat here for the astonishing view of waves crashing on the rocky shoreline just outside the restaurant's long wall of windows. It's one of the best views from any restaurant on the Oregon coast, and is well worth putting up with a less than superb meal. Stick to something simple such as grilled oysters or smoked-salmon fettuccine, and you shouldn't be too disappointed. You can enjoy the setting and save money by stopping here for lunch.

At Adobe Resort, 1555 U.S. 101. **541/547-3141.** www.adoberesort.com. Reservations recommended. Main courses $8.50–$16 lunch, $15–$27 dinner. AE, DC, DISC, MC, V. Daily 8am–2:30pm and 5–9pm.

The Drift Inn AMERICAN/NORTHWEST This unprepossessing place, right on U.S. 101 in the center of Yachats, may seem at first glance to be little more than a modern tavern (albeit a tavern with big windows, wooden booths, and polished wood floors), but looks can be deceiving. The Drift Inn actually has a split personality. Sure, there's the standard beer-and-burgers menu, but at dinner, you can get more creative dishes such as salmon topped with hazelnuts and blackberries, or pan-fried razor clams. There's live music here nightly.

124 U.S. 101 N. **541/547-4477.** www.the-drift-inn.com. Main courses $5–$21. MC, V. Daily 8am–9:30pm.

Luna Sea Fish House ★ 🍴 SEAFOOD   I admit it: I'm a sucker for fish and chips, and I've sampled this simple fare from Astoria to Brookings. The fish and chips at this tiny roadside hole in the wall are the best on the coast. Why? Well, it could be because the owners of the restaurant have a commercial fishing boat and serve fish so fresh you'd have to catch it yourself if you wanted it any fresher. For the ultimate, get the combo, which includes halibut, albacore, and salmon. Breakfasts at Luna Sea are also seafood-centric with seafood Benedict, salmon hash, and a seafood omelet.

153 U.S. 101 N. ⓒ **541/547-4794.** www.lunaseafishhouse.com. Main courses $7–$13. AE, DISC, MC, V. Daily 8am–9pm (8pm in winter).

South to Florence

More wide sandy beaches can be found south of Yachats at (in order from north to south) Stonefield Beach State Recreation Site, Muriel O. Ponsler Memorial State Scenic Viewpoint, and Carl G. Washburne Memorial State Park (ⓒ **541/547-3416;** www.oregon.gov/oprd/parks). The latter offers 5 miles of beach, hiking trails, and a campground.

The next park to the south, **Heceta Head Lighthouse State Scenic Viewpoint,** offers the most breathtaking setting. Situated on a small sandy cove, the park has a stream flowing across the beach and several haystack rocks just offshore. As the name implies, the park is home to **Heceta Head Lighthouse** (ⓒ **541/547-3416**), the most photographed lighthouse on the Oregon coast. The lighthouse will be closed for renovations throughout 2012 and possibly until August of 2013. Heceta (pronounced "huh-*see*-tuh") Head is a rugged headland that's named for Spanish explorer Capt. Bruno Heceta. The old lighthouse keeper's home is now a bed-and-breakfast (see "Where to Stay" under "Yachats" above), which has an interpretive center. Between Memorial Day weekend and Labor Day weekend, free tours are given of the lighthouse keeper's house Thursday through Monday between noon and 5pm. There is a $5 day-use fee to use the park.

At more than 300 feet long and 120 feet high, **Sea Lion Caves** ★★, 91560 U.S. 101 N. (ⓒ **541/547-3111;** www.sealioncaves.com), 1 mile south of Heceta Head Lighthouse, is the largest sea cave in the United States. The cave was discovered in 1880, and since 1932 it has been one of the most popular stops along the Oregon coast. The cave and a nearby rock ledge are the only year-round mainland homes for Steller sea lions, hundreds of which reside here throughout the year. This is the larger of the two species of sea lion that frequent this coast, and bulls can weigh almost a ton. The sea lions spend the day lounging and barking up a storm, and the bickering of the adults and antics of the pups are always entertaining. Although at any time of year you're likely to find quite a few of the sea lions here, it is during the fall and winter that the majority of the sea lions move into the cave. Today a combination of stairs, pathways, and an elevator lead down from the bluff-top gift shop to a viewpoint in the cave wall. The best time to visit is late in the afternoon, when the sun shines directly into the cave and the crowds of people are smaller. Admission is $12 for adults, $11 for seniors, $8 for children 3 to 12. The caves are open daily from 9am to 5pm.

Another 6 miles south is the **Darlingtonia State Natural Site,** a small botanical preserve protecting a bog full of rare *Darlingtonia californica* plants, insectivorous pitcher plants also known as cobra lilies. You'll find this fascinating preserve on Mercer Lake Road.

FLORENCE & THE OREGON DUNES

50 miles S of Newport, 50 miles N of Coos Bay, 60 miles W of Eugene

Florence and the Oregon Dunes National Recreation Area, which stretches south of town for almost 50 miles, have long been popular summer vacation spots for Oregon families. The national recreation area is the longest unbroken, publicly owned stretch of coastline on the Oregon coast, and within its boundaries are 14,000 acres of dunes, some of which stand more than 500 feet tall.

Within this vast area of shifting sands—the largest area of sand dunes on the West Coast—there are numerous lakes both large and small, living forests, and skeletal forests of trees that were long ago "drowned" beneath drifting sands. Many area lakes are ringed with summer homes and campgrounds, and it is these lakes that are the primary destination of many vacationers. Consequently, water-skiing and fishing are among the most popular activities, followed by riding dune buggies and other off-road vehicles (ORVs) through the sand dunes.

The Umpqua River divides the national recreation area roughly at its midway point, and on its banks you'll find the towns of Gardiner, Reedsport, and Winchester Bay, each of which has a very distinct character. Gardiner was founded in 1841 when a Boston merchant's fur-trading ship wrecked near here. An important mill town in the 19th century, Gardiner has several stately Victorian homes. Reedsport is the largest of these three communities and is the site of the Umpqua Discovery Center, a museum focusing on the history and natural history of this region. The town of Winchester Bay is almost at the mouth of the Umpqua River and is known for its large fleet of charter-fishing boats.

Florence is one of the few towns on the Oregon coast with historic character. Set on the banks of the Siuslaw River, it is filled with restored wooden commercial buildings that house restaurants and interesting shops. The charm of the historic downtown is all the more appealing when compared to the unsightly sprawl of U.S. 101.

Essentials

GETTING THERE   Florence is on U.S. 101 at the junction with Ore. 126 from Eugene. Gardiner, Reedsport, and Winchester Bay are all on U.S. 101 at or near the junction with Ore. 38 from Elkton, which in turn is reached from I-5 by taking either Ore. 99 from Drain or Ore. 138 from Sutherlin.

VISITOR INFORMATION   For more information on the dunes, contact the **Oregon Dunes National Recreation Area Visitor Center,** 855 U.S. 101, Reedsport, OR 97467 (© **541/271-6000;** www.fs.fed.us/r6/siuslaw). From mid-May to mid-September, this visitor center is open daily from 8am to 4:30pm; other months, it is closed on Saturday and Sunday.

For more information on Florence, contact the **Florence Area Chamber of Commerce,** 290 U.S. 101, Florence, OR 97439 (© **541/997-3128;** www.florence chamber.com).

There is a $5-per-car day-use fee within the recreation area.

The Oregon Dunes National Recreation Area ★★★

The first Oregon dunes were formed between 12 and 26 million years ago by the weathering of inland mountain ranges, but it was not until about 7,000 years ago, after the massive eruption of the Mount Mazama volcano, that they reached their current size and shape. That volcanic eruption emptied out the entire molten-rock contents of Mount Mazama, and in the process created the caldera that would later become Crater Lake.

Due to water currents and winds, the dunes today are in constant flux. Currents move the sand particles north each winter and south each summer, while constant winds off the Pacific Ocean blow the sand eastward, piling it up into dunes that are slowly marching east. Over thousands of years, the dunes have swallowed up forests, leaving some groves of trees as remnant tree islands.

Freshwater trapped behind the dunes has formed numerous **freshwater lakes,** many of which are now ringed by campgrounds and vacation homes. These lakes are popular for fishing, swimming, and boating. The largest of the lakes lie outside the national recreation area and are, from north to south, Woahink Lake, Siltcoos Lake, Tahkenitch Lake, Clear Lake, Eel Lake, North Tenmile Lake, and Tenmile Lake. Smaller lakes that are within the recreation area include Cleawox Lake, Carter Lake, Beale Lake, and Horsfall Lake.

European beach grass is playing an even greater role in changing the natural dynamics of this region. Introduced to anchor sand dunes and prevent them from inundating roads and river channels, this plant has been much more effective than anyone ever imagined. Able to survive even when buried under several feet of sand, European beach grass has covered many acres of land and formed dunes in back of the beach. These dunes effectively block sand from blowing inland off the beach, and as winds blow sand off the dunes into wet, low-lying areas, vegetation takes hold, thus eliminating areas of former dunes. Aerial photos have shown that where once 80% of the dunes here were open sand, today only 20% are. It is predicted that within 50 years, these dunes will all have been completely covered with vegetation and will no longer be the barren, windswept expanses of sand seen today.

There are numerous options for exploring the dunes. **Jessie M. Honeyman Memorial State Park ★★** (*©* **541/997-3641;** www.oregon.gov/oprd/parks), 3 miles south of Florence, is a unique spot with a beautiful forest-bordered lake and towering sand dunes. The park offers camping, picnicking, hiking trails, and access to Cleawox and Woahink lakes. On Cleawox Lake, there is a swimming area and a boat-rental facility. The dunes adjacent to Cleawox Lake are used by off-road vehicles.

The easiest place to get an overview of the dunes is at the **Oregon Dunes Overlook,** 10 miles south of Florence. Here you'll find viewing platforms high atop a forested sand dune that overlooks a vast expanse of bare sand. Another easy place from which to view the dunes is the viewing platform on the Taylor Dunes Trail, which begins at the **Carter Lake Campground,** 7½ miles south of Florence. It is an easy ½-mile walk to the viewing platform.

There are several places to wander among these sand dunes. If you have time only for a quick walk, head to **Carter Lake Campground,** where you can continue on from the Taylor Dunes viewing platform. The beach is less than a mile beyond the viewing platform, and roughly half this distance is through dunes. From this same campground, you can hike the **Carter Dunes Trail.** The beach is 1½ miles away through dunes, forest, and meadows known as a *deflation plain.* A 3.5-mile loop trail leads from the **Oregon Dunes Overlook** out to the beach by way of Tahkenitch Creek, a meandering stream that flows through the dunes and out to the ocean. Another mile south of the Oregon Dunes Overlook, you'll find the **Tahkenitch Creek Trail Head,** which accesses an 8-mile network of little-used trails that wander through dunes, forest, marshes, and meadows. However, for truly impressive dunes, the best route is the **John Dellenback Dunes Trail ★★**, which has its trail head a half-mile south of **Eel Creek Campground** (11 miles south of Reedsport). This 5.4-mile round-trip trail leads through an area of dunes 2 miles wide by 4 miles long. Don't get lost!

About 30% of the sand dunes are open to **off-road vehicles (ORVs),** which are also known as ATVs (all-terrain vehicles), and throngs of people flock to this area to roar up and down the dunes. If you'd like to do a little off-roading, you can rent a miniature dune buggy or ATV from **Sand Dunes Frontier,** 83960 U.S. 101 S. (✆ **541/997-5363;** www.sanddunesfrontier.com), 4 miles south of Florence. Guided tours of the dunes are offered by Sand Dunes Frontier and **Sandland Adventures,** 85366 U.S. 101 S. (✆ **541/997-8087;** www.sandland.com), 1 mile south of Florence (this company has a little amusement park as well). The tours cost about $12 to $50. One-person dune buggies and ATVs rent for about $45 per hour. Down at the southern end of the recreation area, you can rent vehicles from **Spinreel Dune Buggy Rentals,** 67045 Spinreel Rd., North Bend (✆ **541/759-3313;** www.ridetheoregondunes.com), located just off U.S. 101, about 9 miles south of Reedsport.

Ever heard of sand boarding? It's basically snowboarding in the sand, and at **Sand Master Park,** 87542 U.S. 101 N., Florence (✆ **541/997-6006;** www.sandmaster park.com), you (or your teenage kids) will find 40 acres of sculpted sand dunes designed to mimic a wintertime snowboard park (lots of jumps and rails). June through mid-September, the park is open daily from 9am to 6:30pm; other months, it's open Monday, Tuesday, and Thursday through Saturday from 10am to 5pm, and Sunday noon to 5pm. The park is closed from mid-January through February. Sand boards rent for $10 to $25.

If you'd rather avoid the dune buggies and ORVs, stay away from the dunes between the South Jetty area (just south of Florence) and Siltcoos Lake; the area adjacent to Umpqua Lighthouse State Park just south of Winchester Bay; and the area from Spinreel Campground south to the Horsfall Dune & Beach Access Road, which is just north of the town of North Bend.

Other Activities & Attractions
IN THE FLORENCE AREA

Florence's **Old Town,** on the north bank of the Siuslaw River, is one of the most charming historic districts on the Oregon coast. The restored wood and brick buildings, many of which house interesting shops, galleries, and restaurants, capture the flavor of a 19th-century fishing village. If you want to learn more about the area's history, stop by the **Siuslaw Pioneer Museum,** Maple and Second streets (✆ **541/997-7884**), which is open Tuesday through Sunday from noon to 4pm and charges a $3 admission. The museum is closed from Christmas through January. For evening entertainment, be sure to check the calendar at the **Florence Events Center,** 715 Quince St. (✆ **541/997-1994;** www.eventcenter.org), which often has interesting shows that are sponsored by the **Seacoast Entertainment Association** (www.seatcoasta.org).

If you'd like to ride a horse along the beach, head north to **C&M Stables,** 90241 U.S. 101 N. (✆ **541/997-7540;** www.oregonhorsebackriding.com), which is located 8 miles north of Florence and offers rides on the beach and through the dunes. A 1-hour dune ride costs $40 to $45, and a 2-hour ride on the beach costs $60 to $65.

If golf is your sport, try the 18-hole **Sandpines Golf Links,** 1201 35th St. (© **800/917-4653;** www.sandpines.com), which plays through dunes and pine forest and is one of Oregon's most popular courses. During the summer, you'll pay $79 for 18 holes. Alternatively, try the 18-hole **Ocean Dunes Golf Links,** 3345 Munsel Lake Rd. (© **800/468-4833** or 541/997-3232; www.oceandunesgolf.com), which also plays through the dunes and charges $25 to $42 for 18 holes during the summer.

If you'd like to rent a kayak and paddle around on the Siuslaw River or rent a surfboard and catch some waves, contact **Central Coast Watersports,** 1901 U.S. 101 (© **800/789-3483** or 541/997-1812; www.centralcoastwatersports.com). Kayaks rent for $50 to $60 per day, and surfboards rent for $20 (wetsuits are $15).

IN THE REEDSPORT AREA

In downtown Reedsport on the Umpqua River waterfront, you can visit the **Umpqua Discovery Center,** 409 Riverfront Way (© **541/271-4816;** www.umpquadiscovery center.com). This museum contains displays on the history and ecology of the area. One of the better exhibits focuses on the natural history of the tidewater region. March 15 to October 14, it's open Monday through Saturday from 9:30am to 5pm; October 15 to March 14, it's open Monday through Saturday from 10am to 4pm. Admission is $8 for adults, $7 for seniors, and $4 for children 6 to 15. Outside the discovery center, you'll find an observation tower that is sometimes a good place to do a little bird-watching.

At the **Dean Creek Elk Viewing Area ★,** 1 mile east of town on Ore. 38, you can spot 100 or more elk grazing on 1,040 acres of meadows that have been set aside as a preserve. In summer the elk tend to stay in the forest, where it's cooler.

In Winchester Bay, you can visit the historic **Umpqua River Lighthouse.** The original lighthouse was at the mouth of the Umpqua River and was the first lighthouse on the Oregon coast. It fell into the Umpqua River in 1861 and was replaced in 1894 by the current lighthouse. Adjacent to the lighthouse is the **Visitors Center & Museum,** 1020 Lighthouse Rd. (© **541/271-4631**), which is housed in a former Coast Guard station and contains historical exhibits and an information center. Here at the museum you can arrange to join a tour of the lighthouse. Tours are offered May through October daily between 10am and 4pm and cost $3 for adults and $2 for children 6 to 16. Across the street from the lighthouse is a **whale-viewing platform.** (The best viewing months are Nov–June.) Also nearby is the very pretty **Umpqua Lighthouse State Park** (© **541/271-4118;** www.oregon.gov/oprd/parks), the site of the 500-foot-tall sand dunes that are the tallest in the United States. The park offers picnicking, hiking, and camping amid forests and sand dunes.

Where to Stay

IN FLORENCE

Driftwood Shores Resort & Conference Center ☺   Located several miles north of Florence's Old Town district, this is the only oceanfront lodging in the area. It's popular year-round, so book early. The rooms vary in size and amenities, but all have ocean views and balconies. Most also have kitchens, and the three-bedroom suites are as large as many vacation homes. The hotel's restaurant has ocean views from every table.

88416 First Ave., Florence, OR 97439. www.driftwoodshores.com. © **800/422-5091** or 541/997-8263. Fax 541/997-3253. 125 units. Mid-June to Sept $112–$177 double, $260–$342 suite; Oct to mid-June $97–$147 double, $221–$297 suite. Children 12 and under stay free in parent's room. AE,

DC, DISC, MC, V. **Amenities:** Restaurant; lounge; Jacuzzi; indoor pool. *In room:* TV, fridge, hair dryer, free Wi-Fi.

The Edwin K Bed & Breakfast ★   Located in Old Town Florence only 2 blocks from shops and restaurants, this 1914 Sears Craftsman home is one of the most luxurious B&Bs on the coast. The four upstairs rooms are the most spacious, and two overlook the Siuslaw River, which is just across the street and has a huge sand dune rising up on its far bank. One of these two front rooms has a claw-foot tub, while the other has a double whirlpool tub and a separate double shower. Other rooms, although not as plush, are still comfortable, and one downstairs room opens to the backyard and a 30-foot waterfall. Breakfasts are lavish five-course affairs, and in the afternoon, tea, cookies, and sherry are served.

1155 Bay St. (P.O. Box 2687), Florence, OR 97439. www.edwink.com. © **800/833-9465** or 541/997-8360. Fax 541/997-2423. 7 units. May–Sept $150–$175 double, $175–$200 apt/suite; lower rates other months. Rates include full breakfast (except in apt). DISC, MC, V. Children 14 and over welcome in main house. *In room:* Fridge, hair dryer, no phone, free Wi-Fi.

River House Inn   Overlooking the Siuslaw River drawbridge and sand dunes on the far side of the river, the River House is only 1 block from the heart of Florence's Old Town district. This motel offers comfortable and attractive rooms, most of which have views and balconies. The largest and most expensive have double whirlpool tubs. Riverfront rooms are worth requesting.

1202 Bay St., Florence, OR 97439. www.riverhouseflorence.com. © **888/824-2750** or 541/997-3933. 40 units. Mid-May to mid-Oct $119–$179 double; mid-Oct to mid-May $99–$169 double. Rates include continental breakfast. Children 12 and under stay free in parent's room. AE, DISC, MC, V. *In room:* TV, fridge, hair dryer, free Internet.

Where to Eat
IN FLORENCE

When you need a good cup of espresso, stop in at **Siuslaw River Coffee Roasters,** 1240 Bay St. (© 541/997-3443; www.coffeeoregon.com). For cookies, pastries, and fresh bread, search out **the Shed Bakery,** 182 Laurel St. (© 541/997-9811), which is in an old outboard-motor repair shed in the middle of a block in Old Town. Look for the bakery behind the street-front buildings. You'll find more tasty pastries on the waterfront at **Sweet Magnolia Bakery,** 1277 Bay St. (© 541/997-2959) At **Lovejoy's Restaurant & Tea Room,** 195 Nopal St. (© 541/902-0502; www.lovejoys restaurant.com), you can sit down to a traditional English tea. If you're looking for some gourmet foods or wine, drop by **Grape Leaf,** 1269 Bay St. (© 541/997-1646), which has a small wine bar and also serves light meals. You can also get great crab cocktails to go at the **Krab Kettle,** 280 U.S. 101 (© 541/997-8996), a little seafood market a few blocks from old town Florence.

Maple Street Grille ★ AMERICAN   This little cottage restaurant a half-block off the river in Old Town has just half a dozen tables, but should be your first choice for dinner in Florence. The menu is full of familiar comfort foods, all done well and often with a regional spin. I recommended starting with the bacon-wrapped barbecued shrimp or the Oregon cheese plate. For an entree, nothing is more comforting than mac and cheese, here made with Rogue Creamery blue cheese and topped with apple chutney. The pot roast, however, comes pretty close. There are also seafood cakes made with salmon and Dungeness crab, as well as a good cioppino. The lunch menu includes lots of creative burgers.

165 Maple St. ☎ **541/997-9811.** Reservations recommended. Main courses $10–$12 lunch, $11–$23 dinner. DISC, MC, V. Tues–Sat 11am–9pm.

Waterfront Depot Restaurant & Bar ★ 📷 NEW AMERICAN   This dark, cozy waterfront bar/restaurant is my favorite place to dine in Florence. It's housed in the 1913 Mapleton railroad depot, which was moved here from farther up the Siuslaw River and is one of the many white historic buildings that line Bay Street. Inside, the restaurant is a well-balanced blend of hip bar and old-country-inn dining room. There are battered wooden floors and a beautiful little bar. The menu is on blackboards attached to the depot's old sliding doors, and though the menu is not very long, there's plenty of variety and some of the best values on the coast. Among the appetizers, keep an eye out for the oyster stew, which is a great deal. Among the entrees, the grilled salmon is an equally good deal, as are the lamb shanks. For dessert, get a fat slice of cake.

1252 Bay St. ☎ **541/902-9100.** www.thewaterfrontdepot.com. Reservations recommended. Main courses $8.50–$15. DISC, MC, V. Daily 4–10pm.

IN WINCHESTER BAY

If you're craving some smoked salmon or other fish, drop by **Sportsmen's Cannery & Smokehouse,** 182 Bayfront Loop, Winchester Bay (☎ **541/271-3293;** www. sportsmenscannery.com).

THE COOS BAY AREA

85 miles NW of Roseburg, 50 miles S of Florence, 24 miles N of Bandon

With a population of around 35,000, the Coos Bay area, consisting of the towns of Coos Bay, North Bend, and Charleston, is the largest urban center on the Oregon coast. Coos Bay and North Bend are the bay's commercial districts and have merged into a single large town, while nearby Charleston maintains its distinct character as a small fishing port.

As the largest natural harbor between San Francisco and Puget Sound, Coos Bay has long been an important port. Logs, wood chips, and wood products are the main export. However, shipments of wood products have been down for more than a decade, and in response to the economic downturn of the port, the bay area has been working hard to attract both more tourists and more industry. In downtown Coos Bay, there is an attractive waterfront boardwalk, complete with historical displays, and what was once a huge lumber mill is now the site of the equally large Mill Resort & Casino.

Even if it isn't the most beautiful town on the Oregon coast, Coos Bay has a lot of character and quite a few tourist amenities, including a few decent restaurants, moderately priced motels, and even a few B&Bs. But what makes Coos Bay a town not to be missed is its proximity to a trio of picturesque state parks—Sunset Bay, Shore Acres, and Cape Arago.

Essentials

GETTING THERE   From the north, take Ore. 99 from just south of Cottage Grove. This road becomes Ore. 38. At Reedsport, head south on U.S. 101. From the south, take Ore. 42 from just south of Roseburg.

The **Southwest Oregon Regional Airport,** 1100 Airport Lane, North Bend (✆ **541/756-8531;** www.flyoth.com), is served by **United Express.** The airport code is OTH.

VISITOR INFORMATION   Contact the **Coos Bay Visitor Information Center,** 50 Central Ave., Coos Bay, OR 97420 (✆ **800/824-8486** or 541/269-0215; www.oregonsbayareachamber.com).

GETTING AROUND   Car rentals are available in the Coos Bay area from **Hertz** (✆ **800/654-3131** or 541/756-4416; www.hertz.com) and **Enterprise Rent-a-Car** (✆ **800/261-7331** or 541/751-0298; www.enterprise.com).

A Trio of State Parks & More

Southwest of Coos Bay, you'll find three state parks and a county park that preserves some of the most breathtaking shoreline in the Northwest. The three state parks are connected by an excellent trail that is perfect for a rewarding day hike.

Start your exploration of this beautiful stretch of coast by heading southwest on the Cape Arago Highway. In 12 miles you'll come to **Sunset Bay State Park** ★ (✆ **800/551-6949** or 541/888-4902; www.oregon.gov/oprd/parks). This park has one of the few beaches in Oregon where the water actually gets warm enough for swimming (although folks from warm-water regions may not agree). Sunset Bay is almost completely surrounded by sandstone cliffs, and the entrance to the bay is quite narrow, which means the waters here stay fairly calm. Picnicking and camping are available, and there are lots of tide pools to explore.

Continuing on another 3 miles brings you to **Shore Acres State Park** ★★ (✆ **800/551-6949** or 541/888-4902; www.oregon.gov/oprd/parks), once the estate of local shipping tycoon Louis J. Simpson, who spent years developing his gardens. His ships would bring him unusual plants from all over the world, and eventually the gardens grew to include a formal English garden and a Japanese garden with a 100-foot lily pond. His home, which long ago was torn down, and the gardens were built atop sandstone cliffs overlooking the Pacific and a tiny cove. Rock walls, sculpted by the waves into unusual shapes, rise up from the water. During winter storms, wave-watching is a popular pastime here. The water off the park is often a striking shade of blue, and **Simpson Beach,** in the little cove, just might be the prettiest beach in Oregon. A trail leads down to this beach. There is a $5 day-use fee here.

Cape Arago State Park ★★ (✆ **800/551-6949;** www.oregon.gov/oprd/parks) is the third of this trio of parks. Just offshore from the rugged cape lie the rocks and small islands of Simpson Reef, which provide sunbathing spots for hundreds of seals (including elephant seals) and sea lions. The barking of the sea lions can be heard from hundreds of yards away, and though you can't get very close, with a pair of binoculars you can see the seals and sea lions quite well. The best viewing point is at **Simpson Reef Viewpoint.** On either side of the cape are coves with quiet beaches, although the beaches are closed from March to June to protect young seal pups. Tide pools along these beaches offer hours of fascinating exploration during other months.

Also in the vicinity of these three state parks, you'll find **Bastendorff Beach County Park** (✆ **541/888-5353;** www.co.coos.or.us/ccpark/bastendorff/Bastendorff.html), north of Sunset Bay at the mouth of Coos Bay, which offers a long, wide beach that's popular with surfers.

Four miles down Seven Devils Road from Charleston, you'll find the **South Slough National Estuarine Research Reserve** (✆ **541/888-5558;** www.oregon.gov/dsl/ssnerr). An interpretive center (Tues–Sat 10am–4:30pm) set high above the slough provides background on the importance of estuaries. A hiking trail leads down to the marshes, and there is good canoeing and sea kayaking if you have a boat with you.

Other Area Activities & Attractions

Charleston is the bay area's charter-fishing marina. If you'd like to do some sportfishing, contact **Betty Kay Charters** (© 541/888-9021; www.bettykaycharters.com). Expect to pay around $70 for a 5-hour bottom-fishing trip and $175 for a 12-hour halibut-fishing trip.

In addition to all the outdoor recreational activities around the bay area, there is also a museum well worth visiting. The **Coos Art Museum,** 235 Anderson Ave., Coos Bay (© 541/267-3901; www.coosart.org), is a highly regarded museum that hosts changing exhibits in a wide variety of styles and media. Runners will also be interested to know that up on the second floor of the museum, there is a small exhibit dedicated to long-distance runner Steve Prefontaine, who was from Coos Bay and who died in 1975. The museum is open Tuesday through Friday from 10am to 4pm and Saturday from 1 to 4pm; admission is $5 for adults and $2 for seniors and students.

Also in town, you can visit the **Oregon Coast Historical Railway,** 766 S. First St., Coos Bay (© 541/297-6130; www.orcorail.org), a free open-air exhibit that includes a partially restored 1922 Baldwin steam engine, a restored 1949 diesel switcher, and a couple of cabooses. You'll find the display on the waterfront in downtown Coos Bay.

Part of the renovation of the Coos Bay waterfront has been the construction of the **Mill Casino & Hotel,** 3201 Tremont Ave., North Bend (© 800/953-4800 or 541/756-8800; www.themillcasino.com). Here you can play slot machines, blackjack, poker, and bingo. There are several restaurants and a lounge. Also, you should be sure to check the calendar at the **Egyptian Theatre,** 229 S. Broadway (© 541/269-8650; www.egyptian-theatre.com), a restored historic movie palace that was built in 1925 and now shows both new and vintage movies.

Where to Stay

Coos Bay Manor B&B This B&B, in a historic colonial-style home built in 1912, is unusual for a B&B in that it takes both children and pets. However, with its Victorian decor, it does seem more like the sort of place you'd choose for a vacation away from your kids. Rooms are full of antiques, and there are quilts on the beds. The Barron's Room, with its four-poster bed, is my personal favorite, though the Victorian Room, which also has a four-poster bed, is the largest.

955 S. Fifth St., Coos Bay, OR 97420. www.coosbaymanor.com. © **800/269-1224** or 541/269-1224. 5 units. $135 double; $220 suite. Rates include full breakfast. AE, MC, V. Children and pets accepted. *In room:* TV (some rooms), no phone, free Wi-Fi.

Edgewater Inn This is Coos Bay's only waterfront hotel, and though the water it faces is only a narrow stretch of the back bay, you can sometimes watch ships in the harbor. Guest rooms are large, and deluxe rooms are particularly well designed and spacious. Other deluxe rooms have in-room spas. Most rooms also have balconies overlooking the water (and industrial areas).

275 E. Johnson Ave., Coos Bay, OR 97420. www.edgewater-inns.com. © **800/233-0423** or 541/267-0423. 82 units. $85–$105 double. Rates include continental breakfast. AE, DISC, MC, V. Pets accepted ($10 per night). **Amenities:** Exercise room; Jacuzzi; indoor pool. *In room:* A/C, TV, fridge, hair dryer, free Wi-Fi.

At Coos Bay you enter **myrtlewood** country. The myrtle tree grows only along a short section of coast in southern Oregon and Northern California and is prized by woodworkers for its fine grain and durability. A very hard wood, it lends itself to all manner of platters, bowls, goblets, sculpture, and whatever. All along the south coast, you'll find myrtlewood factories and shops where you can see how the raw wood is turned into finished pieces. At the south end of the town of Coos Bay, watch for **The Oregon Connection,** 1125 S. First St.

(ℂ 800/255-5318 or 541/267-7804; www.oregonconnection.com), which is just off U.S. 101. This is one of the bigger myrtlewood factories. **Myrtlewood Factory Showroom,** 68794 Hauser Depot Rd. at U.S. 101 (ℂ **541/756-2220;** www.realoregongift.com), 5 miles north of North Bend, is another large factory and showroom. Six miles south of Bandon on U.S. 101, watch for **Zumwalt's Myrtlewood Factory,** 47422 U.S. 101 (ℂ **541/347-3654;** www.zumwalts myrtlewood.com), which has a good selection and prices.

Where to Eat

Benetti's Italian Restaurant SOUTHERN ITALIAN   For a city of its size, Coos Bay is surprisingly short of good places to eat, but Benetti's, right in downtown Coos Bay, has long been a local favorite. Large servings of classic southern Italian dishes keep people coming back for more. This is a good choice if you're here with the whole family.

260 S. Broadway, Coos Bay. ℂ **541/267-6066.** www.benettis.com. Reservations recommended. Main courses $11–$25. AE, DISC, MC, V. Sun–Thurs 5–9pm; Fri–Sat 5–10pm.

Blue Heron Bistro INTERNATIONAL   This odd little spot in the heart of downtown Coos Bay is an eclectic international restaurant that specializes in seafood and German fare. The Blue Heron also has one of the largest assortments of imported beers on the coast, and it's the sort of place that's perfect for lunch, dinner, or just a quick bite to eat. Items range from German bratwurst to local oysters to Dutch fisherman's casserole.

100 Commercial Ave., Coos Bay. ℂ **541/267-3933.** www.blueheronbistro.com. Main courses $8–$20. DISC, MC, V. Mon–Fri 11am–8pm; Sat–Sun noon–8pm.

The Portside Restaurant ☺ SEAFOOD   Charleston is home to Coos Bay's charter- and commercial-fishing fleets, so it's no surprise that it's also home to the area's best seafood restaurant. Check the daily fresh sheet to see what just came in on the boat. This place has been around for decades, and preparations tend toward traditional continental dishes, of which the house specialty is a bouillabaisse Marseillaise that's swimming with shrimp, red snapper, lobster, crab legs, butter clams, prawns, and scallops. The restaurant overlooks the boat basin and is popular with families.

63383 Kingfisher Rd., Charleston. ℂ **541/888-5544.** www.portsidebythebay.com. Reservations recommended. Main courses $9–$40. AE, DC, MC, V. Daily 11:30am–9 or 9:30pm.

BANDON ★★★

24 miles S of Coos Bay, 85 miles W of Roseburg, 54 miles north of Gold Beach

Once known primarily as the cranberry capital of Oregon (you can see the cranberry bogs south of town along U.S. 101), Bandon is now better known for its world-class Bandon Dunes Golf Resort. It's also set on one of the most beautiful pieces of coastline in the state. Just south of town, the beach is littered with boulders, monoliths, and haystack rocks that seem to have been strewn by some giant hand. Sunsets are stunning.

Just north of town, the Coquille River empties into the Pacific, and at the river's mouth stands a picturesque lighthouse. The lighthouse is one of only a handful of Bandon buildings to survive a fire in 1936. Even though most buildings downtown date only from the 1930s, Bandon still has the quaint feel of a historic seaside village, and a waterfront boardwalk connects Bandon with the Coquille River. Be sure to take a stroll along the boardwalk while you're in town.

Essentials

GETTING THERE From Roseburg, head west on Ore. 42 to Coquille, where you take Ore. 42S to Bandon, which is on U.S. 101.

VISITOR INFORMATION For more information, contact the **Bandon Chamber of Commerce,** 300 Second St., Bandon, OR 97411 (℗ **541/347-9616;** www. bandon.com).

FESTIVALS Bandon is the cranberry capital of Oregon, and every year in September the harvest is celebrated with the **Bandon Cranberry Festival.**

Outdoor Activities

Head out of Bandon on Beach Loop Road, and you'll soon see why the rocks are a big draw. Wind and waves have sculpted shoreline monoliths into contorted spires and twisted shapes. The first good place to view the rocks and get down to the beach is at **Coquille Point,** at the end of 11th Street. Here you'll find a short, paved interpretive trail atop a bluff overlooking the beach, rock monoliths, and the river mouth. There's also a long staircase leading down to the beach. From here you can see Table Rock and the Sisters. From the **Face Rock State Scenic Viewpoint,** you can see the area's most famous rock, which resembles a face gazing skyward. Nearby are rocks that resemble a dog, a cat, and kittens. A trail leads down to the beach from the viewpoint, so you can go out and explore some of the rocks that are left high and dry by low tide. South of the rocks, along a flat stretch of beach backed by dunes, there are several beach access areas, all of which are within **Bandon State Natural Area.**

Across the river from downtown Bandon, you'll find **Bullards Beach State Park** (℗ **541/347-3501;** www.oregon.gov/oprd/parks). Within the park are beaches, a marsh overlook, hiking and horseback-riding trails, a picnic area, a campground, and a boat ramp. Fishing, crabbing, and clamming are all very popular. In the park you'll also find the 1896 **Coquille River Lighthouse.** This lighthouse is one of the only lighthouses to ever be hit by a ship—in 1903 an abandoned schooner plowed into the light. Early May through mid-October, tours of the lighthouse are offered daily between 11am and 5pm.

At Bandon, as elsewhere on the Oregon coast, **gray whales** migrating between the Arctic and Baja California, Mexico, pass close to the shore and can often be spotted from land. The whales pass Bandon between December and February on their way south and between March and May on their way north. Gray days and early mornings before the wind picks up are the best times to spot whales. Coquille Point, at the end of 11th Street, and the bluffs along Beach Loop Road are the best vantage points.

More than 300 species of birds have been spotted in the Bandon vicinity, making this one of the best sites in Oregon for **bird-watching.** The **Oregon Islands National Wildlife Refuge,** which includes 1,853 rocks, reefs, and islands off the state's coast, includes the famous monoliths of Bandon. Among the birds that nest on these rocks are rhinoceros auklets, storm petrels, gulls, and tufted puffins. The puffins, with their large, colorful beaks, are the most beloved of local birds, and their images show up on all manner of local souvenirs. The **Bandon Marsh National Wildlife Refuge** (*✆* 541/ 347-1470; www.fws.gov/oregoncoast/bandonmarsh/index.htm), at the mouth of the Coquille River, is another good spot for bird-watching. In this area you can expect to see grebes, mergansers, buffleheads, plovers, and several species of raptors.

If you'd like to ride a horse down the beach, contact **Bandon Beach Riding Stables,** 54629 Beach Loop Rd. (*✆* **541/347-3423**), south of Face Rock. A 1-hour ride is $40 and a 1½-hour sunset ride is $50.

The world-class **Bandon Dunes Golf Course,** 57744 Round Lake Dr. (*✆* **888/ 345-6008;** www.bandondunesgolf.com), a classic Scottish-style links course, is Oregon's only oceanfront golf course and has made Bandon a major golfing destination. The course, notorious for its blustery winds, has been compared to Pebble Beach and St. Andrews. The summer greens fees are $225 for resort guests and $275 for nonguests ($110 for your second 18 holes). November to April, you can play here for $75 to $220. This is a walking course, and no golf carts are allowed; caddies are available and will cost you $80 to $100 per bag.

Bandon Crossings Golf Course, 87530 Dew Valley Lane (*✆* **888/465-3218** or 541/347-3232; www.bandoncrossings.com), an 18-hole course 5 miles south of town on U.S. 101, is an economical alternative to Bandon Dunes. Green fees are between $45 and $75 in the summer.

If that's still out of your price range, there's always the **Old Bandon Golf Links,** 3235 Beach Loop Dr. (*✆* **541/329-1927;** www.oldbandongolflinks.com), which offers a scenic 9 holes not far from the famous Face Rock. The green fee is $20 for 9 holes. This course rents 1880s and 1920s vintage golf clubs for golfers who want to play the game the way it used to be.

Other Area Activities & Attractions

The **West Coast Game Park Safari** ★, 46914 U.S. 101 S. (*✆* **541/347-3106;** www.gameparksafari.com), 7 miles south of Bandon, bills itself as America's largest wild-animal petting park and is a must for families. Depending on what young animals they have at the time of your visit, you might be able to play with a leopard, tiger, or bear cub. The park is open daily from 9am to 6pm in summer (call for hours in other months). Admission is $16 for adults, $15 for seniors, $9 for children 7 to 12, and $6 for children 2 to 6.

Shopping is one of Bandon's main attractions, and in **Old Town Bandon,** just off U.S. 101, you'll find some interesting shops and galleries. A couple of galleries sell artworks by regional artists. One of the better ones is the **Bandon Glass Art Studio,** 240 U.S. 101 (*✆* **541/347-4723;** www.bandonglassart.com), which is just across the highway from Old Town. Here you can watch glass directly from the furnace being made into the paperweights and fluted glass bowls the gallery sells.

Where to Stay

Bandon Dunes Golf Resort ★★★

Although this is one of the most tasteful and luxurious accommodations on the Oregon coast, the emphasis is so entirely on the golf course that anyone not interested in the game will feel like an interloper. However, if golf is your game, then you'll adore this place. The lodge sits up on the dunes and looks out over the fairways to the Pacific. Accommodations are also available in a variety of buildings around the vast property. For luxurious hotel rooms, opt for the Inn. For more spacious accommodations, get a suite in one of the Lily Pond Cottages (really multiunit buildings arranged around a pretty pond). Other accommodations include suites in a forest setting. Bear in mind that not all room types have golf-course views, but you can rest assured that all the accommodations here are world class.

57744 Round Lake Dr., Bandon, OR 97411. www.bandondunesgolf.com. ℭ **888/345-6008.** 186 units. May–Oct $200–$390 double; $600–$1,800 suite. Children 12 and under stay free in parent's room. AE, DC, DISC, MC, V. **Amenities:** 5 restaurants; 3 lounges; concierge; executive-level rooms; exercise room; 4 18-hole golf courses and 1 13-hole par-3 course; Jacuzzi; room service; sauna. *In room:* TV, CD player, fridge, hair dryer, MP3 docking station, free Wi-Fi.

Bandon Inn ★

Set atop a hill overlooking Old Town Bandon and the Coquille River, this older hotel has been transformed into a reasonable facsimile of a Cape Cod inn, complete with cedar-shingle siding and white-trimmed windows. With tastefully traditional decor, this is a good in-town alternative to the Best Western or the Sunset Oceanfront Lodging. A walkway leads down the hill from the inn to Old Town, so you can walk to some of Bandon's best restaurants.

355 U.S. 101, Bandon, OR 97411. www.bandoninn.com. ℭ **800/526-0209** or 541/347-4417. Fax 541/347-3616. 57 units. Mid-June to early Oct $124–$155 double; late Apr to mid-June and early Oct to early Nov $99–$135 double; early Nov to late Apr $79–$120 double. Children 6 and under stay free in parent's room. AE, DISC, MC, V. Pets accepted ($15 per night). *In room:* TV, fridge, free Wi-Fi.

Best Western Inn at Face Rock Resort ★

Located about a mile south of Face Rock, this modern hotel is Bandon's original golf resort and is adjacent to the 9-hole Old Bandon Golf Links. Guest rooms here are the best on Beach Loop Drive, and there are plenty of recreational facilities. Although the hotel is across the street from the beach, many of the rooms have ocean views. The views from the hotel restaurant, however, aren't nearly as good as those at the nearby **Lord Bennett's Restaurant** (p. 223). A short path leads down to the beach.

3225 Beach Loop Dr., Bandon, OR 97411. www.innatfacerock.com. ℭ **800/638-3092** or 541/347-9441. Fax 541/347-2532. 74 units. $115–$231 double. Rates include full breakfast. Children 17 and under stay free in parent's room. AE, DC, DISC, MC, V. Pets accepted ($20 fee). **Amenities:** Restaurant; lounge; bikes; exercise room; Jacuzzi; indoor pool; sauna. *In room:* TV, hair dryer, Internet (Wi-Fi in some).

Lighthouse Bed and Breakfast

Located on the road that leads to the mouth of the Coquille River, this riverfront B&B has a view of the historic Bandon Lighthouse, and, with its weathered cedar siding, large decks, and small sunroom, it's the quintessential Oregon beach house. Guest rooms range from a small room with the private bathroom across the hall to a spacious room with views of the ocean and lighthouse, a wood-burning stove, and a double whirlpool tub overlooking the river. Both the beach and Old Town Bandon are within a very short walk.

Throughout the winter, Oregon's rocky shores and haystack rocks feel the effects of storms that originate far to the north in cold polar waters. As these storms slam ashore, sometimes with winds topping 100 mph, their huge waves smash against the rocks with breathtaking force, sending spray flying. The perfect storm-watching days come right after a big storm, when the waves are still big but the sky is clear. This is also the best time to go beachcombing—it's your best chance to find the rare handblown Japanese glass fishing floats that sometimes wash ashore on the Oregon coast.

Among the **best storm-watching spots** on the coast are the South Jetty at the mouth of the Columbia River in Fort

Stevens State Park, Cannon Beach, Cape Meares, Depoe Bay, Cape Foulweather, Devil's Punchbowl on the Otter Crest Scenic Loop, Seal Rock, Cape Perpetua, Shore Acres State Park, Cape Arago State Park, Face Rock Viewpoint outside Bandon, and Cape Sebastian.

Some of the **best lodgings** for storm-watching are the Channel House in Depoe Bay, the Overleaf Lodge Resort in Yachats, and the Sunset Motel in Bandon. The coast's **best restaurants** for storm-watching include the Pelican Pub & Brewery in Pacific City, Tidal Raves and Restaurant Beck in Depoe Bay, Lord Bennett's Restaurant in Bandon, and Redfish in Port Orford.

650 Jetty Rd. SW (P.O Box 24), Bandon, OR 97411. www.lighthouselodging.com. ✆ **541/347-9316.** 5 units. $140–$245 double; lower rates Nov–Apr. Rates include full breakfast. MC, V. Children 12 and over welcome. *In room:* Hair dryer, free Wi-Fi.

Sunset Oceanfront Lodging Dozens of Bandon's famous monoliths rise from the sand and waves in front of this motel, making sunsets from the Sunset truly memorable. The rooms, however, with their dated furnishings and paneled walls, aren't nearly as nice as the views. There are, however, plans to update some of the rooms, so you should be sure to ask about them. On the other hand, since there's everything here from economy motel rooms and kitchen suites to rustic cabins and classic cottages, you should be able to find accommodations to your liking. If you want something rustic and private, try to get one of the cottages. The adjacent **Lord Bennett's Restaurant** (see below) has *the* view in Bandon.

1865 Beach Loop Rd. (P.O. Box 373), Bandon, OR 97411. www.sunsetmotel.com. ✆ **800/842-2407** or 541/347-2453. Fax 541/347-3636. 70 units. May 16–Oct 15 $70–$285 double; Oct 16–May 15 $50–$190 double. Rates include continental breakfast. Children 13 and under stay free in parent's room. AE, DISC, MC, V. Pets accepted ($10 per night). **Amenities:** Restaurant; lounge; Jacuzzi; indoor pool. *In room:* TV, Wi-Fi.

Where to Eat

When it's time for espresso, stop in at **Bandon Coffee Cafe,** 365 Second St. SE (✆ **541/347-1144;** www.bandoncoffee.com), in a cottage on the edge of Old Town. The **Bandon Baking Co. and Deli,** 160 Second St. (✆ **541/347-9440;** www.bandonbakingco.com), is a good bet for pastries and sandwiches. For a quick meal of incredibly fresh fish and chips, you can't beat **Bandon Fish Market,** 249 First St. SE (✆ **541/347-4282;** www.bandonfishmarket.com), which is right on the waterfront and has a few picnic tables. Also here on the waterfront, you can get cooked

Dungeness crab at **Tony's Crab Shack,** 155 First St. (℗ **541/347-2875;** www. tonyscrabshack.com).

Alloro Wine Bar ★★ ITALIAN   This wine bar is stylish and sophisticated, and fills up nightly with golfers in town to play the fabled Bandon Dunes course. With customers from all over the country, Alloro works hard to present creative Italian fare the likes of which you'll find nowhere else on the south coast. You might start your meal with duck empanadas or pan-seared scallops with caramelized pork belly, lemon cream, blood-orange puree, and fava beans. The Dungeness crab bisque should not be missed, and keep an eye out for house-made pastas such as ravioli with two cheeses, almonds, peas, and mint. I tend to go with the fish of the day, but such dishes as lamb *osso buco* with morels and slow-cooked rabbit with chorizo and fava beans can be mighty tempting. The wine list has lots from both Oregon and Italy, and there are also good desserts.

375 Second St. SE. ℗ **541/347-1850.** www.allorowinebar.com. Reservations recommended. Main courses $12–$27. AE, DISC, MC, V. Summer daily 4–9 or 10pm; contact for hours in other months. Closed Jan to mid-Feb.

The Loft Restaurant & Bar ★★ NEW AMERICAN   For a town with a world-class golf course, Bandon is surprisingly short of good places to eat. So, this restaurant on the second floor of the High Dock Building in old town Bandon should definitely be one of your choices while you're in the area. The menu is eclectic and varied, and ingredients are often locally sourced and organic. Familiar fare, such as burgers and pot pie, gets a gourmet spin. The burger comes with truffle aioli, and the pot pie is made with free-range chicken, wild black-trumpet mushrooms, and a porcini mushroom sauce. Of course, seafood dishes, such as grilled wild salmon and Dungeness crab cakes, are mainstays of the menu. To top it all off, there's a pretty view of the town's marina and, in the distance, the Coquille River Lighthouse.

315 First St. SE ℗ **541/329-0535.** www.theloftofbandon.com. Reservations recommended. Main courses $16–$26. AE, DISC, MC, V. Summer Wed–Sun 5–9pm; shorter hours other months.

Lord Bennett's Restaurant and Lounge AMERICAN   Lord Bennett's is the only restaurant in Bandon that overlooks this town's bizarre beachscape of contorted rock spires and sea stacks, and this alone makes it a must for a meal. The sunsets are unforgettable. Since sunsets come late in the day in the summer, you might want to eat a late lunch the day you plan to come here. I suggest starting dinner with some crab cakes before moving on to such main courses as oysters baked with spinach, bacon, and Pernod, or lamb chops with a hazelnut crust. There's a decent wine list, and the desserts are both beautiful and delicious.

1695 Beach Loop Dr. (next to the Sunset Motel). ℗ **541/347-3663.** www.bandonbythesea.com/ lord_ben.htm. Reservations recommended. Main courses $5–$10 lunch, $15–$21 dinner. AE, DISC, MC, V. Daily 11am–3pm and 5–9pm.

THE SOUTHERN OREGON COAST ★★★

Port Orford: 27 miles S of Bandon; 79 miles N of Crescent City, CA; 95 miles W of Grants Pass. Gold Beach: 54 miles N of Crescent City, CA; 32 miles S of Port Orford. Brookings/Harbor: 26 miles N of Crescent City, CA; 35 miles S of Gold Beach

The 60-mile stretch of coast between Port Orford and the California state line is the most beautiful stretch of the entire Oregon coast, yet because of its distance from major metropolitan areas, it attracts surprisingly few visitors.

Anchoring the northern end of this stretch of coast is Port Orford, which is today little more than a wide spot in the road, yet it is the oldest town on the coast other than Astoria. Named by Captain George Vancouver on April 5, 1792, this natural harbor in the lee of Port Orford Heads became the first settlement right on the Oregon coast when settlers and soldiers together constructed Fort Orford in 1851. A fort was necessary because of hostilities with the area's native population. This fort, however, was not sufficient protection for the settlers, and they eventually fled inland, crossing the Siskiyou Mountains.

The first settlers made camp here because there was something of a natural harbor, and today a small commercial-fishing fleet still works out of Port Orford harbor. However, because the harbor is not very protected, a large crane is used to haul the fishing fleet out of the water every night.

Cape Blanco, located just north of Port Orford and discovered and named by Spanish explorer Martín de Aguilar in 1603, once made an even grander claim than Port Orford when it was heralded as the westernmost point of land in the lower 48. Today that claim has been laid to rest by Cape Flattery, Washington, and Cape Blanco now only claims to be the westernmost point in Oregon.

In 19th-century California, gold prospectors had to struggle through rugged mountains in search of pay dirt, but here in Oregon they could just scoop it up off the beach. The black sands at the mouth of the Rogue River were high in gold, and it was this gold that gave Gold Beach its name. The white settlers attracted by the gold soon came in conflict with the local Rogue River (or TuTuNi) Indians. Violence erupted in 1856, but within the year the Rogue River Indian Wars had come to an end, and the TuTuNis were moved to a reservation.

The TuTuNis had for centuries found the river to be a plentiful source of salmon, and when the gold played out, commercial fishermen moved in to take advantage of the large salmon runs. The efficiency of their nets and traps quickly decimated the local salmon population, and a hatchery was constructed to replenish the runs.

Brookings and Harbor together comprise the southernmost community on the Oregon coast. Because of the warm year-round temperatures, this region is known as the Oregon Banana Belt, and you'll see palm trees and other cold-sensitive plants thriving in gardens around town. Farms south of town grow nearly all of the Easter lilies sold in the United States. Other plants that thrive in this climate include coast redwoods, Oregon myrtles, and wild azaleas. Dividing the sister towns of Brookings and Harbor is the Chetco River, one of the purest and most beautiful rivers in the state.

Essentials

GETTING THERE   There is no convenient way to get to this stretch of coast. Coming from the north, the nearest highway connection to I-5 is Ore. 42 from Roseburg to Bandon. Coming from the south, you must either follow U.S. 101 north through California or take U.S. 199 southwest from Grants Pass and then continue north on U.S. 101. There is also a narrow, winding road over the mountains to Gold Beach from Galice (near Grants Pass), but I don't recommend this road, and in winter it is usually closed.

VISITOR INFORMATION   For more information on Port Orford, contact the **Port Orford & North Curry County Chamber of Commerce,** Battle Rock Park, U.S. 101 S. (P.O. Box 637), Port Orford, OR 97465 (© **541/332-8055;** www. portorfordchamber.com). For information on the Gold Beach area, contact the **Gold

Beach Promotion Committee, 94080 Shirley Lane (P.O. Box 375), Gold Beach, OR 97444 (© 800/525-2334 or 541/247-7526; www.goldbeach.org), which has its visitor center in South Beach Park at the south end of town. For more information on the Brookings area, contact the Brookings-Harbor Chamber of Commerce, 16330 Lower Harbor Rd. (P.O. Box 940), Brookings, OR 97415 (© 800/535-9469 or 541/469-3181; www.brookingsor.com).

The Port Orford Area

Cape Blanco is now preserved as Cape Blanco State Park (© 541/332-6774; www.oregon.gov/oprd/parks), where you'll find miles of beaches, hiking trails through windswept meadows, picnic areas, and a campground. This high headland is also the site of the Cape Blanco Lighthouse, which is the most westerly lighthouse in Oregon. Not far from the lighthouse is the Hughes House Museum (© 541/332-0248; www.portorfordoregon.com), a restored Eastlake Victorian home that was built in 1898 and is furnished with period antiques. Both the lighthouse and the Hughes House are open to the public April through October, Tuesday through Sunday from 10am to 3:30pm. Lighthouse admission is $2 for adults and $1 for children 11 and under; Hughes House admission is by donation.

For a good view of Port Orford and this entire section of coast, drive up to Port Orford Heads State Park, which is located on the northern edge of town and has a short trail out to an overlook. The route to the wayside is well marked. Here you can also visit the Port Orford Lifeboat Station (© 541/332-0521; www.portorford lifeboatstation.org), a small museum preserving the history of the Coast Guard on the southern Oregon coast. The museum is open April through October, Thursday through Monday from 10am to 3:30pm; admission is free. Right in town, you can visit Battle Rock Park and learn the history of the rock refuge that rises out of Port Orford's beach. This is a good beach on which to walk, as is the beach at Paradise Point State Recreation Site, just north of town.

In town you'll find several art galleries. One of my favorites is the Cook Gallery, 705 Oregon St. (© 541/332-0045; www.rickcookfurniture.com), which features beautiful handcrafted wood furniture and sculpture. North of town, check out the wood carvings at A&T Myrtlewood, 45683 U.S. 101, Sixes (© 541/348-2586; www.aandtmyrtlewood.com).

Six miles south of Port Orford, you'll find Humbug Mountain State Park (© 541/332-6774; www.oregon.gov/oprd/parks), where Humbug Mountain rises 1,756 feet from the ocean. A pretty campground is tucked into the forest at the base of the mountain, and a trail leads to the summit.

About 12 miles south of Port Orford is a place the kids aren't going to let you pass by. The Prehistoric Gardens & Rainforest, 36848 U.S. 101 S. (© 541/332-4463; http://prehistoricgardens.com), is a lost world of life-size dinosaur replicas. Though they aren't as realistic as those in *Jurassic Park,* they'll make the kids squeal with delight. The gardens are open in the summer daily from 9am to 7pm; other months, call for hours. Admission is $10 for adults, $9 for seniors, and $8 for children 3 to 12.

The Gold Beach Area

There is, of course, a beach at Gold Beach, though it's not really the area's main attraction. That distinction goes to the Rogue River, which empties into the Pacific here at the town of Gold Beach and is the most famous fishing and rafting river in the state. You can tour the river in powerful hydrojet boats, which have a very shallow draft and use water jets instead of propellers. These features allow these boats to cross rapids and riffles only a few inches deep. Along the way you may see deer, black bear, river otters, and bald eagles. A running narration covers the river's colorful history. **Jerry's Rogue Jets,** 29880 Harbor Way (© **800/451-3645** or 541/247-4571; www.roguejets.com), which leaves from the Port of Gold Beach on the south side of the Rogue River Bridge, offers three different trips, ranging in length from 64 to 104 miles. Fares range from $45 to $90 for adults and $20 to $40 for children.

When you want to get out on the beach, head north of town across the Rogue River to Nesika Beach. To reach the best stretch of this beach, take the North Nesika Beach turnoff and then continue north to the end of the road. Alternatively, continue a little farther north to Old Coast Road, where you'll find a steep trail down to the beach.

Jerry's Rogue River Museum, 29880 Harbor Way (© **541/247-4571;** www. roguejets.com), at the Port of Gold Beach and affiliated with Jerry's Jet Boat Tours, is the more modern and informative of the town's two museums. It focuses on the geology and cultural and natural history of the Rogue River. It's open daily in summer from 9am to 9pm and daily in the off season from 9am to 5pm; admission is free. At the diminutive **Curry Historical Museum,** 29419 Ellensburg Ave. (© **541/247-9396;** www.curryhistory.com), you can learn more about the history of the area and see plenty of Native American and pioneer artifacts. The museum is open Tuesday through Saturday from 10am to 4pm. Admission is $2 for adults and 50¢ for children 15 and under. The museum is closed in January.

Golfers can play a round at the 9-hole **Cedar Bend Golf Course,** 34391 Cedar Valley Rd. (© **541/247-6911;** www.cedarbendgolf.com), 12 miles north of Gold Beach off U.S. 101. If you'd like to go horseback riding, contact **Hawk's Rest Ranch,** 94667 N. Bank Pistol River Rd. (© **541/247-6423;** www.siskiyouwest. com), in Pistol River, 10 miles south of Gold Beach. Expect to pay $40 to $50 for a 90-minute ride.

Hikers have an abundance of options in the area. At the **Frances Schrader Old Growth Trail,** 10 miles up Jerry's Flat Road/South Bank Rogue River Road near the Lobster Creek Campground, you can hike through an ancient forest of huge, majestic trees. In this same area, you'll also find the **Myrtle Tree Trail.** Along this .25-mile trail, you'll find the world's largest myrtle tree, which is 88 feet tall and 42 feet in circumference. For more information on hiking in the Gold Beach area, contact the Siskiyou National Forest's **Gold Beach Ranger Station,** 29279 Ellensburg Ave., Gold Beach, OR 97444 (© **541/247-3600;** www.fs.fed.us/r6/rogue-siskiyou).

South to Brookings

Gold Beach itself is a wide sandy beach, but just a few miles to the south, the mountains once again march into the sea, creating what, in my opinion, is Oregon's most spectacular section of coastline. Though it's only 30 miles from Gold Beach to **Brookings,** you can easily spend the whole day making the trip. Along the way are numerous viewpoints, picnic areas, hiking trails, and beaches.

The **Oregon Coast Trail,** which extends (in short sections) from California to Washington, has several segments both north and south of Gold Beach. The most spectacular sections of this trail are south of town at Cape Sebastian and in Samuel H. Boardman State Scenic Corridor.

The first place you'll come to as you drive south from Gold Beach is **Turtle Rock Wayside,** just south of town. Although this is little more than a roadside pull-off, it does have a nice view. The next place to stop is at **Cape Sebastian State Scenic Corridor ★★,** which is 5 miles south of Gold Beach. This headland, which towers 700 feet above the ocean, is a good vantage point for whale-watching between December and March. A 1.5-mile trail leads from the parking area out to the end of the cape and continues down to the beach at Hunter's Cove. This little-visited spot is one of the best places on the south coast for a hike.

Another 2 miles south on U.S. 101, you come to **Meyers Creek ★★,** which is at the **Pistol River State Scenic Viewpoint.** Here, scattered on the beach, you'll find some of the rugged monolithic rock formations that make this coastline so breathtaking. This is the most popular windsurfing and surfing beach on the south coast and is also a good clamming beach. About 2 miles farther south, you'll come to an area of large sand dunes at the mouth of the Pistol River.

South of the Pistol River, you enter the **Samuel H. Boardman State Scenic Corridor,** which has numerous viewpoints, **beaches ★,** picnic areas, and stretches of hiking trail. About 6 miles south of the Pistol River, you come to **Arch Rock Viewpoint ★★,** a picnic area with a beautiful view of an offshore monolith that has been carved into an arch by the action of the waves. Two miles beyond this, you come to the **Natural Bridge Viewpoint.** These two arches were formed when a sea cave collapsed. In 2 more miles you cross the **Thomas Creek Bridge,** which at 345 feet high is the highest bridge in Oregon. In a little more than a mile, you come to **Whale-head Beach Viewpoint,** where a pyramidal rock just offshore bears a striking resemblance to a spy-hopping whale. There's a better view of Whalehead Rock a half-mile south.

In another 1½ miles you'll come to **House Rock Viewpoint,** where sweeping vistas unfold to the north and south. At **Cape Ferrelo Viewpoint** and **Lone Ranch Viewpoint** just to the south, you'll find a grassy headland. Just south of here, watch for **Rainbow Rock Viewpoint,** which has a panorama of a stretch of beach strewn with large boulders. Go another 3 miles to **Harris Beach State Park (𝄕 541/469-2021),** the last stop along this coast. Here you'll find picnicking, camping, and a good view of **Goat Island,** which is the Oregon coast's largest island.

The Brookings Area

The Chetco River is known throughout Oregon as one of the best salmon and steel-head rivers in the state. It is also one of the prettiest rivers and offers opportunities for swimming, rafting, and kayaking. If you want to go out fishing for salmon or steelhead with a guide, contact **Fishawk River Company (𝄕 541-469-2422** or 541/661-0031; www.fishawk.net).

The area's botanical attractions are one of the most interesting reasons to pay a visit to the Brookings area. At **Alfred A. Loeb State Park (𝄕 541/469-2021;** www. oregon.gov/oprd/parks), 8 miles up the Chetco River from Brookings on North Bank Road, you can see old-growth myrtle trees (from which the ubiquitous myrtlewood souvenirs of the south coast are made). Myrtle (*Umbellularia californica*) grows naturally only along the southern Oregon and Northern California coasts. The Brookings area is also the northernmost range of the giant coast redwoods (*Sequoia sempervirens),* and just beyond Loeb State Park, you'll come to one of the largest stands of coast redwoods in Oregon. Here the 1.3-mile **Redwood Nature Trail** loops past numerous big trees. This nature trail is connected to Loeb State Park via the .8-mile

Information, Please

The Oregon state welcome center at **Crissey Field State Recreation Site** (© 800/551-6949), on U.S. 101 just across the state line from California, is big and green, like the state of Oregon itself. The center shares space with the U.S. Forest Service and is a showcase of "green" construction. There are photovoltaic panels on the roof, geothermal radiant floor heat, solar water heaters, and counters made from myrtlewood trees cut down in a nearby state park for safety reasons. All in all, this center makes an appropriate introduction to a state that is as "green" as it is green.

Riverview Trail. The region's wild azaleas, celebrated each year over Memorial Day weekend, come into bloom in May. The best place to see them is at **Azalea Park,** which is a couple of blocks east of U.S. 101 just before the bridge over the Chetco River at the south end of Brookings.

One of the more unusual places to visit in the area is the **Brandy Peak Distillery,** 18526 Tetley Rd. (© 541/469-0194; www.brandypeak.com), which is located north of Brookings off U.S. 101. (Take Carpenterville Rd. for 4 miles up into the hills, and then go right on Tetley Rd. and immediately right into the distillery.) This microdistillery produces varietal marc brandies (unaged brandies), as well as barrel-aged brandies, grappas, and pear brandy. The distillery is open for tours and tastings Tuesday through Saturday from 1 to 5pm between March and early January, and by appointment the rest of the year. If you want to be absolutely sure, call beforehand. Three miles south of Brookings on U.S. 101, be sure to stop at the **Chetco Valley Museum,** 15461 Museum Rd. (© 541/469-6651), if for no other reason than to see the largest Monterrey cypress in the state (perhaps the country), in front of the museum. Memorial Day through Labor Day, the museum is open Saturday and Sunday from noon to 4pm (call for hours in other months).

Where to Stay
PORT ORFORD

Castaway by the Sea ⚐   Situated on a hill high above Port Orford harbor and commanding a sweeping panorama of the southern Oregon coast, this modest motel is far more comfortable than it appears from the outside. All the rooms take in the extraordinary view, and most have comfy little sunrooms from which to gaze off to sea. The rooms are quite large and well maintained, and some have kitchenettes. Out back there is a lawn with a few benches overlooking the harbor. The motel also rents out an adjacent historic house.

545 W. Fifth St. (P.O. Box 844), Port Orford, OR 97465. www.castawaybythesea.com. © **541/332-4502.** Fax 541/332-9303. 13 units. $65–$95 double; $85–$155 suite; $185 house. AE, DISC, MC, V. Pets accepted ($10 per night). *In room:* TV, kitchen, free Wi-Fi.

Home by the Sea ★   Set high atop a bluff overlooking the beach and Battle Rock, this contemporary B&B has large guest rooms (and a downstairs living room) with some of the best views on the coast. The inn is a block off U.S. 101 and within walking distance of several restaurants, art galleries, the beach, and the town's harbor. Owners/innkeepers Alan and Brenda Mitchell are a wealth of information about the area. A garage is available for anyone traveling by motorcycle or bicycle.

444 Jackson St. (P.O. Box 606), Port Orford, OR 97465. http://homebythesea.com/HBSroom.html. *①* **877/332-2855** or 541/332-2855. 2 units. $105–$115 double. Rates include full breakfast. Children 12 and under stay free in parent's room. MC, V. *In room:* TV, fridge, hair dryer, free Wi-Fi.

WildSpring Guest Habitat ★★ With enough tranquility to restore the most frazzled soul, this woodland retreat overlooking the ocean is a blissful hideaway on the outskirts of Port Orford. Accommodations are in beautifully appointed cabins in the woods. With hardwood floors, living and dining areas, and slate-walled showers, these cabins are so comfortably and attractively furnished that you just might forget to go out and explore the beach. A central guest hall has a kitchen you can use and plenty of refreshments for guests. The open-air slate hot tub, with its ocean view, is reason enough to visit Port Orford and stay at this delightful eco-friendly resort. Massages, manicures, and pedicures are available.

92978 Cemetery Loop, Box R, Port Orford, OR 97465. www.wildspring.com. *①* **866/333-9453.** Fax 541/332-0360. 5 units. June–Sept $276–$306 double; May and Oct $238–$278 double; Nov–Apr $198–$248 double. Rates include continental breakfast. AE, DISC, MC, V. Children 13 and older welcome. **Amenities:** Bikes; concierge; Jacuzzi. *In room:* TV/DVD, CD player, fridge, hair dryer, MP3 docking station, no phone, free Wi-Fi.

GOLD BEACH

Ireland's Rustic Lodges 🏕 The name sums it up—rustic cabins set amid shady grounds that are as green as Ireland (and beautifully landscaped, too). Although there are some modern motel rooms here, they just can't compare to the quaint old cabins, which have stone fireplaces, paneled walls, and unusual door handles made from twisted branches. Built in 1922, the cabins are indeed rustic and are not for those who need modern comforts. The mature gardens surrounding the cabins are beautiful any time of year, but particularly in late spring. Ireland's is managed by the adjacent Gold Beach Inn, which has lots of very predictable modern rooms, if that's what you're looking for.

29346 Ellensburg Ave. (U.S. 101), Gold Beach, OR 97444. www.irelandsrusticlodges.com. *①* **877/447-3526** or 541/247-7718. 40 units. Mid-June to mid-Sept $99–$144 double, $110–$169 cabin; mid-Sept to mid-June $58–$105 double, $70–$115 cabin. Rates include full breakfast. Children 12 and under stay free in parent's room. AE, DISC, MC, V. Pets accepted ($10). **Amenities:** 2 Jacuzzis; free Wi-Fi. *In room:* TV.

Jot's Resort ★ ☺ Stretching along the north bank of the Rogue River, Jot's has a definite fishing orientation and is very popular with families. The resort offers a wide variety of room sizes and rates, but every room has a view of the water and the Rogue River Bridge. The deluxe rooms are the most attractively furnished, while the condos are the most spacious (some have spiral staircases that lead up to loft sleeping areas). The dining room and lounge offer reasonably priced meals. Fishing guides and deep-sea charters can be arranged.

94360 Wedderburn Loop (P.O. Box 1200), Gold Beach, OR 97444. www.jotsresort.com. *①* **800/367-5687** or 541/247-6676. Fax 541/247-6716. 140 units. Summer $95–$135 double, $155–$375 suite/condo; off-season rates $50–$60 double, $95–$250 suite/condo. Children 12 and under stay free in parent's room. AE, DISC, MC, V. Pets accepted ($10–$25 per night). **Amenities:** Restaurant; lounge; exercise room; 3 Jacuzzis; indoor and outdoor pools. *In room:* TV, fridge, hair dryer, free Wi-Fi.

Tu Tu Tun Lodge ★★★ Tu Tu Tun Lodge, 7 miles up the Rogue River from Gold Beach, provides the most deluxe lodging on the south coast and has a sophisticated styling and an idyllic setting. The main lodge building, with an immense fireplace, incorporates enough rock and natural wood to give it a rustic feel without sacrificing any modern comforts. On warm days, the patio overlooking the river is a great spot for relaxing, and on cold nights logs crackle in a fire pit. Guest rooms are beautifully furnished, many with Stickley furniture. Each room has a private patio or balcony, and second-floor rooms have excellent river views. Some rooms have wood-burning fireplaces or outdoor soaking tubs. The dining room overlooks the river and serves four-course dinners ($53). There's a 6-hole pitch-and-putt golf course here, and fishing guides and boat excursions can be arranged.

96550 N. Bank Rogue River Rd., Gold Beach, OR 97444. www.tututun.com. ✆ **800/864-6357** or 541/247-6664. Fax 541/247-0672. 21 units. $135–$365 double, $255–$420 suite, $275–$775 house; lower rates in winter. DISC, MC, V. May–Oct Children 10 and older welcome; Nov–Apr all ages welcome. **Amenities:** Restaurant (dining room closed for dinner Nov–Apr); lounge; concierge; access to nearby health club; Jacuzzi; outdoor lap pool; room service; spa services. *In room:* TV, fridge, hair dryer, free Wi-Fi.

THE BROOKINGS AREA

Best Western Beachfront Inn   Located on the edge of the marina in Brookings' sister town of Harbor (on the south side of the Chetco River), the Beachfront Inn has the only oceanfront accommodations in this area. Most rooms are fairly large and all have ocean views and balconies. The more expensive rooms have whirlpool tubs with picture windows. There's also an outdoor pool and whirlpool.

16008 Boat Basin Rd., Brookings, OR 97415. www.bestwesternoregon.com. ✆ **800/468-4081** or 541/469-7779. Fax 541/469-0283. 102 units. June–Sept $179–$250 double; Oct–May $124–$195 double. Children 12 and under stay free in parent's room. AE, DC, DISC, MC, V. Pets accepted ($10 per night). **Amenities:** Jacuzzi; outdoor pool; free Wi-Fi. *In room:* TV, fridge, hair dryer, free Internet.

Brookings South Coast Inn ★   This 1917 Craftsman bungalow was designed by the famous San Francisco architect Bernard Maybeck and is filled with the sort of beautiful architectural details that characterized the Arts and Crafts movement. The inn's most spacious guest room is dedicated to Maybeck. If you want an ocean view, you'll have to stay in the apartment, which also has a full kitchen. The cottage, across the garden from the main house, offers a more private setting. Guests have use of a large living room full of antiques, where a fire often crackles in the stone fireplace (although the weather here never gets very cold).

516 Redwood St., Brookings, OR 97415. www.southcoastinn.com. ✆ **800/525-9273** or 541/469-5557. 6 units. $119–$159 double. Rates include full breakfast (except in apt and cottage). AE, DISC, MC, V. *In room:* A/C, TV/DVD, hair dryer, free Wi-Fi (in main house).

Where to Eat

PORT ORFORD

Crazy Norwegian's Fish and Chips SEAFOOD   This casual roadside diner at the south end of Port Orford serves some of the best fish and chips on the Oregon coast. Best of all, it comes in three sizes, so whether you're starving or just want a snack, you should be sure to stop here. If you're not a fish and chips person, try the crab melt sandwich.

259 Sixth St. (U.S. 101). ✆ **541/332-8601.** Main courses $6.50–$13. AE, DISC, MC, V. Apr–Aug daily 11:30am–8pm; Sept–Mar Wed–Sun 11:30am–7pm.

Redfish ★ NORTHWEST   There simply is nothing else like Redfish anywhere on the southern Oregon coast. The restaurant is a modernist glass cube of an architectural confection overlooking the beach and Battle Rock. The restaurant's unexpected sophistication and elegance and its superb food make a meal here a highlight of a visit to this stretch of the coast. At both lunch and dinner, keep an eye out for the outstanding caramelized sea scallops on white-truffle grits and the crab cakes. While you can get a rib-eye steak, a lamb T-bone, or seared halibut with a grapefruit beurre blanc, you can also get one of the best burgers on the Oregon coast. Brunch is served on the weekends.

517 Jefferson St. © **541/366-2200.** www.redfishportorford.com. Reservations recommended. Main courses $9–$14 lunch, $10–$29 dinner. AE, DC, DISC, MC, V. Mon–Fri 11am–9pm; Sat–Sun 9am–9pm.

GOLD BEACH

The best meals in Gold Beach are served in the dining room at **Tu Tu Tun Lodge** (see "Where to Stay," above). For delicious, filling breakfasts, head up the Rogue River a mile or so to **Indian Creek Café,** 94682 Jerry's Flat Rd. (© **541/247-0680**). The town's other top breakfast place is **Rollin in Dough Bakery & Bistro,** 94257 N. Bank Rd (© **541/247-4438;** www.rollin-in-dough.com), which also makes lots of good pastries. You'll find this place just east of the U.S. 101 bridge. If you want to take home some local seafood, head to the Port of Gold Beach and **Fishermen Direct Seafood,** 29975 Harbor Way (© **888/523-9494** or 541/247-9494; www.fishermendirect.com), which is in the Cannery Building. They sell canned and smoked salmon and albacore tuna.

Anna's by the Sea NEW AMERICAN   In a big red barn of a building a block east of busy U.S. 101, you'll find a tiny little restaurant/wine bar/wine shop serving some of the best food in town. The menu is as short as the restaurant is small (it only seats 14 people), but the chef, who goes by the nickname of Cookie, turns out meals with big flavors. Be sure to start with the cream of tomato soup. After that, you might opt for the wild-caught Mexican shrimp with black truffle oil and potato puffs, local black rock cod with sweet onions, or seared scallops on chanterelle mushroom gravy. This is a far cry from Gold Beach's other tourist-town restaurants.

29672 Stewart St. © **541/247-2100.** www.annasbythesea.com. Reservations recommended. Main course $17–$19. MC, V. Oct–June Wed–Sat 5:30–8:30pm; July–Sept Tues–Sat 5:30–8:30pm.

Nor'wester Seafood ★ SEAFOOD/STEAK   Large portions of simply prepared fresh seafood are the mainstays of the menu at this dockside restaurant, which has long been a local favorite. Fish and chips are good, and the steak-and-seafood combinations are popular choices for big appetites. From the second-floor dining room, you can watch fishing boats on the Rogue River. You'll find the Nor'wester at the north end of town in the port.

10 Harbor Way (in the Port of Gold Beach). © **541/247-2333.** www.norwesterseafood.com. Reservations recommended. Main courses $23–$34. AE, DISC, MC, V. Daily 5–9pm.

THE BROOKINGS AREA

If it's pizza you're craving, **Wild River Pizza Company,** 16279 U.S. 101 S., just south of Brookings (© **541/469-7454;** www.wildriverbrewing.com), turns out a crispy one, accompanied by their own microbrews. Locals swear by the **Hungry Clam,** at the Port of Brookings-Harbor (© **541/469-2526**), for fish and chips; I, however, have not been impressed. For smoked salmon, head south of town to the **Great American Smokehouse,** 15657 U.S. 101 S. (© **800/828-3474** or 541/469-6903; www. smokehouse-salmon.com), which sells a wide variety of smoked and canned seafood.

Café Kitanishi JAPANESE   Something about being on the coast always puts me in the mood for sushi. If you, too, are suddenly struck with a desire for hamachi, ebi, unagi, or any other sort of sushi, head to Café Kitanishi. I always go for such fancy rolls as the dragon roll and the fire engine roll. Of course they have California rolls, but since you're now in Oregon, why not pretend to be an Oregonian and order a Brookings *maki?* Surprisingly, this place has a variety of pastries and cakes for dessert. You'll find the restaurant 2 blocks off U.S. 101 (go west on Wharf Street).

632 Hemlock St. © **541/469-7864.** www.cafekitanishi.com. Reservations recommended at dinner. Sushi $4–$16; main courses $9–$15 lunch, $17–$27 dinner. AE, DISC, MC, V. Tues–Wed 11am–3pm; Thurs–Sat 11am–3pm and 5–9pm.

THE COLUMBIA GORGE

The Columbia Gorge, which begins just a few miles east of Portland and stretches for nearly 70 miles along the shores of the Columbia River, is a dramatic landscape of mountains, cliffs, and waterfalls created by massive ice-age floods.

Flanked by national forests and snow-covered peaks on both the Oregon and Washington sides of the Columbia River, the Gorge is as breathtaking a landscape as you will find anywhere in the West, and the fascinating geology, dramatic vistas, and abundance of recreational opportunities make it a premier vacation destination almost any month of the year. Not only is the area filled with waterfalls, trails, and some of the world's best windsurfing and kiteboarding, but there are also fascinating museums, resort hotels, hot springs, historic B&Bs, and even wineries. Between 1913 and 1922, a scenic highway (one of the first paved roads in the Northwest) was built through the Gorge, and in 1986 much of the area was designated the Columbia Gorge National Scenic Area in an attempt to preserve the Gorge's spectacular and unique natural beauty.

The Columbia River is older than the hills. It's older than the mountains, too, which explains why this river flows not from the mountains but through them. The river was already flowing into the Pacific Ocean when the Cascade Range began rising millions of years ago. However, it was a series of recent events, geologically speaking, that gave the Columbia Gorge its very distinctive appearance. About 15,000 years ago, toward the end of the last ice age, huge dams of ice far upstream collapsed and sent floodwaters racing down the Columbia. As the floodwaters swept through the Columbia Gorge, they were as much as 1,200 feet deep. Ice and rock carried by the floodwaters helped the river to scour out the sides of the once gently sloping valley, leaving behind the steep-walled gorge that we know today. The waterfalls that elicit so many oohs and aahs are the most dramatic evidence of these great floods.

The vast gorge that the Columbia River has formed as it slices through the mountains is effectively a giant bridge between the rain-soaked forests west of the Cascades and the desert-dry sagebrush scrublands of central Oregon. This change in climate is caused by moist air condensing into snow and rain as it passes over the crest of the Cascades. And because most of the air's moisture falls on the western slopes, the eastern slopes and the land stretching for hundreds of miles beyond lie in a rain shadow. Perhaps nowhere else on earth can you witness this rain-shadow effect so easily and in such a short distance. It's so pronounced that as you come around a bend on I-84 just east of Hood River, you can see dry grasslands to the east and dense forests of Douglas fir over your shoulder to the west. In between the two extremes lies a community of plants that's unique to the Columbia Gorge, and consequently, springtime here brings colorful displays of wildflowers.

In North America, the Columbia River is second only to the Mississippi in the volume of water it carries to the sea—but more than just water flows through the Columbia Gorge. As the only break in the entire length of the Cascade Range, the Gorge acts as a massive natural wind tunnel. During the summer, the sun bakes the lands east of the Cascades, causing the air to rise. Cool air from the west side then rushes up the river, at times whipping through Hood River with near gale force. These winds, blowing against the downriver flow of water, set up ideal conditions for windsurfing and kiteboarding on the Columbia. The reliability of the winds, and the waves they kick up, has turned Hood River into something of an Aspen of windsurfing.

For centuries the Columbia River has been an important route between the maritime Northwest and the dry interior. Lewis and Clark canoed down the river in 1805, and pioneers followed the Oregon Trail to its banks at The Dalles. It was here at The Dalles that many pioneers transferred their wagons to boats for the dangerous journey downriver to Oregon City. The set of rapids known as The Dalles and the waterfalls of the Cascades were the two most dangerous sections of the Columbia Gorge, so towns arose at these two points to transport goods and people around the treacherous waters. For a while, locks and a canal helped circumvent some of the treacherous white water, but now the rapids of the Columbia lie flooded beneath the waters behind the Bonneville and The Dalles dams. The ease of navigating the river today has dimmed the importance of the towns of Cascade Locks and The Dalles, but both are steeped in the history of the Gorge.

THE COLUMBIA GORGE ★★★

Columbia Gorge: Begins 18 miles E of Portland

Stretching from the Sandy River in the west to the Deschutes River in the east, the Columbia Gorge National Scenic Area is one of the most breathtakingly dramatic places in the United States. Carved by floods of unimaginable power, this miles-wide canyon is flanked on the north by Mount Adams and on the south by Mount Hood, both of which rise more than 11,000 feet high. With its diaphanous waterfalls, basalt cliffs painted with colorful lichens, and dark forests of Douglas firs rising up from the banks of the Columbia River, the Gorge is a year-round recreational area where hiking trails lead to hidden waterfalls and mountain-top panoramas, mountain-bike trails meander through the forest, and windsurfers race across wind-whipped waters.

The Columbia Gorge National Scenic Area is as controversial as it is beautiful. Over the years since this area received this federal designation, the fights over the use of private land within the Gorge have been constant. The pressure to develop this scenic marvel of the Northwest has been unrelenting, as landowners throughout the Gorge have fought against restrictions on development. To find out more about protecting the Gorge, contact the **Friends of the Columbia Gorge** (© **503/241-3762;** www. gorgefriends.org), which every spring offers numerous guided wildflower hikes.

Essentials

GETTING THERE I-84 and the Historic Columbia River Highway both pass through the Gorge on the Oregon side of the Columbia.

VISITOR INFORMATION   For information on the Gorge, contact the Columbia River Gorge Visitor's Association, P.O. Box 324, Corbett, OR 97019 (© **800/984-6743;** www.crgva.org), or the Columbia River Gorge National Scenic Area, 902 Wasco St., Ste. 200, Hood River, OR 97031 (© **541/308-1700;** www.fs.fed.us/r6/columbia). There's also the Forest Service Visitor Center (© **503/695-2372**) at Multnomah Falls Lodge (take the Historic Columbia River Hwy. or the Multnomah Falls exit off I-84) and another in the lobby of Skamania Lodge, 1131 SW Skamania Lodge Way (© **509/427-2528**), in Stevenson, Washington.

Learning About the Gorge & Its History

Columbia Gorge Interpretive Center Museum ★★   Focusing on the Gorge's early Native American inhabitants and the development of the area by white settlers, this museum is your single best introduction to the Columbia Gorge. Exhibits contain historical photographs by Edward Curtis and others that illustrate the story of portage companies and paddle wheelers that once operated along this stretch of the Columbia River. A 37-foot-high replica of a 19th-century fish wheel gives an understanding of how salmon runs have been threatened in the past and the present. Displays also frankly discuss other problems that the coming of settlers brought to this area, and a slide program tells the history of the formation of the Gorge. When it's not cloudy, the center has an awesome view of the south side of the Gorge. This museum is also home to a large rosary collection.

990 SW Rock Creek Dr., Stevenson, WA. © **800/991-2338** or 509/427-8211. www.columbiagorge. org. Admission $7 adults, $6 seniors and students, $5 children 6–12, free for children 5 and under. Daily 10am–5pm. Closed New Year's day, Thanksgiving, and Christmas.

A Driving Tour

Though I-84 is the fastest road through the Columbia Gorge, it is not the most scenic route. The Gorge is well worth a full day's exploration and is best appreciated at a more leisurely pace on the **Historic Columbia River Highway ★★★,** which begins 16 miles east of downtown Portland at the second Troutdale exit off I-84. Opened in 1915, this highway was a marvel of engineering at the time and, by providing access to automobiles, opened the Gorge to casual visits.

At the western end of the historic highway, you'll find **Lewis & Clark State Park,** which is near the mouth of the Sandy River. This park is popular with anglers and Portlanders looking to cool off in the Sandy River during the hot summer months. There is also a rock-climbing area within the park.

The first unforgettable view of the Gorge comes at the **Portland Women's Forum State Scenic Viewpoint,** which may also be your first encounter with the legendary Columbia Gorge winds. To learn more about the historic highway and how it was built, stop at the **Vista House,** 40700 E. Historic Columbia River Hwy. (© **503/695-2240;** http://vistahouse.com), 733 feet above the river on **Crown Point.** Although you can see displays of historical photos here at Vista House, most visitors can't concentrate on the exhibits, preferring to gaze at the breathtaking 30-mile view. Spring through fall, Vista House is open daily from 9am to 6pm; call for hours in other months.

From Crown Point, the historic highway drops down into the Gorge and passes several picturesque **waterfalls.** The first of these is 249-foot **Latourell Falls ★,** a diaphanous wisp of a waterfall cascading over basalt cliffs stained lime-green by lichen. A 2.3-mile loop trail leads from this waterfall up to the smaller Upper

The Columbia Gorge & Hood River

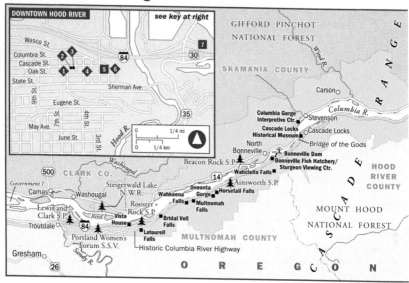

DOWNTOWN HOOD RIVER — see key at right

GIFFORD PINCHOT NATIONAL FOREST

SKAMANIA COUNTY

Latourell Falls. East of these falls, you'll come to Shepherd's Dell Falls, Bridal Veil Falls, Mist Falls, and Wahkeena Falls, all of which are either right beside the road or a short walk away. If you're interested in a longer hike, trails link several of the falls. However, for spectacular views, you can't beat the steep 4.4-mile round-trip hike to Angels Rest. The well-signposted trail head for this hike is on the historic highway near the community of Bridal Veil.

At 620 feet from the lip to the lower pool, **Multnomah Falls ★★★** is the tallest waterfall in Oregon and the fourth tallest in the United States. As the largest and most famous waterfall along the historic highway, this is also the state's most visited natural attraction, so expect crowds. A steep trail leads up to the top of the falls, and partway up there is a picturesque arched bridge that is directly in front of the falls. From the top of the falls, other trails lead off into the **Mount Hood National Forest.** The historic **Multnomah Falls Lodge** (p. 241) has a restaurant, snack bar, and gift shop, as well as a **National Forest Visitor Center** (🕿 **503/695-2372**) with information on the geology, history, and natural history of the Gorge.

East of Multnomah Falls, the scenic highway passes by **Oneonta Gorge ★★**, a narrow rift in the cliffs. Through this tiny gorge flows a stream that serves as a watery pathway for anyone interested in exploring upstream to **Oneonta Falls;** just bear in mind that you'll be walking in the creek if you explore this gorgeous little gorge. Less than a half-mile east of Oneonta Gorge, you'll come to **Horsetail Falls.** From these roadside falls, a trail leads uphill to Upper Horsetail Falls. The trail then passes behind the upper falls and continues another 2 miles to Triple Falls, passing above Oneonta Gorge along the way.

If you'd like to escape the crowds and see a little-visited waterfall, watch for Frontage Road on your right just before the historic highway merges with I-84. Drive east for 2 miles to a gravel parking area at the trail head for **Elowah Falls ★★.** These

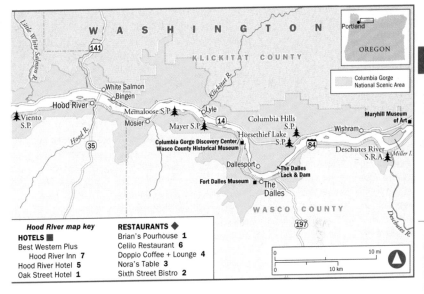

Map labels:

WASHINGTON

141

KLICKITAT COUNTY

Little White Salmon R.
Klickitat R.

White Salmon
Bingen

Hood River
Memaloose S.P.
Mosier
Lyle
Mayer S.P.
14
Columbia Hills S.P.
Horsethief Lake S.P.
Columbia Gorge Discovery Center/
Wasco County Historical Museum

Viento S.P.
Hood R.
35

Maryhill Museum
of Art

Wishram

84
Deschutes River
S.R.A.
Miller I.

Dallesport

Fort Dalles Museum
The Dalles
The Dalles
Lock & Dam

WASCO COUNTY

197

Deschutes R.

Portland
OREGON

Columbia Gorge
National Scenic Area

7

THE COLUMBIA GORGE | The Columbia Gorge

Hood River map key
HOTELS ■
Best Western Plus
Hood River Inn **7**
Hood River Hotel **5**
Oak Street Hotel **1**

RESTAURANTS ◆
Brian's Pourhouse **1**
Celilo Restaurant **6**
Doppio Coffee + Lounge **4**
Nora's Table **3**
Sixth Street Bistro **2**

0   10 mi
0   10 km

289-foot-tall falls are set in a beautiful natural amphitheater less than a mile from the road. Just be aware that this parking area is subject to car break-ins; don't leave any valuables in your vehicle.

Just after the two highways merge, you come to exit 40, the exit for **Bonneville Lock and Dam** (© **541/374-8820;** www.nwp.usace.army.mil/op/b/home.asp). The visitor center here has exhibits on the history of this dam, which was completed in 1938. One of the most important features of the dam is its fish ladder, which allows adult salmon to return upriver to spawn. Underwater windows let visitors see fish as they pass through the ladder. Visit the adjacent **Bonneville Fish Hatchery,** 70543 NE Herman Loop (© **541/374-8393;** www.dfw.state.or.us), to see how trout, salmon, and steelhead are raised before being released into the river. A **Sturgeon Viewing Center ★★** allows you to marvel at several immense sturgeons through an underwater viewing window. At this same exit off I-84 (and at Eagle Creek), you'll find access to a section of the **Historic Columbia River Highway State Trail,** a paved multiuse trail that connects the town of Cascade Locks with Bonneville Dam. This trail incorporates abandoned sections of the Historic Columbia River Highway and is open to hikers and bikers. Near the western trail head for this trail, you'll also find the trail to **Wahclella Falls ★,** a little-visited yet very picturesque waterfall tucked back in a side canyon. The trail to the falls is less than a mile long and relatively flat.

Beyond the dam is Eagle Creek, the single best spot in the Gorge for a hike. The **Eagle Creek Trail ★★** leads past several waterfalls, and if you have time for only one hike in the Gorge, it should be this one. You'll also find a campground and picnic area here.

Not far beyond Eagle Creek is the **Bridge of the Gods,** which connects Oregon and Washington at the site where, according to a Native American legend, once stood a natural bridge used by the gods. Geologists now believe that the legend is based in fact; there is evidence that a massive rock slide may have once blocked the river at this point.

Just beyond the Bridge of the Gods is **Cascade Locks.** It was at this site that cascades once turned the otherwise placid Columbia River into a raging torrent that required boats be portaged a short distance downriver. The Cascade Locks were built in 1896 and allowed steamships to pass unhindered. The locks made traveling between The Dalles and Portland much easier, but the completion of the Columbia River Scenic Highway, in 1915, made the trip even easier by land. With the construction of the Bonneville Lock and Dam, the cascades were flooded, and the locks became superfluous.

There are two small museums here at the locks. The **Cascade Locks Historical Museum,** 1 NW Portage Rd. (© **541/374-8535;** www.portofcascadelocks.org/museum.htm), which is housed in the old lock tender's house, includes displays of Native American artifacts and pioneer memorabilia, as well as the Northwest's first steam engine. The museum is open May through September, Monday to Thursday from noon to 5pm and Friday to Sunday from 10am to 5pm. Admission is by donation.

The **Port of Cascade Locks Visitors Center,** which has displays on river travel in the past, is also the ticket office for the **stern-wheeler *Columbia Gorge* ★★** (© **800/224-3901** or 503/224-3900; www.portlandspirit.com), which makes regular trips on the river. These cruises provide a great perspective on the Gorge. Fares for the 2-hour scenic cruises are $28 for adults and $18 for children; dinner and brunch cruises run $44 to $68 for adults, $39 to $63 for seniors, and $22 to $63 for children. There are also 5-hour cruises twice a week in the summer ($84 for adults, $64 for seniors and children 4–12). These cruises should not be missed on a visit to the Columbia Gorge.

Should you decide not to take the historic highway and stay on I-84, you may want to stop at **Rooster Rock State Park,** especially if it's a hot summer day. This park has a long sandy beach, and in a remote section of the park there's even a clothing-optional beach. From I-84 there's also easy access to Multnomah Falls, the main attraction of the Historic Columbia River Highway.

Another option is to cross to the Washington side of the Columbia River and take Wash. 14 east from Vancouver. This highway actually provides the most spectacular views of both the Columbia Gorge and Mount Hood. If you should decide to take this route, be sure to stop at **Beacon Rock State Park ★★** (© **509/427-8265;** www.parks.wa.gov), which has as its centerpiece an 800-foot-tall monolith that has a trail (mostly stairways and catwalks) leading to its summit. In the early 20th century, there was talk of blasting the rock apart to build jetties at the mouth of the river. Luckily, another source of rock was used, and this amazing landmark continues to guard the Columbia. If you want to make better time, you can cross back to Oregon on the Bridge of the Gods. Continuing east on the Washington side of the river, you'll come to Stevenson, site of the above-mentioned Columbia Gorge Interpretive Center.

In the town of North Bonneville, a few miles west of Stevenson, you can swim in the mineral-water pool and soak in the hot tubs at **Bonneville Hot Springs Resort,** 1252 E. Cascade Dr. (© **866/459-1678** or 509/427-9720; www.bonnevilleresort.com), which charges $15 ($12 for seniors) for the use of its pool and soaking tubs for up to 3 hours. The resort is open to the public daily from 8am to 9pm (children 16 and under limited to Sun–Thurs 1:30–7:30pm). Massages and other spa services are also available. East of Stevenson, in the town of Carson, you can also avail yourself of the therapeutic waters of the **Carson Hot Springs Resort,** 372 St. Martin's Springs Rd. (℃ **800/607-3678** or 509/427-8292; www.carsonhotspringresort.com). This rustic "resort" has been in business since 1897 and has one building that looks every bit its age. However, it's just this old-fashioned appeal that keeps people coming back year after year. It's open Monday through Thursday from 11am to 4pm, Friday and Saturday from 9am to 5pm, and Sunday from 9am to 4pm. A soak and post-soak wrap costs $20, while an hour massage is $60.

Because the Columbia River Gorge is so scenic, you might want to leave the driving to someone else so you can take it all in. If so, contact **Martin's Gorge Tours** (℃ **877/290-8687** or 503/349-1323; www.martinsgorgetours.com). Various tours focus on waterfalls, wildflowers, or wine and cost $49 to $85 per person.

Windsurfing

If you want to launch your sailboard along this stretch of the Gorge, try Rooster Rock State Park, near the west end of the Gorge, or Viento State Park, just west of Hood River. Both parks are right off I-84 and are well marked. Rentals are available in Hood River.

Where to Stay

Best Western Columbia River Inn ★   Located at the foot of the Bridge of the Gods and well situated for exploring the Gorge, this modern motel has splendid river views from its rooms. Many of the rooms also have small balconies, although nearby railroad tracks can make them very noisy; luckily rooms are well insulated. For a splurge, try a spa room.

735 Wanapa St., Cascade Locks, OR 97014. www.bwcolumbiariverinn.com. ℃ **800/595-7108** or 541/374-8777. Fax 541/374-2279. 62 units. $95–$170 double. Rates include full breakfast. Children 17 and under stay free in parent's room. 2-night minimum stay on summer weekends. AE, DC, DISC, MC, V. Pets accepted ($10 fee). **Amenities:** Exercise room; Jacuzzi; indoor pool. *In room:* A/C, TV, fridge, hair dryer, free Wi-Fi.

Bonneville Hot Springs Resort ★   Although this hot-springs resort doesn't have any views to speak of and is not nearly as impressive as the nearby Skamania Lodge (see below), it is still one of the more interesting places to stay in the Columbia Gorge. Unfortunately, the decor has felt dated and uninspired from the moment the resort opened, so don't come expecting gorgeous spaces. There is, however, an 80-foot-long, mineral-water indoor pool, a full-service spa, and a big outdoor hot tub in a courtyard with an unusual stone-wall waterfall. Guest rooms have balconies (ask for one overlooking the courtyard), and some have their own mineral-water soaking tubs. For the kids, there's a miniature golf course.

1252 E. Cascade Dr. (P.O. Box 356), North Bonneville, WA 98639. www.bonnevilleresort.com. ℃ **866/459-1678** or 509/427-7767. Fax 509/427-7733. 78 units. $179–$289 double; $499 suite. Rates include full breakfast. AE, DISC, MC, V. **Amenities:** Restaurant; lounge; exercise room; 2 Jacuzzis; indoor pool; room service; sauna; spa. *In room:* A/C, TV, fridge, hair dryer, MP3 docking station, free Wi-Fi.

McMenamins Edgefield ★★ ⅈ   Ideally situated for exploring the Columbia Gorge and Mount Hood, this flagship of the McMenamins microbrewery empire is the former Multnomah County poor farm. Today the property includes not only tastefully decorated guest rooms with antique furnishings, but also a brewery, a pub, a restaurant, a movie theater, a winery, a wine-tasting room, a distillery, two golf courses, a cigar bar, extensive gardens, and, in summer, a large outdoor dining area. The inn has the feel of a remote retreat, though you are still within 30 minutes of Portland.

2126 SW Halsey St., Troutdale, OR 97060. www.mcmenamins.com. © **800/669-8610** or 503/669-8610. 114 units, 100 with shared bathroom. $70–$115 double with shared bathroom; $120–$175 double with private bathroom; $30 hostel bed per person. Children 6 and under stay free in parent's room. AE, DC, DISC, MC, V. **Amenities:** 3 restaurants; 6 lounges; 2 par-3 golf courses; soaking pool; spa; free Wi-Fi. *In room:* No phone.

Skamania Lodge ★★★   Boasting the most spectacular vistas of any hotel in the Gorge, Skamania Lodge is also the only golf resort around. But it's also well situated for other activities, whether you brought your sailboard, mountain bike, or hiking boots (there's even a hiking trail on the property). The decor is classically rustic, with lots of rock and natural wood, and Northwest Indian art and artifacts are displayed throughout. Huge windows in the lobby have superb views of the Gorge. Riverview guest rooms are more expensive than forest-view rooms (which overlook more parking lot than forest), but are well worth the extra cost. There are also rooms with fireplaces.

1131 SW Skamania Lodge Way, Stevenson, WA 98648. www.skamania.com. © **800/221-7117** or 509/427-7700. Fax 509/427-2547. 254 units. $119–$189 double; $199–$279 suite. Children 17 and under stay free in parent's room. AE, DISC, MC, V. Pets accepted ($50 fee). **Amenities:** 2 restaurants; lounge; bikes; concierge; exercise room; 18-hole golf course; 4 Jacuzzis; indoor pool; room service; sauna; spa; 2 tennis courts. *In room:* A/C, TV, hair dryer, MP3 docking station, free Wi-Fi.

CAMPGROUNDS

Camping in the Gorge isn't quite the wonderful experience you might think. With an interstate highway and a very active railway line paralleling the river on the Oregon side, and another railroad and a secondary highway on the Washington side, the Gorge tends to be quite noisy. However, there are a few camping options between Portland and Hood River, and these campgrounds do what they can to minimize the traffic noises. Ainsworth State Park, 3½ miles east of Multnomah Falls, has showers, and the RV sites are quite nice. At exit 41 off I-84, there is Eagle Creek Campground, the oldest campground in the National Forest system and popular for its access to the Eagle Creek Trail. At exit 51 off of I-84, Wyeth Campground, a U.S. Forest Service campground, sits on the bank of Gordon Creek. Over on the Washington side of the Columbia River, you can camp at Beacon Rock State Park, which is located 7 miles west of the Bridge of the Gods. Because it is tucked back away from the highway and railroad tracks, this is just about the quietest campground in the Gorge.

Where to Eat

The area's best place to eat is the dining room of the Skamania Lodge (see above).

Black Rabbit Restaurant ★★ NORTHWEST/REGIONAL AMERICAN   This casual yet upscale restaurant is located on the grounds of McMenamins Edgefield (see above), and is the ideal place to stop for dinner on the way back to Portland after a day of exploring the Gorge. Start with steamed mussels (perhaps accompanied by a glass of Edgefield wine), and then move on to Northwest cioppino or pan-seared ahi with plum-miso glaze. There is also a less expensive and less formal brewpub here.

In the McMenamins Edgefield, 2126 SW Halsey St., Troutdale. © **800/669-8610** or 503/492-3086. www.mcmenamins.com. Main courses $8–$14 lunch, $14–$24 dinner. AE, DC, DISC, MC, V. Daily 7–10pm.

Multnomah Falls Lodge ★ AMERICAN   Built in 1925 at the foot of Multnomah Falls, the historic Multnomah Falls Lodge may be the most touristy place to
eat in the entire Gorge, but the setting is wonderful and the food isn't half bad.
Breakfast, when the crowds haven't yet arrived, is one of the best times to eat here.
Try the grilled salmon or trout and eggs. At dinner, stick with the prime rib or grilled
salmon. For a peek at the falls, try to get a table in the conservatory room or, in summer, out on the patio.

Historic Columbia River Hwy. (or I-84, exit 31). ℂ **503/695-2376.** www.multnomahfallslodge.com.
Reservations recommended. Main courses $12–$23 lunch, $18–$24 dinner. AE, DISC, MC, V. Daily
8am–9pm.

Tad's Chicken 'n Dumplins ★ 🍴 AMERICAN   Located on the banks of the
Sandy River at the western end of the Historic Columbia River Highway, this rustic
restaurant has been in business since the 1920s and, as its name implies, specializes
in all-American chicken and dumplings. Sure, you can get a steak or salmon, but
you'd be remiss if you passed up the opportunity to fill up on this restaurant's namesake dish. Try to get a seat on the enclosed back porch, which overlooks the river. If
you're coming here after dark, just watch for the classic neon sign out front.

1325 E. Historic Columbia River Hwy., Troutdale. ℂ **503/666-5337.** www.tadschicdump.com. Call-
ahead wait list. Main courses $14–$30. AE, DISC, MC, V. Mon–Fri 5–10pm; Sat–Sun 4–10pm.

HOOD RIVER

62 miles E of Portland, 20 miles W of The Dalles, 32 miles N of Government Camp

Every summer, hot air rising over the desert to the east of the Cascade Range sucks
cool air up the Columbia River Gorge from the Pacific, and the winds howl through
what is basically a natural wind tunnel. The winds are incessant, and gusts can whip
the river into a tumult of whitecaps. They used to curse these winds in Hood River.
Not anymore.

Ever since the first person pulled into town with a sailboard, Hood River has taken
to praying for wind. Hood River is now the windsurfing and kiteboarding capital of
America, which has given this former lumber town a new lease on life. People come
from all over the world to ride the winds that howl up the Gorge. In early summer the
boardheads roll into town in their "Gorge-mobiles," which are equivalent to 1960s
surfers' woodies, and start listening to the wind reports. They flock to riverside parks
on both the Oregon and Washington sides of the Columbia, unfurl their sails and
kites, zip up their wet suits, and launch themselves into the melee of hundreds of
other like-minded souls shooting back and forth across a mile of windswept water.
High waves whipped up by near-gale-force winds provide perfect launching pads for
rocketing skyward. Aerial acrobatics such as flips and 360-degree turns are common
sights. In recent years, kiteboarding has become even more popular than windsurfing.
Kiteboarding replaces the sail with a kite, shortens the board, and enables even more
radical maneuvers and higher speeds than windsurfing, and lots more time in the air
instead of in the water. Even if you're not into this fast-paced sport, you'll get a vicari-
ous thrill from watching the boardheads going for major airtime.

Windsurfing and kiteboarding may be the main events here in Hood River, but this
is certainly not a one-trick town. Sometimes the winds just aren't accommodating,
and even boardheads can get bored sitting on shore waiting for conditions to improve.
For this reason, Hood River has become something of an outdoor sports mecca, with

a rapidly developing reputation for excellent mountain biking, white-water kayaking and rafting, paragliding, rock climbing, hiking, skiing, and snowboarding. In other words, Hood River is full of active people.

Hood River does not exist on sports alone, however; outside town, in the Hood River Valley, are apple and pear orchards, wineries, and vineyards. Hood River also claims a historic hotel and several good restaurants. Most of the town's old Victorian and Craftsman houses have now been restored, giving Hood River a historic atmosphere to complement its lively windsurfing scene. All in all, this town makes a great base, whether you're here for the sports, to explore the Gorge, or to visit nearby Mount Hood.

Essentials

GETTING THERE   Hood River is on I-84 at the junction with Ore. 35, which leads south to connect with U.S. 26 near the community of Government Camp.

Amtrak offers **rail** service to the town of Bingen, Washington, just across the Columbia River from Hood River. The station is at the foot of Walnut Street.

VISITOR INFORMATION   Contact the **Hood River County Chamber of Commerce,** 720 E. Port Marina Dr., Hood River, OR 97031 (🕿 **800/366-3530** or 541/386-2000; www.hoodriver.org), near the river at exit 63 off I-84.

FESTIVALS   The **Hood River Valley Blossom Festival** is held in mid-April and celebrates the flowering of the valley's pear and apple trees. In mid-October the **Hood River Valley Harvest Fest** celebrates the region's bounty of apples and pears.

Windsurfing & Other Outdoor Activities ★★★

If you're here to ride the wind or just want to watch, head to the Columbia Gorge Sailpark at Hood River Marina, the nearby Event Site, or the Hook, all of which are accessible via exit 63 off I-84. Across the river in Washington, try the fish hatchery (the Hatchery), west of the mouth of the White Salmon River, or Swell City, a park about 4 miles west of the bridge. If you're a **windsurfer** or **kiteboarder,** you'll find all kinds of windsurfing- and kiteboarding-related shops in downtown Hood River. Classes are available through **Hood River WaterPlay** (🕿 **800/963-7873** or 541/386-9463; www.hoodriverwaterplay.com) and **Gorge Kiteboard School** (🕿 **541/490-4401;** www.gorgekiteboardschool.com), which teaches only kiteboarding.

When there isn't enough wind for sailing, there's still the option to go **rafting** on the nearby White Salmon River, across the Columbia in Washington. Companies offering raft trips on this river include **Zoller's Outdoor Odysseys** (🕿 **800/366-2004** or 509/493-2641; www.zooraft.com), **Wet Planet Whitewater** (🕿 **877/390-9445;** www.wetplanetrafting.com), and **All Adventures Rafting** (🕿 **800/743-5628;** www.alladventures.net). Although the White Salmon can be rafted anytime of year, the most popular season runs from April through September. A half-day trip will cost around $60 or $65 per person.

Mountain biking is also very popular, and Hood River bike shops can direct you to some fun area rides. Check out **Discover Bicycles,** 210 State St. (🕿 **541/386-4820;** www.discoverbicycles.com), or **Mountain View Cycles,** 205 Oak St. (🕿 **541/386-2453;** www.mtviewcycles.com), both of which rent bikes. Expect to pay between $25 and $60 per day.

Hikers have their choice of trails in Mount Hood National Forest ("Mount Hood," in chapter 8), the **Columbia Gorge** (p. 234), or across the river in Gifford Pinchot National Forest (head up Wash. 141 to Mt. Adams). At 12,276 feet, Mount Adams is the second-highest peak in Washington. For more information about hiking on Mount Adams, contact the Gifford Pinchot National Forest's **Mount Adams Ranger Station,** 2455 Wash. 141, Trout Lake, WA 98650 (✆ **509/395-3400;** www.fs.fed.us/gpnf).

The Fruit Loop (Exploring the Hood River Valley)

Before windsurfing took center stage, the Hood River Valley was known as one of Oregon's top fruit-growing regions, and today the valley is still full of apple and pear orchards. From blossom time (Apr) to harvest season (Sept–Oct), the valley offers quiet country roads to explore. Along the way, you'll find numerous farm stands, wineries, museums, and interesting shops that reflect the valley's rural heritage. Pick up a brochure called Hood River County Fruit Loop Guide to Local Farm Stands at the Hood River County Chamber of Commerce visitor center (see "Visitor Information," under "Essentials," above).

Be sure to start your tour of the Hood River Valley by stopping at **Panorama Point,** off of Ore. 35 just south of town (follow the signs). This hilltop park provides a splendid view of the valley's orchards, with Mount Hood looming in the distance.

In the fall, fruit stands pop up along the roads around the valley. **Rasmussen Farms,** 3020 Thomsen Rd. (✆ **800/548-2243** or 541/386-4622; www.rasmussenfarms.com), is one of the biggest and best farm stands in the valley and is off Ore. 35 about 6 miles south of Hood River. The stand is open mid-April through late December daily from 9am to 6pm. Also not to be missed is the nearby **Apple Valley Country Store,** 2363 Tucker Rd. (✆ **541/386-1971;** www.applevalleystore.com), where you can stock up on homemade jams and jellies and maybe buy one of the store's legendary apple pies. You'll find the store west of Rasmussen's on the opposite side of the valley. Also in the valley are numerous orchards and farms where you can pick your own fruit. Keep an eye out for U-PICK signs. Between June and August, you can also cut lavender at a couple of area farms. With Mount hood for a backdrop, the lavender fields at **Lavender Valley,** 3925 Portland Dr. (✆ **541/386-1906;** www.lavendervalley.com), just north of the Apple Valley Country Store, are among the most beautiful in the state. If you're out this way in July, be sure to stop by. **Hood River Lavender,** 3801 Straight Hill Rd. (✆ **888/528-3276** or 541/354-9917; www.lavenderfarms.net), with views of Mounts Hood and Adams, is toward the middle of the valley just south of the community of Odell.

The little hamlet of Parkdale, at the south end of the Fruit Loop, is home to the fascinating little **Hutson Museum,** 4967 Baseline Dr. (✆ **541/352-6806**), which houses lapidary, archaeology, and anthropology collections, of which the rock collection and exhibits of Native American artifacts are a highlight. The museum is open April through October, and days and hours vary with the seasons, so call ahead.

Any time between February and late December, but especially during fruit-blossom time, the **Mount Hood Railroad** (✆ **800/872-4661** or 541/386-3556; www.mthoodrr.com) offers a great way to see the Hood River Valley. Trains operated by this scenic railroad company depart from the historic 1911 Hood River depot on 2- and 4-hour excursions. The 2-hour excursions go to Odell, and the 4-hour excursions wind their way up the valley to Parkdale, where you can get a snack at a cafe or visit the Hutson Museum. For the 2-hour excursion, fares are $27 for adults, $25 for

7

THE COLUMBIA GORGE

Hood River

seniors, and $17 for children 2 to 12; fares on the 4-hour excursions are $32 for adults, $28 for seniors, and $20 for children. The schedule varies with the season (July–Aug it's Tues–Sun). There are also regularly scheduled dinner and brunch trains and other specialty excursion trains. Reservations are recommended.

Wine Touring

The Hood River Valley is one of Oregon's main wine regions. Because summers here are much hotter than in the Willamette Valley, different varieties of grapes are grown. Stop in at a Hood River winery, and you'll be tasting not only pinot noir and pinot gris, but also merlot, Syrah, zinfandel, Viognier, and other Bordeaux and Rhone varietals.

If you're wine touring in the Hood River valley, be sure to stop by **the Gorge White House,** 2265 U.S. 35 (𝒞 **541/386-2828;** www.thegorgewhitehouse.com), a beautifully restored old farmhouse that now serves as a tasting room for many area wineries. If you're short on time and want to taste wines from several wineries, this is the place to head. The Gorge White House is open June through September daily from 10am to 6pm; April, May, and October, it's open Friday through Monday from 10am to 6pm. It's closed from November to March.

Because there are always new wineries opening in the area, be sure to check the **Columbia Gorge Wine Region** website (www.columbiagorgewine.com) before heading out on a wine tour. If you'd prefer to have someone else do the driving, you can book a wine tour with **Columbia Wine Tours** (𝒞 **541/380-1410;** www.columbiawinetours.com), which charges $125 to $140 for two people.

IN TOWN

Naked Winery   If you think wine should be taken seriously, then you need to get Naked—Naked wine, that is. This downtown Hood River tasting room always offers a long lineup of surprisingly good wines with slightly naughty names: Foreplay chardonnay, Missionary cabernet, Gay rosé, Escort pinot gris. There's even the Oh! series of Orgasmic wines.

102 Second St. 𝒞 **800/666-9303.** www.nakedwinery.com. Tasting fee $5. Daily noon–7pm.

The Pines 1852 ★★   Although this winery is actually in The Dalles, it has a tasting room in downtown Hood River. Because the wines here are produced by Peter Rosback, one of Oregon's top winemakers, they are some of my favorite area wines. Don't miss an opportunity to sample these lush wines, particularly the old-vine zinfandel.

202 State St. 𝒞 **541/993-8301.** www.thepinesvineyard.com. Tasting fee $5. Wed and Sun noon–6pm; Thurs–Sat noon–9pm.

Quenett Winery   If you have only a passing interest in wine, this is the best place in the area to sample a bit of local vino. The conveniently located downtown tasting room is a pretty little wine bar. The winery specializes in red wines, including Zinfandel, Sangiovese, and Barbera. However, several white wines are also produced.

111 Oak St. 𝒞 **541/386-2229.** www.quenett.com. Tasting fee $5. Sun–Thurs noon–6pm; Fri–Sat noon–8pm.

Springhouse Cellar 🍷   Housed in an old building near the Mount Hood Railroad depot, this winery is another great place to visit for outstanding values. White wines, including Chardonnay, Viognier, and Pinot Blanc, are in the $15 to $18 range, while reds, including Sangiovese, Syrah, and Cabernet Sauvignon, are mostly $20 to $24.

13 Railroad Ave. 𝒞 **541/308-0700.** www.springhousecellar.com. Tasting fee $5. Daily noon–6pm.

UP THE VALLEY

Cathedral Ridge Winery This winery produces a good Riesling, as well as Pinot Gris, Chardonnay, a Cabernet-Merlot blend, and several other varietals. There are great views of both Mount Hood and Mount Adams from here.

4200 Post Canyon Dr. ℂ **800/516-8710.** www.cathedralridgewinery.com. Tasting fee $5. June–Oct daily 11am–6pm; Nov–May daily 11am–5pm. From downtown, take Oak St./Cascade St. west to Country Club Rd.

Hood River Vineyards & Winery This winery is best known for its many excellent fruit wines, some of which are sweet and some of which are dry. They also produce a variety of port-style dessert wines.

4693 Westwood Dr. ℂ **541/386-3772.** http://hoodrivervineyardsandwinery.com. Daily 11–5pm. From downtown, take Oak St./Cascade St. west to Country Club Rd.

Marchesi Vineyards This little mid-valley winery has a decidedly Italian feel to it, which is not surprising considering that owner and winemaker Franco Marchesi is from Italy's Piedmont region, which is known for producing some of the world's best red wines. While Marchesi produces Pinot Gris and Pinot Noir, it is the Dolcetto and Barbera that are real standouts.

3955 Belmont Dr. ℂ **541/386-1800.** www.marchesivineyards.com. Tasting fee $5. Spring–fall Fri–Sun 11:30am–6:30pm; by appointment other months.

Mt. Hood Winery With a large tasting room on the edge of several acres of vineyards, this mid-valley winery produces a wide range of wines, including Pinot Noir, Pinot Gris, Chardonnay, Tempranillo, Syrah, and a delicious port-style wine. The wines can be hit or miss, but the location is convenient if you just want to sample some wine on the way up the valley.

2882 Van Horn Dr. ℂ **541/386-8333.** www.mthoodwinery.com. Tasting fee $5. Mar–Nov daily 11am–5pm. Drive Ore. 35 south from Hood River for 4 miles and turn left at blinking yellow light.

Pheasant Valley Winery ★ This winery's vineyard was Oregon's first certified organic vineyard, and it produces both organic Pinot Noir and Pinot Gris. These are some of my favorite area wines. They also produce an organic pear wine.

3890 Acree Dr. ℂ **866/357-9463** or 541/387-3040. www.pheasantvalleywinery.com. Tasting fee $5–$15. Memorial Day to Labor Day Fri–Sun noon–5pm. From downtown, take 13th St. south to Tucker Rd. and follow through several twists and turns to a right turn onto Acree Dr.

Phelps Creek Vineyards With a tasting room right on the Hood River Golf Course, this is one of the prettiest places in the valley to sit outside with a glass of wine. Phelps Creek does several Pinot Noirs and a couple of Chardonnays every year.

1850 Country Club Rd. ℂ **541/386-2607.** www.phelpscreekvineyards.com. Tasting fee $5. Feb–Dec daily 11am–5pm; Jan Fri–Mon 11am–5pm, Tues–Thurs by appointment. From downtown, take Oak St./Cascade St. west to Country Club Rd.

Viento ★ 🍷 Excellent wines at reasonable prices make this one of my favorite Oregon wineries. Look for Grüner Veltliner, a wine most popular in Austria and rarely produced in the Northwest, as well as Rieslings with varying sweetness, Barbera, Sangiovese, and sometimes Cabernet Sauvignon or Syrah from Washington State's famed Pepper Bridge Vineyard.

In the Gorge White House Annex, 2265 U.S. 35. ℂ **541/490-6655.** www.vientowines.com. Tasting fee $5. May–Nov Fri–Mon noon–5pm.

Other Attractions in Hood River

Western Antique Aeroplane and Automobile Museum Housed in a pair of hangars at the Hood River airport, this private museum is packed with restored old planes, primarily from the 1920s and 1930s, and many of them are in flyable condition. There are also some 80 cars, dating from an 1899 Locomobile Steam Car to 1970s hot rods. Throw in some World War II military vehicles, a dozen motorcycles, and a half-dozen old tractors, and you have a wonderfully eclectic museum.

Ken Jernstedt Airfield, 1600 Air Museum Rd. (✆ **541/308-1600.** www.waaamuseum.org. Admission $12 adults, $10 seniors, $6 students, free for children 4 and under. Daily 9am–5pm. Closed New Year's Day, Thanksgiving, and Christmas.

Where to Stay

If you're looking for a bed-and-breakfast and those listed below are full, call Room-finder (✆ **541/386-6767;** www.hoodriverroomfinder.com), a free service provided by the Columbia River Gorge–Hood River Bed & Breakfast Association.

EXPENSIVE

Columbia Cliff Villas Hotel ★★ Located adjacent to the historic Columbia Gorge Hotel (see below), this condominium hotel is designed to resemble its historic neighbor but is far more spacious and luxurious. The suites, with their walls of glass looking out to the basalt cliffs of the Columbia Gorge, are gorgeously decorated, many with Asian accent pieces. Hardwood floors, stone fireplaces, leather furniture, and gorgeous big bathrooms all add to the tasteful luxury here. While there are also standard hotel-style rooms, the suites are so impressive that they are definitely worth a splurge. If you want to recoup some of the cost, you could even do some cooking in the full kitchen. While these accommodations are surrounded primarily by parking lots, the gardens of the Columbia Gorge Hotel are only steps away.

3880 Westcliff Dr., Hood River, OR 97031. www.columbiacliffvillas.com. (✆ **866/912-8366** or 541/436-2660. Fax 541/610-1549. 28 units. $169–$350 double; $229–$895 suite (midweek and multi-night discounts available). Children 6 and under stay free in parent's room. AE, DC, DISC, MC, V. Pets accepted ($25 fee). **Amenities:** Babysitting; bikes; concierge; access to nearby health club; room service. *In room:* A/C, TV/DVD, hair dryer, kitchen (in suites), MP3 docking station, free Wi-Fi.

Columbia Gorge Hotel ★ Just west of Hood River off I-84, and in business since the early 1920s, this little oasis of luxury offers a genteel atmosphere, once enjoyed by Rudolph Valentino and Clark Gable. With its yellow-stucco walls and red-tile roofs, this hotel would be at home in Beverly Hills, and the hotel gardens could hold their own amid the many public gardens of Victoria, British Columbia. The hotel is perched more than 200 feet above the river on a steep cliff, and it is difficult to take your eyes off the view. Be forewarned, though, that most of the rooms are rather cramped, as are the bathrooms.

4000 Westcliff Dr., Hood River, OR 97031. www.columbiagorgehotel.com. (✆ **800/345-1921** or 541/386-5566. Fax 541/386-9141. 39 units. $169–$239 double. Children 18 and under stay free in parent's room. AE, DISC, MC, V. Pets accepted ($20 per night). **Amenities:** Restaurant; lounge; room service; spa. *In room:* A/C, TV, fridge, hair dryer, Wi-Fi.

MODERATE

Best Western Plus Hood River Inn ★ As the only area hotel located right on the water (there's a dock and private beach), the Best Western is popular with wind-surfers. The convention hotel atmosphere (crowds of corporate types busily network-ing) is somewhat constraining, but if you like comfort and predictability, this is a good bet. Riverside, the hotel's restaurant, is Hood River's only waterfront restaurant and serves primarily Mediterranean dishes.

1108 E. Marina Way, Hood River, OR 97031. www.hoodriverinn.com. © **800/828-7873** or 541/386-2200. 158 units. Mid-May to Sept $140–$215 double, $180–$350 suite; Oct to mid-May $111–$160 double, $180–$350 suite. Rates include full breakfast. Children 12 and under stay free in parent's room. AE, DC, DISC, MC, V. Pets accepted ($12 per night). **Amenities:** Restaurant; lounge; exercise room; Jacuzzi; outdoor pool; room service. *In room:* A/C, TV, fridge, hair dryer, free Wi-Fi.

Oak Street Hotel ★ ⅱ   This little hotel in a restored 1909 house in downtown Hood River shares space with a real-estate office. As sort of a cross between a B&B and a small inn, the Oak Street Hotel may not offer a lot of amenities, but it does have loads of contemporary charm. Guest rooms are small but very attractively furnished. Room no. 5, with its views of the Columbia River, is my favorite. One of the best reasons to stay here is for the delicious baked goodies that are served at breakfast. Plus, you'll be within a few blocks of several good restaurants.

610 Oak St., Hood River, OR 97031. www.oakstreethotel.com. © **866/386-3845** or 541/386-3845. Fax 541/387-8696. 9 units. Apr–Oct $129 double, $149 suite; Nov–Mar $119 double, $129 suite. Rates include continental breakfast. AE, DISC, MC, V. *In room:* A/C, TV, fridge, free Wi-Fi.

INEXPENSIVE

Hood River Hotel ★   Built in 1913 and located in downtown Hood River, this hotel has a casual elegance and is an economical alternative to the pricey Columbia Gorge Hotel. Now, don't expect much; this is sort of a historic hotel for young travelers. Canopy beds, ceiling fans, wood floors, and area rugs give the rooms a classic feel, but bathrooms in some rooms are little larger than closets. My favorite rooms are the third-floor rooms with sky-lit bathrooms. The riverview rooms are the most expensive, and there are suites with full kitchens as well. Light sleepers should be aware of the railroad tracks behind the hotel.

102 Oak St., Hood River, OR 97031. www.hoodriverhotel.com. © **800/386-1859** or 541/386-1900. Fax 541/386-6090. 41 units. $99–$154 double; $139–$234 suite. Rates included $10 breakfast voucher. Children 12 and under stay free in parent's room. AE, DISC, MC, V. Self-parking $5. Pets accepted ($25 fee). **Amenities:** Restaurant; lounge; exercise room; Jacuzzi; sauna. *In room:* A/C, TV, free Wi-Fi.

The Mosier House Bed & Breakfast ★ ⅱ   This beautifully restored Victorian home is in the small town of Mosier, 5 miles east of Hood River, and the views of the Columbia Gorge from the inn's front porch are unforgettable. Inside you'll find wood floors and period antiques, and although the four rooms with shared baths are all fairly small, they have the feel of an authentic vintage travelers' hotel. One of the shared bathrooms has a claw-foot tub, as does the room with the private bath. All in all, this inn manages to capture a bygone era without being overly frilly or self-consciously romantic, and it makes an excellent base for exploring the eastern end of the Columbia Gorge.

704 Third Ave. (P.O. Box 476), Mosier, OR 97040. www.mosierhouse.com. © **877/328-0351** or 541/478-3640. 5 units, 1 with private bathroom. $85–$110 double with shared bathroom; $135 double with private bathroom. Rates include full breakfast. MC, V. Children 12 and over welcome. *In room:* A/C, no phone, free Wi-Fi.

Vagabond Lodge ★ ☺   If you've got a banker's tastes but a teller's budget, you can take advantage of the Vagabond Lodge's proximity to the Columbia Gorge Hotel and enjoy the latter's gardens and restaurant without breaking the bank. The back rooms at the Vagabond are some of the best in Hood River simply for their views (some have balconies). There are lots of big old oaks and evergreens, and natural rock outcroppings have been incorporated into the motel's landscaping. If you're in the mood for a splurge, ask for one of the suites. (Some have fireplaces; others, whirlpool tubs.) A playground and lots of grass make this a good choice for families.

4070 Westcliff Dr., Hood River, OR 97031. www.vagabondlodge.com. © **877/386-2992** or 541/386-2992. Fax 541/386-3317. 42 units. May–Oct $77–$98 double, $120 suite; Nov–Apr $56–81 double, $96 suite. Children 12 and under stay free in parent's room. AE, DC, DISC, MC, V. Pets accepted ($5 per night). *In room:* A/C, TV, fridge, free Wi-Fi.

CAMPGROUNDS

Area campgrounds include Tollbridge Park, on Ore. 35, 17 miles south of town, and Tucker Park, on Tucker Road (Ore. 281), just a few miles south of town. Both of these county parks are on the banks of the Hood River. Farther south, you'll find the Sherwood Campground, a national-forest campground also on the banks of the Hood River. (This campground is favored by mountain bikers.) Eight miles west of Hood River off I-84 is Viento State Park, which gets quite a bit of traffic noise both from the interstate and from the adjacent railroad tracks. Eleven miles east of town, you'll find Memaloose State Park, which has the same noise problems. These two state parks are popular with windsurfers.

Where to Eat

For creamy gelato and good espresso, stop in at **Doppio Coffee + Lounge,** 310 Oak St. (© **541/386-3000;** www.doppiocoffeelounge.com).

Brian's Pourhouse ★★ NORTHWEST/AMERICAN   Located in an old house a few blocks up the hill from downtown Hood River, this restaurant is a casual, fun place with very creative food. In summer the big deck is the place to eat, and any time of year, the stylish little bar area is a cozy spot for a cocktail or a local microbrew. The menu is highly eclectic and ranges from fish tacos to sesame-crusted ahi tuna served with a wasabi–mashed potato egg rolls.

606 Oak St. © **541/387-4344.** www.brianspourhouse.com. Reservations recommended. Main courses $8–$23. AE, DISC, MC, V. Sun–Thurs 5–10pm; Fri–Sat 5–11pm (late-night menu daily until midnight).

Celilo Restaurant ★★ NORTHWEST   This restaurant is utterly hip in concept and is a sophisticated alternative to the homey restaurants that have long been popular in Hood River. Think timber-town natural-wood decor meets modern urban design aesthetic, and you'll have a good idea of what this place is like. The concept of fresh and local drives the kitchen here, so you can count on the menu sticking to whatever is in season—luckily, that can cover a lot of territory in this fertile region. Dishes with house-made pasta are always a good bet, and, in the fall, you might get your noodles sauced with fresh chanterelle mushrooms. Fresh herbs flavor many of the dishes here.

16 Oak St. © **541/386-5710.** www.celilorestaurant.com. Reservations recommended. Main courses $7.50–$12 lunch, $9.75–$24 dinner. AE, MC, V. Daily 11:30am–3pm and 5–9:30 or 10pm.

Nora's Table ★★ NORTHWEST   South Indian seafood curry; seared rockfish tacos with mango–red pepper slaw; Hawaiian tombo tuna with coconut–lemongrass risotto cakes, Asian long beans, and citrus-miso vinaigrette: The menu here is as eclectic as the population of Hood River. And everything is so delicious, you just want to keep going back again and again. The wine list here is primarily wines from the Columbia Gorge. Look for Nora's downstairs and just off Oak Street.

110 Fifth St. ☎ **541/387-4000.** www.norastable.com. Reservations recommended. Main courses $12–$26. MC, V. Tues–Sat 5–9pm.

Sixth Street Bistro AMERICAN/INTERNATIONAL   Just a block off Oak Street toward the river, the Sixth Street Bistro has an intimate dining room and patio on the lower floor, and a lounge with a balcony on the second floor. Each has its own entrance, but they share a menu. The menu has numerous international touches, such as coconut red curry and pad thai, as well as juicy burgers. You'll find seasonal specials and vegetarian dishes as well, and the restaurant sources ingredients locally and seasonally as much as possible.

509 Cascade Ave. ☎ **541/386-5737.** www.sixthstreetbistro.com. Reservations recommended. Main courses $7–$12 lunch, $9–$22 dinner. AE, MC, V. Sun–Thurs 11:30am–9:30pm; Fri–Sat 11:30am–10pm.

Hood River After Dark

Double Mountain Brewery & Taproom   This little brewery produces some of the most distinctive brews in Oregon and is one of my favorite brewpubs in the state. If you're a fan of microbrews, be sure to pay a visit. 8 Fourth St. ☎ **541/387-0042.** www.doublemountainbrewery.com.

Full Sail Tasting Room & Pub   Full Sail brews some of the most consistently flavorful and well-rounded beers in the Northwest and has developed a loyal following. You have to walk right past the brewery to get to the pub, which is at the back of an old industrial building a block off Hood River's main drag. Big windows look out over the river. 506 Columbia St. ☎ **541/386-2247.** www.fullsailbrewing.com.

East of Hood River: Wildflowers & Views

East of Hood River, you'll find two more sections of the Historic Columbia River Highway (Ore. 30): One is open only to hikers and bikers, the other to automobiles. The former section, located between Hood River and Mosier and known as the Historic Columbia River Highway State Trail (☎ **800/551-6949;** www.oregon.gov/oprd/parks), was abandoned when I-84 was built and two tunnels on this section of the old highway were filled in. After the tunnels were re-excavated to open up this stretch as a 4.5-mile paved trail, it was discovered that part of the trail was subject to frequent rock falls. Consequently, a large and impressive rock catchment structure was built along part of the route leading up to the tunnels from the west. Although the trail receives some traffic noise from I-84, it is a fascinating and easy hike or bike ride. To reach the western trail head, travel east out of downtown Hood River on State Street and continue east on Old Columbia River Drive. For the eastern trail head, take exit 69 off I-84 and then take the first left. Starting from this latter trail head makes for a much shorter hike if you just want to visit the tunnels. However, the main visitor center for the trail is at the western trail head. There is a $5 fee to use the trail.

The second part of the old highway, beginning at exit 69 off I-84 and stretching from Mosier to The Dalles, climbs up onto the Rowena Plateau, where sweeping vistas take in the Columbia River, Mount Hood, and Mount Adams. Between March and May, the wildflowers are some of the finest in the state. The best place to see them is at the Nature Conservancy's **Tom McCall Preserve** (☎ **503/802-8100;**

www.nature.org/wherewework/northamerica/states/oregon). On spring weekends there are usually volunteers guiding wildflower walks through the preserve. Before leaving Mosier, you can stop for coffee at **10 Speed East,** 1104 First Ave. (© **541/478-2104;** http://10speedeast.com); a bite or a beer at the **Thirsty Woman Pub,** Main Street (© **541/478-0199;** http://thirstywoman.com); or ice cream and displays of vintage Porsches at **Route 30 Classics,** First Avenue (© **541/478-2525;** www.route30classics.com).

THE DALLES

128 miles W of Pendleton, 85 miles E of Portland, 133 miles N of Bend

The Dalles (rhymes with "the pals"), a French word meaning "flagstone," was the name given to this area by early-19th-century French trappers. These explorers may have been reminded of stepping stones or flagstone-lined gutters when they first gazed upon the flat basalt rocks that forced the Columbia River through a long stretch of rapids and cascades here. These rapids, which were a barrier to river navigation, formed a natural gateway to western Oregon.

For more than 10,000 years, Native Americans inhabited this site because of the ease with which salmon could be taken from the river as it flowed through the tumultuous rapids. The annual fishing season at nearby Celilo Falls was a meeting point for tribes from all over the West. Tribes would come to fish, trade, and stockpile supplies for the coming winter.

Although the Lewis and Clark expedition stopped here when they passed through the region in 1805 and 1806, white settlers, the first of whom came to The Dalles as missionaries in 1838, were latecomers to this area. However, by the 1840s, a steady flow of pioneers was passing through the region, which was effectively the end of the overland segment of the Oregon Trail. Pioneers who were headed for the mild climate and fertile soils of the Willamette Valley would load their wagons onto rafts at this point and float downriver to the mouth of the Willamette, and then up that river to Oregon City.

By the 1850s, The Dalles was the site of an important military fort and had become a busy river port. Steamships shuttled from here to Cascade Locks on the run to Portland. However, the coming of the railroad in 1880, and later the flooding of the river's rapids, reduced the importance of The Dalles as a port town. Today the city serves as the eastern gateway to the Columbia Gorge and, as such, is the site of the Columbia Gorge Discovery Center.

Essentials

GETTING THERE The Dalles is on I-84 at the junction of U.S. 197, which leads south to Antelope, where it connects with U.S. 97.

Amtrak passenger **trains** stop across the Columbia River from The Dalles in Wishram, Washington. The station is at the west end of Railroad Avenue.

VISITOR INFORMATION Contact **The Dalles Area Chamber of Commerce,** 404 W. Second St., The Dalles, OR 97058 (© **800/255-3385** or 541/296-2231; www.thedalleschamber.com).

Learning About the Gorge

Columbia Gorge Discovery Center/Wasco County Historical Museum ★

These two museums, housed in one building on the outskirts of The Dalles, serve as the eastern gateway to the Columbia Gorge. In the museum building, constructed to resemble a Northwest Native American longhouse, you'll find exhibits on the geology and history of the Gorge. Among the most fascinating exhibits is a film of Native Americans fishing at Celilo Falls before the rising waters behind The Dalles Dam flooded the falls. There is also a short nature trail that leads past a small pond and links to a trail that stretches for more than 8 miles, passing Lewis & Clark's Rock Fort campsite along its route. In spring the trail is lined with beautiful wildflowers.

5000 Discovery Dr. (© **541/296-8600.** www.gorgediscovery.org. $8 adults, $7 seniors, $4 children 6–16. Daily 9am–5pm.

Exploring The Dalles

Long before settlers arrived in The Dalles, Lewis and Clark's expedition stopped here. The site of their camp is called Rock Fort, and it is one of their only documented campsites. The historic site is on First Street west of downtown, near the Port of The Dalles' industrial area northeast of Webber and Second streets.

Some of The Dalles's most important historic buildings can be seen at the **Fort Dalles Museum and the Anderson Homestead,** 500 W. 15th St. (© **541/296-4547;** www.fortdallesmuseum.org), at the corner of Garrison Street. Established in 1850, Fort Dalles was the only military post between Fort Laramie and Fort Vancouver. By 1867 the fort had become unnecessary, and after several buildings were destroyed in a fire, it was abandoned. Today several of the original buildings, including a Carpenter-Gothic officers' home, are still standing. Though small, this is the oldest history museum in Oregon. Memorial Day through Labor Day, the museum is open daily from 10am to 4pm; call for hours in other months. Admission is $5 for adults, $4 for seniors, and $1 for children 7 to 17.

Not far from the Fort Dalles Museum, at **Sorosis Park,** you get a good view of The Dalles, the Columbia River, and Mount Adams. To reach this park, drive 1 block west from the museum and turn left on Trevitt Street, which becomes Scenic Drive. Continue on this latter street to the park.

Within a decade of the establishment of Fort Dalles, this community became the county seat of what was the largest county ever created in the United States. Wasco County covered 130,000 square miles between the Rocky Mountains and the Cascade Range. The **Original Wasco County Courthouse,** 410 W. Second Pl. (© **541/296-4798;** www.historicthedalles.org/wcoc/original_wasco_co_courthouse. htm), a two-story wooden structure built in 1859, has been preserved, and the inside looks much as it did when it was a functioning courthouse. It's open Memorial Day through Labor Day, Wednesday through Saturday from 11am to 3pm. Admission is free.

The Dalles's other historic landmark is a much more impressive structure. **Old St. Peter's Landmark church** (© **541/296-5686;** www.oldstpeterslandmark.org), at the corner of West Third and Lincoln streets, is no longer an active church, but its 176-foot-tall steeple is a local landmark. The church was built in the Gothic Revival style in 1897, and a 6-foot-tall rooster symbolizing The Dalles tops its spire. The church is open Tuesday through Friday from 11am to 3pm and Saturday and Sunday from 1 to 3pm.

If you're interested in learning more about the history and the historic buildings of The Dalles, pick up a copy of the historic walking tours brochure at the chamber of commerce. As you explore The Dalles, also keep an eye out for the city's many **historical murals.**

At the east end of town rises **The Dalles Lock and Dam** (✆ **541/506-7819;** www.nwp.usace.army.mil/locations/thedalles.asp), which provides both irrigation water and electricity. The dam, which was completed in 1957, stretches for 1½ miles from the Oregon shore to the Washington shore. One of the main reasons this dam was built was to flood the rapids that made this section of the Columbia River impossible to navigate. Among the numerous rapids flooded by the dam were Celilo Falls, which for thousands of years was the most important salmon-fishing area in the Northwest. Every year, thousands of Native Americans would gather here to catch and smoke salmon, putting the dried fish away for the coming winter. The traditional method of catching the salmon was to use a spear or a net on the end of a long pole. Men would build precarious wooden platforms out over the river and catch the salmon as they tried to leap up the falls. You can still see traditional Native American fishing platforms near the Shilo Inn here in The Dalles. The dam's **visitor center,** open May through September daily 9am to 5pm, has displays on both the history of the river and the construction of the dam. To reach the visitor center, take exit 87 off I-84 and turn right on Brett Clodfelter Way.

East of town 17 miles, you'll find the **Deschutes River State Recreation Area** (✆ **541/739-2322**), which is at the mouth of the Deschutes River and is the eastern boundary of the Columbia Gorge National Scenic Area. The park has several miles of hiking trails, and an old railway right-of-way that parallels the Deschutes River for 17 miles has been turned into a gravel mountain-biking and horseback-riding trail.

Wine Tasting

Dry Hollow Vineyards   Set high on a hillside south of The Dalles and surrounded by cherry orchards and vineyards, this little winery has one of the prettiest settings in the Gorge. This is one of the only wineries in the area producing sauvignon blanc, and they also do chardonnay and Riesling. Of course, as at other area wineries, there are Bordeaux-style reds.

3410 Dry Hollow Lane. ✆ **541/296-2953.** www.dryhollowvineyards.com. Tasting fee $5. Feb–Nov Sat–Sun noon–5pm. From the east end of The Dalles, take Brewery Grade Rd. to Dry Hollow Rd. to Dry Hollow Lane.

Historic Sunshine Mill/Quenett Winery   A 100-year-old flour-mill building, complete with huge silos, has been converted into the coolest tasting room in the Gorge. Old gears and belts crowd the ceiling and hint at the activity that once took place here. Quenett Winery, which also has a tasting room in Hood River, specializes in big red wines. This building also serves as the bottling facility for Copa di Vino, which produces unusual single serving packaged glasses of wine.

901 E. Second St. ✆ **541/298-8900.** www.sunshinemill.com. Tasting fee $5. Daily noon–6pm.

East of The Dalles

Maryhill Museum of Art/Stonehenge Monument ★★ 🏛   Between 1914 and 1926, in Washington State atop a remote, windswept bluff overlooking the Columbia River, eccentric entrepreneur Sam Hill built a grand mansion he called Maryhill. Today the mansion is one of the finest, most eclectic, and least visited museums in Washington. There are sculptures and drawings by Auguste Rodin; an extensive collection of Native American baskets and other artifacts; furniture, jewelry, and other items that once belonged to Hill's friend, Queen Marie of Romania; and a collection of post–World War II miniature French fashion mannequins. There's a

sculpture park here, and both a cafe and picnic tables. A few mile
stands Hill's concrete reproduction of Stonehenge, which he buil
local men who died in World War I. Note that the Rodins and fa
are sometimes loaned out to other museums.

35 Maryhill Museum Dr. (Wash. 14), Goldendale, WA. ℂ **509/773-3733.**
org. Admission $9 adults, $8 seniors, $3 children 7–18. Mar 15–Nov 15 daily
Dalles, cross the Columbia River on U.S. 197, and then drive 20 miles east on Wash. 14.

Where to Stay

Although there are a few hotels in The Dalles, you should stay in Hood River, which
is only 20 miles away and has a better selection of accommodations plus lots of great
restaurants.

Celilo Inn ★ 🛏️ This restored and updated motel at the east end of The Dalles,
overlooking The Dalles Dam, may not be in the prettiest of locations, but rooms are
so stylish and the renovation of this old motel so remarkable that the Celilo Inn
makes an excellent base for exploring this end of the Columbia River Gorge. The
inn caters to people who are touring local wineries and offers winery tours and
packages.

3550 E. Second St., The Dalles, OR 97058. ℂ **541/769-0001.** www.celiloinn.com. 46 units. $99–
$149 double; $149–$169 suite. Rates include continental breakfast. AE, DISC, MC, V. Pets accepted
($25 per night). **Amenities:** Exercise room; outdoor pool. *In room:* A/C, TV, fridge, hair dryer, MP3
docking station, free Wi-Fi. Take exit 87 off I-84.

CAMPGROUNDS

If you want to pitch a tent or park an RV, try Deschutes River State Recreation Area,
17 miles east of The Dalles off I-84. For reservations, contact **ReserveAmerica**
(ℂ **800/452-5687;** www.reserveamerica.com). On the Washington side of the
Gorge, there is camping at Columbia Hills State Park (no reservations) near the community of Dallesport (take U.S. 197 N. to Wash. 14 E.).

Where to Eat

For delicious breakfasts, pastries, and sandwiches, don't miss **Petite Provence of
the Gorge,** 408 E. Second St. (ℂ **541/506-0037;** www.provence-portland.com), a
wonderful little French pastry shop.

Baldwin Saloon Historic Restaurant & Bar ★ AMERICAN/CONTINEN-
TAL Built in 1876, the Baldwin Saloon has one of the few remaining cast-iron
facades in town and is one of the only restaurants in The Dalles with much historic
character. Brick walls, wooden booths, and a high ceiling add to the old-time feel, as
does the collection of late-19th-century landscape paintings and large bar nudes. The
eclectic menu has everything from burgers to bouillabaisse.

205 Court St. ℂ**541/296-5666.** www.baldwinsaloon.com. Reservations accepted only for parties
of 5 or more. Main courses $11–$25. DISC, MC, V. Mon–Thurs 11am–9pm; Fri–Sat 11am–10pm.

THE CASCADES

8

From the schussing of January and the kayaking of April to the wildflowers of August and the splashes of fall foliage in October, Oregon's Cascade Range is a year-round recreational magnet. Stretching from the Columbia Gorge in the north to California in the south, the Cascades are a relatively young volcanic mountain range with picture-perfect, snowcapped volcanic peaks rising above lush green forests of evergreens. The Cascades' volcanic heritage sets this mountain range apart from others in the West, and throughout these mountains, signs of past volcanic activity are evident. Crater Lake, formed after a massive volcanic eruption, is the most dramatic evidence of the Cascades' fiery past. But you can also see evidence of volcanic activity in the cones of Mount Hood and Mount Jefferson, and in the lava fields of McKenzie Pass.

Although this volcanic geology is spectacular, it is not what draws most people to these mountains. The main attraction is the wide variety of outdoor sports activities available. Crystal-clear rivers, churned into white water as they cascade down from high in the mountains, provide numerous opportunities for rafting, kayaking, canoeing, and fishing. High mountain lakes hold hungry trout, and throughout the summer, lakeside campgrounds stay filled with anglers. The Pacific Crest Trail winds the entire length of the Cascades, but it is the many wilderness areas scattered throughout these mountains that are the biggest draw for day hikers and backpackers. Mountain bikers also find miles of national-forest trails to enjoy. In winter, skiers and snowboarders flock to more than half a dozen ski areas and countless miles of cross-country ski trails—and because winter lingers late in the high Cascades, the ski season here is one of the longest in the country. Skiing often begins in mid-November and continues on into April, and even May and June at Mount Bachelor. In fact, on Mount Hood, high-elevation snowfields allow a year-round ski season.

The Cascades also serve as a dividing line between the lush evergreen forests of western Oregon and the dry, high desert landscapes of eastern Oregon. On the western slopes, Douglas firs and Western red cedars dominate, while on the east side, the cinnamon-barked ponderosa pine is most common. These trees were the lifeblood of the Oregon economy for much of the 20th century, but with few virgin forests left in the state, a litigious battle to protect the last old-growth forests has been raging here for decades. Today visitors to the Cascades will be confronted at nearly every turn by the sight of clear-cuts scarring the mountainsides, yet it is still possible to find groves of ancient trees beneath which to hike and camp.

MOUNT HOOD ★★★

60 miles E of Portland, 46 miles S of Hood River

At 11,235 feet, Mount Hood, a dormant volcano, is the tallest mountain in Oregon. Located fewer than 60 miles east of downtown Portland, it is also the busiest mountain in the state. Summer and winter, people flock here in search of cool mountain air filled with the scent of firs and pines. Campgrounds, hiking and mountain-biking trails, trout streams and lakes, downhill ski areas, and cross-country ski trails all provide ample opportunities for outdoor recreational activities on Mount Hood.

With five downhill areas and many miles of cross-country trails, the mountain is a ski bum's dream come true. One of the country's largest night-skiing areas is here, and at Timberline you can ski right through the summer. Because even those with a moderate amount of mountain-climbing experience can reach the summit fairly easily, Mount Hood is also the most climbed major peak in the United States.

One of the first settlers to visit Mount Hood was Samuel Barlow, who in 1845 had traveled the Oregon Trail and was searching for an alternative to taking his wagon train down the treacherous waters of the Columbia River. Barlow blazed a trail across the south flank of Mount Hood, and the following year he opened his trail as a toll road. The **Barlow Trail,** though difficult, was cheaper and safer than rafting down the river. The trail is now used for hiking and mountain biking.

During the Great Depression, the Works Progress Administration employed skilled craftsmen to build the rustic **Timberline Lodge** at the tree line on the mountain's south slope. Today the lodge is a National Historic Landmark and is the main destination for visitors to the mountain. The lodge's vista of Mount Hood's peak and of the Oregon Cascades to the south gets my vote for the state's most unforgettable view.

Don't expect to have this mountain all to yourself, though. Because of its proximity to Portland, Mount Hood sees a lot of visitors throughout the year, and, on snowy days, the road back down the mountain from the ski areas can be bumper to bumper and backed up for hours. Also keep in mind that you'll need to have a Sno-Park permit in the winter (available at ski shops around the area) and a Northwest Forest Pass to park at trail heads in the summer (available at ranger stations, visitor centers, and a few outdoors-oriented shops).

Essentials

GETTING THERE   From Portland, Mount Hood is reached by driving east on I-84 to exit 16 (Wood Village) and then continuing east on U.S. 26. From Hood River, drive south on Ore. 35. These two highways meet just east of the community of Government Camp, which is the main tourist town on the mountain.

VISITOR INFORMATION   For more information on Mount Hood, contact the **Hood River Ranger Station,** 6780 Ore. 35, Parkdale, OR 97041 (✆ **541/352-6002;** www.fs.fed.us/r6/mthood). Online you can also check out www.mthood.info.

Summer on the Mountain

In snow-free months, most visitors are heading to historic Timberline Lodge (see "Where to Stay," below). Besides having a fabulous view of Mount Hood, the lodge is surrounded by meadows that burst into bloom in July and August. Here you can access the 41-mile-long Timberline Trail, which circles the mountain. If you just have time for a short hike, head west from the lodge on this trail rather than east. (The route east passes through dusty ash fields and then drops down into the hot, barren

White River Valley.) You'll find snow here year-round, and there's even summer skiing and snowboarding at the Timberline ski area. The lift-accessed ski slopes are high above the lodge on the Palmer Snowfield and are open only in the morning. In summer you can ride the lift even if you aren't skiing. The Magic Mile Skyride, which operates Monday through Thursday from 11am to 2pm and Friday through Sunday from 11am to 3pm, costs $15 for adults and $9 for seniors and children 7 to 14.

In summer you can also ride the lift at the **Mt. Hood Adventure Park at Skibowl,** 87000 E. U.S. 26, Government Camp (© **503/272-3206** or 503/222-2695; www.skibowl.com), where you'll find mountain-biking trails, hiking trails, an alpine slide (sort of a summertime bobsled run), and numerous other rides and activities.

One of the most popular and enjoyable hikes on Mount Hood is the trail to **Mirror Lake ★**, which, as its name implies, reflects the summit of Mount Hood in its mirrorlike waters. The trail is fairly easy and is good for families with young children. If you want to add a bit more challenge, you can continue to the summit of Tom, Dick & Harry Mountain, the back side of which in winter is part of the Mt. Hood Skibowl ski area. The view from the summit is superb, and in late summer there are huckleberries along the trail. You'll find the trail head on U.S. 26, just before you reach Government Camp.

The east side of the mountain, accessed by Ore. 35 from Hood River, is much drier and less visited than the south side. Here on the east side, you'll find good hiking trails in the vicinity of **Mount Hood Meadows,** where the wildflower displays in late July and August are some of the best on the mountain. The loop trail past Umbrella and Sahalie falls is particularly enjoyable. Also on this side of the mountain, you'll find the highest segment of the Timberline Trail. This section of trail climbs up Cooper Spur ridge from historic Cloud Cap Inn (no longer open to the public). The close-up views of the mountain and the distant views of eastern Oregon's dry landscape make this one of my favorite hiking destinations on Mount Hood. To reach the trail head, follow signs off Ore. 35 for Cooper Spur and Cloud Cap. On the east side of Ore. 35, off Forest Service Road 44, you'll also find the best **mountain-biking trails** in the area. Among these are the Surveyor's Ridge Trail and the Dog Mountain Trail.

If you're interested in a little adventure and an alternative route from the west side of the mountain to the Hood River area, try exploring the gravel **Lolo Pass Road,** which is usually in good enough condition for standard passenger cars. However, be sure to check with the Forest Service on road conditions before attempting to drive this road. Also, be sure to have a Forest Service map, since roads out here are not well marked, and it's easy to get lost. Branching off from the Lolo Pass Road are several smaller roads that lead to some of the best hiking trails on Mount Hood. Also off the Lolo Pass Road, you'll find **Lost Lake,** one of the most beautiful (and most photographed) lakes in the Oregon Cascades. When the water is still, the view of Mount Hood and its reflection in the lake is positively sublime. Here you'll find campgrounds, cabins, picnic areas, good fishing, and hiking trails.

Down at the base of the mountain, just west of the community of Welches, you can learn about the forests, rivers, and fish of the Northwest at the Bureau of Land Management's **Wildwood Recreation Site.** Within this 550-acre natural area are 2.5 miles of trails, including a boardwalk that crosses a wetland area. The highlight of the trail is an underwater fish-viewing window on the Cascade Streamwatch Trail. There's also a playground here, which makes this a good stop for families with small children. Fishing and swimming in the Salmon River are popular. There's also access to the steep and strenuous Boulder Ridge Trail, as well as the much easier Old Salmon River Trail. There's a $5 day-use fee.

It's also possible to do some paddling while you're in the area. **Blue Sky White-water Rafting** (© **800/898-6398** or 503/630-3163; www.blueskyrafting.com) operates white-water-rafting trips on the Clackamas River, which has its source on the flanks of Mount Hood. A half-day trip costs $48 and a full-day trip costs $80 per person. **River Drifters** (© **800/972-0430** or 800/226-1001; www.riverdrifters.net) leads similar Clackamas River trips, and also trips on the Sandy River, which is more convenient if you're short on time. Sandy River trips cost $95 and are offered March through mid-June and during October and November.

If you're interested in a more strenuous mountain experience, the Mount Hood area offers plenty of mountain- and rock-climbing opportunities. **Timberline Mountain Guides,** P.O. Box 1167, Bend, OR 97709 (© **541/312-9242;** www.timberline mtguides.com), leads summit climbs on Mount Hood. They also offer ski-mountaineering and rock-climbing courses. A 2-day Mount Hood mountaineering course with summit climb costs $485.

Winter on the Mountain

Although snowpacks that can be slow to reach skiable depths and frequent midwinter rains make the ski season on Mount Hood unpredictable, the regular ski season typically runs from around Thanksgiving right through March or April. Add to this the summer skiing on the Palmer Snowfield at Timberline Ski Area, and you have the longest ski season in the United States. There are five ski areas on Mount Hood, though two of these are tiny operations that attract primarily beginners and families looking for an economical way to all go schussing together. For cross-country skiers, there are many miles of marked ski trails, some of which are groomed.

The single most important thing to know about skiing anywhere in Oregon is that you'll have to have a **Sno-Park permit.** These permits, which sell for $4 a day, $9 for 3 days, or $25 for the season, allow you to park in plowed parking areas on the mountain. You can get permits at ski shops in Sandy and Hood River and at a few convenience stores. Expect to pay a service fee wherever you buy your pass.

Mt. Hood Skibowl (© **800/754-2695,** 503/272-3206, or, or 503/222-2695 for snow report; www.skibowl.com) is located in Government Camp on U.S. 26 and is the closest ski area to Portland. Skibowl offers 1,500 vertical feet of skiing and has more expert slopes than any other ski area on the mountain. This is also one of the largest lighted ski areas in the country. An adult all-day lift ticket costs $49 ($30 for night skiing). Call for hours of operation.

Timberline Ski Area (© **503/272-3158** or 503/222-2211 for snow report; www.timberlinelodge.com) is the highest ski area on Mount Hood and has one slope that is open throughout the summer. This is the site of the historic **Timberline Lodge** (see below). Adult lift-ticket prices range from $25 for night skiing to between $58 and $64 for an all-day pass. Call for hours of operation.

Mount Hood Meadows ★★ (© **503/337-2222** or 503/227-7669 for snow report; www.skihood.com), 12 miles northeast of Government Camp on Ore. 35, is the largest ski resort on Mount Hood, with more than 2,000 skiable acres, 2,777 vertical feet of slopes, five high-speed quad lifts, and a wide variety of terrain. This is the closest Mount Hood comes to having a destination ski resort, and consequently, it is here that you'll find the most out-of-state skiers. An all-day lift ticket costs $74 for adults. Call for hours of operation.

If you're interested in **cross-country skiing,** there are plenty of trails. For views, head to the **White River Sno-Park,** east of Government Camp. The trails at **Glacier View Sno-Park,** across U.S. 26 from Mount Hood Skibowl, are good for beginner and intermediate skiers. The mountain's best-groomed trails are at the **Mount Hood Meadows Nordic Center** ($10 all-day trail pass) on Ore. 35 and at **Teacup Lake** ($8 donation requested), which is across the highway from the turnoff for Mount Hood Meadows. Teacup Lake is maintained by a local ski club (www.teacup nordic.org) and has the best system of groomed trails on the mountain. In the town of Sandy and at Government Camp, numerous ski shops rent cross-country skis.

En Route to the Mountain

If you like sweet wines, watch for the Wasson Brothers wine-tasting room, 17020 Ruben Lane, at U.S. 26 (© **503/668-3124;** www.wassonwine.com), as you drive through Sandy. This winery produces a wide range of fruit wines and also does quite a few dry varietals. The tasting room is open daily from 9am to 5pm.

Where to Stay
ON THE MOUNTAIN

Best Western Mt. Hood Inn Located at the west end of Government Camp right on the highway, this modern budget hotel is a curious mix of log-cabin rustic and urban-loft styling. Although this may sound like an odd mash-up, it's comfortable and, most of the year, a relatively good value (winter holidays are the exception). Pine furnishings give the guest rooms here a contemporary rustic feel. The king spa rooms, with two-person whirlpool tubs beside the king-size beds, are definitely the best rooms. Just across the parking lot, you'll find the Ice Axe Grill, home of the Mt. Hood Brewing Company, which is a good place for an apres-ski pint.

87450 E. Government Camp Loop, Government Camp, OR 97028. www.mthoodinn.com. © **800/780-7234** or 503/272-3205. Fax 503/272-3307. 57 units. $109–$209 double. Rates include continental breakfast. Children 12 and under stay free in parent's room. AE, DC, DISC, MC, V. Pets accepted ($10 per night). **Amenities:** Exercise room; Jacuzzi. *In room:* TV/DVD, fridge, free Wi-Fi.

Collins Lake Resort/Grand Lodges ★★ When it opened a few years ago, this condominium resort development in the heart of Government Camp was the biggest thing to hit Mount Hood since Timberline Lodge was built. Collins Lake and the affiliated Grand Lodges offer by far the most luxurious and spacious accommodations on the mountain. These are condos, so interior decor is up to owners, but don't worry too much. These condos are beautiful, and most have hardwood floors and gorgeous kitchens with granite counters. Be sure to ask about lift-ticket discounts when staying here in the winter. Summer or winter, the lodges have a shuttle that will take you to places to play.

88149 E. Creek Ridge Rd., Government Camp, OR 97028. www.collinslakeresort.com. © **800/234-6288** or 503/928-3498. 74 units. $189–$529 double. Children 12 and under stay free in parent's room. AE, DISC, MC, V. Pets accepted ($50–$100 fee). **Amenities:** Bikes; concierge; exercise room (Grand Lodges); 3 Jacuzzis; 2 outdoor pools; sauna; Wi-Fi. *In room:* A/C (Grand Lodges), TV/DVD, hair dryer, kitchen, free Wi-Fi.

Timberline Lodge ★★ Constructed during the Great Depression of the 1930s as a WPA project, this classic alpine ski lodge overflows with craftsmanship. The grand stone fireplace, huge exposed beams, and wide-plank floors of the lobby impress every first-time visitor. Woodcarvings, imaginative wrought-iron fixtures, hand-hooked rugs, and handmade furniture complete the rustic picture. Unfortunately, guest rooms, which vary considerably in size, are not as impressive as the public areas of the lodge. The smallest rooms lack private bathrooms, and windows in most rooms fail to take advantage of the phenomenal views that could be had here. However, you can always visit the Ram's Head lounge for a better view of Mount Hood.

Timberline Lodge, OR 97028. www.timberlinelodge.com. © **800/547-1406** or 503/272-3311. Fax 503/272-3145. 70 units, 10 with shared bathroom. $125 double with shared bathroom; $165–$300 double with private bathroom. Children 12 and under stay free in parent's room. DISC, MC, V. **Amenities:** 4 restaurants; 3 lounges; children's programs; exercise room; Jacuzzi; year-round outdoor pool; sauna; Wi-Fi. *In room:* TV and hair dryer (rooms without shared bath), no phone (shared-bath rooms).

AT THE BASE OF THE MOUNTAIN

The Resort at The Mountain ★★   It's a bit of a drive to Timberline or Government Camp and the area's hiking trails and ski areas, but if a day at the spa or a round of golf in a gorgeous setting sounds tempting, this resort, set in a large clearing in the dense woods at the base of Mount Hood, is your best choice in the Mount Hood area. Beautifully landscaped grounds hide the resort's many low-rise buildings and make this a tranquil woodsy retreat. The guest rooms, all renovated a few years ago, are large and modern and have either a balcony or a patio. The main lodge has a formal dining room, while a more casual dining room overlooks the golf course. In addition to the amenities listed below, there are horseshoe pits, an 18-hole putting course, croquet and lawn-bowling courts, volleyball and badminton courts, and nature trails.

68010 E. Fairway Ave., Welches, OR 97067. www.theresort.com. © **877/439-6774** or 503/622-3101. 157 units. $129–$279 double; $229–$479 suite; $299–$789 villa. Children 18 and under stay free in parent's room. AE, DISC, MC, V. Pets accepted ($50 fee). **Amenities:** 2 restaurants; 2 lounges; babysitting; bikes; exercise room; 27-hole golf course; Jacuzzi; outdoor pool; room service; full-service spa; 4 tennis courts. *In room:* A/C, TV/DVD, fridge, hair dryer, free Wi-Fi.

NORTHEAST OF THE MOUNTAIN

Cooper Spur Mountain Resort ⚑   If you want to get away from it all, try this surprisingly remote lodge in the off season. (During ski season, it can be difficult to get a reservation.) The inn consists of a main building and a handful of modern log cabins. These latter accommodations should be your first choice here. The cabins have two bedrooms and a loft area reached by a spiral staircase. There are also rooms with full kitchens. The inn's restaurant serves decent, reasonably priced steaks. At the end of the day, you can soak yourself in one of the inn's whirlpool spas.

10755 Cooper Spur Rd., Mt. Hood, OR 97041. www.cooperspur.com. © **541/352-6692.** 16 units. $99–$149 double; $159–$329 cabin or suite; $375–$499 log house. AE, DC, DISC, MC, V. Pets accepted ($35 per day). **Amenities:** Restaurant; lounge; concierge; 2 Jacuzzis; tennis court. *In room:* TV, fridge, free Wi-Fi.

Where to Eat

If you're heading up the mountain from Portland on U.S. 26, you can get good espresso at Cafe Aria, 67211 E. U.S. 26 (© **503/564-9333;** www.cafe-aria.com), in Welches. After a day of hiking or skiing, you can celebrate with a pint of locally brewed beer from the Mt. Hood Brewing Company at the Ice Axe Grill, 87304 E. Government Camp Loop (© **503/272-3172;** www.iceaxegrill.com), which is at the west end of Government Camp.

ON THE MOUNTAIN

Cascade Dining Room ★★ NORTHWEST/INTERNATIONAL   It may seem a bit casual, and there are no stunning views of Mount Hood even though it's right outside the window, but the Cascade Dining Room is still the best restaurant on Mount Hood. The menu, which leans toward alpine flavors (and is somewhat over-priced), changes regularly but might include roasted marrow bones with foie gras mousse, pork-loin schnitzel with huckleberry jam, or herb spaetzle with wild mushrooms and a duck egg poached in Riesling. For dessert, be sure to order the apple-pecan crisp, made with local Hood River apples. There's also a superb wine list, with plenty of Northwest wines.

In Timberline Lodge, Timberline. ✆ **503/272-3391.** www.timberlinelodge.com. Reservations recommended. Main courses $17–$19 lunch, $20–$48 dinner. DISC, MC, V. Mon–Fri 7:30–10:30am, 11am–2pm, and 5:30–8pm; Sat–Sun 7:30–10:30am, 11am–3pm, and 5:30–8pm.

Ram's Head Bar AMERICAN   Although ostensibly just the mezzanine-level bar at the historic Timberline Lodge, the Ram's Head is the best place on the mountain for a casual meal with an in-your-face view of Mount Hood. Keep in mind, though, that this place is crowded on summer and winter weekends, and scoring a primo seat in front of the window can be a challenge. The menu is short, but includes some surprisingly sophisticated dishes for a bar. Try a salad with alder-smoked salmon, mac and cheese made with smoked salmon and Dungeness crab, or some white cheddar fondue. While you wait to snag that perfect seat, you can sip a pint of beer from Timberline Lodge's own Mt. Hood Brewing Company down in Government Camp.

In Timberline Lodge, Timberline. ✆ **503/272-3391.** www.timberlinelodge.com. Reservations not accepted. Main courses $12–$19. DISC, MC, V. Mon–Thurs 2–11pm; Fri–Sun 11am–11pm.

AT THE BASE OF THE MOUNTAIN

Calamity Jane's 👕 BURGERS   Burger lovers won't want to miss this rustic burger joint outside Sandy. Not only are there the usual burgers and cheeseburgers, but there are also such outrageous concoctions as a peanut-butter burger, a George Washington burger (with sour cream and sweet pie cherries), a hot fudge–and-marshmallow burger—even an unbelievably priced inflation burger. Not all the burgers at this entertaining eatery are calculated to turn your stomach; some are just plain delicious. There are even pizza burgers. This place is just east of Sandy on U.S. 26.

42015 U.S. 26, Sandy. ✆ **503/668-7817.** www.calamity-janes.com. Burgers $7.50–$13. AE, DISC, MC, V. Sun–Thurs 11am–9pm; Fri–Sat 11am–10pm.

The Rendezvous Grill & Tap Room ★ MEDITERRANEAN   Located right on U.S. 26 in Welches, this casual, upscale restaurant is a great choice for dinner on your way back to Portland. Although the emphasis is on Mediterranean dishes, other flavors also show up. Don't miss the rigatoni with alder-smoked chicken, topped with toasted hazelnuts and dried cranberries. The pan-fried oysters and the ever-popular crab-and-shrimp cakes, both of which are available at lunch and dinner, are also good bets.

67149 E. U.S. 26, Welches. ✆ **503/622-6837.** www.rendezvousgrill.net. Reservations recommended. Main courses $8.75–$15 lunch, $18–$26 dinner. AE, DISC, MC, V. Daily 11:30am–9pm.

THE SANTIAM PASS & MCKENZIE RIVER

Santiam Pass: 82 miles SE of Salem, 40 miles NW of Bend. McKenzie Pass: 77 miles NE of Eugene, 36 miles NW of Bend

As the nearest mountain recreational areas to both Salem and Eugene, the Santiam Pass, McKenzie Pass, and McKenzie River routes are some of the most popular in the state. Ore. 22, which leads over Santiam Pass, is also one of the busiest routes to the Sisters and Bend areas in central Oregon. Along these highways are some of the state's best white-water-rafting and fishing rivers, some of the most popular and most beautiful backpacking areas, and good downhill and cross-country skiing. In the summer, the Detroit Lake recreation area is the main attraction along Ore. 22 and is a favorite of water-skiers and lake anglers. In winter it's downhill and cross-country skiing at Santiam Pass that brings most people up this way.

Ore. 126, on the other hand, follows the scenic McKenzie River and is favored by white-water rafters and drift-boat anglers fishing for salmon and steelhead. Several state parks provide access to the river. During the summer, Ore. 126 connects to Ore. 242, a narrow road that climbs up and over McKenzie Pass, the most breathtaking pass in the Oregon Cascades.

Essentials

GETTING THERE   Santiam Pass is open year-round and is reached by Ore. 22 from Salem, U.S. 20 from Albany, and Ore. 126 from Eugene. McKenzie Pass, which is closed in winter, is on Ore. 242 and lies to the south of Santiam Pass. It can be reached by all the same roads that lead to Santiam Pass.

VISITOR INFORMATION   For more information on outdoor recreation in this area, contact the **Detroit Ranger District,** 44125 North Santiam Hwy. SE, Detroit, OR 97342 (© **503/854-3366**), or the **McKenzie River Ranger District,** 57600 McKenzie Hwy., McKenzie Bridge, OR 97413 (© **541/822-3381**). Also check the website of the **Willamette National Forest** (www.fs.fed.us/r6/willamette).

Along the Santiam Pass Highway

Detroit Lake is the summertime center of activity on this route—fishing and water-skiing are the most popular activities. North of the lake, you'll find **Breitenbush Hot Springs Retreat & Conference Center** (© **503/854-3320**; www.breitenbush. com), a New Age community/retreat center that has rustic cabins, dorms, and campsites and allows day use of its hot springs by advance reservation. The fee is between $14 and $26 per person, and inexpensive vegetarian meals are available ($12). Breitenbush offers massage, yoga, meditation classes, and a wide range of other programs focusing on holistic health and spiritual growth.

At Santiam Pass, you'll find the **Hoodoo Ski Area** (© **541/822-3799,** or 541/822-3337 for snow report; www.hoodoo.com), which is the best little ski area in Oregon. Hoodoo has five chair lifts and 32 runs for all levels of experience. Lift tickets are $45 to $48 for adults and $31 to $34 for children. Night skiing is available. Here you'll also find an awesome tubing run for the kids and the Hoodoo Nordic Center, which has almost 10 miles of groomed cross-country ski trails and charges $14 for a trail pass. Also in the Santiam Pass area, you'll find several Sno-Parks. The Maxwell, Big Springs, and Lava Lake East Sno-Parks access the best trails in the area. However, these trails are very popular with snowshoers. Consequently, you might want to leave the skinny skis at home and bring snowshoes instead.

Up the McKenzie River

The McKenzie River is one of Oregon's most popular white-water-rafting rivers, and the cold blue waters challenge a wide range of experience levels. **Oregon Whitewater Adventures** (© **800/820-7238**; www.oregonwhitewater.com) and **A Helfrich Outfitter** (© **800/328-7688** or 541/726-5039; www.raft2fish.com) both offer half- and full-day trips. Expect to pay $60 to $65 for a half day of rafting and $80 to $90 for a full day, with lower rates for children.

The McKenzie River town of Blue River is home to one of the best golf courses in Oregon. **Tokatee Golf Club,** 54947 McKenzie Hwy., McKenzie Bridge (© **800/452-6376** or 541/822-3220; www.tokatee.com), gets consistently high ratings and has a spectacular setting with views of snowcapped Cascade peaks and lush forests. The green fee is $42 ($30 for electric cart) for 18 holes.

Off Ore. 126, between the towns of Blue River and McKenzie Bridge, you'll find the turnoff for the **West Cascades Scenic Byway** (Forest Service Rd. 19). This road meanders for 54 miles through the foothills of the Cascades, first following the South Fork McKenzie River (and Cougar Reservoir) and then following the North Fork of the Middle Fork Willamette River, which offers excellent fly-fishing and numerous swimming holes. Along the route, you'll find several hiking trails and, toward the south end of Cougar Reservoir, a .25-mile trail that leads to the very popular **Terwilliger Hot Springs.** This undeveloped, clothing-optional hot spring is something of a counterculture mecca, and, though absolutely enchanting, it is extremely popular. Arrive very early to avoid the crowds. There is a $5 per person day-use fee here. The southernmost stretch of Forest Service Road 19 is the most scenic portion and passes through a deep, narrow gorge formed by the North Fork of the Middle Fork Willamette River. At the southern end of the scenic byway is the community of Westfir, which is the site of the longest covered bridge in Oregon.

Between the turnoff for McKenzie Pass and the junction of Ore. 126 and U.S. 20, you'll find some of the Cascades' most enchanting water features. Southernmost of these is **Belknap Resort and Hot Springs,** 59296 Belknap Springs Rd., McKenzie Bridge (© **541/822-3512;** www.belknaphotsprings.com), where, for $7 for 1 hour or $12 for the day, you can soak in a hot mineral swimming pool. Just north of Trail Bridge Reservoir, on a side road off the highway, a 4-mile round-trip hike on a section of the McKenzie River Trail leads to the startlingly blue waters of the **Tamolitch Pool ★★**. This pool is formed by the McKenzie River welling up out of the ground after flowing underground for 3 miles. Five miles south of the junction with Ore. 20, you'll come to two picturesque waterfalls, **Sahalie Falls** and **Koosah Falls.** Across the highway from these falls is **Clear Lake,** the source of the McKenzie River. This spring-fed lake truly lives up to its name, and the rustic **Clear Lake Resort,** 60700 Ore. 126 (© **541/967-3917**), rents rowboats ($15 per hr. or $30 per day) so you can get out on the water and see for yourself. Be sure to hike the trail on the east side of the lake; it leads to the turquoise waters of **Great Springs,** which is connected to the lake by a 100-yard stream.

One of the most breathtaking sections of road in the state begins just east of **Belknap Hot Springs.** Ore. 242, which is open only in the summer, is a narrow, winding road that climbs up through forests and lava fields to **McKenzie Pass ★★★**, from which there's a sweeping panorama of the Cascades and some of the youngest lava fields in Oregon. An observation building made of lava rock provides sighting tubes so that you can identify all the visible peaks, and a couple of trails will lead you out into this otherworldly landscape. In autumn this road has some of the best fall color in the state. On the west side of the pass, the short **Proxy Falls** trail leads through old lava flows to a waterfall that in late summer has no outlet stream. The water simply disappears into the porous lava.

Where to Stay

Belknap Lodge & Hot Springs 🎁 Set on the banks of the McKenzie River, this lodge is one of the most enjoyable mountain retreats in the state. Extensive lawns and flower gardens have been planted, turning this clearing in the forest into a burst of color in the summer. Guest rooms vary in size, but all have comfortable furnishings. Some also have whirlpool tubs or decks overlooking the roaring river. Cabins with fireplaces and air-conditioning are also available. Water from the hot springs, which are on the far side of the river and reached by a footbridge, is pumped into two small pools. The lodge also has sites for tents and RVs ($25–$35).

59296 Belknap Springs Rd. (P.O. Box 2001), McKenzie Bridge, OR 97413. www.belknaphotsprings. com. 📞 **541/822-3512.** Fax 541/822-3327. 25 units. $100–$135 double; $155–$185 suite; $130– $400 cabin. 2-night minimum on weekends and holidays. Rates for lodge include continental breakfast. DISC, MC, V. Pets accepted in some cabins ($20 fee). **Amenities:** 2 hot springs–fed outdoor pools; free Wi-Fi. *In some rooms:* A/C, TV/VCR/DVD, fridge, hair dryer, no phone.

Eagle Rock Lodge ★ This bed-and-breakfast on the banks of the McKenzie River has the best rooms in the area and should be your first choice for a luxurious outdoors-oriented escape. Several of the rooms have gas fireplaces and two-person whirlpool tubs, both of which can be very welcoming after a long day of hiking.

49198 McKenzie Hwy, Vida, OR 97488. www.eaglerocklodge.com. 📞 **888/773-4333** or 541/822- 3630. 8 units. $130–$185 double; $225 suite. Rates include full breakfast. Children 12 and under stay free in parent's room. MC, V. **Amenities:** Free Wi-Fi. *In room:* A/C, fridge, hair dryer, no phone.

Holiday Farm Resort ★ 🎁 This beautifully situated getaway is a collection of renovated cottages and cabins perched on the edge of the McKenzie River, and the setting under the big trees is as idyllic as you'll find in Oregon. Grab a book and a seat on your private riverside deck, and you may never give a thought to pulling on your hiking boots. Holiday Farm started out as a stagecoach stop and has been around long enough to have hosted U.S. President Herbert Hoover. A formal dining room and a more casual lounge serve meals. Guests have 800 feet of riverfront to enjoy and two private lakes for fishing and swimming.

54455 McKenzie River Dr., Blue River, OR 97413. www.holidayfarmresort.com. 📞 **541/822-3725.** 6 units. Mid-May to Sept $225–$350 cottage double; lower rates other months. AE, MC, V. Pets accepted. **Amenities:** Restaurant; lounge; spa. *In room:* Kitchen, free Wi-Fi.

Inn at the Bridge ★ The privately owned modern cabins here are set right on the banks of the McKenzie River and are as clean and comfortable as any accommodations you'll find in the area. Although the cabins are close to the highway, the sound of the river is all you'll hear most of the time. Summer or winter, these cedar-shingled two-bedroom cabins are a great choice.

56393 McKenzie Hwy., McKenzie Bridge, OR 97413. www.mckenzie-river-cabins.com. 📞 **541/822-6006.** 10 units. $199 double. 2-night minimum stay. MC, V. *In room:* A/C, TV, kitchen.

CAMPGROUNDS

There are several campgrounds along the McKenzie River on Ore. 126. Of these the Delta Campground, set under huge old-growth trees between Blue River and McKenzie Bridge, and Paradise, on the banks of the McKenzie, are two of the finest. If you are up this way to hike, mountain bike, or do some flat-water canoeing, there is no better choice than Clear Lake's Coldwater Cove Campground on Ore. 126 just south of Santiam Pass junction. For reservations at this campground (and Paradise), contact the National Recreation Reservation Service (*C* **877/444-6777**; www. recreation.gov).

Along the West Cascades Scenic Byway, you'll find several campgrounds. **Cougar Crossing,** toward the north end of the scenic byway, is the closest campground to Terwilliger Hot Springs. South of here, you'll find **Frissell Crossing** and **French Pete,** both of which are on the banks of the South Fork of the McKenzie River.

Where to Eat

For burgers and pies, stop at the **Vida Cafe,** 45641 McKenzie Hwy., Vida (*C* **541/896-3289**), near milepost 26; or, at milepost 38, the **Finn Rock Grill,** 50660 McKenzie Hwy., Vida (*C* **541/822-6080**), which has a deck beside the river.

THE WILLAMETTE PASS ROUTE

Oakridge: 41 miles SE of Eugene. Willamette Pass: 68 miles SE of Eugene

Ore. 58, which connects Eugene with U.S. 97 north of Crater Lake, is the state's fastest and straightest route over the Cascades. This is not to imply, however, that there isn't anything along this highway worth slowing down for. Flanked by two wilderness areas, Waldo Lake and Diamond Peak, and three major lakes—Waldo, Odell, and Crescent—Ore. 58 provides access to a wide range of recreational activities, chief among which are mountain biking, fishing, and boating in summer and both downhill and cross-country skiing in winter.

The sister towns of Oakridge and Westfir are the only real towns on this entire route and are the only places where you'll find much in the way of services. Westfir is also the southern terminus of the West Cascades Scenic Byway, which winds through the Cascade foothills to just outside the town of McKenzie Bridge on Ore. 126.

Essentials

GETTING THERE   Ore. 58 begins just south of Eugene off I-5 and stretches for 92 miles to U.S. 97.

VISITOR INFORMATION   For more information on recreational activities in this area, contact the **Middle Fork Ranger Station,** 46375 Ore. 58, Westfir, OR 97492 (*C* **541/782-2283**; www.fs.fed.us/r6/willamette). Another source of information is the **Oakridge/Westfir Area Chamber of Commerce,** P.O. Box 217, Oakridge, OR 97463 (*C* **541/782-4146**; www.oakridgechamber.com).

What to See & Do: Hot Springs to Snow Skiing

In the Willamette National Forest outside the logging town of Oakridge are miles and miles of great mountain-biking trails that have turned the Oakridge area into one of Oregon's top mountain-biking regions. Stop by the ranger station in Westfir to get maps and information on riding these trails. One of the most scenic rides is the 22-mile trail around Waldo Lake. You'll also find trails at Willamette Pass Ski Area (*C* **541/345-7669**; www.willamettepass.com), where, in summer, ski trails become mountain-biking trails. On summer weekends, this ski area operates a gondola that will carry you and your bike up to the top of the mountain. An all-day pass costs $28 for adults, $18 for children. If you're not here to mountain bike but want to ride the gondola to the top of the mountain, it will cost you $14 for adults, $8 for seniors and youths ages 6 to 10, and $1 for children ages 1 to 5.

If you're interested in exploring this area on a guided mountain-bike tour, contact **Oregon Adventures** (📞 **541/968-5397;** www.oregon-adventures.com), which offers a variety of 3- to 5-day mountain bike trips, for $450 to $669 per person. This company can also arrange car shuttles for one-way bike rides. Bikes can be rented from **Willamette Mountain Mercantile,** 48080 Ore. 58, Oakridge (📞 **541/782-1800;** www.oakridgebikeshop.com), which charges $35 to $75 per day for its mountain bikes.

After a day of mountain biking, you can soak your sore muscles in a natural hot spring. Right beside Ore. 58 about 10 miles east of Oakridge, you'll find **McCredie Hot Springs.** However, this hot spring is neither the hottest nor the most picturesque in the state, and with traffic noise and crowds, it isn't the most pleasant either. But if you want a quick soak without having to go wandering down gravel roads, this hot spring will do the trick.

Just before reaching Willamette Pass, you'll see signs for **Salt Creek Falls,** which are well worth a stroll down the short trail to the falls overlook. At 286 feet high, these are the second-highest falls in the state. Longer hiking trails also lead out from the falls parking area.

Also just before Willamette Pass is the turnoff for Forest Service Road 5897, which leads 10 miles north to **Waldo Lake,** one of the purest lakes in the world. The lake, which is just more than a mile high, covers 10 square miles and is 420 feet deep. When the waters are still, it is possible to see more than 100 feet down into the lake. Because this is such a large lake, and because there are reliable afternoon winds, it is popular for sailboating and windsurfing. Powerboaters, canoeists, and sea kayakers also frequent the lake. There are several campgrounds along the east shore of the lake, while the west shore abuts the Waldo Lake Wilderness Area. The 22-mile loop trail around the lake is popular with mountain bikers and backpackers, but shorter day hikes, particularly at the south end, are rewarding. The mosquitoes here are some of the worst in the state, so before planning a trip, be sure to get a bug report from the Middle Fork Ranger Station.

Just over Willamette Pass lie two more large lakes. **Odell Lake** is best known by anglers who come to troll for kokanee salmon and Mackinaw trout. However, it's also a good windsurfing lake. Though the waters never get very warm, **Crescent Lake** is the area's best for swimming, notably at Symax Beach, on the lake's northeast corner.

At **Willamette Pass Ski Area** (📞 **541/345-7669;** www.willamettepass.com), 69 miles southeast of Eugene on Ore. 58, you'll find 29 downhill runs and 12 miles of groomed cross-country trails. The ski area is open daily from around Thanksgiving to mid-April. Night skiing is available on Friday and Saturday nights from mid-December to late March. Adult lift tickets are $49 per day.

Where to Stay

While there are rustic cabin resorts on Odell and Crescent lakes, both of which are just east of Willamette Pass, none are particularly recommendable.

CAMPGROUNDS

On Waldo Lake, the North Waldo Campground, with its swimming area and boat launch, should be your first choice. Second choice on the lake should be Islet Campground or, at the south end of the lake, Shadow Bay Campground. Just over Willamette Pass, there are several campgrounds on Odell Lake. The campground at the

Odell Lake Lodge & Resort (*© **800/434-2540** or 541/433-2540; www.odelllake resort.com), at the east end of the lake, is the quietest campground on this lake.

Where to Eat

Most people heading up this way plan to be self-sufficient when mealtime rolls around, whether they're camping or staying in a cabin. If you don't happen to have a full ice chest, you'll find a few basic restaurants in Oakridge. Although none are particularly memorable, they're the only places to get a meal other than in the dining room of the Odell Lake Lodge or at the Willamette Pass Ski Area. However, there is one exception in the town of Oakridge. **Brewers Union Local 180,** 48329 E. First St. (*© **541/782-2024;** www.brewersunion.com), is an English-style brewpub serving cask-conditioned ales and basic pub grub.

THE NORTH UMPQUA RIVER

Diamond Lake: 76 miles E of Roseburg, 80 miles NE of Medford

Ore. 138, which heads east out of Roseburg and leads to Diamond Lake and the north entrance to Crater Lake National Park, is one of the state's most scenic highways. Along much of its length, the highway follows the North Umpqua River, which is famed among fly anglers for its fighting steelhead and salmon. As far as I'm concerned, this deep aquamarine stream is the most beautiful river in Oregon and is well worth a visit even if you don't know a woolly bugger from a muddler minnow (that's fly talk, for the uninitiated). Between Idleyld Park and Toketee Reservoir, you'll find numerous picnic areas, boat launches, swimming holes, and campgrounds.

As Ore. 138 approaches the crest of the Cascades, it skirts the shores of Diamond Lake, which is a major recreational destination (though it's certainly not as beautiful as nearby Crater Lake). Almost a mile in elevation, Diamond Lake is set at the foot of jagged Mount Thielsen, a spire-topped pinnacle known as the "lightning rod of the Cascades." The lake offers swimming, boating, fishing, camping, hiking, biking, and, in winter, snowmobiling and cross-country skiing. Just beyond Diamond Lake is the north entrance to Crater Lake National Park.

The 24-mile-long Ore. 230 connects the Diamond Lake area with the valley of the upper Rogue River at the community of Union Creek. Although this stretch of the Rogue is not as dramatic as the North Umpqua or the lower Rogue River, it has its charms, including a natural bridge, a narrow gorge, and some grand old trees.

Essentials

GETTING THERE   The North Umpqua River is paralleled by Ore. 138, which connects Roseburg, on I-5, with U.S. 97, which parallels the Cascades on the east side of the mountains. This highway leads to the north entrance of Crater Lake National Park.

VISITOR INFORMATION   For information on recreational activities in this area, contact the **North Umpqua Ranger District,** 18782 North Umpqua Hwy., Glide, OR 97443 (*© **541/496-3532**), or the **Diamond Lake Ranger District,** 2020 Toketee Ranger Station Rd., Idleyld Park, OR 97447 (*© **541/498-2531**). Also check the websites of the **Rogue River–Siskiyou National Forest** (www.fs.fed.us/ r6/rogue-siskiyou) and the **Umpqua National Forest** (www.fs.fed.us/r6/umpqua).

What to See & Do: Rafting & a Waterfall

Oregon abounds in waterfalls and white-water rivers, but in the town of Glide, 12 miles east of Roseburg, you'll find the only place in the state where rivers collide. At the interesting Colliding Rivers Viewpoint, the North Umpqua River, rushing in from the north, slams into the white water of the Little River, which flows from the south, and the two rivers create a churning stew. However, this phenomenon is really only impressive during times of winter rains or during spring snowmelt season.

If you'd rather just paddle the river in a kayak or raft, contact **North Umpqua Outfitters** (*C* **888/454-9696;** www.nuorafting.com), which charges $105 to $125 for its rafting trips.

At the turnoff for Toketee Reservoir, you'll find the trail head for the .5-mile hike to **Toketee Falls ★**. This double cascade plummets 120 feet over a wall of columnar basalt and is one of the most picturesque waterfalls in the state. The viewing area is on a deck perched out on the edge of a cliff. Also in this same area, past the Toketee Lake Campground, you'll find **Umpqua Hot Springs,** which are down a short trail. These natural hot springs perch high above the North Umpqua River, on a hillside covered with mineral deposits. For longer hikes, consider the many segments of the 79-mile **North Umpqua Trail,** which parallels the river from just east of Glide all the way to the Pacific Crest Trail. The lower segments of this trail are also popular mountain-biking routes.

At **Diamond Lake,** just a few miles north of Crater Lake National Park, you'll find one of the most popular mountain recreation spots in the state. In summer the popular and somewhat run-down **Diamond Lake Resort** (*C* **800/733-7593** or 541/793-3333; www.diamondlake.net) is the center of area activities. Here you can rent boats, swim at a small beach, and access the 11-mile paved hiking/biking trail that circles Diamond Lake.

Near the community of Union Creek, west of Crater Lake National Park on Ore. 62, are the Rogue River Gorge and a small natural bridge formed by a lava tube. The gorge, though only a few feet wide in places, is quite dramatic and has an easy trail running alongside.

In winter Diamond Lake Resort serves as the region's main snowmobiling destination, but it's also a decent area for cross-country skiers, who will find rentals and groomed trails at Diamond Lake Resort. There are also many more miles of marked, but not groomed, cross-country ski trails in the area; the more interesting trails are found at the south end of the lake. Snowmobile rentals and tours are also available. You can also do some downhill skiing on untracked nearby slopes through Diamond Lake Resort's **Cat Ski Mt. Bailey** (*C* **800/733-7593;** www.catskimtbailey.com), which charges $350 for a day of skiing and also offers multiday packages. For more information on these activities, contact **Diamond Lake Resort** (*C* **800/733-7593** or 541/793-3333; www.diamondlake.net).

Where to Stay & Eat

Prospect Historical Hotel ★ 🏨 This combination historic hotel and adjoining modern motel is in the tiny hamlet of Prospect, 30 miles from Crater Lake's Rim Village. The hotel, built in the 1880s, is a big white building with a wraparound porch, and although the small rooms are rather spartan, their country styling lends them a bit of charm. If you stay in one of these rooms, you'll get period furnishings, hand-made quilts, air-conditioning, and a full breakfast. The motel rooms are much larger and have TVs, telephones, and coffeemakers; some also have kitchenettes. The elegant dining room, which is open May through October, serves excellent prime rib.

391 Mill Creek Dr. (P.O. Box 50), Prospect, OR 97536. www.prospecthotel.com. © **800/944-6490** or 541/560-3664. Fax 541/560-3825. 24 units. May–Sept $90–$150 double, $205 suite; Oct–Apr $70–$130 double, $185 suite. Rates include full breakfast (in historic hotel). DC, DISC, MC, V. Pets accepted in motel ($15 per night). **Amenities:** Restaurant; lounge; concierge. *In room:* A/C, TV (in motel), fridge (in motel), free Wi-Fi.

Steamboat Inn ★★ Located midway between Roseburg and Crater Lake, this inn on the banks of the North Umpqua River is the finest lodging on the river. The beautiful gardens, luxurious guest rooms, and gourmet meals attract people looking for a quiet getaway in the forest and a base for hiking and biking. If you aren't springing for one of the suites, which have their own soaking tubs overlooking the river, your best bets will be the streamside rooms, misleadingly referred to as cabins. These have gas fireplaces and open onto a long deck that overlooks the river. The hideaway cottages are more spacious but don't have river views and are half a mile from the lodge (and the cozy dining room). There are also three-bedroom houses that are great for families. Dinners ($50) are multicourse affairs and are open to the public by reservation. There's a fly-fishing shop on the premises.

42705 North Umpqua Hwy., Steamboat, OR 97447. www.thesteamboatinn.com. © **800/840-8825** or 541/498-2230. Fax 541/498-2411. 20 units, including 5 cottages and 5 houses. Mid-May to Oct $175 cabin, $210–$245 cottages and houses, $300 suites; lower rates midweek Nov to mid-May. Children 3 and under stay free in parent's room. MC, V. Closed Jan–Feb. Pets accepted. **Amenities:** Restaurant; babysitting; free Wi-Fi. *In room:* A/C (some rooms), hair dryer, no phone (most rooms).

CAMPGROUNDS

Along the North Umpqua River, between Idleyld Park and Diamond Lake, you'll find the Bureau of Land Management's Susan Creek Campground, the most upscale public campground along the North Umpqua. (It even has hot showers.) The large Horseshoe Bend Campground, near Steamboat, is popular with rafters and kayakers on weekends and has well-separated campsites, big views of surrounding cliffs, and access to the North Umpqua Trail. Toketee Campground, at Toketee Reservoir, is situated back from the lake, but there are a few sites on the river.

Diamond Lake has three U.S. Forest Service campgrounds—Diamond Lake, Broken Arrow, and Thielsen View—with a total of more than 400 campsites. Here you'll also find the **Diamond Lake RV Park,** 3500 Diamond Lake Loop (© **541/793-3318;** www.diamondlakervpark.com), which is the closest RV park to Crater Lake National Park.

Southwest of Crater Lake National Park, on Ore. 62, you'll find **Farewell Bend Campground,** which is set amid big trees on the Rogue River. The next campgrounds are **Union Creek** and **Natural Bridge,** both of which are also along the Rogue River near the town of Prospect. North of Ore. 62, on Ore. 230, you'll find the **Hamaker Campground,** on a pretty bend in the Rogue River with big trees and meadows across the river.

CRATER LAKE NATIONAL PARK ★★★

71 miles NE of Medford, 83 miles E of Roseburg, 60 miles N of Klamath Falls

There simply is nothing in the forests of the southern Oregon Cascades to prepare you for Crater Lake. There are no preliminaries, no teasing glimpses through the trees. You drive through a rather unremarkable mountain forest, wondering why this place was ever made into a national park, and then, with little warning, you arrive at the edge of a cliff and gaze down 1,000 feet to a circular bowl of water a mesmerizing shade of sapphire blue. The view takes your breath away (or is it the elevation?), and you quickly understand why this lake became a national park way back in 1902.

At 1,932 feet deep, Crater Lake is the deepest lake in the United States (and the seventh deepest in the world). The crater (or, more accurately, the caldera) that holds the serene lake was born in an explosive volcanic eruption 7,700 years ago. When the volcano, now known as Mount Mazama, erupted, its summit (thought to have been around 12,000 ft. high) collapsed, leaving a crater 4,000 feet deep. Thousands of years of rain and melting snow turned the empty heart of this volcano into today's cold, clear lake, which today is surrounded by crater walls that in places are nearly 2,000 feet tall. At one end of the lake, the cone of Wizard Island rises from the deep blue waters of the lake. The island is the tip of a new volcanic peak that has been building slowly since Mount Mazama's last eruption.

Essentials

GETTING THERE   If you're coming from the south on I-5, take exit 62 in Medford and follow Ore. 62 for 75 miles. If you're coming from the north, take exit 124 in Roseburg and follow Ore. 138. From Klamath Falls, take U.S. 97 N. to Ore. 62. In winter only the south entrance is open. Due to deep snowpack, the north entrance usually doesn't open until sometime in late July.

VISITOR INFORMATION   For more information, contact **Crater Lake National Park**, P.O. Box 7, Crater Lake, OR 97604 (© **541/594-3000**; www.nps.gov/crla).

ADMISSION   Park admission is $10 per vehicle.

Seeing the Highlights

After your first breathtaking view of the lake, stop by one of the park's two visitor centers. The Steel Visitor Center is between the south park entrance and Rim Village, which is where you'll find the smaller and less thorough Rim Visitor Center. Although the park is open year-round, in winter, when deep snows blanket the park, only the road to Rim Village is kept clear. During the summer (usually beginning in late June, though sometimes later), **Rim Drive ★★★** provides many viewing points along its 39-mile length.

Narrated boat trips ★★★ around the lake are the park's most popular activity. These tours last 2 hours and begin at Cleetwood Cove, at the bottom of a very steep 1-mile trail that descends 700 feet from the rim to the lakeshore. Before deciding to take a boat tour, be sure you're in good enough physical condition to make the steep climb back up to the rim. Bring warm clothes because it can be quite a bit cooler on the lake than it is on the rim. A naturalist on each boat provides a narrative on the ecology and history of the lake, and all tours include a stop on Wizard Island. Tours are offered from late July to mid-September and cost $29 to $39 for adults and $19 to $25 for children ages 3 to 11. Reservations can be made in advance through Crater Lake Lodge (© **888/774-2728**; www.craterlakelodges.com).

Of the many miles of **hiking trails** within the park, the mile-long Cleetwood Trail is the only trail that leads down to the lakeshore, and it's a steep and tiring hike back up from the lake. The trail to the top of Mount Scott, although it's a rigorous 2.5 miles, is the park's most rewarding hike. Shorter trails with good views include the .8-mile trail to the top of the Watchman, which overlooks Wizard Island, and the

1.7-mile trail up Garfield Peak. The short Castle Crest Wildflower Trail is best hiked in late July or early August. Backpackers can hike the length of the park on the Pacific Crest Trail (PCT) or head out on a few other trails that lead into more remote, though less scenic, corners of the park.

Other summertime park activities include children's programs, ranger talks, history lectures, guided hikes, and trolley tours. To find out about these, check the park's website or, once you get to the park, in *Reflections,* a free park newspaper given to all visitors when they enter the park.

In winter, **cross-country skiing** and snowshoeing are popular on the park's snow-covered Rim Drive and in the backcountry. At Rim Village, you'll find several miles of well-marked ski trails, affording some of the best views in the state, weather permitting. Skiers in good shape can usually make the entire circuit of the lake in 2 days but must be prepared to camp in the snow. Spring, when the weather is warmer and there are fewer severe storms, is actually the best time to ski around the lake. December through April, there are ranger-led snowshoe hikes on Saturdays and Sundays at 1pm. Snow-shoes are available free of charge for these hikes. Because space is limited on these snowshoe hikes, try to sign up in advance at the Steel Visitor Center (© **541/594-3100**).

Where to Stay & Eat

The Cabins at Mazama Village   Though the Mazama Village Motor Inn isn't on the rim of the crater, it's just a short drive away and should be your second choice of lodging on a Crater Lake vacation. The modern motel-style guest rooms are housed in 10 steep-roofed buildings that look much like traditional mountain cabins. A laundromat, gas station, and general store make Mazama Village a busy spot in the summer.

Mailing address: 1211 Ave. C, White City, OR 97503. www.craterlakelodges.com. © **888/774-2728** or 541/594-2255. Fax 303/297-3175. 40 units. $132 double. Children 11 and under stay free in parent's room. AE, DC, DISC, MC, V. Closed late Sept to late May. *In room:* No phone.

Crater Lake Lodge ★★★   Perched on the edge of the rim overlooking Crater Lake, this lodge is the finest national-park lodge in the Northwest. The views are breathtaking, and the amenities are modern without sacrificing the rustic atmosphere (a stone fireplace and ponderosa-pine-bark walls in the lobby). Slightly more than half of the guest rooms overlook the lake, and although most rooms have modern bathrooms, eight have claw-foot bathtubs. The very best accommodations are the corner rooms on the lake side of the lodge. The lodge's dining room provides a view of both Crater Lake and the Klamath River basin. Reservations are hard to come by, so plan as far in advance as possible.

Mailing address: 1211 Ave. C, White City, OR 97503. www.craterlakelodges.com. © **888/774-2728** or 541/594-2255. Fax 303/297-3175. 71 units. $158–$218 double; $282 suite. Children 11 and under stay free in parent's room. AE, DC, DISC, MC, V. Closed mid-Oct to late May. **Amenities:** Restaurant; lounge. *In room:* No phone.

CAMPGROUNDS

Tent camping and RV spaces are available on the south side of the park at the Mazama Campground, where there are more than 213 sites ($21–$29 per night). This campground is open mid-June through mid-September. There are also 16 tent sites available at Lost Creek Campground ($10 per night) on the park's east side. This campground is open early July through early October. For reservations at Mazama Campground, contact Crater Lake National Park Lodges (📞 **888/774-2728;** www.craterlake lodges.com). For information on campgrounds outside the park, see "Campgrounds" in "The North Umpqua–Upper Rogue River," earlier in this chapter.

THE KLAMATH FALLS AREA

65 miles E of Ashland, 60 miles S of Crater Lake

Unless you are an avid bird-watcher or are looking for a cheap place to stay close to Crater Lake National Park, you won't find too much to attract you to the Klamath Falls area. However, this region, a wide, windswept expanse of lakes, high desert, and mountain forests just north of the California line, has a history of human presence that stretches back more than 14,000 years. The large lakes in this dry region have long attracted a wide variety of wildlife (especially waterfowl), which once provided a food source for the area's Native American population. The prehistoric residents of the region lived on the shores of the Klamath Basin's lakes and harvested fish, birds, and various marsh plants. Today two local museums exhibit extensive collections of Native American artifacts that have been found in this area.

Upper Klamath Lake and adjacent Agency Lake have shrunk considerably over the years as shallow, marshy areas have been drained to create pastures and farmland. Today, however, as the lake's native fish populations have become threatened and migratory bird populations in the region have plummeted, there is a growing movement to restore some of the region's drained marshes to more natural conditions. Although large portions of the area are now designated as national wildlife areas that offer some of the best bird-watching in the Northwest, farming and ranching are still considered the primary use of these wildlife lands. Conflicts between local farmers and environmentalists over how best to manage this region's limited water supply often occur during the summer dry season.

The region's shallow lakes warm quickly in the hot summers here, and partly because of the excess nutrients in the waters from agricultural runoff, they support large blooms of blue-green algae. Although the algae blooms deprive the lake's fish of oxygen, they provide the area with its most unusual agricultural product. The harvesting and marketing of Upper Klamath Lake's blue-green algae as a dietary supplement has become big business throughout the country as people have claimed all manner of health benefits from this chlorophyll-rich dried algae.

Essentials

GETTING THERE   Klamath Falls is on U.S. 97, which leads north to Bend and south to I-5 near Mount Shasta in California. The city is also connected to Ashland by the winding Ore. 66 and to Medford by Ore. 140, which continues east to Lakeview in eastern Oregon. The Klamath Falls Airport, 6775 Arnold Ave. (📞 **541/883-5372;** http://flykfalls.com), is served by United Express from Portland and San Francisco. Amtrak's Coast Starlight trains stop here en route between San Francisco and Portland.

VISITOR INFORMATION   For more information on the region, contact **Discover Klamath,** 205 Riverside Dr., Ste. B, Klamath Falls, OR 97601 (📞 **800/445-6728** or 541/882-1501; www.discoverklamath.com).

GETTING AROUND   Rental cars are available at Klamath Falls Airport from Budget (© **800/527-0700;** www.budget.com), Enterprise (© **800/261-7331;** www. enterprise.com), and Hertz (© **800/654-3131;** www.hertz.com).

Delving Into Local History

In addition to the two museums listed here, you might want to drive by the historic **Ross Ragland Theater & Cultural Center,** 218 N. Seventh St. (© **541/884-0651;** www.rrtheater.org), an impressive Art Deco theater in downtown Klamath Falls. Better yet, catch a show here. The theater stages a wide variety of performances throughout the year. If you'd like to learn more about the area's logging history, drive 30 miles north of Klamath Falls to **Collier Memorial State Park,** 46000 U.S. 97 N., Chiloquin (© **541/783-2471;** www.oregon.gov/oprd/parks), where you'll find an outdoor logging museum filled with antique logging equipment. Behind this museum, a pretty picnic area sits on the banks of Spring Creek, one of the clearest and most beautiful little streams in the state.

Favell Museum of Western Art & Indian Artifacts ★ 🎒   Anyone with an interest in Native American artifacts or Western art will be fascinated by a visit to this unusual museum, considered one of the best Western museums in the country. On display are thousands of arrowheads (including one made from fire opal), obsidian knives, spear points, stone tools of every description, baskets, pottery, and even ancient shoes and pieces of matting and fabric. Though the main focus is on the Native Americans of the Klamath Basin and Columbia River, there are artifacts from Alaska, Canada, other regions of the U.S., and Mexico. Few museums anywhere in the country have such an extensive collection on display, and the cases of artifacts can be overwhelming, so take your time. There's also a collection of Western art by more than 300 artists, including members of the famous Cowboy Artists of America Association. You'll also find one of the world's largest publicly displayed collections of miniature guns.

125 W. Main St. ©**541/882-9996.** www.favellmuseum.org. Admission $8 adults, $5 children 6–16. Tues–Sat 10am–5pm.

Klamath County Museum   More Native American artifacts, this time exclusively from the Klamath Lakes area, are on display in this museum, while a history of the Modoc Indian Wars chronicles the most expensive campaign of the American West. Also of particular interest are the early-20th-century photos by local photographer Maud Baldwin.

1451 Main St. ©**541/883-4208.** www.co.klamath.or.us/museum/index.htm. Admission $5 adults, $4 seniors and students, $3 for ages 5–12, free for children 4 and under. Tues–Sat 9am–5pm.

Bird-Watching & Other Outdoor Activities

In this dry region between the Cascades and the Rocky Mountains, there are few large bodies of water, so the lakes and marshes of the Klamath Basin are a magnet for birds. White pelicans, great blue herons, sandhill cranes, egrets, grebes, bitterns, and osprey can all be seen here. However, the main attraction for many human visitors is the annual winter gathering of bald eagles. In winter the region is home to as many as 500 bald eagles, making this the largest concentration of bald eagles in the lower 48. Each winter morning, starting about 30 minutes before sunrise, 100 or more eagles can be seen heading out from their roosting areas in the Bear Valley National Wildlife Refuge near the town of Worden, 11 miles south of Klamath Falls. To find the eagle-viewing area, drive south out of Klamath Falls on U.S. 97 through the community of Worden and almost to the California state line. Turn west onto the Keno-Worden Road, and just after the railroad tracks, turn left onto a dirt road. Follow this road for a half mile or so and pull off on the shoulder. Now start scanning the skies for eagles heading east to the marshlands. For more information on bird-watching in the area, contact the Klamath Basin National Wildlife Refuges Complex, 4009 Hill Rd., Tulelake, CA 96134 (℡ 530/667-2231; www.fws.gov/klamathbasinrefuges).

If, on the other hand, you want to paddle yourself around one of the local lakes, check out the **Upper Klamath Canoe Trail,** which begins near the junction of Ore. 140 and West Side Road northwest of Klamath Falls. The canoe trail wanders through marshlands on the edge of Upper Klamath Lake. For more information, contact the Fremont-Winema National Forests' **Klamath Falls Ranger District,** 2819 Dahlia St., Klamath Falls, OR 97601 (℡ 541/883-6714; www.fs.fed.us/r6/frewin). Canoes and kayaks can be rented at the Upper Klamath Lake's **Rocky Point RV Resort,** 28121 Rocky Point Rd. (℡ 541/356-2287), for $45 for half a day or $50 for a full day.

About 35 miles northwest of Klamath Falls on Ore. 140, you'll find the region's main mountain recreation area. Here, in the vicinity of **Lake of the Woods** and **Fish Lake,** you'll find the fun High Lakes mountain-bike trail, which leads through a rugged lava field. Also in the area is the hiking trail to the summit of Mount McLoughlin. In winter this same area has cross-country ski trails. There are rustic cabin resorts and campgrounds on both Lake of the Woods and Fish Lake.

Where to Stay

Lake of the Woods Resort ★ ☺   Lake of the Woods is one of the prettiest lakes in southern Oregon and a great spot for families. This rustic resort's log cabins, with their red doors and green trim, look as though they belong in a national park, and the Saturday night barbecues, outdoor movie nights, and wildlife shows give this place the feel of an old-fashioned summer camp for the whole family. Most cabins, although rustic, have full kitchens or kitchenettes, as well as an old-time mountain-cabin decor. You can rent motorboats and canoes for exploring the lake and mountain bikes for riding area trails (one of which leads through an ancient lava flow). Or you can just swim in the lake.

950 Harriman Rte., Klamath Falls, OR 97601. www.lakeofthewoodsresort.com. ℡ 866/201-4194 or 541/949-8300. 26 units. Memorial Day weekend to Sept $139–$325 cabin. 2-night minimum. AE, DISC, MC, V. Pets accepted ($5 per day). **Amenities:** Restaurant; lounge; bikes; watersports rentals; free Wi-Fi. In room: Kitchen (most cabins), no phone.

Rocky Point RV Resort 🎣   This rustic fishing resort on the west shore of Upper Klamath Lake may conjure childhood memories of summer vacations by the lake. While this is primarily an RV resort, it also has rooms and cabins for rent. While they are quite basic, the setting is bewitching. Shaded by huge old ponderosa pine trees and partly built atop the rocks for which this point is named, the resort has a great view across the waters and marshes of the Upper Klamath National Wildlife Refuge. Green lawns set with Adirondack chairs go right down to the water, where there is a small boat-rental dock. The rustic restaurant and lounge have the best views on the property. The Upper Klamath Lake canoe trails originate here, and the bird-watching is excellent, but fishing is still the most popular pastime.

28121 Rocky Point Rd., Klamath Falls, OR 97601. www.rockypointoregon.com. ℡ **541/356-2287.** Fax 541/356-2222. 9 units. $85 double; $140–$160 cabin. 2-night minimum in cabins weekends and holidays. Children 5 and under stay free in parent's room. DISC, MC, V. Closed Nov–Mar. Pets accepted in cabins ($10 per night). **Amenities:** Restaurant; lounge; watersports equipment rentals; free Wi-Fi. *In room:* Fridge, no phone.

Running Y Ranch Resort ☺ With an Arnold Palmer–designed golf course and lots of houses for sale, this remote resort is clearly geared toward golfers buying second homes. Yet with horseback riding, canoe rentals, bike trails, a game room, a winter ice-skating rink, and other kid-oriented activities, golfers should definitely bring the family along as well. The Running Y is located northwest of Klamath Falls off Ore. 140 close to the shore of Upper Klamath Lake and set amid ponderosa pines. The hotel has a mountain-lodge feel, and although some rooms have balconies, the rooms feel a bit like those of a chain motel. Dining options are limited and not too reliable.

5500 Running Y Rd., Klamath Falls, OR 97601. www.runningy.com. ✆ **800/851-6013** or 541/850-5500. 82 units. $89–$139 double; $129–$139 suite. AE, DC, DISC, MC, V. Pets accepted. **Amenities:** 2 restaurants; lounge; 18-hole golf course; health club; Jacuzzi; indoor pool; sauna; spa; 2 tennis courts. *In room:* A/C, TV, hair dryer, free Wi-Fi.

CAMPGROUNDS

Along Ore. 140 between Klamath Falls and Medford are several national forest campgrounds. On Fish Lake, Fish Lake Campground and Doe Point Campground have nice locations, but they both get a lot of traffic noise. Just west of Fish Lake on Forest Service Road 37, the North Fork Campground provides a quieter setting on a trout stream and a scenic mountain-bike trail. Sunset Campground and Aspen Point Campground on Lake of the Woods are popular in summer with the boating, fishing, and water-skiing crowd. The latter campground is near Great Meadow Recreation Area, has a swimming beach, and is right on the High Lakes mountain-bike trail.

Where to Eat

For dinner with the best view in the area, head to Rocky Point RV Resort (see above), 30 minutes outside Klamath Falls and open Wednesday to Sunday in summer and on weekends in spring and fall.

SOUTHERN OREGON

Roughly defined as the area from the California state line in the south to a little way north of Roseburg, southern Oregon is a mountainous region that has far more in common with Northern California than it has with the rest of Oregon. The landscape is much drier than in northwestern Oregon, and dominating the region are the Siskiyou Mountains, a jumble of rugged peaks and rare plants that link the Cascades and the Coast Range.

It was gold that first brought European settlers to this area, and it was timber that kept them here. The gold is all played out now, but the legacy of the gold-rush days, when stagecoaches traveled the rough road between Sacramento and Portland, can be seen in picturesque towns such as Jacksonville and Oakland.

Although southern Oregon is a long drive from the nearest metropolitan areas, it is relatively easy to plan a multiday trip from San Francisco or Portland. From Ashland, the southernmost city in the region, it's roughly a 6-hour drive to either Portland or San Francisco.

Ashland is the region's most popular destination and is renowned for its **Oregon Shakespeare Festival,** which attracts tens of thousands of theatergoers annually. The festival, which now stretches through most of the year, has turned what was once a sleepy mill town into a facsimile of Tudor England. Not to be outdone, the **Britt Festivals** in the nearby historic town of **Jacksonville** offer summer performances by internationally recognized musicians and dance companies.

However, it isn't just the Bard that attracts visitors to this region. The rugged beauty of the Siskiyous and the wild waters of the Rogue and Umpqua rivers are big draws as well, with rafting and jet-boat tours providing options for getting out on the water. In recent years, this region has also seen a proliferation of wineries in both the Umpqua Valley west of Roseburg and the Applegate Valley west of Jacksonville. Because this region is so much warmer than the Willamette Valley wine country, it grows a wide variety of Bordeaux, Rhone, Italian, and Spanish varieties of grapes. So even if you've got a trunk full of pinot noir, you might want to do a little more wine touring in this region so you can pick up some cabernet sauvignon or tempranillo.

ASHLAND ★★

285 miles S of Portland, 50 miles W of Klamath Falls, 350 miles N of San Francisco

With classy cocktail bars and upscale restaurants, live jazz in the clubs and cafes, lots of art galleries, and day spas that take advantage of Ashland's famed Lithia Springs mineral waters, Ashland has become the most cosmopolitan community in southern Oregon. Sure, this is still a small town 5 to 6 hours by car from San Francisco or Portland, but more than 75 years of staging Shakespeare plays has turned Ashland into Oregon's preeminent arts community, which in turn has attracted the city's diverse population. Because this is one of the best little arts towns in America, come prepared to fall in love.

Ashland's rise to stardom began on a midsummer's night back in 1935. In a small Ashland theater built as part of the Chautauqua movement, Angus Bowmer, an English professor at what is now Southern Oregon University, staged a performance of Shakespeare's *As You Like It*. Despite the hard times that the Great Depression had brought to this quiet mill town in the rugged Siskiyou Mountains, the show was a success. Although the Depression had dashed any hopes local businessman Jesse Winburne had of turning Ashland into a mineral-springs resort, the hard times did not hit until after he had built beautiful **Lithia Park.** Luckily, each man's love's labor was not lost, and today their legacies have turned the town into one of Oregon's most popular destinations.

The **Oregon Shakespeare Festival,** born of Bowmer's admiration for the Bard, has become a world-class repertory festival that stretches across 9 months, and although Ashland never became a mineral-springs resort, Lithia Park, through which still flow the clear waters of Winburne's dreams, has become the town's centerpiece. When not wandering the park's pathways, you can go wine tasting or check out one of the state's best shopping districts. Head farther afield and you can hike and bike in the mountains and forests that surround Ashland. In other words, even after the curtains go down and the stages go dark, there's still plenty to do in this town.

Essentials

GETTING THERE   Ashland is located on I-5. From the east, Ore. 66 connects Ashland with Klamath Falls.

The nearest airport is Medford's **Rogue Valley International–Medford Airport (MFR),** 1000 Terminal Loop Pkwy., Medford (© 541/772-8068), which is served by Allegiant Air, Alaska/Horizon Air, and Skywest Airlines (Delta Connection and United Express).

VISITOR INFORMATION   Contact the **Ashland Chamber of Commerce,** 110 E. Main St. (P.O. Box 1360), Ashland, OR 97520 (© 541/482-3486; www.ashland chamber.com). You can also check the website of the **Southern Oregon Visitors Association** (http://southernoregon.org).

GETTING AROUND   If you need a taxi, call **TLC Yellow Cab** (© 541/482-3065). Car-rental companies with offices at the Rogue Valley International–Medford Airport are **Avis** (© 800/331-1212; www.avis.com), **Budget** (© 800/527-0700; www. budget.com), **Enterprise** (© 800/261-7331; www.enterprise.com), **Hertz** (© 800/654-3131; www.hertz.com), and **National** (© 877/222-9058; www.nationalcar.com). **Rogue Valley Transportation District** (© 541/779-2877; www.rvtd.org) provides public bus service in the Ashland area.

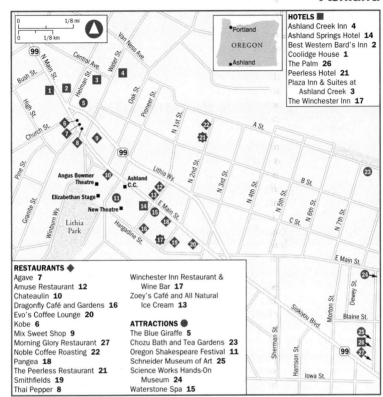

HOTELS
Ashland Creek Inn **4**
Ashland Springs Hotel **14**
Best Western Bard's Inn **2**
Coolidge House **1**
The Palm **26**
Peerless Hotel **21**
Plaza Inn & Suites at
  Ashland Creek **3**
The Winchester Inn **17**

RESTAURANTS ◆
Agave **7**
Amuse Restaurant **12**
Chateaulin **10**
Dragonfly Café and Gardens **16**
Evo's Coffee Lounge **20**
Kobe **6**
Mix Sweet Shop **9**
Morning Glory Restaurant **27**
Noble Coffee Roasting **22**
Pangea **18**
The Peerless Restaurant **21**
Smithfields **19**
Thai Pepper **8**
Winchester Inn Restaurant &
  Wine Bar **17**
Zoey's Café and All Natural
  Ice Cream **13**

ATTRACTIONS ●
The Blue Giraffe **5**
Chozu Bath and Tea Gardens **23**
Oregon Shakespeare Festival **11**
Schneider Museum of Art **25**
Science Works Hands-On
  Museum **24**
Waterstone Spa **15**

9

SOUTHERN OREGON | Ashland

FESTIVALS   The month-long Yuletide **Holiday Festival of Light** held each year in December is Ashland's other big annual festival.

The Oregon Shakespeare Festival

The Oregon Shakespeare Festival, the raison d'être of Ashland, is an internationally acclaimed theater festival that runs from February through October or early November. The season typically includes three or four works by Shakespeare, plus eight other classic or contemporary plays. These plays are performed in repertory, with as many as four staged on any given day.

The festival complex, often referred to as "the bricks" because of its brick courtyard, is in the center of town and contains three theaters. The visually impressive outdoor **Elizabethan Theatre,** modeled after England's 17th-century Fortune Theatre, is used only in the summer and early fall. The **Angus Bowmer Theatre** is the festival's largest indoor theater. The **New Theatre** is a small, state-of-the-art venue used primarily for contemporary and experimental plays.

In addition to the plays, there are **backstage tours** (tickets $12 for adults and $9 for children). Throughout the festival season there are also talks and special performances.

The opening of the Elizabethan Theatre is celebrated each June in Lithia Park with the elaborate Feast of Will. Between June and early October, the Green Show provides 35 minutes of free preperformance entertainment outside the doors of the Elizabethan Theatre.

For more information and upcoming schedules, contact the **Oregon Shakespeare Festival,** 15 S. Pioneer St., Ashland, OR 97520 (✆ **800/219-8161** or 541/482-4331; www.osfashland.org). Ticket prices range from $20 to $93; children's and preview tickets are less expensive.

Exploring Ashland & Its Surroundings

The **Schneider Museum of Art,** 1250 Siskiyou Blvd. (✆ **541/552-6245;** www.sou.edu/sma), on the campus of Southern Oregon University, mounts art exhibits of a quality you'd expect in a museum in a major city. The museum is open Monday through Saturday from 10am to 4pm. Admission is by $5 suggested donation.

Ashland's first claim to fame was its healing mineral waters, and today you can still relax and be pampered at one of the city's day spas. **The Phoenix,** 2425 Siskiyou Blvd. (✆ **541/488-1281;** www.thephoenixspa.com); **The Blue Giraffe,** 51 Water St. (✆ **541/488-3335;** www.bluegiraffespa.com); and **Waterstone Spa,** 236 E. Main St. (✆ **541/488-0325;** www.waterstonespa.com), all offer various body treatments, skin care, and massages. However, for the most unusual spa experience in town, plan a visit to the **Chozu Bath and Tea Gardens,** 832 A St. (✆ **541/552-0202;** www.chozugardens.com), where you can experience the Japanese tea ceremony, soak in a hot salt-water pool in the bath gardens, or get a massage.

If you happen to have the kids along, you may want to schedule time for a visit to the **Science Works Hands-On Museum,** 1500 E. Main St. (✆ **541/482-6767;** www.scienceworksmuseum.org), which is filled with fun interactive science exhibits. In summer the museum is open Wednesday through Saturday from 10am to 5pm and Sunday from noon to 5pm (other months it closes at 4pm). Admission is $7.50 for adults and $5 for seniors and children ages 2 to 12.

Wine Touring

For a map and more information on southern Oregon wineries, contact the **Southern Oregon Winery Association** (www.sorwa.org). If you'd like to have someone else take you around to area wineries, book a wine tour with **Main Street Adventure Tours** (✆ **541/482-9852;** www.ashland-tours.com), which has tours starting at $70 per person with a two-person minimum.

Agate Ridge Vineyard   Although this small winery on the route from Crater Lake to Medford is a bit out of the way, Agate Ridge is worth a stop if you happen to be driving this way. They do a surprisingly wide range of wines, include such rarely seen whites as Roussanne, Marsanne, Viognier, and Semillon.

1098 Nick Young Rd., Eagle Point. ✆ **541/830-3050.** www.agateridgevineyard.com. Tasting fee $3–$5. May–Oct daily 11am–5pm; Nov–Apr Tues–Sun 11am–5pm. Take exit 30 off I-5 and drive north on Ore. 62 toward Eagle Point, and then turn left on Nick Young Rd.

EdenVale Wines ★   This winery tasting room, beside a historic mansion on the outskirts of Medford, sells not only wines under its own EdenVale Winery label but also wines from other small wineries in southern Oregon. Between July and mid-September, there's live jazz in the gardens here on Thursday evenings.

2310 Voorhies Rd., Medford. ✆ **541/512-2955.** www.edenvalleyorchards.com. Tasting fee $5–$10. Mon–Sat 11am–6pm; Sun noon–4pm. From Ore. 99 north of Phoenix, turn west on S. Stage Rd. and left again on Voorhies Rd.

RoxyAnn Winery ★   RoxyAnn started out as the Hillcrest Orchard, which has been producing fruit for more than a century. Today this winery is producing some of the best southern Oregon wines. A wide variety of wines are produced here under several different labels. Although this winery is actually on the east side of Medford, it is close enough to Ashland to make it an appropriate stop on an afternoon's wine tasting in the area. The tasting room is in a big old barn.

3285 Hillcrest Rd., Medford. ✆ **541/776-2315.** www.roxyann.com. Tasting fee $3–$5. Daily 11am–6pm. From exit 27 off I-5, drive east on Barnett Rd., turn left on Phoenix Rd., and right on Hillcrest Rd.

Trium ★★   Trium is a tiny winery, and in the past it has produced some of the best wines in southern Oregon. Wines, primarily from estate-grown grapes, include Pinot Gris, Viognier, and Cabernet Sauvignon. This winery is quite close to Ashland and is worth searching out.

7112 Rapp Lane, Talent. ✆ **541/535-4015.** www.triumwines.com. Tasting fee $5. Apr–Oct daily 11am–5:30pm; Nov–Dec Sat–Sun 11am–5:30pm; Jan–Mar by appointment. From Ore. 99 north of Ashland, take E. Rapp Rd. west and turn left on Rapp Lane.

Weisinger's   Just south of town, this family-owned winery has a great view over the hills and valleys. Dry whites are a strong point, though if you're looking for age-worthy wines with a lot of tannin, you may like Weisinger's Merlot and Petite Pompadour, a Bordeaux-style blend of Cabernet Franc, Merlot, Malbec, and Cabernet Sauvignon.

3150 Siskiyou Blvd., Ashland. ✆ **800/551-9463** or 541/488-5989. www.weisingers.com. Tasting fee $3–$8. May–Sept daily 11am–5pm; Oct–Apr Wed–Sun 11am–5pm. Take Ore. 99 (Siskiyou Blvd.) south from downtown Ashland.

Enjoying the Great Outdoors

No visit to Ashland is complete without taking a long, leisurely stroll through beautiful **Lithia Park.** This 100-acre park follows the banks of Ashland Creek starting at the plaza. Shade trees, lawns, flowers, ponds, fountains, and, of course, the babbling brook are reminiscent of an English garden.

Summertime thrill seekers shouldn't pass up the chance to do some **white-water rafting** ★ on the Rogue or Klamath rivers while in southern Oregon. Try **Noah's River Adventures,** 53 N. Main St. (✆ **800/858-2811;** www.noahsrafting.com), which has trips lasting from half a day to 4 days. Prices range from $89 for a half-day trip to between $139 and $159 for a full day, depending on the length and type of the trip. Noah's also offers salmon- and steelhead-fishing trips.

Bikes ($10–$15 per hr. or $35–$45 per day) can be rented at **Bear Creek Bicycle,** 1988 Ore. 99 N. (✆ **541/488-4270;** www.bearcreekbicycle.com), which is just around the corner from the Bear Creek path. This paved path is a great, easy route to ride.

If you'd rather go horseback riding before the play, get in touch with **City Slickers Trail Rides** (✆ **541/951-4611;** www.oregontrailrides.com), which charges $50 for a 1-hour ride and $85 for a 2-hour ride.

Miles of **hiking trails,** including the Pacific Crest Trail, can be found up on Mount Ashland in the Rogue River–Siskiyou National Forest. Another stretch of the

Pacific Crest Trail lies within the **Cascade-Siskiyou National Monument,** which is located south and east of Ashland. This monument was created to preserve an area of outstanding botanical diversity but is limited in its recreational opportunities. For more information, contact the Medford office of the **Bureau of Land Management,** 3040 Biddle Rd., Medford (© **541/618-2200;** www.blm.gov/or/resources/recreation/csnm).

In winter there's good downhill and cross-country **skiing** at **Mount Ashland** (© **541/482-2897;** www.mtashland.com), a small downhill ski area 15 miles south of Ashland. All-day lift tickets for adults are $33 to $39. You can rent cross-country skis and pick up ski-trail maps at **Ashland Outdoor Store,** 37 Third St. (© **541/488-1202;** www.outdoorstore.com).

Shopping

Ashland has the best shopping in southern Oregon. Interesting and unusual shops line East Main Street, so when the curtains are down on the stages, check the windows of downtown.

Art galleries abound in Ashland, and on the first Friday of the month, many are open late. My all-around favorite place to check out works by local artists is at **Ashland Art Works,** 291 Oak St. (© **541/488-4735;** www.ashlandartworks.com), an artists' cooperative of five separate galleries all housed in a collection of cottages on the banks of Ashland Creek. For contemporary art, check out the **Hanson Howard Gallery,** 89 Oak St. (© **541/488-2562;** www.hansonhowardgallery.com). **Davis & Cline,** 525 A St., Ste. 1 (© **877/482-2069** or 541/482-2069; www.davisandcline.com), which is located in the historic Railroad District about 8 blocks from the plaza, is another of my favorite contemporary art galleries here in town. This gallery even sells Dale Chihuly art glass.

For wearable art, stop by **The Websters,** 11 N. Main St. (© **800/482-9801** or 541/482-9801; www.yarnatwebsters.com), a knitting and weaving store carrying beautiful sweaters, woven jackets, and accessories. You'll find name-brand women's fashions at a discount at **Thread Hysteria,** 19 N. Main St. (© **541/488-3982;** www.threadhysteria.net), and a wide range of fun hats at **Hatsetera,** 300 E. Main St. (© **541/488-6755**). Between the April and November, be sure to stop by the **Lithia Artisan's Market of Ashland** (© **888/303-2826;** www.lithiaartisansmarket.com) on Calle Guanajuato. The location is on the banks of Ashland Creek behind the stores on the north side of the plaza. Market hours are Saturday from 10am to 6pm and Sunday from 11am to 5pm.

Where to Stay

It seems Shakespeare and B&Bs go hand in hand. At last count, there were more than 25 bed-and-breakfasts in town. If your reason for coming to Ashland is to attend the Shakespeare Festival and you plan to stay at a B&B, you'll find it most convenient to choose an inn within walking distance of the theaters. By doing so, you'll also be within walking distance of the town's best restaurants and shopping and won't have to deal with finding a parking space before the show. For a comprehensive list of Ashland inns, contact **Ashland's Bed & Breakfast Network** (© **800/944-0329;** www.abbnet.com).

EXPENSIVE

Ashland Creek Inn ★★   As the name implies, this luxurious B&B is located on the shady banks of Ashland Creek, and the decks here are wonderful places to spend a hot summer afternoon or have a glass of wine before heading off to the theater. The rooms, mostly large suites, have fun themes, including the Caribbean, Morocco, Denmark, and Taos. All are very tastefully decorated with antiques and art, and all but one have a kitchen or kitchenette. Although this inn is only 2 blocks from the heart of downtown, it feels like a remote forest retreat. Breakfasts are multicourse affairs, which you can enjoy on a deck or in the garden when the weather is good.

70 Water St., Ashland, OR 97520. www.ashlandcreekinn.com. © **541/482-3315.** 10 units. Mid-May to Oct $240–$395 suite; Nov to mid-Feb $120–$200 suite; mid-Feb to mid-May $140–$300 suite. Rates include full breakfast. 3-night minimum May–Oct. MC, V. Pets accepted ($10 per night). Children 12 and over welcome. **Amenities:** Concierge; access to nearby health club. *In room:* A/C, TV, CD player, fridge, hair dryer, kitchen (some rooms), free Wi-Fi.

Ashland Mountain House ★★★

Built in 1852, the Ashland Mountain House served as a stagecoach stop for 25 years and today is Oregon's most beautiful historic inn. The impeccable restoration job and attention to detail by owners Kathy and John Loram have turned what was little more than a run-down heap of a house into a gorgeous B&B. Today this old yellow farmhouse 5 miles from town is once again welcoming weary travelers with its gracious hospitality and beautiful setting on 6 acres overlooking hills and valleys. Inside the inn, you'll find a library with an antique Steinway piano and floor-to-ceiling shelves of books. Gorgeous wood floors and original woodwork give the interior a classic feel, while silk-screened wallpapers do a great job of conjuring this old house's early years. My favorite room here is the two-story Brick Building, a little cottage next door to the main house.

1148 Old Hwy. 99 S., Ashland, OR 97520. www.ashlandmountainhouse.com. © **866/899-2744** or 541/482-2744. 4 units. Apr–Oct $180–$250 double; Nov–Mar $140–$200 double. MC, V. Rates include full breakfast and afternoon dessert. Children 12 and over welcome. **Amenities:** Concierge. *In room:* A/C, TV, hair dryer, free Wi-Fi.

Ashland Springs Hotel ★★ 🏨

First opened in 1925, this nine-story historic hotel is one of the finest hotels between Portland and San Francisco. In the light-filled lobby, there are cases full of Victorian-era natural-history displays, and, on the mezzanine overlooking the lobby, a continental breakfast is served every morning. Guest rooms are luxuriously appointed and beds sport crisp white linens, feather pillows, and down comforters. Although all the rooms have large windows, the corner rooms are worth requesting, as are rooms facing east over the city and the valley. Be sure to notice the fascinating collection of pressed plants on display behind the reception desk, in the elevator, and in guest rooms.

212 E. Main St., Ashland, OR 97520. www.ashlandspringshotel.com. © **888/795-4545** or 541/488-1700. Fax 541/488-1701. 70 units. Mid-May to early Oct $179–$269 double; early Oct to mid-May $89–$199 double. Rates include continental breakfast. Children 6 and under stay free in parent's room. AE, DC, DISC, MC, V. Pets accepted ($30 per night). **Amenities:** Restaurant; lounge; concierge; exercise room and access to nearby health club; sauna; spa. *In room:* A/C, TV, fridge, hair dryer, free Wi-Fi.

Lithia Springs Resort & Gardens

With its white fences and collection of cottages surrounded by colorful perennial gardens and wide lawns, this little resort on the edge of town has the feel of an English country estate. However, the hillsides that rise up from the edge of the property are purely southern Oregon. Guest accommodations include large suites with double whirlpool tubs, cottages, and even a converted water tower. Fans of mineral springs will definitely want to stay here; the water that flows from the taps here is supersoft mineral water that has a strong smell but feels great on your skin.

2165 W. Jackson Rd., Ashland, OR 97520. www.ashlandinn.com. ✆ **800/482-7128.** 27 units. $179–$219 double; $219–$249 suite; $226–$329 cottage. Rates include full breakfast. Children 12 and under stay free in parent's room. AE, DISC, MC, V. Pets accepted ($25 per night). **Amenities:** Concierge; spa services. *In room:* A/C, TV/DVD, CD player, fridge, hair dryer, no phone, free Wi-Fi.

Mt. Ashland Inn ★

Located on 160 acres on the side of Mount Ashland, this massive log home commands distant panoramas from its forest setting, and though the inn is only 20 minutes from downtown Ashland, you're in a different world up here. The Pacific Crest Trail, which stretches from Canada to Mexico, passes through the front yard, and just a few miles up the road is the Mt. Ashland Ski Area. Whether you're in the area for an active vacation or a few nights of theater, this lodge makes a very special base of operations. The decor is straight out of an Eddie Bauer catalog, and every room has a Jacuzzi and a gas fireplace. One guest bathroom even has a stone wall with a built-in waterfall. The Sky Lakes Wilderness Suite has views of Mount Shasta and is the best room in the house.

550 Mt. Ashland Rd., Ashland, OR 97520. www.mtashlandinn.com. ✆ **800/830-8707** or 541/482-8707. 5 units. $155–$230 suite. Rates include full breakfast. 2-night minimum on weekends. Children 5 and under stay free in parent's room. DISC, MC, V. Pets accepted ($30 fee). **Amenities:** Concierge; sauna. *In room:* CD player, fridge, hair dryer, free Wi-Fi.

Peerless Hotel ★★

Located in the historic Railroad District and 7 blocks from the festival theaters, this restored 1900 brick boardinghouse is one of Ashland's most interesting lodgings. With the feel of a small historic hotel rather than a B&B, the Peerless is filled with antiques and an eclectic array of individually decorated guest rooms. Of these, the West Indies Suite, with its balcony, double whirlpool tub, and view of Ashland, is by far the most luxurious. However, all other rooms feature lush fabrics, unusual murals, stenciling, and tile work that add up to unexpected luxury. Most rooms have either a whirlpool tub or a claw-foot tub. (One even has two side-by-side claw-foot tubs.) The hotel's restaurant (see below) is one of the finest in Ashland.

243 Fourth St., Ashland, OR 97520. www.peerlesshotel.com. ✆ **800/460-8758** or 541/488-1082. 6 units. June–Oct $160–$219 double, $249–$269 suite; Nov to mid-Feb $83–$112 double, $150–$170 suite; mid-Feb to May $122–$161 double, $199–$219 suite. Midseason and high season rates include full breakfast (breakfast not included in winter). DISC, MC, V. Children 12 and over welcome. **Amenities:** Restaurant; lounge; access to nearby health club; room service. *In room:* A/C, fridge, hair dryer, free Wi-Fi.

Plaza Inn & Suites at Ashland Creek

A bold and colorful decor imbues this luxurious hotel with a distinctly theatrical character, making this one of the most enjoyable lodgings in Ashland. In the guest rooms, the beds are triple sheeted, and carpets have a bold black-and-blue diamond pattern. It all inspires you to make a grand entrance. In summer you can breakfast on the patio beside a small pond. There are also evening appetizers and late-night snacks. The Plaza Suites are only 2 blocks from the plaza itself.

98 Central Ave., Ashland, OR 97520. www.plazainnashland.com. ✆ **888/488-0358** or 541/488-8900. Fax 541/488-8906. 91 units. June to mid-Oct $189–$249 double, $279–$304 suite; mid-Oct to Mar $89–$129 double, $129 suite; Apr–May $109–$159 double, $159–$189 suite. Rates include continental breakfast. Children 18 and under stay free in parent's room. AE, DC, DISC, MC, V. Pets accepted ($25 per night). **Amenities:** Exercise room; Jacuzzi; free Wi-Fi. *In room:* A/C, TV, CD player, fridge, hair dryer, Internet.

MODERATE

Best Western Bard's Inn

If you prefer motels to B&Bs and want to be within walking distance of downtown, the Bard's Inn is a good economical choice in

Ashland. This motel's best feature is that it's only 2 blocks from the festival theaters. The rooms are large and comfortable, and those in the annex have patios or balconies, though they get a bit of traffic noise.

132 N. Main St., Ashland, OR 97520. www.bardsinn.com. © **800/533-9627** or 541/482-0049. 92 units. Mid-May to mid-Oct $130–$225 double; mid-Oct to mid-May $99–$160 double. Rates include continental breakfast. Children 12 and under stay free in parent's room. AE, DC, DISC, MC, V. Pets accepted ($15 fee). **Amenities:** Jacuzzi; small outdoor pool. *In room:* A/C, TV, fridge, hair dryer, free Wi-Fi.

Coolidge House ★   Located right on busy North Main Street only 3 blocks from the theaters, this 1875 Victorian sits high above the street on a hill with commanding views across the valley. Although this is one of the oldest homes in Ashland, inside you'll find not only interesting antiques but also some decidedly modern amenities. Guest suites have sitting rooms and large luxurious bathrooms, most of which come with either a whirlpool tub or a claw-foot tub. The Parlor Suite, with its draped window seat, is the inn's most romantic room. However, if views and space are what you seek, opt for the Sun Suite or the Grape Arbor. There is a pleasant patio in the back garden.

137 N. Main St., Ashland, OR 97520. www.coolidgehouse.com. © **800/655-5522** or 541/482-4721. 6 units. June–Oct $155–$210 double; Nov–Mar $105–$135 double; Apr–May $130–$170 double. Rates include full breakfast. 2-night minimum on weekends Apr–Oct. MC, V. Children 13 and over are welcome. **Amenities:** Concierge. *In room:* A/C, no phone, Wi-Fi.

Country Willows Inn ★   Located just outside town and surrounded by 5 acres of rolling hills and pastures, the Country Willows B&B offers the tranquillity of a farm only minutes by car from Ashland's theaters and excellent restaurants. If you're looking for a very special room, consider the Sunrise Suite, which is in a renovated barn behind the main house: It has pine paneling, a high ceiling, a king-size bed, a gas fireplace, and, best of all, an old-fashioned tub for two with its very own picture window and skylight. Rooms in the restored farmhouse are smaller, but some offer excellent views across the valley. Geese and goats call the farm home, and there are two hiking trails that start at the back door.

1313 Clay St., Ashland, OR 97520. www.countrywillowsinn.com. © **800/945-5697** or 541/488-1590. Fax 541/488-1611. 9 units. May–Oct $140–$190 double, $240–$275 suite; Nov–Feb $120–$155 double, $175–$210 suite; Mar–Apr $130–$175 double, $205–$250 suite. Rates include full breakfast. AE, DISC, MC, V. Children 12 and over welcome. **Amenities:** Bikes; outdoor pool. *In room:* A/C, hair dryer, free Wi-Fi.

The Winchester Inn ★★   With its massive old shade trees, English tea gardens, and elegant, international restaurant (see below), the Winchester is Ashland's premier historic inn, and the location, within a few blocks of the theaters, makes it a superb choice. The rooms are very comfortably furnished with antiques and modern bath fixtures, including sinks built into old bureaus in some rooms. I prefer the upstairs rooms, which get quite a bit more light than those on the ground floor. There are also rooms in the building next door. If you want a bit more space, stay in one of the eight suites, two of which are in the old carriage house. Throughout the year, special events are held here, including winemaker dinners and a Christmas Dickens feast.

35 S. Second St., Ashland, OR 97520. www.winchesterinn.com. © **800/972-4991** or 541/488-1113. Fax 541/488-4604. 19 units. Mid-Feb to Apr $145–$215 double, $255–$299 suite; May–Oct $195–$230 double, $315–$330 suite; Nov to mid-Feb $140 double, $195 suite. Rates include full breakfast. Children 8 and under stay free in parent's room. AE, DISC, MC, V. **Amenities:** Restaurant; lounge; concierge. *In room:* A/C, TV, hair dryer, free Wi-Fi.

INEXPENSIVE

The Palm Located about a mile from the theaters of the Shakespeare Festival, this older but upgraded motor court is an excellent value. The collection of little Cape Cod cottages is surrounded by colorful perennial gardens, and there's even a tiny swimming pool on the grounds. All the old cottages have been completely redone and have a classic cottage feel. Some rooms have kitchens. The Palm goes out of its way to be eco-friendly.

1065 Siskiyou Blvd., Ashland, OR 97520. www.palmcottages.com. (© **800/691-2360** or 541/482-2636. 15 units. Spring–fall $84–$179 double, $159–$249 suite; winter $59–$129 double, $85–$149 suite. AE, MC, V. **Amenities:** Outdoor pool. *In room:* A/C, TV, free Wi-Fi.

Where to Eat

If you're headed to the theater after dinner, let your waitstaff know. They will usually do whatever they can to make sure you aren't late. For a light post-theater meal, try Chateaulin (see below).

EXPENSIVE

Amuse Restaurant ★★ NORTHWEST/FRENCH   Ashland may be a long way from Seattle or Portland, but that doesn't mean you can't have an extremely urban dining experience. Amuse is by far the most contemporary restaurant in town and is thoroughly stylish. The food here comes to your table looking almost too good to eat. The menu changes regularly, but you might start with the crispy veal sweetbreads or some grilled prawns. From there it might be truffle-roasted game hen or poached king salmon. In summer, request a table on the patio.

15 N. First St. (© **541/488-9000.** www.amuserestaurant.com. Reservations recommended. Main courses $22–$34. AE, DISC, MC, V. Wed–Sun 5:30–9pm.

Chateaulin ★ FRENCH   Located just around the corner from the festival theaters, this has long been one of the finest restaurants in town. Exposed brick walls and old champagne bottles give Chateaulin a casually elegant appearance that's accented by Art Nouveau touches and dark-wood furnishings. The menu is almost as traditional as the decor; you can start your meal with escargots or house pâté, and then move on to coq au vin or filet mignon bordelaise. A separate bistro provides a more casual atmosphere and caters to smaller or après-theater appetites. The restaurant's award-winning wine list features French wines, as well as lots of hard-to-find wines from Oregon, Washington, and California.

52 E. Main St. (© **541/482-2264.** www.chateaulin.com. Reservations recommended. Main courses $9–$15 bistro, $16–$35 restaurant. DISC, MC, V. Restaurant: Mon 5:30–9pm; Tues–Thurs and Sun 5–9pm; Fri–Sat 5–10pm. Bistro: Mon 11:30am–9pm; Tues–Sun 11:30am–midnight.

Sweet Treats!

As you meander around southern Oregon, keep your eyes out for local gourmet foods made by these two companies, or visit their factory stores. Ashland's **Dagoba Organic Chocolate,** 1105 Benson Way ((© **541/482-2001;** www.dagobachocolate.com), makes outstanding chocolate bars and has a tasting room and factory store. **Lillie Belle Farms,** 211 N. Front St., Central Point ((© **888/899-2022** or 541/664-2815; www.lilliebellefarms.com), makes some of the most creative, delicious, and unusual chocolate confections you will ever taste.

New Sammy's Cowboy Bistro ★★★ NORTHWEST   This roadside restaurant between Ashland and Talent is the sort of place foodies dream about. Using seasonal organic ingredients, many of which come from the garden beside the restaurant, owners Charlene and Vernon Rollins prepare some of the most creative food in the state. You might start with a chowder made with lobster mushrooms and have quail wrapped in grape leaves and pork belly, perhaps accompanied by lemon-basil flan. The Rollins' cooking credentials extend back to Berkeley's legendary Chez Panisse, so it's no wonder that this tiny place has a loyal following. The wine list here is the best in southern Oregon, and lunch here just might be the best value in the state.

2210 S. Pacific Hwy., Talent. ✆**541/535-2779.** Reservations recommended at lunch, required at dinner. Main courses $15–$17 lunch, $25–$34 dinner; fixed-price dinner $48. DISC, MC, V. Wed–Sun noon–1:30pm and 5–9pm.

The Peerless Restaurant ★★ NORTHWEST   With its warehouse/tropical decor, this upscale small-plates restaurant a few blocks from the plaza seems decidedly out of place in the southern Oregon hills, but good food is good food no matter where it's served. Flavor combinations are often complex, and one bite will convince you that this is not just good food—it's great. You might find blue cheese–stuffed lamb meatballs, a wild-mushroom risotto, or seafood cakes with preserved-lemon aioli. With lots of small plates on the menu, this is a good place for light eaters or groups that have difficulty agreeing on what sort of food everyone wants for dinner. The Peerless tends to work just a little bit harder to satisfy its customers, so dinners here are among the best in town. In summer, ask for a table out on the garden patio.

265 Fourth St. ✆**541/488-6067.** www.peerlessrestaurant.com. Reservations recommended. Main courses $11–$26. AE, DISC, MC, V. Tues–Sat 5:30–9pm.

The Winchester Inn Restaurant & Wine Bar ★ MEDITERRANEAN Located on the ground floor of Ashland's premier inn, this restaurant and wine bar melds a historic Victorian setting with an ambitious menu that is primarily Mediterranean, but that sometimes wanders into other corners of the culinary world. Starters here tend toward such delectable preparations as mini–beef Wellingtons made with wild mushrooms and ahi tuna tartare. For an entree, you might find such dishes as filet mignon with caramelized shallots and blue cheese, or smoked sturgeon with a roasted ratatouille tart. Sunday brunch is the perfect way to finish a weekend of theater before heading home. The dining rooms overlook the inn's English gardens, and in summer you can dine on the porch and deck as well. During the Christmas season, the restaurant serves a special Dickens feast.

35 S. Second St. ✆**541/488-1113.** www.winchesterinn.com. Reservations recommended. Main courses $14–$29; Sun brunch $8–$14. AE, DISC, MC, V. Mon–Sat 5:30–8:30pm; Sun 9:30am–12:30pm and 5:30–8:30pm. Closed early to mid-Jan.

MODERATE
Dragonfly Café & Gardens ★ 🍴 LATIN-ASIAN FUSION   With good prices and great food three meals a day, this restaurant is an all-around winner. Start the day with the coconut French toast or the banana-blackberry pancakes. At lunch, try the carne asada sandwich or an Asian-influenced bonsai burrito. At dinner, be sure to start with the crispy shoestring plantains or the plantains with caviar. Follow up with one of the big bowls of soup or the grilled salmon with papaya-mango-mint salsa. Vegetarians have lots of choices here.

241 Hargadine St. ☎ **541/488-4855.** www.dragonflyashland.com. Reservations accepted for parties of 6 or more. Main courses $7.50–$13 lunch, $10–$22 dinner. AE, DISC, MC, V. Daily 8am–3pm and 5–9pm.

Kobe ★ JAPANESE   Affiliated with Thai Pepper (see below), this stylish little sushi bar is also set on the banks of Ashland Creek and has a pleasant deck for summer dining. While you'll find all your favorite traditional Japanese dishes on the menu, Kobe bills itself as serving modern Japanese food, which means you'll find a bit of food fusion going on. I like the various ceviches and carpaccios they serve here, which, because they're made with raw fish, are in keeping with the sushi theme. Be sure to try one of the sake cocktails.

96 N. Main St. ☎ **541/488-8058.** http://thaipepper-kobe.com. Reservations recommended. Sushi $4–$16; small plates and platters $9–$24. AE, DISC, MC, V. Sun–Thurs 5–10pm; Fri–Sat 5–11pm.

Smithfields ★ NEW AMERICAN   This meat-centric restaurant a few blocks from the "bricks" has the feel of a neighborhood steakhouse and a menu that draws on both classic cooking traditions and southern flavors. As much as possible, ingredients are sourced locally, so you might tuck into a pork chop from nearby Willow Witt farm or snack on black-pepper bread from a local bakery. While there are several simply prepared steaks and chops on the menu, Smithfields is definitely the kind of place where you want to go heavy on the appetizers, which might include roasted bone marrow, salt-cod fritters, Scotch quail eggs, or a house-made charcuterie plate.

36 S. Second St. ☎ **541/488-9948.** http://smithfieldsashland.com. Reservations recommended. Main courses $13–$30. AE, DISC, MC, V. Tues–Fri 5–10pm; Sat–Sun 10am–2:30pm and 5–10pm.

INEXPENSIVE

For the best breakfasts in town, head to **Morning Glory Restaurant,** 1149 Siskiyou Blvd. (☎ 541/488-8636; www.morninggloryrestaurant.com), which is across from Southern Oregon University and is immensely popular with college students. For delicious wraps with international influences, head to **Pangea,** 272 E. Main St. (☎ 541/552-1630; www.pangeaashland.com). If you're in need of a latte and a pastry, stop by **Mix Sweet Shop,** 57 N. Main St. (☎ 541/488-9885). For the best espresso in town, head to **Noble Coffee Roasting,** 281 Fourth St. (☎ 541/488-3288; www. noblecoffeeroasting.com), a large coffeehouse in the Railroad District. If you want to sip a latte with some left-leaning SOU students, stop by **Evo's Coffee Lounge,** 376 E. Main St. (☎ 541/482-2261; www.evoscoffee.com). On hot summer days, you shouldn't miss the ice cream at **Zoey's Café and All Natural Ice Cream,** 199 E. Main St. (☎ 541/482-4794).

Agave MEXICAN   If you're looking for someplace cheap and quick to grab a bite before going to a show, try this casual Mexican place a block off the plaza. The menu is primarily tacos and tamales, but these are far from your standard renditions of these simple foods. The taco might have shredded duck confit or lobster, and the tamale might have winter squash and portobello mushroom. There are even sweet tamales for dessert.

92 N. Main St. ☎ **541/488-1770.** www.agavetaco.net. Main courses $2.50–$10. MC, V. Tues–Sun 11am–9pm.

Thai Pepper ★ THAI   If menu prices around Ashland have left you wondering how you're going be able to afford dinner *and* a show, search out this elegant little Thai restaurant. Thai Pepper has long been a local favorite for its spicy, fragrant food and its great location on the banks of Ashland Creek. I like to start with the lime-beef salad with mango chutney, but the rather nontraditional tiger rolls, made with cream cheese and crab, are a perennial favorite here. The menu includes lots of vegetarian dishes. You'll find the restaurant down a flight of stairs from the street. In summer, try to get a seat on the deck.

84 N. Main St. (C) **541/482-8058.** www.thaipepperkobe.com. Reservations recommended. Main courses $9–$14 lunch, $14–$18 dinner. AE, DISC, MC, V. Mon–Thurs 5–9pm; Fri 11:30am–2pm and 5–9pm; Sun 5–8:30pm.

Ashland After Dark

The Oregon Shakespeare Festival may be the main draw, but Ashland is overflowing with talent. From experimental theater to Broadway musicals, the town sees an amazing range of theater productions. To find out what's going on while you're in town, pick up a free copy of *The Sneak Preview.* If you've had enough Shakespeare or happen to be in town when the Oregon Shakespeare Festival is not staging performances, check out the performance calendars of the **Oregon Cabaret Theatre,** First and Hargadine streets ((C) **541/488-2902;** www.oregoncabaret.com), a professional dinner theater, or the town of Talent's little **Camelot Theatre Company,** 101 Talent Ave. ((C) **541/535-5250;** www.camelottheatre.org), which specializes in making live theater affordable.

For a glass of wine before or after a show, **Liquid Assets Wine Bar,** 96 N. Main St. ((C) **541/482-9463;** www.liquidassetswinebar.com), is the place to go. They serve some tasty, light meals here, too. Alternatively, you can sample and sip local wines at **EdenVale's Enoteca,** 17 N. Main St. ((C) **541/482-3377;** www.edenvaleenoteca. com), which is conveniently located right on the plaza. If you're just looking for someplace to heft a pint of local microbrew, stop by **Standing Stone Brewing,** 101 Oak St. ((C) **541/482-2448;** www.standingstonebrewing.com). Or to keep with the merrie olde England theme of Ashland, head to **The Black Sheep,** 51 N. Main St. ((C) **541/482-6414;** www.theblacksheep.com), an English pub on the plaza. On Saturday nights, you can do a little dancing at the Nuevo Latino restaurant **Tabu,** 76 N. Pioneer St. ((C) **541/482-3900;** www.taburestaurant.com).

JACKSONVILLE ★★ & MEDFORD

16 miles N of Ashland, 24 miles E of Grants Pass

Jacksonville is a snapshot from southern Oregon's past. After the Great Depression, it became a forgotten backwater, and more than 80 buildings from its glory years as a gold-mining boomtown in the mid-1800s were left untouched. The entire town has been restored to much the way it looked in the late 19th century, thanks in large part to the photos of pioneer photographer Peter Britt, who moved to Jacksonville in 1852 and operated the first photographic studio west of the Rockies. His photos of 19th-century Jacksonville have provided preservationists with invaluable 150-year-old glimpses of many of the town's historic buildings. Where Britt's home once stood, visitors now attend the performances of the **Britt Festivals,** another southern Oregon cultural binge that rivals the Oregon Shakespeare Festival in its ability to stage first-rate entertainment.

Though thousands of eager gold seekers were lured into California's Sierra Nevada by the **gold rush** of 1849, few struck it rich. Many of those who were smitten with gold fever and were unwilling to give up the search for the mother lode headed out across the West in search of golder pastures. In 1851 at least two prospectors hit pay dirt in the Siskiyou Mountains of southern Oregon at a spot that would soon be known as Rich Gulch. Within a year, Rich Gulch had become the site of booming Jacksonville, and within another year, the town had become the county seat and commercial heart of southern Oregon. Over the next 30 years, Jacksonville developed into a wealthy town with brick commercial buildings and elegant Victorian homes. However, in the 1880s, the railroad running between Portland and San Francisco bypassed Jacksonville in favor of an easier route 5 miles to the east. It was at this spot that the trading town of **Medford** developed.

Despite a short-rail line into Jacksonville, more and more businesses migrated to the main railway in Medford. Jacksonville's fortunes began to decline, and by the time of the Depression, residents were reduced to digging up the streets of town in search of any overlooked gold. In 1927 the county seat was moved to Medford, and Jacksonville was left with its faded grandeur and memories of better times.

Off the beaten path, forgotten by developers and modernization, Jacksonville inadvertently preserved its past in its buildings. In 1966 the entire town was listed on the National Register of Historic Places, and Jacksonville, with the aid of Britt's photos, underwent a renaissance that has left it a historical showcase. Together the Britt Festivals and Jacksonville's history combine to make this one of the most fascinating towns anywhere in the Northwest.

Essentials

GETTING THERE   Medford is right on I-5, 30 miles north of the California state line, and Jacksonville is 5 miles west on Ore. 238.

Allegiant Air, Alaska/Horizon Air, and SkyWest Airlines (Delta Connection and United Express) serve the **Rogue Valley International–Medford Airport (MFR),** 1000 Terminal Loop Pkwy. (✆ **541/772-8068**).

VISITOR INFORMATION   Contact the **Jacksonville Chamber of Commerce,** 185 N. Oregon St. (P.O. Box 33), Jacksonville, OR 97530 (✆ **541/899-8118;** www. jacksonvilleoregon.org), or the **Medford Visitor & Convention Bureau's Visitor Center,** 1314 Center Dr., Medford, OR 97501 (✆ **800/469-6307** or 541/779-4847; www.visitmedford.org), which is inside the Harry & David Country Village.

The Britt Festivals & Other Performances

The Britt Festivals are a celebration of music and the performing arts featuring internationally renowned performers, and each summer between early June and mid-September, people gather in Jacksonville several nights a week for classical, jazz, international, and popular-music concerts. The setting for most of the performances is an amphitheater on the grounds of Peter Britt's estate. Located only a block from historic California Street, the ponderosa pine–shaded amphitheater provides not only a great setting for the performances but a view that takes in distant hills and the valley far below.

Both reserved and general-admission tickets are available for most shows. If you opt for a general-admission ticket, arrive early to claim a prime spot on the lawns behind the reserved seats—and be sure to bring a picnic. For information, contact the festival at 216 W. Main St., Medford (✆ **800/882-7488,** 541/899-9924, or 541/773-6077; www.brittfest.org). Tickets range from $9 to $86, with most performances in the $20 to $50 range.

Not wanting to lose out to its better known neighbors, Medford has a renovated old downtown theater known as the **Craterian Ginger Rogers Theater,** 23 S.

Central Ave. (© **541/779-3000;** www.craterian.org), in honor of the famous dancer who lived in the area after her retirement. The theater stages everything from performances by the Rogue Opera (© **541/608-6400;** www.rogueopera.com) to touring Broadway shows and classical music performances.

Museums & Historic Homes

With more than 80 buildings listed on the National Register of Historic Places, Jacksonville claims it's the most completely preserved historic town in the nation. Whether or not this is true, the many restored old buildings make the town a genuine step back in time. Along California Street, you'll find restored brick commercial buildings that now house dozens of interesting shops, art galleries, and boutiques, and on the side streets, you'll see the town's many Victorian homes.

Butte Creek Mill In nearby Eagle Point, you can visit one of Oregon's only operating water-powered flour mills. The Butte Creek Mill was built in 1873, and its millstones are still grinding out flour. After looking around at the workings of the mill, you can stop in at the mill store and buy a bag of flour or cornmeal. Also on this same block is the **Eagle Point Museum,** 301 N. Royal Ave. (© **541/826-4166**), which unfortunately has very limited hours (Fri–Sun 9am–5pm; call for winter hours). The Antelope Creek covered bridge is also here in Eagle Point.

402 N. Royal Ave., Eagle Point. © **541/826-3531.** www.buttecreekmill.com. Free admission. Mon–Sat 9am–5pm; Sun 11am–5pm.

More to See & Do

Pears and roses both grow well in the Jacksonville and Medford area, and these crops have given rise to two of the country's best known mail-order businesses. **Harry & David Country Village,** 1314 Center Dr., Medford (© **877/322-8000** or 541/ 864-2278; www.harryanddavid.com), is the retail outlet of a fruit company specializing in mail-order gift baskets. You'll find the store just 1 mile south of Medford at exit 27 off I-5. You can tour the Harry & David kitchens and then wander through the store in search of bargains. In summer the store is open Monday through Saturday from 9am to 8pm, and Sunday from 9am to 7pm. Associated with this store is the **Jackson & Perkins rose test garden.** Not far away, in the town of Central Point, you can see how cheese is made at the **Rogue Creamery,** 311 N. Front St. (© **866/665-1155** or 541/665-1155; www.roguecreamery.com), which is known for its blue cheeses, including the delicious Oregonzola. The creamery is open Monday through Saturday from 9am to 5pm and Sunday from noon to 5pm. Both Harry & David and the Rogue Creamery are part of the **Southern Oregon Wine and Farm Tour** (www.oregonwineandfarmtour.com).

Outdoor Activities

Rafting and **fishing** on the numerous fast-flowing, clear-water rivers of southern Oregon are two of the most popular sports in this region, and Medford makes a good base for doing a bit of either, or both. **Arrowhead River Adventures** (© **800/830-3388** or 541/830-3388; www.arrowheadadventures.com), **Momentum River Expeditions** (© **541/488-2525;** www.momentumriverexpeditions.com), and **Rogue Excursions** (© **800/797-4293** or 541/923-3836; www.fishandraft.com) all offer both rafting and fishing trips. A half day of rafting will cost $69 to $79, and fishing trips cost about $175 to $250 per person per day (with a minimum of two people).

If you're here in the spring, you can catch the colorful **wildflower displays** at Table Rocks. These mesas are just a few miles northeast of Medford, and because of their great age and unique structure, they create a variety of habitats that allow the area to support an unusual diversity of plants. For more information, contact the **Bureau of Land Management,** Medford Office, 3040 Biddle Rd., Medford, OR 97504 (© **541/618-2200;** www.blm.gov/or/districts/medford/index.php).

Information on **hiking** and **backpacking** is available from the Rogue River–Siskiyou National Forest's **Siskiyou Mountains Ranger District,** 6941 Upper Applegate Rd., Jacksonville, OR 97530 (© **541/899-3800;** www.fs.fed.us/r6/rogue-siskiyou).

Wine Touring

The Applegate Valley is one of the best places in southern Oregon to spend a day wine touring. There are more than a dozen wineries in the area that you can now visit on a regular basis. For more information on area wineries, contact **Applegate Valley Wine Trail** (www.applegatewinetrail.com).

Wine connoisseurs also won't want to miss perusing the wine racks at the **Jacksonville Inn Wine Shop,** 175 E. California St., Jacksonville (© **541/899-1900;** www.jacksonvilleinn.com), where you might find a bottle of 1811 Tokay Essencia or a bottle of Chateau Lafite-Rothschild. Oregon wines (and beef jerky) can also be tasted at the **Gary West Tasting Room,** 690 N. Fifth St., Jacksonville (© **800/833-1820;** www.garywest.com).

Bridgeview Applegate Tasting Room ★   Bridgeview has its main facility near Cave Junction, but this tasting room is a bit more convenient if you are staying in Ashland or Jacksonville and are out for a day of wine tasting. Bridgeview is best known for its inexpensive white wines, several of which come in distinctive blue bottles.

16995 N. Applegate Rd., Grants Pass. © **541/846-1039.** www.bridgeviewwine.com. Memorial Day to Labor Day daily 11am–5pm; mid-Mar to May and Labor Day to Nov Sat–Sun 11am–5pm. From Jacksonville, drive west on Ore. 238 and turn right onto N. Applegate Rd.

Devitt Winery & Vineyards ★★ 🍴   This tiny, family-run winery is the retirement occupation of Jim Devitt and his wife, Sue. Devitt had a winery in the Napa Valley area more than 20 years ago and has now brought to his Applegate Valley operation the winemaking skills he developed in California. Look for good Cabernet Sauvignon and Cabernet Franc in the $25 to $30 range. There are also plenty of less expensive wines.

11412 Ore. 238, Jacksonville. © **541/899-7511.** www.devittwinery.com. Tasting fee $5. Daily noon–5pm. From Jacksonville, drive west on Ore. 238 past the community of Ruch.

Quady North   This tasting room is right in downtown Jacksonville, and if you're a fan of dessert wines, you're probably already familiar with the Quady wines of California. Here in Oregon, son Herb Quady is carving out his own niche, though you can also sample dad's wines here.

255 California St., Jacksonville. © **541/702-2123.** www.quadynorth.com. Tasting fee $5. Thurs–Sun 11am–7pm (until 6pm in winter).

Schmidt Family Vineyards   This winery has one of the prettiest settings and tasting rooms in the valley. Wines are produced from estate-grown grapes, and its red wines have been garnering some acclaim. A good variety of white wines is also produced.

330 Kubli Rd., Grants Pass. © **541/846-9985.** www.sfvineyards.com. Tasting fee $5. Daily noon–5pm. From Jacksonville, drive west on Ore. 238, turn right onto N. Applegate Rd. and then right again on Kubli Rd.

Serra Vineyards ★   This vineyard and winery are set on a particularly warm site, which allows Serra to produce outstanding red wines, including Syrah and a Bordeaux blend. From Syrah grapes, they also make a Rosé. Surprisingly, they also produce good Pinot Noir.

222 Missouri Flat Rd., Grants Pass. © **541/846-9223.** www.serravineyard.com. Tasting fee $5. Daily 11am–5pm.

South Stage Cellars   This in-town tasting room pours the wines of not only South State Cellars, but those of more than half a dozen other wineries, all of which make wine from the grapes of Quail Run Vineyards. This 280-acre vineyard produces 27 grape varietals, so you're sure to find something appealing being poured in the tasting room.

125 S. Third St., Jacksonville. © **541/899-9120.** www.southstagecellars.com. Tasting fee $5. Sat–Thurs noon–7pm, Fri noon–9pm.

Valley View Winery   This is the oldest winery in the area and is the first you'll come to as you head out into the Applegate Valley from Jacksonville. Valley View is known for its big red wines, but also produces good dry whites.

1000 Upper Applegate Rd., Jacksonville. © **800/781-9463** or 541/899-8468. www.valleyview winery.com. Tasting fee $5–$10. Daily 11am–5pm. From Jacksonville, drive west on Ore. 238 to Ruch, and turn left onto Upper Applegate Rd.

Where to Stay
IN JACKSONVILLE

Elan Guest Suites ★   In a town full of historic homes and B&Bs full of antiques, this little inn stands out for its sophisticated, contemporary styling. The accommodations are all large suites with plush beds, full kitchens, balconies, and large bathrooms. Because these suites are so spacious, Elan makes a great base for several days of exploring southern Oregon. The inn also doubles as an art gallery, with art displayed in the guest rooms. Perhaps best of all, Elan is only a block from the grounds of the Britt Festivals.

245 W. Main St. (P.O. Box 1229), Jacksonville, OR 97530. www.elanguestsuites.com. © **877/789-1952** or 541/899-8000. 3 units. May–Oct $220–$250 double; Nov–Apr $180–$200 double. Rates include continental breakfast. AE, DISC, MC, V. *In room:* A/C, TV/DVD, CD player, hair dryer, kitchen, MP3 docking station, free Wi-Fi.

Jacksonville Inn ★★   Located in the heart of the town's historic business district in a two-story brick building, the Jacksonville Inn is best known for its gourmet restaurant (see below). Upstairs, however, eight antiques-filled rooms offer traditional elegance mixed with modern amenities. Rooms are elegantly furnished, and several have exposed brick walls that conjure the inn's past (part of the inn was built in 1861). Room 1, with its queen-size canopy bed and whirlpool tub for two, is the most popular. If you're looking for more privacy and greater luxury, consider the cottages, which are a couple of blocks away and have whirlpool tubs, steam showers, and entertainment centers.

175 E. California St. (P.O. Box 359), Jacksonville, OR 97530. www.jacksonvilleinn.com. © **800/321-9344** or 541/899-1900. Fax 541/899-1373. 12 units, including 4 cottages. $159–$199 double;

$270–$465 cottage. Rates include full breakfast. AE, DC, DISC, MC, V. Pets accepted ($10 fee). **Amenities:** Restaurant; lounge; room service. *In room:* A/C, TV, fridge, hair dryer, free Wi-Fi.

McCully House Inn ★★   Built in 1861, the McCully house is one of the oldest buildings in Oregon being used as an inn, and with its classic, symmetrical lines and simple pre-Victorian styling, it looks as if it could easily be an 18th-century New England inn. If you like being steeped in local history, this is one of Jacksonville's best choices. Surrounding the inn and enclosed by a white picket fence is a formal rose garden with an amazing variety of roses. This inn also rents out several nearby cottages, as well as suites in the nearby Reames House.

240 E. California St., Jacksonville, OR 97530. www.mccullyhouseinn.com. © **800/367-1942** or 541/899-2050. Fax 541/899-7556. 13 units. $139–$179 double; $195–$295 suite, cottage, and carriage house. Rates include continental breakfast. AE, DC, DISC, MC, V. *In room:* A/C, no phone, free Wi-Fi.

Touvelle House ★   This luxurious B&B is located just a few blocks from downtown and the Britt Festival grounds, and is one of the town's prettiest inns. Built in 1916, the three-story Craftsman bungalow sits a bit above and well back from the street and is surrounded by more than an acre of attractive gardens. The grand feel of this old house never fails to impress first-time guests. The inn's great room is furnished with Stickley and other Arts and Crafts furniture, while the guest rooms are a mix of sophisticated Victorian and new furnishings. The three second-floor rooms all have remodeled bathrooms with "rainfall" shower heads. If you have trouble with stairs, be sure to ask for the Judge's Chambers room.

455 N. Oregon St. (P.O. Box 1891), Jacksonville, OR 97530. www.touvellehouse.com. © **800/846-8422** or 541/899-8938. 6 units. $129–$199 double. Rates include full breakfast. DISC, MC, V. Children 13 and over welcome. **Amenities:** Concierge; access to nearby health club; outdoor pool; sauna. *In room:* A/C, hair dryer, MP3 docking station, no phone, free Wi-Fi.

Wine Country Inn ★   Jacksonville has several bed-and-breakfast inns, but it's short on moderately priced motels. Filling the bill in the latter category is this motel designed to resemble a 19th-century stage stop, with gables, clapboard siding, and turned-wood railings along two floors of verandas. These details allow the lodge to fit right in with all the original buildings in town. The rooms are spacious, comfortable, and done up in a country style.

830 N. Fifth St., Jacksonville, OR 97530. http://countryhouseinnsjacksonville.com. © **800/367-1942** or 541/899-2050. Fax 541/899-7556. 27 units. $126 double; $175 suite. Rates include continental breakfast. AE, DC, DISC, MC, V. Pets accepted ($15 per night). *In room:* A/C, TV, free Wi-Fi.

IN THE APPLEGATE VALLEY

Applegate Lodge ★★ 🍴   Situated on the bank of the Applegate River 16 miles outside Jacksonville, this lodge has one of the prettiest settings in southern Oregon and is a masterpiece of woodworking, with burnished woods (including rare fiddleback redwood paneling) and unique wooden details throughout. The high-ceilinged great room with a river-rock fireplace features a wall of glass looking out on the river, and across the length of the lodge is a deck where you can sit and listen to the river. The guest rooms are all very large, and several of them have loft sleeping areas. Lots of peeled-log furniture gives the inn a solidly western feel. Right next door is the **Applegate River Ranch House** (see below). The river here is great for swimming.

15100 Ore. 238, Applegate, OR 97530. www.applegateriverlodge.com. © **541/846-6690**. 7 units. $110–$145 double; lower rates in winter. Rates include continental breakfast. AE, DISC, MC, V. Pets accepted ($10 per night). **Amenities:** Restaurant; lounge. *In room:* A/C, CD player, free Wi-Fi.

Where to Eat

IN JACKSONVILLE

Good Bean Coffee, 165 S. Oregon St. (© **541/899-8740;** www.goodbean.com), is *the* place in Jacksonville for a cup of espresso. **MacLevin's Whole Foods Deli,** 150 W. California St. (© **541/899-1251;** www.maclevinsonline.com), will pack up a deli-style picnic for a Britt performance (or any other occasion). If, after an afternoon of wine tasting, you want to sip a wine from, say, Walla Walla or the Willamette Valley, drop by **Corks Wine Bar and Bottle Shoppe,** 150 S. Oregon St. (© **541/899-3005**)

Bella Union Restaurant & Saloon ★ ITALIAN/AMERICAN
For casual dining or someplace to just toss back a cold beer or sip an Italian soda, Bella Union is Jacksonville's top choice. The lounge evokes the days when Bella Union was one of Jacksonville's busiest saloons, but in the back of the building is a pretty little garden patio. However, it's the main dining room up front that's most popular. Old wood floors, storefront windows, and exposed brick walls bring to mind images of gold miners out on the town. Pizzas and pastas make up the bulk of the menu. At lunch, the sandwich with chicken marinated in Gorgonzola and walnut pesto is a good bet. Bella Union also sells boxed meals for picnicking at the Britt Festivals.

170 W. California St. © **541/899-1770.** www.bellau.com. Reservations accepted for parties of 5 or more. Main courses $10–$25. AE, DISC, MC, V. Mon–Wed 11:30am–9pm; Thurs–Sat 11:30am–9pm; Sun 10am–2pm and 4–9pm.

Gogi's Restaurant ★★ REGIONAL AMERICAN
With an ambience somewhere between the casual atmosphere of Bella Union and the formality of the Jacksonville Inn Dinner House, this restaurant is a gleaming and comfortable little bistro. The small plates, such as the pan-fried calamari with saffron aioli or tuna carpaccio with crispy capers, make good choices for sharing around the table. Other tasty standouts include pan-seared salmon with truffled fennel-orange salad and rack of lamb with truffle-infused demi-glace. Gogi's also does picnic baskets for festival attendees.

235 W. Main St. © **541/899-8699.** www.gogis.net. Reservations recommended. Main courses $20–$28. AE, DISC, MC, V. Wed–Sat 5–9pm; Sun 10am–2pm and 5–9pm.

Jacksonville Inn Dinner House ★★ 🗡 CONTINENTAL/MEDITERRANEAN
Old-world atmosphere, either in the cozy and cellarlike downstairs or in the airier upstairs dining room, sets the mood for reliable continental fare. Together the cuisine and the decor attract well-heeled families and retirees that favor well-prepared, though familiar, dishes such as lamb chops, veal scaloppini, and prime rib. The bistro menu is lighter and leans toward Mediterranean influences, with such dishes as hazelnut prawns and roasted garlic pasta. Pears are a mainstay of the local economy and show up frequently in both entrees and desserts. The inn's wine shop gives diners access to a cellar boasting more than 2,000 wines. In summer, ask for a table on the patio. As at other restaurants, picnic meals are also available.

175 E. California St. © **541/899-1900.** www.jacksonvilleinn.com. Reservations recommended. Main courses $7–$16 lunch, $10–$35 dinner. MC, V. Mon–Sat 7:30–10:30am, 11:30am–2pm, and 5–9 or 10pm; Sun 7:30am–2pm and 5–9pm. Bistro menu served daily 4pm–closing.

IN THE APPLEGATE VALLEY

Applegate River Ranch House ★ 🍖 STEAK/SEAFOOD
With a deck overlooking the beautiful Applegate River, the location here just can't be beat. I like to enjoy the view with a plate of succulent oak wood–broiled mushrooms and a glass of

chardonnay. From the chicken to various cuts of beef, anything broiled over the local red-oak wood is delicious. For dessert, top it all off with a piece of the Hula Pie, a mocha-almond-fudge ice-cream pie.

15100 Ore. 238, Applegate. © **541/846-6082.** www.applegateriverlodge.com. Reservations recommended. Main courses $13–$19. DISC, MC, V. Wed–Thurs 5–9pm; Fri–Sun 11am–3pm and 5–9pm.

GRANTS PASS & THE ROGUE RIVER VALLEY

63 miles S of Roseburg, 40 miles NW of Ashland, 82 miles NE of Crescent City

"It's the climate," proclaims a sign at the entrance to Grants Pass, and with weather almost as reliably pleasant as California's, the town has become a popular base for outdoor activities of all kinds. The Rogue River runs through the center of town, so it's not surprising that most local recreational activities revolve around the waters of this famous river. Grants Pass is located at the junction of I-5 and U.S. 199, and is the last large town in Oregon if you're heading over to the redwoods, which are about 90 miles southwest on the Northern California coast. About the same distance to the northeast, you'll find Crater Lake National Park, so Grants Pass makes a good base if you're trying to see a lot of this region in a short time.

The city is slowly reviving its few blocks of historic commercial buildings, and it's worth wandering down SW G Street to see what's new along the historic blocks.

Essentials

GETTING THERE Grants Pass is at the junction of I-5 and U.S. 199. Allegiant Air, Alaska/Horizon Air, and SkyWest Airlines (Delta Connection and United Express) serve the nearby **Rogue Valley International–Medford Airport (MFR),** 1000 Terminal Loop Pkwy. (© **541/772-8068**).

VISITOR INFORMATION Contact the **Grants Pass Tourism,** 1995 NW Vine St., Grants Pass, OR 97526 (© **800/547-5927** or 541/476-7717; www.visitgrantspass. org).

FESTIVALS Boatnik (www.boatnik.com), held Memorial Day weekend, is Grants Pass's biggest annual festival and includes jet-boat and hydroplane races on the Rogue River, as well as lots of festivities at Riverside Park.

Outdoor Activities

Grants Pass is midway between the source of the Rogue River and the river's mouth, and it's an ideal base for river-oriented activities. The Rogue, first made famous by Western novelist and avid fly-fisherman Zane Grey, is now preserved for much of its length as a National Wild and Scenic River. Originating in Crater Lake National Park, the river twists and tumbles through narrow gorges and steep mountains as it winds its way to the coast at Gold Beach. The most famous section of the river is 250-foot-deep **Hellgate Canyon,** where the river narrows and rushes through a cleft in the rock. The canyon can be seen from an overlook on Merlin-Galice Road, which begins at exit 61 off I-5. From I-5 it's about 10 miles to the canyon overlook.

Several area companies offer **river trips** of varying length and in a variety of watercraft. You can spend the afternoon paddling the Rogue in an inflatable kayak or several days rafting the river with stops each night at riverside lodges. If you have only enough time for a short trip on the river, I'd recommend a jet-boat trip down to Hellgate Canyon, which, as mentioned above, is the most scenic spot on this section of the river. **Hellgate Jetboat Excursions,** 966 SW Sixth St., Grants Pass (🕿 **800/648-4874** or541/479-7204; www.hellgate.com), operates five different jet-boat trips (three of which include a meal at a riverside ranch). Adult ticket prices range from $38 to $63.

Local **white-water-rafting** companies offer half-day, full-day, and multiday trips, with the latter stopping either at rustic river lodges or at campsites along the river-banks. Area rafting companies include **Rogue Wilderness Adventures** (🕿 **800/ 336-1647** or 541/479-9554; www.wildrogue.com); **Galice Resort,** 11744 Galice Rd., Merlin (🕿 **541/476-3818;** www.galice.com); **Orange Torpedo Trips,** 210 Merlin Rd., Merlin (🕿 **866/479-5061** or 541/479-5061; www.orangetorpedo.com); and **Rogue River Raft Trips,** Morrison's Lodge, 8500 Galice Rd., Merlin (🕿 **800/ 826-1963** 541/476-3825; www.rogueriverraft.com). Expect to pay around $70 to $80 for a half day and $85 to $95 for a full day. Three-day lodge or camping trips are in the $650 to $929 range.

At several places near Merlin, you can rent rafts and kayaks of different types and paddle yourself downriver. Try **White Water Cowboys,** 210 Merlin Rd., Merlin (🕿 **866/479-5061** or 541/479-5061; www.whitewatercowboys.com); **Galice Resort Store,** 11744 Galice Rd., Merlin (🕿 **541/476-3818;** www.galice.com); or **Ferron's Fun Trips** (🕿 **800/404-2201;** www.roguefuntrips.com). Rental rates range from $20 to $45 for inflatable kayaks and from $55 to $95 for rafts.

Other Things to See & Do

Though most people visiting Grants Pass are here to enjoy the mountains and rivers surrounding the town, history buffs can pick up a free map of the town's historic build-ings at the Tourist Information Center. Two small art museums—the **Grants Pass Museum of Art,** 229 SW G St. (🕿 **541/479-3290;** www.gpmuseum.com), and Rogue Community College's **Wiseman Gallery,** 3345 Redwood Hwy. (🕿 **541/956-7339;** www.roguecc.edu/galleries/wiseman.asp)—offer changing exhibits of classical and contemporary art by local and national artists. Rogue Community College also operates the **Fire House Gallery,** 214 SW Fourth St. (🕿 **541/956-7489;** www. roguecc.edu/galleries/firehouse.asp), in downtown Grants Pass. On the first Friday of each month (except Jan), art galleries and other stores in downtown stay open until 9pm. During this roving gallery party, there's always live entertainment of some sort.

Wildlife Images Rehabilitation & Education Center ★, 11845 Lower River Rd. (🕿 **541/476-0222;** www.wildlifeimages.org), is dedicated to nurturing injured birds of prey and other wild animals back to health and then releasing them back into the wild, if possible. The center is 14 miles south of Grants Pass and is open for tours daily by reservation only. Tours cost $10 for adults and $5 for children 4 to 17. One of the best things about this place is that you can get closer to the animals than you can at a zoo.

Riverside Park, in the center of town, is a popular place to play, especially in the warmer months when people come to cool off in the river.

About midway between Medford and Grants Pass and about 6 miles off I-5 (take exit 40), you'll find one of Oregon's most curious attractions: the **Oregon Vortex,** 4303 Sardine Creek Left Fork Rd., Gold Hill (🕿 **541/855-1543;** www.oregon vortex.com). Straight out of *Ripley's Believe It or Not!,* this classic tourist trap is guar-anteed to have the kids, and many adults, oohing and aahing in bug-eyed amazement at the numerous strange phenomena that defy the laws of physics. People grow taller as they recede. You, and the trees surrounding the House of Mystery, lean toward magnetic north rather than stand upright. Seeing is believing—or is it? It's open March through May and September through October daily from 9am to 4pm, and June through August daily from 9am to 5pm. Admission is $9.75 for adults, $8.75 for seniors, and $7 for children 6 to 11.

Also in Gold Hill, you'll find the large **Del Rio Vineyards & Winery,** 52 N. River Rd. (© **541-855-2062;** www.delriovineyards.com), which is just off I-5 at exit 43. With more than 200 acres of vineyards, Del Rio is one of Oregon's largest vineyards and sells grapes to wineries across the state. In the winery's tasting room, housed in a historic stagecoach stop built in 1864, you can sample both Del Rio wines and wines produced at other wineries from Del Rio grapes. The tasting room is open daily 11am to 5pm (11am–6pm June–Aug). You can also taste local wines in downtown Grants Pass at the **Oregon Outpost,** 137 SW G St. (© **541/474-2918;** www.oregon outpostgifts.com), which also sells a wide variety of gourmet foods from Oregon.

Where to Stay

IN TOWN

The Lodge at Riverside ★★   You'll likely do a double take when you see the log-cabin lodge fronting this riverside hotel. The building is painted brown with green trim and looks as if it belongs in a national park. The log-walled lobby is decorated with mounted trophy animals, including a black bear and an elk head. Guest rooms are large and quite plush, with a sort of modern cabin decor. There are overstuffed wicker easy chairs, plus more wicker chairs on the balconies. All the rooms have river views, and most have patios or balconies facing the Rogue. If you can ignore the traffic noise from the adjacent bridge, you can almost imagine you're out in the wilderness.

955 SE Seventh St., Grants Pass, OR 97526. www.thelodgeatriverside.com. © **877/955-0600** or 541/955-0600. Fax 541/955-0611. 33 units. $130–$195 double; from $325 suite. Rates include continental breakfast and evening wine reception. Children 12 and under stay free in parent's room. AE, DC, DISC, MC, V. **Amenities:** Jacuzzi; outdoor pool. *In room:* A/C, TV/VCR, hair dryer, free Wi-Fi.

OUTSIDE OF TOWN

Morrison's Rogue River Lodge ★★   If you're in the area to do a bit of fishing or rafting, I can think of no better place to stay than at Morrison's. Perched on the banks of the Rogue, this fishing lodge epitomizes the Rogue River experience. The main lodge is a massive log building that's rustic yet comfortable, with a wall of glass that looks across wide lawns to the river. Although there are B&B-style accommodations in the main lodge, the cabins seem more appropriate in this setting. The spacious cabins stand beneath grand old trees, and all have good views of the river. Fireplaces will keep you warm and cozy in the cooler months. The dining room serves surprisingly creative four-course dinners ($38–$42). Fishing and rafting trips are the specialty here, and, in addition to amenities listed below, there is also a private beach and a putting green.

8500 Galice Rd., Merlin, OR 97532. www.morrisonslodge.com. © **800/826-1963** or 541/476-3825. Fax 541/476-4953. 17 units. $240–$420 double. Rates include full breakfast. Children 3 and under stay free in parent's room. AE, DC, DISC, MC, V. Closed mid-Nov to Apr. Pets accepted ($15 per night). **Amenities:** Restaurant; lounge; bikes; concierge; exercise room; outdoor pool; room service (breakfast only); 2 tennis courts; watersports equipment rentals. *In room:* A/C, TV/VCR/DVD, fridge, hair dryer, kitchen (some rooms), free Wi-Fi.

Weasku Inn ★★ 🛏 Located a few miles out of Grants Pass and set beneath towering trees on the banks of the Rogue River, this inn is one of the most memorable lodgings in the state, the quintessential mountain/fishing lodge. The log lodge was built in 1924 and was once *the* area fishing lodge. That was back in the days when Clark Gable, Carole Lombard, Walt Disney, Zane Grey, Bing Crosby, and Herbert Hoover used to stay here. Today the lodge is still the sort of place where such luminaries would feel comfortable. Guest rooms, on the second floor of the old log lodge, are spacious and modern and have interesting details such as bent-willow furnishings. The riverside cabins are in a modern lodge style with whirlpool tubs, fireplaces, and private decks.

5560 Rogue River Hwy., Grants Pass, OR 97527. www.weasku.com. ☎ **800/493-2758** or 541/471-8000. 17 units. $199–$299 double; $225–$329 suite/cabin; $445 3-bedroom house. Rates include continental breakfast and evening appetizers. 3-night minimum in house. Children 12 and under stay free in parent's room. AE, DISC, MC, V. *In room:* A/C, TV, fridge, hair dryer, free Wi-Fi.

Wolf Creek Inn ★ 🛏 Originally opened in 1883 on the old stagecoach road between Sacramento and Portland, the Wolf Creek Inn is a two-story clapboard building with wide front verandas along both floors. Today the inn, which is 25 miles north of Grants Pass and just off I-5, is the oldest hotel in Oregon and is owned and managed by the Oregon State Parks and Recreation Division. The interior is furnished in period antiques dating from the 1870s to the 1930s. On a winter's night, there's no cozier spot than by the fireplace in the downstairs "ladies parlor." The guest rooms are small and comfortably furnished, much as they might have been in the early 1900s. Meals are available in the inn's dining room. All in all, this inn has a genuinely timeless feel. Nearby are hiking trails and a small ghost town.

100 Front St., Wolf Creek, OR 97497. www.historicwolfcreekinn.com. ☎ **541/866-2474.** Fax 541/866-2692. 9 units. May to mid-Oct $95–$105 double, $125 suite; mid-Oct to Apr $85–$95 double, $110 suite. Rates include full breakfast. Children 5 and under stay free in parent's room. DISC, MC, V. **Amenities:** Restaurant; lounge. *In room:* A/C, no phone, free Wi-Fi.

CAMPGROUNDS

Along the Rogue River east of Grants Pass, you'll find the very busy **Valley of the Rogue State Park** (☎ **541/582-1118;** www.oregon.gov/oprd/parks) just off I-5 near the town of Rogue River. West of Grants Pass, there are several county-operated campgrounds, of which **Indian Mary Park,** 7100 Merlin Galice Rd., in the Hellgate Canyon area near Galice, is the nicest. Near Indian Mary Park, you'll also find **Almeda Park,** 14800 Merlin Galice Rd., which is close to the Grave Creek trail head of the Rogue River Trail. Reservations for these campgrounds can be made through **Reserve America** (☎ **800/452-5687;** www.reserveamerica.com).

Where to Eat

For tasty sandwiches and panini, don't miss **Rosso's Trattoria,** 225 SE Sixth St. (☎ **541/476-8708;** www.rossos.biz), in downtown Grants Pass. If all you need is a pizza and a microbrew, try **Wild River Brewing & Pizza Company,** 595 NE E St. (☎ **541/471-7487;** www.wildriverbrewing.com). Alternatively, check out the same company's **Wild River Pub,** 533 NE F St. (☎ **541/474-4456**). For espresso drinks and light meals, visit the **Bluestone Bakery,** 412 NW Sixth St. (☎ **541/471-1922;** www.bluestonebakery.com). **Morrison's Rogue River Lodge,** 8500 Galice Rd., Merlin (☎ **800/826-1963;** www.morrisonslodge.com), serves the best meals on the river. Dinners are $38, and reservations are required. See the review (above) for details.

Summer Jo's ★★ 🍴 STEAK/SEAFOOD   Located out in the country on an organic farm growing flowers, herbs, and vegetables, this casual restaurant provides a glimpse of the good life, Grants Pass style. The cafe also uses organically grown herbs and produce from the surrounding farm. The food here is among the most creative in Grants Pass, and such dishes as housemade gnocchi with smoked red pepper and spinach often highlight fresh produce from the farm. Meals are served inside or outside in the garden, and if you're a gardener, you'll especially enjoy a meal here in high summer when the gardens are bursting with life and color.

2315 Upper River Rd. Loop. © **541/476-6882.** www.summerjo.com. Reservations recommended. Main courses $9–$14 breakfast/lunch, $15–$29 dinner. DISC, MC, V. Thurs–Sun 9:30am–2pm and 5–8:30pm. Closed Jan to mid-Feb. Drive west on G St. and look for the sign; it's 1½ miles from downtown Grants Pass.

Taprock Northwest Grill AMERICAN   The menu here doesn't break any new ground, but the log-lodge styling and the riverside setting together make this your best choice for a meal in downtown. There are burgers, steaks, and seafood platters, and you can even start with Ivar's clam chowder from Seattle. The breakfasts here are huge; definitely the way to start the day if you plan to go out hiking.

971 SE Sixth St. © **541/955-5998.** www.taprock.com. Main courses $9–$21. AE, DISC, MC, V. Sun–Thurs 8am–10pm; Fri–Sat 8am–11pm.

OREGON CAVES & THE ILLINOIS VALLEY

Cave Junction: 30 miles SW of Grants Pass, 56 miles NE of Crescent City

For many people, U.S. 199 is simply the road to the redwoods from southern Oregon. However, this remote stretch of highway passes through the Illinois Valley and skirts the Siskiyou Mountains, two areas that offer quite a few recreational activities. The Illinois River, which flows into the Rogue River, is an even wilder river than the Rogue, and experienced paddlers looking for real white-water adventures often run its Class V waters. Because the Siskiyou Mountains are among the oldest in Oregon, they support a unique plant community. These mountains are also known for their rugged, rocky peaks, which, though not very high, can be very impressive.

In 2002, a huge fire ravaged much of the forest in this area. However, in some areas, the fire only cleared out the underbrush and left the mature trees undamaged. If you are planning on going hiking around here, be sure to check the status of the area in which you plan to hike.

Essentials

GETTING THERE   Cave Junction is on U.S. 199 between Grants Pass and the California state line. Oregon Caves National Monument is 20 miles outside Cave Junction on Ore. 46.

VISITOR INFORMATION   For more information on this area, contact the **Illinois River Valley Visitor Center,** 201 Caves Hwy., Cave Junction, OR 97523 (© **541/592-4076;** http://ivcdo.projecta.com/sectionindex.asp?sectionid=8).

Big Caves & Big Cats

Great Cats World Park   With tigers, leopards, cougars, and other exotic wild cats, this 10-acre wildlife park is one of the most interesting family attractions in southern Oregon. Interactive programs allow visitors to watch as big cats demonstrate their hunting skills. Species here include lions, tigers (including a white tiger), leopards, and other smaller wild cats.

27919 Redwood Hwy., Cave Junction. © **541/592-2957.** www.greatcatsworldpark.com. Admission $14 adults, $12 seniors, $10 children ages 4–12. June–Aug daily 10am–6pm; Sept daily 11am–5pm; mid-Mar to May and Oct daily 11am–4pm; Nov and Feb Sat–Sun 11am–4pm. Located 1¼ miles south of Cave Junction on U.S. 199.

Oregon Caves National Monument ★   High in the rugged Siskiyou Mountains, a clear mountain stream cascades through a narrow canyon, and here stands one of southern Oregon's oldest attractions. Known as the marble halls of Oregon and first discovered in 1874, the caves, which stretch for 3 miles under the mountain, were formed by water seeping through marble bedrock. The slight acidity of the water dissolves the marble, which is later redeposited as beautiful stalactites, stalagmites, draperies, soda straws, columns, and flowstone. Guided tours of the caves take about 1½ hours, and aboveground there are several miles of hiking trails that start near the cave entrance. Bear in mind that children under 42 inches tall are not allowed on tours. In summer, "off-trail" tours ($30), which are essentially introductions to spelunking, are available by reservation. To reach the monument, take Ore. 46 out of Cave Junction and follow the signs.

19000 Caves Hwy., Cave Junction. © **541/592-2100.** www.nps.gov/orca. Admission $8.50 adults, $6 children 16 and under. Cave tours mid-Mar to late May and mid-Oct to late Oct daily 10am–4pm; late May to early Sept daily 9am–6pm; early Sept to mid-Oct daily 9am–5pm.

Other Things to See & Do in the Illinois Valley

The Illinois River, when it isn't raging through rock-choked canyons, creates some of the best **swimming holes** in the state. Try the waters at Illinois River Forks State Park, just outside Cave Junction, or ask at the **Wild Rivers Ranger District,** 26568 Redwood Hwy., Cave Junction, OR 97523 (© **541/592-4000;** www.fs.fed.us/r6/rogue-siskiyou), for directions to other good swimming holes in the area. At this ranger station, you can also pick up information and directions for **hiking trails** in the Siskiyous, where the 180,000-acre Kalmiopsis Wilderness is a destination for backpackers. Unfortunately, this wilderness was the site of the huge Biscuit Fire in 2002. This massive blaze burned the entire wilderness and other adjacent forests. Because some areas survived the fire better than others, it is important to check with the ranger station about conditions of trails before heading out hiking.

WINE TOURING

The Cave Junction area is one of the warmest regions of Oregon and consequently produces some of the best cabernet sauvignon and merlot in the state. This is about as far south as you can get and still claim to be producing Oregon wines—just a few more miles and you're in California (though it's still a long way to Napa Valley).

Bridgeview Vineyard & Winery ★   Best known for its distinctive blue bottles, Bridgeview is one of the largest wineries in the state and produces primarily inexpensive white wines. This place is not for wine snobs, but rather for those who enjoy a pleasant glass of wine with dinner. The tasting room boasts an idyllic setting beside a large pond that is stocked with trout. (Don't forget to feed them.) Most whites and some reds are under $10, making these wines some of the best values in the state.

4210 Holland Loop Rd., Cave Junction. © **877/273-4843** or 541/592-4688. www.bridgeviewwine.com. Daily 11am–5pm. From Cave Junction, go east on Ore. 46 and turn right on Holland Loop Rd.

Foris Vineyards ★ Full-bodied and complex red wines are the hallmark of Foris Vineyards. The pinot noir and cabernet sauvignon/merlot/cabernet franc blend can be outstanding. They also do very good chardonnay, a popular and inexpensive pinot gris, and even a port. Lots of good values here.

654 Kendall Rd., Cave Junction. ℭ **800/843-6747.** www.foriswine.com. Daily 11am–5pm.

Where to Stay

Chateau at the Oregon Caves ★ A narrow road winds for 20 miles south from Cave Junction into the Rogue River–Siskiyou National Forest, climbing through deep forests before finally coming to an end in a narrow, steep-walled canyon. At the very head of this canyon stands the Oregon Caves Chateau, a rustic six-story lodge built in 1934. The lodge has thick bark siding, and inside the lobby there is a two-sided marble fireplace and huge fir beams supporting the ceiling. Unfortunately, due to the wooded canyon setting, the lodge doesn't have the sweeping vistas you would expect. Guest rooms aren't nearly as grand as the lobby, but they do have the original Monterey-style furnishings and a rustic mountain-lodge character. A 1930s-style soda fountain (an absolute classic) serves burgers, shakes, and other simple meals, while in the main dining room steak and seafood dinners are available.

201 Caves Hwy. (P.O. Box 1824), Cave Junction, OR 97523. www.oregoncavesoutfitters.com. ℭ **877/245-9022** or 541/592-3400. Fax 541/592-4075. 23 units. $99–$150 double; $160–$180 suite. Children 12 and under stay free in parent's room. DISC, MC, V. Closed mid-Oct to Apr. **Amenities:** 2 restaurants. *In room:* No phone.

Out 'n' About Treehouse Treesort ★ ☺ These are by far the most unusual accommodations in southern Oregon: a complex of treehouses. Choices include a Tree Room Schoolhouse, the Swiss Family Complex (complete with swinging bridge to the kids' room), the Peacock Perch, the Cabintree (actually a landlocked cabin), a saloon-style treehouse, and a "Cavaltree" fort (big hit with kids). The Tree Room Schoolhouse has a bathroom, and the Treezebo and Forestree have a toilet and sink. The resort offers a variety of fun activities, including a network of zip lines. Despite the address, Out 'n' About is actually located in the community of Takilma.

300 Page Creek Rd., Cave Junction, OR 97523. www.treehouses.com. ℭ **541/592-2208.** 16 units. Summer $130–$280 double; other months $90–$240 double. 2- to 3-night minimum in summer. Rates include full breakfast in summer, continental breakfast other months. MC, V. **Amenities:** Outdoor pool; free Wi-Fi. *In room:* No phone.

Where to Eat

Wild River Brewing & Pizza Company PIZZA/DELI If you're a fan of brewpubs, a pleasant surprise awaits you in the crossroads community of Cave Junction. This very casual combination pizza parlor/deli also happens to be a respectable microbrewery specializing in British and German styles of beer. The rich and flavorful ales go great with the pizzas. For fans of the unusual, there's a pizza with smoked sausage and sauerkraut and another with avocado and alfalfa sprouts.

249 N. Redwood Hwy. ℭ **541/592-3556.** www.wildriverbrewing.com. Sandwiches $5–$7; pizzas $5–$25. DISC, MC, V. Mon–Thurs 11am–9pm; Fri–Sat 11am–10pm; Sun noon–9pm.

THE ROSEBURG AREA

68 miles N of Grants Pass, 68 miles S of Eugene, 83 miles W of Crater Lake National Park

Although primarily a logging mill town, Roseburg is set at the mouth of the North Umpqua River and, consequently, is well situated for exploring one of the prettiest valleys in Oregon. The surrounding countryside bears a striking resemblance to parts of Northern California, so it should come as no surprise that there are a half-dozen wineries in the area. The hills south of town also look a bit like an African savanna, which may be why the Wildlife Safari park is located here. Today this drive-through wildlife park is one of the biggest attractions in southern Oregon. In downtown Roseburg, you'll find numerous old Victorian homes, and a drive through the town's old neighborhoods will be interesting for fans of late-19th-century architecture.

Essentials

GETTING THERE   Roseburg is right on I-5 at the junction with Ore. 138, which leads east up the North Umpqua River to Crater Lake National Park.

VISITOR INFORMATION   For more information on this area, contact the **Roseburg Visitors & Convention Bureau,** 410 SE Spruce St. (P.O. Box 1262), Roseburg, OR 97470 (© **800/444-9584** or 541/672-9731; www.visitroseburg.com).

What to See & Do

Douglas County Museum ★   South of town at the Douglas County Fairgrounds, you'll find this surprisingly well-designed museum. It is housed in an unusual, large building that resembles an old mining structure or mill. Inside are displays on the history and natural history of the region. Pioneer farming and mining displays interpret the settlement of the region, and there's even an exhibit on the history of wine. Interesting traveling exhibits often show up here, so it's worth checking to see what is scheduled.

123 Museum Dr. (exit 123 off I-5), Roseburg. © **541/957-7007.** www.co.douglas.or.us/museum. Admission $5 adults, $4 seniors, free for children 17 and under. Apr–Sept daily 10am–5pm; Oct–Mar Mon–Sat 10am–5pm.

Wildlife Safari ★★ ☺   This 600-acre drive-through nature park is home to wild animals from around the world. You'll come face to face with curious bears, grazing gazelles and zebras, ostriches, and even lumbering elephants and rhinos. You can also visit the educational center or attend an animal show. Convertibles are not allowed in the lion, cheetah, or bear enclosures. For additional fees, the park also offers lots of fun animal activities, including an elephant car wash, camel rides, giraffe feedings, and even lion tug of war.

1790 Safari Rd. (off Ore. 42, south of Roseburg), Winston. © **541/679-6761.** www.wildlifesafari. net. Admission $18 adults, $15 seniors, $12 children 4–12, free for children 3 and under. Daily 9am–5pm.

Wine Touring

The Roseburg area is home to more than a dozen wineries, most of which are located within a short drive of I-5. Wherever you start your wine tour of the area, pick up a copy of the local wineries map that's produced by the **Umpqua Valley Winegrowers Association** (www.umpquavalleywineries.org).

Abacela ★★   This winery produces some of the best red wines in Oregon. If you're patient and can cellar these wines for a few years, you'll be well rewarded. Tempranillo is the specialty, but they also do an excellent Syrah, and their Dolcetto always sells out quickly. Don't miss this one.

12500 Lookingglass Rd., Roseburg. © **541/679-6642.** www.abacela.com. Tasting fee $5–$15. Daily 11am–6pm. Take exit 119 off I-5, drive west 2 miles, turn right on Lookingglass Rd., and continue 2 miles.

Girardet Wine Cellars & Vineyard ★ This winery is known for its big, bold red wines and is one of the state's only wineries producing baco noir. This red wine is made from a hybrid grape that produces wines of deep, inky color. Soft and silky and with low tannins, these wines are very easy drinkers even when they're young.

895 Reston Rd., Roseburg. ✆ **541/679-7252.** www.girardetwine.com. Daily 11am–5pm. Take Ore. 42 W. (exit 119) from I-5, south of Roseburg; go 9 miles, and turn right on Reston Rd. (before Tenmile).

Henry Estate Winery This winery on the bank of the Umpqua River produces a wide range of wines, some of which, especially the whites, can be good values. On occasion they also have produced decent pinot noir. Grapes are grown on a special trellising system known as a Scott Henry trellis, named for the winery's founder and now used all over the world.

687 Hubbard Creek Rd., Umpqua. ✆ **800/782-2686** or 541/459-5120. www.henryestate.com. Daily 11am–5pm. From exit 136 off I-5 at Sutherlin, go west through Umpqua and cross the Umpqua River.

HillCrest Vineyard ★★ This winery is worth seeking out if for no other reason than that it's Oregon's oldest continuously operating winery producing wines from vinifera (European) grapes. Vineyards here were first planted in 1961. The current owners of the winery, Dyson and Susan DeMara, are producing the best wines in southern Oregon.

240 Vineyard Lane, Roseburg. ✆ **541/673-3709.** www.hillcrestvineyard.com. Tasting fee $5. Mar–Dec daily 11am–5pm. From Roseburg, go west on Garden Valley Rd. and turn left on Melrose Rd., right on Doerner Rd., right onto Elgarose Rd., and left onto Vineyard Lane.

MarshAnne Landing Winery Located outside the historic town of Oakland on the site of a former stagecoach stop, this winery specializes in Bordeaux and Rhone varietals. Despite the flying saucers on the labels, the winery's name is a reference to owners Gregory Marsh Cramer and Frances Anne Cramer.

175 Hogan Rd., Oakland. ✆ **541/459-8497.** www.marshannelanding.com. Tasting fee $5. May–Oct Wed–Sun 11am–5pm; Mar–Apr and Nov–Dec Sat–Sun 11am–5pm; other times by appt. Take exit 142 (Metz Hill) off I-5, drive east on Goodrich Hwy. and take a right onto Hogan Rd.

Melrose Vineyards With its tasting room in a converted 100-year-old barn, this vineyard has long sold grapes to other Oregon wineries. Today they also produce decent wines from their own grapes. Prices are reasonable for most of their wines.

885 Melqua Rd., Roseburg. ✆ **541/672-6080.** www.melrosevineyards.com. Tasting fee free–$10. Daily 10am–5:30pm. From Roseburg, go west on Garden Valley Rd., turn left on Melrose Rd., continue almost to the community of Melrose, and turn right on Melqua Rd.

Misty Oaks Vineyard This little family-run winery regularly produces outstanding and award-winning wines and is well worth searching out. The 2006 Gobbler's Knob red blend was particularly good, and the 2007 won several awards as well. Misty Oaks also does good (and reasonably priced) pinot blanc, pinot gris, and Gewürztraminer. The setting is beautiful.

1310 Misty Oaks Lane, Oakland. ✆ **541/459-3558.** www.mistyoaksvineyard.com. Tasting fee $4. Wed–Sun 11am–5pm. Closed Jan-Feb. Take exit 136 off I-5, drive west on Fort McKay Rd., and make a right turn on Cole Rd.

Reustle Prayer Rock Vineyards ★ With its impressive wine cave built into the side of a hill, this winery, which has adopted a Christian theme throughout its facility, is the most impressive and unexpected winery in the region. Tastings are held in private rooms within the wine cave, and wines are accompanied by food pairings. Look for Viognier and Grüner Veltliner.

960 Cal Henry Rd., Roseburg. ✆ **541/459-6060.** www.reustlevineyards.com. Tasting fee $10. Tues–Sat 10am–5pm. Take exit 136 off I-5, drive west on Fort McKay Rd., make a left turn on Garden Valley Rd., and then another left onto Cal Henry Rd.

Sienna Ridge Estate   This is the northernmost of the Umpqua Valley wineries and makes a convenient introduction to the area if you are driving south on I-5. With more than 300 acres of vineyards, this is also one of the largest wine estates in Oregon. The winery produces both pinot noir and cabernet sauvignon, and plenty of whites and dessert wines as well.

1876 John Long Rd., Oakland. ✆ **541/849-3300.** www.siennaridgeestate.com. Tasting fee $5–$10. Daily noon–6pm. Take exit 148 or 150 off I-5 (25 miles north of Roseburg), and drive south.

Spangler Vineyards   This small winery just off I-5 is very convenient if you just want to make a quick foray into the world of Oregon wines. They produce a wide range of reds and whites, and their reserve cabernet can be excellent (though it can also cost as much as $50).

491 Winery Lane, Roseburg. ✆ **541/679-9654.** www.spanglervineyards.com. Tasting fee free–$5. Daily 11am–5pm. Take exit 119 off I-5 (5 miles south of Roseburg), and go west a half mile.

Where to Stay

IN ROSEBURG

Holiday Inn Express   Although it's located just off I-5, this modern economy hotel also happens to sit on the banks of the Umpqua River, and every room has a balcony and a view of the river. The Jacuzzi is set in a gazebo amid green lawns between the hotel building and the river. Downtown Roseburg and a couple of good restaurants are a short walk away.

375 W. Harvard Blvd., Roseburg, OR 97470. www.hiexpress.com. ✆ **888/465-4329** or 541/673-7517. Fax 541/673-8331. 100 units. $129–$148 double. Rates include full breakfast. Children 18 and under stay free in parent's room. AE, DC, DISC, MC, V. Pets accepted ($15 per night). **Amenities:** Exercise room; Jacuzzi; indoor pool. *In room:* A/C, TV, fridge, hair dryer, free Wi-Fi.

Where to Eat

IN ROSEBURG

For espresso, breakfast, or lunch, check out **Brix 527,** 527 SE Jackson St. (✆ **541/440-4901**), in downtown Roseburg.

Dino's Ristorante Italiano ★ ITALIAN   Ask anyone in Roseburg where to get the best meal in town, and they'll invariably send you to Dino's, a little Italian restaurant in downtown Roseburg. This is a good place for a romantic dinner or simply to satisfy your Italian-food cravings with the likes of gnocchi with Gorgonzola cream sauce, linguine with clams, or lasagna Bolognese.

404 SE Jackson St. ✆ **541/673-0848.** www.dinosristorante.com. Reservations recommended. Main courses $13–$20. AE, DISC, MC, V. Tues–Thurs 5–9pm; Fri–Sat 5–9:30pm.

Roseburg Station Pub & Brewery ★ PUB   Another jewel in the McMenamins brewpub crown, the Roseburg Station Pub is a good example of the way McMenamins breathes new life into historic buildings. This restored train station celebrates Roseburg's rail culture and is a casual place for dinner and a microbrew. An eclectic collection of chandeliers decorates the 16-foot ceiling, and street signs from around the world hang all around the dining room. A straightforward menu features burgers, sandwiches, and a handful of more creative entrees. Be sure to accompany your meal with one of the craft ales for which the McMenamins pubs are famous.

700 SE Sheridan St. ℂ **541/672-1934.** www.mcmenamins.com. Main courses $7.75–$18. AE, DISC, MC, V. Mon–Thurs 11am–11pm; Fri–Sat 11am–midnight; Sun noon–10pm.

IN OAKLAND

Tolly's Restaurant & Soda Fountain ★ ☺SODA FOUNTAIN/REGIONAL
AMERICAN   Housed in a historic storefront in downtown Oakland, Tolly's has a timeless feel that conjures images of *Saturday Evening Post* magazine covers. Since 1964, folks from all over the region have been stopping at Tolly's in downtown Oakland for ice-cream sundaes, root-beer floats, and other classic fountain dinks and treats. Drop by if you're passing through the area. Order a burger and a cold malted milkshake in a tall glass, and you'll quickly forget that it's the 21st century.

115 Locust St. ℂ **541/459-3796.** www.tollys-restaurant.com. Reservations recommended. Main courses $4–$15. AE, DISC, MC, V. Daily 11am–3pm.

NORTH OF ROSEBURG: A SERIOUS ICE-CREAM STOP

Consider yourself very lucky if you happen to be driving north from Roseburg on I-5 on a hot summer day. Respite from the heat lies just off the interstate in the town of Rice Hill (exit 148), at legendary **K&R Drive Inn** (ℂ **541/849-2570;** www.krdrive inn.com), where every scoop of ice cream you order is actually a double scoop. Remember this before you order two scoops of Rocky Road. In summer, the K&R is open Monday through Wednesday from 10am to 8pm and Thursday through Sunday from 10am to 9pm; spring and fall, it's open daily from 10:30am to 8pm; and in winter, it's open daily from 11am to 7pm.

CENTRAL OREGON

O n the west side of the Cascade Range, rain is as certain as death and taxes. But cross the dividing line formed by the mountains, and you leave the deluge behind and enter the region known as Central Oregon. The term "Central Oregon" is a bit of a misnomer. It does not so much refer to a geographical area as to a recreational region, and it doesn't actually lie in the central part of the state. It does, however, bask under blue skies nearly 300 days of the year—in fact, Central Oregon gets so little rain that parts of the region are considered high desert. Such a natural attraction is a constant enticement for Oregonians living west of the Cascades. In summer people head to Central Oregon for golfing, hiking, fishing, mountain biking, rafting, and camping, and in winter they descend on the ski slopes of Mount Bachelor, Oregon's best ski resort.

10

All this popularity is due to the Cascade Range, which causes a climatological rain-shadow effect that creates a distinct and visible dividing line between the wet west side and the dry east side. Ponderosa pines, rather than Douglas firs and Western red cedars, dominate the eastern foothill forests of this region. Farther east, where there is even less annual rainfall, juniper and sagebrush country takes over. It is this classically Western environment that has in part led to the adoption of a Wild West theme in the town of Sisters, which has covered wooden sidewalks and false-fronted buildings (albeit in modern pastel colors).

On closer inspection, however, it becomes evident that it is more than just a lack of rainfall that sets this region apart. Central Oregon's unique volcanic geography provides the scenic backdrop to the region's many recreational activities. Obsidian flows, lava caves, cinder cones, pumice deserts—these are the sorts of features that make the Central Oregon landscape unique.

Despite the region's volcanic legacy, the greens and fairways of the region's many golf courses are what come to mind when many people think of Central Oregon. The abundant sunshine here has made this area home to most of the state's golf resorts. Between Kah-Nee-Ta in the north and Sunriver in the south, there are half a dozen major golf resorts and dozens of golf courses.

Despite the dryness of the landscape here, water is one of the region's primary recreational draws. The Deschutes River is the state's most popular rafting river and is fabled among fly anglers for its steelhead runs and its wild red-side rainbow trout. West of Bend, a scenic highway loops past a dozen or so lakes, each with its own unique character and appeal. Closer to Bend, the Deschutes River cascades over ancient lava flows, forming impressive waterfalls that are favorite destinations of area hikers.

However, for solitude and scenic grandeur, most hikers and backpackers head out from Sisters and Bend into the Three Sisters Wilderness, which encompasses its snow-clad namesake peaks. Outside the wilderness, many miles of trails have made the Bend and Sisters areas the best mountain-biking destinations in the state.

Although the open slopes of Mount Bachelor ski area attract the most visitors in the winter, the area also has many miles of cross-country ski trails, including the state's finest Nordic center (at Mount Bachelor, of course). Snowmobiling is also very popular.

NORTH CENTRAL OREGON

Maupin: 95 miles N of Bend, 100 miles E of Portland, 40 miles S of The Dalles

Dominated by two rivers—the Deschutes and the John Day—north Central Oregon is the driest, most desertlike part of this region. It is also the closest sunny-side destination for rain-soaked Portlanders, which has long made it a popular spot for weekend getaways.

Hot springs, canyon lands, and some of the best rafting and fishing in the state are the main draws in this part of Central Oregon. For many visitors, the high-desert landscape is a fascinating change from the lushness of the west side of the Cascades. For others it is just too bleak and barren. But there is no denying that the Deschutes River, which flows through this high desert, is one of the busiest rivers in the state. Rafters and anglers descend en masse throughout the year—especially in summer—to challenge the rapids and the red-side trout.

Even if the Deschutes is not your primary destination, this region has several unusual attractions that make it worthwhile for a weekend's exploration. First and foremost of these is Kah-Nee-Ta Resort, which, with its warm-spring swimming pool and its proximity to Portland, is a powerful enticement after several months of gray skies and constant drizzle west of the Cascades.

Not far from the resort, in the town of Warm Springs, is a fascinating museum dedicated to the cultures of Northwest Native Americans. A forgotten page of pioneer days can be found at nearby Shaniko, a ghost town that once made it big as a wool-shipping town. Much older history, up to 40 million years of it, is laid bare in the three units of the John Day Fossil Beds National Monument. If the stark hills of the national monument don't give you enough sense of being in the desert, be sure to visit The Cove Palisades State Park, where three steep-walled canyons have been flooded by the waters of Lake Billy Chinook.

Essentials

GETTING THERE Maupin, which is the staging site for most rafting and fishing trips on the lower Deschutes River, is at the junction of U.S. 197, the main route from The Dalles south to Bend, and Ore. 216, which connects to U.S. 26 east of Mount Hood.

VISITOR INFORMATION For more information on this area, contact the **Maupin Area Chamber of Commerce,** P.O. Box 220, Maupin, OR 97037 (© **541/993-1708;** www.maupinoregon.com).

Rafting, Fishing & Other Aquatic Activities

Flowing through a dry sagebrush canyon lined with basalt cliffs, the lower Deschutes River, from the U.S. 26 bridge outside Warm Springs down to the Columbia River, is one of the most popular stretches of white water in Oregon. This section of the river provides lots of Class III rapids, and 1-day rafting trips here are very popular. However, at almost 100 miles in length, the lower Deschutes also provides several options for multiday rafting trips.

Popular 1-day splash-and-giggle trips, which are offered by dozens of rafting companies, usually start just upstream from Maupin and end just above the impressive Sherar's Falls. Some companies also offer 2- and 3-day trips. Rafting companies operating on the lower Deschutes River include **All Star Rafting** (✆ 800/909-7238; www.asrk.com), which also rents rafts and offers kayaking lessons; **Imperial River Co.** (✆ 800/395-3903 or 541/395-2404; www.deschutesriver.com), which operates a bed-and-breakfast inn for rafters in Maupin; and **Rapid River Rafters** (✆ 800/962-3327 or 541/382-1514; www.rapidriverrafters.com). Expect to pay around $75 to $95 for a day trip and around $345 to $445 for a 3-day trip.

If you're just passing through the region but would like to catch a glimpse of some of the lower Deschutes River's more dramatic sections, you can visit **Sherar's Falls,** which are at the Sherar Bridge on Ore. 216, between Tygh Valley and Grass Valley. Native Americans can sometimes be seen dipnetting salmon from the waters of these falls, which can also be reached by following the river road north from Maupin for 8 miles. Just west of Sherar Bridge, you'll also find **White River Falls State Park** (✆ 800/551-6949; www.oregon.gov/oprd/parks), where there are more waterfalls.

Twelve miles south of Madras, you'll find one of the most unexpected and unlikely settings in the state. **Lake Billy Chinook,** a reservoir created by the construction of Round Butte Dam in 1964, fills the canyons of the Metolius, Crooked, and Deschutes rivers, and seems lifted straight out of the canyon lands of Arizona or Utah. Here nearly vertical basalt cliffs rise several hundred feet above the lake waters, and sagebrush and junipers cling to the rocky hillsides. The lake is most popular with water-skiers and anglers who come to fish for kokanee (landlocked sockeye salmon) and bull trout (also known as Dolly Vardens). **The Cove Palisades State Park** (✆ 541/546-3412; www.oregon.gov/oprd/parks) provides access to the lake's south shore. On summer Sundays, the park offers easy 2½-hour sea-kayak tours. Reservations are recommended. Here at the state park, you'll also find boat ramps, a marina, campgrounds, picnic areas, and swimming beaches. There are even houseboats for rent (see "Where to Stay & Eat," below), and at the marina you'll find a restaurant atop a hill overlooking the lake. The park day-use fee is $5.

A Native American Heritage Museum

The Museum at Warm Springs ★★ 🏛 For thousands of years, the Warm Springs, Wasco, and Paiute tribes have inhabited this region and adapted to its environment. At this fascinating, not-to-be-missed museum, you'll learn the history of these peoples. Designed to resemble a traditional encampment and accented by architectural details drawn from the cultures of the three tribes, the museum houses an outstanding collection of regional Native American artifacts. Various styles of traditional houses have been reconstructed at the museum and serve as backdrops for displays on everything from basketry and beadwork to fishing and root gathering. Temporary exhibits fill out the main collection and focus on specific topics.

2189 U.S. 26, Warm Springs. ☏ **541/553-3331.** www.museumatwarmsprings.org. Admission $7 adults, $6 seniors, $4.50 students, $3.50 children 5–12. Early Apr to Oct daily 9am–5pm; Nov to early Apr Tues–Sun 9am–5pm. Closed New Year's Day, Thanksgiving, and Christmas.

A Ghost Town & a Fossil Excursion

Between 1900 and 1911, the Central Oregon town of Shaniko was the largest wool-shipping center in the country, and it claims to have been the site of the last range war between cattle ranchers and sheepherders. However, when the railroad line from the Columbia River down to Bend bypassed Shaniko, the town fell on hard times. Eventually, when a flood washed out the railroad spur into town, Shaniko nearly ceased to exist. Today the false-fronted buildings and wooden sidewalks make this Oregon's favorite and liveliest ghost town. Antiques shops and a historic hotel make for a fun excursion or overnight getaway.

The **John Day Fossil Beds National Monument,** 32651 Ore. 19, Kimberly, OR 97848 (☏ **541/987-2333;** www.nps.gov/joda), consisting of three individual units separated by as much as 85 miles, preserves a 40-million-year fossil record indicating that this region was once a tropical or subtropical forest. From tiny seeds to extinct relatives of rhinoceroses and elephants, an amazing array of plants and animals has been preserved in one of the world's most extensive and unbroken fossil records.

To see fossil leaves, twigs, branches, and nuts in their natural state, visit the **Clarno Unit** (☏ **541/763-2203**), 23 miles southeast of Shaniko and U.S. 97. Here ancient mudflows inundated a forest, and today these ancient mudflows appear as eroding cliffs. At the base of these cliffs, a .25-mile trail leads past numerous fossils. From the Clarno Unit, it is an 85-mile drive on Ore. 218 and Ore. 19 to the national monument's **Sheep Rock Unit,** which is the site of the monument's **Thomas Condon Paleontology Center** and the **James Cant Ranch House** historical museum. Here you can get a close-up look at numerous fossils and sometimes watch a paleontologist at work. The paleontology center is open daily from 9am to 5pm (closed holidays Thanksgiving to Presidents' Day). The James Cant Ranch House museum is open daily from 9am to 5pm in summer and Monday through Friday from 10am to 4pm in winter. Just north of the visitor center you'll pass **Blue Basin,** where there's an interpretive trail.

From the Sheep Rock Unit, the monument's **Painted Hills Unit** (☏ **541/987-2333, ext. 1240**), along the John Day River 9 miles northwest of Mitchell, is another 30 miles west on U.S. 26. You won't see any fossils here, but you will see strikingly colored rounded hills that are favorites of photographers. The weathering of volcanic ash under different climatic conditions created the bands of color on these hills.

Although you can't collect fossils in the national monument, you can dig them up behind Wheeler High School in the small town of **Fossil,** 20 miles east of the monument's Clarno Unit. If you want to turn a visit to the John Day Fossil Beds into a learning vacation, check out the classes, workshops, field trips, and multiday adventure trips of the **Oregon Paleo Lands Institute,** 333 W. Fourth St., Fossil (☏ **541/763-4480;** www.paleolands.org). The institute's Field Center also has museum exhibits on geology and paleontology. Call for hours. Eleven miles north of Madras, off U.S. 97, you can also dig thundereggs (baseball-like rock spheres similar to geodes) at **Richardson's Rock Ranch,** 6683 NE Haycreek Road, Madras (☏ **541/475-2680;** www.richardsonrockranch.com). They charge by the pound and will cut your thundereggs for you.

Where to Stay & Eat

In addition to the accommodations listed below, you'll find three modern log cabins for rent on the shore of Lake Billy Chinook at The Cove Palisades State Park. These cabins rent for $80 per night for up to five people ($59 Oct–Apr) and are right beside the water. For reservations, contact **ReserveAmerica** (𝄞 **800/452-5687**; www.reserveamerica.com). Houseboats are also available for rent at Lake Billy Chinook. Contact **Cove Palisades Resort & Marina,** 5700 SW Marina Dr., Culver (𝄞 **877/546-7171** or 541/546-9999; www.covepalisadesresort.com), for houseboats from $1,875 to $6,075 per week in summer (lower rates in spring and fall), or **Lake Billy Chinook Houseboats,** P.O. Box 1921, Redmond, OR 97756 (𝄞 **866/546-2939** or 541/504-5951; www.lakebillychinook.com), for rates from $1,975 to $2,725 per week.

Hotel Condon Although the town of Condon is way off the beaten path, it is fairly convenient if you have spent the day visiting different units of the John Day Fossil Beds National Monument. This restored historic hotel in downtown Condon has a classic small-town feel, but guest rooms have modern furnishings and good beds.

202 S. Main St., Condon, OR 97823. www.hotelcondon.com. 𝄞 **800/201-6706** or 541/384-4624. 18 units. $100 double; $145–$199 suite. Rates include continental breakfast and evening beer-and-wine reception. Children 12 and under stay free in parent's room. AE, DISC, MC, V. *In room:* A/C, TV, hair dryer, free Wi-Fi.

Imperial River Company 🛉 Popular primarily with people heading out rafting on the Deschutes River, this lodge may not be your classic B&B, but it is the most comfortable place for many miles around. Guest rooms, all of which have private entrances, are decorated in Oregon themes and have handmade quilts on the beds. The riverview rooms are the best and have whirlpool tubs. Dinner is available, and meals feature local beef and lamb. Imperial River Company also offers a rafting trips.

304 Bakeoven Rd., Maupin, OR 97037. www.deschutesriver.com. 𝄞 **800/395-3903** or 541/395-2404. 25 units. Late Apr to Oct $89–$169 double, $229–$279 suite; Nov to late Apr $59–$89 double, $149 suite. Rates include continental breakfast. Children 12 and under stay free in parent's room. AE, DISC, MC, V. Pets accepted ($15/night). **Amenities:** Restaurant; lounge. *In room:* A/C, fridge, free Wi-Fi.

Kah-Nee-Ta High Desert Resort & Casino ★★ ☺ Located 120 miles from Portland in a remote canyon, Kah-Nee-Ta Resort, operated by the Confederated Tribes of the Warm Springs Reservation, is the closest sunny-side resort to Portland. The main attractions here are the casino and the huge warm springs–fed swimming pool. Because Kah-Nee-Ta offers a wide range of accommodations and activities (including kayak trips and horseback riding), it is popular with families, who tend to stay in the resort's large mountain lodge–style "Village" rooms beside the main pool. Couples should opt for rooms in the main lodge, which is high on a hillside adjacent to the resort's casino. By the main pool, you'll also find teepees for rent. Salmon bakes and Native American dance performances are often scheduled.

P.O. Box 1240, Warm Springs, OR 97761. www.kahneeta.com. 𝄞 **800/554-4786** or 541/553-1112. 170 units, plus 20 teepees. $89–$166 double; $179–$335 suite or cottage; $75 teepee (for 3 people). Children 13 and under stay free in parent's room. AE, DC, DISC, MC, V. Pets accepted ($15 per night). **Amenities:** 2 restaurants; lounge; bikes; children's programs; exercise room; 18-hole golf course and miniature golf; 3 Jacuzzis; 2 outdoor pools; spa; 2 tennis courts. *In room:* A/C, TV/DVD, CD player, fridge, hair dryer, free Wi-Fi.

Service Creek Stage Stop 🛎 This rustic lodge with simply furnished little rooms is the most centrally located accommodations for anyone exploring all the units of the John Day Fossil Beds National Monument. The lodge is also on the John Day River and rents rafts and operates river shuttles, so when you aren't marveling at geology, you can float the river. There's also a convenience store here that sells fishing supplies, and the lodge owners can put you in touch with local fishing guides.

38686 Ore. 19, Fossil, OR 97830. www.servicecreekresort.com. © **541/468-3331.** 6 units. $85–$95 double. Rates include full breakfast Apr to mid-Sept. AE, DISC, MC, V. **Amenities:** Restaurant; watersports equipment rentals. *In room:* A/C, no phone, free Wi-Fi.

CAMPGROUNDS

Downriver from Sherar's Falls, there are many undeveloped campsites along the Deschutes River. At Lake Billy Chinook, west of U.S. 97 between Madras and Redmond, are several campgrounds. The most developed are the two at The Cove Palisades State Park. Reservations can be made through ReserveAmerica (© **800/452-5687;** www.reserveamerica.com). Farther west, up the Metolius arm of the reservoir on Forest Service Road 64, you'll find the Forest Service's primitive Perry South Campground. A little bit farther west is the Monty Campground, which is the lowermost campground on the Metolius River's free-flowing waters.

THE SISTERS AREA

108 miles SE of Salem, 92 miles NE of Eugene, 21 miles NW of Bend

Lying at the eastern foot of the Cascades, the small town of Sisters takes its name from the nearby Three Sisters mountains, which loom majestically over the town. Ponderosa pine forests, aspen groves, and wide meadows and pastures surround Sisters, giving it a classic Western setting that the town has taken to heart. Today Sisters is designed to resemble an old cow town, and the modern buildings sport false fronts and old-timey covered sidewalks. However, the predominantly pastel color schemes are more 1990s than 1890s and make the town feel as though the school marms took control away from the cowboys.

Once just a place to stop for gas on the way to Bend, Sisters has now become a destination in itself. A few miles outside of town is the Black Butte Ranch resort, one of the state's top golf resorts, and also nearby is the tiny community of Camp Sherman, which has been a vacation destination for more than a century. Sisters is also Oregon's llama capital, with numerous large llama ranches around the area.

Essentials

GETTING THERE Sisters is at the junction of U.S. 20 (which connects I-5 near Corvallis with Bend), Ore. 126 (which links Redmond with Eugene), and Ore. 242 (the McKenzie Pass scenic highway). From the Portland area, take I-5 S. to Salem and then take Ore. 22 E. Allegiant Air, Alaska/Horizon Air, and SkyWest Airlines (United Express and Delta Airlines) serve **Roberts Field/Redmond Municipal Airport,** 2522 SE Jesse Butler Circle (© **541/548-0646,** ext. 3499; www.flyrdm. com), 20 miles east of Sisters.

VISITOR INFORMATION Contact the **Sisters Area Chamber of Commerce,** 291 E. Main St. (P.O. Box 430), Sisters, OR 97759 (© **866/549-0252** or 541/549-0251; www.sisterscountry.com).

FESTIVALS During the annual **Sisters Outdoor Quilt Show** (www.sisters outdoorquiltshow.org) on the second Saturday in July, buildings all over town are hung with quilts. The **Sisters Rodeo** (℃ **800/827-7522** or 541/549-0121; www. sistersrodeo.com), held the second weekend of June, also attracts large crowds. In early September, the weekend after Labor Day, American music, from blues to bluegrass, is celebrated during the **Sisters Folk Festival** (℃ **541/549-4979**; www. sistersfolkfestival.com).

Enjoying the Outdoors

Although shopping may be the number-one recreational activity right in Sisters, the surrounding lands are the town's real main attraction. Any month of the year, you'll find an amazing variety of possible activities within a few miles of town. Northwest of Sisters, in the community of Camp Sherman, is one of the area's most unusual outdoor attractions—the springs that form the headwaters of the Metolius River. Cold, crystal-clear waters bubble up out of the ground and, within only a few hundred yards, produce a respectable river. Follow signs from the Camp Sherman turnoff on U.S. 20.

GOLFING With its red-cinder sand traps, **Aspen Lakes Golf Course,** 16900 Aspen Lakes Dr. (℃ **541/549-4653**; www.aspenlakes.com), is the area's most distinctive golf course (green fees $49–$75 in summer). At **Black Butte Ranch** (℃ **866/901-2961** or 541/595-1500; www.blackbutteranch.com), west of Sisters, you'll find two courses surrounded by ponderosa pines and aspens (green fees $53–$73 in summer). The Glaze Meadow course has been completely renovated for 2012. At **Eagle Crest,** 1522 Cline Falls Rd., Redmond (℃ **866/583-5212**; www.eagle-crest.com), east of Sisters, you get a more desertlike experience with junipers and sagebrush surrounding the fairways (green fees $44–$69 in summer). There are great views at both resorts.

HIKING West and south of Sisters, several excellent scenic trails lend themselves to both day hikes and overnight trips. Many of these trails lead into the Mount Washington, Mount Jefferson, and Three Sisters wilderness areas. Near Camp Sherman, you can hike to the summit of Black Butte for 360-degree views or hike along the spring-fed Metolius River (try starting at the beautiful blue section of river beside the Wizard Falls Fish Hatchery). Farther west off U.S. 20, you'll find trails leading up to the base of craggy Three Fingered Jack. South of town, trails head into the Three Sisters Wilderness (the Chambers Lakes area is particularly scenic). The hike up Tam McArthur Rim is another good one for spectacular views. Stop by the **Sisters Ranger District,** Pine Street and U.S. 20 (℃ **541/549-7700**; www.fs.fed.us/r6/centraloregon), at the west end of town, for information and maps.

To the east of Sisters outside the town of Terrebonne, several miles of very scenic hiking trails wind through **Smith Rock State Park** (℃ **800/551-6649** or 541/548-7501; www.oregon.gov/oprd/parks), a park known primarily for its superb rock climbing. The park's 400-foot crags and the meandering Crooked River provide the backdrops for hikes through high desert scrublands. Hiking trails lead through the canyon and up to the top of the rocks. The view of the Cascades framed by Smith Rock is superb. There is a $5 day-use fee here.

HORSEBACK RIDING If Sisters has put you in a cowboy or cowgirl state of mind, you can saddle up a palomino and go for a ride at **Black Butte Stables,** 13892 Bishop's Cap Rd., Black Butte Ranch (℃ **541/595-2061**; www.blackbuttestables.com), which has stables at Black Butte Ranch west of Sisters. These stables offer a variety of rides, with an hour ride costing $43.

MOUNTAIN BIKING   Sisters makes an excellent base for mountain bikers, who will find dozens of miles of trails of all skill levels within a few miles of town. In fact, one fun, easy ride, the Peterson Ridge Trail, starts on Elm Street only a few blocks south of downtown's many shops. Other fun rides include the Butte Loops Trail around Black Butte and the strenuous Green Ridge Trail. Stop by the Sisters Ranger District, Pine Street and U.S. 20 (✆ **541/549-7700**), at the west end of town, for information and trail maps. You can rent bikes in town at **Eurosports,** 182 E. Hood Ave. (✆ **541/549-2471;** www.eurosports.us), for $20 to $40 per day.

ROCK CLIMBING   Located east of Terrebonne, Smith Rock State Park is one of Central Oregon's many geological wonders. Jagged rock formations tower above the Crooked River here and attract rock climbers from around the world. A couple of shops in the area cater primarily to climbers. If you want to learn how to climb, contact First Ascent Climbing Services (✆ **800/325-5462** or 541/318-7170; www.goclimbing.com), which offers classes ($250 for an all-day private class).

Other Area Attractions

Fans of folk art should be sure to stop by the **Petersen Rock Gardens & Museum,** 7930 SW 77th St., Redmond (✆ **541/382-5574**), 9 miles north of Bend just off U.S. 97. This 4-acre folk-art creation consists of buildings, miniature bridges, terraces, and tiny towers all constructed from rocks. The gardens, built between 1935 and 1952 by a Danish immigrant farmer, are open daily from 9am to 5pm (call to confirm hours in winter). Admission is $4.50 for adults, $3 for seniors, $2 for children 12 to 16, and $1 for children 6 to 11.

   If, after a hard day of playing in the outdoors, you need a massage (or a facial or detox wrap), make a reservation at **Shibui,** 720 Buckaroo Trail (✆ **541/549-6164;** www.shibuispa.com), a beautiful Asian-inspired day spa affiliated with the luxurious FivePine Lodge (see below).

Where to Stay

Black Butte Ranch ★ ☺   Located 8 miles west of Sisters, the Black Butte Ranch resort community is set amid aspen-ringed meadows and has the most breathtaking mountain views of any central Oregon resort. Add a pair of golf courses (one of which was remodeled in 2011), 18 miles of paved biking/jogging paths, and lots of recreational activities, and you have a great family vacation resort. However, because this is a condominium development, rooms and vacation homes here are very hit or miss. The accommodations are set amid open lawns between the forest and the meadows, and most have fireplaces and kitchens. In the majority of rooms, large decks and sliding glass doors let you enjoy the views. In the resort's main dining room, which serves good steaks, large windows provide nearly every table with a view of the mountains or adjacent lake.

P.O. Box 8000, Black Butte Ranch, OR 97759. www.blackbutteranch.com. ✆ **866/901-2961** or 541/595-1252. 124 units. May–Oct $110–$235 condo, $200–$250 cabin, $175–$390 home; Nov–Apr $85–$190 condo, $150–$200 cabin, $150–$295 home. Seasonal minimum-night requirements. AE, DISC, MC, V. Pets accepted ($60 fee). **Amenities:** 2 restaurants; 2 lounges; bikes; children's programs; exercise room; 2 18-hole golf courses; Jacuzzi; 4 outdoor pools and 1 indoor pool; full-service spa; 20 tennis courts; watersports equipment rentals; free Wi-Fi. *In room:* A/C, TV/VCR/DVD, CD player, kitchen, free Wi-Fi (some rooms).

FivePine Lodge & Conference Center ★★   Set beneath shady ponderosa pines on 15 acres on the edge of Sisters, this collection of Craftsman-style, eco-friendly cabins is a modern classic. The main building, with its stone walls, grand fireplace, and mission-style furnishings, is the quintessential mountain lodge, while the large cabins offer space, luxury, and more Arts and Crafts styling. In all the cabins and lodge rooms, you'll find fireplaces and huge bathrooms with big soaking tubs and tiled showers. Patios and balconies, with their Adirondack chairs, are the perfect place to linger over a glass of wine at the end of a summer day. On the pretty grounds, through which winds a man-made stream, you'll find an outdoor pool, spa, health club, movie theater, fine-dining restaurant, and a brewpub.

1021 Desperado Trail, Sisters, OR 97759. www.fivepinelodge.com. 🕐 **866/974-5900** or 541/549-5900. Fax 541/549-5200. 32 units. June–Sept $189–$219 suite or cabin; Oct–May $149–$189 suite or cabin. Rates include continental breakfast and nightly wine reception. Children 17 and under stay free in parent's room. AE, DISC, MC, V. Pets accepted ($25 per night). **Amenities:** 2 restaurants; 2 lounges; babysitting; bikes; concierge; health club w/indoor pool; outdoor pool; spa. *In room:* A/C, TV/DVD, fridge, hair dryer, free Wi-Fi.

Lake Creek Lodge ★★ 👪   This rustic cabin resort not far from the Metolius River is utterly timeless. Stay here once and you'll likely want to spend all future family vacations here. Set on 45 acres of ponderosa pine forest and neatly manicured lawns along the banks of crystal-clear Lake Creek, this lodge has both 1930s vintage cabins and retro-feeling modern cabins. While the newer and larger modern cabins (ideal for families) are my favorites here, the older cabins, with their knotty-pine paneling, have all been remodeled and upgraded. These older cabins are not luxurious, but they are very comfortable and have full kitchens. With a pool, tennis courts, horseshoe pits, a basketball court, and billiards and Ping-Pong tables, this place feels a lot like a summer camp.

13375 SW Forest Service Rd. 1419, Camp Sherman, OR 97730. www.lakecreeklodge.com. 🕐 **800/797-6331** or 541/516-3030. Fax 541/516-3029. 19 units. Late May to Sept $145–$310 double; Oct to late May $99–$250 double. 3-night minimum in summer. Children 3 and under stay free in parent's room. MC, V. Pets accepted ($15 per day). **Amenities:** Restaurant (summer only); seasonal outdoor pool; 2 tennis courts; free Wi-Fi. *In room:* Kitchen, free Wi-Fi (in some cabins).

The Lodge at Suttle Lake ★   Set on the shores of Suttle Lake, just east of Santiam Pass, this mountain lodge sports a classic Adirondack decor. Throw in an ornately carved front door and some very detailed chain-saw art in the lodge lobby, and you have the quintessential Cascadian mountain lodge. In the main lodge, the large lakeview rooms are the ones to ask for, or, for even more space, go for a cabin with a loft sleeping area and complete kitchen. While some of the cabins go a bit overboard with the cutesy cabin decor, these are still immensely comfortable accommodations, the best you'll find at any lakeside setting in the state.

13300 U.S. 20, Sisters, OR 97759. www.thelodgeatsuttlelake.com. 🕐 **541/595-2628.** Fax 541/595-2267. 24 units. $59 rustic cabin; $149–$269 double; $159–$399 cabin. Rates include continental breakfast (except in cabins). 2-night minimum in summer; 3-night minimum on holidays. AE, DISC, MC, V. Pets accepted ($20 per night). No children 14 and under in lodge. **Amenities:** Restaurant (p. 314); lounge; spa; watersports equipment rentals. *In room:* TV (DVD in lodge rooms and 1 cabin), hair dryer (lodge rooms), kitchen (some cabins), free Wi-Fi (lodge rooms and some cabins).

Metolius River Resort ★   Despite the name, this hardly ranks as a resort. However, it's perfect for those seeking peace and quiet or a romantic getaway. Set on the banks of the crystal-clear, spring-fed Metolius River 14 miles west of Sisters, the contemporary, cedar-shingled two-story cabins are exceptional, offering modern amenities and styling with a bit of a rustic feel. Peeled-log beds, wood paneling, river-stone fire-places, and green roofs give the cabins a quintessentially Western appeal. The Metolius River is legendary as the most difficult trout-fishing stream in Oregon, and the cabins here are particularly popular with trout anglers. Not far away, you'll find the springs of the Metolius, where the river comes welling up out of the ground.

25551 SW Forest Service Rd. 1419, Camp Sherman, OR 97730. www.metoliusriverresort.com. © **800/81-TROUT** (818-7688). 11 cabins. $235 double. 2- to 3-night minimum. MC, V. **Amenities:** Restaurant. *In room:* TV/DVD, hair dryer, kitchen, free Wi-Fi.

Where to Eat

No visit to Sisters is complete without a stop at the **Sisters Bakery,** 251 E. Cascade St. (© **541/549-0361**), for marionberry pastries and bear claws. On a hot day, you can't leave town without stopping at the **Sno Cap,** 380 W. Cascade St. (© **541/549-6151**), an old-fashioned drive-in, for some ice cream or one of the legendary marion-berry milk shakes. Good sandwiches, salads, and baked goodies (including gluten-free treats) can be had at **Angeline's Bakery,** 121 W. Main St. (© **541/549-9122;** www.angelinesbakery.com). For local microbrews, head to **Three Creeks Brewing Co.,** 721 Desperado Court (© **541/549-1963;** www.threecreeksbrewing.com), which is adjacent to the FivePine Lodge. For light meals or just a glass of wine, stop by **Cork Cellars,** 161A N. Elm St. (© **541/549-2675;** www.corkcellars.com), a combination wine bar/wine shop. For meals with a view of the mountain, you can't beat the Lodge Restaurant at Black Butte Ranch (see above).

The Boathouse Restaurant AMERICAN   As this restaurant's name implies, it is located right on the water, with views across Suttle Lake to the forested hills of the Cascades. In summer, the deck here is so delightful, you'll want to linger as long as possible over your meal or one of the restaurant's excellent lemon-drop cocktails. The menu is pretty straightforward. You can build your own burger (adding ancho-chili ranch dressing, goat cheese, wild mushrooms, or any of almost 20 toppings). For something a little out of the ordinary, try the crayfish cakes (made with crayfish from Suttle Lake) or the lake trout fish and chips. Although this place is a bit of a drive out from Sisters, it's worth it for the beautiful setting.

At The Lodge at Suttle Lake, 13300 U.S. 20. © **541/595-2628.** www.thelodgeatsuttlelake.com. Reservations recommended for dinner. Main courses $9–$22. AE, DISC, MC, V. Daily 8:30 or 9am–8 or 9pm.

Jen's Garden ★★★ NORTHWEST   This is the best restaurant in Central Oregon and should not be missed if you are staying in Sisters or Bend. I recommend opting for the prix-fixe menu with wine pairings so you can sample whatever the chef is highlighting the evening you visit. Every course is likely to have some sort of delightful flavor surprise, and every wine will be distinctive. Flavors in such dishes as parmesan-curry–crusted escargot with chickpea-crusted vegetables and sweet-corn puree, Champagne-cardamom-melon soup, and marionberry-barbecue sauce–glazed quail stuffed with juniper-scented duck confit are both complex and subtle. While the dining room is wonderfully romantic, I love the back patio.

403 E. Hood Ave., Sisters. © **541/549-2699.** www.intimatecottagecuisine.com. Reservations recommended. Main courses $26; 3-course fixed-price dinner $39, 5-course fixed-price dinner $52. AE, MC, V. Memorial Day to mid-Sept daily 5–8 or 9pm; mid-Sept to Memorial Day Wed–Sun 5–8 or 9pm.

Kokanee Cafe ★★ 🔥 NORTHWEST   This out-of-the-way place, located about 14 miles west of Sisters and adjacent to the Metolius River Resort (see above) in

Camp Sherman, is one of the best restaurants in the region. The interior of the cedar-shingled building is contemporary rustic with an open-beamed ceiling and a wrought-iron chandelier, and out back there's a deck under the ponderosa pines. The menu is short and almost always includes some sort of fresh rainbow trout entree, as well as such interesting dishes as duck breast with mushroom risotto or lamb shanks braised with chamomile and apricots. There are also daily specials, often seafood prepared in whatever style is currently the rage. Lots of reasonably priced wines are available by the bottle or glass, with the emphasis on Oregon wines.

25551 SW Forest Service Rd. 1419, Camp Sherman. (℃ **541/595-6420.** www.kokaneecafe.com. Reservations recommended. Main courses $19–$28. AE, DISC, MC, V. Summer Mon–Fri 5–8 or 9pm, Sat–Sun 11:30am–8 or 9pm; call for hours other months.

BEND & SUNRIVER ★★

160 miles SE of Portland, 241 miles SW of Pendleton

Situated on the banks of the Deschutes River, Bend is the largest city east of the Oregon Cascades, and the surrounding area has more resorts than any other region in the state. To understand why a small city on the edge of a vast high desert could attract so many vacationers, just look to the sky. It's blue. And the sun is shining. For the webfoots who spend months under gray skies west of the Cascades, that's a powerful attractant.

However, Bend doesn't end with sunny skies. It is also home to Mount Bachelor, the biggest and best ski area in the Northwest. The pine-covered slopes of several other mountains—the Three Sisters and Broken Top among them—provide a breathtaking backdrop for the city, and out amid the forests on the flanks of those mountains are trails, trout streams, and lakes that attract hikers, mountain bikers, anglers, and paddlers. A lively downtown filled with interesting shops, art galleries, excellent restaurants, and attractive Drake Park (which is named for the city's founder, A. M. Drake, and not for the ducks that are the park's major attraction) complements the outdoor offerings of the area.

For more than a decade, Bend has been one of the fastest-growing cities in Oregon, and it has attracted lots of well-heeled new residents. Many Oregonians complain that Bend now feels more like a California town than an Oregon community, and, what with the pricey restaurants and fancy furniture stores, it's hard to argue this point. Still, all the new upscale amenities make this a very pleasant town for a vacation.

Essentials

GETTING THERE   Bend is at the junction of U.S. 97, which runs north and south, and U.S. 20, which runs east to west across the state. From the Portland area, the most direct route is by way of U.S. 26 to Madras and then south on U.S. 97.

Allegiant Air, Horizon Air, and SkyWest Airlines (United Express and Delta Airlines) serve **Roberts Field/Redmond Municipal Airport,** 2522 SE Jesse Butler Circle (℃ **541/548-0646,** ext. 3499; www.flyrdm.com), 16 miles north of Bend. The **Central Oregon Breeze** (℃ **800/847-0157** or 541/389-7469; www.cobreeze. com) is a shuttle that operates between Portland and Bend, with a stop at the Redmond Airport. Round-trip tickets between Bend and Portland are $88 for adults and $78 for seniors and students; round-trip tickets between the Redmond airport and Bend are $23 for adults and $20 for seniors and students. There are also **taxis** operating from the Redmond Airport.

SEEING stars

Central Oregon's clear skies not only provide the region with abundant sunshine but also allow the stars to shine brightly at night. At the small **Pine Mountain Observatory** (☎ 541/382-8331; http://pmo-sun.uoregon.edu), 26 miles southeast of Bend off U.S. 20, you can gaze at the stars and planets through 15- to 32-inch telescopes. Admission is a $3 suggested donation, and the observatory is open from late May through late September on Friday and Saturday nights, with programs starting between 8 and 9pm, depending on the month.

In the resort community of Sunriver, south of Bend, the **Sunriver Nature Center & Observatory,** 57245 River Rd. (☎ **541/593-4394;** www.sunrivernaturecenter.org), has stargazing programs, with days and hours varying with the seasons. The observatory can be found by following the Nature Center signs through Sunriver. Admission is $6 for adults and $4 for children. There are also daytime solar-viewing programs here.

VISITOR INFORMATION Contact **Visit Bend,** 917 NW Harriman St., Ste. 101, Bend, OR 97701 (☎ **877/245-8484** or 541/382-8048; www.visitbend.org). You can also contact the **Central Oregon Visitors Association,** 661 SW Powerhouse Dr., Ste. 1301, Bend, OR 97702 (☎ **800/800-8334;** www.visitcentraloregon.com).

FESTIVALS The **Sunriver Music Festival** (☎ **541/593-1084;** www.sunrivermusic.org) is a big classical-music binge that takes place in mid-August. In late August, **Art in the High Desert** (☎ **541/322-6272;** www.artinthehighdesert.com) brings many of the Northwest's top artists to Bend.

Exploring the Bend Area

If you'd like to have a guide show you around the area, contact **Wanderlust Tours** (☎ **800/962-2862** or 541/389-8359; www.wanderlusttours.com), which offers summer canoe trips, winter snowshoe walks, volcano hikes, and even a cave-exploration outing. Most tours cost between $45 to $55 per person.

The High Desert Museum ★★★ ☺ Bend lies on the westernmost edge of the Great Basin, a region that stretches from the Cascade Range to the Rocky Mountains and is often called the high desert. Through the use of historical exhibits, live animal displays, and reconstructions of pioneer buildings, this combination museum and zoo, one of the finest in the Northwest, brings the cultural and natural history of the region into focus. In the main building, there is a walk-through timeline of Western history, as well as a fascinating exhibit on the region's Native American tribes. The natural history of the region comes alive in the Desertarium, where live animals of the region can be observed in a very natural setting. Outside frolicking river otters and slow-moving porcupines are the star attractions, but the birds of prey center is just as interesting. A pioneer homestead and a forestry exhibit with a steam-driven sawmill round out the outdoor exhibits. Informative talks are scheduled throughout the day.

59800 S. U.S. 97. ☎ **541/382-4754.** www.highdesertmuseum.org. Admission May–Oct $15 adults, $12 seniors, $9 children 5–12; Nov–Apr $10 adults, $9 seniors, $6 children 5–12. May–Oct daily 9am–5pm; Nov–Apr daily 10am–4pm. Take U.S. 97 3½ miles south of Bend.

Bend

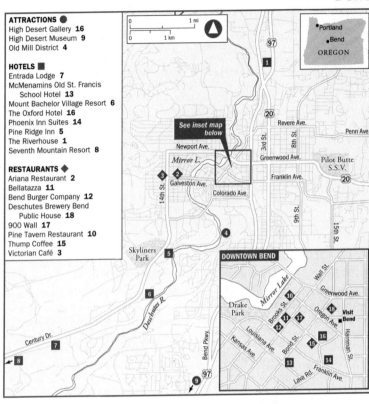

ATTRACTIONS ●
High Desert Gallery **16**
High Desert Museum **9**
Old Mill District **4**

HOTELS ■
Entrada Lodge **7**
McMenamins Old St. Francis
    School Hotel **13**
Mount Bachelor Village Resort **6**
The Oxford Hotel **16**
Phoenix Inn Suites **14**
Pine Ridge Inn **5**
The Riverhouse **1**
Seventh Mountain Resort **8**

RESTAURANTS ◆
Ariana Restaurant **2**
Bellatazza **11**
Bend Burger Company **12**
Deschutes Brewery Bend
    Public House **18**
900 Wall **17**
Pine Tavern Restaurant **10**
Thump Coffee **15**
Victorian Café **3**

Exploring Central Oregon's Volcanic Landscape

From snow-covered peaks to lava caves, past volcanic activity and geologic history are visible everywhere around Bend. For a sweeping panoramic view of the Cascade Range, head up to the top of Pilot Butte at the east end of Greenwood Avenue. From the top of this cinder cone, you can see all of the Cascades' major peaks—from Mount Hood to Mount Bachelor—every one of which is volcanic in origin.

To the south of Bend lies a region of relatively recent volcanic activity that has been preserved as the **Newberry National Volcanic Monument** (☎ **541/593-2421;** www.fs.fed.us/r6/centraloregon/newberrynvm/index.shtml). The best place to start an exploration of the national monument is at the **Lava Lands Visitor Center,** 58201 S. U.S. 97 (☎ **541/593-2421**), 13 miles south of Bend and open from mid-May through mid-October. Here you can learn about the titanic forces that sculpted this region. An interpretive trail outside the center wanders through a lava flow at the base of 500-foot-tall **Lava Butte ★**, an ominous black cinder cone, and a road leads to the top. From the summit of the cinder cone, you have an outstanding view of the

Cascades. A $5 Northwest Forest Pass is necessary to visit Newberry National Volcanic Monument. If you don't already have one, you can purchase one at the visitor center. As you leave the parking lot of the Lava Lands Visitor Center, the side road (Forest Service Rd. 9702) to the right leads to the trail head for the impressive **Benham Falls ★★**, which are an easy .8-mile walk. Be sure to bring mosquito repellant if you visit the falls during the summer.

A mile to the south, you'll find **Lava River Cave**, which is actually a long tube formed by lava flows. The cave is more than a mile long and takes about an hour to explore. A $5 Northwest Forest Pass is necessary to visit the cave; lanterns rent for $4. From early May to June and early September to early October, the cave is open Thursday to Monday from 9am to 5pm, and July to early September daily from 9am to 5pm (no lantern rentals after 4pm). Be sure to bring warm clothes!

When lava flowed across this landscape, it often inundated pine forests, leaving in its wake only molds of the trees. At **Lava Cast Forest,** 9 miles down a very rough road off U.S. 97 south of Lava River Cave, a paved trail leads past such molds. Continuing farther south on U.S. 97 will bring you to the turnoff for the **Newberry Caldera** area, the centerpiece of the monument. Covering 500 square miles, the caldera contains Paulina and East lakes and numerous volcanic features, including an astounding flow of obsidian. There are rental cabins and campgrounds within the national monument, and 150 miles of hiking trails.

10 Hitting the Slopes & Other Winter Sports

If downhill skiing is your passion, you probably already know about the fabulous skiing conditions and myriad runs of **Mount Bachelor ★★★**, 1300 SW Century Dr. (© **800/829-2442** or 541/382-7888 for snow report; www.mtbachelor.com), 22 miles west of Bend on the Cascades Lakes Highway. With more than 3,600 acres of lift-accessed terrain, a 3,365-foot vertical drop, 71 runs, 11 lifts, 4 day lodges, and 8 terrain parks, it's no wonder this place is so popular. All-day lift tickets are $50 to $70 for adults, $40 to $60 for seniors and teenagers 13 to 18, $29 to $43 for children 6 to 12, and free for children 5 and under. There's also a tubing park for families. The ski area's Mount Bachelor Shuttle ($7 each way) operates to and from Bend and leaves from a lot on the west side of town, on Columbia Street between Galveston and Simpson streets.

Cross-country skiers will also find plenty of trails to choose from. Just be sure to stop by a ski shop and buy a **Sno-Park** permit before heading up to the cross-country trails, the best of which are along the Cascades Lakes Highway leading to Mount Bachelor ski area. At the ski area itself, there are 35 miles of groomed trails. Passes to use these trails are $14 to $17 for adults and $9 to $10 for children 6 to 18 years old. Ski shops abound in Bend, and nearly all of them rent both downhill and cross-country equipment. If you're heading to Mount Bachelor, you can rent equipment there, or try the **Powder House,** 311 SW Century Dr. (© **541/389-6234;** www.powderhousebend.com), on the way out of Bend heading toward Mount Bachelor.

If you've had enough skiing, how about a **dogsled ride?** At **Mount Bachelor** (© **800/829-2442** or 541/382-2442), you can participate in 1-hour programs that include a dogsled ride and an orientation on the care of sled dogs. Rates are $75 for adults, $30 for children under 80 pounds. All-day trips to Elk Lake ($450) are also available.

Easy 1-hour free **snowshoe walks** are led by ranger-naturalists on weekends and holidays starting from the **West Village Guest Services Building** at Mount Bachelor. For more information, call ℂ **541/383-4055.**

Summer Activities

If you want to do some mountain hiking without all that uphill slogging, head to **Mount Bachelor** (ℂ **800/829-2442** or 541/382-2442; www.mtbachelor.com), where from July to early September a chair lift operates partway up the mountain to the Pine Marten Lodge. The fare is $16 for adults, $13 for seniors, and $10 for children ages 6 to 12. From here you may either ride the chair or hike down. The lift also operates Thursday through Saturday evenings for access to Scapolo's.

GOLF   For many of Central Oregon's visitors, Bend's abundance of sunshine means only one thing: plenty of rounds of golf at the area's many golf courses. Of the resort courses in the area, the four courses at **Sunriver** (ℂ **541/593-4402**; www.sunriver-resort.com)—Meadows, Woodlands, Crosswater (open to hotel guests and members only), and the 9-hole Caldera Links—are the most highly regarded. Expect to pay anywhere from $49 to $175 for 18 holes.

Right in Bend, you'll find more reasonable prices at the Riverhouse Resort's **River's Edge Golf Course,** 3075 N. Business U.S. 97 (ℂ **541/389-2828;** www.riverhouse.com), where 18 holes will cost you $39 to $59 in the summer. **Widgi Creek Golf Club,** 18707 Century Dr. (ℂ **541/382-4449;** www.widgi.com), is another of the area's highly regarded semiprivate clubs. Green fees range from $35 to $75 in the summer.

HIKING   Hiking is one of the most popular summer activities here, but keep in mind that high-country trails may be closed by snow until late June or early July.

My favorite trail in the Bend area is the **Deschutes River Trail ★★**, which parallels the Deschutes for nearly 9 miles. Any stretch of this trail is beautiful. To reach the trail, drive the Cascades Lakes Highway 6 miles west from Bend, turn left at a sign for the Meadow Picnic Area, and continue 1⅓ miles to the trail head at the picnic area. Another enjoyable, though strenuous, hike is to the summit of **Pilot Butte,** a cinder cone within the Bend city limits. To find the trail head, drive east from downtown on Greenwood Avenue and watch for signs. For a few more recommended hikes, see "A Scenic Drive Along the Cascade Lakes Highway," below.

The **Three Sisters Wilderness,** which begins just more than 20 miles from Bend and Sisters, offers secluded hiking among rugged volcanic peaks. Permits are required for overnight trips in the wilderness area and are available at trail heads. Currently, you'll also need a Northwest Forest Pass (available at the Bend and Sisters ranger stations) to park at area trail heads. Contact the **Bend/Fort Rock Ranger District,** 1230 NE Third St., Ste. A-262, Bend, OR 97701 (ℂ **541/383-4000;** www.fs.fed.us/r6/centraloregon), or the **Sisters Ranger Station,** Pine Street and U.S. 20, Sisters, OR 97759 (ℂ **541/549-7700;** www.fs.fed.us/r6/centraloregon), for trail maps and other information.

HORSEBACK RIDING   Down in Sunriver, you can get saddled up at **Sunriver Stables,** 57215 River Rd. (ℂ **541/593-6995;** www.sunriver-resort.com/stables.php), and ride the meadows and ponderosa pine forests, which offers a variety of rides, with an hour's ride costing $55. Be sure to call for a reservation.

KAYAKING & WHITE-WATER RAFTING   The Deschutes River, which passes through Bend, is the most popular river in Oregon for white-water rafting, although the best sections of river are 100 miles north of here (see "North Central Oregon," earlier in this chapter). However, numerous local companies offer trips on both the lower section of the Deschutes and the stretch of the upper Deschutes between Sunriver and Bend. This latter stretch of the river is known as the Big Eddy run, and though it is short and really has only one major rapid, it offers a quick introduction to rafting. **Sun Country Tours** (© **800/770-2161** or 541/382-6277; www.suncountry tours.com) does both the Big Eddy run ($46) and the lower Deschutes ($103–$108). **Rapid River Rafters,** 500 SW Bond St., Ste. 160 (© **800/962-3327** or 541/382-1514; www.rapidriverrafters.com), also offers full-day trips on the lower Deschutes ($75–$85).

For a much mellower experience, rent a canoe or kayak from **Tumalo Creek Kayak & Canoe,** 805 SW Industrial Way, Ste. 6 (© **541/317-9407;** www.tumalo creek.com), and, if you can load the boat on top of your car, head out on the Cascade Lakes Highway to Sparks or Hosmer lakes. Rental rates start at $40 for 2 hours. Tumalo Creek also offers classes and canoe and kayak tours on the upper Deschutes River ($65 for a half-day tour and $95 for a full-day tour). Sparks Lake and Hosmer Lake are my two favorite paddling spots. You can also do an easy flat-water paddle through the community of Sunriver. At **Sunriver Marina,** 57235 River Rd. (© **541/593-3492**), which is west of Circle 3, you can take a self-guided 2-hour canoe or kayak tour on a beautiful, meandering stretch of the Deschutes River. Tours cost $75. Tumalo Creek also rents stand-up paddleboards, which are all the rage these days. Looking much like huge surfboards, paddleboards are, well, boards that you paddle. Boards rent for $40 for 2 hours or $50 for the day. You can also rent from **StandUp Paddle Bend,** 550 SW Industrial Way, no. 115 (© **541/639-2655;** www.standuppaddleflatwater.com), which charges $15 per hour or $45 per day.

MOUNTAIN BIKING ★★ Mountain biking is one of the most popular activities in Central Oregon, partly because when the snow melts, the cross-country ski trails become mountain-bike trails. Contact the Bend/Fort Rock Ranger District, 1230 NE Third St., Ste. A-262, Bend, OR 97701 (© **541/383-4000;** www.fs.fed.us/r6/ centraloregon), to find out about trails open to mountain bikes. The most scenic mountain-bike trail is the Deschutes River Trail (see "Hiking," above). Mountain bikes (and touring bikes) can be rented from Hutch's Bicycles, 725 NW Columbia St. (© **541/382-9253;** www.hutchsbicycles.com), which charges $35 to $55 per day for mountain bikes.

The **Paulina Plunge** (© **800/296-0562** or 541/389-0562; www.paulinaplunge. com) offers guided mountain-bike rides in Newberry National Volcanic Monument. The outing is an easy downhill ride that includes stops at waterfalls and a natural water slide. These tours, which cost $60, are outrageously fun and should not be missed if you're at all athletic. A much wider range of mountain-bike tours is offered by **Cog Wild Bicycle Tours** (© **866/610-4822** or 541/385-7002; www.cogwild. com). Tours vary in length and degree of difficulty, so there's something for every level of rider and a wide range of prices.

A Scenic Drive Along the Cascade Lakes Highway ★★

During the summer, the Cascade Lakes Highway is the most popular excursion out of Bend. This National Scenic Byway is an 87-mile loop that packs in some of the finest scenery in the Oregon Cascades. Along the way are a dozen major lakes and frequent views of the jagged Three Sisters peaks and the rounded Mount Bachelor. The lakes provide ample opportunities for boating, fishing, swimming, and picnicking. At the **Bend Visitor Center,** 917 NW Harriman St. (☎ **877/245-8484** or 541/382-8048; www.visitbend.org), you can pick up a guide to the Cascade Lakes Scenic Byway. Keep in mind that from mid-November to late May, this road is closed west of Mount Bachelor due to snow.

The first area of interest along the highway is **Dutchman Flat,** just west of Mount Bachelor. A thick layer of pumice produces desertlike conditions that support only a few species of hardy plants. A little farther and you come to **Todd Lake,** a pretty little lake a bit off the highway; it's reached by a short trail. Swimming, picnicking, and camping are all popular here.

Sparks Lake, the next lake along this route, is shallow and marshy and has lava fields at its southern end. An easy trail with frequent glimpses of the lake meanders through these forested lava fields. To find this trail, drive to the end of the Sparks Lake access road. The lake is a popular canoeing spot, though you'll need to bring your own boat. At the north end of the lake, closer to the highway, you'll also find the trail head for a popular mountain-biking trail that heads south to Lava Lake. Across the highway from the marshes, at the north end of the lake, is the trail head for **Green Lakes,** a series of small lakes that are in the Three Sisters Wilderness at the foot of Broken Top Mountain. This is one of the most popular backpacking routes in the region and offers spectacular scenery. The hike to Green Lakes can also be done as a long (and challenging) day hike. West of the Green Lakes trail head is an area known as **Devils Garden,** where several springs surface on the edge of a lava flow. On a boulder here you can still see a few **Native American pictographs.**

With its wide-open waters and reliable winds, **Elk Lake** is popular for sailing and windsurfing. There are cabins, a lodge, and campsites around the lake. **Hosmer and Lava lakes** are both known as good fishing lakes, while spring-fed **Little Lava Lake** is the source of the Deschutes River. **Cultus Lake,** with its sandy beaches, is a popular swimming lake. At **Crane Prairie Reservoir,** you can observe osprey between May and October. The **Twin Lakes** are examples of volcanic maars (craters) that have been filled by springs. These lakes have no inlets or outlets.

In-Town Exploring

Downtown Bend is full of great shops, women's clothing boutiques, and art galleries, and it's easy to spend an afternoon shopping here. To see work by Central Oregon artists, stop by the **High Desert Gallery,** 10 NW Minnesota Ave. (☎ **541/388-8964;** www.highdesertgallery.com). On the first Friday of each month, Bend galleries stay open from 5 to 9pm for a gallery walk. Also be sure to check out the shops in the **Old Mill District** (☎ **541/312-0131;** www.theoldmill.com), a redeveloped area of town that once housed several lumber mills. Today the old mill buildings have been converted into shopping arcades, and new buildings with the look of old mill buildings have been added. You'll find the Old Mill District south of downtown.

Where to Stay
EXPENSIVE
The Oxford Hotel A sophisticated eco-chic boutique hotel in Bend? My, how this town has changed, and wow, what a gorgeous place this is. Located right downtown within walking distance of some of Bend's best restaurants and nightlife, the

Oxford blends urban loft styling with woodsy touches such as floor lamps made from aspen trunks, desk lamps made to resemble sheep skulls (much cooler than they sound), and, in the lobby, a chandelier that looks as if it were cast from tree branches and silvered tree-stump tables. Rooms are much larger than you would find at a comparable hotel in a big city. Some rooms have balconies, and these are definitely worth requesting. Other rooms have big window seats, and some also have kitchenettes. Cork floors in guest room entryways, locally roasted in-room coffee, and organic bath products are just some of the sustainable features of this green-built hotel.

10 NW Minnesota Ave., Bend, OR 97701. www.oxfordhotelbend.com. © **877/440-8436** or 541/382-8436. Fax 541/382-8437. 59 units. $189–$219 double; $239–$259 suite. Children 12 and under stay free in parent's room. AE, DISC, MC, V. Valet parking $10; self-parking $5. Pets accepted ($55 fee). **Amenities:** Restaurant; lounge; free airport shuttle; babysitting; bikes; exercise room; Jacuzzi; room service; sauna. In room: A/C, TV, fridge, hair dryer, MP3 docking station, free Wi-Fi.

Pine Ridge Inn ★★ This small luxury inn on the outskirts of town provides alternative accommodations for anyone who wants first-class surroundings but doesn't need all the facilities (and crowds) of the area's family-oriented resorts. This is an ideal choice for romantic vacations and honeymoons, but it is also a favorite of business travelers who need to be close to town. The inn is set on a bluff high above the Deschutes River, though you'll pay extra for a river view. Whether you book a minisuite or a suite, you'll have tons of space that includes features such as sunken living rooms and fireplaces. Lots of antiques and artworks by regional artists add a distinctive style. Although the inn doesn't have a restaurant, there are complimentary appetizers, wine, and microbrews in the afternoon.

1200 SW Mount Bachelor Dr., Bend, OR 97702. www.pineridgeinn.com. © **800/600-4095** or 541/389-6137. 20 units. $169–$189 minisuite; $239–289 suite. Rates include full breakfast. Children 5 and under stay free in parent's room. AE, DISC, MC, V. Pets accepted ($75 fee). **Amenities:** Concierge; access to nearby health club. In room: A/C, TV/DVD, fridge, hair dryer, free Wi-Fi.

MODERATE

McMenamins Old St. Francis School Hotel ★ 🛍 Attention, lapsed Catholics (and anyone else who attended parochial school): You can finally sleep in class without getting your knuckles smacked by a ruler. McMenamins, the Portland-based brewpub empire, has converted this former Catholic school into the coolest hotel in Central Oregon. Guest rooms are simply furnished and, with their wood paneling, feel like cabins. There are also four cute cottages available. What makes this place really special, though, are all the great little bars and garden spaces scattered around the property. There's a pub, of course, plus a cigar bar in an old garage, a billiards room, and free live music on Thursday nights. There's also a very comfy movie theater that serves food and beer. After a long day of hiking or skiing, you can soak your muscles in the mosaic-tiled soaking pool.

700 NW Bond St., Bend, OR 97701. www.mcmenamins.com. © **877/661-4228** or 541/382-5174. Fax 541/330-8561. 23 units. $125–$185 double; $185–$395 cottage. Children 6 and under stay free in parent's room. AE, DC, DISC, MC, V. Pets accepted ($15 per night). **Amenities:** Restaurant; 4 lounges; hot soaking pool; room service. In room: A/C, TV, hair dryer, free Wi-Fi.

Mount Bachelor Village Resort ★★ Set along the top of a ridge overlooking the Deschutes River, this manicured resort on the road to Mount Bachelor is a more relaxed version of the family resorts so common in Central Oregon. The resort is close enough to town to make going out for dinner convenient, but deep enough in the pine forests to feel away from it all. Keep in mind that this is a condominium resort; most of the accommodations have separate bedrooms, and many have fireplaces and kitchens. For the best views, request a River Ridge condo, right on the edge of the bluff. These rooms are quite simply some of the nicest places to stay in the area, with private outdoor hot tubs on the view decks and whirlpool tubs in the bathrooms. A 2-mile nature trail surrounding the property leads down to the banks of the Deschutes River.

19717 Mount Bachelor Dr., Bend, OR 97702. www.mtbachelorvillage.com. © **888/224-0844** or 541/389-5900. Fax 541/388-7401. 140 units. $119–$229 double; $139–$440 suite/condo/home. 2-night minimum stay. Children 18 and under stay free in parent's room. AE, DISC, MC, V. Pets accepted ($75 per night). **Amenities:** Restaurant; lounge; bikes; concierge; access to nearby health club; 2 Jacuzzis; 2 outdoor pools; 6 tennis courts. *In room:* A/C, TV, fridge, hair dryer, kitchen (some rooms), free Wi-Fi.

Phoenix Inn Suites ★ Set on a low bluff above downtown Bend, this modern hotel is your best bet for comfortable, modern accommodations within walking distance of downtown's many restaurants, bars, and shops. Accommodations are all large suites, so you'll get plenty of space to spread out. This place feels more geared toward business travelers than vacationers, but the location is great. This hotel is just high enough above the rest of downtown that some of the rooms have mountain views, so be sure to request one of these when checking in.

300 NW Franklin Ave., Bend, OR 97701. www.phoenixinn.com. © **888/291-4764** or 541/317-9292. Fax 541/317-9090. 117 units. $139–$159 double; $169–$219 suite. Rates include full breakfast. Children 17 and under stay free in parent's room. AE, DC, DISC, MC, V. **Amenities:** Bikes; exercise room; Jacuzzi; indoor pool. *In room:* A/C, TV, fridge, hair dryer, free Wi-Fi.

Seventh Mountain Resort ★★ ☺ Offering the closest accommodations to Mount Bachelor, this sprawling resort is especially popular with skiers. But summer is still the high season here, and during the warm months, families descend on the property to take advantage of the seemingly endless array of recreational activities. The guest rooms come in a wide range of sizes (most with balconies and/or kitchens). My favorites are the rooms perched on the edge of the wooded Deschutes River canyon. Golfers should note that Widgi Creek Golf Course (p. 319) is adjacent to the resort. In addition to the amenities listed below, the resort also has an ice-skating rink, hiking/jogging trails, a miniature golf course, playgrounds and playing fields, and more. All in all, this is the best place to stay in the immediate Bend vicinity.

18575 SW Century Dr., Bend, OR 97702. www.seventhmountain.com. © **877/765-1501** or 541/382-8711. Fax 541/382-3517. 240 units. $99–$139 double; $129–$369 suite or condo. Children 18 and under stay free in parent's room. AE, DISC, MC, V. **Amenities:** 2 restaurants; lounge; bikes; children's programs; exercise room; 3 Jacuzzis; 3 outdoor pools; sauna; 4 tennis courts. *In room:* A/C, TV/DVD, hair dryer, kitchen, free Wi-Fi.

INEXPENSIVE

Entrada Lodge ◢ Located on 42 acres a few miles west of Bend, on the road to the Mount Bachelor ski area, this motel is in a tranquil setting shaded by tall pine trees. Stay here and you'll be just a little bit closer to Mount Bachelor in winter and the region's many lakes and hiking and mountain-biking trails in summer. Although you'll have to drive back into town or to a nearby resort for meals, it's worth that small inconvenience to get such a pleasant setting at economical rates. The Deschutes National Forest borders the property, and a trail leads from the parking lot to the popular Deschutes River Trail (p. 319), which is only a mile away.

19221 Century Dr., Bend, OR 97702. www.entradalodge.com. © **888/505-6343** or 541/382-4080. 79 units. Summer $89–$129 double; other months $79–$89 double. Rates include continental breakfast. AE, DISC, MC, V. Pets accepted ($10 per day). **Amenities:** Jacuzzi; outdoor pool. *In room:* A/C, TV, hair dryer, free Wi-Fi.

The Riverhouse ★ 🗲   Located at the north end of town on the banks of a narrow stretch of the Deschutes River, the Riverhouse is one of the best hotel deals in the state. And with its golf course and other amenities, it's an economical choice for anyone who wants resort amenities without the high prices. Try to get a ground-floor room; these allow you to step off your patio and almost jump right into the Deschutes. The rooms on the upper floor, however, have a better view of this rocky stretch of river. The hotel's main dining room also has a view of the river and a lounge that features a variety of live entertainment. There's also a poolside cafe. Without a doubt, this is the best deal in Bend. Book early.

3075 N. Business U.S. 97, Bend, OR 97701. www.riverhouse.com. 📞 **866/453-4480** or 541/389-3111. Fax 541/389-0870. 220 units. $89–$189 double; $135–$265 suite. Rates include full breakfast. Children 6 and under stay free in parent's room. AE, DISC, MC, V. Pets accepted. **Amenities:** 2 restaurants; lounge; exercise room; 18-hole golf course; Jacuzzi; indoor and outdoor pool; room service; saunas; 2 tennis courts. *In room:* A/C, TV/DVD, fridge, hair dryer, free Wi-Fi.

IN SUNRIVER

The resort community of Sunriver is Oregon's most popular summer destination resort and has hundreds of condos, cabins, and vacation homes at a wide range of prices. **Sunset Realty** (📞 **800/541-1756**; www.sr-sunset.com) is one of the area's biggest rental companies.

Sunriver Lodge & Resort ★★★ ☺   This sprawling resort is less a hotel than a town unto itself, and with a wealth of activities available for active vacationers, it is the first choice of many families vacationing in Central Oregon. Most of the lodge accommodations overlook both the golf course and the mountains. My favorite rooms are the Lodge Village suites, which have stone fireplaces, high ceilings, and rustic log furniture, although the River Lodge rooms are the most luxurious. Pine trees shade the grounds, and 35 miles of paved bicycle paths connect the resort with the surrounding community. However, no matter how impressive the other facilities are, it is the four golf courses and nearby Mount Bachelor ski area that attract the most business. The resort's main dining room features creative Northwest cuisine and has superb views of the mountains. A complimentary shuttle runs to Bend and Mount Bachelor.

17600 Center Dr. (P.O. Box 3609), Sunriver, OR 97707. www.sunriver-resort.com. 📞 **800/801-8765.** Fax 541/593-5458. 640 units. $139–$239 double; $194–$324 suite. DISC, MC, V. Pets accepted ($75 fee). **Amenities:** 4 restaurants; 2 lounges; babysitting; bikes; children's programs; concierge; 1 9-hole and 3 18-hole golf courses; health club; 2 Jacuzzis; 3 outdoor pools, 1 indoor pool; room service; sauna; spa; 29 tennis courts (3 indoor courts); watersports equipment rentals. *In room:* A/C, TV, CD player, hair dryer, kitchen (some rooms), free Wi-Fi.

CAMPGROUNDS

The closest campground to Bend is Tumalo State Park, 5 miles northwest of Bend off U.S. 20. The biggest campground in the area is La Pine State Park, which is accessible from U.S. 97 between Sunriver and La Pine. Reservations can be made at these parks through **Reserve America** (📞 **800/452-5687**; www.reserveamerica.com).

Of the many campgrounds along the Cascade Lakes Highway, the walk-in **Todd Lake Campground,** 25 miles west of Bend, is my favorite because it is enough of a walk from the parking lot to keep things pretty quiet. **Devil's Lake Campground,** also a walk-in campground, is another favorite of mine. Two others are the **Mallard Marsh** and **South** campgrounds, both of which are on beautiful Hosmer Lake. The campgrounds at **Lava Lake** and **Little Lava Lake** are also fairly quiet, and the view from Lava Lake is the finest at any campground on this stretch of road.

Where to Eat

IN BEND

For the best espresso in Bend, head to **Thump Coffee,** 25 NW Minnesota Ave. (© **541/388-0226;** www.thumpcoffee.com), which is a block off Bond Street in downtown. Alternatively, try **Bellatazza,** 869 NW Wall St., no. 101 (© **541/318-0606;** www.bellatazza.com), for good espresso. If it happens to be summer and you're craving a meal with an unforgettable view, head to **Mount Bachelor** (© **541/382-1709;** www.mtbachelor.com) and take the chair lift up to the Pine Marten Lodge, where you can have lunch, dinner, or just drinks at Scapolo's, an Italian restaurant.

Expensive

Ariana Restaurant ★★ MEDITERRANEAN   In a little Craftsman bungalow a short drive west of downtown Bend, you'll find my favorite Bend restaurant. Cozy and romantic, Ariana is just far enough off the tourist path to feel like a real discovery. The menu leans to Mediterranean dishes, which emphasize sustainable, organic, and seasonal ingredients. You might start with house-made burrata cheese (cream-stuffed mozzarella) or Sicilian-style calamari simmered in a tomato sauce with capers, currants, and pasta. For an entree, there might be soy-glazed salmon with roasted shiitake mushrooms and truffle creamed corn, or scallops served over Dungeness crab and herb risotto. To finish off, I recommend whatever seasonal dessert is coming out of the kitchen.

1304 NW Galveston Ave. © **541/330-5539.** www.arianarestaurantbend.com. Reservations recommended. Main course $17–$29. AE, DISC, MC, V. Tues–Sat 5–9 or 10pm.

900 Wall ★★ NEW AMERICAN   Bend is solidly part of the New West, and this restaurant reflects that with its fresh, local ingredients and commitment to sustainable practices. The last time I ate here, I had house-made salami that was made from a pig that the chef raised on a nearby farm, and both beef and lamb served here comes from a Central Oregon ranch. The presence of both a rotisserie and a grill in the open kitchen should clue you in as to what to order: rotisserie chicken, grilled wild shrimp, grilled pork shoulder, or maybe the burger with sun-dried tomato aioli and Gorgonzola cheese. In summer, try to snag one of the sidewalk tables. Happy hour here offers some great deals.

900 NW Wall St. © **541/323-6295.** www.900wall.com. Reservations recommended. Main courses $14–$29. AE, MC, V. Sun–Thurs 11:30am–9 or 10pm; Fri–Sat 11:30am–10 or 11pm.

Pine Tavern Restaurant AMERICAN/NORTHWEST   Opened in 1936, the Pine Tavern Restaurant has been a local favorite for generations, and neither the decor nor the view has changed much over the years. Knotty pine and cozy booths give the restaurant an old-fashioned feel, while a 250-year-old ponderosa pine growing up through the center of one dining room provides a bit of grandeur. The menu is designed to appeal to a wide range of tastes and includes such comfort foods as meatloaf and grilled salmon, but the prime rib and the sourdough scones with honey butter are what this place is best known for. Try to get a table in the back room, which overlooks Mirror Pond.

967 NW Brooks St. © **541/382-5581.** www.pinetavern.com. Reservations recommended. Main courses $11–$18 lunch, $15–$34 dinner. AE, DISC, MC, V. Mon–Sat 11:30am–2:30pm and 5:30–9:30pm; Sun 5:30–9:30pm (also open for Sun brunch in summer).

Moderate

Deschutes Brewery Bend Public House ✦ REGIONAL AMERICAN   For good handcrafted ales (I'm partial to the Mirror Pond Pale Ale and the Obsidian Stout) and a range of pub food more creative and tastier than you'd expect, this bustling pub is the place. The buffalo wings are some of the best I've ever had and are available in two different renditions. Not only do the cooks do an exemplary job on the normal pub menu, but they also prepare more complex daily specials, and there are daily sausage specials as well. Bring the family—even the ones who don't drink beer.

1044 NW Bond St. ℂ **541/382-9242.** www.deschutesbrewery.com. Main courses $11–$25. AE, DISC, MC, V. Mon–Thurs 11am–11pm; Fri–Sat 11am–midnight; Sun 11am–10pm.

Victorian Café ★ 🎁 AMERICAN   The owner of this popular breakfast and lunch spot is always quick to tell new customers that this place is all about the Benedicts and the specials. The Victorian Cafe takes eggs Benedict to new levels, with creative renditions of the breakfast classic, so be sure to heed the owner's advice. These meals are so filling that you likely won't need to eat again until dinner. Because this place is especially popular on weekends, it is also known for its bloody marys, which are meals unto themselves. On summer mornings, the patio, shaded by aspens and pine trees, is absolutely idyllic, the quintessential Central Oregon breakfast spot.

1404 NW Galveston Ave. ℂ **541/382-6411.** http://victoriancafebend.com. Reservations not accepted. Main courses $10–$20. AE, MC, V. Daily 7am–2pm.

Inexpensive

Bend Burger Company AMERICAN   After a long day of shredding the slopes, grinding gears, or pounding the trail, sometimes you just have to have a burger. If today is that day, then this little hole in the wall in downtown Bend is the place. For a Bend original, try the Bachelor Brat, a burger made with beef, German sausage, sauerkraut, bacon, cheese, and grilled onions.

718 NW Franklin Ave. ℂ **541/306-6166.** http://bendburger.com. No reservations. Main courses $4–$10. DISC, MC, V. Sun–Thurs 11am–8pm; Fri–Sat 11am–9pm.

IN SUNRIVER

For the best views and food in Sunriver, make a reservation at the **Meadows at the Lodge** restaurant (ℂ **541/593-3740**) at Sunriver Lodge (see above).

IN SILVER LAKE

Cowboy Dinner Tree 🎁 AMERICAN   Would you drive 75 miles for a steak? Out in this neck of the high desert, plenty of people do. Since the 1870s, when cowboys on cattle drives used to stop for meals under a shady tree here in Silver Lake, people have been journeying this way for filling meals. What makes this place so popular is not just its remote location, but also the hefty 26- to 30-ounce steaks. These ginormous slabs of beef come with salad, soup, baked potato, and sweet rolls that are legendary around these parts. If you're not a steak eater, you can order a roast chicken. That's right, you get a whole bird. Of course, the whole point of these gargantuan meals is that everyone goes home with enough food for another meal or two.

C.R. 4-12/Forest Service Rd. 28, Silver Lake. ℂ **541/576-2426.** http://cowboydinnertree.net. Reservations required. Full dinner $25. No credit cards. June–Oct Thurs–Sun 4–8:30pm; Nov–May Fri–Sun 4–8:30pm. From La Pine, drive 46 miles on Ore. 31 and turn right in Silver Lake.

Bend After Dark

Bend rivals Portland for its number of brewpubs per capita, so, after a long day of hiking, biking, or skiing, check out one or more of the city's excellent brewpubs. Bend's most creative beers are being brewed at **10 Barrel Brewing,** 1135 NW Galveston Ave. (© **541/678-5228;** www.10barrel.com). On any given night, they might be pouring raspberry sour beer (served with a shot of simple syrup) or a strong ale aged in a bourbon barrel. This pub has a fabulous patio and an open-air bar. There are also good handcrafted ales and pub food at the **Bend Brewing Co.,** 1019 NW Brooks St. (© **541/383-1599;** www.bendbrewingco.com), which is a good downtown alternative to the Deschutes Brewery Bend Public House (see above), as is **Silver Moon Brewing,** 24 NW Greenwood Ave. (© **541/388-8331;** www.silvermoonbrewing.com). In downtown Bend, you'll also find **McMenamins Old St. Francis School Hotel,** 700 NW Bond St. (p. 322; © **541/382-5174;** www.mcmenamins.com), which is home to a pub, several small bars, and a movie theater where you can get McMenamins beers.

If you're not a beer geek, don't despair, you can get good cocktails at the **Astro Lounge,** 939 Bond St. (© **541/388-0116;** www.astroloungebend.com), and **Velvet,** 805 NW Wall St. (© **541/728-0303;** www.velvetbend.com), a bi-level bar that often has live music. Although it's a bit of out of town, on the road to Sisters, the **Bendistillery,** 19330 Pinehurst Rd. (© **541/318-0200;** www.bendistillery.com), offers tastes of its different liquors (including a delicious hazelnut-espresso vodka). You can get a martini made with this microdistillery's own gin (made with local juniper berries) or vodka (filtered through lava rock).

If wine is more your style, head to the **Maragas Winery Taverna,** 643 NW Colorado Ave. (© **541/306-6552;** www.maragaswinery.com), south of downtown. Wine labels at this winery tasting room sport beatnik-theme cartoon art, and zinfandel is a specialty. The taverna is open Tuesday through Thursday from noon to 7pm and Friday and Saturday from noon to 9pm.

Be sure to check the calendar for downtown Bend's **Tower Theatre,** 835 NW Wall St. (© **541/317-0700;** www.towertheatre.org), a restored 1940 movie palace that now stages live theater performances and a wide variety of concerts, as well as screenings of everything from the Marx Brothers' *A Night at the Opera* to *The Big Lebowski.* The **Les Schwab Amphitheater,** 344 SW Shevlin Hixon Dr. (© **541/322-9383;** www.bendconcerts.com), in the Old Mill District, books all kinds of great music each summer, and there are usually free concerts on Sunday afternoons.

EASTERN OREGON

So different is eastern Oregon from the wet west side of the Cascades that it is often difficult to remember that it is still the same state. Indeed, the dry eastern ranch lands, deserts, canyons, and mountain ranges of this region have more in common with the landscapes of neighboring Idaho and Nevada. Yet Oregon it is, and though it is remote, the fascinating geography makes it an interesting region to explore.

With huge cattle ranches sprawling across the countryside (cattle greatly outnumber people in these parts), the arts community of Joseph casting Western-art bronze statues, and the **Pendleton Round-Up** attracting cowboys and cowgirls from around the country, eastern Oregon is the state's Wild West. This part of the state is also steeped in the history of the Oregon Trail, and although it was to the Willamette Valley that most wagon trains were heading, it is here that signs of their passing 150 years ago still abound. All across this region, **wagon ruts** can still be seen, and the history of the Oregon Trail is chronicled at several regional museums. Although the first pioneers never thought to stop and put down roots in this region, when gold was discovered in the Blue Mountains in the 1860s, fortune seekers flocked to the area. Boom towns flourished and just as quickly disappeared, leaving the land to the cattle ranchers and wheat farmers who still call this area home.

Today, however, the region also attracts outdoors enthusiasts. They come to hike and horseback ride in the Eagle Cap Wilderness of the Wallowa Mountains, to bird-watch in the Malheur National Wildlife Refuge, to ski in the Blue Mountains, to explore the deepest canyon in the United States, and to raft and fish the Snake, Owyhee, and Grande Ronde rivers.

Because this region is so far from the state's population centers, it is little visited by west-siders, who rarely venture farther east than the resorts of central Oregon. Eastern Oregon is also so vast, and the road distances so great, that it does not lend itself to quick weekend trips. At the very least, it takes a 3-day weekend to get out to Joseph and the Wallowa Mountains or the Malheur National Wildlife Refuge. Should you travel to this part of the state, leave yourself plenty of time for getting from point A to point B.

PENDLETON

125 miles E of The Dalles, 52 miles NW of La Grande, 40 miles S of Walla Walla, WA

If not for its famous woolen mills, few people outside the Northwest would be familiar with the Pendleton name. But because the blankets and clothing long manufactured by the Pendleton Woolen Mills (here and at other mills around the region) have
gained such a reputation, the name has become as much a part of the West as Winchester, Colt, and Wells Fargo. Today Pendleton blankets and clothing are as popular
as ever, and this town's mill is one of its biggest attractions.

But what brings even more visitors to town than the mill is a single annual event—
the **Pendleton Round-Up.** Located at the western foot of the Blue Mountains in
northeastern Oregon, Pendleton prides itself on being a real Western town; and as the
site of one of the largest and oldest rodeos in the West, it has a legitimate claim. Each
year in mid-September, the round-up fills the town with cowboys and cowgirls, both
real and urban. For the rest of the year, Pendleton sinks back into its quiet small-town
character and begins preparing for the next round-up.

Once the homeland of the Cayuse, Umatilla, Walla Walla, and Nez Perce Indians,
the Pendleton area began attracting settlers in the 1840s, as pioneers who had traveled the Oregon Trail started farming along the Umatilla River. In the 1850s, gold
strikes created boom towns in the nearby mountains, and Pendleton gained greater
regional significance. Sheep ranching and wheat farming later became the mainstays
of the local economy, and by the turn of the century, Pendleton was a rowdy town
boasting dozens of saloons and bordellos. Today Pendleton is a much quieter place,
one that few people notice as they rush by on the interstate. But those who do pull
off find a quiet town whose downtown historic district is filled with attractive brick
buildings and some stately old Victorian homes.

Essentials

GETTING THERE I-84 runs east to west through Pendleton. From the south, take
U.S. 395; from the north, take Ore. 11, which leads to Walla Walla, Washington.
Seaport Airlines (✆ **888/573-2767;** www.seaportair.com) has service to the **East-
ern Oregon Regional Airport,** 2016 Airport Rd. (www.pendleton.or.us), from
Portland. The airport is located about 4 miles west of downtown Pendleton.

VISITOR INFORMATION Contact the **Pendleton Chamber of Commerce,**
501 S. Main St., Pendleton, OR 97801 (✆ **800/547-8911** or 541/276-7411; www.
pendletonchamber.com).

GETTING AROUND Hertz (✆ **800/654-3131;** www.hertz.com) rents cars at
the Eastern Oregon Regional Airport.

The Pendleton Round-Up

The Pendleton Round-Up and Happy Canyon Pageant, held the second week of
September each year, is one of the biggest rodeos in the country and has been held
since 1910. In addition to daily rodeo events, there's a nightly pageant that presents
a history of Native American and pioneer relations in the area. After the pageant, live
country-and-western music gets things hopping in the Happy Canyon Dance Hall; a
country-music concert and a parade round out the events. The Hall of Fame, 1114

SW Court Ave., holds a collection of cowboy and Indian memorabilia. The city is packed to overflowing during round-up week, so if you plan to attend, reserve early. Tickets sell for $15 to $25, and some types of tickets sell out a year in advance. For more information, contact the **Pendleton Round-Up Association,** 1114 SW Court Ave. (P.O. Box 609), Pendleton, OR 97801 (✆ **800/457-6336** or 541/276-2553; www.pendletonroundup.com).

Exploring Pendleton

If you happen to be in town any other week of the year, there are still a few things worth doing. This is the hometown of **Pendleton Woolen Mills,** 1307 SE Court Place (✆ **541/276-6911;** www.pendleton-usa.com), the famed manufacturer of Native American–inspired blankets and classic wool sportswear. At the mill here in Pendleton, the raw wool is turned into yarn and then woven into fabric before being shipped off to other factories to be made into clothing. This mill is also where the famed Indian blankets are woven. Tours are offered Monday through Friday at 9 and 11am and 1:30 and 3pm. Also at the mill is a salesroom that's open Monday through Saturday from 8am to 6pm and Sunday from 9am to 5pm.

At one time, there were supposedly 10 miles of underground passages and rooms beneath the streets of Pendleton, where gamblers, drinkers, and Chinese laborers rubbed shoulders. Over the years, these spaces were home to speakeasies and saloons, opium dens, and the living quarters of Chinese laborers who were forbidden to be above ground after dark. On 90-minute walking tours operated by **Pendleton Underground Tours,** 31 SW Emigrant Ave. (✆ **541/276-0730;** www.pendleton undergroundtours.org), you can learn all about old Pendleton's shady underside. After exploring the underground, you'll visit a former bordello, whose rooms have been decorated much the way they once might have looked. Between March and October, tours are offered Monday and Wednesday through Saturday; call for a schedule in other months. Tickets are $15. Reservations are strongly recommended.

At the Umatilla County Historical Society's **Heritage Station Museum,** 108 SW Frazer Ave. (✆ **541/276-0012;** www.heritagestationmuseum.org), you can learn about the region's more respectable history. The museum is partly housed in the city's 1909 railway depot and contains changing exhibits that focus on regional history, including the Oregon Trail, Pendleton Woolen Mills, and Native American culture. This little museum is worth a visit, and is open Tuesday through Saturday from 10am to 4pm; admission is $5 for adults, $4 for seniors, and $2 for children.

In business since 1883, **Hamley's,** 30 SE Court Ave. (✆ **541/278-1100;** www. hamley.com), is one of the nation's top saddleries, but this huge store is now far more than just someplace to buy a saddle that will fit like a glove. You'll find everything a rodeo star or urban cowboy or cowgirl could ever need to look and feel like the real thing. There are boots and hats, belts and buckles, bits and spurs, all in a fascinating old building. Don't leave town without dropping by.

If you're looking for glimpses of the **Oregon Trail,** head 20 miles west of Pendleton to the town of Echo, where you can see wagon ruts left by early pioneers. There's an interpretive exhibit in town at Fort Henrietta Park on Main Street, and a mile of ruts can also be seen about 5½ miles west of town north of Ore. 320.

East of Town

East of Pendleton, at exit 216 off I-84, you'll find a complex of attractions operated by the Confederated Tribes of the Umatilla Indian Reservation. Included here is the

Wildhorse Casino Resort, 72777 Ore. 331 (© **800/654-9453** or 541/278-2274; www.wildhorseresort.com), a golf course, a motel, an RV park, and the following museum.

Tamástslikt Cultural Institute ★★ This modern museum focuses on the impact the Oregon Trail had on the Native Americans of this region. The exhibits incorporate artifacts, life-size dioramas, and audio and video presentations, which document the effect pioneer settlement had on the indigenous Cayuse, Walla Walla, and Umatilla Indians who were living in the region when the first settlers arrived. Exhibits are well done and quite interesting. Between Memorial Day and Labor Day, there is a living-history village. It's worth a stop.

47106 Wildhorse Blvd. © **541/966-9748.** www.tamastslikt.com. Admission $8 adults; $6 seniors, students, and children; and free for children 5 and under. Apr–Oct daily 9am–5pm; Nov–Mar Mon–Sat 9am–5pm.

Where to Stay

The Pendleton House Bed & Breakfast ★ Built in 1917, this Italiante villa is only 2 blocks from downtown Pendleton and is surrounded by colorful perennial gardens. As befits the villalike surroundings, a formal atmosphere reigns. The Gwendolyn Room, with its fireplace and semiprivate balcony, is the best room in the house; in the Mandarin Room, you'll find the original Chinese wallpaper and Asian styling. Throughout the inn, there are plenty of antiques. Guest rooms share a bathroom, but what a bathroom it is, with the original multiple-head shower and lots of big old porcelain fixtures.

311 N. Main St., Pendleton, OR 97801. www.pendletonhousebnb.com. © **541/276-8581.** Fax 541/276-2827. 6 units, all with shared bathroom. $95–$135 double. Rates include full breakfast. AE, DISC, MC, V. In room: A/C, no phone, free Wi-Fi.

Wildhorse Casino Resort Whether or not you're interested in gambling, the Wildhorse Casino Resort is a good place to stay in the area. Not only is this 10-story hotel the biggest and most contemporary hotel in eastern Oregon, with big comfortable and very modern rooms, but it also has plenty of recreational amenities, including the casino, two pools, a golf course, and a movie theater. The Tamástslikt Cultural Institute (see above) is also nearby. The hotel is 4 miles east of Pendleton and has nice views of the nearby foothills of the Blue Mountains.

72777 Ore. 331, Pendleton, OR 97801. www.wildhorseresort.com. © **800/654-9453** or 541/278-2274. 300 units. $69–$109 double; $119–$159 suite. AE, DISC, MC, V. **Amenities:** 4 restaurants; lounge; children's center; 18-hole golf course; Jacuzzi; indoor pool; room service. In room: A/C, TV, fridge (in tower rooms), hair dryer.

Working Girls Hotel 🛏 Pendleton likes to play up its Wild West heritage, and there was a time when brothels were legal here. The historic building that now houses the Working Girls Hotel was just such an establishment, and although female companionship doesn't come with the rooms anymore, you will get comfortable accommodations. The rooms all have private bathrooms, but only one of these is actually in the room; all others have their bathrooms directly across the hall. The hotel is operated in conjunction with Pendleton Underground Tours.

17 SW Emigrant Ave., Pendleton, OR 97801. www.pendletonundergroundtours.org. © **541/276-0730.** 5 units. $75–$95 double. MC, V. No children permitted. In room: A/C, no phone.

Where to Eat

If you're looking for someplace to get a sandwich or a bowl of soup, drop by the **Great Pacific Wine and Coffee Company,** 403 S. Main St. ((©) **541/276-1350;** www. greatpacific.biz). Cookies, muffins, truffles, and other sweets round out the menu.

Hamley Steakhouse and Cafe STEAKS/AMERICAN   Since Pendleton has made its name on cow punchin', you just can't leave town without sitting down to a steak dinner, and Hamley's is the place to have that meal. Associated with the famous Hamley and Co. saddlery and store, which is on this same block, this restaurant opened in 2007 but feels as if it has been here for a century or more. Before or after dinner, be sure to mosey into the saloon, where you can toss back some Pendleton Whiskey at the 100-year-old mahogany bar. During the day, you can get breakfast and lunch at the affiliated cafe.

8 SE Court St. (©) **541/278-1100.** http://hamleysteakhouse.com. Reservations recommended. Main courses $5–$10 lunch, $10–$41 dinner. AE, DISC, MC, V. Cafe daily 8am–3pm; steak house Sun–Mon 5–8pm, Tues–Thurs 5–9pm, Fri–Sat 5–9:30pm.

Prodigal Son Brewery and Pub ★ ☺ 👕 AMERICAN   When the owners of this brewpub moved back to their hometown of Pendleton to open the town's first brewpub, the name seemed like a natural. My advice is that you, too, should welcome the Prodigal Son. Not only are there plenty of good beers on tap, but the food menu could hold its own in trendy Portland. The Prodigal Reuben, stuffed with house-made corned beef and house-fermented sauerkraut, served on locally made rye bread, should not be missed. There are also plenty of good burgers (made with local beef) and other pub mainstays such as Scotch eggs, fish and chips, and mac and cheese. A children's play area makes this a good family restaurant, too.

230 SE Court St. (©) **541/276-6090.** http://prodigalsonbrewery.com. Main courses $7–$11. DISC, MC, V. Tues–Thurs 11am–10pm; Fri–Sat 11am–11pm; Sun noon–9pm.

LA GRANDE, BAKER CITY & THE BLUE MOUNTAINS

La Grande: 260 miles E of Portland, 52 miles SE of Pendleton. Baker City: 41 miles SE of La Grande, 75 miles NW of Ontario

Though pioneers traveling the Oregon Trail in the 1840s found good resting places in the Powder River and Grande Ronde valleys, where Baker City and La Grande now stand, few stayed to put down roots in this remote region. It would not be until the 1860s that pioneers actually looked on these valleys as places to live and make a living. However, even those first pioneers who just passed through left signs of their passage that persist to this day. Wagon ruts of the Oregon Trail can still be seen in this region, and outside of Baker City stands the most interesting and evocative of the state's museums dedicated to the Oregon Trail experience.

By 1861, however, the Blue Mountains, which had been a major impediment to wagon trains, were crawling with people—gold prospectors, though, not farmers. A gold strike in these mountains started a small gold rush that year, and soon prospectors were flocking to the area. The gold didn't last long, and when mining was no longer financially feasible, the miners left the region. In their wake, they left several ghost towns, but the prosperity of those boom times also gave the region's larger towns an enduring legacy of stately homes and opulent commercial buildings, many built of stone that was quarried in the region. Today the historic commercial buildings of Baker City, the ornate Victorian homes of Union, and the Elgin Opera House are reminders of past prosperity. Although the gold has played out, signs of those raucous days, from gold nuggets to ghost towns, are now among the region's chief attractions.

One of the most arduous and dangerous sections of the Oregon Trail—the crossing of the Blue Mountains—lies just west of present-day La Grande. These mountains are no longer the formidable obstacles they once were, but they are still among the least visited in Oregon. The Blues, as they are known locally, offer a wide variety of recreational activities, including skiing, hiking, mountain biking, fishing, camping, and even soaking in hot springs. With their numerous hotels and restaurants, both La Grande and Baker City make good bases for exploring this relatively undiscovered region.

Essentials

GETTING THERE   Both La Grande and Baker City are on I-84. La Grande is at the junction of Ore. 82, which heads northeast to Joseph and Wallowa Lake. Baker City is at the junction of Ore. 7, which runs southwest to John Day, and Ore. 86, which runs east to the Hells Canyon National Recreation Area.

VISITOR INFORMATION   Contact the **Baker County Chamber of Commerce and Visitors Bureau,** 490 Campbell St., Baker City, OR 97814 (© **800/523-1235** or 541/523-5855; www.visitbaker.com), or **Union County Tourism,** 207 Depot St., La Grande, OR 97850 (© **800/848-9969** or 541/963-8588; www.visit lagrande.com).

Oregon Trail Sites

Oregon Trail history is on view west of La Grande, in downtown Baker City, and just north of Baker City. At the **Oregon Trail Interpretive Park at Blue Mountain Crossing** (© **541/963-7186**) at the Spring Creek exit (exit 248) off I-84, you'll find a .5-mile trail that leads past wagon ruts in the forest. Informational panels explain the difficulties pioneers encountered crossing these rugged mountains. Between Memorial Day and Labor Day, there are occasional living-history programs here. There is a $5 day-use fee.

Baker Heritage Museum   In a large building that once housed Baker City's public swimming pool, you'll find lots of pioneer memorabilia, as well as an extensive mineral collection. This museum also operates the historic Adler House (see "Exploring La Grande & Baker City," below).

2480 Grove St., Baker City. © **541/523-9308.** www.bakerheritagemuseum.com. Admission $6 adults, $5 seniors. Mid-Mar to Oct daily 9am–4pm.

National Historic Oregon Trail Interpretive Center ★★   Atop sagebrush-covered Flagstaff Hill, just north of Baker City, stands a monument to the largest overland migration in North American history. Between 1842 and 1860, an estimated 300,000 people loaded all their worldly belongings onto wagons and set out to cross the continent to the promised land of western Oregon. Their route took them through rugged, inhospitable landscapes, and many of the pioneers perished along the way. This museum commemorates the journeys of these hardy souls, who endured drought, dysentery, and starvation in the hopes of a better life. Through the use of diary quotes, a life-size wagon-train scene, artifacts, and interactive exhibits, the center takes visitors through every aspect of life on the trail. Outside a trail leads to ruts left by the wagons on their journey west.

22267 Ore. 86, Baker City. 📞 **541/523-1843**. www.blm.gov/or/oregontrail. Admission Apr–Oct $8 adults, $4.50 seniors, free for children 15 and under; Nov–Mar $5 adults, $3.50 seniors, free for children 15 and under. Apr–Oct daily 9am–6pm; Nov–Mar daily 9am–4pm. Closed New Year's Day, Thanksgiving, and Christmas.

Exploring La Grande, Baker City & Union

At the Baker County Chamber of Commerce and Visitors Bureau, you can pick up a brochure that outlines a **walking tour** of the town's most important historic buildings, including the restored **Geiser Grand Hotel** (see below), which, when it first opened, was one of the finest hotels in the West.

If you'd like to take a look inside one of Baker City's restored old homes, drop by the **Adler House Museum,** 2305 Main St. (📞 **541/523-9308**), a stately Victorian structure. Everything on the second floor, from the wallpaper to the furniture, is original, dating to the 1890s. The first floor has been refurbished and decorated to look the way it might have more than 100 years ago. The museum is open from Memorial Day to Labor Day, Friday through Monday from 10am to 2pm. Admission is $6 per adult.

Baker City's fortunes were made by gold mines in the Blue Mountains, and if you'd like to see some samples from those golden years, stop in at the **U.S. Bank** on Main Street in Baker City. The gold collection here includes a nugget that weighs in at 80.4 ounces.

Five miles east of La Grande, you'll find the steaming waters of Hot Lake, on the banks of which local sculptor David Manuel and his family have a bronze foundry, sculpture park, art gallery, and museums honoring fire trucks, wagons, Native American artifacts, and military artifacts. The Manuels have restored the historic hospital building that stands on the shores of Hot Lake, and the building now houses a bed-and-breakfast, a restaurant, and a spa. Self-guided tours of the property cost $10. For information, contact **Hot Lake Springs,** 66172 Ore. 203, La Grande (📞 **541/963-4685**; www.hotlakesprings.com). Also see the listing for the inn in this section.

A few miles beyond Hot Lake, you'll come to the historic town of Union, which is full of restored Victorian homes. At the **Union County Museum,** 333 S. Main St. (📞 **541/562-6003;** www.unioncountymuseum.org), you can learn about the history of the area and also see an interesting exhibit on the history of cowboys. The museum is open Monday through Saturday from 10am to 4pm, and admission is $4 for adults, $3 for seniors, and $2 for students.

Not far from Union, in the community of Cove, you can sample locally made wines at the **Gilstrap Brothers Vineyard and Winery,** 69789 Antles Lane, Cove (📞 **866/568-4200** or 541/568-4646; www.gilstrapbrothers.com). This winery makes a wide range of red wines and the occasional white. Call for hours.

Outdoor Activities

SPRING THROUGH FALL

If you're interested in bird-watching, head out to the **Ladd Marsh Wildlife Area,** 59116 Pierce Rd. (📞 **541/963-4954;** www.dfw.state.or.us), 5 miles south of La Grande off I-84 at the Foothill Road exit (exit 268). March through May, the refuge has lots of waterfowl, and in summer the wetland is home to sandhill cranes, geese, ducks, avocets, black-necked stilts, and numerous raptors. Also keep an eye out for

In the town of **Elgin**, 18 miles north of La Grande on Ore. 82, you can take in a play or concert at the restored **Elgin** **Opera House Theater**, 104 N. Eighth St. (℃ **541/437-1918;** www.elginopera house.com), which was built in 1912.

elk. The best way to visit this area is by walking the 1-mile nature trail east of I-84 near exit 268.

In summer there are plenty of nearby trails for hiking or mountain biking. My favorite trails are those that radiate out from Anthony Lake, high in the Elkhorn Mountains 45 minutes from Baker City. These trails start at an elevation of more than 7,000 feet and meander through open forests with views of craggy granite peaks. The 8-mile loop hike from Anthony Lake up the Elkhorn Crest Trail to Dutch Flat Saddle and back to Anthony Lake via Crawfish Basin Trail makes a good day hike. By the way, the campground at Anthony Lake might just be my favorite campground in the state. Contact the Wallowa-Whitman National Forest's **La Grande Ranger Station,** 3502 Ore. 30, La Grande, OR 97850 (℃ **541/963-7186**), or the **Whitman Ranger Station,** 3285 11th St., Baker City, OR 97814 (℃ **541/523-4476**), for more information. Online, visit www.fs.fed.us/r6/w-w.

WINTER

With the highest base elevation and the most powderlike snow in the state, **Anthony Lakes** (℃ **541/856-3277;** www.anthonylakes.com), 45 minutes west of Baker City, is a good ski area—small, but with a nice variety of terrain. Daily lift tickets are $35. You'll also find good, groomed cross-country ski trails here, and the area is very popular with snowmobilers.

Winter is also the best time of year to see some of the region's Rocky Mountain elk. Every year from December through February, the Oregon Department of Fish & Wildlife feeds a large herd of elk at the **Elkhorn Wildlife Area,** 61846 Powder River Lane, North Powder (℃ **541/898-2826;** www.dfw.state.or.us), about halfway between La Grande and Baker City. You can usually see between 100 and 150 elk. Between mid-December and the end of February, **T & T Wildlife Tours** (℃ **541/ 856-3356;** www.tnthorsemanship.com) takes visitors out to the feeding area by horse-drawn wagon. Tours last about a half hour and cost $7 for adults and $5 for children. To reach Elkhorn, take exit 285 off I-84 and follow the WILDLIFE VIEWING signs.

The Elkhorn Mountain Scenic Loop

Rising on the outskirts of Baker City is the Elkhorn Range of the Blue Mountains. A paved loop road winding up and around the south side of these mountains features scenic vistas, access to the outdoors throughout the year, and even a couple of sparsely inhabited ghost towns. Start this loop by heading south out of Baker City on Ore. 245, and then take Ore. 7 west to Sumpter, 30 miles from Baker City.

As you approach Sumpter, you'll notice that the valley floor is covered with large piles of rocks. These are the tailings (the refuse left after the mining operations have worked over the land) from the Sumpter Dredge, preserved as the **Sumpter Valley Dredge State Heritage Area** (℃ **541/894-2486;** www.oregon.gov/oprd/parks). Between 1935 and 1954, the ominous-looking dredge laid waste to the valley floor as it sat in its own little pond sifting through old streambed gravel for gold. Although you can stop and view the dredge any time of year, between May and October it is possible to board the strange machine (daily 8am–5pm), which has a few interpretive exhibits on board. Admission is by donation, and tours of the dredge are offered.

In its wake, the dredge left 6 miles of tailings that formed hummocks of rock and gouged-out areas that have now become small ponds. Although such a mining-scarred landscape isn't usually scenic, the Sumpter Valley is surprisingly alive with birds attracted to the ponds.

A favorite way of visiting the Sumpter Dredge is aboard the **Sumpter Valley Railway** (© **866/894-2268** or 541/894-2268; www.svry.com), which operates a classic steam train on a 5-mile run from west of Phillips Reservoir to the Sumpter Valley Dredge. This railway first began operation in 1890 and was known as the stump dodger. Excursions are operated on Saturday, Sunday, and holidays from Memorial Day weekend through September; round-trip fares are $15 for adults, $14 for seniors, and $9 for children 6 to 16.

Gold kept Sumpter alive for many decades, and a bit of gold-mining history is still on display in this rustic mountain town, which, though it has a few too many people to be called a ghost town, is hardly the town it once was. In the boom days of the late 19th and early 20th centuries, Sumpter boasted several brick buildings, hotels, saloons, and a main street crowded with large buildings. However, when a fire destroyed the town in 1917, it was never rebuilt. Today only one brick building and a few original wooden structures remain.

Continuing west on a winding county road for 14 miles will bring you to **Granite ★**, another ghost town with a few flesh-and-blood residents. The weather-beaten old buildings on a grassy hillside are the epitome of a Western ghost town, and most buildings are marked. You'll see the old school, general store, saloon, bordello, and other important town buildings.

Beyond Granite, the road winds down to the North Fork of the John Day River and then heads back across the mountains by way of the Anthony Lakes area. Although Anthony Lakes is best known for its small ski area, in summer there are hiking trails and fishing in the area's small lakes. The vistas in this area are the best on this entire loop drive, with rugged, rocky peaks rising above the forest. Also in this same area, you'll catch glimpses of the irrigated pastures of the Powder River Valley far below.

Coming down onto the valley floor, you reach the tiny farming community of Haines, which is the site of the **Eastern Oregon Museum,** 610 Third St. (© **541/856-3233;** www.hainesoregon.com/eomuseum.html), a small museum cluttered with all manner of artifacts of regional historic significance. It's open mid-May to mid-September, Wednesday through Sunday from 11am to 4:30pm; admission is $2.

Where to Stay
IN LA GRANDE
Hot Lake Springs Bed & Breakfast   This sprawling hot-springs hotel, a few miles outside La Grande, was in an advanced state of decay when it was purchased in 2003 by local bronze sculptor David Manuel and his family. After a years-long restoration, the hotel reopened in 2010 with guest rooms decorated by area families who donated funds and furnishings. These rooms vary considerably in style of decor and quality, so be sure to look at rooms on the website before booking. Be forewarned that the waters of Hot Lake are high in sulfur, and consequently the grounds are quite pungent. There are also large numbers of geese and peacocks running free on the

property, and their droppings are everywhere. Although there is a restaurant here, no alcohol is served nor is it allowed on the grounds.

66172 Ore. 203 (P.O. Box 1043), La Grande, OR 97850. www.hotlakesprings.com. © **541/963-4685.** Fax 541/963-4876. 22 units. $125–$245 double. Rates include full breakfast. **Amenities:** Restaurant; hot tubs; spa. In room: No phone. Take exit 265 off I-5 and drive 5 miles east on Ore. 203.

IN UNION

The Union Hotel ★ 💰 Although Union today is a sleepy town, it was once the county seat and a booming place. This grand little hotel first opened its doors in 1921, and now, after an extensive renovation, it has become one of eastern Oregon's more interesting historic hotels. Surrounded by lawns and shade trees, the three-story brick hotel goes a long way toward conjuring up Union's lively past. The lobby, with its white-tile floor, could be straight out of a movie set, while the upstairs guest rooms are decorated in various themes. To make the most of a visit here, try to stay in the room with the whirlpool tub. Although Union is 14 miles from La Grande, the location is still fairly convenient for exploring this region.

326 N. Main St., Union, OR 97883. www.theunionhotel.com. © **541/562-6135.** 16 units. $39–$119 double. DC, DISC, MC, V. Pets accepted ($20 fee). **Amenities:** Free Wi-Fi. In room: A/C, no phone.

IN BAKER CITY

Geiser Grand Hotel ★★ 🏨 Built in 1889 at the height of the region's gold rush, the Geiser Grand is by far the grandest hotel in eastern Oregon. With its corner turret and clock tower, the hotel is a classic 19th-century Western luxury hotel. In the center of the hotel is the Geiser Grill (see below) dining room, above which is suspended the largest stained-glass ceiling in the Northwest. Throughout the hotel, including in all the guest rooms, ornate crystal chandeliers add a crowning touch. Guest rooms also feature 10-foot windows, most of which look out to the Blue Mountains. The two cupola suites are the most luxurious and also have whirlpool tubs. Meals are served both in the formal dining room and in the much more relaxed 1889 saloon. No trip to eastern Oregon is complete without a stay at this grande dame of the old West.

1996 Main St., Baker City, OR 97814. www.geisergrand.com. © **888/434-7374** or 541/523-1889. Fax 541/523-1800. 30 units. $99–$119 double; $129–$229 suite. Children 12 and under stay free in parent's room. AE, DISC, MC, V. Pets accepted ($15 per night). **Amenities:** 2 restaurants; lounge; babysitting; bikes; concierge; access to nearby health club; room service. In room: A/C, TV/VCR/ DVD, CD player; hair dryer, free Wi-Fi.

CAMPGROUNDS

You'll find several national-forest campgrounds along the Elkhorn National Scenic Byway, including **Union Creek Campground** (© **541/523-4476;** www.fs.fed.us/ r6/w-w), which is on the shore of Phillips Reservoir southeast of Baker City. Others can be found near Anthony Lakes.

Where to Eat

IN LA GRANDE

For good pastries and fresh-baked bread, stop in at **Kneads,** 1113 Adams Ave. (© **541/963-5413;** www.kneadsbakery.com). For locally brewed beers, drop by **Mt. Emily Ale House,** 1202 Adams Ave. (© **541/962-7711**), which also serves pizzas and sandwiches.

Foley Station ★ AMERICAN Located in a historic building in downtown La Grande, Foley Station is the city's most sophisticated restaurant. While the restaurant has long been known for its Sunday brunch (especially the Belgian waffles), it's also a good place for lunch and dinner. Long menus at every meal ensure that everyone in your party will find something to tempt them. At lunch, try the Reuben or the quiche of the day. For dinner, good steaks and pasta dishes highlight the main menu; however, do check out the more creative dishes on the chef's seasonal menu.

1114 Adams Ave. ☎ **541/963-7473.** www.foleystation.com. Reservations recommended. Main courses $6–$12 lunch, $15–$42 dinner. MC, V. Wed–Fri 11am–9pm; Sat 3–9pm; Sun 9am–9pm.

Ten Depot Street 🍴 STEAK/SEAFOOD   Housed in a historic brick commercial building, this restaurant has a classic 19th-century feel, complete with a saloon on one side. Although the steaks and prime rib are what most people order, the salads are large and flavorful, and there are even some vegetarian dishes. There's live music (usually rock) in the bar on Tuesday and Thursday.

10 Depot St. ☎ **541/963-8766.** www.tendepotstreet.com. Reservations recommended. Main courses $8–$29. AE, MC, V. Mon–Sat 5–10pm.

IN THE BAKER CITY AREA

For pub food and microbrews, there's **Barley Brown's Brew Pub,** 2190 Main St. (☎ **541/523-4266;** www.barleybrowns.com). For espresso, try **Mad Matilda's Coffee House,** 1705 Main St. (☎ **541/519-2991**). If it's a hot day, stop in at **Charlie's Ice Cream Parlor,** 2101 Main St. (☎ **541/524-9307**).

Geiser Grill ★ AMERICAN   Located in the central court of the historic Geiser Grand Hotel (see above), this restaurant, with its stained-glass ceiling, conjures a gold rush–era elegance. Mesquite-smoked prime rib and the wide variety of steaks are always good bets, but this restaurant is also committed to serving excellent fresh seafood dishes, including line-caught wild salmon. There are also plenty of pasta dishes. Before or after dinner, you'll need to spend a little time in the 1889 Saloon just to complete your historical evening. At lunch, you can order a buffalo burger.

In the Geiser Grand Hotel, 1996 Main St. ☎ **541/523-1889.** www.geisergrand.com. Reservations recommended. Main courses $6–$12 lunch, $11–$38 dinner. AE, DISC, MC, V. Mon–Fri 11am–2pm and 4:30–9pm; Sat–Sun 7–9am, 11am–2pm, and 4:30–9pm.

chinese history IN EASTERN OREGON

In the town of John Day, the fascinating little **Kam Wah Chung State Heritage Site ★★** (☎ **541/575-2800**), on Northwest Canton Street adjacent to City Park, is well worth a visit. It preserves the home and shop of a Chinese doctor who for much of the first half of the 20th century ministered to his fellow countrymen laboring here. The building looks much as it might have at the time of the doctor's death and contains an office, a pharmacy, a general store, and living quarters. It's open May through October daily from 9am to 5pm. Admission is free.

You'll find more Chinese history in Baker City, where an old Chinese cemetery can be seen on Allen Street, just east of exit 304 off of I-84. This cemetery has a modern Chinese pavilion that was built in Souzhou, China, designed by the same company that built Portland's Lan Su Chinese Garden. The Pendleton Underground Tours in Pendleton (p. 330) also focus on the region's Chinese history.

JOSEPH & THE WALLOWA MOUNTAINS

Joseph: 355 miles E of Portland, 80 miles E of La Grande, 125 miles N of Baker City

The Wallowa Mountains, which stand just south of the town of Joseph, are a glacier-carved range of rugged beauty that has been called both the Alps of Oregon and the Little Switzerland of America. Though the range is small enough in area to drive around in a day, it is big on scenery and contains the largest designated wilderness area in the state: the Eagle Cap Wilderness.

In the northeast corner of the mountains lies Wallowa Lake, which was formed when glacial moraines blocked a valley that had been carved by the glaciers. With blue waters reflecting the rocky peaks, the lake has long attracted visitors. In the fall, the lake also attracts bald eagles that come to feed on spawning kokanee salmon, which turn a bright red in the spawning season.

The town of Joseph, just north of Wallowa Lake, is a center for the casting of Western-themed **bronze sculptures,** and there are several art galleries and found-ries in the area. The town of Enterprise, 6 miles west of Joseph, is the less touristy of the area's main towns, but it also has a bronze foundry (and one of the best brewpubs in Oregon). With its natural beauty, recreational opportunities, and artistic bent, this corner of the state today has more to offer than any other area in eastern Oregon.

Essentials

GETTING THERE   Ore. 82 connects Joseph to La Grande in the west, and Ore. 3 heads north from nearby Enterprise to Lewiston, Idaho, by way of Wash. 129.

VISITOR INFORMATION   For more information, contact the **Wallowa County Chamber of Commerce,** 309 S. River St., Suite B (P.O. Box 427), Enterprise, OR 97828 (© **800/585-4121** or 541/426-4622; www.wallowacountychamber.com).

FESTIVALS   Check out the rowdy **Chief Joseph Days Rodeo** (© **541/432-1015;** www.chiefjosephdays.com), over the last full weekend in July. In mid-July the Nez Perce hold their annual **TamKaLiks Celebration** (© **541/886-3101;** www.wallowanezperce.org) and powwow in the nearby town of Wallowa.

Exploring Joseph

Though the lake and mountains are the main attractions of this area, the presence of several bronze foundries in Joseph and Enterprise has turned the area into something of a Western art community. Along Main Street in Joseph, you'll find several galleries that specialize in bronze statues and Western art. You'll also find more than half a dozen life-size bronze wildlife and Western-art sculptures in sidewalk gardens along Main Street. **Joseph's Valley Bronze of Oregon** has a gallery at 18 S. Main St. (© **541/432-7445;** www.valleybronze.com), and is one of the largest bronze found-ries in the country. Tours of the foundry ($15 per person) are offered daily during the summer and begin at the gallery. **Parks Bronze,** 331 Golf Course Rd., Enterprise (© **541/426-4595;** www.parksbronze.com), offers foundry tours Monday through Thursday at 10:30am. Tours are $10 per person, with a $30 minimum. For more information on area artists, visit the website of Joseph Oregon Artists (www.joseph oregonartists.com).

At the **Wallowa County Museum,** 110 S. Main St., Joseph (© **541/432-6095;** www.co.wallowa.or.us/community_services/museum/index.html), you can see pioneer artifacts, displays on the Nez Perce Indians, and other items donated to the museum by local families. This old-fashioned community museum is housed in a former bank building and is open daily from 10am to 5pm between Memorial Day and the third weekend in September. Admission is $2.50 for adults.

On most Saturdays between June and mid-October (and a few other dates between Mother's Day and early Sept), you can go for a 3½-hour train ride on the **Eagle Cap Excursion Train** (© **800/323-7330** or 541/963-9000; www.eaglecap train.com). Trains run between Elgin and Minam, and fares are $75 for adults, $65 for seniors, and $35 for children.

Outdoor Activities

Down at the south end of Wallowa Lake, you'll find **Wallowa Lake State Park** (© **541/432-4185;** www.oregon.gov/oprd/parks), where there is a swimming beach, picnic area, and campground. Adjacent to the park is the **Wallowa Lake Marina** (© 541/**432-9115;** www.wallowalakemarina.com), where you can rent canoes, kayaks, rowboats, paddleboats, and motorboats (first weekend in May to mid-Sept). This end of the lake has an old-fashioned mountain-resort feel, with pony and kiddy rides, go-cart tracks, miniature golf courses, and the like. It is also the trail head for several trails into the Eagle Cap Wilderness. The park is home to numerous large deer, which have become accustomed to begging for handouts from campers. Although the deer are entertaining, they are still wild animals and can be dangerous.

For a different perspective on the lake, ride the **Wallowa Lake Tramway,** 59919 Wallowa Lake Hwy., Joseph (© **541/432-5331;** www.wallowalaketramway.com), to the summit of 8,200-foot Mount Howard. This is the steepest tramway in America and provides great views both from the gondolas and from the top of the mountain. The views take in Wallowa Lake and the surrounding jagged peaks. The tramway operates between Memorial Day and early October daily from 10am to 4pm; the fare is $26 for adults, $23 for seniors, $21 for students 12 to 17, and $17 for children 4 to 11. Food is available at the **Summit Grill & Alpine Patio.**

Because most hikes on the north side of the Wallowas start out in valleys and can take up to a dozen miles or so to reach the alpine meadows of the higher elevations, there aren't a lot of great day hikes here. The **backpacking,** however, is excellent. If you're looking for **day hikes,** try taking the tramway to the top of Mount Howard, where great views unfold on the 2 miles of easy walking trails. If you'd like to head into the **Eagle Cap Wilderness** to the popular **Lakes Basin** or anywhere else in the Wallowas, you'll find the trail head less than a mile past the south end of the lake. For more information on hiking in the Wallowas, contact the **Wallowa Valley Ranger Station,** 201 E. Second St., Joseph, OR 97846 (© **541/426-4978;** www. fs.fed.us/r6/w-w).

Horse packing into the Wallowas is a popular activity, and rides of a day or longer can be arranged through **Eagle Cap Wilderness Pack Station,** 59761 Wallowa Lake Hwy., Joseph, OR 97846 (© **541/432-4145;** www.eaglecapwildernesspack station.com), which offers trips into the Eagle Cap Wilderness during the summer. These stables also offer 1-hour ($30), 2-hour ($60), half-day ($90), and full-day ($150) rides.

This region also offers some of the best **trout fishing** in Oregon, and if you're looking for a guide to take you to the best holes, contact **Eagle Cap Fishing Guides,**

💬 "I WILL fight no more, FOREVER"

The Wallowa Mountains and Hells Canyon areas were once the homeland of the **Nez Perce people.** Sometime in the early 1700s, the Nez Perce acquired horses that were descended from Spanish stock and that had been traded northward from the American Southwest. The Nez Perce land proved to be ideal for raising horses, and the tribe began selectively breeding animals. Their horses became far superior to those used by other tribes and came to be known as **Appaloosas.** Eventually, the hills in southeast Washington where these horses were first bred became known as the **Palouse Hills.**

The Nez Perce had befriended explorers Lewis and Clark in 1805 and remained friendly to white settlers when other Indian tribes were waging wars. This neutrality was "rewarded," however, with treaties that twice cut the size of their reservation in half. When one band refused to sign a new treaty and relinquish its land, it began one of the great tragedies of Northwest history.

En route to a reservation in Idaho, several Nez Perce men ignored orders from the tribal elders and attacked and killed four white settlers to exact revenge for the earlier murder by whites of the father of one of these Nez Perce men. This attack angered settlers, and the cavalry was called to hunt down the Nez Perce. Tribal elders decided to flee to Canada, and, led by Chief Joseph (also known as Young Joseph), 700 Nez Perce, including 400 women and children, began a 2,000-mile march across Idaho and Montana on a retreat that lasted 4 months.

Along the way, several skirmishes were fought, and the Nez Perce were defeated only 40 miles from Canada. At their surrender, Chief Joseph spoke his famous words: "Hear me my Chiefs, I am tired; my heart is sick and sad. From where the sun now stands, I will fight no more, forever."

The town of Joseph is named after Chief Joseph, and on the town's outskirts, you'll find the grave of his father, Old Joseph. Young Joseph is buried on the Colville Indian Reservation in central Washington. In town you can view historic photos and read quotes from Chief Joseph at the **Nez Perce Wallowa Homeland Exhibit,** 302 N. Main St. (📞 **541/886-3101**). Not far from Joseph, in Spalding, Idaho (near Lewiston), is the **Nez Perce National Historical Park** (📞 **208/843-7001;** www.nps.gov/nepe).

P.O. Box 865, Joseph, OR 97846 (📞 **800/940-3688;** www.eaglecapfishing.com), or **Winding Waters River Expeditions,** P.O. Box 566, Joseph, OR 97846 (📞 **877/426-7238** or 541/432-0747; www.windingwatersrafting.com). Expect to pay anywhere from $385 to $450 for a day of fishing for one or two people. For fishing supplies, stop by the **Joseph Fly Shoppe,** 203 N. Main St., Joseph (📞 **541/432-4343;** www.josephflyshop.com).

In winter the Wallowas are popular with cross-country and backcountry skiers. Check at the ranger station in Joseph for directions to trails. You'll also find a small downhill ski area and groomed cross-country trails at **Ferguson Ridge** (www.skifergi.com), which is 9 miles southeast of Joseph on Tucker Down Road.

Wing Ridge Ski Tours, P.O. Box 714, Joseph, OR 97846 (📞 **800/646-9050** or 541/432-0712; www.wingski.com), rents backcountry huts for $50 per person per night. This company also offers a guide service.

Bronze Antler Bed & Breakfast ★   This beautifully restored Craftsman bungalow is Joseph's finest B&B and has by far the best view of any lodging in the area. Throughout the 1925 vintage home, you'll see lots of beautiful architectural details, and furnishings are in keeping with the style of the period. Guest rooms have fluffy down comforters and European antiques collected by the innkeepers Bill Finney and Heather Tyreman during their travels in Europe. Joseph's restaurants and art galleries are within a few blocks of the inn, which makes this a very convenient place to stay if you're in town to soak up Joseph's artistic atmosphere.

309 S. Main St. (P.O. Box 74), Joseph, OR 97846. www.bronzeantler.com. © **866/520-9769** or 541/432-0230. 4 units. $84–$164 double; $125–$259 suite. Rates include full breakfast. AE, DISC, MC, V. Children 12 and over welcome by prior arrangement. **Amenities:** Concierge. *In room:* A/C, CD player, hair dryer, no phone, free Wi-Fi.

Eagle Cap Chalets ☺   Set under tall pines just a short walk from hiking trails and the lake, Eagle Cap Chalets has a wide variety of rooms, as well as an indoor pool and Jacuzzi and a miniature golf course. Consequently, this place is very popular with families and groups. The rooms here vary from motel style to rustic-though-renovated cabins, and most have phones. Siding on all the buildings makes them appear to be built of logs. Cabins and condos have kitchens. In the early fall, there always seem to be deer hanging out on the lawns.

59879 Wallowa Lake Hwy., Joseph, OR 97846. www.eaglecapchalets.com. © **541/432-4704**. 34 units. $65–$120 double; $90–$150 suite; $65–$200 cabin; $115–$185 1- and 2-bedroom condos. DISC, MC, V. Pets accepted ($30–$50 fee). **Amenities:** Espresso bar; Jacuzzi; outdoor pool. *In room:* TV.

Imnaha River Inn ★   Located 35 miles northeast of Joseph on the edge of Hells Canyon, this remote log inn is set deep in the Imnaha River Canyon. The sprawling modern inn is filled with animal hides and trophy heads, and the log construction conjures the wild pioneering spirit of this region. The lofty, high-ceilinged living room, with its big stone fireplace, is the perfect place to relax after a day in the outdoors. However, the deck overlooking the river is equally enticing. Fishing, hunting, rafting, and hiking are the primary pursuits, but if you just want to get away from it all in an awe-inspiring setting, this is the best choice in all of eastern Oregon. Lunches ($12) and dinners ($18) are available.

73946 Rimrock Rd., Imnaha, OR 97842. www.imnahariverinn.com. © **866/601-9214** or 541/577-6002. 7 units, all with shared bathroom. $130–$140 double. Rates include full breakfast. No credit cards. **Amenities:** Dining room; free Wi-Fi. *In room:* A/C, no phone.

Wallowa Lake Lodge ★   This rustic two-story lodge at the south end of Wallowa Lake was built in 1923 and is surrounded by big pines and a wide expanse of lawn that attracts deer in late summer and early fall. Big comfortable chairs fill the lobby, where folks often sit by the stone fireplace in the evening. The guest rooms are divided between those with carpeting and modern bathrooms and those with hardwood floors, original bathroom fixtures, and antique furnishings (my favorites). All but two of the latter have two bedrooms each, and two rooms have balconies overlooking the lake. The cabins are rustic but comfortable and have full kitchens. The dining room is one of the better places in the area for dinner.

60060 Wallowa Lake Hwy., Joseph, OR 97846. www.wallowalakelodge.com. © **541/432-9821**. Fax 541/432-4885. 30 units, including 8 cabins. Mid-May to mid-Oct $99–$170 double, $150–$235 cabin; mid-Oct to mid-May $80–$120 double, $100–$140 cabin. DISC, MC, V. **Amenities:** Restaurant; lounge; free Wi-Fi. *In room:* No phone.

CAMPGROUNDS

At the south end of Wallowa Lake, you'll find a campground under the trees at **Wallowa Lake State Park** (© 541/432-4185; www.oregon.gov/oprd/parks). In addition to campsites, the park also has yurts for rent. For campsite reservations, contact **ReserveAmerica** (© 800/452-5687; www.reserveamerica.com).

Where to Eat

As befits a town that revels in its Wild West character, Joseph has a little brewpub. The **Mutiny Brewing Company,** 600 N. Main St. (© 541/432-5274; http://mutinybrewing.com), brews its own beers and has some cheap eats.

Calderas ★ ▮▮ NEW AMERICAN   A block off Main Street, in a building full of beautiful Art Nouveau woodwork by a local artisan, Calderas is a stylish bistro that also doubles as a gift shop. The menu is short and eclectic, with a half-dozen appetizers that are often large enough to be a meal on their own. The Mediterranean flat bread, which is basically a small (and delicious) pizza, is a personal favorite. There's also cheese fondue and pesto shrimp skewers. The ginger-teriyaki tri-tip beef is so popular that it shows up both as an appetizer and an entree. Much of the produce in the summer comes from the owners' farm, and during the warmer months there is a pretty patio for al fresco dining.

300 N. Lake St., Joseph © **541/432-0585.** www.calderasofjoseph.com. Main courses $13–$30. AE, DC, DISC, MC, V. Wed–Mon 2–9:30pm; winter Thurs–Sat 4–8pm.

Summit Grill & Alpine Patio AMERICAN   While this restaurant's view of the Wallow Mountains, Wallowa Lake, and seemingly all of northeastern Oregon is absolutely breathtaking, you're more likely to find yourself short of breath due to the 8,150-foot elevation. Set atop Mount Howard and accessed by an aerial tram, this casual restaurant justifiably calls itself "the Northwest's highest restaurant." The menu is pretty straightforward, with a variety of sandwiches and burgers, but your best bet is the sausage plate, which comes with kielbasa or bratwurst, German potato salad, and sauerkraut. To eat here, you'll first have to pay to ride the tram up the mountain.

59919 Wallowa Lake Hwy. © **541/432-5331.** http://wallowalaketramway.com. Reservations not necessary. Main courses $6.50–$9.75. MC, V. Daily 10am–4pm. Closed early Oct to late May.

Terminal Gravity Brewery & Public House ★ INTERNATIONAL   Although it's small, this brewery on the east side of Enterprise gets raves across the state for its excellent beers. The beer alone would be worth a stop, but this place, housed in an old Craftsman bungalow, also serves some of the best food in this corner of the state. There are only a couple of tables and a few barstools in the main dining room, but there are a few more tables upstairs and out on the veranda, plus some picnic tables in the front yard. Although the regular menu includes a few sandwiches and a handful of basic entrees, you can expect a couple of dinner specials each night.

803 SE School St., Enterprise. © **541/426-3000.** www.terminalgravitybrewing.com. Main courses $7.25–$12. DISC, MC, V. Mon–Sat 11am–10pm; Sun 11am–9pm.

Vali's Alpine Restaurant & Delicatessen EASTERN EUROPEAN   Just past the Wallowa Lake Lodge, you'll find this little restaurant, which specializes in the hearty fare of Eastern Europe. Only one dish is served each evening, so if you like to have options, you won't want to eat here. Cabbage rolls or Hungarian goulash (Wed), chicken paprika (Thurs), beef kabobs (Fri), steak (Sat), and schnitzel (Sun) should help you stay warm on cold mountain evenings. On Saturday and Sunday mornings, there are fresh homemade doughnuts.

59811 Wallowa Lake Hwy., Joseph. ℂ **541/432-5691.** www.valisrestaurant.com. Reservations required. Main courses $11–$16. No credit cards. Memorial Day to Labor Day Wed–Sun 5–8pm, Sat–Sun 9–11am and 5–8pm; Apr to Memorial Day Sat–Sun 9–11am and 5–8pm.

HELLS CANYON & THE SOUTHERN WALLOWAS

South access: 70 miles NE of Baker City. North access: 20 to 30 miles E of Joseph

Sure, the Grand Canyon is an impressive sight, but few people realize that it isn't the deepest canyon in the United States. That distinction goes to Hells Canyon, which forms part of the border between Oregon and Idaho. Carved by the Snake River and bounded on the east by the Seven Devils Mountains and on the west by the Wallowa Mountains, Hells Canyon is as much as 8,000 feet deep. Although it's not quite as spectacular a sight as the Grand Canyon, neither is it as crowded. Because there is so little road access to Hells Canyon, it is one of the least visited national recreation areas in the West.

The Hells Canyon area boasts a range of outdoor activities, but because of blazing-hot temperatures in summer, when this rugged gorge lives up to its name, spring and fall are the best times to visit. Despite the heat, though, boating, swimming, and fishing are all popular in the summer.

Essentials

GETTING THERE   The south access to Hells Canyon National Recreation Area is reached off of Ore. 86 between 9 and 48 miles northeast of the town of Halfway, depending on which route you follow. Northern sections of the national recreation area, including the Hat Point Overlook, are reached from Joseph on Ore. 82, which begins in La Grande.

VISITOR INFORMATION   For more information, contact the **Hells Canyon National Recreation Area,** 201 E. Second St. (P.O. Box 905), OR 97846 (ℂ **541/ 426-5546;** www.fs.fed.us/hellscanyon).

Exploring the Region

Much of **Hells Canyon ★★** is wilderness and accessible only by boat, horseback, or foot. Few roads lead into the canyon, and most of these are recommended only for four-wheel-drive vehicles. If you are driving a car without high clearance, you'll have to limit your exploration of this region to the road to Hells Canyon Dam and the scenic byway that skirts the eastern flanks of the Wallowa Mountains. If you don't mind driving miles on gravel, you can also head out to the Hat Point Overlook east of Joseph.

From the south, river-level access begins in the community of Oxbow, but the portion of the Snake River that has been designated a National Wild and Scenic River starts 27 miles farther north, below Hells Canyon Dam. Below the dam, the Snake River is turbulent with white water and provides thrills for jet-boaters and rafters. To get this bottom-up view of the canyon, take Ore. 86 to Oxbow, cross the river into Idaho, and continue 22 miles downriver to **Hells Canyon Creek Visitor Center**

(© **541/785-3395**), which is located 1 mile past the Hells Canyon Dam. This center has informative displays on the natural history of Hells Canyon and is open daily 8am to 4pm from early May to early October. The Stud Creek Trail leads 1 mile down the river from the visitor center and is an easy way to get a sense of what it's like to hike in the canyon.

To get a top-down overview of the canyon, drive to the **Hells Canyon Overlook,** 30 miles northeast of Halfway on Forest Road 39. From here you can gaze down into the canyon, but you won't be able to see the river.

You'll find many miles of **hiking trails** within the national recreation area, but summer heat, rattlesnakes, and poison oak keep all but the most dedicated hikers at bay. However, in early June, the wildflowers in Hells Canyon can be spectacular. For information on trails here, contact the information center for the recreation area.

The best way to see Hells Canyon is by **white-water raft** or in a **jet boat. Hells Canyon Adventures,** P.O. Box 159, Oxbow, OR 97840 (© **800/422-3568** or 541/785-3352; www.hellscanyonadventures.com), specializes in jet-boat tours, with tours ranging in price from $55 to $75 per adult for a 2-hour tour ($30–$50 for children) to $160 per adult for a 6-hour tour ($74 for children). Overnight tours are also available. If you'd rather float the river in a raft, contact **Hells Canyon Raft,** P.O. Box 4610, McCall, ID 83638 (© **800/523-6502** or 208/634-6366; www.hells canyonraft.com), which operates 3- to 6-day raft trips through Hells Canyon. Rates range from $995 to $1,745 for adults ($830–$1,510 for children).

Multiday horseback trips into the southern Wallowas are offered by **Cornucopia Wilderness Pack Station,** P.O. Box 568, Union, OR 97883 (© **866/562-8075** or 541/562-1181; www.cornucopiapackstation.com), which charges $125 to $250 per person per day for most of its trips.

You can also opt to explore the southern Wallowas with a llama carrying your gear. Contact **Wallowa Llamas,** 36678 Allstead Lane, Halfway, OR 97834 (© **541/742-2961;** www.wallowallamas.com), for more information. Trips range in price from $695 to $1,295.

Where to Stay & Eat

Pine Valley Lodge ★★ 🍴 This little lodge, composed of three old buildings in downtown Halfway, is a Wild West fantasy of an inn and is owned by a local cattle ranch. With handmade furniture and Western collectibles scattered about, the main lodge is a fascinating place to wander around. The main house has a large suite on the ground floor and two smaller rooms upstairs. Next door is the Blue Dog, a four-bedroom cottage. Outdoorsy types will like the Main Street Shack, which truly is a shack, albeit a charming one.

163 N. Main St. (P.O. Box 609), Halfway, OR 97834. www.pvlodge.com. © **541/742-2027.** 8 units. $80–$160 double. Rates include continental breakfast on weekends. MC, V. Pets accepted ($10). **Amenities:** Free Wi-Fi. *In room:* A/C, no phone.

ONTARIO & THE OWYHEE RIVER REGION

Ontario: 72 miles SE of Baker City, 63 miles NW of Boise, 130 miles NE of Burns

Ontario, the easternmost town in Oregon, lies in the Four Rivers region, at the confluence of the Owyhee, Snake, Malheur, and Payette rivers. Irrigated by waters from the massive Owyhee Reservoir, these wide, flat valleys are prime agricultural lands that produce onions, sugar beets, and, as in Idaho, plenty of potatoes. This region is also where most of the world's zinnia seeds are grown. During the summer, zinnia fields color the landscape in bold swaths. If you're curious to see the flower fields, head south out of Ontario on Ore. 201.

The biggest attraction in the region is the **Four Rivers Cultural Center,** which focuses on the various cultures that have made the region what it is today. However, there is also some Oregon Trail history to be seen nearby, and south of Ontario lies one of Oregon's most rugged and remote regions. This corner of the state is a vast untracked high desert, and along the banks of the Owyhee River and Succor Creek, you can see canyons and cliffs that seem far more suited to a Southwestern landscape.

Essentials

GETTING THERE   Ontario is on the Idaho line at the junction of I-84 and U.S. 20/26, all of which link the town to western Oregon.

VISITOR INFORMATION   For more information on the Ontario area, contact the **Ontario Chamber of Commerce,** 876 SW Fourth Ave., Ontario, OR 97914 (✆ **866/ 989-8012** or 541/889-8012; www.ontariochamber.com).

Note: Ontario is on Mountain Standard Time, not Pacific Standard Time.

A Cultural Museum

Four Rivers Cultural Center & Museum ★   Although this remote corner of Oregon may seem an unlikely place for a multicultural museum, that is exactly what you'll find here. The museum focuses on four very distinct cultures that have called this region home. The Paiutes were the original inhabitants of the area, and an exploration of their hunting-and-gathering culture is the first exhibit. In the mid-19th century, the first pioneers began arriving in the area and quickly displaced the Paiutes. By the late 19th century, many Mexican cowboys, known as vaqueros or buckaroos, had come north to the region to work the large cattle ranches. At the same time, Basque shepherds settled in the area and tended large herds of sheep in the more remote corners of the region. The fourth culture is that of the Japanese, who were forced to live in internment camps in the area during World War II. The museum also has a Japanese garden.

676 SW Fifth Ave. ✆ **541/889-8191.** www.4rcc.com. Admission $4 adults, $3 seniors and children 6–14. Mon–Sat 10am–5pm.

More to See & Do: Exploring the Region

For more Oregon Trail history, head 18 miles west of Ontario to the small farming community of Vale. Here you'll find the **Rinehart Stone House Museum,** 255 Main St. S. (✆ **541/473-2070**), which was built in 1872 and was a stagecoach stop and an important wayside along the route of the Oregon Trail. Today it houses a small historical museum, open from March through October, Tuesday through Saturday from 12:30 to 4:30pm; admission is free. Six miles south of Vale, at Keeney Pass, you can see wagon ruts left by pioneers traveling the Oregon Trail.

South of Ontario 15 miles, you'll find **Nyssa,** the "Thunderegg Capital of Oregon." **Rockhounding** is the area's most popular pastime, and thundereggs (also known as geodes) are the prime find. These round rocks look quite plain until they are cut open to reveal the agate or crystals within. You'll find plenty of cut-and-polished thundereggs in the rock shops around town. If you'd like to do a bit of rockhounding yourself, you can head south to **Succor Creek State Natural Area ★**, a rugged canyon where you'll find a campground, picnic tables, and thundereggs waiting to be unearthed.

If you have a four-wheel-drive or high-clearance vehicle, you can continue another 30 minutes to **Leslie Gulch ★★**, an even more spectacular canyon with walls of naturally sculpted sandstone. If you're lucky, you might even see bighorn sheep here. Few places in Oregon have more of the feel of the desert than these two canyons, just as in the desert Southwest, here, too, rivers have been dammed to provide irrigation water and aquatic playgrounds. **Lake Owyhee,** 45 miles south of Ontario off Ore. 201, is the longest lake in Oregon and offers boating, fishing, and camping. The Owyhee River above the lake is a designated State Scenic Waterway and is popular for **white-water rafting ★★**. If you're interested in running this remote stretch of river, contact **Oregon Whitewater Adventures** (✆ **800/820-7238;** www.oregon whitewater.com). A 4-day trips costs $820 for adults and a 5-day trip is $975.

Where to Stay

For the most part, Ontario is a way station for people traveling along I-84, and as such, the city's accommodations are strictly off-ramp budget motels. Motel options include **Best Western Plus Inn & Suites,** 251 NE Goodfellow St., Ontario, OR 97914 (✆ **800/780-7234** or 541/889-2600), charging $90 to $150 for a double; **America's Best Value Inn,** 266 NE Goodfellow St., Ontario, OR 97914 (✆ **888/315-2378** or 541/889-8282), charging $66 to $85 for a double; and **Motel 6,** 275 NE 12th St., Ontario, OR 97914 (✆ **800/466-8356** or 541/889-6617), charging $48 to $53 for a double.

At nearby **Farewell Bend State Recreation Area** (✆ **541/869-2365;** www. oregon.gov/oprd/parks), 25 miles northwest of Ontario on I-84, you'll find not only campsites but also cabins ($42 per night). For reservations, contact **ReserveAmerica** (✆ **800/452-5687;** www.reserveamerica.com).

Where to Eat

In downtown Ontario, you'll find a couple of basic Mexican restaurants and some places specializing in steaks, but that's about it.

SOUTHEASTERN OREGON

Burns: 130 miles SE of Bend, 130 miles SW of Ontario, 70 miles S of John Day

Southeastern Oregon, the most remote and least populated region of the state, is a region of extremes. Vast marshlands, the most inhospitable desert in the state, and a mountain topped with aspen groves and glacial valleys are among the most prominent features of this landscape. Although cattle outnumber human inhabitants, and the deer and the antelope play, it's birdlife that's the region's number-one attraction. At Malheur National Wildlife Refuge, birds abound almost any month of the year, attracting flocks of bird-watchers, binoculars and bird books in hand.

Because this is such an isolated region (Burns and Lakeview are the only towns of consequence), it is not an area to be visited by the unprepared. Always keep your gas tank topped off, and carry water for both you and your car. Two of the region's main attractions, **Steens Mountain** and the **Hart Mountain National Antelope Refuge,** are accessible only by way of gravel roads more than 50 miles long. A visit to the Alvord Desert will also require spending 60 or more miles on a gravel road.

Essentials

GETTING THERE   The town of Burns is midway between Bend and Ontario on U.S. 20. Malheur National Wildlife Refuge, Steens Mountain, and Hart Mountain National Antelope Refuge are all located south of Burns off Ore. 205.

VISITOR INFORMATION   For more information on this area, contact the **Harney County Chamber of Commerce,** 484 N. Broadway, Burns, OR 97720 (© **541/573-2636;** www.harneycounty.com).

Exploring the Region

Because water is scarce here in the high desert, it becomes a magnet for wildlife wherever it appears. Three marshy lakes—Malheur, Harney, and Mud—south of Burns cover such a vast area and provide such an ideal habitat for birdlife that they have been designated the **Malheur National Wildlife Refuge ★.** The shallow lakes, surrounded by thousands of acres of marshlands, annually attract more than 300 species of birds, including waterfowl, shorebirds, songbirds, and raptors. Some of the more noteworthy birds that are either resident or migratory at Malheur are trumpeter swans, sandhill cranes, white pelicans, great blue herons, and great horned owls. Of the more than 58 mammals that live in the refuge, the most visible are mule deer, pronghorn antelope, and coyotes, but I once saw a bobcat near the visitor center.

The refuge headquarters is 32 miles south of Burns on Ore. 205, but the refuge stretches for another 30 miles south to the crossroads of Frenchglen. The refuge is open daily from dawn to dusk. The **visitor center,** where you can find out about recent sightings and current birding hot spots, is open weekdays and most weekends during the spring and summer, while a **museum** housing a collection of nearly 200 stuffed-and-mounted birds is open daily. About 6 miles north of the visitor center, you can visit **Historic Sod House Ranch,** which at one time was the northern head-quarters for the huge ranch created by 19th-century rancher Peter French (for whom the nearby community of Frenchglen is named). The ranch preserves several historic buildings, including a 116-foot-long barn. The ranch, which is part of the wildlife refuge, is open August 15 to October 15 daily from 8am to 4pm, and there are guided interpretive tours when volunteers are available. Camping is available at the Bureau of Land Management's Page Springs Campground near Frenchglen (© **541/573-4400;** www.blm.gov/or/districts/burns/index.php). For more information on the refuge, contact **Malheur National Wildlife Refuge,** 36391 Sodhouse Lane, Princeton, OR 97721 (© **541/493-2612;** www.fws.gov/malheur). Bird-watchers may also want to make their way west from Malheur to Summer Lake, which is roughly midway between Lakeview and Bend on Ore. 31. The birding here can be as good as at Malheur.

East of the wildlife refuge, you can drive through the scenic **Diamond Craters Outstanding Natural Area.** Along a 40-mile route, partially on gravel roads, you can explore a bizarre landscape of lava domes, volcanic craters, and lava flows. The route begins at Diamond Junction on Ore. 205 north of Frenchglen and winds its way toward New Princeton on Ore. 78. For more information, contact the **Bureau of Land Management Burns Office,** 28910 U.S. 20 W., Hines, OR 97738 (© **541/573-4400;** www.blm.gov/or/districts/burns).

Steens Mountain, at 9,733 feet high, is a different sort of desert oasis. This mountain rises so high that it creates its own weather, and on the upper slopes the

It takes hours to get anywhere in this neck of the woods, and at the end of a long drive, nothing feels better than getting up to your neck in hot water. Out here in the wilds of the Oregon outback, there are a couple of developed, though rustic, hot springs where you can have a soak and rent a cabin, park an RV, or pitch a tent. **Summer Lake Hot Springs**, 41777 Ore. 31, Paisley, OR 97636 (*✆* **541-943-3931;** www.summerlake hotsprings.com), 125 miles southeast of Bend on Ore. 31, has rock-lined, open-air soaking pools and a hot swimming pool inside an old barn. There are also two houses ($130–$165 per night) and two adorable cabins done in a sort of architectural salvage/shabby-chic styling ($85 per night). This place is something of a counterculture resort and is particularly busy during summer music festivals and before and after the Burning Man festival (late Aug–early Sept) in Nevada.

Crystal Crane Hot Springs, 59315 Ore. 78, Burns, OR 97720 (*✆* **541/493-2312;** www.cranehotsprings.com), 25 miles east of Burns on Ore. 78, is a bit less off the beaten path if you happen to be out this way birding at Malheur National Wildlife Refuge. Here you'll find a hot-springs-fed pond for swimming ($3.50 day-use fee) and several indoor private soaking tubs that can be rented by the hour ($7.50 per person per hour; reservations recommended). Crystal Crane rents out five tiny cabins, one of which has a half bathroom (the others share bathroom facilities). Cabin rates are $45 to $60 for a double.

sagebrush of the high desert gives way to juniper and aspen forests. From Frenchglen, there's a 66-mile loop road that leads to the summit and back down by a different route. Due to early snows and lingering snow in the spring, this road is usually open only between July and October. Even then the road is not recommended for cars with low clearance, but if you have the appropriate vehicle, it's well worth a visit.

Steens Mountain is a fault-block mountain that was formed when the land on the west side of a geological fault line rose in relationship to the land on the east side of the fault. This geologic upheaval caused the east slope of Steens Mountain to form a precipitous escarpment that falls away to the Alvord Desert a mile below. From the summit of Steens Mountain, the panorama across southeastern Oregon is spectacular. The road leads almost to the summit, but then you'll have to walk 5 or 10 minutes to the very top of the peak. Stretched out below you when you stand on the summit, or at the nearby East Rim Overlook, are four glacier-carved gorges—Kiger, Little Blitzen, Big Indian, and Wildhorse. From near the summit, a steep and strenuous trail leads down into Wildhorse Gorge to Wildhorse Lake. Although the round-trip hike is only 2.6 miles in length, it involves descending and then ascending 1,100 feet to and from the floor of the gorge. There are wild horses in the area, known as Kiger mustangs.

For more information on Steens Mountain or the Alvord Desert, which is only accessible via a 64-mile gravel road, contact the **Bureau of Land Management Burns Office,** 28910 U.S. 20 W., Hines, OR 97738 (*✆* **541/573-4400;** www.blm. gov/or/districts/burns/index.php).

More wildlife-viewing opportunities are available at the **Hart Mountain National Antelope Refuge ★**, which is a refuge for both pronghorns, the fastest land mammal in North America, and California bighorn sheep. The most accessible location for viewing pronghorns is the refuge headquarters, 49 miles southwest of Frenchglen on gravel roads. Bighorn sheep are harder to spot and tend to keep to the steep cliffs west of the refuge headquarters. Primitive camping is available near the headquarters at **Hot Springs Campground,** where there is a hot spring. For more information, contact the **Sheldon-Hart Mountain Refuge Complex,** 20995 Rabbit Hill Rd., Lakeview, OR 97630 (© **541/947-2731;** www.fws.gov/sheldonhart mtn/Hart/index.html).

If you'd like to learn more about the history of this region, I recommend stopping by the **Round Barn Visitor Center,** 51955 Lava Beds Rd., Diamond (© **888/493-2420;** www.roundbarn.net), which also operates **Jenkins Tours.** The tour company offers several different tours, including trips to Steens Mountain and heritage tours. Call for rates.

Where to Stay & Eat

If bird-watching in Malheur National Wildlife Refuge has left you famished, you can get a simple meal at **The Narrows,** 33468 Sod House Lane, Princeton (© **541/495-2006;** www.narrowsrvpark.com), a combination restaurant, minimart, and RV park about 5 miles west of the refuge headquarters.

Frenchglen Hotel ★   This historic two-story hotel 60 miles south of Burns on the edge of Malheur National Wildlife Refuge is in the middle of nowhere, so for decades the Frenchglen Hotel (now owned by Oregon State Parks) has been an important way station for travelers passing through this remote region. Today the hotel is most popular with bird-watchers. There are small, simply furnished guest rooms on the second floor of the hotel. For more spacious and modern accommodations, book a room in the affiliated Drovers' Inn, a four-unit new building that has rooms with attached bathrooms ($100–$110 double). This hotel is often booked up months in advance. Three meals a day will cost $30 to $45 per person, and the hearty dinners are quite good.

39184 Ore. 205, Frenchglen, OR 97736. www.oregonstateparks.org/park_3.php. © **800/551-6949** or 541/493-2825. 8 units, all with shared bathroom. $70–$75 double. DISC, MC, V. Closed Nov–Mar 15. **Amenities:** Restaurant. *In room:* No phone.

Hotel Diamond ★   With a big screen porch, an old stone barn, poplars and shade trees, and a green lawn that attracts deer, the Hotel Diamond, built in 1898, is a delightfully timeless place. Rooms in the historic hotel have hand-stitched quilts and a simple country flavor. Family-style dinners are available for around $19 (make reservations at least 24 hr. in advance). Located 54 miles south of Burns off Ore. 205, the hotel is on the opposite side of Malheur National Wildlife Refuge from Frenchglen.

10 Main St., Diamond, OR 97722. www.central-oregon.com/hoteldiamond. © **541/493-1898.** 8 units, 3 with private bathroom. $74 double with shared bathroom; $97 double with private bathroom. Rates include continental breakfast. MC, V. Closed Nov–Mar. **Amenities:** 2 restaurants. *In room:* A/C, no phone.

PLANNING YOUR TRIP TO OREGON

I know trying to find a good deal on a car rental isn't as fun as picking the gorgeous central Oregon mountain lodge you'll stay in, but it's one of those travel-planning basics that needs to be addressed. In this chapter you'll find information not only on renting a car but on lots of other topics that are important in planning a vacation.

GETTING THERE

Portland is the gateway to Oregon. In addition, driving directions throughout this book often use Portland as a reference point, assuming that you'll be flying into Portland and then driving to your destination.

By Plane

Portland International Airport (PDX) is Oregon's biggest and busiest airport and is served by most major national and many international airlines. For most people visiting Oregon, this should be the airport of choice. However, if you are heading to the central or southern Oregon coast, you might consider flying into either the **Eugene Airport (EUG)**, which is served by Allegiant Air, Delta Connection, Alaska/Horizon Air, and United Express. If you are headed to Bend or Sunriver, flying into **Roberts Field/Redmond Municipal Airport (RDM)** might work for you. This airport is served by Allegiant Air, Alaska/Horizon Air, and SkyWest Airlines (United Express and Delta Airlines). If you are headed to Ashland for some Shakespeare, you could consider the **Rogue Valley International–Medford Airport (MFR),** which is served by Allegiant Air, Alaska/Horizon Air, and Skywest Airlines (Delta Connection and United Express).

To find out which airlines travel to Oregon, please see "Airline Websites," p. 364.

By Car

The distance to Portland from Seattle is 175 miles; from Spokane, 350 miles; from Vancouver, British Columbia, 285 miles; from San Francisco, 640 miles; and from Los Angeles, 1,015 miles.

If you're driving from California, I-5 runs up through the length of the state and continues north toward the Canadian border, passing through the heart of Portland. If you're coming from the east, I-84 runs from Idaho and points east into Oregon, eventually ending in Portland.

By Train

Amtrak's (© **800/872-7245;** www.amtrak.com) *Coast Starlight* train connects Portland with Seattle, San Francisco, Los Angeles, and San Diego, and stops at historic **Union Station,** 800 NW Sixth Ave., about 10 blocks from the heart of downtown Portland. Between Portland and Seattle there are both regular trains and modern European-style Talgo trains, which make the trip in 3½ to 4 hours versus 4½ hours for the regular train. On either type of train, one-way fares between Seattle and Portland are usually between $31 and $44. The Talgo train, called *Cascades,* runs between Eugene, Oregon, and Vancouver, British Columbia.

By Bus

Greyhound (© **800/231-2222** in the U.S.; © **001/214/849-8100** outside the U.S.; www.greyhound.com) is the sole nationwide bus line. International visitors can obtain information about the **Greyhound North American Discovery Pass.** The pass, which offers unlimited travel and stopovers in the U.S. and Canada, can be obtained outside the United States from travel agents or through www.discoverypass.com.

GETTING AROUND

By Car

A car is by far the best way to see Oregon. There just isn't any other way to get to the more remote natural attractions or to fully appreciate such regions as the Oregon coast or eastern Oregon. It takes about 1½ hours to drive from Portland to Cannon Beach on the Oregon coast; from Portland to Mount Hood, about 1 hour; from Portland to Bend, about 3 hours; and from Portland to Ashland or Crater Lake, about 5 hours.

Major rental-car companies with offices in Oregon include Alamo, Avis, Budget, Dollar, Enterprise, Hertz, National, and Thrifty, and all of these companies have offices in Portland at or near Portland International Airport. Rates for rental cars vary considerably among companies and with the model you want to rent, the dates you rent, and your pickup and drop-off points. If you contact the same company three times to check on renting the same model car, you may get three different quotes, depending on current availability of vehicles. It pays to shop early. At press time, weekly rates for a compact car in July (high-season rates) were running anywhere from $250 ($320 with taxes and fees) to $340 ($440 with taxes and fees) at Portland International Airport. Expect lower rates in the rainy months.

Insurance and taxes are almost never included in quoted rental car rates in the U.S.; be sure to find out what the total car-rental bill will be with all taxes and additional fees included. These surcharges can add a significant cost to your car rental. Drivers under the age of 25 can expect to pay an additional "younger driver" fee that can add $100 to $150 to the cost of a car rental. Drivers under the age of 20 may not be able to rent a car at all. If you're visiting from abroad and plan to rent a car in the United States, keep in mind that foreign driver's licenses are usually recognized in the U.S., but you may want to consider obtaining an international driver's license.

Maps are available at most highway tourist information centers, at the tourist information offices listed earlier in this chapter and throughout this book, and at gas stations throughout the region. For a map of Oregon, contact **Travel Oregon** (© **800/547-7842;** www.traveloregon.com). One of the most important benefits of belonging to the **American Automobile Association** (© **800/222-4357;** www. aaa.com) is that it supplies members with both free maps and emergency road service. In Portland, AAA is located at 600 SW Market St. (© **800/452-1643** or 503/222-6767; www.aaaorid.com). Members of AAA also can get detailed road maps of Oregon by calling their local AAA office.

In Oregon, you may turn right on a red light after a full stop, and if you are in the far-left lane of a one-way street, you may turn left into the adjacent left lane of a one-way street at a red light after a full stop. Everyone in a moving vehicle is required to wear a seat belt. Also, keep in mind that Oregon is a big state, so keep your gas tank as full as possible when traveling in the mountains or on the sparsely populated east side of the Cascades. In the event of a breakdown, stay with your car, lift the hood, turn on your emergency flashers, and wait for a police patrol car. *Do not leave your vehicle.*

Oregon is an anachronism when it comes to gas stations; there are no self-service gas stations in the state. So when you pull into a gas station, just sit back and let the attendant fill your tank. Taxes are already included in the printed price of gasoline. One U.S. gallon equals 3.8 liters or .85 imperial gallons.

By Train

International visitors can buy a **USA Rail Pass,** good for 15, 30, or 45 days of unlimited travel on **Amtrak** (© **800/USA-RAIL** [872-7145] in the U.S. or Canada; 001/215-856-7953 outside the U.S.; www.amtrak.com). The pass is available online or through many overseas travel agents. See Amtrak's website for the cost of travel within the western, eastern, or northwestern United States. Reservations are generally required and should be made as early as possible. Regional rail passes are also available.

By Plane

Although there are airports with regular commercial service in Redmond, Eugene, and Medford, flying isn't usually a very appropriate way to get around Oregon.

Note: Some major airlines offer transatlantic or transpacific passengers special discount tickets under the name **Visit USA,** which allows mostly one-way travel from one U.S. destination to another at very low prices. Unavailable in the U.S., these discount tickets must be purchased abroad in conjunction with your international fare. This system is the easiest, fastest, cheapest way to see the country. Inquire with your air carrier.

By Bus

See "Getting There: By Bus," above.

By Recreational Vehicle (RV)

An economical way to tour Oregon is with a recreational vehicle. They can be rented for a weekend, a week, or longer. In Portland contact **Cruise America,** 8400 SE 82nd Ave. (© **800/671-8042** or 503/777-9833; www.cruiseamerica.com). If you're going to be traveling in the peak season of summer, it's important to make reservations for your RV at least 2 to 3 months ahead of time.

TIPS ON ACCOMMODATIONS

From boutique hotels to B&Bs, golf resorts to mountain lodges, hipster hotels to rustic cabins, Oregon has as wide a variety of accommodations as it has landscapes. For the most part, summer is the high season in Oregon, so if you plan to visit any time between June and September, you'll be paying top dollar for your room. To save money, you'll have to put up with a little rain or snow, which isn't necessarily a reason to avoid a rainy-season Oregon vacation. Winter brings great skiing and snowboarding to the Cascades and storm watching on the coast, and in Portland, plenty of cozy cafes, bookstores, museums, and theaters will keep you busy.

It's always a good idea to make hotel reservations as soon as you know your trip dates. During the summer, Portland and the Oregon coast are particularly busy, and hotels book up well in advance—especially on holiday and festival weekends. Major downtown hotels, which cater primarily to business travelers, commonly offer weekend discounts of as much as 50% to entice vacationers to fill up the empty rooms. However, resorts and hotels near tourist attractions tend to have higher rates on weekends. If you don't want to pay a premium for a downtown business hotel or an oceanfront lodge, try the budget chain motels, which are well represented throughout the state but which are rarely in memorable locations.

For information on B&Bs in Oregon, contact the **Oregon Bed and Breakfast Guild,** P.O. Box 12702, Salem, OR 97309 (© **800/944-6196;** www.obbg.org). If the great outdoors are your main interest, consider staying in a yurt, cabin, or teepee at a state park. For information, contact **Oregon State Parks** (© **800/452-5687;** www.oregon.gov/oprd/parks).

If you're looking for places to camp, you'll find great campgrounds all across Oregon. Those along the coast are the most popular, followed by campgrounds on lakes. During the summer, campground reservations are almost a necessity at most state parks, especially those along the coast. For information on making campsite reservations, see the box "Serious Reservations," above.

 ## SERIOUS reservations

The days of spontaneous summer weekends are a thing of the past in Oregon. If you want to be assured of getting a room or a campsite at some of the busier destinations, you'll need to make your reservations months in advance, especially if you're going on a weekend.

To be sure that you get the state-park campsite, cabin, or houseboat you want, you'll need to make your reservations as much as 9 months in advance (that's the earliest you can reserve) through **ReserveAmerica** (© **800/452-5687** or 503/731-3411; www.reserveamerica.com).

While National Forest Service campgrounds are generally less developed and less in demand than state-park campgrounds, many do stay full throughout the summer months, especially those at the beach. For reservations at forest-service campgrounds, contact the **National Recreation Reservation Service** (© **877/444-6777** or 518/885-3639; www.recreation.gov). These sites can be reserved up to 6 months in advance.

The same sort of advance planning also applies to just about any lodging on the coast on a summer weekend. Making rooms even more difficult to come by are the many festivals scheduled around the state throughout the summer. Be sure to check whether your schedule might coincide with some popular event.

Various state parks also offer a variety of camping alternatives. Top among these are yurts (circular domed tents with electricity, plywood floors, and beds), which make camping in the rain a bit easier. Yurts, which rent for $35 to $76 a night, can be found at 14 coastal parks, as well as at four inland state parks (Champoeg, Valley of the Rogue, Tumalo, and Wallowa Lake). Cabins are available at 15 state parks. Nightly rates range from $24 to $85. A couple of state parks also have teepees for rent ($36–$39 per night). On central Oregon's Lake Billy Chinook at The Cove Palisades State Park, you can even rent a houseboat for $1,685 to $6,075 per week. Contact **Cove Palisades Resort & Marina** (✆ 877/546-7171 or 541/546-9999; www.covepalisadesresort.com).

FAST FACTS: OREGON

Area Codes Oregon has three area codes. In the Portland area, where 10-digit dialing is required for local calls, 503 is the main area code. However, you may occasionally encounter the 971 area code. Outside of the northwest corner of the state (roughly Mount Hood and Portland to the coast and south to Salem), the area code is 541.

Business Hours The following are general hours; specific establishments' hours may vary. Banks are open Monday through Friday from 9am to 5pm (some also Sat 9am–noon). Stores are open Monday through Saturday from 10am to 6pm, and Sunday from noon to 5pm (malls usually stay open Mon–Sat until 9pm). Bars are legally allowed to be open until 2am.

Car Rental See "Getting Around: By Car," above.

Cellphones See "Mobile Phones," below.

Crime See "Safety," later in this section.

Customs Every visitor 21 years of age or older may bring in, free of duty, the following: (1) 1 liter of alcohol; (2) 200 cigarettes, 100 cigars (but not from Cuba); and (3) $100 worth of gifts. These exemptions are offered to travelers who spend at least 72 hours in the United States and who have not claimed them within the preceding 6 months. It is forbidden to bring into the country almost any meat products (including canned, fresh, and dried meat products, such as bouillon and soup mixes). Generally, condiments including vinegars, oils, pickled goods, spices, coffee, tea, and some cheeses and baked goods are permitted. Avoid rice products, as rice can often harbor insects. Bringing fruits and vegetables is prohibited since they may harbor pests or disease. International visitors may carry in or out up to $10,000 in U.S. or foreign currency with no formalities; larger sums must be declared to U.S. Customs on entering or leaving, which includes filing form FinCEN 105. For details regarding U.S. Customs and Border Protection, consult your nearest U.S. embassy or consulate, or **U.S. Customs** (www.customs.gov).

Disabled Travelers Most disabilities shouldn't stop anyone from traveling in the U.S. Thanks to provisions in the Americans with Disabilities Act, most public places are required to comply with disability-friendly regulations. Almost all public establishments (including hotels, restaurants, museums, and such, but not including certain National Historic Landmarks) and at least some modes of public transportation provide accessible entrances and other facilities for those with disabilities.

Because it has few steep streets, Portland is a particularly wheelchair-friendly city. Downtown hotels have handicapped accessible rooms, and buses, light rail, and streetcars are also wheelchair accessible. For information on these transit options, contact **TriMet** (✆ 503/962-2455 or (TTY) 503/962-5811; http://trimet.org/access/index.htm). In state parks and national forests throughout Oregon, you'll find many paved trails designed to accommodate those in wheelchairs. At **Yaquina Head Outstanding Natural Area** (p. 200), on the Oregon coast outside of Newport, there are even wheelchair-accessible tide pools.

The **America the Beautiful—National Park and Federal Recreational Lands Pass— Access Pass** gives travelers with visual impairments or those with permanent disabilities (regardless of age) free lifetime entrance to federal recreation sites administered by the National Park Service, including the Fish and Wildlife Service, the Forest Service, the Bureau of Land Management, and the Bureau of Reclamation. This includes national parks, monuments, historic sites, recreation areas, and national wildlife refuges.

The America the Beautiful Access Pass can only be obtained in person at a National Park Service facility that charges an entrance fee, such as Crater Lake National Park or Lewis & Clark National Historical Park. You need to show proof of a medically determined disability. Besides free entry, the pass also offers a 50% discount on some federal-use fees charged for such facilities as camping, swimming, parking, boat launching, and tours. For more information, go to www.nps.gov/fees_passes.htm, or call the United States Geological Survey/USGS (℡ **888/275-8747**), which issues the passes.

Doctors   To find a doctor, check with the front desk or concierge at your hotel or look in the yellow pages of the local telephone book under "Physician." Also see the "Doctor" and "Hospitals" listings in the Fast Facts section of the Portland chapter (chapter 4).

Drinking Laws   The legal age for purchase and consumption of alcoholic beverages is 21; proof of age is required and often requested at bars, nightclubs, and restaurants, so it's always a good idea to bring ID when you go out. Do not carry open containers of alcohol in your car or any public area that isn't zoned for alcohol consumption. The police can fine you on the spot. Don't even think about driving while intoxicated.

Aside from on-premises sales of cocktails in bars and restaurants, hard liquor can be purchased only in liquor stores. Beer and wine are available in convenience stores and grocery stores. Brewpubs tend to sell only beer and wine, but some also have licenses to sell hard liquor.

Driving Rules   See "Getting Around," above.

Electricity   Like Canada, the United States uses 110 to 120 volts AC (60 cycles), compared to 220 to 240 volts AC (50 cycles) in most of Europe, Australia, and New Zealand. Downward converters that change 220–240 volts to 110–120 volts are difficult to find in the United States, so bring one with you.

Embassies & Consulates   All embassies are in the nation's capital, Washington, D.C. Some consulates are in major U.S. cities, and most nations have a mission to the United Nations in New York City. If your country isn't listed below, call for directory information in Washington, D.C. (℡ **202/555-1212**), or check **www.embassy.org/embassies**.

The embassy of **Australia** is at 1601 Massachusetts Ave. NW, Washington, DC 20036 (℡ **202/797-3000;** www.usa.embassy.gov.au). Consulates are in New York, Honolulu, Houston, Los Angeles, and San Francisco.

The embassy of **Canada** is at 501 Pennsylvania Ave. NW, Washington, DC 20001 (℡ **202/682-1740;** www.canadainternational.gc.ca/washington). Other Canadian consulates are in Buffalo (New York), Detroit, Los Angeles, New York, and Seattle.

The embassy of **Ireland** is at 2234 Massachusetts Ave. NW, Washington, DC 20008 (℡ **202/462-3939;** www.embassyofireland.org). Irish consulates are in Boston, Chicago, New York, San Francisco, and other cities.

The embassy of **New Zealand** is at 37 Observatory Circle NW, Washington, DC 20008 (℡ **202/328-4800;** www.nzembassy.com). New Zealand consulates are in Los Angeles, Salt Lake City, San Francisco, and Seattle.

The embassy of the **United Kingdom** is at 3100 Massachusetts Ave. NW, Washington, DC 20008 (℡ **202/588-6500;** http://ukinusa.fco.gov.uk). Other British consulates are in

Atlanta, Boston, Chicago, Cleveland, Houston, Los Angeles, New York, San Francisco, and Seattle.

Emergencies Call ℂ **911** to report a fire, call the police, or get an ambulance anywhere in the U.S. This is a toll-free call. (No coins are required at public telephones.)

Family Travel Because the weather in much of Oregon is cool and rainy for much of the year and because the Pacific Ocean waters of the Oregon coast are too cold and often too rough for swimming, Oregon may not at first seem like a great spot for a family vacation. However, with the giant sand dunes of Oregon Dunes National Recreation Area, perfect kite-flying conditions, and whale-watching excursions, the Oregon coast has plenty of possibilities for keeping the kids busy. There's plenty more family fun to be had at central Oregon's many family resorts, where horse-back riding, swimming, biking, boating, hiking, and golfing are all popular activities. On the flanks of Mount Hood, which is a dormant volcano, the Skibowl ski area operates a summertime action park with alpine sleds (sort of like summertime bobsleds), bungee jumping, a zip line, and lots of other fun activities.

Families traveling in Oregon should be sure to take note of family admission fees at many museums and other attractions. These admission prices are often less than what it would cost for individual tickets for the whole family. At hotels and motels, children usually stay free if they share their parent's room and no extra bed or crib is required, and sometimes they also get to eat for free in the hotel dining room. Be sure to ask.

For recommendations of kid-friendly attractions and activities, see "The Best Family Attractions" and "The Best Family Activities" in chapter 1, where you'll also find a list of the best family-oriented hotels and resorts in the state. To locate accommodations, restaurants, and attractions that are particularly kid-friendly, see the "Kids" icon throughout this guide, and in the Portland chapter (chapter 4), see the "Family-Friendly Hotels" and "Family-Friendly Restaurants" boxes. Also, check out the "Especially for Kids" section of the Portland chapter. Many of the resorts in central Oregon offer children's programs, although these programs may only be available during the summer months. In the absence of children's programs, many hotel and resort concierges throughout the state can recommend babysitters.

Gasoline Please see "Getting Around: By Car," earlier in this chapter.

Health The best medical facilities in the state are in Portland, Salem, and Eugene. See "Emergencies" and "Hospitals" in the "Fast Facts" section of chapter 4 (Portland) for details. If you suffer from a chronic illness, consult your doctor before your departure. Pack prescription medications in your carry-on luggage, and carry them in their original containers, with pharmacy labels—otherwise they may not make it through airport security. Visitors from outside the U.S. should carry generic names of prescription drugs. For U.S. travelers, most reliable healthcare plans provide coverage if you get sick away from home. Foreign visitors may have to pay all medical costs up front and be reimbursed later.

Insurance For information on traveler's insurance, trip cancelation insurance, and medical insurance while traveling, please visit www.frommers.com/planning.

Internet & Wi-Fi Nearly anywhere you go in Oregon, even in small towns, you can find some way to connect to the Internet. Among the more common places to get access to the Internet are cafes, public libraries, and in hotel lobbies, where computers are often available for guests' use. See "Fast Facts," in chapter 4, for details on Internet access in Portland.

Legal Aid While driving, if you are pulled over for a minor infraction (such as speeding), never attempt to pay the fine directly to a police officer; this could be construed as attempted bribery, a much more serious crime. Pay fines by mail, or directly into the hands of the clerk of the court. If accused of a more serious offense, say and do nothing before consulting a lawyer. In the U.S., the burden is on the state to prove a person's guilt beyond a reasonable doubt, and everyone has the right to remain silent, whether he or she is suspected of a crime or actually arrested. Once arrested, a person can make one telephone call to a party of his or her choice. The international visitor should call his or her embassy or consulate.

LGBT Travelers Oregon cities such as Portland and Eugene are notoriously liberal, and gay and lesbian travelers will generally feel very welcome in these cities. In Portland, look for **Portland's LGBTQ Community Yellow Pages** (☎ 503/230-7701; www.pdxgay yellowpages.com), which is usually available at **Powell's Books,** 1005 W. Burnside St.

For a list of gay-friendly accommodations in Oregon, go to the **Purple Roofs** website (www.purpleroofs.com).

Mail At press time, domestic postage rates were 32¢ for a postcard and 45¢ for a letter. For international mail, a first-class letter of up to 1 ounce costs 90¢ (85¢ to Canada and Mexico); a first-class postcard costs the same as a letter. For more information, go to **www.usps.com**.

If you aren't sure what your address will be in the United States, mail can be sent to you, in your name, c/o General Delivery at the main post office of the city or region where you expect to be. (Call ☎ 800/275-8777 for information on the nearest post office.) The addressee must pick up mail in person and must produce proof of identity (driver's license, passport, for example). Most post offices will hold mail for up to 1 month, and are open Monday to Friday from 8am to 6pm, and Saturday from 9am to 3pm.

Always include zip codes when mailing items in the U.S. If you don't know your zip code, visit www.usps.com/zip4.

Medical Requirements Unless you're arriving from an area known to be suffering from an epidemic (particularly cholera or yellow fever), inoculations or vaccinations are not required for entry into the United States. Also see "Health."

Mobile Phones Just because your cellphone works at home doesn't mean it'll work everywhere in the U.S. (thanks to the fragmented cellphone system in the United States). If you live in the U.S., it's a good bet that your phone will work in Oregon's major cities, but take a look at your wireless company's coverage map on its website before heading out; T-Mobile, Sprint, and Nextel are particularly weak in rural areas. (To see where GSM phones work in the U.S., check out www.t-mobile.com/coverage.) If you're visiting from another country, be sure to find out about international calling rates and roaming charges before using your phone in the United States. You could ring up a huge phone bill with just a few calls.

Options for staying connected in the U.S. include renting a mobile phone from a company such as **Roberts Rent-A-Phone** (☎ 800/964-2468; www.roberts-rent-a-phone.com). However, you can also buy an inexpensive phone and prepaid minutes from such companies as **TracFone** (www.tracfone.com). These phones are readily available in such stores as Walmart and Target and usually cost less than $20. Prepaid minutes might cost $20 for 60 minutes, though double-minute plans can lower this cost. Another alternative if you are traveling with your laptop computer or have a smart phone is to install **Skype** (www.skype.com), a VoIP (Voice over Internet Protocol) program/app that allows you to use your computer or smart phone as an Internet-based telephone. Doing this allows you to call other Skype users at no charge.

THE VALUE OF THE U.S. DOLLAR VS. OTHER POPULAR CURRENCIES

$	Aus$	Can$	Euro (€)	NZ$	UK£
$1	A$0.94	C$0.96	€0.69	NZ$1.27	£0.61

Frommer's lists exact prices in the local currency. The currency conversions quoted above were correct at press time. However, rates fluctuate, so before departing consult a currency exchange website such as **www.oanda.com/currency/converter** to check up-to-the-minute rates.

Money & Costs   The most common U.S. bills are the $1 (a "buck"), $5, $10, and $20 denominations. There are also $2 bills (seldom encountered), $50 bills, and $100 bills (the last two are usually not welcome as payment for small purchases).

Coins come in seven denominations: 1¢ (1 cent, or a penny); 5¢ (5 cents, or a nickel); 10¢ (10 cents, or a dime); 25¢ (25 cents, or a quarter); 50¢ (50 cents, or a half dollar); and the gold-colored Sacagawea coin, the new release of Presidential coins, and the rare silver dollar, all worth $1.

What will a vacation in Oregon cost? Of course, that depends on what level of luxury you crave on your vacation. If you make like a local and camp out, whether in a tent or in an RV, and cook your own food or eat at fast-food places, you can probably get by on less than $50 per day per person. On the other hand, if you want to stay in a luxe hotel in downtown Portland, a waterfront hotel, a historic B&B, or a central Oregon golf resort, you can spend upwards of $200 per night for a hotel room alone. You can cut that cost substantially by visiting during the rainy season, but, then, of course, the weather isn't nearly as pleasant as it is in the summer. If you're looking to save some money on your vacation (aren't we all?), book a room away from downtown Portland or off the beach.

Credit cards are the most widely used form of payment in the U.S. It's highly recommended that you travel with at least one major credit card; options include **Visa** (Barclaycard in Britain), **MasterCard** (Eurocard in Europe), **American Express, Diners Club,** and **Discover.** MasterCard and Visa are the two most commonly accepted credit cards. You must have a credit card to rent a car, and hotels and airlines usually require a credit card imprint as a deposit against expenses.

You can withdraw cash advances from your credit cards at banks or ATMs, but high fees make credit card cash advances a pricey way to get cash. Keep in mind that you'll pay interest from the moment of your withdrawal, even if you pay your monthly bills on time. Also, note that many banks now assess a 1% to 3% "transaction fee" on **all** charges you incur abroad (whether you're using the local currency or your native currency).

The easiest and best way to get cash in the United States is from an ATM (automated teller machine), sometimes referred to as a "cash machine" or "cashpoint." The **Cirrus** (© **800/424-7787;** www.mastercard.com) and **PLUS** (www.visa.com) networks span the country; you can find them even in remote regions. Go to your bank card's website to find ATM locations at your destination. Be sure you know your daily withdrawal limit before you depart. Four-digit PINs work fine in Oregon.

In Oregon, you'll find ATMs at banks in even the smallest towns. You can also usually find them at gas station minimarts, although these machines usually charge a slightly higher fee than banks. You can sometimes avoid a fee by searching out a small community bank, a savings and loan, or a credit union ATM. To avoid fees, you can also go into a grocery store, make a purchase, and ask for cash back on your debit card.

Beware of hidden credit card fees while traveling. Check with your credit or debit card issuer to see what fees, if any, will be charged for overseas transactions. Recent reform legislation in the U.S., for example, has curbed some exploitative lending practices. But many banks have responded by increasing fees in other areas, including fees for customers who use credit and debit cards while out of the country—even if those charges were made in U.S. dollars. Fees can amount to 3% or more of the purchase price. Check with your bank before departing to avoid any surprise charges on your statement.

For help with currency conversions, tip calculations, and more, download Frommer's convenient Travel Tools app for your mobile device. Go to www.frommers.com/go/mobile and click on the "Travel Tools To Go" icon.

WHAT THINGS COST IN OREGON	U.S. $
Taxi from the airport to downtown Portland	35.00–40.00
Double room, moderate	125.00–200.00
Double room, inexpensive	65.00–125.00
Three-course dinner for one without wine, moderate	20.00–30.00
Bottle of beer	3.00–3.50
Cup of coffee	1.50–1.75
1 gallon/1 liter of regular gas	3.75 / 1.00
Admission to most museums	10.00–15.00
Admission to Crater Lake National Park	10.00

Newspapers & Magazines

PLANNING YOUR TRIP TO OREGON

Newspapers & Magazines The *Oregonian* is the Portland daily paper and is available throughout most of the state. *Portland Monthly* is a good lifestyle monthly that offers plenty of coverage of what's hot in Portland. *Oregon Coast* magazine is another publication worth picking up.

Packing For the most part, Oregon is a very casual place. Sure, there are a few high-end restaurants in Portland and the wine country where you might want to get dressed up, but for the most part, you can get by with business casual in almost any restaurant in the state. The only really important articles of clothing to pack for a vacation in Oregon are a rain jacket and a sweater or fleece jacket. Even in the middle of summer, it gets cool at night almost anywhere in the state, and August on the Oregon coast is notoriously cool and foggy. You can leave your umbrella at home, hardly anyone here uses them. The rain in Oregon is more often just a constant drizzle rather than the sorts of downpours common in other parts of the United State. For more helpful information on packing for your trip, download our convenient Travel Tools app for your mobile device. Go to www.frommers.com/go/mobile and click on the "Travel Tools To Go" icon.

Passports Virtually every air traveler entering the U.S. is required to show a passport. All persons, including U.S. citizens, traveling by air between the United States and Canada, Mexico, Central and South America, the Caribbean, and Bermuda are required to present a valid passport. **Note:** U.S. and Canadian citizens entering the U. S. at land and sea ports of entry from within the Western Hemisphere must now also present a passport or other documents compliant with the Western Hemisphere Travel Initiative (WHTI; see www.getyouhome.gov for details). Children 15 and under may continue entering with only a U.S. birth certificate, or other proof of U.S. citizenship.

Australia **Australian Passport Information Service** (📞 131-232, or visit www.passports.gov.au).

Canada **Passport Office,** Department of Foreign Affairs and International Trade, Ottawa, ON K1A 0G3 (📞 **800/567-6868;** www.ppt.gc.ca).

Ireland **Passport Office,** Setanta Centre, Molesworth Street, Dublin 2 (📞 **01/671-1633;** www.foreignaffairs.gov.ie).

New Zealand **Passports Office,** Department of Internal Affairs, 47 Boulcott St., Wellington, 6011 (📞 **0800/225-050** in New Zealand or 04/474-8100; www.passports.govt.nz).

United Kingdom Visit your nearest passport office, major post office, or travel agency, or contact the **Identity and Passport Service (IPS),** 89 Eccleston Square, London, SW1V 1PN (📞 **0300/222-0000;** www.ips.gov.uk).

United States To find your regional passport office, check the U.S. State Department website (http://travel.state.gov/passport) or call the **National Passport Information Center** (☎ **877/487-2778**) for automated information.

Petrol Please see "Getting Around: By Car," earlier in this chapter.

Police Call ☎ **911** for emergencies. If 911 doesn't work, dial 0 (zero) for the operator and state your reason for calling.

Safety Oregon's tourist spots are generally quite safe. Portland is also a relatively safe city, but you should take some precautions. For further information on safety in Portland, see "Safety" under "Fast Facts," in chapter 4. As a general precaution, avoid deserted areas, especially at night, and don't go into public parks at night unless there is some special event going on. In theaters, restaurants, and other public places, keep your possessions in sight. If you plan to go hiking or participate in outdoor activities, don't leave anything valuable in your car. This is particularly important to remember at the waterfall parking lots in the Columbia River Gorge area. These parking lots are all subject to frequent car break-ins (known as car clouting).

Senior Travel Don't be shy about asking for discounts, but always carry some kind of identification, such as a driver's license, that shows your date of birth—especially if you've kept your youthful glow. In Portland, most attractions, theaters, and tour companies offer senior discounts. These can add up to substantial savings, but you have to remember to ask.

The U.S. National Park Service offers an **America the Beautiful–National Park and Federal Recreational Lands Pass–Senior Pass** (formerly the **Golden Age Passport**), which gives seniors 62 years and older lifetime entrance to all properties administered by the National Park Service—national parks, monuments, historic sites, recreation areas, and national wildlife refuges—for a one-time processing fee of $10. The pass must be purchased in person at any NPS facility that charges an entrance fee. Besides free entry, the America the Beautiful Senior Pass also offers a 50% discount on some federal-use fees charged for such facilities as camping, swimming, parking, boat launching, and tours. For more information, contact the **United States Geological Survey (USGS; ☎ 888/275-8747;** www.nps.gov/fees_passes.htm), which issues the passes.

Smoking Smoking is prohibited in restaurants and bars in Oregon.

Taxes The United States has no value-added tax (VAT) or other indirect tax at the national level. Every state, county, and city may levy its own local tax on all purchases, including hotel and restaurant checks and airline tickets. These taxes will not appear on price tags. Luckily for anyone visiting Oregon, this state is a shopper's paradise—there's no sales tax. However, you may have to pay taxes on a rental car or hotel room (even some campgrounds charge a "bed tax").

Telephones Many convenience groceries and packaging services sell **prepaid calling cards** in denominations up to $50. Many public pay phones at airports now accept American Express, MasterCard, and Visa. **Local calls** made from most pay phones cost either 25¢ or 35¢. Most long-distance and international calls can be dialed directly from any phone. **To make calls within the United States and to Canada,** dial 1 followed by the area code and the seven-digit number. **For other international calls,** dial 011 followed by the country code, city code, and the number you are calling.

Calls to area codes **800, 888, 877,** and **866** are toll-free. However, calls to area codes **700** and **900** (chat lines, bulletin boards, "dating" services, and so on) can be expensive—charges of 95¢ to $3 or more per minute. Some numbers have minimum charges that can run $15 or more.

For **reversed-charge or collect calls,** and for person-to-person calls, dial the number 0 then the area code and number; an operator will come on the line, and you should specify whether you are calling collect, person-to-person, or both. If your operator-assisted call is international, ask for the overseas operator.

For **directory assistance** ("Information"), dial 411 for local numbers and national numbers in the U.S. and Canada. For dedicated long-distance information, dial 1, then the appropriate area code plus 555-1212.

Time The continental United States is divided into **four time zones:** Eastern Standard Time (EST), Central Standard Time (CST), Mountain Standard Time (MST), and Pacific Standard Time (PST). Alaska and Hawaii have their own zones. For example, when it's 9am in Los Angeles (PST), it's 7am in Honolulu (HST), 10am in Denver (MST), 11am in Chicago (CST), noon in New York City (EST), 5pm in London (GMT), and 2am the next day in Sydney. With the exception of a thin strip along the eastern edge of the state, Oregon is on Pacific Standard Time.

Daylight saving time (summer time) is in effect from 1am on the second Sunday in March to 1am on the first Sunday in November, except in Arizona, Hawaii, the U.S. Virgin Islands, and Puerto Rico. Daylight saving time moves the clock 1 hour ahead of standard time.

For help with time translations, and more, download our convenient Travel Tools app for your mobile device. Go to www.frommers.com/go/mobile and click on the "Travel Tools To Go" icon.

Tipping In hotels, tip **bellhops** at least $1 per bag ($2–$3 if you have a lot of luggage) and tip the **chamber staff** $1 to $2 per day (more if you've left a big mess for him or her to clean up). Tip the **doorman** or **concierge** only if he or she has provided you with some specific service (for example, calling a cab for you or obtaining difficult-to-get theater tickets). Tip the **valet-parking attendant** $1 every time you get your car.

In restaurants, bars, and nightclubs, tip **service staff** and **bartenders** 15% to 20% of the check, tip **checkroom attendants** $1 per garment, and tip **valet-parking attendants** $1 per vehicle.

As for other service personnel, tip **cab drivers** 15% of the fare; tip **skycaps** at airports at least $1 per bag ($2–$3 if you have a lot of luggage); and tip **hairdressers** and **barbers** 15% to 20%.

For help with tip calculations, currency conversions, and more, download our convenient Travel Tools app for your mobile device. Go to www.frommers.com/go/mobile and click on the "Travel Tools To Go" icon.

Toilets You won't find public toilets or restrooms on the streets in most U.S. cities, but they can be found in hotel lobbies, bars, restaurants, museums, department stores, railway and bus stations, and service stations. Large hotels and fast-food restaurants are often the best bet for clean facilities. Restaurants and bars in resorts or heavily visited areas may reserve their restrooms for patrons.

VAT See "Taxes" above.

Visas The U.S. State Department has a **Visa Waiver Program (VWP)** allowing citizens of the following countries to enter the United States without a visa for stays of up to 90 days: Andorra, Australia, Austria, Belgium, Brunei, Czech Republic, Denmark, Estonia, Finland, France, Germany, Greece, Hungary, Iceland, Ireland, Italy, Japan, Latvia, Liechtenstein, Lithuania, Luxembourg, Malta, Monaco, the Netherlands, New Zealand, Norway, Portugal, San Marino, Singapore, Slovakia, Slovenia, South Korea, Spain, Sweden, Switzerland, and the United Kingdom. (**Note:** This list was accurate at press time; for the most up-to-date list of countries in the VWP, consult http://travel.state.gov/visa.) Even though a visa isn't necessary, in an effort to help U.S. officials check travelers against terror watch lists before they arrive at U.S. borders, visitors from VWP countries must register online through the Electronic System for Travel Authorization (ESTA) before boarding a plane or a boat to the U.S. Travelers must complete an electronic application providing basic personal and travel eligibility information. The Department of Homeland Security recommends filling out the form at least 3 days before traveling. Authorizations will be valid for up to 2 years or until the traveler's passport expires, whichever comes first. Currently, there is a US$14 fee for the online application. Existing ESTA registrations remain valid through their expiration dates. **Note:** Any passport issued on or after October 26, 2006, by a VWP country must be an **e-Passport** for VWP travelers to be eligible to enter the U.S. without a visa. Citizens of these nations also need to present a round-trip air or cruise ticket upon arrival. E-Passports contain computer chips capable of storing biometric information, such as the required digital photograph of the holder. If your passport doesn't have this feature, you can still travel without a visa if the valid passport was issued before October 26, 2005, and includes a machine-readable zone; or if the valid passport was issued between October 26, 2005, and October 25, 2006, and includes a digital photograph. For more information, go to **http://travel.state.gov/visa**. Canadian citizens may enter the United States without visas, but will need to show passports and proof of residence.

Citizens of all other countries must have (1) a valid passport that expires at least 6 months later than the scheduled end of their visit to the U.S.; and (2) a tourist visa. For information about U.S. Visas go to **http://travel.state.gov** and click on "Visas." Or go to one of the following websites:

Australian citizens can obtain up-to-date visa information from the **U.S. Embassy Canberra,** Moonah Place, Yarralumla, ACT 2600 (✆ **02/6214-5600**), or by checking the U.S. Diplomatic Mission's website at http://canberra.usembassy.gov/visas.html.

British subjects can obtain up-to-date visa information by calling the **U.S. Embassy Visa Information Line** (✆ **09042-450-100** from within the U.K. at £1.20 per minute; or ✆ **866-382-3589** from within the U.S. at a flat rate of $16, payable by credit card only) or by visiting the "Visas to the U.S." section of the American Embassy London's website at http://london.usembassy.gov/visas.html.

Irish citizens can obtain up-to-date visa information through the **U.S. Embassy Dublin,** 42 Elgin Rd., Ballsbridge, Dublin 4 (✆ **1580-47-VISA** [8472] from within the Republic of Ireland at €2.40 per minute; http://dublin.usembassy.gov).

Citizens of **New Zealand** can obtain up-to-date visa information by contacting the **U.S. Embassy New Zealand,** 29 Fitzherbert Terrace, Thorndon, Wellington (✆ **644/462-6000**; http://newzealand.usembassy.gov).

Visitor Information   Contact **Travel Oregon** (✆ **800/547-7842**; www.traveloregon. com) or **Travel Portland,** 701 SW Sixth Ave., Portland, OR 97205 (✆ **877/678-5263** or 503/275-9293; www.travelportland.com).

Most cities and towns in Oregon have either a tourist office or a chamber of commerce that provides information. When approaching cities and towns, watch for signs along the highway directing you to these information centers. See the individual chapters for addresses.

For Oregon regional websites, try the Travel **Oregon Tourism Commission**'s website at **www.traveloregon.com**, where you can also check out blog postings. Learn about local Oregon news, sports, and entertainment at **www.oregonlive.com**, the *Oregonian* newspaper's website. This latter website also has lots of great blogs. My favorites are "The Beer Here," "Wine Bytes," and "Travels with Terry." For general Oregon travel blogs, visit www. travelblog.org.

For information on camping in Oregon state parks, contact the **Oregon State Parks Information Center,** 725 Summer St. NE, Ste. C, Salem, OR 97301 (✆ **800/551-6949** or 503/986-0707; www.oregon.gov/oprd/parks).

Wi-Fi   See "Internet & Wi-Fi," earlier in this section.

AIRLINE WEBSITES

MAJOR AIRLINES

Air Canada
www.aircanada.com

Alaska Airlines
www.alaskaair.com

American Airlines
www.aa.com

Budget Airlines
www.budgetair.com

Continental Airlines
www.continental.com

Delta Air Lines
www.delta.com

Frontier Airlines
www.frontierairlines.com

Hawaiian Airlines
www.hawaiianair.com

JetBlue Airways
www.jetblue.com

Southwest Airlines
www.southwest.com

United Airlines
www.united.com

US Airways
www.usairways.com

Index